REF 823.8 D548zx P616 2006
Pierce, Gilbert A. (Gilbert
Ashville), 1841-1901
The Dickens dictionary

WITHDRAWN

D1527352

Faithfully Yours
Charles Dickens

# THE DICKENS DICTIONARY

GILBERT A. PIERCE

*WITH ADDITIONS BY*
WILLIAM A. WHEELER

*REVISED EDITION*
*WITH BIBLIOGRAPHY*

ILLUSTRATED

REF
823.8
D548zx
P616
2006

2/07

DOVER PUBLICATIONS, INC.
Mineola, New York

CUYAHOGA COMMUNITY COLLEGE
EASTERN CAMPUS LIBRARY

MAR - 9 2007

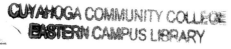

*Bibliographical Note*

This Dover edition, first published in 2006, is an unabridged republication of the revised edition (with bibliography) of the work originally published in 1900 by Houghton Mifflin Company, Boston, under the title, *The Dickens Dictionary: A Key to the Plots and Characters in the Tales of Charles Dickens.* The work was originally published in 1872.

*International Standard Book Number: 0-486-44739-1*

Manufactured in the United States of America
Dover Publications, Inc., 31 East 2nd Street, Mineola, N.Y. 11501

# PREFACE

The Dickens Dictionary first appeared in 1872. The compilers placed on the title-page the apt quotation from Oldys: "If he be ignorant, who would not wish to enlarge his knowledge? If he be knowing, who would not willingly refresh his memory?" As a short cut to the abundant riches of Dickens it has served a most useful turn, and still more has it been an invaluable quickener of the memory and index to the great multitude of Dickens's creations.

The book has been enlarged for this edition so as to cover a number of newly collected stories by Dickens. Certain changes in the arrangement have also been made. In place of the Principal Incidents which followed the list of Characters Introduced under the head of each of the works, an Outline of the story has been prepared to precede the Index to Characters, and in that Outline have been introduced some of the illustrative excerpts which were used to fill out the sketches of the characters. The order of tales has also been changed to conform to that followed in the new Library Edition of Dickens's works. In addition to the indexes, alphabetical and classified, previously given, a bibliography of Dickens's writings has been provided.

Mr. Pierce, in his preface to the earlier edition of the Dictionary, makes the following statements, which should be included in any account of the work:—

"In three or four cases, the extracts from Dickens are taken from his 'Readings, as condensed by Himself,' and not directly from his novels. In the case of other extracts, omissions and explanatory additions are always carefully indicated. . . .

"On the completion of this Dictionary, it was placed in the hands of Mr. William A. Wheeler, as a 'scholar of critical habits and approved experience,' to be revised and corrected for the press; and he has read every page of it with scrupulous care, both in the manuscript and the proofs, suggesting many alterations which have materially improved the work, besides furnishing contributions of his own, which have given it still greater interest, value, and completeness."

Perhaps nothing will at once give so striking an illustration of the fertility of the creative genius of Charles Dickens, and so fully justify the preparation of this volume, as the statement that the Directory of the Inhabitants of Dickens-Land, which points back to the indexes to characters, contains eighteen hundred and ninety-nine entries.

# CONTENTS

# ILLUSTRATIONS



**With the exception of the frontispiece portrait, the illustrations are from drawings by Sol Eytinge, Jr.**

*Sol Eytinge Jr., Del.*

PI

TION.

# POSTHUMOUS PAPERS OF THE PICKWICK CLUB

## OUTLINE

Chapter I At a meeting of the Pickwick Club in London four members of the club were constituted a Corresponding Society, charged with the duty of travel and observation and subsequent report to the club, each member being carefully instructed to pay his own expenses. The four were Samuel Pickwick, the founder of the club, Tracy Tupman — the too susceptible Tupman — Augustus Snodgrass, a man of poetic turn, and Nathaniel Winkle, a sportsman.

II The four companions set out on their adventures on the 13th of May, 1827. Their rendezvous was the Golden Cross, and Mr. Pickwick, in his eagerness to begin the accumulation of wisdom, succeeded in drawing down upon himself the wrath of his cab driver. The altercation which followed was broken up by the interference of a volatile and voluble young man, Mr. Alfred Jingle, who rescued Mr. Pickwick, attached himself to the whole party, and went with them on the coach to Rochester, entertaining them with his frivolous tales by the way.

At the Bull Inn, where they put up, they found there was to be a ball in the evening, and after dinner, to which Mr. Jingle had been invited, Mr. Tupman fell an easy prey to the stranger and his own susceptibility, purchased tickets to the ball, and abstracted Mr. Winkle's coat, which he lent to Mr. Jingle.

"It 's a new coat," said Mr. Tupman, as the stranger surveyed himself with great complacency in a cheval glass. "The first that 's been made with our club button," — and he called his companion's attention to the large gilt button which displayed a bust of Mr. Pickwick in the centre, and the letters "P. C." on either side.

"'P. C.,'" said the stranger, — "queer set out — old fellow's likeness and 'P. C.'— What does 'P. C.' stand for — Peculiar Coat, eh?" Mr. Tupman, with rising indignation, and great importance, explained the mystic device.

"Rather short in the waist, ain't it?" said the stranger, screwing himself round, to catch a glimpse in the glass of the waist buttons which were half way up his back. "Like a general postman's coat — queer coats those — made by contract — no measuring — mysterious dispensations of Providence — all the short men get long coats — all the long men short ones." Running on in this way, Mr. Tupman's new companion adjusted his dress, or rather the dress of Mr. Winkle; and, accompanied by Mr. Tupman, ascended the staircase leading to the ball-room.

There was a certain Dr. Slammer, surgeon to the Ninety-seventh, present, a general favorite, who was paying great attention to a widow whose whole air was that of a rich woman.

Upon the doctor and the widow the eyes both of Mr. Tupman and his companion had been fixed for some time, when the stranger broke silence.

"Lots of money — old girl — pompous doctor — not a bad idea — good fun," were the intelligible sentences which issued from his lips. Mr. Tupman looked inquisitively in his face.

"I'll dance with the widow," said the stranger.

"Who is she?" inquired Mr. Tupman.

"Don't know — never saw her in all my life — cut out the doctor — here goes." And the stranger forthwith crossed the room; and, leaning against a mantel-piece, commenced gazing with an air of respectful and melancholy admiration on the fat countenance of the little old lady. Mr. Tupman looked on in mute astonishment. The stranger progressed rapidly. The little doctor danced with another lady — the widow dropped her fan; the stranger picked it up, and presented it, — a smile, a bow, a courtesy, a few words of conversation. The stranger walked boldly up to, and returned with, the master of the ceremonies, a little introductory pantomime, and the stranger and Mrs. Budger took their places in a quadrille.

The surprise of Mr. Tupman at this summary proceeding, great as it was, was immeasurably exceeded by the astonishment of the doctor. The stranger was young, and the widow was flattered. The doctor's attentions were unheeded by the widow; and the doctor's indignation was wholly lost on his imperturbable rival. Doctor Slammer was paralyzed. He, Doctor Slammer of the Ninety-seventh, to be extinguished in a moment by a man whom nobody had ever seen before, and whom nobody knew even now. Doctor Slammer, — Doctor Slammer of the Ninety-seventh rejected! Impossible! It could not be! Yes, it was: there they were. What! introducing his friend! Could he believe his eyes! He looked again, and was under the painful necessity of

THE PICKWICK CLUB.

admitting the veracity of his optics. Mrs. Budger was dancing with Mr. Tracy Tupman: there was no mistaking the fact. There was the widow before him, bouncing bodily here and there with unwonted vigor; and Mr. Tracy Tupman hopping about with a face expressive of the most intense solemnity, dancing (as a good many people do) as if a quadrille were not a thing to be laughed at, but a severe trial to the feelings, which it requires inflexible resolution to encounter.

Silently and patiently did the doctor bear all this, and all the handings of negus, and watching for glasses, and darting for biscuits, and coquetting, that ensued; but, a few seconds after the stranger had disappeared to lead Mrs. Budger to her carriage, he darted swiftly from the room, with every particle of his hitherto-bottled-up indignation effervescing from all parts of his countenance, in a perspiration of passion.

The stranger was returning, and Mr. Tupman was beside him. He spoke in a low tone, and laughed. The little doctor thirsted for his life. He was exulting. He had triumphed.

"Sir!" said the doctor in an awful voice, producing a card, and retiring into an angle of the passage, "my name is Slammer, Doctor Slammer, sir — Ninety-seventh regiment — Chatham Barracks — my card, sir, my card." He would have added more; but his indignation choked him.

"Ah!" replied the stranger coolly, "Slammer — much obliged — polite attention — not ill now, Slammer — but when I am — knock you up."

"You — you 're a shuffler, sir," gasped the furious doctor, "a poltroon, a coward, a liar, a — a — will nothing induce you to give me your card, sir?"

"Oh! I see," said the stranger, half aside, "negus too strong here — liberal landlord — very foolish — very — lemonade much better — hot rooms — elderly gentleman — suffer for it in the morning — cruel — cruel;" and he moved on a step or two.

"You are stopping in this house, sir," said the indignant little man: "you are intoxicated now, sir; you shall hear from me in the morning, sir. I shall find you out."

"Rather you found me out than found me at home," replied the unmoved stranger.

Doctor Slammer looked unutterable ferocity as he fixed his hat on his head with an indignant knock; and the stranger and Mr. Tupman ascended to the bedroom of the latter to restore the borrowed plumage to the unconscious Winkle.

That gentleman was fast asleep: the restoration was soon made. The stranger was extremely jocose; and Mr. Tracy Tupman, being quite bewildered with wine, negus, lights, and ladies, thought the whole affair an exquisite joke. His new friend departed; and after experiencing some slight difficulty in finding the orifice in his night-cap originally intended for the reception of his head, and finally overturning his candlestick in his struggles to put it on, Mr. Tracy Tupman managed to get into bed by a series of complicated evolutions, and shortly afterwards sank into repose.

Early on the following morning, inquiry was made at the inn for a gentleman wearing a bright blue dress-coat with a gilt button with "P. C." on it; and as Mr. Winkle answered to the description, he was awakened out of a sound sleep, dressed himself hastily, and went down stairs to the coffee-room.

An officer in undress uniform was looking out of the window. He turned round as Mr. Winkle entered, and made a stiff inclination of the head. Having ordered the attendants to retire, and closed the door very carefully, he said, "Mr. Winkle, I presume?"

"My name *is* Winkle, sir."

"You will not be surprised, sir, when I inform you that I have called here this morning on behalf of my friend, Doctor Slammer of the Ninety-seventh."

"Doctor Slammer!" said Mr. Winkle.

"Doctor Slammer. He begged me to express his opinion, that your conduct of last evening was of a description which no gentleman could endure, and (he added) which no one gentleman would pursue towards another."

Mr. Winkle's astonishment was too real and too evident to escape the observation of Doctor Slammer's friend: he therefore proceeded. "My friend, Doctor Slammer, requested me to add, that he is firmly persuaded you were intoxicated during a portion of the evening, and possibly unconscious of the extent of the insult you were guilty of. He commissioned me to say, that, should this be pleaded as an excuse for your behaviour, he will consent to accept a written apology, to be penned by you from my dictation."

"A written apology!" repeated Mr. Winkle in the most emphatic tone of amazement possible.

"Of course you know the alternative," replied the visitor coolly.

"Were you intrusted with this message to me by name?" inquired Mr. Winkle, whose intellects were hopelessly confused by this extraordinary conversation.

"I was not present myself," replied the visitor; "and, in consequence of your firm refusal to give your card to Doctor Slammer, I was desired by that gentleman to identify the wearer of a very uncommon coat, — a bright blue dress-coat, with a gilt button displaying a bust, and the letters 'P. C.'"

Mr. Winkle actually staggered with astonishment as he heard his own costume thus minutely described. Doctor Slammer's friend proceeded: —

"From the inquiries I made at the bar just now, I was convinced that the owner of the coat in question arrived here, with three gentlemen, yesterday afternoon. I immediately sent up to the gentleman who was described as appearing the head of the party; and he at once referred me to you."

If the principal tower of Rochester Castle had suddenly walked from its foundation, and stationed itself opposite the coffee-room-window, Mr. Winkle's surprise would have been as nothing, compared with the profound astonishment with which he had heard this address. His first impression was that his coat had been stolen. "Will you allow me to detain you one moment?" said he.

"Certainly," replied the unwelcome visitor.

Mr. Winkle ran hastily up stairs, and with a trembling hand opened the bag. There was the coat in its usual place, but exhibiting, on a close inspection, evident tokens of having been worn on the preceding night.

"It must be so," said Mr. Winkle, letting the coat fall from his hands. "I took too much wine after dinner, and have a very vague recollection of walking about the streets, and smoking a cigar afterwards. The fact is I was very drunk. I must have changed my coat, gone somewhere, and insulted somebody, — I have no doubt of it, — and this message is the terrible consequence." Saying which, Mr. Winkle retraced his steps in the direction of the coffee-room, with the gloomy and dreadful resolve of accepting the challenge of the warlike Doctor Slammer, and abiding by the worst consequences that might ensue.

To this determination Mr. Winkle was urged by a variety of considerations; the first of which was his reputation with the club. He had always been looked up to as a high authority on all matters of amusement and dexterity, whether offensive, defensive, or inoffensive; and if, on this very first occasion of being put to the test, he shrunk back from the trial, beneath his leader's eye, his name and standing were lost forever. Besides, he remembered to have heard it frequently surmised by the uninitiated in such matters, that, by an understood arrangement between the seconds, the pistols were seldom loaded with ball; and, furthermore, he reflected, that if he applied to Mr. Snodgrass to act as his second, and depicted the danger in glowing terms, that gentleman might possibly communicate the intelligence to Mr.

Pickwick, who would certainly lose no time in transmitting it to the local authorities, and thus prevent the killing or maiming of his follower.

Such were his thoughts when he returned to the coffee-room, and intimated his intention of accepting the doctor's challenge. . . .

That morning's breakfast passed heavily off. Mr. Tupman was not in a condition to rise after the unwonted dissipation of the previous night; Mr. Snodgrass appeared to labor under a poetical depression of spirits; and even Mr. Pickwick evinced an unusual attachment to silence and soda-water. Mr. Winkle eagerly watched his opportunity. It was not long wanting. Mr. Snodgrass proposed a visit to the castle; and, as Mr. Winkle was the only other member of the party disposed to walk, they went out together.

"Snodgrass," said Mr. Winkle when they had turned out of the public street, — "Snodgrass, my dear fellow, can I rely upon your secrecy?" As he said this, he most devoutly and earnestly hoped he could not.

"You can," replied Mr. Snodgrass. "Hear me swear — "

"No, no!" interrupted Winkle, terrified at the idea of his companion's unconsciously pledging himself not to give information. "Don't swear, don't swear, it 's quite unnecessary."

Mr. Snodgrass dropped the hand which he had, in the spirit of poesy, raised towards the clouds as he made the above appeal, and assumed an attitude of attention.

"I want your assistance, my dear fellow, in an affair of honor," said Mr. Winkle.

"You shall have it," replied Mr. Snodgrass, clasping his friend's hand.

"With a doctor, — Doctor Slammer of the Ninety-seventh," — said Mr. Winkle, wishing to make the matter appear as solemn as possible: "an affair with an officer, seconded by another officer, at sunset this evening, in a lonely field beyond Fort Pitt."

"I will attend you," said Mr. Snodgrass.

He was astonished, but by no means dismayed. It is extraordinary how cool any party but the principal can be in such cases. Mr. Winkle had forgotten this. He had judged of his friend's feelings by his own.

"The consequences may be dreadful," said Mr. Winkle.

"I hope not," said Mr. Snodgrass.

"The doctor, I believe, is a very good shot," said Mr. Winkle.

"Most of these military men are," observed Mr. Snodgrass calmly; "but so are you; a'n't you?"

Mr. Winkle replied in the affirmative; and, perceiving that he had not alarmed his companion sufficiently, changed his ground.

"Snodgrass," he said in a voice tremulous with emotion, "if I fall, you will find in a packet which I shall place in your hands a note for my — for my father."

This attack was a failure also. Mr. Snodgrass was affected; but he undertook the delivery of the note as readily as if he had been a two-penny postman.

"If I fall," said Mr. Winkle, "or, if the doctor falls, you, my dear friend, will be tried as an accessory before the fact. Shall I involve my friend in transportation, — possibly for life!"

Mr. Snodgrass winced a little at this; but his heroism was invincible. "In the cause of friendship," he fervently exclaimed, "I would brave all dangers."

How Mr. Winkle cursed his companion's devoted friendship internally, as they walked silently along, side by side, for some minutes, each immersed in his own meditations! The morning was wearing away: he grew desperate.

"Snodgrass," he said, stopping suddenly, "do not let me be balked in this matter; do not give information to the local authorities; do *not* obtain the assistance of several peace-officers to take either me, or Doctor Slammer of the Ninety-seventh Regiment, at present quartered in Chatham Barracks, into custody, and thus prevent this duel, — I say, do *not*."

Mr. Snodgrass seized his friend's hand warmly, as he enthusiastically replied, "Not for worlds!"

A thrill passed over Mr. Winkle's frame, as the conviction that he had nothing to hope from his friend's fears, and that he was destined to become an animated target, rushed forcibly upon him. . . .

It was a dull and heavy evening when they again sallied forth on their awkward errand. Mr. Winkle was muffled up in a huge cloak to escape observation; and Mr. Snodgrass bore under his the instruments of destruction. . . .

"We are in excellent time," said Mr. Snodgrass as they climbed the fence of the first field: "the sun is just going down." Mr. Winkle looked up at the declining orb, and painfully thought of the probability of his "going down" himself, before long.

"There 's the officer," exclaimed Mr. Winkle, after a few minutes' walking.

"Where?" said Mr. Snodgrass.

"There, — the gentleman in the blue cloak." Mr. Snodgrass looked in the direction indicated by the forefinger of his friend, and observed a figure muffled up as he had described. The officer evinced his consciousness of their presence by slightly beckoning with his hand; and the two friends followed him at a little distance as he walked away. . . .[He] turned suddenly from the path; and after climbing a paling, and scaling a hedge, entered a secluded field. Two gentlemen were waiting in it: one was a little fat man with black hair; and the other — a portly personage in a braided surtout — was sitting with perfect equanimity on a camp-stool.

"The other party, and a surgeon, I suppose," said Mr. Snodgrass; "take a drop of brandy." Mr. Winkle seized the wicker bottle which his friend proffered, and took a lengthened pull at the exhilarating liquid.

"My friend, sir, Mr. Snodgrass," said Mr. Winkle, as the officer approached. Doctor Slammer's friend bowed, and produced a case similar to that which Mr. Snodgrass carried.

"We have nothing further to say, sir, I think," he coldly remarked, as he opened the case: "an apology has been resolutely declined."

"Nothing, sir," said Mr. Snodgrass, who began to feel rather uncomfortable himself. . . .

"We may place our men, then, I think," observed the officer, with as much indifference as if the principals were chess-men, and the seconds players.

"I think we may," replied Mr. Snodgrass, who would have assented to any proposition, because he knew nothing about the matter. The officer crossed to Dr. Slammer, and Mr. Snodgrass went up to Mr. Winkle.

"It 's all ready," he said, offering the pistol. "Give me your cloak."

"You have got the packet, my dear fellow?" said poor Winkle.

"All right," said Mr. Snodgrass. "Be steady, and wing him." . . .

Mr. Winkle was always remarkable for extreme humanity. It is conjectured that his unwillingness to hurt a fellow-creature intentionally was the cause of his shutting his eyes when he arrived at the fatal spot; and that the circumstance of his eyes being closed prevented his observing the very extraordinary and unaccountable demeanor of Doctor Slammer. That gentleman started, stared, retreated, rubbed his eyes, stared again, and finally shouted, "Stop, stop!"

"What 's all this?" said Doctor Slammer, as his friend and Mr. Snodgrass came running up. "That 's not the man."

"Not the man!" said Doctor Slammer's second.

"Not the man!" said Mr. Snodgrass.

"Not the man!" said the gentleman with the camp-stool in his hand.

"Certainly not," replied the little doctor. "That 's not the person who insulted me last night." . . .

Now, Mr. Winkle had opened his eyes, and his ears too, when he heard his adversary call out for a cessation of hostilities; and perceiving, by what he had afterwards said, that there was, beyond all question, some mistake in the matter, he at once foresaw the increase of reputation he should inevitably acquire by concealing the real motive for his coming out: he therefore stepped boldly forward, and said:—

"I am not the person. I know it."

"Then, that," said the man with the camp-stool, "is an affront to Doctor Slammer, and a sufficient reason for proceeding immediately."

"Pray, be quiet, Payne!" said the doctor's second. "Why did you not communicate this fact to me this morning, sir?"

"To be sure, to be sure!" said the man with the camp-stool indignantly.

"I entreat you to be quiet, Payne," said the other. "May I repeat my question, sir?"

"Because, sir," replied Mr. Winkle, who had time to deliberate upon his answer,—"because, sir, you described an intoxicated and ungentlemanly person as wearing a coat which I have the honor, not only to wear, but to have invented,—the proposed uniform, sir, of the Pickwick Club in London. The honor of that uniform I feel bound to maintain; and I therefore, without inquiry, accepted the challenge which you offered me."

"My dear sir," said the good-humored little doctor, advancing with extended hand, "I honor your gallantry. Permit me to say, sir, that I highly admire your conduct, and extremely regret having caused you the inconvenience of this meeting, to no purpose."

"I beg you won't mention it, sir," said Mr. Winkle.

"I shall feel proud of your acquaintance, sir," said the little doctor.

"It will afford me the greatest pleasure to know you, sir," replied Mr. Winkle. Thereupon, the doctor and Mr. Winkle shook hands; and then Mr. Winkle and Lieutenant Tappleton (the doctor's second); and then Mr. Winkle and the man with the camp-stool; and, finally, Mr. Winkle and Mr. Snodgrass,—the last-named gentleman in an excess of admiration at the noble conduct of his heroic friend.

"I think we may adjourn," said Lieutenant Tappleton.

"Certainly," added the doctor. . . .

The two seconds adjusted the cases; and the whole party left the ground in a much more lively manner than they had proceeded to it.

III Before Mr. Winkle and his second, Mr. Snodgrass, had returned, Mr. Pickwick had made a new acquaintance, known as Dismal Jemmy, who was entertaining the whole party at dinner with The Stroller's Tale, when Dr. Slammer and his military friends came in, on the invitation of Mr. Winkle, and discovering Mr. Tupman and Mr. Jingle, came near precipitating a fresh quarrel. Mr. Jingle proved to be a cheap actor, and disappeared for a short time from the scene.

IV The next day there was a military review to which Mr. Pickwick and his companions repaired. But they got very much in the way and were greatly relieved when rescued by a stout gentleman in top boots who already had a slight acquaintance with Mr. Tupman. This gentleman, Mr. Wardle, had driven to the ground in his barouche with his sister, Miss Rachael Wardle, a spinster, and his two daughters, Isabella and Emily. He had a goodly hamper of provisions, and was attended by Joe, a fat boy with inordinate powers of sleep. In the course of the review and the eating and drinking which went on, the two parties came to be on the best of terms.

V On the day following the review, the Pickwickians set out for Manor Farm at Dingley Dell by invitation of Mr. Wardle. Winkle was to ride, the other three to drive a chaise. At an early hour, the carriage was brought to the door.

It was a curious little green box on four wheels, with a low place like a wine-bin for two behind, and an elevated perch for one in front, drawn by an immense brown horse, displaying great symmetry of bone. An hostler stood near it, holding by the bridle another immense horse — apparently a near relative of the animal in the chaise — ready saddled for Mr. Winkle.

"Bless my soul!" said Mr. Pickwick, as they stood upon the pavement while the coats were being put in, — "bless my soul! who 's to drive? I never thought of that!"

"Oh! you, of course," said Mr. Tupman.

"Of course," said Mr. Snodgrass.

"I!" exclaimed Mr. Pickwick.

"Not the slightest fear, sir," interposed the hostler. "Warrant him quiet, sir, a hinfant in arms might drive him."

"He don't shy; does he?" inquired Mr. Pickwick.

"Shy, sir? He would n't shy if he was to meet a vaggin-load of monkeys with their tails burnt off."

The last recommendation was indisputable. Mr. Tupman and Mr. Snodgrass got into the bin; Mr. Pickwick ascended to his perch, and deposited his feet on a floor-clothed shelf erected beneath it for that purpose.

"Now, Shiny Villiam," said the hostler to the deputy hostler, "give the gen'lm'n the ribbins." "Shiny Villiam"—so called, probably, from his sleek hair and oily countenance—placed the reins in Mr. Pickwick's left hand; and the upper hostler thrust a whip into his right.

"Woo!" cried Mr. Pickwick, as the tall quadruped evinced a decided inclination to back into the coffee-room window.

"Wo—o!" echoed Mr. Tupman and Mr. Snodgrass from the bin. "Only his playfulness, gen'lm'n," said the head hostler encouragingly; "jist kitch hold on him, Villiam." The deputy restrained the animal's impetuosity, and the principal ran to assist Mr. Winkle in mounting.

"T' other side, sir, if you please."

"Blowed if the gen'lm'n worn't a gettin' up on the wrong side!" whispered a grinning post-boy to the inexpressibly gratified waiter.

Mr. Winkle, thus instructed, climbed into his saddle with about as much difficulty as he would have experienced in getting up the side of a first-rate man-of-war.

"All right?" inquired Mr. Pickwick, with an inward presentiment that it was all wrong.

"All right!" replied Mr. Winkle faintly.

"Let 'em go!" cried the hostler, "hold him in, sir;" and away went the chaise and the saddle-horse, with Mr. Pickwick on the box of the one, and Mr. Winkle on the back of the other, to the delight and gratification of the whole inn-yard.

"What makes him go sideways?" said Mr. Snodgrass in the bin to Mr. Winkle in the saddle.

"I can't imagine," replied Mr. Winkle. His horse was going up the street in the most mysterious manner,—side first, with his head towards one side of the way, and his tail to the other.

Mr. Pickwick had no leisure to observe either this or any other particular; the whole of his faculties being concentrated in the management of the animal attached to the chaise, who displayed various peculiarities highly interesting to a bystander, but by no means equally amusing to any one seated behind him. Besides constantly jerking his head up in a very unpleasant and uncomfortable manner, and tugging at the reins to an extent which rendered it a matter of great difficulty for Mr. Pickwick to hold them, he had a singular propensity for darting suddenly, every now and then, to the side of the road, then stopping short, and then rushing forward for some minutes, at a speed which it was wholly impossible to control.

"What *can* he mean by this?" said Mr. Snodgrass, when the horse had executed this manœuvre for the twentieth time.

"I don't know," replied Mr. Tupman; "it *looks* very like shying, don't it?" Mr. Snodgrass was about to reply, when he was interrupted by a shout from Mr. Pickwick.

"Woo!" said that gentleman. "I have dropped my whip."

"Winkle," cried Mr. Snodgrass, as the equestrian came trotting up on the tall horse, with his hat over his ears, and shaking all over, as if he would shake to pieces with the violence of the exercise,—"pick up the whip; there 's a good fellow." Mr. Winkle pulled at the bridle of the tall horse till he was black in the face; and having, at length, succeeded in stopping him, dismounted, handed the whip to Mr. Pickwick, and, grasping the reins, prepared to remount.

Now, whether the tall horse, in the natural playfulness of his disposition, was desirous of having a little innocent recreation with Mr. Winkle, or whether it occurred to him that he could perform the journey as much to his own satisfaction without a rider as with one, are points upon which, of course, we can arrive at no definite and distinct conclusion. By whatever motives the animal was actuated, certain it is, that Mr. Winkle had no sooner touched the reins than he slipped them over his head, and darted backwards to their full length.

"Poor fellow!" said Mr. Winkle soothingly, "poor fellow, good old horse!" The "poor fellow" was proof against flattery: the more Mr. Winkle tried to get nearer him, the more he sidled away; and, notwithstanding all kinds of coaxing and wheedling, there were Mr. Winkle and the horse going round and round each other for ten minutes, at the end of which time each was at precisely the same distance from the other as when they first commenced,—an unsatisfactory sort of thing under any circumstances, but particularly so in a lonely road, where no assistance can be procured.

"What am I to do?" shouted Mr. Winkle, after the dodging had been prolonged for a considerable time. "What am I to do? I can't get on him!"

"You had better lead him till we come to a turnpike," replied Mr. Pickwick from the chaise.

"But he won't come," roared Mr. Winkle. "Do come and hold him."

Mr. Pickwick was the very personation of kindness and humanity; he threw the reins on the horse's back, and, having descended from his seat, carefully drew the chaise into the hedge, lest any thing should come along the road, and stepped back to the assistance of his distressed companion, leaving Mr. Tupman and Mr. Snodgrass in the vehicle.

The horse no sooner beheld Mr. Pickwick advancing towards him, with the chaise-whip in his hand, than he exchanged the rotary motion in which he had previously indulged, for a retrograde movement, of so very determined a character, that it at once drew Mr. Winkle, who was still at the end of the bridle, at a rather quicker rate than fast walking, in the direction from which they had just come. Mr. Pickwick ran to his assistance; but, the faster Mr. Pickwick ran forward, the faster the horse ran backward. There was a great scraping of feet, and kicking up of the dust; and at last Mr. Winkle, his arms being nearly pulled out of their sockets, fairly let go his hold. The horse paused, stared, shook his head, turned round, and quietly trotted home to Rochester, leaving Mr. Winkle and Mr. Pickwick gazing on each other with countenances of blank dismay. A rattling noise at a little distance attracted their attention. They looked up.

"Bless my soul!" exclaimed the agonized Mr. Pickwick: "there 's the other horse running away!"

It was but too true. The animal was startled by the noise, and the reins were on his back. The result may be guessed. He tore off with the four-wheeled chaise behind him, and Mr. Tupman and Mr. Snodgrass in the four-wheeled chaise. The heat was a short one. Mr. Tupman threw himself into the hedge; Mr. Snodgrass followed his example; the horse dashed the four-wheeled chaise against a wooden bridge, separated the wheels from the body, and finally stood stock still to gaze upon the ruin he had made.

After extricating themselves, the party are compelled to walk and to lead the horse; and it is not until late in the afternoon that they reach Manor Farm, tired, dusty, and foot-sore;

VI A company of neighbors had been invited to meet the guests, and the evening was passed in getting acquainted, playing cards, and listening to two recitations from an old gentleman present, one a poem, The Ivy Green, the other a tale, The Convict's Return.

VII After a good night's rest, Mr. Wardle takes the party of four out for rook-shooting before breakfast, as a special compliment to Mr. Winkle, the sportsman, who covers himself with confusion, for he peppers Mr. Tupman instead of the rooks.

The susceptible Tupman, meanwhile, has been shot by another archer whose second arrow was aimed at the heart of Miss Rachael Wardle. He remained at Dingley Dell on the excuse of his gun-shot wounds, while the rest went to Muggleton to witness a cricket match. Here Mr. Jingle turned up again, having, in some mysterious fashion, got into the good graces of the cricketers, and in the supper which followed the game, he corkscrewed himself into the Wardle party.

VIII In the absence of the rest of the party at Muggleton, Tracy Tupman made rapid approaches to the heart of Rachael Wardle; had indeed nearly entered the citadel, when the two were thrown into consternation by discovering that they were discovered by Joe, the Fat Boy, who, however, looked so absolutely vacant as he announced that supper was ready, as to deceive this elect couple. It was late in the evening before Mr. Wardle and the Pickwickians returned, Mr. Jingle with them, all somewhat discomposed by their hilarious feasting, but Mr. Jingle in full possession of all his faculties. This lively visitor at once ingratiated himself by his anecdotes and his good nature, to the great alarm of Mr. Tupman, who was seized with vague fears as to what he might do. Mr. Jingle had his wits about him. Early the next morning, he overheard Joe revealing the secret of the lovers to old Mrs. Wardle, who was terribly indignant. He laid his plans accordingly; getting Rachael by herself he disclosed Joe's perfidy, and then in a series of explosive sentences gave her to understand that Tupman was really making love to her niece Emily. He offered to prove it, and the price of his proof was to be the substitution of himself in the affections of Miss Rachael. That done, he repaired to Tupman and made him believe that Miss Rachael wished him to deceive the rest by pretending to make love to Emily. This the wretched Tupman did to the best of his ability, to the decided estrangement of the affections of Miss Rachael Wardle, who at once transferred them to the artful Jingle.

IX This farce was kept up for three or four days, and then came the climax. Jingle eloped with Rachael Wardle in a post chaise. Their flight was quickly made known by one of the household servants, and Mr. Wardle and Mr. Pickwick set off in pursuit in a gig. The chase was an exciting one; it lasted through the night, and came to an end only by the most unfortunate upset of the pursuers' gig, which went all to pieces, while Mr. Jingle dashed forward derisively.

X The house at which Mr. Jingle put up was the White Hart Inn, High Street, Borough, and early in the morning the next scene disclosed the yard of the inn, with a new and important personage in the foreground. This was Sam Weller, the boots of the inn. Sam carries Mr. Jingle's boots to him, and being asked where Doctors' Commons is, at once divines that the owner of the boots wants to procure a marriage-license.

"My father," said Sam in reply to a question, "vos a coachman. A vidower he vos, and fat enough for anything, — uncommon fat, to be sure! His missus dies, and leaves him four hundred pound. Down he goes to the Commons, to see the lawyer and draw the blunt, — wery smart, top-boots on, nosegay in his button-hole, broad-brimmed tile, green shawl, — quite the gen'lm'n. Goes through the archvay, thinking how he should inwest the money; up comes the touter, touches his hat, — 'License, sir, license?' — 'What 's that?' says my father. 'License, sir,' says he. 'What license?' says my father. 'Marriage-license,' says the touter. 'Dash my veskit!' says my father, 'I never thought o' that.' — 'I think you wants one, sir,' says the touter. My father pulls up, and thinks a bit. 'No,' says he, 'damme, I 'm too old; b'sides, I 'm a many sizes too large,' says he. 'Not a bit on it, sir!' says the touter. 'Think not?' says my father. 'I 'm sure not,' says he. 'We married a gen'lm'n twice your size last Monday.' — 'Did you, though?' says my father. 'To be sure ve did!' says the touter: 'you 're a babby to him. This vay, sir, — this vay!' And, sure enough, my father walks arter him, like a tame monkey behind a horgan, into a little back-office vere a feller sat among dirty papers and tin boxes, making believe he was busy. 'Pray take a seat vile I makes out the affidavit, sir,' says the lawyer. 'Thankee, sir!' says my father; and down he sat, and stared vith all his eyes, and his mouth vide open, at the names on the boxes. 'What 's your name, sir?' says the lawyer. 'Tony Weller,' says my father. 'Parish?' says the lawyer. 'Belle Savage,' says my father; for he stopped there ven he drove up; and he know'd nothing about parishes, he did n't. 'And what 's the lady's name?' says the lawyer. My father was struck all of a heap. 'Bless'd if I know!' says he. 'Not know!' says the lawyer. 'No more nor you,' says my father. 'Can't I put that in arterwards?' — 'Impossible!' says the lawyer. 'Wery well,' says my father, after he 'd thought a moment, 'put down Mrs. Clarke.' — 'What Clarke?' says the lawyer, dipping his pen in the ink. 'Susan Clarke, Markis o' Granby, Dorking,' says my father: 'she 'll have me, if I ask her, I des-say. I never said nothing to her; but she 'll have me, I know.' The license was made out, and she *did* have him; and, what 's more, she 's got him now; and *I* never had any of the four hundred pound, worse luck! Beg your pardon, sir," said Sam when he had concluded, "but, vhen I gets on this here grievance, I runs on like a new barrow vith the vheel greased."

To Sam appeared Mr. Perker, a lawyer of Gray's Inn, with Pickwick and Wardle, the three being on the search for Jingle. Sam showed them the way, and they came upon Miss Wardle, just as her Jingle returned. A violent scene followed, which was brought to an end by the diplomacy of the lawyer, who succeeded in getting rid of Jingle by the payment of a round sum out of the pocket of Mr. Wardle; whereupon Wardle, Pickwick, and the disconsolate Rachael returned to Dingley Dell.

XI Tracy Tupman could not bear his bitter disappointment, and so stole away from Dingley Dell, but left behind him tolerably clear advice as to his whereabouts. So Pickwick and his two companions also took leave openly, and followed Tupman to his retreat at the Leather Bottle, Cobham, Kent. It was here that Pickwick made his notable antiquarian discovery, which caused a great sensation in the Pickwick Club when it was disclosed and discussed; for the party all returned now for a short stay in London.

XII Mr. Pickwick's lodgings were with a certain widow, Mrs. Bardell, and he had conceived the idea that he could greatly increase his comfort by attaching to himself a body servant. Remembering Sam Weller, the boots of the White Hart, he satisfied himself that Sam was the man for him, and despatched a message to him by Mrs. Bardell's small son. While the little boy was gone, he broached the matter to Mrs. Bardell, but so circumspectly that before he could make his meaning absolutely clear, Mrs. Bardell had misinterpreted her lodger's meaning into a proposal of marriage. In her agitation, she fell on Mr. Pickwick's neck and fainted. It was a most inopportune moment, for just then the door opened, and Master Bardell, Mr. Tupman, Mr. Snodgrass, and Mr. Winkle entered, to the embarrassment of the last three. After them came shortly Sam Weller, and arrangements were satisfactorily made, by which he became Mr. Pickwick's man servant.

XIII The next journey of the Pickwickians was to Eatanswill, whither they had been invited by Mr. Perker, the agent of one of the candidates in an approaching parliamentary election. They found the town torn in two by the opposing parties, with their candidates and their party papers, the Gazette and the Independent. Mr. Pott was the editor of the Gazette, the organ of Mr. Perker's candidate, and acted as host to the Pickwickians, who found themselves involved in the fine fury of an election contest.

XIV All of the Pickwick party could not be housed at Mr. Pott's, and they made their headquarters at the Peacock,

where they listened to the Bagman's story; but the next day they
XV were the attendants upon a reception given by Mrs. Leo Hunter, whither they went in costume, — Mr. Tupman as a brigand, Mr. Snodgrass as a troubadour, Mr. Winkle as a sportsman, or possibly postman, and Mr. Pickwick in his own classic gaiters and spectacles. Here, to their amazement, they encountered the irrepressible Jingle, figuring as Mr. Charles Fitz Marshall. Jingle, not quite ready for explanation, disappeared, and Pickwick, full of moral ardor, set off for his last known abiding-place, Bury St. Edmunds, accompanied by Sam.

XVI At the Angel in Bury, Sam managed to fall in with Jingle's servant, one Job Trotter, and to extract from him the information that his master was that night to elope with a young lady from a neighboring boarding-school. Mr. Pickwick at once resolved to thwart this nefarious design, and proceeded in the dark of night to the spot, to act as a private detective. Unhappily, he was found, and not Alfred Jingle, and was released by the incensed mistress of the boarding-school only when Mr. Wardle, who was known to her, turned up and vouched for his friend. The wrath of Mr. Pickwick and Sam when they found they had been cozened by Jingle and Job was profound.

XVII Mr. Pickwick had an attack of rheumatism in consequence of this adventure, and amused himself with editing a story of Sam's entitled The Parish Clerk. He wished his companions to
XVIII rejoin him, and they came accordingly, but not without first undergoing some mortification of their own, due to Mr. Pott's green jealousy. All these mishaps, however, were thrown into the shade by the reception of a missive addressed to Mr. Pickwick by Messrs. Dodson & Fogg of London, attorneys, in behalf of Mrs. Martha Bardell, who brought an action for breach of promise.

XIX Such serious business could not interfere with pleasure, so the next day they all went off to a shooting-party. Mr. Pickwick, however, was so stiff with rheumatism, that he could not have gone, except by a happy thought which produced a wheelbarrow and made that his vehicle, with Sam to wheel it.

The gamekeeper having been coaxed and feed, and having, moreover, eased his mind by "punching" the head of the inventive youth who had first suggested the use of the machine, Mr. Pickwick was placed in it, and off the party set, — Wardle and the long gamekeeper leading the way; and Mr. Pickwick in the barrow, propelled by Sam, bringing up the rear.

"Stop, Sam!" said Mr. Pickwick, when they had got half across the first field.

"What 's the matter now?" said Wardle.

"I won't suffer this barrow to be moved another step," said Mr. Pickwick resolutely, "unless Winkle carries that gun of his in a different manner."

"How *am* I to carry it?" said the wretched Winkle.

"Carry it with the muzzle of it to the ground," replied Mr. Pickwick.

"It 's so unsportsman-like," reasoned Winkle.

"I don't care whether it 's unsportsman-like, or not," replied Mr. Pickwick. "I am not going to be shot in a wheelbarrow, for the sake of appearances, to please anybody."

"I know the gentleman 'll put that 'ere charge into somebody afore he 's done," growled the long man.

"Well, well, I don't mind," said poor Winkle, turning his gun-stock uppermost: "there!"

"Any thin' for a quiet life," said Mr. Weller; and on they went again.

"Stop!" said Mr. Pickwick after they had gone a few yards farther.

"What now?" said Wardle.

"That gun of Tupman's is not safe: I know it is n't!" said Mr. Pickwick.

"Eh? What! not safe?" said Mr. Tupman in a tone of great alarm.

"Not as you are carrying it," said Mr. Pickwick. "I am very sorry to make any further objections; but I cannot consent to go on unless you carry it as Winkle does his."

"I think you had better, sir," said the long gamekeeper, "or you 're quite as likely to lodge the charge into your own vestcoat as in anybody else's."

Mr. Tupman, with the most obliging haste, placed his piece in the position required, and the party moved on again; the two amateurs marching with reversed arms, like a couple of privates at a royal funeral.

The dogs came suddenly to a dead stop; and the party, advancing stealthily a single pace, stopped too.

"What 's the matter with the dogs' legs?" whispered Mr. Winkle. "How queer they 're standing!"

"Hush! can 't you?" replied Wardle softly. "Don't you see they 're making a point?"

"Making a point!" said Mr. Winkle, staring about him, as if he expected to discover some particular beauty in the landscape, which the sagacious animals were calling special attention to,—"making a point! What are they pointing at?"

"Keep your eyes open," said Wardle, not heeding the question in the excitement of the moment. "Now, then!"

There was a sharp whirring noise, that made Mr. Winkle start back as if he had been shot himself. Bang, bang, went a couple of guns. The smoke swept quickly away over the field, and curled into the air.

"Where are they?" said Mr. Winkle in a state of the highest excitement, turning round and round in all directions, — "where are they? Tell me when to fire. Where are they? where are they?"

"Where are they?" said Wardle, taking up a brace of birds which the dogs had deposited at his feet, — "where are they? Why, here they are."

"No, no! I mean the others," said the bewildered Winkle.

"Far enough off by this time," replied Wardle, coolly reloading his gun.

"We shall very likely be up with another covey in five minutes," said the long gamekeeper. "If the gentleman begins to fire now, perhaps he 'll just get the shot out of the barrel by the time they rise."

"Ha, ha, ha!" roared Mr. Weller.

"Sam," said Mr. Pickwick, compassionating his follower's confusion and embarrassment.

"Sir."

"Don't laugh."

"Certainly not, sir." So, by way of indemnification, Mr. Weller contorted his features from behind the wheelbarrow, for the exclusive amusement of the boy with the leggings, who thereupon burst into a boisterous laugh, and was summarily cuffed by the long gamekeeper, who wanted a pretext for turning round to hide his own merriment.

"Bravo, old fellow!" said Wardle to Mr. Tupman: "you fired that time, at all events."

"Oh, yes!" replied Mr. Tupman with conscious pride. "I let it off."

"Well done. You'll hit something next time if you look sharp. Very easy; ain't it?"

"Yes, it 's very easy," said Mr. Tupman. "How it hurts one's shoulder, though! It nearly knocked me backwards. I had no idea these small fire-arms kicked so."

"Ah!" said the old gentleman, smiling. "You'll get used to it in time. Now, then — all ready, all right with the barrow there?"

"All right, sir," replied Mr. Weller.

"Come along, then."

"Hold hard, sir," said Sam, raising the barrow.

"Ay, ay!" replied Mr. Pickwick; and on they went as briskly as need be.

"Keep that barrow back, now," cried Wardle, when it had been hoisted over a stile into another field, and Mr. Pickwick had been deposited in it once more.

"All right, sir," replied Mr. Weller, pausing.

"Now, Winkle," said the old gentleman, "follow me softly, and don't be too late this time."

"Never fear," said Mr. Winkle. "Are they pointing?"

"No, no! not now. Quietly now, quietly." On they crept, and very quietly they would have advanced, if Mr. Winkle, in the performance of some very intricate evolutions with his gun, had not accidentally fired, at the most critical moment, over the boy's head, exactly in the very spot where the tall man's brain would have been, had he been there instead.

"Why, what on earth did you do that for?" said old Wardle, as the birds flew unharmed away.

"I never saw such a gun in my life!" replied poor Winkle, looking at the lock, as if that would do any good. "It goes off of its own accord. It *will* do it."

"Will do it!" echoed Wardle, with something of irritation in his manner. "I wish it would kill something of its own accord."

"It 'll do that afore long, sir," observed the tall man in a low, prophetic voice.

"What do you mean by that observation, sir?" inquired Mr. Winkle angrily.

"Never mind, sir, never mind," replied the long gamekeeper. "I 've no family myself, sir; and this here boy's mother will get something handsome from Sir Geoffrey, if he 's killed on his land. Load again, sir; load again."

"Take away his gun!" cried Mr. Pickwick from the barrow, horror-stricken at the long man's dark insinuations. "Take away his gun! do you hear, somebody?"

Nobody, however, volunteered to obey the command; and Mr. Winkle, after darting a rebellious glance at Mr. Pickwick, reloaded his gun, and proceeded onwards with the rest.

We are bound, on the authority of Mr. Pickwick, to state that Mr. Tupman's mode of proceeding evinced far more of prudence and deliberation than that adopted by Mr. Winkle. . . .

With the quickness and penetration of a man of genius, he had at once observed that the two great points to be attained, were first to discharge his piece without injury to himself, and, secondly, to do so without danger to the bystanders. Obviously the best thing to do, after surmounting the difficulty of firing at all, was to shut his eyes firmly, and fire into the air.

On one occasion, after performing this feat, Mr. Tupman, on opening his eyes, beheld a plump partridge in the very act of falling wounded to the ground. He was just on the point of congratulating Wardle on his invariable success, when that gentleman advanced towards him, and grasped him warmly by the hand.

"Tupman," said the old gentleman, "you singled out that particular bird?"

"No," said Mr. Tupman, — "no."

"You did," said Wardle. "I saw you do it; I observed you pick him out; I noticed you as you raised your piece to take aim: and I will say this, that the best shot in existence could not have done it more beautifully. You are an older hand at this than I thought you, Tupman; you have been out before."

It was in vain for Mr. Tupman to protest, with a smile of self-denial, that he never had. The very smile was taken as evidence to the contrary; and, from that time forth, his reputation was established. It is not the only reputation that has been acquired as easily; nor are such fortunate circumstances confined to partridge-shooting.

Meanwhile, Mr. Winkle flashed and blazed and smoked away without producing any material results worthy of being noted down; sometimes expending his charge in mid-air, and at others sending it skimming along so near the surface of the ground as to place the lives of the two dogs on a rather uncertain and precarious tenure. As a display of fancy shooting, it was extremely varied and curious; as an exhibition of firing with any precise object, it was, upon the whole, perhaps a failure. . . .

"Well," said Wardle, walking up to the side of the barrow, and wiping the streams of perspiration from his jolly red face; "smoking day, is n't it?"

"It is, indeed," replied Mr. Pickwick. "The sun is tremendously hot, even to me. I don't know how you must feel it."

"Why," said the old gentleman, "pretty hot. It 's past twelve, though. You see that green hill there?"

"Certainly."

"That 's the place where we are to lunch; and, by Jove! there 's the boy with the basket, punctual as clock-work."

It chanced that after dinner Mr. Pickwick fell asleep in his barrow, and the rest left him temporarily for more hunting. When they were gone the owner of the place, highly irate at the intrusion of a party, came upon him, and at his orders Mr. Pickwick, still asleep, was trundled into the village pound. He was relieved from his most unfortunate predicament by the timely arrival of Mr. Wardle and Sam.

XX The business of Mrs. Bardell's suit could not longer be postponed, and Mr. Pickwick, accompanied by Sam, called at the office of Dodson & Fogg, which he left presently in a high state of indignation because of the treatment he received. His sober second thought took him where his first should have taken him, to Mr. Perker's, and on the way he fell in with an estimable old stage driver, Mr. Tony Weller, own father to Sam.

XXI Mr. Pickwick does not at first find Mr. Perker, but is hospitably entertained by Perker's clerks at a tavern, where he hears The Old Man's Tale about the Queer Client.

XXII Mr. Weller, senior, drove the Ipswich coach, and Mr. Pickwick and Sam were his passengers shortly after, along with Mr. Peter Magnus, whose errand was to make a proposal to a lady of the neighborhood. The two dined together. On being left alone in his chamber afterward, Mr. Pickwick remembered that he had left his watch below, and went after it. So tortuous were the passages it was no wonder that on returning he missed his way.

A dozen times did he softly turn the handle of some bedroom door which resembled his own, when a gruff cry from within of "Who the devil's that?" or "What do you want here?" caused him to steal away, on tiptoe, with a perfectly marvelous celerity. He was reduced to the verge of despair, when an open door attracted his attention. He peeped in—right at last! There were the two beds, whose situation he perfectly remembered, and the fire still burning. His candle, not a long one when he first received it, had flickered away in the draughts of air through which he had passed, and sunk into the socket just as he closed the door after him. "No matter," said Mr. Pickwick: "I can undress myself just as well by the light of the fire."

The bedsteads stood one on each side of the door; and on the inner side of each was a little path, terminating in a rush-bottomed chair, just wide enough to admit of a person's getting into or out of bed on that side, if he or she thought proper. Having carefully drawn the curtains of his bed on the outside, Mr. Pickwick sat down on the rush-bottomed chair, and leisurely divested himself of his shoes and gaiters. He then took off and folded up his coat, waistcoat, and neckcloth, and, slowly drawing on his tasselled night-cap, secured it firmly on his head by tying beneath his chin the strings which he had always attached to that article of dress. It was at this moment that the absurdity of his recent bewilderment struck upon his mind; and, throwing himself back in the rush-bottomed chair, Mr. Pickwick laughed to himself so heartily, that it would have been quite delightful to any man of well-constituted mind to have watched the smiles which expanded his amiable features as they shone forth from beneath the night-cap.

"It is the best idea," said Mr. Pickwick to himself, smiling till he almost cracked the night-cap strings, — "it is the best idea, my losing myself in this place, and wandering about those staircases, that I ever heard of. Droll, droll, very droll!" Here Mr. Pickwick smiled again, a broader smile than before, and was about to continue the process of undressing, in the best possible humor, when he was suddenly stopped by a most unexpected interruption; to wit, the entrance into the room of some person with a candle, who, after locking the door, advanced to the dressing-table, and set down the light upon it.

The smile that played on Mr. Pickwick's features was instantaneously lost in a look of the most unbounded and wonder-stricken surprise. The person, whoever it was, had come in so suddenly, and with so little noise, that Mr. Pickwick had no time to call out, or oppose their entrance. Who could it be? A robber! Some evil-minded person who had seen him come up stairs with a handsome watch in his hand, perhaps. What was he to do!

The only way in which Mr. Pickwick could catch a glimpse of his mysterious visitor, with the least danger of being seen himself, was by creeping on to the bed, and peeping out from between the curtains on the opposite side. To this manœuvre he accordingly resorted. Keeping the curtains carefully closed with his hands, so that nothing more of him could be seen than his face and night-cap, and putting on his spectacles, he mustered up courage and looked out.

Mr. Pickwick almost fainted with horror and dismay. Standing before the dressing-glass was a middle-aged lady in yellow curl-papers, busily engaged in brushing what ladies call their "back hair." However the unconscious middle-aged lady came into that room, it was quite clear that she contemplated remaining there for the night; for she had brought a rushlight and shade with her, which, with praiseworthy precaution against fire, she had stationed in a basin on the floor, where it was glimmering away, like a gigantic lighthouse in a particularly small piece of water.

"Bless my soul," thought Mr. Pickwick, "what a dreadful thing!"

"Hem!" said the old lady; and in went Mr. Pickwick's head with automaton-like rapidity.

"I never met with anything so awful as this!" thought poor Mr. Pickwick, the cold perspiration starting in drops upon his night-cap,—"never! This is fearful!"

It was quite impossible to resist the urgent desire to see what was going forward. So out went Mr. Pickwick's head again. The prospect was worse than before. The middle-aged lady had finished arranging her hair, and carefully enveloped it in a muslin night-cap with a small plaited border; and was gazing pensively on the fire.

"This matter is growing alarming," reasoned Mr. Pickwick with himself. "I can't allow things to go on in this way. By the self-possession of that lady, it 's clear to me that I must have come into the wrong room. If I call out, she 'll alarm the house; but, if I remain here, the consequence will be still more frightful."

Mr. Pickwick, it is quite unnecessary to say, was one of the most modest and delicate-minded of mortals. The very idea of exhibiting his night-cap to a lady overpowered him; but he had tied these confounded strings in a knot, and, do what he would, he could n't get it off. The disclosure must be made. There was only one other way of doing it. He shrunk behind the curtains, and called out very loudly:—

"Ha, hum!"

That the lady started at this unexpected sound was evident by her falling up against the rushlight-shade; that she persuaded herself it must have been the effect of imagination was equally clear; for when Mr. Pickwick, under the impression that she had fainted away, stone-dead, from fright, ventured to peep out again, she was gazing pensively on the fire as before.

"Most extraordinary female this!" thought Mr. Pickwick, popping in again. "Ha, hum!"

These last sounds, so like those in which, as legends inform us, the ferocious giant Blunderbore was in the habit of expressing his opinion that it was time to lay the cloth, were too distinctly audible to be again mistaken for the workings of fancy.

"Gracious Heaven!" said the middle-aged lady, "what 's that!"

"It 's—it 's—only a gentleman, ma'am," said Mr. Pickwick from behind the curtains.

"A gentleman!" said the lady with a terrific scream.

"It 's all over," thought Mr. Pickwick.

"A strange man!" shrieked the lady. Another instant, and the house would be alarmed. Her garments rustled as she rushed towards the door.

"Ma'am," said Mr. Pickwick, thrusting out his head, in the extremity of his desperation,—"ma'am."

Now, although Mr. Pickwick was not actuated by any definite object in putting out his head, it was instantaneously productive of a good effect. The lady, as we have already stated, was near the door. She must pass it to reach the staircase, and she would most undoubtedly have done so by this time, had not the sudden apparition of Mr. Pickwick's night-cap driven her back into the remotest corner of the apartment, where she stood staring wildly at Mr. Pickwick, while Mr. Pickwick, in his turn, stared wildly at her.

"Wretch!" said the lady, covering her eyes with her hands, "what do you want here?"

"Nothing, ma'am, — nothing whatever, ma'am," said Mr. Pickwick earnestly.

"Nothing!" said the lady, looking up.

"Nothing, ma'am, upon my honor," said Mr. Pickwick, nodding his head so energetically, that the tassel of his night-cap danced again. "I am almost ready to sink, ma'am, beneath the confusion of addressing a lady in my night-cap (here the lady hastily snatched off hers); but I can 't get it off, ma'am (here Mr. Pickwick gave it a tremendous tug in proof of the statement). It is evident to me, ma'am, now, that I have mistaken this bedroom for my own. I had not been here five minutes, ma'am, when you suddenly entered it."

"If this improbable story be really true, sir," said the lady, sobbing violently, "you will leave it instantly."

"I will, ma'am, with the greatest pleasure," replied Mr. Pickwick.

"Instantly, sir," said the lady.

"Certainly, ma'am," interposed Mr. Pickwick very quickly, — "certainly, ma'am. I — I — am very sorry, ma'am," said Mr. Pickwick, making his appearance at the bottom of the bed, "to have been the innocent occasion of this alarm and emotion, — deeply sorry, ma'am."

The lady pointed to the door. One excellent quality of Mr. Pickwick's character was beautifully displayed at this moment under the most trying circumstances. Although he had hastily put on his hat over his night-cap, after the manner of the old patrol; although he carried his shoes and gaiters in his hand, and his coat and waistcoat over his arm, — nothing could subdue his native politeness.

"I am exceedingly sorry, ma'am," said Mr. Pickwick, bowing very low.

"If you are, sir, you will at once leave the room," said the lady.

"Immediately, ma'am, — this instant, ma'am," said Mr. Pickwick, opening the door, and dropping both his shoes with a loud crash in so doing.

"I trust, ma'am," resumed Mr. Pickwick, gathering up his shoes, and turning round to bow again, — "I trust, ma'am, that my unblemished character, and the devoted respect I entertain for your sex, will plead as some slight excuse for this" — But, before Mr. Pickwick could conclude the sentence, the lady had thrust him into the passage, and locked and bolted the door behind him. Mr. Pickwick finally encountered Sam Weller, his valet, who led him to his room; but this night-adventure disturbed him considerably.

XXIII By good chance Sam Weller ran against Job Trotter in Ipswich, and made ready to get even with him. Mr. Winkle, Mr. Snodgrass, and Mr. Tupman also came to the ren-
XXIV dezvous, and all would have gone off well, except that Mr. Magnus having been successful in his venture, enthusiastically introduced Mr. Pickwick to the lady of his choice, who proved to be no other than the heroine of the contretemps of the night before.

"Miss Witherfield," said Mr. Magnus, "allow me to introduce my very particular friend, Mr. Pickwick. Mr. Pickwick, I beg to make you known to Miss Witherfield."

The lady was at the upper end of the room; and, as Mr. Pickwick bowed, he took his spectacles from his waistcoat-pocket, and put them on, — a process which he had no sooner gone through, than, uttering an exclamation of surprise, Mr. Pickwick retreated several paces, and the lady, with a half-suppressed scream, hid her face in her hands, and dropped into a chair; whereupon Mr. Peter Magnus was struck motionless on the spot, and gazed from one to the other with a countenance expressive of the extremities of horror and surprise.

This certainly was, to all appearance, very unaccountable behavior: but the fact was, that Mr. Pickwick no sooner put on his spectacles than he at once recognized in the future Mrs. Magnus the lady into whose room he had so unwarrantably intruded on the previous night; and the spectacles had no sooner crossed Mr. Pickwick's nose than the lady at once identified the countenance which she had seen surrounded by all the horrors of a night-cap. So the lady screamed, and Mr. Pickwick started.

"Mr. Pickwick!" exclaimed Mr. Magnus, lost in astonishment, "what is the meaning of this, sir? What is the meaning of it, sir?" added Mr. Magnus, in a threatening and a louder tone.

"Sir," said Mr. Pickwick, somewhat indignant at the very sudden manner in which Mr. Peter Magnus had conjugated him.

self into the imperative mood, "I decline answering that question."

"You decline it, sir?" said Mr. Magnus.

"I do, sir," replied Mr. Pickwick. "I object to saying anything which may compromise that lady, or awaken unpleasant recollections in her breast, without her consent and permission."

"Miss Witherfield," said Mr. Peter Magnus, "do you know this person?"

"Know him!" repeated the middle-aged lady, hesitating.

"Yes, know him, ma'am. I said know him," replied Mr. Magnus with ferocity.

"I have seen him," replied the middle-aged lady.

"Where?" inquired Mr. Magnus,—"where?"

"That," said the middle-aged lady, rising from her seat, and averting her head,—"that I would not reveal for worlds."

"I understand you, ma'am," said Mr. Pickwick, "and respect your delicacy. It shall never be revealed by *me*, depend upon it."

This, of course, makes Mr. Magnus very angry; and he proceeds to work himself into a red-hot, scorching, consuming passion, and indulges freely in threats of a duel. Miss Witherfield, however, contrives to settle matters by informing the mayor that Mr. Pickwick is about to fight a duel, in which Mr. Tupman proposes to act as his second, and that the other party has absconded. The sequel is, that Mr. Pickwick and Mr. Tupman are arrested, and taken before the mayor, George Nupkins, Esquire, a proceeding attended by great legal ceremony.

XXV Mr. Pickwick might have fared hardly at the hands of Mr. Nupkins, if Sam had not made a discovery which he whispered to his master. Captain Fitz Marshall, alias Jingle, together with Job Trotter, had succeeded in making themselves at home with the Nupkins's, as elsewhere, and with the same general matrimonial intentions. An exposure followed, and in the course of it began Sam's own experiences with Mary, the pretty housemaid.

XXVI After this, Mr. Pickwick returned to London to look after his case, and Sam to pick up such valuable information as he could from Mrs. Bardell, and there being an interval of two days
XXVII before the Pickwickians were all to meet at Dingley Dell for the holidays, Sam got leave to visit his father, whom he found in the toils of his second wife, formerly a widow, aided and abetted by the Rev. Mr. Stiggins.

XXVIII Just before Christmas the Pickwickians and Sam set off for Dingley Dell, where the main party was most hospitably received and entertained above stairs, the humbler contingent making himself most agreeable in the servants' quarters.

XXIX Among the stories told this Christmas Eve was that of the Goblins who stole a sexton, named Gabriel Grub.

XXX Christmas Day brought an addition to the party in two medical students, Benjamin Allen, brother to Arabella Allen who was visiting the Wardles and had made inroads upon the heart of Mr. Winkle, and Mr. Allen's friend, Bob Sawyer. They all went skating, where again the unhappy Mr. Winkle was forced to display an accomplishment he did not possess. Mr. Pickwick, in sliding, broke through the ice, but maintained his courage and good cheer, and the next day they all went back to London.

XXXI Mr. Pickwick found himself at once in the toils of the law. The clerks of Messrs. Dodson & Fogg invaded his social domain with subpœnas, and his own lawyer, Mr. Parker, introduced him to the great Sergeant Snubbin, who consented to take his
XXXII case. Meanwhile, *inter leges non cenæ silent*, and Mr. Bob Sawyer invites Mr. Pickwick to supper, with the consequence of bringing into unhappy prominence his own difficulties with his landlady.

XXXIII The day before the trial began was a busy one for Sam Weller, who was kept running back and forth between the George and Vulture, where Mr. Pickwick now put up, and Mr. Perker's office. Sam had leave of absence at last to visit his father, Tony Weller. While waiting for his father at the Blue Boar, he determines to write Mary a letter.

> To ladies and gentlemen who are not in the habit of devoting themselves practically to the science of penmanship, writing a letter is no very easy task, it being always considered necessary in such cases for the writer to recline his head on his left arm, so as to place his eyes as nearly as possible on a level with the paper, and, while glancing sideways at the letters he is constructing, to form with his tongue imaginary characters to correspond. These motions, although unquestionably of the greatest assistance to original composition, retard, in some degree, the progress of the writer; and Sam had unconsciously been a full hour and a half writing words in small text, smearing out wrong letters with his little finger, and putting in new ones, which required going over very often to render them visible through the old blots, when he was roused by the opening of the door and the entrance of his parent.
>
> "Vell, Sammy," said the father, . . . "wot 's that you 're a doin' of, — pursuit of knowledge under difficulties? eh, Sammy?"
>
> "I 've done now," said Sam, with slight embarrassment. "I 've been a writin'."
>
> "So I see," replied Mr. Weller. "Not to any young 'ooman, I hope, Sammy."

"Why, it 's no use a sayin' it ain't," replied Sam. "It 's a walentine."

"A what!" exclaimed Mr. Weller, apparently horror-stricken by the word.

"A walentine," replied Sam.

"Samivel, Samivel," said Mr. Weller in reproachful accents, "I did n't think you 'd ha' done it. Arter the warnin' you 've had o' your father's wicious propensities; arter all I 've said to you upon this here wery subject; arter actiwally seein' and bein' in the company o' your own mother-in-law (vich I should ha' thought wos a moral lesson as no man could ever ha' forgotten to his dyin' day),— I did n't think you 'd ha' done it, Sammy, I did n't think you 'd ha' done it." These reflections were too much for the good old man. He raised Sam's tumbler to his lips, and drank off the contents.

"Wot 's the matter now?" said Sam.

"Nev'r mind, Sammy," replied Mr. Weller. "It 'll be a wery agonizin' trial to me at my time of life; but I 'm pretty tough, that 's vun consolation, as the wery old turkey remarked ven the farmer said he wos afeered he should be obliged to kill him for the London market."

"Wot 'll be a trial?" inquired Sam.

"To see you married, Sammy; to see you a deluded wictim, and thinkin' in your innocence that it 's all wery capital," replied Mr. Weller. "It 's a dreadful trial to a father's feelin's — that 'ere, Sammy."

"Nonsense!" said Sam. "I ain't a goin' to get married, don't you fret yourself about that: I know you 're a judge of these things. Order in your pipe, and I 'll read you the letter — there!"

We cannot distinctly say whether it was the prospect of the pipe, or the consolatory reflection that a fatal disposition to get married ran in the family, and could n't be helped, which calmed Mr. Weller's feelings, and caused his grief to subside. We should be rather disposed to say that the result was attained by combining the two sources of consolation; for he repeated the second in a low tone very frequently, ringing the bell, meanwhile, to order in the first. He then divested himself of his upper coat; and lighting the pipe, and placing himself in front of the fire with his back towards it, so that he could feel its full heat, and recline against the mantel-piece at the same time, turned towards Sam, and, with a countenance greatly modified by the softening influence of tobacco, requested him to "fire away."

Sam dipped his pen into the ink to be ready for any corrections, and began with a very theatrical air: —

"'Lovely'"—

"Stop," said Mr. Weller, ringing the bell. "A double glass of the inwariable, my dear."

"Very well, sir," replied the girl, who with great quickness appeared, vanished, returned, and disappeared.

"They seem to know your ways here," observed Sam.

"Yes," replied his father, "I've been here before in my time. Go on, Sammy."

"'Lovely creetur,'" repeated Sam.

"'T ain't in poetry, is it?" interposed the father.

"No, no," replied Sam.

"Wery glad to hear it," said Mr. Weller. "Poetry's unnat'ral: no man ever talked in poetry 'cept a beadle on boxin'-day, or Warren's blackin', or Rowland's oil, or some of them low fellows. Never you let yourself down to talk poetry, my boy. Begin again, Sammy."

Mr. Weller resumed his pipe with critical solemnity; and Sam once more commenced, and read as follows:—

"'Lovely creetur i feel myself a dammed'"—

"That ain't proper," said Mr. Weller, taking his pipe from his mouth.

"No, it ain't 'dammed,'" observed Sam, holding the letter up to the light; "it's 'shamed:' there's a blot there. 'I feel myself ashamed.'"

"Wery good," said Mr. Weller. "Go on."

"'Feel myself ashamed, and completely cir'— I forget wot this here word is," said Sam, scratching his head with the pen, in vain attempts to remember.

"Why don't you look at it, then?" inquired Mr. Weller.

"So I *am* a lookin' at it," replied Sam; "but there's another blot. Here's a 'c,' and a 'i,' and a 'd.'"

"Circumwented, p'rhaps," suggested Mr. Weller.

"No, it ain't that," said Sam,—"circumscribed; that's it!"

"That ain't as good a word as circumwented, Sammy," said Mr. Weller gravely.

"Think not?" said Sam.

"Nothin' like it!" replied his father.

"But don't you think it means more?" inquired Sam.

"Vell, p'rhaps it is a more tenderer word," said Mr. Weller, after a few moments' reflection. "Go on, Sammy."

"'Feel myself ashamed and completely circumscribed in a dressin' of you, for you *are* a nice gal, and nothin' but it.'"

"That's a wery pretty sentiment," said the elder Mr. Weller, removing his pipe to make way for the remark.

"Yes, I think it is rayther good," observed Sam, highly flattered.

"Wot I like in that 'ere style of writin'," said the elder Mr. Weller, "is, that there ain't no callin' names in it, — no Wenuses, nor nothin' o' that kind. Wot 's the good o' callin' a young 'ooman a Wenus or a angel, Sammy?"

"Ah! what, indeed?" replied Sam.

"You might jist as vell call her a griffin, or a unicorn, or a king's arms at once, which is wery well known to be a col-lection o' fabulous animals," added Mr. Weller.

"Just as well," replied Sam.

"Drive on, Sammy," said Mr. Weller.

Sam complied with the request, and proceeded as follows; his father continuing to smoke with a mixed expression of wisdom and complacency which was particularly edifying.

"'Afore I see you, I thought all women was alike.'"

"So they are," observed the elder Mr. Weller parenthetically.

"'But now,'" continued Sam, — "'now I find what a reg'lar soft-headed, inkred'lous turnip I must ha' been; for there ain't nobody like you, though *I* like you better than nothin' at all.' I thought it best to make that rayther strong," said Sam, looking up.

Mr. Weller nodded approvingly, and Sam resumed: —

"'So I take the privilidge of the day, Mary, my dear, — as the gen'lem'n in difficulties did, ven he valked out of a Sunday, — to tell you that the first and only time I see you your likeness was took on my hart in much quicker time and brighter colors than ever a likeness was taken by the profeel macheen (wich p'r'aps you may have heerd on Mary my dear) altho it *does* finish a portrait and put the frame and glass on complete with a hook at the end to hang it up by and all in two minutes and a quarter.'"

"I am afeered that werges on the poetical, Sammy," said Mr. Weller dubiously.

"No, it don't," replied Sam, reading on very quickly to avoid contesting the point.

"'Except of me Mary my dear as your walentine and think over what I 've said. My dear Mary I will now conclude.' That 's all," said Sam.

"That 's rayther a sudden pull up; ain't it, Sammy?" inquired Mr. Weller.

"Not a bit on it," said Sam. "She 'll vish there wos more, and that 's the great art o' letter-writin'."

"Well," said Mr. Weller, "there 's somethin' in that; and I wish your mother-in-law 'ud only conduct her conwersation on the same gen-teel principle. Ain't you a goin' to sign it?"

"That 's the difficulty," said Sam. "I don't know what *to* sign it."

"Sign it 'Veller,'" said the oldest surviving proprietor of that name.

"Won't do," said Sam. "Never sign a walentine with your own name."

"Sign it 'Pickwick,' then," said Mr. Weller: "it 's a wery good name, and a easy one to spell."

"The wery thing!" said Sam. "I *could* end with a werse: what do you think?"

"I don't like it, Sam," rejoined Mr. Weller. "I never know'd a respectable coachman as wrote poetry, 'cept one, as made an affectin' copy o' werses the night afore he wos hung for a highway robbery; and *he* wos only a Cambervell man: so even that 's no rule."

But Sam was not to be dissuaded from the poetical idea that had occurred to him, so he signed the letter, —

"Your love-sick
Pickwick."

And, having folded it in a very intricate manner, squeezed a downhill direction in one corner, — "To Mary, House-maid, at Mr. Nupkins's Mayors, Ipswich, Suffolk," — and put it into his pocket, wafered, and ready for the general post.

Mr. Weller, senior, had his own experience to relate, and at last carried Sam off to a meeting of the Brick Lane Branch of the United Grand Junction Ebenezer Temperance Association, whose subsequent proceedings were somewhat turbulent.

XXXIV St. Valentine's Day was the ominous one chosen for the trial of the case of Bardell *vs.* Pickwick, and this memorable case, here faithfully recorded, ended in the award of damages to the plaintiff to the amount of seven hundred and fifty pounds, which Mr. Pickwick firmly declared he never would pay.

XXXV It would be two months before the legal process of execution could be issued, and Mr. Pickwick resolved with his native cheerfulness to make the most of his freedom. He chose Bath as his next place of entertainment, and there the Pickwickians found themselves in gay society at once, while Sam entered similar high life by the area door.

XXXVI Mr. Pickwick and his friends took lodgings with a new acquaintance they had scraped, and Sam Weller as a gentle-
XXXVII man's gentleman tasted of the pleasures of Bath at a "swarry." Matters had not gone altogether smoothly, however, for Mr. Winkle by an unlucky series of accidents had found it most prudent to leave Bath precipitately and secretly.

After him Mr. Pickwick now sent Sam with orders to bring him back, willy nilly.

XXXVIII Mr. Winkle had selected Bristol for his retreat, and here he fell in with Mr. Bob Sawyer, who had established his practice in Bristol, at a safe distance from pressing creditors. He also met with Mr. Benjamin Allen, and from what he learned strongly suspected that the lovely Arabella Allen was choosing him, him! Nathaniel Winkle, in place of her brother's friend, Bob Sawyer. Moreover, Mr. Dowler, the enraged husband from whom he had fled, also turned up, fleeing from Mr. Winkle himself, and the two men oozed courage instead of blood.

XXXIX Sam had found Mr. Winkle, and kept vigilant watch over him until Mr. Pickwick himself appeared on the scene, when he was despatched with a missive to Arabella who was somewhere, no one knew exactly where, on Clifton Downs. In searching for her Sam had the great good fortune to fall in with his own sweetheart, Mary, who was able to direct him to Miss Allen's abode and to renew her own pleasant relations with him. As a result Mr. Pickwick and Mr. Winkle made an evening visit with a dark lantern, Mr. Winkle assured himself of his happiness, and Mr. Pickwick occasioned a new problem in the science of physics.

XL When the two months at Bath were up, the Pickwickians returned to London, and Mr. Pickwick with great promptness received a visit from the sheriff's deputy, and firmly refusing to make any payment of damages or costs, was committed to the debtors' prison in the Fleet.

XLI Here he made the acquaintance of a now extinct hostelry; he saw new companions and was introduced into a society
XLII which was new to him, though his own private means enabled him to escape much of the common misery.

XLIII His residence in the Fleet brought him one surprise in the discovery that two of his fellow prisoners were Jingle and Job Trotter. He was so firm in his resolution to remain indefinitely in the prison rather than yield to what he regarded as an iniquitous proceeding, that he dismissed the faithful Sam.

XLIV But Sam had his own view of the situation. If he could not get into the Fleet by one door he would by another, and accordingly concocted a subtle scheme by which he got himself committed to the Fleet by his own father.

XLV Mr. Pickwick was greatly touched by his servant's fidelity, and somewhat embarrassed, since Sam's account of his own obstinacy was a distant parody of what he himself was displaying. He received his old companions; and he had a new experience of the world he had entered, in the death of one of the prisoners.

XLVI Sam also received a visit from his father, his mother-in-law, and her spiritual adviser; both he and Mr. Pickwick renewed acquaintance with Jingle and Trotter, but Mr. Pickwick, depressed by the misery and squalor which he saw, determined to withdraw more into the privacy of his own apartment.

XLVII There is no saying how long he might have remained incarcerated, if the very sharp attorneys Messrs. Dodson & Fogg had not proceeded with an action against Mrs. Bardell for not paying their costs, and so clapped her also into the debtors' prison.

XLVIII Sam saw in an instant a way out for his master, and at once sent for Mr. Perker. While that gentleman was explaining to Mr. Pickwick that the only way to release Mrs. Bardell was by his paying all the costs, in walked Mr. Winkle and the lady who had been Arabella Allen, but had suddenly been carried off a willing captive by her lover, and was now Mrs. Winkle. Presently Mr. Snodgrass and Mr. Tupman also arrived, and, borne down on by the united force of his friends, Mr. Pickwick's obstinacy gave way, and he turned his back on the Fleet.

XLIX The first matter to which he gave his attention on returning to the world was the love affair of his friend Winkle; and with great diplomacy he succeeded in allaying the wrath of Mrs. Winkle's brother Benjamin on behalf of his friend Bob Sawyer,
L and of reconciling that gentleman to his fate. Returning to the Bush, he sought the company in the travellers' room, and there heard the tale of the Bagman's Uncle.

LI He had still, however, to make peace between Mr. Winkle and his father; so he set out for Birmingham, accompanied by Messrs. Allen and Sawyer, who had recovered their customary good spirits and were quite sure they would be of great service on this delicate errand. Mr. Pickwick met Mr. Winkle, senior, and found him distinctly a man of business.

LII On their way back to London they were overtaken by so heavy a storm that they were fain to put up for the night at the Saracen's Head, Towcester, and here they encountered Mr. Pott, their old acquaintance, the editor of the Eatanswill Gazette, and Mr. Slurk, the editor of the rival Independent, who had temporarily changed their skies but kept their humors.

LIII Upon returning to London, the most important incident brought to the notice of the travellers was the death of Tony Weller's second wife; and Sam, upon visiting his father, had the opportunity of helping him pay off old scores upon Mrs. Weller's spiritual adviser.

LIV Mr. Pickwick's benevolence was clearly shown not only in his fatherly interest in Mr. Winkle and his wife, but in the fact that he had secured a place for Alfred Jingle in Demerara; and Job Trotter showed his own fidelity in accompanying his old master thither, in spite of a better offer made by Mr. Perker. While Mr. Pickwick was receiving this last information in Mr. Perker's office, Messrs. Dodson & Fogg were ushered in, for the settlement of accounts. They got their money, and in addition Mr. Pickwick's unequivocal opinion of their characters, which was hurled after them.

LV Scarcely had they gone before Mr. Wardle appeared, announced by the sleepy Joe, and inviting Mr. Pickwick to dine with him intimated that his daughter Emily had lost her heart to Mr. Snodgrass. By a series of embarrassing situations, that gentleman was forced to make a public avowal of this upon the occasion of the dinner that evening.

LVI Mr. Weller, having lost his wife, suddenly discovered that she had, by her habits of saving, left him and Sam a respectable little property; and in settling the estate in company with other portly coachmen he became somewhat initiated into the mysteries of the law.

LVII Having secured his money at last, he proceeded to place it in the hands of Mr. Pickwick, as the safest place he knew; and upon the occasion, it became evident to all concerned that Sam was ready to marry Mary, the pretty housemaid, but would remain unflinchingly devoted to Mr. Pickwick. Now arrived also the senior Mr. Winkle, who was quickly won over by the charms of his new daughter-in-law.

LVIII The affairs of all being happily arranged, Mr. Pickwick provided a home for himself, with Sam and Mary in attendance; dedicated it at once by the marriage there of Mr. Snodgrass and Emily Wardle, "and now the whole 'Pickwick Club' is dissolved, which was an image of the 'cockney' world."

---

## INDEX TO CHARACTERS

**Allen, Arabella.** Sister of Benjamin Allen; afterwards the wife of Mr. Winkle. xxviii, xxx, xxxix, xlviii, liii, liv, lvi, lvii.

**Allen, Benjamin.** A medical student, and the devoted friend of Mr. Bob Sawyer to whom he purposes marrying his sister Arabella. xxx, xxxii, xxxviii, xlviii, l, li, lii, liv, lvii.

**Ayresleigh, Mr.** A prisoner for debt, whom Mr. Pickwick meets in the "coffee-room" at Coleman Street. xl.

**Bagman, The one-eyed.** A stout, jovial, middle-aged man with a "lonely eye," whom Mr. Pickwick meets, first at the Peacock

Inn, Eatanswill, and afterwards at the Bush, in Bristol. He is the narrator of "The Bagman's Story," and of "The Story of the Bagman's Uncle." xiv, xlviii, xlix.

**Bail, The professional.** xl.

**Bamber, Jack.** A little, high-shouldered, keen-eyed old man, whom Mr. Pickwick casually meets at the Magpie and Stump. He relates "The Old Man's Tale about a Queer Client." xx.

**Bantam, Angelo Cyrus, Esq., M. C.** A charming young man of not much more than fifty, whom Mr. Pickwick meets at Bath; friend to Capt. Dowler, and master of ceremonies at the ball which Mr. Pickwick attends. xxxv.

**Bardell, Mrs. Martha.** Mr. Pickwick's landlady. When in London, Mr. Pickwick made his home at her lodging-house, and found her a very accommodating landlady. He determines, however, to take a servant; and, desiring to consult Mrs. Bardell in relation to the matter, he sends for her.

"Mrs. Bardell," said Mr. Pickwick. . . .

"Sir," said Mrs. Bardell. . . .

"Do you think it 's a much greater expense to keep two people than to keep one?"

"La, Mr. Pickwick!" said Mrs. Bardell, coloring up to the very border of her cap, as she fancied she observed a species of matrimonial twinkle in the eyes of her lodger, — "la, Mr. Pickwick, what a question!"

"Well, but *do* you?" inquired Mr. Pickwick.

"That depends," said Mrs. Bardell, . . . "that depends a good deal upon the person, you know, Mr. Pickwick; and whether it 's a saving and careful person, sir."

"That 's very true," said Mr. Pickwick; "but the person I have in my eye (here he looked very hard at Mrs. Bardell) I think possesses these qualities, and has, moreover, a considerable knowledge of the world, and a great deal of sharpness, Mrs. Bardell, which may be of material use to me."

"La, Mr. Pickwick!" said Mrs. Bardell, the crimson rising to her cap-border again.

"I do," said Mr. Pickwick, growing energetic, as was his wont in speaking of a subject which interested him, — "I do, indeed; and, to tell you the truth, Mrs. Bardell, I have made up my mind."

"Dear me, sir!" exclaimed Mrs. Bardell.

"You 'll think it not very strange now," said the amiable Mr. Pickwick, with a good-humored glance at his companion, "that I never consulted you about this matter, and never mentioned it till I sent your little boy out this morning — eh?"

Mrs. Bardell could only reply by a look. She had long worshipped Mr. Pickwick at a distance; but here she was all at once raised to a pinnacle to which her wildest and most extravagant hopes had never dared to aspire. Mr. Pickwick was going to propose — a deliberate plan, too, — sent her little boy away.

After a few words more, Mrs. Bardell, overcome by her feelings, goes off into ecstatic hysterics, and throws herself into the arms of Mr. Pickwick, who vehemently protests, and begs her to desist.

"Mrs. Bardell, my good woman — dear me, what a situation! Pray consider, Mrs. Bardell; don't — if anybody should come" —

"Oh! let them come," exclaimed Mrs. Bardell frantically. "I'll never leave you — dear, kind, good soul!" And with these words Mrs. Bardell clung the tighter.

"Mercy upon me!" said Mr. Pickwick, struggling violently. "I hear somebody coming up the stairs. Don't, don't, there's a good creature, don't!" But entreaty and remonstrance were alike unavailing: for Mrs. Bardell had fainted in Mr. Pickwick's arms; and, before he could gain time to deposit her on a chair, Master Bardell entered the room, ushering in Mr. Tupman, Mr. Winkle, and Mr. Snodgrass.

Mr. Pickwick was struck motionless and speechless. He stood with his lovely burden in his arms, gazing vacantly on the countenances of his friends, without the slightest attempt at recognition or explanation. They, in their turn, stared at him; and Master Bardell, in his turn, stared at everybody.

The astonishment of the Pickwickians was so absorbing, and the perplexity of Mr. Pickwick was so extreme, that they might have remained in exactly the same relative situations until the suspended animation of the lady was restored, had it not been for a most beautiful and touching expression of filial affection on the part of her youthful son. Clad in a tight suit of corduroy spangled with brass buttons of a very considerable size, he at first stood at the door astounded and uncertain; but, by degrees, the impression that his mother must have suffered some personal damage pervaded his partially-developed mind, and, considering Mr. Pickwick as the aggressor, he set up an appalling and semi-earthly kind of howling, and, butting forward with his head, commenced assailing that immortal gentleman about the back and legs, with such blows and pinches as the strength of his arm and the violence of his excitement allowed.

"Take this little villain away!" said the agonized Mr. Pickwick. "He's mad!"

"What *is* the matter?" said the three tongue-tied Pickwickians.

"I don't know," replied Mr. Pickwick pettishly. "Take away the boy (here Mr. Winkle carried the interesting boy, screaming and struggling, to the farther end of the apartment). Now help me to lead this woman down stairs."

"Oh! I am better now," said Mrs. Bardell faintly.

"Let me lead you down stairs," said the ever gallant Mr. Tupman.

"Thank you, sir; thank you!" exclaimed Mrs. Bardell hysterically. And down stairs she was led accordingly, accompanied by her affectionate son.

"I cannot conceive," said Mr. Pickwick, when his friend returned, — "I cannot conceive what has been the matter with that woman. I had merely announced to her my intention of keeping a man-servant, when she fell into the extraordinary paroxysm in which you found her. Very extraordinary thing!"

"Very!" said his three friends.

"Placed me in such an extremely awkward situation," continued Mr. Pickwick.

"Very!" was the reply of his followers, as they coughed slightly, and looked dubiously at each other.

This behavior was not lost upon Mr. Pickwick. He remarked their incredulity. They evidently suspected him.

The result of this unfortunate incident was a trial for breach of promise, the celebrated case of Bardell *vs.* Pickwick. xii, xxvi, xxxiv, xlvi.

**Bardell, Master Tommy.** The hopeful son of Mrs. Bardell. xii, xxvi, xlvi.

**Bar-maid at the Town Arms**, open to bribery. xiii.

**Bar-maid wounded at the post of duty, The**, ii.

**Beller, Henry.** Member of the Brick Lane Branch. xxxiii.

**Betsey.** Servant-girl at Mrs. Raddle's. xxxii.

**Bilson & Slum.** A great commercial house. xiv.

**Bladud, Prince.** Mythical founder of Bath; hero of the "True Legend" discovered by Mr. Pickwick. xxxvi.

**Blazo, Sir Thomas.** A West Indian cricketer, invented by Mr. Jingle. vii.

**Blotton, Mr.** (of Aldgate). A member of the Pickwick Club. i, xi.

**Boldwig, Captain.** A fierce little man, very consequential and imperious; owner of the premises on which Mr. Pickwick and his friends trespass while hunting. xix.

**Bolo, Miss.** A fashionable lady at Bath. xxxv.

**Boots at the Bull Inn, The.** A messenger of war. ii.

**Brooks.** The pieman of Sam Weller's acquaintance. xix.

**Budger, Mrs.** A little old widow, with plenty of money; Mr.

Serjeant Buzfuz began by saying, that never, in the whole course of his professional experience, — never, from the very first moment of his applying himself to the study and practice of the law, had he approached a case with such a heavy sense of the responsibility imposed upon him, — a responsibility he could never have supported, were he not buoyed up and sustained by a conviction, so strong that it amounted to positive certainty, that the cause of truth and justice, or, in other words, the cause of his much-injured and most-oppressed client, *must* prevail with the high-minded and intelligent dozen of men whom he now saw in that box before him.

Counsel always begin in this way, because it puts the jury on the best terms with themselves, and makes them think what sharp fellows they must be. A visible effect was produced immediately; several jurymen beginning to take voluminous notes.

"You have heard from my learned friend, gentlemen," continued Serjeant Buzfuz, well knowing, that, from the learned friend alluded to, the gentlemen of the jury had heard nothing at all, — "you have heard from my learned friend, gentlemen, that this is an action for a breach of promise of marriage, in which the damages are laid at one thousand five hundred pounds. But you have not heard from my learned friend, inasmuch as it did not come within my learned friend's province to tell you, what are the facts and circumstances of this case. Those facts and circumstances, gentlemen, you shall hear detailed by me, and proved by the unimpeachable female whom I will place in that box before you.

"The plaintiff is a widow; yes, gentlemen, a widow. The late Mr. Bardell, after enjoying for many years the esteem and confidence of his sovereign, as one of the guardians of his royal revenues, glided almost imperceptibly from the world to seek elsewhere for that repose and peace which a custom-house can never afford."

This was a pathetic description of the decease of Mr. Bardell, who had been knocked on the head with a quart-pot in a public-house cellar.

"Some time before Mr. Bardell's death he had stamped his likeness upon a little boy. With this little boy, the only pledge of her departed exciseman, Mrs. Bardell shrunk from the world, and courted the retirement and tranquillity of Goswell Street; and here she placed in her front-parlor window a written placard bearing this inscription: 'Apartments furnished for a single gentleman. Inquire within.'" Here Serjeant Buzfuz paused, while several gentlemen of the jury took a note of the document.

"There is no date to that, is there, sir?" inquired a juror.

"There is no date, gentlemen; but I am instructed to say that it was put in the plaintiff's parlor-window just this time three years. Now I entreat the attention of the jury to the wording of this document: 'Apartments furnished for a single gentleman'! 'Mr. Bardell,' said the widow, — 'Mr. Bardell was a man of honor; Mr. Bardell was a man of his word; Mr. Bardell was no deceiver; Mr. Bardell was once a single gentleman himself; *in* single gentlemen I shall perpetually see something to remind me of what Mr. Bardell was when he first won my young and untried affections; to a single gentleman shall my lodgings be let.' Actuated by this beautiful and touching impulse (among the best impulses of our imperfect nature, gentlemen), the desolate widow dried her tears, furnished her first floor, caught her innocent boy to her maternal bosom, and put the bill up in her parlor window. Did it remain there long? No. Before the bill had been in the parlor window three days, — three days, gentlemen, — a being erect upon two legs, and bearing all the outward semblance of a man, and not of a monster, knocked at Mrs. Bardell's door. He inquired within; he took the lodgings; and on the very next day he entered into possession of them. This man was Pickwick — Pickwick the defendant."

Serjeant Buzfuz here paused for breath. The silence awoke Mr. Justice Stareleigh, who immediately wrote down something with a pen without any ink in it, and looked unusually profound, to impress the jury with the belief that he always thought most deeply with his eyes shut.

"Of this man Pickwick I will say little: the subject presents but few attractions; and I, gentlemen, am not the man, nor are you, gentlemen, the men, to delight in the contemplation of revolting heartlessness and of systematic villainy."

Here Mr. Pickwick, who had been writhing in silence, gave a violent start, as if some vague idea of assaulting Serjeant Buzfuz, in the august presence of justice and law, suggested itself to his mind.

"I say systematic villainy, gentlemen," said Serjeant Buzfuz, looking through Mr. Pickwick, and talking *at* him; "and, when I say systematic villainy, let me tell the defendant, Pickwick,— if he be in court, as I am informed he is, — that it would have been more decent in him, more becoming, in better judgment, and in better taste, if he had stopped away.

"I shall show you, gentlemen, that, for two years, Pickwick continued to reside, without interruption or intermission, at Mrs. Bardell's house. I shall show you, that on many occasions he gave halfpence, and on some occasions even sixpences, to her little boy; and I shall prove to you, by a witness whose testimony it will be impossible for my learned friend to weaken or controvert, that, on one occasion, he patted the boy on the head, and, after inquiring whether he had won any *alley tors* or *commoneys* lately (both of which I understand to be a particular species of marbles much prized by the youth of this town), made use of this remarkable expression: 'How should you like to have another father?' I shall prove to you, gentlemen, on the testimony of three of his own friends, — most unwilling witnesses, gentlemen, most unwilling witnesses, — that on that morning he was discovered by them holding the plaintiff in his arms, and soothing her agitation by his caresses and endearments.

"And now, gentlemen, but one word more. Two letters have passed between these parties, — letters which are admitted to be in the handwriting of the defendant. Let me read the first: — 'Garraway's, twelve o'clock. Dear Mrs. B. — Chops and tomato-sauce. Yours, PICKWICK.' Gentlemen, what does this mean? Chops! Gracious heavens! and tomato-sauce! Gentlemen, is the happiness of a sensitive and confiding female to be trifled away by such shallow artifices as these? The next has no date whatever, which is in itself suspicious. 'Dear Mrs. B., I shall not be at home till to-morrow. Slow coach.' And then follows this very remarkable expression. 'Don't trouble yourself about the warming-pan.' Why, gentlemen, who *does* trouble himself about a warming-pan? Why is Mrs. Bardell so earnestly entreated not to agitate herself about this warming-pan, unless it is, as I assert it to be, a mere cover for hidden fire, — a mere substitute for some endearing word or promise, agreeably to a preconcerted system of correspondence, artfully contrived by Pickwick with a view to his contemplated desertion, and which I am not in a condition to explain?

"Enough of this. My client's hopes and prospects are ruined.

But Pickwick, gentlemen, — Pickwick, the ruthless destroyer of this domestic oasis in the desert of Goswell Street, — Pickwick, who has choked up the well, and thrown ashes on the sward, — Pickwick, who comes before you to-day with his heartless tomato-sauce and warming-pans, — Pickwick still rears his head with unblushing effrontery, and gazes without a sigh on the ruin he has made. Damages, gentlemen, heavy damages, are the only punishment with which you can visit him, the only recompense you can award to my client. And for those damages she now appeals to an enlightened, a high-minded, a right-feeling, a conscientious, a dispassionate, a sympathizing, a contemplative jury of her civilized countrymen."

With this beautiful peroration, Mr. Sergeant Buzfuz sat down, and Mr. Justice Stareleigh woke up.

**Cabman, The.** The first person Mr. Pickwick encountered in his exploration of the world. ii.

**Chambermaid at the White Hart, The.** x.

**Chancery Prisoner, The.** An old man whose acquaintance Mr. Pickwick makes in the Fleet. He has been confined there for twenty years, but gets his release at last from the hands of his Maker, and accepts it with a smile of quiet satisfaction. xlii, xliv.

**Charley, the pot boy.** xx.

**Christina, Donna.** Daughter of Don Bolaro Fizzgig. ii.

**Clarke, Mrs. Susan.** Preempted by Tony Weller. x.

**Clergyman, The.** One of the guests at Mr. Wardle's. He sings the song of "The Ivy Green," and relates the story of "The Convict's Return." vi, xi, xxviii.

**Clubber, Sir Thomas.** A fashionable gentleman at Rochester, commissioner at the head of the dock-yard there. ii.

**Clubber, Lady.** His wife. ii.

**Clubbers, The Miss.** His daughters. ii.

**Cluppins, Mrs. Betsey.** A bosom-friend of Mrs. Bardell's. xxvi, xxxiv, xlvi. *See* PICKWICK, SAMUEL.

**Cobbler, The bald-headed.** xliv.

**Craddock, Mrs.** Mr. Pickwick's landlady at Bath. xxxvi, xxxvii.

**Crawley, Mr.** An objectionable partner. xxxv.

**Cripps, Bob.** Bob Sawyer's boy. xxxviii.

**Crookey.** An attendant at the sponging-house in Coleman Street. xl.

**Crumpets, The man addicted to.** xliv.

**Crushton, The Honorable Mr.** A gentleman whom Mr. Pickwick meets at Bath; a friend of Capt. Dowler's. xxxv.

**Dirty-faced man at the Peacock, The.** xiv.

**Dismal Jemmy.** *See* Hutley, Jem.

**Dodson and Fogg.** Attorneys for Mrs. Bardell. xx, xxxiv, liii.

**Dowler, Captain.** A blustering coward, formerly in the army, whom Mr. Pickwick meets at the travellers' room at the White Horse Cellar. xxxv, xxxvi, xxxviii.

**Dowler, Mrs.** Wife of Capt. Dowler. xxxv, xxxvi.

**Dubbley.** One of the special officers of the Mayor's Court at Ipswich; a dirty-faced man, over six feet high, and stout in proportion. xxiv. *See* Nupkins, George.

**Dumkins, Mr.** A member of the All-Muggleton Cricket Club. vii.

**Edmunds, John.** Hero of the story of "The Convict's Return." vi.

**Edmunds, Mr.** His father; a morose, dissolute, and savage-hearted man. vi.

**Edmunds, Mrs.** His mother; a gentle, ill-used, and heart-broken woman. vi.

**Emma.** A servant-girl at Mr. Wardle's. xxviii.

**Fat boy.** See Joe.

**Fitz-Marshall, Charles.** *See* Jingle, Alfred.

**Fizkin, Horatio, Esq.** (of Fizkin Lodge, near Eatanswill). A candidate for parliament, defeated by the honorable Samuel Slumkey. xiii. *See* Slumkey, The Honorable Samuel.

**Fizzgig, Don Bolaro.** A Spanish grandee, invented by Mr. Jingle on the spur of the moment. ii.

**Flasher, Wilkins.** A stock-broker. lv.

**Fogg, Mr.** *See* Dodson and Fogg.

**George.** Mr. Weller's coachman friend. xciii.

**Goodwin.** Servant to Mrs. Pott. xviii.

**Groffin, Thomas.** One of the jury in the case of Bardell *vs* Pickwick. He desires to be excused from attendance on the ground that he is a chemist, and has no assistant. xxxiv.

"I can't help that, sir," replied Mr. Justice Stareleigh: "you should hire one."

"I can't afford it, my lord," rejoined the chemist.

"Then you ought to be able to afford it, sir," said the judge, reddening; for Mr. Justice Stareleigh's temper bordered on the irritable, and brooked not contradiction. . . . "Swear the gentleman." . . .

"Very well, my lord," replied the chemist in a resigned manner. "Then there 'll be murder before this trial 's over: that 's all. Swear me, if you please, sir." And sworn the chemist was before the judge could find words to utter.

"I merely wanted to observe, my lord," said the chemist, taking his seat with great deliberation, "that I 've left nobody but an errand-boy in my shop. He is a very nice boy, my lord; but he is not acquainted with drugs; and I know that the prevailing impression on his mind is, that Epsom salts mean oxalic acid; and syrup of senna, laudanum. That 's all, my lord."

**Grub, Gabriel.** Hero of Mr. Wardle's "Story of the Goblins who stole a Sexton;" a cross-grained, surly, solitary fellow, who is made good-natured and contented by his remarkable experiences on Christmas Eve. xxix.

**Grummer, Daniel.** A constable in attendance upon the Mayor's Court at Ipswich. xxiv, xxv. *See* NUPKINS, GEORGE.

**Grundy, Mr.** A friend of Mr. Lowten's, and a frequenter of the Magpie and Stump Inn. xx.

**Gunter, Mr.** A friend of Mr. Bob Sawyer's. xxxii.

**Gwynn, Miss.** Writing and ciphering governess at Westgate House Establishment for Young Ladies, at Bury St. Edmunds. xvi.

**Hairy Cap, The boy with the.** An embryo hostler. xxxiii.

**Harris.** A green-grocer. xxxviii.

**Henry.** A character in "The Parish Clerk;" cousin to Maria Lobbs, whom he finally marries. xvii.

**Heyling, George.** Hero of "The Old Man's Tale about a Queer Client." xxi.

**Heyling, Mary.** His wife. xxi.

**Hopkins, Jack.** A medical student, whom Mr. Pickwick meets at Mr. Bob Sawyer's party. xxxii.

"I hope that 's Jack Hopkins," said Mr. Bob Sawyer. "Hush! Yes: it is. Come up, Jack; come up!"

A heavy footstep was heard upon the stairs, and Jack Hopkins presented himself. He wore a black velvet waistcoat with thunder-and-lightning buttons, and a blue striped shirt with a white false collar.

"You 're late, Jack," said Mr. Benjamin Allen.

"Been detained at Bartholomew's," replied Hopkins.

"Anything new?"

"No: nothing particular. Rather a good accident brought into the casualty ward."

"What was that, sir?" inquired Mr. Pickwick.

"Only a man fallen out of a four-pair-of-stairs window; but it 's a very fair case, — very fair case, indeed."

"Do you mean that the patient is in a fair way to recover?" inquired Mr. Pickwick.

"No," replied Hopkins carelessly. "No, I should rather say he would n't. There must be a splendid operation though, to-morrow, — magnificent sight if Slasher does it!"

"You consider Mr. Slasher a good operator?" said Mr. Pickwick.

"Best alive!" replied Hopkins. "Took a boy's leg out of the socket last week, — boy ate five apples and a gingerbread-cake. Exactly two minutes after it was all over, boy said he would n't lie there to be made game of; and he 'd tell his mother if they did n't begin."

"Dear me!" said Mr. Pickwick, astonished.

"Pooh! that 's nothing, — that ain't," said Jack Hopkins. "Is it, Bob?"

"Nothing at all," replied Mr. Bob Sawyer.

"By the bye, Bob," said Hopkins, with a scarcely perceptible glance at Mr. Pickwick's attentive face, "we had a curious accident last night. A child was brought in who had swallowed a necklace."

"Swallowed what, sir?" interrupted Mr. Pickwick.

"A necklace," replied Jack Hopkins. "Not all at once: you know that would be too much. *You* could n't swallow that, if the child did, — eh, Mr. Pickwick? Ha, ha!" Mr. Hopkins appeared highly gratified with his own pleasantry, and continued, "No, the way was this: child's parents were poor people who lived in a court. Child's eldest sister bought a necklace, — common necklace, made of large black wooden beads. Child, being fond of toys, cribbed the necklace, hid it, played with it, cut the string, and swallowed a bead. Child thought it capital fun; went back next day, and swallowed another bead."

"Bless my heart," said Mr. Pickwick, "what a dreadful thing! I beg your pardon, sir. Go on."

"Next day, child swallowed two beads; the day after that, he treated himself to three; and so on, till in a week's time he had got through the necklace, — five-and-twenty beads in all. The sister, who was an industrious girl, and seldom treated herself to a bit of finery, cried her eyes out at the loss of the necklace; looked high and low for it; but, I need n't say, did n't find it. A few days after, the family were at dinner: the child, who was n't hungry, was playing about the room, when suddenly there was heard a devil of a noise, like a small hailstorm. 'Don't do that, my boy,' said the father. 'I ain't a doin nothin',' said the child. 'Well, don't do it again,' said the father. There was a short silence, and then the noise began again worse than ever. 'If you don't mind what I say, my boy,' said the father, 'you 'll find yourself in bed in something less than a pig's whisper.' He gave the child a shake to make him obedient; and such a rattling ensued as nobody ever heard before. 'Why, damme, it 's *in* the child!' said the father. 'He's got the croup in the wrong place!'—'No, I haven't, father,' said the child, beginning to cry. 'It's the necklace: I swallowed it, father.' The father caught the child up, and ran with him to the hospital; the beads in the boy's stomach rattling all the way with the jolting, and the people looking up in the air, and down in the cellars, to see where the unusual sound came from. He's in the hospital now," said Jack Hopkins; "and he makes such a devil of a noise when he walks about, that they're obliged to muffle him in a watchman's coat, for fear he should wake the patients."

**Humm, Anthony.** Chairman of the Brick Lane Branch of the United Grand Junction Ebenezer Temperance Association. xxxiii.

**Hunt.** Gardener to Captain Boldwig. xix.

**Hunter, Mrs. Leo.** A literary lady whom Mr. Pickwick meets at Eatanswill. xv. One morning, Sam Weller hands Mr. Pickwick a card bearing the following inscription:—

| |
|---|
| Mrs. Leo Hunter. |
| *The Den, Eatanswill.* |

"Person's a waitin'," said Sam epigrammatically.

"Does the person want me, Sam?" inquired Mr. Pickwick.

"He wants you partickler; and no one else'll do, as the Devil's private secretary said ven he fetched avay Dr. Faustus," replied Mr. Weller.

"*He?* Is it a gentleman?" said Mr. Pickwick.

"A wery good imitation o' one, if it ain't," replied Mr. Weller.

"But this is a lady's card," said Mr. Pickwick.

"Given me by a gen'lm'n, hows'ever," replied Sam; "and he's a waitin' in the drawing-room—said he'd rather wait all day than not see you."

Mr. Pickwick, on hearing this determination, descended to the drawing-room, where sat a grave man, who started up on his entrance, and said with an air of profound respect:—

"Mr. Pickwick, I presume?"

"The same."

"Allow me, sir, the honor of grasping your hand—permit me, sir, to shake it," said the grave man.

"Certainly," said Mr. Pickwick.

The stranger shook the extended hand, and then continued:—

"We have heard of your fame, sir. The noise of your antiquarian discussion has reached the ears of Mrs. Leo Hunter,—my wife, sir: *I* am *Mr.* Leo Hunter." The stranger paused, as if he expected that Mr. Pickwick would be overcome by the disclosure; but, seeing that he remained perfectly calm, proceeded:—

"My wife, sir,—Mrs. Leo Hunter,—is proud to number among her acquaintance all those who have rendered themselves celebrated by their works and talents. Permit me, sir, to place in a conspicuous part of the list the name of Mr. Pickwick, and his brother-members of the club that derives its name from him."

"I shall be extremely happy to make the acquaintance of such a lady, sir," replied Mr. Pickwick.

"You *shall* make it, sir," said the grave man. "To-morrow morning, sir, we give a public breakfast—a *fête champêtre*—to a great number of those who have rendered themselves celebrated by their works and talents. Permit Mrs. Leo Hunter, sir, to have the gratification of seeing you at the Den."

"With great pleasure," replied Mr. Pickwick.

"Mrs. Leo Hunter has many of these breakfasts, sir," resumed the new acquaintance,—"'feasts of reason, sir, and flows of soul,' as somebody who wrote a sonnet to Mrs. Leo Hunter on her breakfasts, feelingly and originally observed."

"Was *he* celebrated for his works and talents?" inquired Mr. Pickwick.

"He was, sir," replied the grave man. "All Mrs. Leo Hunter's acquaintance are: it is her ambition, sir, to have no other acquaintance."

"It is a very noble ambition," said Mr. Pickwick.

"When I inform Mrs. Leo Hunter that that remark fell from *your* lips, sir, she will indeed be proud," said the grave man. "You have a gentleman in your train who has produced some beautiful little poems, I think, sir."

"My friend Mr. Snodgrass has a great taste for poetry," replied Mr. Pickwick.

"So has Mrs. Leo Hunter, sir. She dotes on poetry, sir. She adores it; I may say that her whole soul and mind are wound up and intwined with it. She has produced some delightful pieces herself, sir. You may have met with her 'Ode to an Expiring Frog,' sir."

"I don't think I have," said Mr. Pickwick.

"You astonish me, sir," said Mr. Leo Hunter. "It created an immense sensation. It was signed with an 'L' and eight stars, and appeared originally in a Lady's Magazine. It commenced:—

"'Can I view thee panting, lying
On thy stomach, without sighing;
Can I unmoved see thee dying
On a log,
Expiring frog!'"

"Beautiful!" said Mr. Pickwick.

"Fine," said Mr. Leo Hunter; "so simple!"

"Very," said Mr. Pickwick.

"The next verse is still more touching. Shall I repeat it?"

"If you please," said Mr. Pickwick.

"It runs thus," said the grave man still more gravely:—

"'Say, have fiends in shape of boys,
With wild halloo and brutal noise,
Hunted thee from marshy joys,
With a dog,
Expiring frog?'"

"Finely expressed," said Mr. Pickwick.

"All point, sir, all point," said Mr. Leo Hunter; "but you shall hear Mrs. Leo Hunter repeat it. *She* can do justice to it, sir."

**Hunter, Mr. Leo.** Mrs. Leo Hunter's husband. xv.

**Huntley, Jem,** *called* "DISMAL JEMMY." An itinerant actor, who "does the heavy business;" brother to Job Trotter, and friend of Mr. Alfred Jingle, who introduces him to Mr. Pickwick. He relates to them "The Stroller's Tale," in which he himself figures. iii, v. *See* JOHN.

**Isaac.** A friend of Mr. Jackson's. xlvi.

**Jackson, Mr.** A clerk in the office of Dodson and Fogg. xx, xxxi, xlvi.

**Jane**, a servant girl at Mr. Pott's. xiii.

**Jane**, a servant girl at Mr. Wardle's. xxviii.

**Jem**, a man servant at Mr. Wardle's. xxviii.

**Jemmy, Dismal.** *See* HUNTLEY, JEM.

**Jingle, Alfred.** An impudent strolling actor, who palms himself off on Mr. Pickwick and his travelling-companions of the club as a gentleman of consequence, sponges good dinners and borrows money from them, and finally gets into the Fleet prison, where, some time afterwards, Mr. Pickwick finds him in great destitution and distress, and benevolently pays his debts and releases him, on satisfactory evidence of penitence, and on promise of reformation, which is faithfully kept. Mr. Jingle is a very loquacious person, talking incessantly; rarely speaking a connected sentence, however, but stringing together mere disjointed phrases, generally without verbs. He first meets Mr. Pickwick and his party at the coach-stand in Saint Martin's-le-Grand. ii, iii, vii–x, xv, xxv, xlii, xlv, xlvii, liii.

"Heads, heads; take care of your heads!" cried the loquacious stranger, as they came out under the low archway, which in those days formed the entrance to the coach-yard. "Terrible place—dangerous work—other day—five children—mother—tall lady, eating sandwiches — forgot the arch — crash — knock — children look round — mother's head off — sandwich in her hand — no mouth to put it in — head of a family off — shocking, shocking! Looking at Whitehall, sir? — fine place — little window — somebody else's head off there, eh, sir? — he did n't keep a sharp look-out enough, either — eh, sir, eh?"

"I was ruminating," said Mr. Pickwick, "on the strange mutability of human affairs."

"Ah! I see — in at the palace-door one day, out at the window the next. Philosopher, sir?"

"An observer of human nature, sir," said Mr. Pickwick.

"Ah, so am I. Most people are when they 've little to do, and less to get. Poet, sir?"

"My friend Mr. Snodgrass has a strong poetic turn," said Mr. Pickwick.

"So have I," said the stranger. "Epic poem — ten thousand lines — revolution of July — composed it on the spot — Mars by day, Apollo by night — bang the field-piece, twang the lyre."

**Jinks, Mr.** A pale, sharp-nosed, half-fed, shabbily-clad clerk of the Mayor's Court at Ipswich. xxiv, xxv.

**Jinkins, Mr.** A character in "The Bagman's Story;" a rascally adventurer with a wife and six babes, — all of them small ones, — who tries to marry a buxom widow, the landlady of a roadside inn, but is prevented by Tom Smart, who marries her himself. xiv.

**Joe, the Fat Boy.** Servant to Mr. Wardle; a youth of astonishing obesity and voracity, who has a way of going to sleep on the slightest provocation, and in all sorts of places and attitudes. Mr. Wardle, having met Mr. Pickwick and his friends at a grand review at Rochester, invites them into his carriage for a lunch. iv–ix, xxviii, liv, lvi.

"Joe, Joe," said the stout gentleman, when the citadel was taken, and the besiegers and besieged sat down to dinner. "Damn that boy! he 's gone to sleep again. Be good enough to pinch him, sir, — in the leg, if you please, nothing else wakes him. Thank you! Undo the hamper, Joe."

The fat boy, who had been effectually roused by the compression of a portion of his leg between the finger and thumb of Mr. Winkle, rolled off the box once again, and proceeded to unpack the hamper, with more expedition than could have been expected from his previous inactivity.

"Now, we must sit close," said the stout gentleman. After a great many jokes about squeezing the ladies' sleeves, and a vast quantity of blushing at sundry jocose proposals that the ladies should sit in the gentlemen's laps, the whole party were stowed down in the barouche; and the stout gentleman proceeded to hand the things from the fat boy (who had mounted up behind for the purpose) into the carriage.

"Now, Joe, knives and forks!" The knives and forks were handed in; and the ladies and gentlemen inside, and Mr. Winkle on the box, were each furnished with those useful implements.

"Plates, Joe, plates!" A similar process employed in the distribution of the crockery.

"Now, Joe, the fowls.—Damn that boy! he 's gone to sleep again. Joe, Joe!" (Sundry taps on the head with a stick, and the fat boy, with some difficulty, roused from his lethargy.) "Come, hand in the eatables."

There was something in the sound of the last word, which roused the unctuous boy. He jumped up; and the leaden eyes, which twinkled behind his mountainous cheeks, leered horribly upon the food as he unpacked it from the basket.

"Now, make haste," said Mr. Wardle; for the fat boy was hanging fondly over a capon, which he seemed wholly unable to part with. The boy sighed deeply, and, bestowing an ardent gaze upon its plumpness, unwillingly consigned it to his master.

**John.** A low pantomime actor, and an habitual drunkard, whose death is described in "The Stroller's Tale," related to Mr. Pickwick and his friends by Mr. Hutley. iii.

**Kate.** A character in the story of "The Parish Clerk;" cousin to Maria Lobbs. xvii.

**Laundress, Mr. Perker's unwashed.** xx.

**Lobbs, Maria.** A character in Mr. Pickwick's story of "The Parish Clerk;" a pretty girl, beloved by Nathaniel Pipkin, and also by her cousin Henry, whom she marries. xvii.

**Lobbs, Old.** Father to Maria Lobbs; a rich saddler, and a terrible old fellow when his pride is injured, or his blood is up. xvii.

**Lord Chancellor, The late**, complimentary to Mr. Pell. xliii.

**Lowten, Mr.** A puffy-faced young man, clerk to Mr. Perker. xx, xxi, xxxi, xxxiv, xl, xlvii, liii, liv.

**Lucas, Solomon.** A costumer. xv.

**Luffey, Mr.** Vice-president of the Dingley Dell Cricket Club. vii.

**Magnus, Peter.** A red-haired man, with an inquisitive nose and blue spectacles, who is a fellow-traveller with Mr. Pickwick from London to Ipswich. He is fiancé of Miss Witherfield, into whose chamber Mr. Pickwick innocently intrudes. xxii, xxiv.

**Mallard, Mr.** Clerk to Mr. Serjeant Snubbin. xxxi, xxxiv.

**Martin, Betsy.** Member of the Brick Lane Branch. xxxiii.

**Martin, Mr.** A prisoner confined in the Fleet prison. xlii.

THE FAT BOY.

**Martin.** A coachman. xlviii.

**Martin.** A gamekeeper. xix.

**Martin, Jack.** Hero of "The Story of the Bagman's Uncle." xlix.

**Mary.** A servant girl at Mr. Nupkins's; afterwards married to Sam Weller. xxv, xxxix, xlvii, lii, liv, lvi.

**Mary.** A servant girl at Mr. Wardle's. v.

**Mary.** A servant girl at the Peacock. xiv.

**Matinters, The Two Miss.** Ladies attending the ball at Bath. xxxv.

**Miller, Mr.** A guest at Mr. Wardle's. A hard-headed, Ripstone pippin-faced man. vi, xxviii.

**Mivins, Mr.** *Called* "THE ZEPHYR." A fellow-prisoner with Mr. Pickwick in the Fleet. xli, xlii.

**Mudberry, Mrs.** Neighbor of Mrs. Bardell. xxxiv.

**Mudge, Mr. Jonas.** Secretary of the Brick Lane Branch of the United Grand Junction Ebenezer Temperance Association. xxxiii.

**Mutanhed, Lord.** A fashionable gentleman whom Mr. Pickwick meets at a ball in Bath; a friend of Captain and Mrs. Dowler. xxxv.

**Muzzle, Mr.** An undersized footman, with a long body and short legs, in the service of George Nupkins, Esq. xxiv, xxv.

**Namby, Mr.** A sheriff's officer who arrests Mr. Pickwick. xl.

**Necklace-swallowing child.** xxxii.

**Neddy.** A prisoner for debt, confined in the Fleet; a phlegmatic and taciturn man. xlii, xliii.

**Noddy, Mr.** A friend of Mr. Bob Sawyer. xxxii.

**Nupkins, George, Esq.** Mayor of Ipswich. Mr. Pickwick and his friend Mr. Tupman are brought before him on a charge preferred by Miss Witherfield, that they are about to engage in a duel, — Mr. Pickwick as principal, and Mr. Tupman as his second. xxiv, xxv.

**Nupkins, Mrs.** Wife of George Nupkins, Esq. xxv.

**Nupkins, Miss Henrietta.** Their daughter. xxv.

**Payne, Doctor.** Surgeon of the Forty-third regiment, and a friend of Doctor Slammer's. ii, iii.

**Pell, Mr. Solomon.** An attorney at the Insolvent Court in Portugal Street; a fat, flabby, pale man, with a narrow forehead, wide face, large head, short neck, and wry nose. xliii, lv.

**Perker, Mr.** Agent for the Honorable Samuel Slumkey in his race for parliament; afterwards Mr. Pickwick's attorney, — a little, high-dried man, with a dark, squeezed-up face, small, restless black eyes, and the air of one in the habit of propounding regular posers. x, xiii, xxxi, xxxiv, xxxv, xlvii, liii, liv.

**Phunky, Mr.** Associate counsel with Serjeant Snubbin in the case of Bardell *vs* Pickwick; regarded as "an infant barrister," as he has not been at the bar quite eight years. xxxi, xxxiv.

**Pickwick, Moses.** A Perkin Warbeck. xxxv. The veritable family of this name, living at Bath, changed their name, after it had become too intimately associated with the novel, to Sainsbery.

**Pickwick, Samuel.** Founder of the Pickwick Club. i–xxviii, xxx–xxxii, xxxiv–xxxvii, xxxix–xlviii, l–lvi.

**Pike-keeper,** The evasive. ix. — The lonely. xxii.

**Pipkin, Nathaniel.** The "Parish Clerk" in Mr. Pickwick's tale of that name. He is a harmless, good-natured little being, of a very nervous temperament, and with a cast in his eye, and a halt in his gait. He falls in love with the beautiful Maria Lobbs, but sees her married to another. xvii.

**Podder, Mr.** A member of the All-Muggleton Cricket Club. vii.

**Ponto.** Mr. Jingle's intelligent dog. ii.

**Porkenhams, The.** Bosom friends of the Nupkins family. xxv.

**Pott, Mr.** Editor of "The Eatanswill Gazette." xiii, xv, xviii.

**Pott, Mrs.** Wife of the editor of "The Eatanswill Gazette." xiii, xv, xviii, li.

**Price, Mr.** A coarse, vulgar young man, with a sallow face and a harsh voice; a prisoner for debt, whom Mr. Pickwick encounters in the "coffee-room" of the sponging-house in Coleman Street. xl.

**Prosee, Mr.** The eminent counsel. xlvii.

**Pruffle.** A servant to a scientific gentleman at Bath. xxxix.

**Quanko, Samba.** A persistent cricketer. vii.

**Raddle, Mr.** Husband to Mrs. Raddle. xxxii, xlvi.

**Raddle, Mrs. Mary Ann.** Mr. Bob Sawyer's landlady; sister to Mrs. Cluppins, and a thorough shrew. xxxii, xlvi.

**Ramsey.** In the clutches of Dodson and Fogg. xx.

**Rogers, Mrs.** A lodger at Mrs. Bardell's. xlvi.

**Roker, Mr. Tom.** A turnkey at the Fleet prison. xl–xlv.

**Rook-boys, The.** vii.

**Sam.** A cab-driver. ii.

**Sanders, Mrs. Susannah.** A bosom-friend of Mrs. Bardell's. xxvi, xxxiv.

**Sarah.** A servant girl at Westgate House. xvi.

**Sausage Maker, The,** who mysteriously disappeared. xxxi.

**Sawyer, Bob.** A medical student whom Mr. Pickwick meets at Mr. Wardle's. He afterwards hangs out his sign (Sawyer, late Nockemorf) as a medical practitioner, in Bristol, where Mr. Winkle meets him.

**Scorbutic youth, The.** xxxii.

**Secretary of the Pickwick Club, The.** lvi, lvii.

**Shepherd, The.** *See* STIGGINS, THE REVEREND MR.

**"Shiny Villiam."** Deputy hostler at the Bull. v, xxii.

**Simmery, Frank, Esq.** A smart young stock-broker. lv.

**Simpson, Mr.** A prisoner in the Fleet. xlii.

**Skimpin, Mr.** Junior counsel with Serjeant Buzfuz for Mrs. Bardell, in her suit against Mr. Pickwick. xxxiv.

**Slammer, Doctor.** Surgeon of the Ninety-seventh Regiment, present at a charity ball at the Bull Inn, Rochester. ii, iii.

**Slasher, Mr.** An expert operator. xxxii.

**Slumkey, The Honorable Samuel.** Candidate for parliament from the borough of Eatanswill. He is successful in the contest, beating his opponent, Horatio Fizkin, Esq. xiii.

**Slurk, Mr.** Editor of "The Eatanswill Independent." i.

**Smangle.** A fellow-prisoner with Mr. Pickwick in the Fleet. xli, xlii, xliv.

**Smart, Tom.** Hero of "The Bagman's Story." xiv.

**Smauker, John.** Footman in the service of Angelo Cyrus Bantam, Esq. xxxv, xxxvii.

**Smiggers, Joseph.** Perpetual Vice-President of the Pickwick Club. i.

**Smithers, Miss.** A young lady-boarder at Westgate House, Bury St. Edmunds. xvi.

**Smithie, Mr.** A gentleman present at the charity ball at the Bull Inn, Rochester. ii.

**Smithie, Mrs.** His wife. ii.

**Smithie, The Misses.** His daughters. ii.

**Smorltork, Count.** A famous foreigner whom Mr. Pickwick meets at Mrs. Leo Hunter's fancy-dress breakfast. xv.

**Smouch, Mr.** A sheriff's assistant, who takes Mr. Pickwick to the Fleet Prison. xl.

**Snicks, Mr.** The Life Office Secretary. xlvii.

**Snipe, The Honorable Wilmot.** Ensign of the Ninety-seventh: one of the company at the ball in Rochester attended by Mr. Tupman. ii.

**Snodgrass, Augustus.** A poetic member of the Corresponding Society of the Pickwick Club. i–vi, viii, xi–xv, xviii, xxiv–xxvi, xxviii, xxx–xxxii, xxxiv–xxxvi, xliv, xlvii, liv, lvii.

**Snubbin, Serjeant.** Senior counsel for Mr. Pickwick in his suit with Mrs. Bardell. xxxi, xxxiv.

Mr. Serjeant Snubbin was a lantern-faced, sallow-complexioned man, of about five and forty. . . . He had that dull-looking, boiled eye, which is so often to be seen in the heads of people who have applied themselves during many years to a weary and laborious course of study, and which would have been sufficient, without the additional eye-glass which dangled from a broad black ribbon round his neck, to warn a stranger that he was very near-sighted. His hair was thin and weak, which was partly attributable to his having never devoted much time to its arrangement, and partly to his having worn for five and twenty years the forensic wig, which hung on a block beside him. The marks of hair-powder on his coat-collar, and the ill-washed and worse-tied white neckerchief round his throat, showed that he had not found leisure since he left the court to make any alteration in his dress; while the slovenly style of the remainder of his costume warranted the inference that his personal appearance would not have been very much improved if he had.

**Snuphanuph, Lady.** A fashionable lady whom Mr. Pickwick meets at a party at Bath. xxxv, xxxvi.

**Staple, Mr.** A little cricket-player who makes a big speech at the dinner which succeeds the match-game at Dingley Dell. vii.

**Stareleigh, Mr. Justice.** The judge who presides, in the absence of the chief justice, at the trial of Bardell *vs* Pickwick; xxxiv.

**Stiggins, The Reverend Mr.,** *called* THE SHEPHERD. An intemperate, canting, and hypocritical parson, who ministers to a fanatical flock, composed largely of women, at Emanuel Chapel. xxvii, xxxiii, xlv, lii.

**Stout gentleman, The, on the cricket field.** vii.

**Struggles, Mr.** A cricketer of Dingley Dell. vii.

**Stumps, Bill, Owner of.** xi.

**Tadger, Brother.** A member of the Brick Lane Branch of the United Grand Junction Ebenezer Temperance Association. xxxiii.

**Tappleton, Lieutenant.** Doctor Slammer's second. ii, iii.

**Tomkins, Miss.** Principal of a boarding-school for young ladies, called Westgate House, at Bury St. Edmunds. xvi.

**Tomlinson, Mrs.** Postmistress at Rochester, and one of the company at the charity ball at the Bull Inn there. ii.

**Tommy.** A waterman. ii.

**Trotter, Job.** The confidential servant of Mr. Alfred Jingle, and the only man who proves too sharp for Sam Weller. xvi, xx, xxiii, xxv, xlii, xlv–xlvii, liii, lvii.

**Trundle, Mr.** A young man who marries Isabella Wardle. He is repeatedly brought upon the scene as an actor, but not once as an interlocutor. iv, vi, viii, xvi, xvii, xix, xxviii, lvii.

**Tuckle.** A footman at Bath. xxxvii.

**Tupman, Tracy.** One of the Corresponding Society of the Pickwick Club; of so susceptible a disposition, that he falls in love with every pretty girl he meets. i–ix, xi–xv, xviii, xiv, xxiv–xxvi, xxviii, xxx, xxxii, xxxiv, xxxv, xliv, xlvii, lvii.

**Upwitch, Richard.** A green-grocer; one of the jurymen in the case of Bardell *vs* Pickwick. xxxiv.

**Waiter at the Bull Inn, The.** An expensive object to look at. ii.

**Walker, H.** Member of the Brick Lane Branch. xxxii.

**Wardle, Mr.** (of Manor Farm, Dingley Dell). A friend of Mr. Pickwick and his companions; a stout, hearty, honest old gentleman, who is most happy when he is making others so. iv, vi–xi, xvi–xix, xxviii, xxx, liv, lvi.

**Wardle, Miss Emily.** One of his daughters. iv, vi–xi, xxviii, xxx, liv, lvii.

**Wardle, Miss Isabella.** Another daughter. iv, vi–viii, xxviii, lvii.

**Wardle, Miss Rachael.** His sister; a spinster of doubtful age, with a peculiar dignity in her air, majesty in her eye, and touch-me-not-ishness in her walk. The "too susceptible" Mr. Tupman falls in love with her, only to be circumvented by the adroit Mr. Jingle, who steals her heart away from him, and elopes with her, but is pursued, overtaken, and induced to relinquish his prize in consideration of a check for a hundred and twenty pounds. iv, vi–ix.

**Wardle, Mrs.** Mother of Mr. Wardle and Miss Rachael; very old and very deaf. vi–ix, xxviii, lvii.

**Watty, Mr.** A bankrupt client of Mr. Perker, whom he keeps pestering about his affairs, although they have not been in chancery for years. xxxi.

**Weller, Samuel.** Mr. Pickwick's valet; an inimitable compound of wit, simplicity, quaint humor, and fidelity, who may be regarded as an embodiment of London low life in its most agreeable and entertaining form. Master and servant first meet at a public-house, whither Mr. Pickwick goes with Mr. Wardle in search of that gentleman's sister, who has eloped with Mr. Alfred Jingle. Mr. Weller first appears on the scene busily employed in brushing a pair of boots, and "habited in a coarse striped waistcoat, with black calico sleeves and blue glass buttons; drab breeches and leggings. A bright red handkerchief was wound in a very loose and unstudied style round his neck, and an old white hat was thrown carelessly on one side of his head. There were two rows of boots before him; one cleaned, and the other dirty; and, at every addition he made to the clean row, he stopped in his work, and contemplated its results with evident satisfaction." In the famous trial of Bardell *vs* Pickwick, Sam was an interesting witness. x, xii, xiii, xv, xvi, xviii–xx, xxii–xxviii, xxx–xxxv, xxxvi–xlviii, l–lii, lv–lvii.

Serjeant Buzfuz now rose with more importance that he had yet exhibited, if that were possible, and said, "Call Samuel Weller."

It was quite unnecessary to call Samuel Weller; for Samuel Weller stepped into the box the instant his name was pronounced; and placing his hat on the floor, and his arms on the rail, took a bird's-eye view of the bar and a comprehensive survey of the bench, with a remarkably cheerful and lively aspect.

COURT. — "What 's your name, sir?"

"Sam Weller, my lord."

COURT. — "Do you spell it with a 'V,' or with a 'W'?"

"That depends upon the taste and fancy of the speller, my lord. I never had occasion to spell it more than once or twice in my life; but I spells it with a 'V.'"

Here a voice in the gallery exclaimed, "Quite right too, Samivel; quite right. Put it down a we, my lord, put it down a we."

COURT. — "Who is that who dares to address the court? Usher."

"Yes, my lord."

COURT. — "Bring that person here instantly."

"Yes, my lord."

But as the usher did n't find the person, he did n't bring him; and, after a great commotion, all the people who had got up to look for the culprit sat down again. The little judge turned to the witness as soon as his indignation would allow him to speak, and said: —

COURT. — "Do you know who that was, sir?"

"I rayther suspect it was my father, my lord."

COURT. — "Do you see him here now?"

Sam stared up into the lantern in the roof of the court, and said, "Wy, no, my lord, I can't say that I *do* see him at the present moment."

COURT. — "If you could have pointed him out, I would have sent him to jail instantly."

Sam bowed his acknowledgments.

"Now, Mr. Weller," said Serjeant Buzfuz.

"Now, sir."

"I believe you are in the service of Mr. Pickwick, the defendant in this case. Speak up, if you please, Mr. Weller."

"I mean to speak up, sir. I am in the service o' that 'ere gen'l'man, and a wery good service it is."

"Little to do, and plenty to get, I suppose?"

"Oh! quite enough to get, sir, as the soldier said ven they ordered him three hundred and fifty lashes."

OLD WELLER AND THE COACHMEN.

COURT. — "You must not tell us what the soldier said, unless the soldier is in court, and is examined in the usual way: it's not evidence."

"Wery good, my lord."

"Do you recollect anything particular happening on the morning when you were first engaged by the defendant? Eh, Mr. Weller?"

"Yes, I do, sir."

"Have the goodness to tell the jury what it was."

"I had a reg'lar new fit-out o' clothes that mornin', gen'l'men of the jury; and that was a wery partickler and uncommon circumstance vith me in those days."

The judge looked sternly at Sam; but Sam's features were so perfectly serene that the judge said nothing.

"Do you mean to tell me, Mr. Weller, that you saw nothing of this fainting on the part of the plaintiff in the arms of the defendant, which you have heard described by the witnesses?"

"Certainly not, sir. I was in the passage till they called me up; and then the old lady as you call the plaintiff, — she war n't there, sir."

"You were in the passage, and yet saw nothing of what was going forward? Have you a pair of eyes, Mr. Weller?"

"Yes, I have a pair of eyes; and that's just it. If they wos a pair o' patent double million magnifyin' gas microscopes of hextra power, p'r'aps I might be able to see through two flights o' stairs and a deal-door; but bein' only eyes, you see, my wision's limited."

"Now, Mr. Weller, I'll ask you a question on another point, if you please."

"If you please, sir."

"Do you remember going up to Mrs. Bardell's house one night in November?"

"Oh, yes! wery well."

"Oh! you *do* remember that, Mr. Weller. I thought we should get at something at last."

"I rayther thought that, too, sir."

"Well, I suppose you went up to have a little talk about the trial, — eh, Mr. Weller?"

"I went up to pay the rent; but we *did* get a talkin' about the trial."

"Oh! you did get a talking about the trial. Now, what passed about the trial? Will you have the goodness to tell us, Mr. Weller?"

"Vith all the pleasure in life, sir. Arter a few unimportant observations from the two wirtuous females as has been examined here to-day, the ladies gets into a wery great state o' admiration at the honorable conduct of Mr. Dodson and Mr. Fogg, — them two gen'l'men as is settin' near you now."

"The attorneys for the plaintiff. Well, they spoke in high praise of the honorable conduct of Messrs. Dodson and Fogg, the attorneys for the plaintiff, did they?"

"Yes: they said what a wery gen'rous thing it was o' them to have taken up the case on spec, and not to charge nothin' at all for costs unless they got 'em out of Mr. Pickwick."

"It 's perfectly useless, my lord, attempting to get at any evidence through the impenetrable stupidity of this witness. I will not trouble the court by asking him any more questions. Stand down, sir. That 's my case, my lord."

**Weller, Tony.** Father to Samuel Weller; one of the old plethoric, mottled-faced, great-coated, many-waistcoated stage-coachmen that flourished in England before the advent of railways. xx, xxii, xxiii, xxvii, xxxiii, xxxiv, xliii, xlv, lii, lv, lvi.

**Weller, Mrs. Susan.** His wife, formerly Mrs. Clarke. xxvii, xlv.

**Whiffers.** A footman at Bath. xxxvii.

**Whiffin.** The Eatanswill crier. xiii.

**Wicks, Mr.** Clerk in office of Dodson and Fogg. xx.

**Wilkins.** Gardener to Captain Boldwig. xix.

**Winkle, Mr., senior.** Father of Nathaniel Winkle; an old wharfinger at Birmingham, and a thorough man of business, having the most methodical habits, and never committing himself hastily in any affair. He is greatly displeased at his son's marriage to Miss Arabella Allen, but finally forgives him, and admits that the lady is "a very charming little daughter-in-law, after all." l, lvi.

**Winkle, Nathaniel.** A member of the Corresponding Society of the Pickwick Club, and a cockney pretender to sporting skill. i–v, vii, ix, xi–xiii, xv, xviii, xix, xxiv–xxvi, xxviii, xxx–xxxii, xxxiv–xxxvi, xxxviii, xxxix, xliv, xlvii, liv, lvi, lvii.

**Witherfield, Miss.** A middle-aged lady, affianced to Mr. Magnus. xxii, xxiv.

**Wugsby, Mrs. Colonel.** A fashionable lady whom Mr. Pickwick meets at Bath. xxxv, xxxvi.

**Zephyr, The.** *See* MIVINS, MR.

# SKETCHES BY BOZ

## ILLUSTRATIVE OF EVERY-DAY LIFE AND EVERY-DAY PEOPLE

## INDEX TO CHARACTERS

### OUR PARISH

#### THE BEADLE

**Simmons.** Parish beadle, and prototype of Mr. Bumble in "Oliver Twist."

#### THE FOUR SISTERS

**Lawson, Mr.** A surgeon, &c., in attendance on Mrs. Robinson at the time of her confinement.

**Robinson, Mr.** A gentleman in a public office, who marries the youngest Miss Willis, though he has to court her three sisters also, as they are all completely identified one with another.

**Willises, The four Miss.** Four sisters in "our parish," who seem to have no separate existence, and who drive the neighborhood distracted by keeping profoundly secret the name of the fortunate one who is to marry Mr. Robinson.

#### ELECTION FOR BEADLE

**Bung, Mr.** A man of thirty-five years of age, with five small children; a candidate for the office of beadle, which he obtains by a large majority.

**Purday, Captain.** A bluff and unceremonious old naval officer on half-pay (first introduced, though not mentioned by name, in the sketch entitled "The Curate"). He is a determined opponent of the constituted authorities, whoever they may chance to be, and zealously supports Bung for beadle.

**Spruggins, Mr. Thomas.** Defeated candidate for beadle; a little thin man, fifty years old, with a pale face expressive of care and fatigue, owing, perhaps, to the fact of his having ten small children ( two of them twins) and a wife.

**Spruggins, Mrs.** His wife. She solicits votes for her husband, and increases the general prepossession which at first prevails in his favor by her personal appearance, which indicates the probability of a still further addition, at no remote period, to his already large family.

THE BROKER'S MAN

**Bung, Mr.** A broker's assistant, afterwards the parish beadle. (*See above.*) One of those careless, good-for-nothing, happy fellows who float cork-like on the surface for the world to play at hockey with.

**Fixem.** A broker, who assumes the alias of Smith; Bung's master.

**John.** A servant.

THE LADIES' SOCIETIES

**Browns, The three Miss.** Members of various visitation committees and charitable societies, and admirers of the curate, who is a young man, and unmarried. They are opposed to —

**Parker, Mrs. Johnson.** The mother of seven extremely fine girls, — all unmarried, — and the founder of a Ladies' Bible and Prayer-Book Distribution Society, from which the Miss Browns are excluded.

OUR NEXT-DOOR NEIGHBOR

**William.** A young man who overtasks himself to earn a support for himself and his widowed mother, and at last dies in her arms.

## SCENES

THE STREETS — NIGHT

**Macklin, Mrs.** An inhabitant of No. 4 in one of the little streets in the suburbs of London.

**Peplow, Mrs.** A neighbor of Mrs. Macklin.

**Peplow, Master.** Her son.

**Smuggins, Mr.** A little round-faced man, in the comic line, with a mixed air of self-denial and mental consciousness of his own powers.

**Walker, Mrs.** An inhabitant of No. 5 in the same street with Mrs. Macklin.

SEVEN DIALS

**Mary.** A woman who has taken "three-outs" enough of gin and bitters to make her quarrelsome.

**Sarah.** A vixen who falls out with her, and settles the difficulty by a resort to blows.

DOCTORS' COMMONS

**Bumple, Michael.** Promoter, or complainant, against Mr. Sludberry, in a brawling case.

**Sludberry, Thomas.** A little red-faced, sly-looking ginger-beer seller, defendant in the case of "Bumple against Sludberry;"

sentenced to excommunication for a fortnight and payment of costs.

LONDON RECREATIONS

**Bill, Uncle.** One of a party of Sunday pleasurers at a tea-garden; considered a great wit by his friends.

**Sally.** His niece, joked by Uncle Bill about her marriage, and her first baby, because a certain young man is "keeping company" with her.

THE RIVER

**Dando.** A boatman.

ASTLEY'S

**Woolford, Miss.** A circus-rider.

PRIVATE THEATRES

**Larkins, Jem.** An amateur actor in the genteel comedy line, known to the public as Mr. Horatio St. Julian.

**Loggins, Mr.** A player who takes the part of Macbeth, and is announced on the bills as Mr. Beverley.

VAUXHALL GARDENS BY DAY

**Green, Mr.** An aeronaut.

**Green, Mr., jun.** His son and assistant.

THE LAST CAB-DRIVER AND THE FIRST OMNIBUS-CAD

**Barker, Mr. William**, *commonly called* BILL BOORKER *or* AGGERAWATIN BILL. An omnibus-cad, with a remarkable talent for enticing the youthful and unwary, and shoving the old and helpless, into the wrong 'bus.

A PARLIAMENTARY SKETCH

**Captain, The.** A spare, squeaking old man, always damning his own eyes or "somebody else's," and a complete walking-reservoir of spirits and water.

**Jane.** The Hebe of "Bellamy's," or the refreshment-room of the Houses of Parliament. She has a thorough contempt for the great majority of her visitors, and a great love of admiration.

**Nicholas.** The butler of "Bellamy's." He has held the same place, dressed exactly in the same manner, and said precisely the same things, ever since the oldest of its present visitors can remember.

**Tom, Honest.** A metropolitan member of the House of Commons.

THE FIRST OF MAY

**Sluffen, Mr.**, of Adam-and-Eve Court. A speaker at the anniversary dinner given to the chimney-sweeps on May Day at White Conduit House.

### THE PAWNBROKER'S SHOP

**Henry, Mr.** A pawnbroker, whose shop is near Drury Lane.

**Jinkins.** A customer, dirty, intoxicated, and quarrelsome.

**Mackin, Mrs.** Another customer, slipshod and abusive.

**Tatham, Mrs.** An old woman who tries to borrow eighteen pence or a shilling on a child's frock and "a beautiful silk ankecher."

## CHARACTERS

### THOUGHTS ABOUT PEOPLE

**Smith, Mr.** A poor clerk, a mere passive creature of habit and endurance.

### A CHRISTMAS DINNER

**George, Aunt.** The hostess at whose house the Christmas family party assemble.

**George, Uncle.** Her husband.

**Jane, Aunt.** Another member of the family.

**Margaret, Aunt.** Married to a poor man, and treated coldly by her relations in consequence.

**Robert, Uncle.** Husband to Aunt Jane.

### THE NEW YEAR

**Dobble, Mr.** A clerk in a public office, who gives a quadrille party on New Year's eve.

**Dobble, Mr., jun.** His son.

**Dobble, Miss Julia.** His eldest daughter.

**Dobble, Mrs.** His wife.

**Tupple, Mr.** A junior clerk in the same office with Mr. Dobble; a young man with a tendency to cold and corns, but "a charming person," and "a perfect ladies' man."

### MISS EVANS AND THE EAGLE

**Evans, Miss Jemima** (*called* "J'mima Ivins" by her acquaintances). A shoe-binder and straw-bonnet-maker, affianced to Mr. Samuel Wilkins.

**Evans, Miss Tilly.** One of her sisters.

**Evans, Mrs.** Her mother.

**Wilkins, Mr. Samuel.** A journeyman carpenter of small dimensions, "keeping company" with Miss Jemima Evans.

### THE PARLOR ORATOR

**Ellis, Mr.** A sharp-nosed man with a very slow and soft voice, who considers Mr. Rogers "such improving company."

**Rogers, Mr.** A stoutish man of about forty, with a red face and a confident oracular air, which marks him as a leading politician, general authority, and universal anecdote-relater. Proof is what he requires — proof, not assertions — in regard to anything and everything whatsoever.

**Tommy.** A little chubby-faced green-grocer, of great good sense, who opposes Mr. Rogers, and is denounced by him, in consequence, "as a willing slave."

THE HOSPITAL PATIENT

**Jack.** A young fellow who treats his paramour so brutally as to cause her death, and yet is so loved by her, even to the last, that she cannot be persuaded to swear his life away, but dies praying God to bless him.

THE MISPLACED ATTACHMENT OF MR. JOHN DOUNCE

**Dounce, Mr. John.** A fat, red-faced, white-headed old boy, a retired glove and braces maker, and a widower. He falls in love with a bewitching bar-maid, who trifles with his affections, and at last tells him plainly that she "would n't have him at no price;" whereupon he offers himself successively to a schoolmistress, a landlady, a feminine tobacconist, a housekeeper, and his own cook, by the last of whom he is accepted, married, — and thoroughly henpecked.

**Harris, Mr.** A law-stationer and a jolly old fellow; a friend of Mr. Dounce.

**Jennings, Mr.** A robe-maker; also a friend of Mr. Dounce, and a sad dog in his time.

**Jones, Mr.** Another friend, a barrister's clerk, and a rum fellow, — capital company, — full of anecdote.

THE MISTAKEN MILLINER

**Martin, Miss Amelia.** A milliner and dressmaker who has an ambition to "come out" as a public singer, and tries it, but fails miserably.

**Rodolph, Mr. and Mrs. Jennings.** Her friends and counsellors.

THE DANCING ACADEMY

**Billsmethi, Signor.** A popular dancing-master.

**Billsmethi, Master.** His son.

**Billsmethi, Miss.** His daughter, a young lady with her hair curled in a crop all over her head, and her shoes tied in sandals all over her ankles. She sets her cap for Mr. Cooper, and, not succeeding in securing him for a husband, brings a suit for breach of promise, but finally compromises the matter for twenty pounds, four shillings, and sixpence.

**Cooper, Mr. Augustus.** A young gentleman of Fetter Lane, in the oil-and-color business, just of age, with a little money, a little business, and a little mother.

### MAKING A NIGHT OF IT

**Potter, Mr. Thomas.** A clerk in the city, with a limited income, and an unbounded friendship for Mr. Smithers.

**Smithers, Mr. Robert.** Also a clerk in the city, knit by the closest ties of intimacy and friendship to Mr. Potter. On the receipt of their quarter's salary, these two "thick-and-thin pals," as they style themselves, spend an evening together, and proceeding by degrees from simple hilarity to drunkenness, commit various breaches of the peace; are locked up in the station-house for the night; brought before the police court in the morning, and each fined five shillings for being drunk, and thirty-four pounds for seventeen assaults at forty shillings a head.

### THE PRISONERS' VAN

**Bella.** A young girl, not fourteen, forced by a sordid and rapacious mother to a life of vice and crime, which she loathes, but cannot escape from.

**Emily.** Her sister, hardened in depravity by two additional years' experience of the debauchery of London street-life, and priding herself on being "game."

## TALES

### THE BOARDING-HOUSE

**Agnes.** Mrs. Bloss's maid.

**Bloss, Mrs.** The wealthy widow of a cork-cutter, whose cook she had been. Having nothing to do, she imagines she must be ill, but eats amazingly, and has the appearance of being remarkably well. She makes the acquaintance of Mr. Gobler, and marries him.

**Calton, Mr.** A superannuated beau, exceedingly vain, inordinately selfish, and the very pink of politeness. He makes himself agreeable to Mrs. Maplesone, and agrees to marry her; but, failing to do so, she sues him for breach of promise, and recovers a thousand pounds.

**Evenson, Mr. John.** A stern, morose, and discontented man, a thorough radical, and a universal fault-finder.

**Gobler, Mr.** A lazy, selfish hypochondriac, whose digestion is so much impaired, and whose interior so deranged, that his stomach is not of the least use to him.

**Hicks, Mr. Septimus.** A tallish, white-faced, spectacled young man, who has the reputation of being very talented. He falls in love with Miss Matilda Maplesone, whom he marries, but afterwards deserts.

**James.** A servant to Mrs. Tibbs.

**Maplesone, Mrs.** An enterprising widow of fifty, shrewd, scheming, and good-looking, with no objection to marrying again, if it would benefit her dear girls.

**Maplesone, Miss Julia.** Her younger daughter; married to Mr. Septimus Hicks.

**Maplesone, Miss Matilda.** Her elder daughter; married to Mr. Simpson.

**O'Bleary, Mr. Frederick.** A patriotic Irishman recently imported in a perfectly wild state; in search of employment and ready to do or be anything that might turn up.

**Robinson.** A female servant to Mrs. Tibbs.

**Simpson, Mr.** One of the "walking gentlemen" of society; an empty-headed young man, always dressed according to the caricatures published in the monthly fashions.

**Tibbs, Mr.** A short man, with very short legs, but a face peculiarly long, by way of indemnification. He is to his wife what the 0 is in 90, — of some importance with her, but nothing without her.

**Tibbs, Mrs.** His wife, mistress of the boarding-house; the most tidy, fidgety, thrifty little person that ever inhaled the smoke of London.

**Tompkins, Mr. Alfred.** Clerk in a wine-house; a connoisseur in paintings, and with a wonderful eye for the picturesque.

**Wisbottle, Mr.** A clerk in the Woods and Forests office, and a high Tory; addicted to whistling, and having a great idea of his singing powers.

**Wosky, Doctor.** Mrs. Bloss's medical attendant, who has amassed a fortune by invariably humoring the worst fancies of his female patients.

MR. MINNS AND HIS COUSIN.

**Brogson, Mr.** An elderly gentleman visiting at Mr. Budden's.

**Budden, Mr. Octavius.** A retired corn-chandler, residing at Amelia Cottage, Poplar Walk, Stamford Hill. He is a cousin to Mr. Minns.

**Budden, Mrs. Amelia.** His wife.

**Budden, Master Alexander Augustus.** Their son, a precocious child, and the pride of his parents.

**Jones, Mr.** A little man with red whiskers, a visitor at Mr. Budden's and a "devilish sharp fellow," who talks equally well on any subject.

**Minns, Mr. Augustus.** A clerk in Somerset House, and a precise, tidy, retiring old bachelor, who is always getting into trouble when he leaves his own snug and well-ordered apartments, and who is thoroughly disgusted with a visit which he is compelled to make to his cousin, Mr. Octavius Budden.

SENTIMENT

**Butler, Mr. Theodosius.** A very wonderful genius, author of a pamphlet entitled "Considerations on the Policy of Removing the Duty on Beeswax." This he presents to Cornelius Brook Dingwall, Esq., M. P., under the assumed name of Edward M'Neville Walter, and thus gains admission to his house, and an opportunity of winning the heart of his supersentimental daughter.

**Crumpton, Miss Amelia.** A very tall, thin, skinny, upright, yellow, and precise maiden lady, with the strictest possible idea of propriety.

**Crumpton, Miss Maria.** The exact counterpart of her sister, in conjunction with whom she carries on a finishing-school for young ladies, called "Minerva House."

**Dadson, Mr.** Writing-master at the Miss Crumptons' school.

**Dadson, Mrs.** His wife.

**Dingwall, Cornelius Brook, Esq., M. P.** A very haughty, solemn, and portentous man, having a great opinion of his own abilities, and wonderfully proud of being a member of parliament.

**Dingwall, Mrs. Brook.** His wife.

**Dingwall, Frederick.** Son of Mr. and Mrs. Brook Dingwall; one of those public nuisances, — a spoiled child.

**Dingwall, Miss Lavinia Brook.** Their daughter, the most romantic of all romantic young ladies; in love with Edward M'Neville Walter (otherwise Mr. Theodosius Butler), a young man much her inferior in life. She is therefore sent to the Miss Crumptons' educational establishment, to eradicate the sentimental attachment from her young mind, on the supposition that she can have no opportunity of meeting him there. She does meet him, however, and runs away with and marries him in haste, only to repent at leisure.

**Hilton, Mr.** Master of ceremonies at a ball at Minerva House.

**James.** Servant to Mr. Brook Dingwall.

**Lobskini, Signor.** A singing-master, with a splendid tenor voice.

**Parsons, Miss Lætitia.** A brilliant musical performer.

**Smithers, Miss Emily.** The belle of Minerva House.
**Wilson, Miss Caroline.** Her bosom-friend, and the ugliest girl in Hammersmith, — or out of it.

THE TUGGSES AT RAMSGATE

**Amelia, Jane, and Mary Ann.** Young ladies who take part in games of chance in a concert-room at Ramsgate.
**Slaughter, Lieutenant.** A friend of Captain Waters.
**Tippin, Mr.** A comic singer at Ramsgate.
**Tippin, Mrs.** His wife; a concert-singer from the London theatres.
**Tippin, Master.** Their son.
**Tippin, Miss.** Their daughter; a performer on the guitar.
**Tuggs, Mr. Joseph.** A little pursy London grocer, with shiny hair, twinkling eyes, and short legs. By the unexpected decision of a long-pending lawsuit he comes into possession of twenty thousand pounds, whereupon he incontinently puts on airs, closes his shop, and starts with his family for Ramsgate, that being a fashionable watering-place.
**Tuggs, Mrs.** His wife; in charge of the cheesemongery department while her husband is a shop-keeper.
**Tuggs, Miss Charlotte.** Their only daughter. When her father becomes rich, she calls herself Charlotta.
**Tuggs, Mr. Simon.** Their only son; a young gentleman with that elongation in his thoughtful face, and that tendency to weakness in his interesting legs, which tell so forcibly of a great mind and romantic disposition. At first, he is a book-keeper in his father's shop; but, when a large fortune suddenly falls to the family, he changes the orthographical architecture of his name, and styles himself Cymon; attempts to play the gentleman; and roundly abuses his father for not appearing aristocratic. Going to Ramsgate, he is neatly taken in and swindled by Captain Waters and his wife, whom he meets there, and greatly admires, — especially the wife. He escapes with the loss of his veneration for appearances, and of fifteen hundred pounds in money.
**Waters, Captain Walter.** A pretended military man, and a sharper.
**Waters, Mrs. Belinda.** His wife; a young lady with long black ringlets, large black eyes, brief petticoats, and unexceptionable ankles.

HORATIO SPARKINS

**Barton, Mr. Jacob.** Brother of Mrs. Malderton; a large grocer, who never scrupled to avow that he was n't above his business. "He 'd made his money by it, and he did n't care who know'd it."
**Flamwell, Mr.** A little spoffish toad-eater, with green spectacles,

always pretending to know everybody, but in reality knowing nobody; a friend of Mr. Malderton.

**John.** A man in Mr. Malderton's service, half groom, half gardener, but, on great occasions, touched up and brushed to look like a second footman.

**Malderton, Mr.** (of Oak Lodge, Camberwell). A man who has become rich in consequence of a few successful speculations, and who is hospitable from ostentation, illiberal from ignorance, and prejudiced from conceit. The whole scope of his ideas is limited to Lloyds, the Exchange, the India House, and the Bank.

**Malderton, Mrs.** His wife; a little fat woman, with a great aversion to anything *low.*

**Malderton, Miss Marianne.** Their younger daughter; a sentimental damsel.

**Malderton, Miss Teresa.** Their elder daughter; a young lady of eight and twenty, who has flirted for ten years in vain, but is still on the lookout for a husband.

**Malderton, Mr. Frederick.** Their elder son; the very *beau idéal* of a smart waiter, and the family authority on all points of taste, dress, and fashionable arrangement.

**Malderton, Mr. Thomas.** Their younger son; snubbed by his father on all occasions, with a view to prevent his becoming "sharp," — a very unnecessary precaution.

**Sparkins, Mr. Horatio.** A young man whose dashing manners and gentlemanlike appearance so dazzle the Maldertons, that they think he must be a man of large fortune and aristocratic family. They even go so far as to suspect that he may be a nobleman, and are greatly mortified at last to discover that he is a mere clerk in a linen-draper's shop, and owns to the plebeian name of Smith.

### THE STEAM EXCURSION

**Briggs, Mrs.** A widow-lady; a rival of Mrs. Taunton.

**Briggs, Miss.** One of her three daughters.

**Briggs, Miss Julia.** Another daughter.

**Briggs, Miss Kate.** Another daughter.

**Briggs, Mr. Alexander.** Her younger son, articled to his brother. He is remarkable for obstinacy.

**Briggs, Mr. Samuel.** Her elder son; an attorney, and a mere machine; a sort of self-acting, legal walking-stick.

**Edkins, Mr.** (of the Inner Temple). A pale young gentleman in a green stock and green spectacles, who makes a speech on every occasion on which one can possibly be made.

**Fleetwood, Mr.** One of the excursion party.

**Fleetwood, Mrs.** His wife, who accompanies him.

**Fleetwood, Master.** Their son; an unfortunate innocent of about four years of age.

**Hardy, Mr.** A stout, middle-aged gentleman, with a red face, a somewhat husky voice, and a tremendous laugh. He is a practical joker, is immensely popular with married ladies, and a general favorite with young men.

**Helves, Captain.** A military gentleman with a bass voice and an incipient red moustache; a friend of the Tauntons.

**Noakes, Mr. Percy.** A law-student, smart, spoffish, and eight and twenty. With a few friends he attempts to get up an excursion party to which no one shall be invited who has not received the unanimous vote of a committee of arrangements. But the obstinate Mr. Alexander Briggs being a member of this committee, and blackballing everybody who is proposed by Mr. Noakes or his friends, the original plan is abandoned; and every gentleman is allowed to bring whom he pleases. The party start on a Wednesday morning for the Nore, and reach it after a pleasant trip; but on the return a violent squall comes up; the pitching and tossing of the boat bring on a general seasickness; and, when they get back to the wharf at two o'clock the next morning, every one is thoroughly dispirited and worn out.

**Stubbs, Mrs.** A dirty old laundress, with an inflamed countenance.

**Taunton, Mrs.** A good-looking widow of fifty, with the form of a giantess and the mind of a child. The sole end of her existence is the pursuit of pleasure, and some means of killing time. She is a particular friend of Mr. Percy Noakes, and a mortal enemy of the Briggses.

**Taunton, Miss Emily.** Her daughter; a frivolous young lady.

**Taunton, Miss Sophia.** Another daughter, as light-minded as her sister.

### THE GREAT WINGLEBURY DUEL

**Brown, Miss Emily.** A young lady beloved by both Mr. Trott and Mr. Hunter, but finally married to the latter.

**Hunter, Mr. Horace.** Rival of Mr. Trott for the hand of Miss Emily Brown.

**Manners, Miss Julia.** A buxom and wealthy woman of forty, formerly engaged to be married to a Mr. Cornberry, who died leaving her a large property unencumbered with the addition of himself. Being in want of a young husband, she falls in love with a certain wild and prodigal nobleman, Lord Peter, who falls in love with her handsome fortune of three thousand pounds a year; but in the end she marries plain Mr. Trott.

**Overton, Joseph, Esq.** Solicitor, and mayor of Great Winglebury.

**Peter, Lord.** A dissipated sprig of nobility, attached to Miss Manners (or her money); killed by being thrown from his horse in a steeple-chase.

**Thomas.** A waiter at the Winglebury Arms.

**Trott, Mr. Alexander.** A cowardly young tailor (or umbrella-maker). He desires to marry Miss Emily Brown, but is deterred by the hostile attitude of Mr. Horace Hunter, who challenges him to mortal combat for daring to think of such a thing. He accepts the challenge in a bloodthirsty note, but immediately sends another, and an anonymous one, to the mayor of Great Winglebury, urging that Mr. Trott be forthwith arrested. By a ludicrous blunder he is mistaken for Lord Peter, who is expected at the Winglebury Arms for the purpose of meeting Miss Julia Manners, his intended, and who is to be seized and carried off as an insane person in order that his relatives may not discover him. Thus it happens that Trott is taken away in a carriage with Miss Manners, and, mutual explanations having been made, that he marries her instead of the adorable Miss Emily Brown.

**Williamson, Mrs.** Landlady of the Winglebury Arms.

### MRS. JOSEPH PORTER

**Balderstone, Mr. Thomas,** *called* "UNCLE TOM." A rich brother of Mrs. Gattleton, always in a good temper, and always talking and joking.

**Brown, Mr.** A performer on the violoncello at the private theatricals.

**Cape, Mr.** A violinist.

**Evans, Mr.** A tall, thin, and pale young gentleman, with lovely whiskers, and a remarkable talent for writing verses in albums, and for playing the flute. He is the *Roderigo* of the private theatricals.

**Gattleton, Mr.** A retired stockbroker, living at Rose Villa, Clapham Rise. He is infected, as are the other members of his family, with a mania for private theatricals, acting himself as prompter.

**Gattleton, Mrs.** His wife; a kind-hearted, good-tempered, vulgar soul, with a natural antipathy to other people's unmarried daughters, a bodily fear of ridicule, and a great dislike for Mrs. Joseph Porter.

**Gattleton, Miss.** One of their three daughters.

**Gattleton, Miss Caroline.** Another daughter; the *Fenella* of the private theatricals.

**Gattleton, Miss Lucina.** Another daughter, who plays the part of *Desdemona*.

**Gattleton, Mr. Sempronius.** Their son, at once stage-manager and *Othello.*

**Harleigh, Mr.** A singer, who takes the part of *Masaniello.*

**Jenkins, Miss.** A piano-player.

**Porter, Mrs. Joseph.** A sarcastic scandal-monger, who delights in making other people uncomfortable. At the private theatricals of the Gattletons, she indulges her propensity to mischief-making by setting on Mr. Thomas Balderstone (who prides himself on his accurate knowledge of Shakespeare) to interrupt the performers in the very midst of the play by correcting their numerous mistakes.

**Porter, Miss Emily.** Her daughter.

**Wilson, Mr.** The *Iago* of the private theatricals.

A PASSAGE IN THE LIFE OF MR. WATKINS TOTTLE

**Ikey.** The factotum of Mr. Solomon Jacobs's sponging-house.

**Jacobs, Mr. Solomon.** A bailiff, living in Cursitor Street.

**Jem.** A sallow-faced, red-haired, sulky boy in charge of the door of Mr. Jacobs's private lock-up.

**John.** Servant to Mrs. Parsons.

**Lillerton, Miss.** A prim spinster of uncertain age, with a complexion as clear as that of a wax doll, and a face as expressive.

**Martha.** Servant to Mrs. Parsons.

**Parsons, Mr. Gabriel.** An elderly and rich sugar-baker, who mistakes rudeness for honesty, and abrupt bluntness for an open and candid manner.

**Parsons, Mrs. Fanny.** His wife.

**Timson, The Reverend Charles.** A friend of Mr. Parsons. He marries Miss Lillerton.

**Tottle, Mr. Watkins.** A plump, clean, rosy bachelor of fifty; a compound of strong uxorious inclinations and an unparalleled degree of anti-connubial timidity. Having been arrested for debt, and confined in a sponging-house, his friend Parsons engages to pay the debt, and take him out, if he will agree to marry Miss Lillerton, who has five hundred pounds a year in her own right. On being released, he offers himself to that lady, but after such an awkward and ambiguous fashion, that she quite mistakes his meaning, and answers him in a way that makes him think himself accepted. On being sent by her with a note — respecting their marriage, as he supposes — to the Reverend Mr. Timson, it transpires that she has been engaged to that gentleman for several weeks. The upshot of the whole affair is that Mr. Parsons renounces the friendship and acquaintance of Mr. Tottle, who takes refuge from "the slings and arrows of outrageous fortune' by walking into the Regent's Canal.

**Walker, Mr.** An imprisoned debtor, inmate of Mr. Solomon Jacobs's private lock-up.

**Willis, Mr.** Another inmate of the same establishment.

THE BLOOMSBURY CHRISTENING

**Danton, Mr.** A young man with a considerable stock of impudence, and a very small share of ideas, who passes for a wit. He is a friend of Mr. Kitterbell's, and a great favorite generally, especially with young ladies.

**Dumps, Mr. Nicodemus,** *called* "LONG DUMPS." An old bachelor, never happy but when he is miserable, and always miserable when he has the best reason to be happy, and whose only real comfort is to make everybody about him wretched. He is uncle to Mr. Charles Kitterbell, and, having been invited to stand as godfather to that gentleman's infant son, reluctantly does so, but takes his revenge by suggesting the most dismal possibilities of sickness and accident, as altogether likely to happen to the child, and by making a speech at the supper after the christening, so lugubrious and full of gloomy forebodings as to throw Mrs. Kitterbell into violent hysterics, thus breaking up the party, and enabling him to walk home with a cheerful heart.

**Kitterbell, Mr. Charles.** A small, sharp, spare man, with an extraordinarily large head and a cast in his eye; very credulous and matter-of-fact.

**Kitterbell, Mrs. Jemima.** His wife; a tall, thin young lady with very light hair, a particularly white face, a slight cough, and a languid smile.

**Kitterbell, Master Frederick Charles William.** Their first baby.

THE DRUNKARD'S DEATH

**Tom.** One of the officers who arrest young Warden.

**Warden.** A confirmed and irreclaimable drunkard. Remorse, fear, and shame; the loss of friends, happiness, and station; the death of his wife from grief and care; the murder of one of his sons, whom he had driven from home in a drunken fit; his own betrayal of another son into the hangman's hands from a like cause; his final desertion by his daughter, who has stayed by him and supported him for years; the utmost extremity of poverty, disease, and houseless want, — do not avail to conquer his fierce rage for drink, which drives him remorselessly on, until at last he seeks release in death by drowning himself in the Thames.

**Warden, Mary.** His daughter.

**Warden, William.** His son. He avenges his brother's death by killing the gamekeeper who shot him; flees from justice to his father's solitary attic room in the obscurest portion of Whitefriars; is discovered by the officers in consequence of his father's getting intoxicated and betraying his hiding-place; and is seized, handcuffed, carried off, and made to suffer the penalty of his crime.

# THE ADVENTURES OF OLIVER TWIST

## OUTLINE

Chapter The hero of this tale was born in a workhouse; his mo-
I ther, brought in the night before from the street, died on giving him birth, without making known her own history. In this forlorn substitute for a home the child was brought up. The
II parish beadle, Mr. Bumble, who named the foundlings in alphabetical order, presented him with the name of Oliver Twist, and for nine years Oliver knew no other home than the workhouse. At the end of that time the authorities proposed to let him out, as the phrase runs, as an apprentice, and were ready to pay
III three pounds ten to Mr. Gamfield, a chimney sweep, if he would thus take Oliver off their hands. Mr. Gamfield, who was not without a reputation for hard dealings with youngsters, and bore his reputation in his face, might have carried his point, if Oliver, terrified at the prospect, had not pleaded so piteously that a more humane member of the workhouse board refused to have the bargain carried out.

IV Bumble presently discovered a new chance to be rid of Oliver, and after a short consideration the little orphan was turned over to Mr. Sowerberry, the undertaker. Far below Mr.
V Sowerberry, but far above Oliver, were a charity-boy, Mister Noah Claypole, and a maid of all work, Charlotte, who rejoiced in having a lowlier worm than themselves to turn upon, and Oliver soon learned his situation. His master also began to make him useful, and was particularly pleased with the effect produced by the little chap as a mute or professional mourner.

VI A month of probation passed, and then Oliver was regularly apprenticed. He was a meek, downtrodden creature, but one day Noah brutally taunted the memory of Oliver's dead mother, and the apprentice, stung into spirit, flew at the hulking coward and thrashed him to the content of the reader.

VII Although Mrs. Sowerberry and Charlotte immediately pounced on Oliver like a couple of hawks, his spirit had so enlarged the boy in their eyes that Noah Claypole was sent off for Mr. Bumble, rolling his story like a snowball into a mountainous mass, so that Mr. Bumble came back with him and administered an official beating, after which Oliver was shut up on bread and water. At night the boy, thus flung away by his kind, crept out into the darkness and stole away, his only blessing the good-by of little Dick, one of his workhouse companions.

VIII For five miles Oliver ran and stealthily eluded any chance passer-by. Then he stopped to rest by a mile-stone which told him he was seventy miles from London. To the little fellow, frantically eager to escape, that great city seemed to offer the only final hiding-place, and he pushed on his way, footsore and hungry, helped by some, driven off by others, until he reached in the early morning the village of Barnet. Here he fell in with a swaggering youngster named Jack Dawkins, otherwise known as The Artful Dodger, who offered to escort him to London and make him acquainted with a very respectable old gentleman.

IX The very respectable old gentleman was one Fagin, a Jew, and his occupation was nothing other than that of a professional thief, who was, so to speak, at the head of a school of thieves, for he was surrounded by youngsters whom he was training in the art of pilfering and picking pockets.

When the breakfast was cleared away, the merry old gentleman and the two boys played at a very curious and uncommon game, which was performed in this way. The merry old gentleman, placing a snuff-box in one pocket of his trousers, a note-case in the other, and a watch in his waistcoat pocket, with a guard-chain round his neck, and sticking a mock diamond pin in his shirt, buttoned his coat tight round him, and putting his spectacle-case and handkerchief in his pockets, trotted up and down the room with a stick, in imitation of the manner in which old gentlemen walk about the streets any hour in the day. Sometimes he stopped at the fireplace, and sometimes at the door, making belief that he was staring with all his might into shop windows. At such times, he would look constantly round him, for fear of thieves, and keep slapping all his pockets in turn, to see that he had n't lost anything, in such a very funny and natural manner, that Oliver laughed till the tears ran down his face. All this time, the two boys followed him closely about; getting out of his sight, so nimbly, every time he turned round, that it was impossible to follow their motions. At last, the Dodger trod upon his toes, or ran upon his boot accidentally, while Charley Bates stumbled up against him behind; and in that one moment they took from him, with the most extraordinary rapidity, snuff-box, note-case, watch, guard-chain, shirt-pin, pocket-handkerchief — even the spectacle-case. If the old gentleman felt a hand in any one of his pockets, he cried out where it was; and then the game began all over again.

When this game had been played a great many times, a couple of young ladies called to see the young gentlemen; one of whom was named Bet, and the other Nancy. They wore a good deal of hair, not very neatly turned up behind, and were rather untidy about the shoes and stockings. They were not exactly pretty, perhaps; but they had a great deal of color in their faces, and looked quite stout and hearty. Being remarkably free and agreeable in their manners, Oliver thought them very nice girls indeed. As there is no doubt they were.

These visitors stopped a long time. Spirits were produced, in consequence of one of the young ladies complaining of a coldness in her inside; and the conversation took a very convivial and improving turn. At length, Charley Bates expressed his opinion that it was time to pad the hoof. This, it occurred to Oliver, must be French for going out; for, directly afterwards, the Dodger, and Charley, and the two young ladies, went away together, having been kindly furnished by the amiable old Jew with money to spend.

"There, my dear," said Fagin. "That 's a pleasant life, is n't it? They have gone out for the day."

"Have they done work, sir?" inquired Oliver.

"Yes," said the Jew; "that is, unless they should unexpectedly come across any, when they are out; and they won't neglect it, if they do, my dear: depend upon it."

"Make 'em your models, my dear. Make 'em your models," said the Jew, tapping the fire-shovel on the hearth to add force to his words; "do everything they bid you, and take their advice in all matters — especially the Dodger's, my dear. He 'll be a great man himself, and will make you one too, if you take pattern by him — Is my handkerchief hanging out of my pocket, my dear?" said the Jew, stopping short.

"Yes, sir," said Oliver.

"See if you can take it out, without my feeling it, — as you saw them do, when we were at play this morning."

Oliver held up the bottom of the pocket with one hand, as he had seen the Dodger hold it, and drew the handkerchief lightly out of it with the other.

"Is it gone?" cried the Jew.

"Here it is, sir," said Oliver, showing it in his hand.

"You 're a clever boy, my dear," said the playful old gentleman, patting Oliver on the head approvingly. "I never saw a sharper lad. Here 's a shilling for you. If you go on in this way, you 'll be the greatest man of the time. And now come here, and I 'll show you how to take the marks out of the handkerchiefs."

Oliver wondered what picking the old gentleman's pocket in play had to do with his chances of being a great man. But, thinking that the Jew, being so much his senior, must know best, he followed him quietly to the table, and was soon deeply involved in his new study.

X For a while Oliver innocently took part in what he supposed to be a lively game, until, on being sent out with two of the boys, he was horrified to discover in a flash what all this training meant, when the boys made off with the handkerchief of an old gentleman who was poring over some books in a bookstall. Just as the old gentleman discovered his loss, Oliver made his own discovery, and in the confusion of the moment turned and fled. After him, with the cry of "Stop thief!" went every one in the neighborhood, and in a trice he was knocked down and picked up bruised and stunned, an object of derision to the crowd and of pity to the old gentleman.

XI There was a police-office near by, presided over by an insolent petty magistrate, and Oliver was brought before him, while Mr. Brownlow, the old gentleman, appeared reluctantly as prosecutor. Mr. Fang, the police-justice, after abusing the law, Mr. Brownlow, and Oliver, was about to commit the last to prison, when the keeper of the bookstall rushed in and made it clear that the two boys who had been with Oliver were the sinners, and that Oliver himself was innocent. Mr. Brownlow, who had been puzzled at some obscure reminder in Oliver's face, now took charge of the boy, who had fainted away, called a coach, and drove off with him to his own home in Pentonville.

XII When Oliver began to recover from a fever, and found himself in the home of his new friend, he was strangely drawn toward a picture in the room in which he slept, and Mr. Brownlow himself was struck by the extraordinary likeness between the boy's face and that of the lady in the picture. Mr. Brownlow appeared to be on the point of tracing a possible real connection, when his plans were suddenly thwarted in an unexpected manner. For when the Artful Dodger and Charley Bates
XIII returned to Fagin and told their story, the old Jew was fearful that Oliver might disclose the secret of his school of crime. One of his companions in wickedness, Bill Sikes, accompanied by his dog, entered just then, and between them they persuaded Nancy, a girl who was Bill's companion, to impersonate the heart-broken sister of Oliver, to make inquiries at the police-office,

and if possible to secure the boy. A singular chance threw Oliver in Nancy's way.

XIV Mr. Brownlow had invited an irascible, warm-hearted, skeptical old friend of his, Mr. Grimwig, to visit Oliver in preparation for the discovery which he hoped to make regarding his origin. As they were talking together, a package of books was brought from the bookstall, which was the scene of Oliver's adventure a little time before. The messenger got away before Mr. Brownlow could stop him to send the money and return another parcel of books, and Oliver, who had quite recovered, was eager to run the errand. Mr. Grimwig was ready "to eat his head" if the boy came back, and to his surprise, as well as Mr. Brownlow's, the boy did not come back.

XV He was walking along, thinking how happy and contented he ought to feel, and how much he would give for only one look at poor little Dick, who, starved and beaten, might be lying dead at that very moment, when he was startled by a young woman screaming out very loud, "Oh, my dear brother!" and he had hardly looked up to see what the matter was, when he was stopped by having a pair of arms thrown tight round his neck.

"Don't!" cried Oliver, struggling. "Let go of me! Who is it? What are you stopping me for?"

The only reply to this was a great number of loud lamentations from the young woman who had embraced him, and who had got a little basket and a street-door-key in her hand.

"Oh, my gracious!" said the young woman, "I've found him! Oh, Oliver, Oliver! Oh, you naughty boy, to make me suffer such distress on your account. Come home, dear, come. Oh, I've found him! Thank gracious goodness heavins, I've found him!" With these incoherent exclamations the young woman burst into another fit of crying, and got so dreadfully hysterical, that a couple of women who came up at the moment asked a butcher's boy with a shiny head of hair anointed with suet, who was also looking on, whether he did n't think he had better run for the doctor. To which the butcher's boy, who appeared of a lounging, not to say indolent disposition, replied that he thought not.

"Oh, no, no! never mind," said the young woman, grasping Oliver's hand; "I'm better now. Come home directly, you cruel boy, come!"

"What's the matter, ma'am?" inquired one of the women.

"Oh, ma'am!" replied the young woman, "he ran away near a month ago from his parents, who are hard-working and respectable people, and joined a set of thieves and bad characters, and almost broke his mother's heart."

"Young wretch!" said one woman.

"Go home, do, you little brute!" said the other.

"I'm not," replied Oliver, greatly alarmed. "I don't know her. I haven't got any sister, or father and mother, either. I'm an orphan; I live at Pentonville."

"Oh, only hear him! how he braves it out!" cried the young woman.

"Why, it's Nancy!" exclaimed Oliver, who now saw her face for the first time, and started back in irrepressible astonishment.

"You see he knows me," cried Nancy, appealing to the bystanders. "He can't help himself. Make him come home, there's good people, or he'll kill his dear mother and father, and break my heart!"

"What the devil's this?" said a man, bursting out of a beershop, with a white dog at his heels. "Young Oliver! Come home to your poor mother, you young dog! come home directly."

"I don't belong to them; I don't know them. Help, help!" cried Oliver, struggling in the man's powerful grasp.

"Help!" repeated the man. "Yes; I'll help you, you young rascal! What books are these? You've been stealing 'em, have you? Give 'em here!" With these words the man tore the volumes from his grasp, and struck him violently on the head.

"That's right!" cried a looker-on, from a garret-window. "That's the only way of bringing him to his senses!"

"To be sure!" cried a sleepy-faced carpenter, casting an approving look at the garret window.

"It'll do him good!" said the two women.

"And he shall have it too!" rejoined the man, administering another blow, and seizing Oliver by the collar. "Come on, you young villain! Here, Bull's-eye, mind him, boy! mind him!"

Weak with recent illness, stupefied by the blows and the suddenness of the attack, terrified by the fierce growling of the dog and the brutality of the man, and overpowered by the conviction of the bystanders that he was really the hardened little wretch he was described to be, what could one poor child do? Darkness had set in; it was a low neighborhood; no help was near; resistance was useless. In another moment he was dragged into a labyrinth of dark, narrow courts, and forced along them at a pace which rendered the few cries he dared give utterance to wholly unintelligible. It was of little moment, indeed, whether they were intelligible or not; for there was nobody to care for them had they been ever so plain.

XVI Nancy and Bill dragged the terrified boy back to Fagin's, where he was stripped of his new clothes, robbed of books

and money, and set upon by the boys; but all this was not without
a passionate protest from Nancy, in whose heart the forlorn boy had
awakened a slumbering pity.

XVII Oliver's real friends had not lost him without an effort to
recover him. They had posted notices, offering a reward for
information, and one of these posters met the eye of Mr. Bumble,
who had come up to London on parochial business. The beadle at
once sought Mr. Brownlow, but sadly disappointed that gentleman
by the tale of Oliver's baseness which his worm-eaten head had
concocted.

XVIII Meanwhile Oliver was in very sooth shut up in prison, for
the wily Jew was intent on making him useful, and as a
preparation kept him close under his eye, and by all the arts he
knew attempted to undermine his conscience and convert him into
a supple if not a willing tool. He was indeed concocting with Bill
XIX Sikes and Nancy a plan for a midnight robbery, and they
had decided that they needed the aid of Oliver. Nancy had
not lost her sense of guardianship of the boy, and it was partly to
protect him now that she fell in with the plan of the men, and drew
XX Oliver with her one night to the home of Bill Sikes, who
was to take the chief part in the proposed robbery. Bill
threatened Oliver with instant death if he hesitated to do whatever
he was bidden, and in the early morning Bill and Oliver took their
XXI way into the city proper, then to Smithfield, and finally at
night reached a place called Shepperton.

XXII Here in a lonely house they found two of Bill's companions,
Barney and Toby Crackit, and in the dead of night the
whole party stealthily sought a gentleman's house in the neighborhood, which was to be the scene of their burglary. The use to be
made of Oliver was apparent. As a small boy he could be pushed
through a narrow opening and made to open the outer door to the
robbers. In the moment when he discovered how he was to be
used Oliver determined to rush up the staircase and rouse the
house. But at that moment the thieves were seen from within, and
the shot that was fired took effect upon Oliver.

XXIII The mystery of this poor boy's origin came near solution
when he was in this plight, for as Mr. Bumble was taking
tea with Mrs. Corney, matron of the workhouse, and pleasantly
occupying himself with schemes on that thrifty person's heart and
purse, word was brought that old Sally lay a-dying; and Mrs.
XXIV Corney, reluctantly leaving Mr. Bumble, reached the old
woman's bedside in time only to hear her confession that
when Oliver was brought into the world she was in attendance, and
stole from the dying mother — what, old Sally's own death forbad
her disclosing.

XXV But Oliver's own fate was for a time quite as uncertain as
his origin. As Fagin and the boys were in their room,
Toby Crackit appeared. He did not need to tell them what the
papers had already revealed, that the attempt at burglary had
failed and the robbers had escaped, but it was news to him that
Bill Sikes had not returned. The last Toby had seen of him, Bill
was making off with the wounded Oliver on his back. Nor could
XXVI Fagin learn anything when he went in search of Nancy, but
before he returned he fell in with a mysterious acquaintance
named Monks, who returned with him and seemed to have strong
reasons for wishing to secure the safety of Oliver.

XXVII Meanwhile, Mrs. Corney, having seen the last of old Sally,
returned to her apartment and her Bumble, who extracted
from her "the one little, little, little word ye-ye-yes," and then
bidding her good night stopped on his way home to give Sowerberry
an order for Sally's coffin. There the virtuous and indignant
beadle came suddenly upon Noah and Charlotte repeating without
authority his own recent performance with Mrs. Corney.

XXVIII In point of fact, Bill Sikes had carried Oliver off, and had
commanded Toby Crackit to keep him, but as their pursuers
drew near with dogs, Toby took to his heels with all the risks of
Bill's pistol in his rear, and Bill Sikes himself at last let Oliver lie
in a ditch and made his own escape. When Oliver came to himself
he crept confused and trembling out of the ditch, and stumbled
back to the very house which he had been forced to enter. Here he
was discovered on the doorstep by the servants who had been the
frightened heroes of the night, and, better yet, was brought in
XXIX and cared for by Miss Rose Maylie and her aunt, who were
the occupants of the house, and who sent for the neighboring
surgeon.

XXX The whole party, who had expected from Giles the butler's
account to find a brawny villain, were much surpised
at finding a pale, feeble boy, scarcely more than a child in appearance.
Between them they determined to save the little fellow, and
though the servants with unheard-of promptness had sent for Bow
XXXI Street officers, Mr. Losberne, the surgeon, succeeded in convincing
these officers and even Giles himself that the boy
was not the supposed housebreaker's boy.

XXXII Under the care of his friends Oliver throve apace, but all
attempts at substantiating his story failed. The surgeon
drove with him to the house where Oliver had spent the night of
the robbery, but he threw away all his chances of catching any
accomplice of the thieves by blurting out his errand to the villainous-looking
hunchback whom he found there. They drove to Mr.

Brownlow's house only to find that he had gone to the West Indies, and his house was closed.

XXXIII For several months peace reigned; then an unexpected alarm fell on the house. Rose Maylie was taken ill and her life was despaired of. It chanced that one day there was need of the utmost haste in reaching Mr. Losberne. Oliver was dispatched on the errand, and at the inn encountered the stranger who had shown such exceeding interest in him when talking with Fagin. Oliver himself was ignorant of the significance of the encounter. His only thought was for Rose, and his fears were allayed by a favorable turn to the disease.

XXXIV The recovery of Rose was accompanied by the appearance on the scene of Mrs. Maylie's son Harry, who was Rose's lover, and it transpired from his conversation with his mother that a mystery hung over Rose's birth. What most concerned Oliver, however, was that one day as he sat by himself there looked in upon him through the window for one moment of mutual recognition the faces of Fagin the Jew and Monks the stranger. In vain he
XXXV raised the alarm; the two men disappeared as mysteriously as they came, and the other mystery appeared no nearer solution, for earnestly as Harry pleaded Rose would not consent to bestow herself on him, when there was a stain apparently resting on
XXXVI her name. Harry left the place, but made a secret compact with Oliver that the boy should write him regularly.

XXXVII It will be remembered that Mr. Bumble, after a secret inventory of Mrs. Corney's property, decided that it would be a step upward in life for him to marry her, resign his beadle's truncheon, and become master of the workhouse. This he did, but unhappily for his peace he found he was not master of Mrs. Bumble. That lady, on the contrary, made him a mere attachment to her authority. It was after the first pitched battle between them, in which he was made to know his place, that Mr. Bumble, repairing to the public house, fell into the hands of Monks, who had come down to see if he could get word with the woman who had been with Oliver's mother when she died.

XXXVIII Accordingly Bumble, Mrs. Bumble, and Monks met in an old mill near by, with a thunder storm rolling over them, and there Mrs. Bumble disclosed all she knew, which was that old Sally died with a pawnbroker's ticket in her hand, that this ticket was for a trinket, and that Mrs. Bumble redeemed the trinket, a locket with the name Agnes upon it. This she produced, and for her information received twenty-five pounds from Monks. As for the locket, that he flung down a trap-door into the roaring stream below.

XXXIX Monks returned to London and sought Fagin, whom he
found just returned from Bill Sikes, who was recovering
from a fever and had sent Nancy to the Jew's to get some money.
Monks drew off into another room with Fagin, but Nancy, who had
already learned something of the plot that was hatching against
Oliver, succeeded in following them without being discovered, and
in learning more of Monks's secret. She carried her secret straight
XL to Rose Maylie, who had come up to London, and conveyed
so much as she had learned, to wit, that Monks was Oliver's
evil brother, who was fired with an unholy hatred of him, a desire
to secure the fortune which otherwise would belong to the poor boy,
and if possible to disgrace him by making him in Fagin's hands a
thief and an outcast.

XLI Rose was much perplexed over the disclosure, more especially as Nancy had enjoined on her not to reveal her part in
the business. As she was deliberating over the matter, Oliver suddenly burst into the room. He had been out with Giles and had,
without being seen himself, set eyes on his old benefactor, Mr.
Brownlow. He had noted the house at which he stopped, and Rose
at once called a carriage and drove with him to the place. She
found Mr. Brownlow and Mr. Grimwig together, told them Oliver's
story and what she had learned from Nancy, and then produced
Oliver himself. As a consequence, Mrs. Maylie, Rose, Harry, Mr.
Brownlow, Mr. Grimwig, and Mr. Losberne formed themselves into
a sort of committee to bring Monks to justice and give Oliver
his own.

XLII Meantime an early acquaintance of Oliver's had appeared
on the scene. Noah Claypole had with Charlotte's assistance
robbed Sowerberry's till, and the two had come up to London.
As luck would have it they put up at The Three Cripples, which
was one of the resorts of Fagin and his friends, and Fagin overhearing their conversation and learning their history introduced
himself to them, and invited them to join his band. The Artful
XLIII Dodger had just been caught at pocket-picking, and Noah
Claypole, who now called himself Morris Bolter, was set
upon his first duty of going in disguise to the police court and
learning the fate of young Dawkins.

XLIV His second mission was a more significant one, for Fagin,
discovering that Nancy had some secret errand away from
Bill Sikes, employed Noah to dog her steps. Fagin fancied that
Nancy had formed a new attachment, and that by possessing him-
XLV self of it he could get her into his own power, and perhaps
with her connivance get rid of the ruffian Bill Sikes, whom
he greatly feared. In point of fact Nancy had made an appoint-

ment with Mr. Brownlow and Rose Maylie, and met them in one
of the dark recesses under London Bridge. Here Noah Claypole
hid himself and overheard the conference, in which Nancy
XLVI disclosed to them the place where they were likely to find
Monks, but refused to have any part in giving up Fagin or Bill
Sikes. She told them that she had failed to keep her appointment
the week before because Bill had suspected her and secured her
against going out, and that she succeeded this time only by
XLVII drugging him. It was this fact told by Fagin to Sikes which
so infuriated him that, rushing back to his room, he beat her and
left her dead on the floor.

The murderer, whose evil life had brought him no remorse
XLVIII hitherto, was now dazed by his foul deed. He wandered
forth with his dog. Wherever he went he seemed to cross the path
of some one who was about to detect his crime. At last, turning
back to London as by some fatal instinct, he resolved to flee the
country. He determined first to kill his dog, since he was in
danger of being discovered by means of that faithful comrade; but
even his dog seemed to have his eye on him, and eluded capture
himself.

While Sikes was thus trying to escape from himself, a
XLIX principal in the business had been taken; for Mr. Brownlow,
acting through Nancy's information, had with the aid of others
entrapped Monks and brought him to his own house. Then he
confronted him with the knowledge he had of the man's villainy,
and, under threat of delivering him over to the law, wrested from
him a signature to a document which was to be a clear recital of
his brother's rights; for Mr. Brownlow had been the faithful friend
of the father of these two. While they were thus engaged, Mr.
Losberne interrupted them with the news that the officers
L were upon the heels of Sikes and Fagin. Sikes was indeed
hard pressed. As the young accomplices of Fagin were huddled
together, telling of the misfortune which was overtaking their master, Bill's dog came bounding into the room from an open window. Then knocks were heard below. Bill himself had come. Of the party gathered there, one, the boy Charley Bates, was seized with a frenzied desire to deliver Bill up, and attacked him. While they were struggling, the officers came nearer. Bill made one terrible effort to escape. He wrenched himself loose from the boy, and with a rope essayed to lower himself from the roof into a dark corner in the rear of the building. Suddenly he seemed to see Nancy in a vision, he threw up his arms, the rope formed a noose, he lost his balance, and fell strangled from the building. After him with a howl went his dog, dashing his faithful brains out.

LI Two days after this event, Mr. Brownlow, Mrs. Maylie, Mr. Grimwig, Rose, and Oliver all went to Oliver's native town, where they had before them Monks, Mr. Bumble, and Mrs. Bumble, and little by little the whole mystery was solved, carrying with it the knowledge now first disclosed of Rose's parentage.

LII All that remained was to secure certain papers which Monks had deposited with the Jew for safe keeping, and a visit to the cell where Fagin was confined wrested the secret from the trembling old wretch.

LIII And thus each got his deserts. The Jew was hanged. Rose and Harry were married. Monks betook himself to a distant part of the new world, where his evil courses brought him to a death in prison. Mr. Brownlow adopted Oliver. Noah and Charlotte became degraded informants. Mr. and Mrs. Bumble ended their days as paupers in the workhouse where once they had tyrannized over the weak and helpless.

---

## INDEX TO CHARACTERS

**Anny.** A pauper. xxiv, li.

**Artful Dodger, The.** *See* DAWKINS, JOHN.

**Barney.** A villainous young Jew, with a chronic catarrh, employed at The Three Cripples Inn, Little Saffron Hill. xv, xxii, xlii, xlv.

**Bates, Charley.** A thief; one of Fagin's "apprentices." ix, x, xii, xiii, xvi, xviii, xxv.

**Bayton.** One of the poor of the parish. v.

**Becky.** Bar-maid at the Red Lion Inn. xxi.

**Bedwin, Mrs.** Mr. Brownlow's housekeeper. xii, xiv, xvii, xli, li.

**Bet,** *or* **Betsy.** A thief in Fagin's service, and a companion of Nancy. ix, xiii, xvi, xviii.

**Bill.** A grave-digger. v.

**Blathers** *and* **Duff.** Bow Street officers. xxxi.

**Bolter, Morris.** *See* CLAYPOLE, NOAH.

**Brittles.** A servant at Mrs. Maylie's. xxviii, xxx, xxxi, liii.

**Brownlow, Mr.** A benevolent old gentleman, who takes Oliver into his house, and treats him kindly. x–xii, xvi, xli, xlvi, xlix, li–liii.

**Bull's-eye.** Bill Sikes's dog. xiii, xv, xvi, xix, xxxix, xlviii, l.

**Bumble, Mr.** A beadle puffed up with the insolence of office. i, iii–v, vii, xvii, xxiii, xxxvii, xxxviii, li. He visits the branch workhouse where Oliver Twist is "farmed," and is received with great attention by Mrs. Mann, the matron.

Mrs. Mann ushered the beadle into a small parlor with a brick floor, placed a seat for him, and officiously deposited his cocked hat and cane on the table before him. Mr. Bumble wiped from his forehead the perspiration which his walk had engendered, glanced complacently at the cocked hat, and smiled. Yes, he smiled. Beadles are but men; and Mr. Bumble smiled.

"Now, don't you be offended at what I'm a going to say," observed Mrs. Mann with captivating sweetness. "You've had a long walk, you know, or I would n't mention it. Now, will you take a little drop of something, Mr. Bumble?"

"Not a drop, not a drop," said Mr. Bumble, waving his right hand in a dignified but still placid manner.

"I think you will," said Mrs. Mann, who had noticed the tone of the refusal and the gesture that had accompanied it, —"just a *leetle* drop, with a little cold water, and a lump of sugar."

Mr. Bumble coughed.

"Now, just a little drop," said Mrs. Mann persuasively.

"What is it?" inquired the beadle.

"Why, it's what I'm obliged to keep a little of in the house, to put in the blessed infants' daffy when they ain't well, Mr. Bumble," replied Mrs. Mann, as she opened a corner cupboard, and took down a bottle and glass. "It's gin."

"Do you give the children daffy, Mrs. Mann?" inquired Bumble, following with his eyes the interesting process of mixing.

"Ah, bless 'em! that I do, dear as it is," replied the nurse. "I could n't see 'em suffer before my eyes, you know, sir."

"No," said Mr. Bumble approvingly; "no, you could not. You are a humane woman, Mrs. Mann." (Here she set down the glass.) "I shall take an early opportunity of mentioning it to the Board, Mrs. Mann." (He drew it towards him.) "You feel as a mother, Mrs. Mann." (He stirred the gin and water.) "I—I drink your health with cheerfulness, Mrs. Mann;" and he swallowed half of it.

"And now about business," said the beadle, taking out a leathern pocket-book. "The child that was half-baptized, Oliver Twist, is eight years old to-day."

"Blees him!" interposed Mrs. Mann, inflaming her left eye with the corner of her apron.

"And notwithstanding an offered reward of ten pound, which was afterwards increased to twenty pound; notwithstanding the most superlative, and I may say, supernatural exertions on the part of this parish," said Bumble, "we have never been able to discover who is his father, or what is his mother's settlement, name, or condition."

Mrs. Mann raised her hands in astonishment, but added, after a moment's reflection, "How comes he to have any name at all, then?"

The beadle drew himself up with great pride, and said, "I inwented it."

"You, Mr. Bumble?"

"I, Mrs. Mann. We name our foundlin's in alphabetical order. The last was a S, — Swubble: I named him. This was a T, — Twist: I named *him*. The next one as comes will be Unwin, and the next Vilkins. I have got names ready made to the end of the alphabet, and all the way through it again, when we come to Z."

"Why, you 're quite a literary character, sir," said Mrs. Mann.

"Well, well," said the beadle, evidently gratified with the compliment; "perhaps I may be, perhaps I may be, Mrs. Mann." He finished the gin and water, and added, "Oliver being now too old to remain here, the Board have determined to have him back into the house; and I have come out myself to take him there: so let me see him at once."

Mrs. Corney being matron of the workhouse, and the death of Mr. Slout, the master of the establishment, being daily expected, Mr. Bumble, who stands next in the order of succession, thinks it might be a good opportunity for "a joining of hearts and housekeepings." With this idea in his mind, he pays the lady a visit, and, while she is out of the room for a few moments, counts the spoons, weighs the sugar-tongs, closely inspects the silver milk-pot, takes a mental inventory of the furniture, and makes himself acquainted with the contents of a chest of drawers. Upon her return, after some billing and cooing, she says "the one little, little little word" he begs to hear, and bashfully consents to become Mrs. Bumble as soon as ever he pleases. But the course of Mr. Bumble's love does not run smooth after marriage; for his wife turns out to be a thorough shrew. When the first tiff occurs, Mrs. Bumble bursts into tears, but they do not serve to soften the heart of Mr. Bumble; for he smilingly bids her keep on. "It opens the lungs," he tells her, "washes the countenance, exercises the eyes, and softens the temper: so cry away." When, however, she changes her tactics, boldly flies at him, and gives him a sound and well-merited drubbing, he yields incontinently, and indulges in sad and solitary reflections. "I sold myself," he says, "for six tea-spoons, a pair of sugar-tongs, and a milk-pot, with a small quantity of second-hand furniter, and twenty pound in money. I went very reasonable, cheap, — dirt cheap."

This precious pair are afterwards guilty, — first, of selling certain articles which were left in the workhouse by the mother of Oliver Twist, and which are necessary to his identification; and, secondly, of witnessing what they suppose to be the destruction of these articles. Brought before Mr. Brownlow, they are confronted with proofs and witnesses of their rascality; but Bumble excuses himself by saying, "It was all Mrs. Bumble. She *would* do it."

"That is no excuse," replied Mr. Brownlow. "You were present on the occasion of the destruction of these trinkets, and, indeed, are the more guilty of the two, in the eye of the law; for the law supposes that your wife acts under your direction."

"If the law supposes that," said Mr. Bumble, squeezing his hat emphatically in both hands, "the law is a ass, a idiot. If that 's the eye of the law, the law 's a bachelor; and the worst I wish the law is, that his eye may be opened by experience,—by experience."

Notwithstanding this disclaimer of any personal responsibility in the matter, Mr. Bumble loses his situation, and retires with his wife to private life.

**Charlotte.** Servant to Mrs. Sowerberry; afterwards married to Noah Claypole. iv–vi, xxvii, xlii, liii.

**Chitling, Tom.** An "apprentice" of Fagin's; a "half-witted dupe," who makes a rather unsuccessful thief. xviii, xxv, xxxix, l.

**Claypole, Noah.** A chuckle-headed charity-boy, apprenticed to Mr. Sowerberry the undertaker. He afterwards goes to London, and becomes a thief. v, vi, xxvii, xlii, xliii, xlv–xlvii, liii.

**Corney, Mrs.** Matron of a workhouse; afterwards married to Mr. Bumble. xxiii, xxiv, xxvii, xxxvii, xxxviii, li.

**Crackit, Toby.** A housebreaker. xxiii, xxv, xxviii, xxxix, l.

**Dawkins, John,** *called* THE ARTFUL DODGER. A young pickpocket in the service of Fagin the Jew. viii–x, xii, xiii, xvi, xviii, xix, xxv, xxxix, xliii. When Oliver Twist runs away from his master, and sets out for London, he meets the Artful Dodger on the road, who gives him something to eat, and afterwards takes him to Fagin's den.

"Don't fret your eyelids," . . . said the young gentleman. "I 've got to be in London to-night, and I know a 'spectable old genelman as lives there, wot 'll give you lodgings for nothink, and never ask for the change; that is, if any genelman he knows interduces you. And don't he know me? Oh, no! Not in the least! By no means! Certainly not!"

Although the Dodger is an adept in thieving and knavery, he is detected at last in attempting to pick a gentleman's pocket, and is sentenced to transportation for life. While in court, he maintains

THE ARTFUL DODGER AND CHARLEY BATES.

his accustomed coolness, impudently chaffs the police officers, asking the jailer to communicate "the names of them two files as was on the bench," and generally "doing full justice to his bringing-up, and establishing for himself a glorious reputation." When brought into court, he requests to know what he is "placed in that 'ere disgraceful sitivation for."

"Hold your tongue; will you?" said the jailer.

"I'm an Englishman, ain't I?" rejoined the Dodger. "Where are my privileges?"

"You'll get your privileges soon enough," retorted the jailer, "and pepper with 'em."

"We'll see wot the Secretary of State for the Home Affairs has got to say to the beaks, if I don't," replied Mr. Dawkins. "Now, then, wot is this here business? I shall thank the madg-'strates to dispose of this here little affair, and not to keep me while they read the paper; for I've got an appointment with a gentleman in the city: and as I'm a man of my word, and wery punctual in business matters, he'll go away if I ain't there to my time, and then, p'r'aps there won't be an action for damage against those as kept me away. Oh, no, certainly not!"

The evidence against him is direct and conclusive; but the Dodger continues unabashed; and, when the magistrate asks him if he has anything to say, he affects not to hear the question.

"Do you hear his worship ask you if you've anything to say?" inquired the jailer, nudging the silent Dodger with his elbow.

"I beg your pardon," said the Dodger, looking up with an air of abstraction. "Did you redress yourself to me, my man?"

"I never see such an out-and-out young wagabond, your worship," observed the officer with a grin. "Do you mean to say any thing, you young shaver?"

"No," replied the Dodger, "not here; for this ain't the shop for justice; besides which, my attorney is a breakfasting this morning with the wice-president of the house of commons. But I shall have something to say elsewhere, and so will he, and so will a wery numerous and 'spectable circle of acquaintance, as'll make them beaks wish they'd never been born, or that they'd got their footmen to hang 'em up to their own hat-pegs afore they let 'em come out this morning to try it on upon me. I'll"—

"There! he's fully committed," interposed the clerk. "Take him away."

"Come on," said the jailer.

"Oh, ah! I'll come on," replied the Dodger, brushing his hat with the palm of his hand. "Ah," (to the bench) "it 's no use your looking frightened: I won't show you no mercy, — not a ha'porth of it. *You 'll* pay for this, my fine fellers. I would n't be you for something! I would n't go free, now, if you was to fall down on your knees and ask me. Here, carry me off to prison! Take me away!"

With these last words the Dodger suffered himself to be led off by the collar, threatening, till he got into the yard, to make a parliamentary business of it, and then grinning in the officer's face with great glee and self-approval.

**Dick, Little.** Companion of Oliver Twist at a branch workhouse where infant paupers are tended with parochial care. vii, xvii.

**Dodger, The Artful.** *See* DAWKINS, JOHN.

**Duff.** A Bow Street officer. *See* BLATHERS and DUFF.

**Fagin.** A crafty old Jew, a receiver of stolen goods, with a number of confederates of both sexes. He also employes several boys (styled "apprentices") to carry on a systematic trade of pilfering. After a long career of villainy, he is sentenced to death for complicity in a murder. Having been taken to prison, he is placed in one of the "condemned cells," and left there alone. viii, ix, xii, xiii, xv, xvi, xix, xx, xxv, xxvi, xxxiv, xxxix, xlii–xlv, liii.

He sat down on a stone bench opposite the door, which served for seat and bedstead, and, casting his bloodshot eyes upon the ground, tried to collect his thoughts. After a while, he began to remember a few disjointed fragments of what the judge had said, though it had seemed to him at the time that he could not hear a word. These gradually fell into their proper places, and, by degrees, suggested more; so that in a little time he had the whole almost as it was delivered. To be hanged by the neck till he was dead: that was the end, — to be hanged by the neck till he was dead.

As it came on very dark, he began to think of all the men he had known who had died upon the scaffold, — some of them through his means. They rose up in such quick succession that he could hardly count them. He had seen some of them die, and joked, too, because they died with prayers upon their lips. With what a rattling noise the drop went down! and how suddenly they changed from strong and vigorous men to dangling heaps of clothes!

Some of them might have inhabited that very cell, — sat upon that very spot. It was very dark: why did n't they bring a light? The cell had been built for many years. Scores of men must have passed their last hours there. It was like sitting in a vault strewn with dead bodies, — the cap, the noose, the pinioned arms, the faces that he knew even beneath that hideous veil. — Light, light!

At length, when his hands were raw with beating against the heavy door and walls, two men appeared, — one bearing a candle, which he thrust into an iron candlestick fixed against the wall, and the other dragging in a mattress on which to pass the night; for the prisoner was to be left alone no more.

Then came night, — dark, dismal, silent night. Other wretches are glad to hear the church-clocks strike; for they tell of life and coming day: to the Jew they brought despair. The boom of every iron bell came laden with the one deep, hollow sound, — death. What availed the noise and bustle of cheerful morning, which penetrated even there, to him? It was another form of knell, with mockery added to the warning.

The day passed off. Day! — there was no day: it was gone as soon as come: and night came on again, — night so long, and yet so short; long in its dreadful silence, and short in its fleeting hours. At one time he raved and blasphemed; and at another howled, and tore his hair. Venerable men of his own persuasion had come to pray beside him; but he had driven them away with curses. They renewed their charitable efforts, and he beat them off.

Saturday night. He had only one night more to live; and, as he thought of this, the day broke, — Sunday.

It was not until the night of this last awful day that a withering sense of his helpless, desperate state came in its full intensity upon his blighted soul; not that he had ever held any defined or positive hope of mercy, but that he had never been able to consider more than the dim probability of dying so soon. He had spoken little to either of the two men who relieved each other in their attendance upon him; and they, for their parts, made no effort to rouse his attention. He had sat there, awake, but dreaming. Now he started up every minute, and, with gasping mouth and burning skin, hurried to and fro, in such a paroxysm of fear and wrath, that even they — used to such sights — recoiled from him with horror. He grew so terrible, at last, in all the tortures of his evil conscience, that one man could not bear to sit there eyeing him alone; and so the two kept watch together.

He cowered down upon his stone bed, and thought of the past. He had been wounded with some missiles from the crowd on the day of his capture, and his head was bandaged with a linen cloth. His red hair hung down upon his bloodless face; his beard was torn, and twisted into knots; his eyes shone with a terrible light; his unwashed flesh crackled with the fever that burnt him up.

Eight — nine — ten. If it was not a trick to frighten him, and those were the real hours treading on each other's heels, where would he be when they came round again! Eleven! Another struck before the voice of the previous hour had ceased to vibrate. At eight he would be the only mourner in his own funeral-train; at eleven —

Those dreadful walls of Newgate, which have hidden so much misery and such unspeakable anguish, not only from the eyes, but, too often and too long, from the thoughts of men, never held so dread a spectacle as that. The few who lingered as they passed, and wondered what the man was doing who was to be hung to-morrow, would have slept but ill that night if they could have seen him.

**Fang, Mr.** A violent and overbearing police-magistrate; intended as a portrait of one A. S. Laing, the senior magistrate of Hatton Garden Police Office at the time "Oliver Twist" was in course of publication, who was notorious for his arrogant and brutal treatment of witnesses, and, indeed, of all who came before him. So true a likeness was it, that Lord John Russell, the home secretary, felt compelled to remove Mr. Justice Laing from office. xi.

Oliver Twist, charged with stealing a handkerchief from Mr. Brownlow as he stands quietly reading at a book-stall, is brought before Mr. Fang for trial; Mr. Brownlow appearing as witness.

Mr. Fang was a middle-sized man, with no great quantity of hair, and what he had, growing on the back and sides of his head. His face was stern, and much flushed. If he were really not in the habit of drinking rather more than was exactly good for him, he might have brought an action against his countenance for libel, and have recovered heavy damages.

The old gentleman bowed respectfully, and advancing to the magistrate's desk, said, suiting the action to the word: "That is my name and address, sir." He then withdrew a pace or two, and, with another polite and gentlemanly inclination of the head, waited to be questioned.

Now, it so happened that Mr. Fang was at that moment perusing a leading article in a newspaper of the morning, adverting to some recent decision of his, and commending him, for the three hundred and fiftieth time, to the special and particular notice of the secretary of state for the home department. He was out of temper, and he looked up with an angry scowl.

"Who are you?" said Mr. Fang.

The old gentleman pointed with some surprise to his card.

"Officer," said Mr. Fang, tossing the card contemptuously away with the newspaper, "who is this fellow?"

"My name, sir," said the old gentleman, speaking *like* a gentleman, and consequently in strong contrast to Mr. Fang, — "my name, sir, is Brownlow. Permit me to inquire the name of the magistrate who offers a gratuitous and unprovoked insult to a respectable man, under the protection of the bench." Saying this, Mr. Brownlow looked round the office as if in search of some person who could afford him the required information.

"Officer," said Mr. Fang, throwing the paper on one side, "what 's this fellow charged with?"

"He 's not charged at all, your worship," replied the officer. "He appears against the boy, your worship."

His worship knew this perfectly well; but it was a good annoyance, and a safe one.

"Appears against the boy, does he?" said Fang, surveying Mr. Brownlow contemptously from head to foot. "Swear him."

"Before I am sworn, I must beg to say one word," said Mr. Brownlow; "and that is, that I never, without actual experience, could have believed" —

"Hold your tongue, sir!" said Mr. Fang peremptorily.

"I will not, sir!" replied the spirited old gentleman.

"Hold your tongue this instant, or I 'll have you turned out of the office!" said Mr. Fang. "You 're an insolent, impertinent fellow. How dare you bully a magistrate?"

"What?" exclaimed the old gentleman, reddening.

"Swear this person!" said Fang to the clerk. "I 'll not hear another word. Swear him!"

Mr. Brownlow's indignation was greatly roused; but, reflecting that he might injure the boy by giving vent to it, he suppressed his feelings, and submitted to be sworn at once.

"Now," said Fang, "what 's the charge against this boy? What have you got to say, sir?"

"I was standing at a book-stall," Mr. Brownlow began.

"Hold your tongue, sir!" said Mr. Fang. "Policeman! — Where 's the policeman? Here, swear this man. Now, policeman, what is this?"

The policeman, with becoming humility, related how he had taken the charge; how he had searched Oliver, and found nothing on his person; and how that was all he knew about it.

"Are there any witnesses?" inquired Mr. Fang.

"None, your worship," replied the policeman.

Mr. Fang sat silent for some minutes, and then, turning round to the prosecutor, said in a towering passion: —

"Do you mean to state what your complaint against this boy is, fellow, or do you not? You have been sworn. Now, if you stand there, refusing to give evidence, I'll punish you for disrespect to the bench: I will, by" —

By what or by whom nobody knows; for the clerk and jailer coughed very loud just at the right moment, and the former dropped a heavy book on the floor; thus preventing the word from being heard, — accidentally, of course.

With many interruptions and repeated insults, Mr. Brownlow contrived to state his case; observing that in the surprise of the moment he had run after the boy because he saw him running away; and expressing his hope that if the magistrate should believe him, although not actually the thief, to be connected with thieves, he would deal as leniently with him as justice would allow.

"He has been hurt already," said the old gentleman in conclusion. "And I fear," he added with great energy, looking towards the bar, "I really fear that he is very ill."

"Oh, yes! I dare say," said Mr. Fang with a sneer. "Come, none of your tricks here, you young vagabond: they won't do. What 's your name?"

Oliver tried to reply; but his tongue failed him. He was deadly pale; and the whole place seemed turning round and round.

"What 's your name, you hardened scoundrel?" thundered Mr. Fang. "Officer, what 's his name?"

This was addressed to a bluff old fellow in a striped waistcoat, who was standing by the bar. He bent over Oliver, and repeated the inquiry; but finding him really incapable of understanding the question, and knowing that his not replying would only infuriate the magistrate the more, and add to the severity of his sentence, he hazarded a guess.

"He says his name 's Tom White, your worship," said this kind-hearted thief-taker.

"How do you propose to deal with the case, sir?" inquired the clerk in a low voice.

"Summarily," replied Mr. Fang. "He stands committed for three months, — hard labor, of course. Clear the office."

The keeper of the book-stall, however, who saw the affair, and knows that Oliver is not guilty, just at this moment hastily enters the room, demands to be heard, and testifies that it was not Oliver, but his companion (the "Artful Dodger"), who picked Mr. Brownlow's pocket; and that Oliver, apparently much terrified and astonished by the proceeding, ran off, was pursued, knocked down, arrested, and taken away by a police-officer. This evidence, though unwillingly received by the magistrate, acquits the boy, who is compassionately taken by Mr. Brownlow to his own house, where he is laid up with fever, and is carefully nursed till he recovers.

**Fleming, Agnes.** Mother of Oliver Twist. i, liii.

**Fleming, Rose.** *See* MAYLIE, ROSE.

**Gamfield.** A chimney-sweep. iii.

**Giles, Mr.** Mrs. Maylie's butler and steward. xxviii–xxxi, xxxiv, xxxv, liii. Two burglars, Sikes and Crackit, attempt to break into Mrs. Maylie's house, one night, but, being alarmed, retreat in haste, and are followed in a most valiant manner by Giles and his fellow-servants. When a short distance from the house, however, they stop very suddenly, under instructions from Giles.

"My advice, or, leastways, I should say, my *orders*, is," said the fattest man of the party, "that we 'mediately go home again."

"I am agreeable to anything which is agreeable to Mr. Giles," said a shorter man, who was by no means of a slim figure, and who was very pale in the face, and very polite, as frightened men frequently are.

"I should n't wish to appear ill-mannered, gentlemen," said the third, who had called the dogs back. "Mr. Giles ought to know."

"Certainly," replied the shorter man; "and, whatever Mr. Giles says, it is n't our place to contradict him. No, no, I know my sitiwation, — thank my stars, I know my sitiwation." To tell the truth, the little man *did* seem to know his situation, and to know perfectly well that it was by no means a desirable one, for his teeth chattered in his head as he spoke.

"You are afraid, Brittles," said Mr. Giles.

"I ain't," said Brittles.

"You are," said Giles.

"You 're a falsehood, Mr. Giles," said Brittles.

"You 're a lie, Brittles," said Mr. Giles.

Now, these four retorts arose from Mr. Giles's taunt: and Mr. Giles's taunt had arisen from his indignation at having the responsibility of going home again imposed upon himself under cover of a compliment. The third man brought the dispute to a close most philosophically.

"I 'll tell you what it is, gentlemen," said he, "we 're all afraid."

"Speak for yourself, sir," said Mr. Giles, who was the palest of the party.

"So I do," replied the man. "It 's natural and proper to be afraid under such circumstances: *I* am."

"So am I," said Brittles; "only there 's no call to tell a man he is, so bounceably."

These frank admissions softened Mr. Giles, who at once owned that *he* was afraid; upon which they all three faced about, and ran back again with the completest unanimity, till Mr. Giles (who had the shortest wind of the party, and was encumbered with a pitchfork) most handsomely insisted upon stopping to make an apology for his hastiness of speech.

"But it 's wonderful," said Mr. Giles, when he had explained, "what a man will do when his blood is up. I should have committed murder, I know I should, if we 'd caught one of the rascals."

As the other two were impressed with a similar presentiment, and their blood, like his, had all gone down again, some speculation ensued upon the cause of this sudden change in their temperament.

"I know what it was," said Mr. Giles: "it was the gate!"

"I should n't wonder if it was!" exclaimed Brittles, catching at the idea.

"You may depend upon it," said Giles, "that that gate stopped the flow of the excitement. I felt all mine suddenly going away as I was climbing over it."

By a remarkable coincidence the other two had been visited with the same unpleasant sensation at that precise moment: so that it was quite conclusive that it was the gate, especially as there was no doubt regarding the time at which the change had taken place, because all three remembered that they had come in sight of the robbers at the very instant of its occurrence.

**Grimwig, Mr.** An irascible but warm-hearted friend of Mr. Brownlow's. xiv, xvii, xli, li, liii. He is thus introduced: —

At this moment there walked into the room, supporting himself by a thick stick, a stout old gentleman, rather lame in one leg, who was dressed in a blue coat, striped waistcoat, nankeen breeches and gaiters, and a broad-brimmed white hat with the sides turned up with green. A very small-plaited shirt-frill stuck out from his waistcoat, and a very long steel watch-chain, with nothing but a key at the end, dangled loosely below it. The ends of his white neckerchief were twisted into a ball about the size of an orange: the variety of shapes into which his countenance was twisted defy description. He had a manner of screwing his head round on one side when he spoke, and looking out of the corners of his eyes at the same time, which irresistibly reminded the beholder of a parrot. In this attitude he fixed himself the moment he made his appearance, and, holding out a small piece of orange-peel at arm's length, exclaimed in a growling, discontented voice: —

"Look here! do you see this? Is n't it a most wonderful and extraordinary thing that I can't call at a man's house, but I find a piece of this cursed poor surgeon's friend on the staircase? I've been lamed with orange-peel once; and I know orange-peel will be my death at last. It will, sir: orange-peel will be my death, or I'll be content to eat my own head, sir!" This was the handsome offer with which Mr. Grimwig backed and confirmed nearly every assertion that he made; and it was the more singular in his case, because, even admitting, for the sake of argument, the possibility of scientific improvements being ever brought to that pass which will enable a gentleman to eat his own head, in the event of his being so disposed, Mr. Grimwig's head was such a particularly large one, that the most sanguine man alive could hardly entertain a hope of being able to get through it at a sitting, to put entirely out of the question a very thick coating of powder.

**Kags.** A returned transport. l.

**Leeford, Edward.** *See* MONKS.

**Limbkins, Mr.** Chairman of the workhouse board. ii, iii.

**Lively, Mr.** A salesman in Field Lane, and a dealer in stolen goods. xxvi.

**Losberne, Mr.**, called "THE DOCTOR." A friend of the Maylie family; a surgeon, fat rather from good humor than good living, and an eccentric bachelor, but kind and large-hearted withal. xxix–xxxvi, xli, xlix, li, liii.

**Mann, Mrs.** Matron of the branch workhouse where Oliver Twist is "farmed." i, xvii.

**Martha.** A pauper. xxiii, xxiv, li.

**Maylie, Mrs.** A lady who befriends Oliver Twist. xxix–xxxi, xxxiii, xxxiv, xli, li, liii.

**Maylie, Harry.** Son of Mrs. Maylie; afterwards married to his foster-sister, Rose. xxxiv–xxxvi, li, liii.

**Maylie, Rose.** Her adopted daughter; an orphan, whose true name is Rose Fleming, and who turns out to be Oliver Twist's aunt. xxviii, xxix, xxx–xxxiii, xxxv, xxxvi, xl, xli, xlvi, li, liii.

**Monks.** A half-brother of Oliver Twist. His real name is Edward Leeford. His father, while living apart from his wife, from whom he has long been separated, sees and loves Agnes Fleming, daughter of a retired naval officer. The result of their intimacy is a child (Oliver), who is born while Mr. Leeford is in Rome, where he is suddenly taken ill and dies. His wife and her son join him as soon as they hear of his illness, that they may look after his large property, which they take possession of immediately upon his death, destroying a will, which leaves the great bulk of it to Agnes Fleming and her unborn child. Believing that this child will yet appear to claim his rights, young Leeford, under the assumed name of Monks, endeavors to find him out, and, after a long search, discovers that he was born in a workhouse, but has left there. He pursues the boy, and finds him at last in London, in the den of Fagin the Jew, whom he makes his accomplice and confidant, giving him a large reward for keeping the boy insnared. The proofs of Monks' villainy are discovered by Mr. Brownlow; and he is compelled to give up one-half (three thousand pounds) of the wreck of the property remaining in his hands, after which he leaves the country, and ultimately dies in prison. xxvi, xxxiii, xxxiv, xxxvii–xxxix, xlix, li, liii.

**Nancy.** A thief in Fagin's service, and mistress to Sikes, to whom, brutal as he is, she is always faithful and devoted. ix, xiii, xv, xvi, xix, xx, xxvi, xxxix, xl, xliv-xlvii.

**Sally, Old.** An inmate of the workhouse, who robs Agnes Fleming (Oliver's mother) when on her death-bed. xxiv.

**Sikes, Bill.** A brutal thief and housebreaker, with no gleam of light in all the blackness of his character. He first appears on the scene during a squabble between Fagin and the Artful Dodger, in which Fagin throws a pot of beer at Charley Bates. The pot misses its mark; and the contents are sprinkled over the face of Sikes, who just then opens the door. xiii, xv, xvi, xix–xxii, xxviii, xxxix, xliv, xlvii, xlviii, l.

"Why! what the blazes is in the wind now?" growled a deep voice. "Who pitched that 'ere at me? It 's well it 's the beer, and not the pot, as hit me, or I 'd have settled somebody. . . Wot 's it all about, Fagin? D— me, if my neckankecher ain't lined with beer! — Come in, you sneaking warmint: wot are you stopping outside for, as if you was ashamed of your master? Come in!"

The man who growled out these words was a stoutly-built fellow of about five and forty, in a black velveteen coat, very soiled drab breeches, lace-up half-boots, and gray cotton stockings, which enclosed a very bulky pair of legs, with large swelling calves, — the kind of legs which in such costume always look in an unfinished and incomplete state without a set of fetters to garnish them. He had a brown hat on his head, and a dirty belcher handkerchief round his neck, with the long frayed ends of which he smeared the beer from his face as he spoke, disclosing, when he had done so, a broad heavy countenance with a beard of three days' growth, and two scowling eyes, one of which displayed various party-colored symptoms of having been recently damaged by a blow.

"Come in, d' ye hear?" growled this engaging-looking ruffian. A white shaggy dog, with his face scratched and torn in twenty different places, skulked into the room.

"Why did n't you come in afore?" said the man. "You 're getting too proud to own me afore company, are you? Lie down!"

This command was accompanied with a kick which sent the animal to the other end of the room. He appeared well used to it, however; for he coiled himself up in a corner very quietly, without uttering a sound, and, winking his very ill-looking eyes about twenty times in a minute, appeared to occupy himself in taking a survey of the apartment.

"What are you up to? Ill-treating the boys, you covetous, avaricious, in-sa-ti-a-ble old fence?" said the man, seating himself deliberately. "I wonder they don't murder you: *I* would if I was them. If I 'd been your 'prentice, I 'd have done it long ago; and — No, I could n't have sold you arterwards, though; for you 're fit for nothing but keeping as a curiosity of ugliness in a glass bottle; and I suppose they don't blow them large enough."

"Hush, hush! Mr. Sikes," said the Jew, trembling. "Don't speak so loud."

"None of your mistering," replied the ruffian: "you always mean mischief when you come that. You know my name: out with it. I shan't disgrace it when the time comes."

"Well, well, then, Bill Sikes," said the Jew with abject humility. "You seem out of humor, Bill."

"Perhaps I am," replied Sikes. "I should think *you* were rather out of sorts too, unless you mean as little harm when you throw pewter pots about, as you do when you blab and" —

"Are you mad?" said the Jew, catching the man by the sleeve, and pointing towards the boys.

Mr. Sikes contented himself with tying an imaginary knot under his left ear, and jerking his head over on the right shoulder; a piece of dumb show which the Jew appeared to understand perfectly. He then in cant terms, with which his whole conversation was plentifully besprinkled, but which would be quite unintelligible if they were recorded here, demanded a glass of liquor.

"And mind you don't poison it," said Mr. Sikes, laying his hat upon the table.

This was said in jest; but, if the speaker could have seen the evil leer with which the Jew bit his pale lip as he turned round to the cupboard, he might have thought the caution not wholly unnecessary, or the wish, at all events, to improve upon the distiller's ingenuity not very far from the old gentleman's merry heart.

**Sowerberry, Mr.** A parochial undertaker, to whom Oliver Twist is apprenticed. iv, v, vii.

**Sowerberry, Mrs.** His wife, "a short, thin, squeezed-up woman, with a vixenish countenance" and disposition. iv–vii.

**Thingummy, Mrs.** An old nurse at the workhouse, who assists Oliver Twist into the world. i.

**Twist, Oliver.** A poor, nameless orphan boy, born in the workhouse of an English village, whither his young mother, an outcast and a stranger, had come to lie down and die. He is "brought up by hand," and "farmed out" at a branch establishment, where twenty or thirty other juvenile offenders against the poor-laws are starved, beaten, and abused by an elderly woman named Mrs. Mann. On his ninth birthday, Mr. Bumble, the beadle, visits the branch, and removes him to the workhouse, to be taught a useful trade. i–xii, xiv–xvi, xviii, xx–xxii, xxviii–xxxvi, xli, li–liii.

The room [in the workhouse] in which the boys were fed was a large stone hall, with a copper at one end, out of which the master, dressed in an apron for the purpose, and assisted by one or two women, ladled the gruel at meal-times; of which composition each boy had one porringer, and no more, — except on festive occasions, — and then he had two ounces and a quarter of bread besides. The bowls never wanted washing: the boys polished them with their spoons till they shone again; and, when they had performed this operation (which never took very long, the spoons being nearly as large as the bowls), they would sit staring at the copper with such eager eyes, as if they could devour the very bricks of which it was composed; employing themselves meanwhile in sucking their fingers most assiduously, with the view of catching up any stray splashes of gruel that might have been cast thereon. Boys have generally excellent appetites. Oliver Twist and his companions suffered the tortures of slow starvation for three months: at last they got so voracious and wild with hunger, that one boy, who was tall for his age, and had n't been used to that sort of thing (for his father had kept a small cook's shop), hinted darkly to his companions, that, unless he had another basin of gruel *per diem*, he was afraid he should some night eat the boy who slept next him, who happened to be a weakly youth of tender age. He had a wild, hungry eye; and they implicitly believed him. A council was held. Lots were cast who should walk up to the master after supper that evening, and ask for more; and it fell to Oliver Twist.

The evening arrived. The boys took their places; the master, in his cook's uniform, stationed himself at the copper; his pauper assistants ranged themselves behind him: the gruel was served out, and a long grace was said over the short commons. The gruel disappeared; and the boys whispered to each other, and winked at Oliver, while his next neighbors nudged him. Child as he was, he was desperate with hunger, and reckless with misery. He rose from the table, and advancing, basin and spoon in hand, to the master, said, somewhat alarmed at his own temerity: —

"Please, sir, I want some more."

The master was a fat, healthy man; but he turned very pale. He gazed in stupefied astonishment on the small rebel for some seconds; and then clung for support to the copper. The assistants were paralyzed with wonder, and the boys with fear.

"What!" said the master at length in a faint voice.

"Please, sir," replied Oliver, "I want some more."

The master aimed a blow at Oliver's head with the ladle, pinioned him in his arms, and shrieked aloud for the beadle.

The Board were sitting in solemn conclave, when Mr. Bumble rushed into the room in great excitement, and, addressing the gentleman in the high chair, said: —

"Mr. Limbkins, I beg your pardon, sir! Oliver Twist has asked for more." There was a general start. Horror was depicted on every countenance.

"For *more!*" said Mr. Limbkins. "Compose yourself, Bumble, and answer me distinctly. Do I understand that he asked for more after he had eaten the supper allotted by the dietary?"

"He did, sir," replied Bumble.

"That boy will be hung," said the gentleman in the white waistcoat. "I know that boy will be hung."

Nobody controverted the prophetic gentleman's opinion. An animated discussion took place. Oliver was ordered into instant confinement; and a bill was next morning pasted on the outside of the gate, offering a reward of five pounds to anybody who would take Oliver Twist off the hands of the parish: in other words, five pounds and Oliver Twist were offered to any man or woman who wanted an apprentice to any trade, business, or calling.

# THE LIFE AND ADVENTURES OF NICHOLAS NICKLEBY

## OUTLINE

Chapter I The pedigree of the Nickleby family so far as regards the hero of this tale was very simple. One Godfrey Nickleby, who had been in sore straits most of his life, but enjoyed a modest property toward the end, left two sons, Ralph and Nicholas. The oft-told tale of their father's struggle with ill fortune had the effect in the case of Ralph of stimulating all his money-getting powers, while Nicholas was made timid and cautious. Ralph went to the city to make a fortune. Nicholas retired to a little country place and kept what he could, marrying and bringing up two children, a son Nicholas, and a daughter Kate. Egged on by his wife, who was ill-satisfied with their small income, the elder Nicholas speculated with his small fortune, with the result that he lost it all, and dying bequeathed his widow and two children to an indifferent world.

II It had fared quite otherwise with Mr. Ralph Nickleby. He had established himself in Golden Square, London, and conducted what business he had in an office in his house, aided by a sallow-faced man in rusty brown, his clerk Newman Noggs. Some notion of the kind of business which occupied Mr. Nickleby is seen by his attendance with a friend as promoter at a meeting called to petition Parliament in favor of The United Metropolitan Improved Hot Muffin and Crumpet Baking and Punctual Delivery Company, of which said company Mr. Nickleby was an active director.

III On his way home from luncheon after the meeting, Ralph Nickleby was met by his clerk Newman Noggs, who brought him a letter announcing the death of his brother and the presence in London of Mrs. Nickleby and her son and daughter. The letter contained information of their whereabouts, and Ralph Nickleby with sourness in his face and at his heart made his way to the house in the Strand where he was to look for them. Before coming into their apartment he encountered Miss La Creevy, a miniature painter who at fifty had not parted with her sentiment. She was the landlady of the unfortunate Nicklebys, and Ralph endeavored at once to instill an unhealthy suspicion of their ability to pay their rent, since his first thought was to get them out of London again as quickly as possible. He then presented himself to his sister-in-law and her young family, and, after hectoring them all, offered to obtain a position for Nicholas as usher in a Yorkshire school kept by a Mr. Squeers, where he would receive a munificent salary of five pounds a year; with an equivocal show of surly kindness he undertook to provide for Mrs. Nickleby and Kate after Nicholas was out of the way.

IV Mr. Wackford Squeers was at this time in London picking up boys for his school, and Ralph Nickleby, who had had previous dealings with him, at once escorted Nicholas to his inn. They found Mr. Squeers just closing a bargain with Mr. Snawley, a stepfather who wished to get rid of his new wife's two boys, and Ralph Nickleby quickly turned over Nicholas to Mr. Squeers, readily persuading the schoolmaster by some private logic, and giving Nicholas to understand that his acceptance of the post and his steady adherence to it were the price to be paid for the support of his mother and sister. This business despatched, Nicholas was sent to Golden Square with a package of papers to be delivered to Newman Noggs, who received this nephew of his employer with such enigmatic grimaces and cracking of finger-joints as quite disconcerted the youngster.

V The next morning Nicholas, leaving his mother and sister asleep, that they might not have the pain of parting, stole out of the house, saying only a good-bye to the good-natured Miss La Creevy, whom he charged to look after his dear ones, and went with his box to the inn from which the party was to go by coach to Yorkshire. Here he found Squeers eating breakfast for the little boys as well as for himself, and haranguing them on the duty of conquering their animal passions. Just before the coach started Mrs. Nickleby and Kate arrived, followed by Ralph Nickleby. The mother and sister had hastened to see Nicholas off, and Ralph had wished to make sure that he got away. Kate was greatly troubled over the most unengaging appearance of her brother's master, but there was no help now. At the last moment Newman Noggs suddenly arrived and secretly handed Nicholas a letter with impressive secrecy. Off went the coach on its cold and wearisome journey.

VI The journey was not without adventure, for in the gray of the next day the coach broke down, and while waiting at an inn for an opportunity to go forward, two of the company regaled the rest with the tales of The Five Sisters of York and The Baron of Grogzwig. Finally the coach again set forth, and deposited Mr. Squeers, Nicholas, and the boys at the George and New Inn, Greta

Bridge. Thence they were taken by a cart and chaise in attend-
VII ance to Dotheboys Hall, the name given by Squeers to his establishment. Here Nicholas, on his first evening, when he remained with Mr. and Mrs. Squeers, had an uncomfortable presentiment from the conversation of this unworthy couple that he had fallen upon evil things, rendered greater by what he saw of a miserable boy named Smike, who appeared as a drudge in the service of the schoolmaster.

Mr. Squeers was emptying his great-coat pockets of letters to different boys, and other small documents which he had brought down in them. The boy glanced with an anxious and timid expression at the papers, as if with a sickly hope that one among them might relate to him. The look was a very painful one, and went to Nicholas's heart at once; for it told a long and very sad history.

It induced him to consider the boy more attentively; and he was surprised to observe the extraordinary mixture of garments which formed his dress. Although he could not have been less than eighteen or nineteen, and was tall for that age, he wore a skeleton suit such as was then usually put upon a very little boy. In order that the lower part of his legs might be in perfect keeping with this singular dress, he had a very large pair of boots, originally made for tops, which might have been once worn by some stout farmer, but were now too patched and tattered for a beggar. God knows how long he had been there; but he still wore a tattered child's frill, only half concealed by a coarse man's neckerchief. He was lame; and, as he feigned to be busy in arranging the table, glanced at the letters with a look so keen, and yet so dispirited and hopeless, that Nicholas could hardly bear to watch him.

"What are you bothering about there, Smike?" cried Mrs Squeers. "Let the things alone, can't you?"

"Eh!" said Squeers, looking up. "Oh! it's you; is it?"

"Yes, sir. Is there" —

"Well! what are you stammering at?"

"Have you — did anybody — has nothing been heard — about me?"

"Devil a bit, not a word; and never will be. Now, this is a pretty sort of thing, is n't it, — that you should have been left here all these years, and no money paid after the first six, nor no notice taken, nor no clue to be got who you belong to? It's a pretty sort of thing that I should have to feed a great fellow like you, and never hope to get one penny for it; is n't it?"

The boy put his hand to his head as if he were making an

effort to recollect something, and then, looking vacantly at his questioner, gradually broke into a smile, and limped away.

"I 'll tell you what, Squeers," remarked his wife, as the door closed, "I think that young chap 's turning silly."

"I hope not; for he 's a handy fellow out of doors, and worth his meat and drink any way. Hows'ever, I should think he 'd have wit enough for us if he *was* silly. But come! Let 's have supper; for I 'm hungry and tired, and want to get to bed."

This reminder brought in an exclusive steak for Mr. Squeers; and Nicholas had a tough bit of cold beef. Mr. Squeers then took a bumper of hot brandy and water of a stiff nature; and Mrs. Squeers made the new young man the ghost of a small glassful of that compound.

Then Mr. Squeers yawned again, and opined that it was time to go to bed; upon which signal Mrs. Squeers and the girl dragged in a straw mattress and a couple of blankets, and arranged them into a couch for Nicholas.

"We 'll put you into your regular bedroom to-morrow, Nickleby. Let me see. Who sleeps in Brooks's bed, my dear?"

"In Brooks's there 's Jennings, little Bolder, Graymarsh, and What's-his-name."

"So there is. Yes: Brooks is full."

"There 's a place somewhere, I know; but I can't at this moment call to mind where. However, we 'll have that all settled to-morrow. Good-night, Nickleby. Seven o'clock in the morning, mind."

"I shall be ready, sir. Good-night!"

"I don't know, by the by, whose towel to put you on; but, if you 'll make shift with something to-morrow morning, Mrs. Squeers will arrange that in the course of the day. My dear, don't forget."

Mr. Squeers then nudged Mrs. Squeers to bring away the brandy bottle, lest Nicholas should help himself in the night; and, the lady having seized it with great precipitation, they retired together.

Nicholas went to bed with a heavy heart, but first read his communication from Newman Noggs, who mysteriously offered him aid whenever he should need it, in return for some service which Nicholas's father had once done him.

VIII In the morning Nicholas was to have a glimpse of the internal economy of the school. The most significant part of the early exercise was the breakfast of brimstone and treacle which Mrs. Squeers administered. The schoolroom itself was full of vicious, neglected, and down-trodden boys, and Squeers, having just returned from London, proceeded to render the boys still more wretched by the manner of his communication of such home news as he thought it judicious to convey. Once more Nicholas had his heart wrung by the misery of poor Smike.

It was Mr. Squeers's custom to call the boys together, and make a sort of report, after every half-yearly visit to the metropolis: so, in the afternoon, the boys were recalled from house-window, garden, stable, and cow-yard; and the school were assembled in full conclave.

"Let any boy speak a word without leave," said Mr. Squeers mildly, "and I'll take the skin off his back."

Death-like silence immediately prevailed.

"Boys, I've been to London, and have returned to my family and you as strong and as well as ever."

The boys gave three feeble cheers at this refreshing intelligence. Such cheers!

"I have seen the parents of some boys," continued Squeers, turning over his papers; "and they're so glad to hear how their sons are getting on, that there's no prospect at all of their sons going away, which, of course, is a very pleasant thing to reflect upon for all parties."

Two or three hands went to two or three eyes; but the greater part of the young gentlemen—having no particular parents to speak of—were wholly uninterested in the thing, one way or other.

"I have had disappointments to contend against. Bolder's father was two pound ten short. Where is Bolder? Come here, Bolder!"

An unhealthy-looking boy, with warts all over his hands, stepped from his place to the master's desk, and raised his eyes to Squeers's face; his own quite white from the rapid beating of his heart.

"Bolder," said Squeers, speaking very slowly; for he was considering, as the saying goes, where to have him,—"Bolder, if your father thinks, that, because— Why! what's this, sir?"

He caught up the boy's hand by the cuff of the jacket.

"What do you call this, sir?"

"I can't help the warts, indeed, sir. They will come. It's the dirty work, I think, sir,—at least, I don't know what it is, sir; but it's not my fault."

"Bolder, you're an incorrigible young scoundrel; and, as the last thrashing did you no good, we must see what another will do towards beating it out of you."

Mr. Squeers fell upon the boy, and caned him soundly.

"There, rub away as hard as you like: you won't rub that off in a hurry. Now let us see. A letter for Cobbey. Stand up, Cobbey!"

Another boy stood up, and eyed the letter very hard, while Squeers made a mental abstract of the same.

"Oh! Cobbey's grandmother is dead, and his Uncle John has took to drinking, which is all the news his sister sends, except eighteenpence, which will pay for that broken square of glass. Mrs. Squeers, my dear, will you take the money?

"Graymarsh, — he 's the next. Stand up, Graymarsh!"

Another boy stood up.

"Graymarsh's maternal aunt is very glad to hear he 's so well and happy, and sends her respectful compliments to Mrs. Squeers, and thinks she must be an angel. She likewise thinks Mr. Squeers is too good for this world, but hopes he may long be spared to carry on the business. Would have sent the two pair of stockings, as desired, but is short of money, so forwards a tract instead. Hopes, above all things, that Graymarsh will study to please Mr. and Mrs. Squeers, and look upon them as his only friends; and that he will love Master Squeers; and not object to sleeping five in a bed, which no Christian should. Ah, a delightful letter; very affecting, indeed."

It was affecting in one sense; for Graymarsh's maternal aunt was strongly supposed by her more intimate friends to be his maternal parent.

"Mobbs's mother-in-law took to her bed on hearing that he would n't eat fat, and has been very ill ever since. She wishes to know by an early post where he expects to go to, if he quarrels with his vittles; and with what feelings he *could* turn up his nose at the cow's-liver broth, after his good master had asked a blessing on it. This was told her in the London newspapers, — not by Mr. Squeers; for he is too kind and too good to set anybody against anybody. Mobbs's mother-in-law is sorry to find Mobbs is discontented (which is sinful and horrid), and hopes Mr. Squeers will flog him into a happier state of mind; with this view she has also stopped his halfpenny a week pocket-money, and given a double-bladed knife, with a corkscrew in it, which she had bought on purpose for him, to the missionaries. A sulky state of feeling won't do. Cheerfulness and contentment must be kept up. — Mobbs, come to me!"

The unhappy Mobbs moved slowly towards the desk, rubbing his eyes in anticipation of good cause for doing so; and soon afterwards retired by the side door, with as good cause as a boy need have.

Mr. Squeers then proceeded to open a miscellaneous collection of letters, — some enclosing money, which Mrs. Squeers "took care of;" and others referring to small articles of apparel, as caps, and so forth, all of which the same lady stated to be too large or too small for everybody but young Squeers, who would appear to have had most accommodating limbs; since everything that came into the school fitted him.

In course of time, Squeers retired to his fireside, leaving Nicholas to take care of the boys in the schoolroom, which was very cold, and where a meal of bread and cheese was served out shortly after dark.

There was a small stove at that corner of the room which was nearest to the master's desk; and by it Nicholas sat down, depressed and self-degraded. As he was absorbed in meditation, he encountered the upturned face of Smike, on his knees before the stove, picking a few cinders from the hearth, and planting them on the fire. When he saw that he was observed, he shrunk back, expecting a blow.

"You need not fear me. Are you cold?"

"N–n–o."

"You are shivering."

"I am not cold. I am used to it."

"Poor, broken-spirited creature!"

If he had struck the wretched object, he would have slunk away without a word. But now he burst into tears.

"Oh, dear! oh, dear! My heart will break! It will, it will!"

"Hush! Be a man; you are nearly one by years. God help you!"

"By years! Oh, dear, dear! how many of them! How many of them since I was a little child, younger than any that are here now? Where are they all?"

"Whom do you speak of?"

"My friends, myself, my — Oh! what sufferings mine have been!"

"There is always hope."

"No, no; none for me. Do you remember the boy that died here?"

"I was not here, you know; but what of him?"

"I was with him at night; and, when it was all silent, he cried no more for friends he wished to come and sit with him, but began to see faces round his bed, that came from home: he said they smiled and talked to him; and he died at last, lifting his head to kiss them. What faces will smile on me when I die? Who will talk to me in those long, long nights? They cannot come from home: they would frighten me if they did; for I don't know what home is. Pain and fear, pain and fear, for me, alive or dead. No hope, no hope!"

The bell rang to bed, and the boy crept away. With heavy heart Nicholas soon afterwards retired — no, not retired; there was no retirement there — followed to the dirty and crowded dormitory.

IX Nicholas, however, had so far seen only one side of the Squeers family. The other members were young Wackford, who looked forward to the day when he should make his little finger felt more heavily than his father's loins, and Miss Fanny Squeers, who had been visiting her friend 'Tilda Price when Nicholas arrived. Fanny's curiosity was aroused by the malignity with which her mother spoke of this upstart son of a gentleman, and it needed only a coy approach to Nicholas to inflame her with passion for him. She took the first opportunity that offered when her father and mother were away to make a little *partie carrée*, consisting of herself and Nicholas, 'Tilda Price and 'Tilda's young man, John Browdie, a big Yorkshireman. Alas for human hopes! The giddy 'Tilda took to flirting with the innocent Nicholas, and the party broke up with threats and tears.

X While Nicholas was thus beginning to make his way in the world, his sister Kate was initiated into her first acquaintance with the pleasure of earning one's living. Miss La Creevy found her a delightful companion, and a good sitter, and one morning as the two were together, Mr. Ralph Nickleby walked in, and, carrying Kate back to her mother, informed them that he had found a situation for Kate at the establishment of a milliner and dressmaker. This was presided over by Mrs. Mantalini and ornamented by Mr. Mantalini. As before, Ralph Nickleby had some financial dealings with the Mantalinis, which made them particularly anxious to do his bidding, and Kate was installed, with her hours from nine to nine, but with the great privilege of spending her nights with her mother. They were not to remain in their lodgings, however, for their highly prudential guardian, Mr. Ralph Nickleby, had provided them with the use of an old dingy house in

XI Thames Street, whither Newman Noggs conducted them, concealing his own provision for their needs, and allowing the volatile Mrs. Nickleby to dress up Mr. Ralph Nickleby's character.

XII It fared worse and worse with Nicholas, for on the day after the tea-party, when Fanny Squeers was returning from a visit to 'Tilda Price, after some squaring of emotional accounts between the two young women, he chanced to meet them both, and being driven into a corner by their wiles, escaped out of it only by the violent method of declaring that the one hope of his life was to escape from his accursed place. Naturally Miss Squeers received

this declaration in the spirit of her family and immediately joined her mother's side, so that Nicholas's life was rendered still more a burden, and poor Smike suffered with him. Indeed, Smike, driven
XIII to desperation, slipped away one night, hoping to escape his torment. In the morning, when the flight was discovered, Mr. and Mrs. Squeers were quite beside themselves with wrath, but they lost little time in pursuing the wretch with such success that Mrs. Squeers brought him back tied hand and foot.

With hands trembling with delight, Squeers unloosened the cord; and Smike, more dead than alive, was brought in, and locked up in a cellar until such time as Mr. Squeers should deem it expedient to operate upon him.

The news that the fugitive had been caught and brought back ran like wildfire through the hungry community; and expectation was on tiptoe all the morning. On tiptoe it remained until the afternoon; when Squeers, having refreshed himself with his dinner and an extra libation or so, made his appearance (accompanied by his amiable partner) with a fearful instrument of flagellation, strong, supple, wax-ended, and new.

"Is every boy here?"

Every boy was there; but every boy was afraid to speak; so Squeers glared along the lines to assure himself.

There was a curious expression in the usher's face; but he took his seat without opening his lips in reply. Squeers left the room, and shortly afterwards returned, dragging Smike by the collar, or, rather, by that fragment of his jacket which was nearest the place where his collar ought to have been.

"Now, what have you got to say for yourself?— Stand a little out of the way, Mrs. Squeers, my dear: I've hardly got room enough."

"Spare me, sir!"

"Oh! that's all you've got to say; is it? Yes, I'll flog you within an inch of your life, and spare you that."

One cruel blow had fallen on him, when Nicholas Nickleby cried, "Stop!"

"Who cried stop?"

"I did. This must not go on!"

"Must not go on?"

"No! Must not! Shall not! I will prevent it! You have disregarded all my quiet interference in this miserable lad's behalf; you have returned no answer to the letter in which I begged forgiveness for him, and offered to be responsible that he would remain quietly here. Don't blame me for this public interference. You have brought it upon yourself, not I."

"Sit down, beggar!"

"Wretch, touch him again at your peril! I will not stand by and see it done. My blood is up, and I have the strength of ten such men as you. By Heaven! I will not spare you if you drive me on. I have a series of personal insults to avenge; and my indignation is aggravated by the cruelties practised in this foul den. Have a care; for, if you raise the devil in me, the consequences will fall heavily upon your head."

Squeers spat at him, and struck him a blow across the face. Nicholas instantly sprang upon him, wrested his weapon from his hand, and, pinning him by the throat, beat the ruffian till he roared for mercy.

He flung him away with all the force he could muster; and the violence of his fall precipitated Mrs. Squeers over an adjacent form; Squeers, striking his head against the same form in his descent, lay at his full length on the ground, stunned and motionless.

Having brought affairs to this happy termination, and having ascertained, to his satisfaction, that Squeers was only stunned, and not dead (upon which point he had had some unpleasant doubts at first), Nicholas packed up a few clothes in a small valise, and, finding that nobody offered to oppose his progress, marched boldly out by the front door, and struck into the road. Then such a cheer arose as the walls of Dotheboys Hall had never echoed before, and would never respond to again. When the sound had died away, the school was empty; and of the crowd of boys not one remained.

As Nicholas made his way down the road, he met to his dismay John Browdie, prepared to take satisfaction out of the young man who had come between him and his sweetheart; but a word of frank apology turned the good-natured Yorkshireman into a friend, and the account which Nicholas gave of his late adventure made him at once an enthusiastic partisan of the young hero, so that he forced money upon him. In the morning after his first night on the road Nicholas was joined by the unhappy Smike, who had fled in the darkness to his one friend in the world.

XIV Nicholas, remembering the offer of the mysterious Newman Noggs, and not desiring to alarm his mother and sister, had resolved to present himself at the door of this friend as soon as he reached London with Smike. It chanced to be on an evening when the decayed gentleman, as his compassionate neighbors termed him, was engaged in helping out the wedding anniversary of two of these neighbors, Mr. and Mrs. Kenwigs, who with their children, Mrs. Kenwigs's uncle, a water-rates collector, Mr.

Lillyvick, supposed to have Mrs. Kenwigs down in his will, Miss Petowker of the Theatre Royal, Drury Lane, and other friends, were holding high festival, including a figure dance by Morleena Kenwigs and a recitation of the "Blood Drinker's Burial" by Miss Petowker. From this scene Newman Noggs was called to meet two strangers.

XV They were of course Nicholas and Smike, and Nicholas having told his story pressed Newman Noggs to tell him what his uncle had heard. In response Newman showed him the copy he had hastily made of a letter from Fanny Squeers to Ralph Nickleby. It tortured the truth to such an extent that Nicholas was scarcely restrained from rushing out at once to tell his uncle exactly what had happened. In the course of the evening Nicholas had one further adventure, very slight in itself, but capable of making a great impression on the Kenwigs family, for he rescued the Kenwigs infant from an imitation danger.

XVI Nicholas Nickleby lost no time in making ready to support himself and Smike and relieve Newman Noggs of a willing care of them. He secured an empty apartment in the same house, and visited a General Agency Office to see if he could find work suited to his capacity. He fancied he should like to be a secretary to some gentleman, and getting the address of a Mr. Gregsbury, a member of Parliament, he waited on him just as a committee of that gentleman's constituents were calling to express their disapproval of his parliamentary conduct. Nicholas was forced to listen to an interview which showed the difference between a member of Parliament before and after he was elected, and then he offered his services as secretary, only to find that for fifteen shillings a week he was to bring enormous information to the service and a willingness to black the gentleman's boots, as the metaphor has it. Declining this broken step-ladder to fortune, Nicholas returned somewhat disconsolate, to find that Newman Noggs had by his representations secured him as a teacher of French to the young Kenwigses at five shillings a week, taking the precaution to remove Nicholas's name as too good for the purpose, and concealing him under the alias of Mr. Johnson. And so Nicholas began his duties at once under the dampening supervision of Mr. Lillyvick.

XVII Nicholas had not made himself known to his mother and sister, and Kate, supposing him happy in Yorkshire, had already begun her own unpromising efforts at self-support, by presenting herself at the Mantalinis', where she was the forced listener to a conjugal discussion which resulted in Mr. Mantalini's extorting money from his wife for his indulgence in horseflesh. Kate herself was set to work under the forewoman of the establishment, Miss Knag, and returned at the end of the first day, dispirited, to

her mother, who had been more agreeably engaged in building houses of cards, in which frail structures she had bestowed Kate and Nicholas, the one as partner to Madame Mantalini, the latter as Dr. Nickleby of Westminster School. Kate had no such illu-
XVIII sions, and even the intimate affection with which Miss Knag at first regarded her and which enchanted Mrs. Nickleby, as the forewoman, walking home with Kate and meeting Mrs. Nickleby, insisted on their both taking tea at her house with her brother, an unhappy rejected lover of Madame Mantalini, — even this affection was turned to gall when the spinster forewoman was suddenly supplanted by the young girl in the duty of waiting upon some of Madame Mantalini's noble customers.

XIX With Mrs. Nickleby's agile mind it was an easy matter to move out of one castle in Spain into another, and when after several days of torture by Miss Knag, whose K turned out to be a superfluous letter, Kate, coming home, met her mother in conversation on the street corner with Mr. Ralph Nickleby, that ingenious old lady had built an entirely new structure from Mr. Nickleby's fortune in consequence of his inviting Kate to preside at his dinner-table the next evening, when he was to entertain a party of gentlemen. This party proved on close acquaintance to consist of Lord Frederick Verisopht, Sir Mulberry Hawk, Mr. Pyke and Mr. Pluck, two hangers-on of Sir Mulberry who was a vicious old rake and older but perhaps not therefore a better man than Lord Frederick Verisopht, and finally Mr. Snobb and Colonel Chowser. All these ornaments of society were geese for Ralph Nickleby to pluck, and he designed to use Kate especially in taking the feathers from Lord Frederick Verisopht. The dinner with its sly allusions was insufferable to Kate, but even the dinner was less terrible than the sudden intrusion into the drawing-room afterward of the baleful old brute, Sir Mulberry Hawk. Ralph Nickleby came in, in time to save Kate from the desecration of Sir Mulberry's touch, and for a moment showed a gleam of compassion for his niece.

XX The effect of this social experience on Kate was so disturbing that the next morning Miss La Creevy carried a message to the haughty Miss Knag, excusing Kate from attendance that day. — On her return she was greatly surprised by a visit from Nicholas, who thus far had failed to find his uncle at home, and now, preceded by Miss La Creevy, found him at his mother's, where he had been reading Fanny Squeers's note, and passing his own saturnine comments on it. Nicholas with vigor rather than discretion denounced his uncle, tried to set his mother up on some firm understanding of the situation, and then left, determined not to be a burden on the family, and found poor Smike at his room, vainly essaying to cut loose from the one source of comfort he possessed.

XXI It was by no means certain that had Nicholas been willing to live on Kate's earnings he could well have done so, for on her returning to Madame Mantalini's, and setting to work after being an unwilling witness to an altercation between Mantalini and his wife upon the financial outlook, she was surprised by the intrusion of a sheriff's deputy, who proceeded to put in a writ of execution on the goods in payment of Mr. Mantalini's just and unjust debts. So the establishment closed. Kate was out of work; but taking note of an advertisement for a companion to a lady, she applied to Mrs. Wititterly, and was received into the household of that languid and too highly organized nature. Once more the undaunted Mrs. Nickleby proceeded to build her daughter's fortune, this time on the Wititterly sand.

XXII Nicholas, with the hopefulness of youth, determined not to remain in London, but to set out on his travels in hopes of bettering his fortune. Accompanied by the faithful Smike he trudged over the road which led to Portsmouth, with the vague notion, if all else failed, of going to sea. By the way he burrowed in the dark places of Smike's confused memory, hoping to rescue some remains of fact. Twelve miles short of Portsmouth, the two, well tired out, stopped for the night at a roadside inn, and there fell in with a company of strolling players under the management of Mr. Vincent Crummles, also on the way to Portsmouth. Mr. Crummles at once discovered great latent dramatic possibilities in Nicholas and Smike, declaring the latter would be an immense success as the apothecary in Romeo and Juliet, and without more ado added them to his company. The next day the party
XXIII joined Mrs. Crummles and others in Portsmouth. Nicholas and Smike were introduced to the theatre and all the queerly assorted members of the company, the infant phenomenon, Miss Ninetta Crummles, being particularly dazzling, and were received practically into the Crummles household. Nicholas was at once invested with the character of play-wright to the company, and given half a dozen leading parts in old plays for his varied powers.

XXIV He had an opportunity very soon of trying all his wits, for not only was he bidden to prepare a play adapted from the French, for Miss Snevellicci's benefit, and take a leading part in it himself, but he had beforehand to go through the trying ordeal of accompanying that lady and the infant phenomenon on a canvassing tour through the town. The success of the play, however, atoned
XXV for any small discomfort. There was a surprise in store for him, a sort of *coup de théatre*, when, the next day, Mr.

Crummles with great pride announced that the company was to be strengthened by the addition of Miss Henrietta Petowker of the Theatre Royal, Drury Lane, and Miss Petowker herself appearing on the stage was rapturously applauded by a gentleman with an umbrella, who revealed himself to Nicholas as Mr. Lillyvick. Then it transpired that Mr. Lillyvick, having won Miss Petowker's affections, and being in considerable alarm over the effect of his proceedings on the Kenwigs family, had come down into the provinces to marry Miss Petowker on the sly. The wedding came off almost as an additional play, and was followed shortly by "Romeo and Juliet," with Smike, under the training of Nicholas, an irreproachable apothecary.

XXVI While Nicholas was thus doing his best to get the better of the world he lived in, poor Kate had an even more difficult task, for the two dissipated scoundrels, Lord Frederick Verisopht and Sir Mulberry Hawk, became more hot on her trail as the chase developed difficulties. Each sought to out-manœuvre the other. Both went to see Ralph Nickleby, and he, usurer as he was and ready to coin money out of hearts if he could, told Lord Frederick where she now lived. Sir Mulberry, meanwhile, encountering Mrs. Nickleby, discovered from that incoherent lady her home, and shortly after the two pimps Pyke and Pluck visited her with an
XXVII invitation from the noble rascals to attend the theatre with them. At the play, by a most fortunate accident for the intriguers, Mrs. Wititterly appeared with Kate in a neighboring box. It was easy to bring the two parties together, and Mrs. Wititterly,
XXVIII with her twittering after society, became the dupe, and through her means the rakes persecuted the girl until in desperation she had recourse to her uncle. Small comfort she received from him, but Newman Noggs gave his apparently rather ineffectual blessing and took his own satisfaction in making up faces at Ralph Nickleby behind the door.

XXIX Nevertheless Newman Noggs was the guardian angel of the young Nicklebys, for it was his letter, mysteriously conveying the knowledge of some impending trouble for Kate, which determined Nicholas, who had won a place quite at the head of the company, thereby exciting most unreasonable jealousy and envy,
XXX to retire from the boards and return to London; but this he did not do without first a dinner with the Snevelliccis and Lillyvicks, at which Mr. Lillyvick made some discoveries as to his wife's nature, and an affecting parting with Mr. Crummles, who seized the opportunity of the starting of the coach for a public embrace of Nicholas.

XXXI Nicholas would have found Newman Noggs at once, or

failing him, Miss La Creevy, if those two conspirators had not taken good care to be out of the way in the evening, that he might not, upon receiving the intelligence they had for him, precipi-
XXXII tately do some rash thing. As it was, not finding either of them, or his mother, whom Miss La Creevy had sagaciously carried off to the theatre, he impatiently walked the streets, and, going into a hotel to get some refreshment, he caught the name of his sister from the lips of some body in a neighboring box. The conversation waxed insolent about her. Nicholas, infuriated, sprang up and made himself known to Sir Mulberry Hawk, who treated him with contempt and refused to give his name. Nicholas followed him to his quarters, and as a parting compliment received a cut of his whip from Sir Mulberry, but immediately repaid it with a violence which temporarily put an end to that nobleman's career.

XXXIII The next morning Nicholas went at once to the Witit-terly's and brought Kate away. He had some difficulty in readjusting his mother to new conditions, but none whatever in writing a brief note to his Uncle Ralph in which he cast off that relationship. While Ralph Nickleby was holding this note, in came
XXXIV Mantalini to borrow money at usurious rates on papers stolen from his wife, and after him Madame Mantalini, all resolves to extinguish her husband, and under his blandishments anon condoning his offence. Scarcely had they gone, leaving a single gleam of comfort with Ralph in the news they brought of Nicholas's encounter with Hawk, which Ralph hoped meant mischief for Nicholas, when Squeers was ushered in, attended by the cub Wackford. Ralph, full of his malignant feelings towards his nephew, listened to Squeers as he related the abduction by Nicholas of Smike, with the thought of possibly wounding the young man through his affection for his forlorn comrade.

XXXV For the present, at any rate, Smike had nothing to fear. Nicholas, having established his mother and sister with Miss La Creevy, made haste to bring his poor defendant into the household, and with some difficulty brought him and his history into focus with Mrs. Nickleby. Then he set out to find employment, and bethought himself of the same agency he had visited before. As he stood before the window, his eye caught a benevolent-looking gentleman also looking in, and presently they fell into conversation. Something in the old gentleman's benevolence drew out the young man's story, and as he told it the attraction seemed to be reversed, and now it was Nicholas who drew the old gentleman to himself. In a trice, Mr. Charles Cheeryble, for such was his name, had carried Nicholas off to his office in the city, and there introduced him to his twin brother, Edwin, who was twin also in nature, and to Mr. Tim Linkinwater, their right hand man, an obstinate piece of fidelity and affection. It took but a short time not only to install Nicholas as a clerk in the office, but to establish the family in a vacant cottage at Bow.

XXXVI Nicholas had not forgotten his friends the Kenwigses. Indeed, he was forced to visit them on a somewhat painful errand, but taking his courage in both hands he called upon the family in Golden Square shortly after a new child had arrived, with great expectations of wealth from the family uncle. Into the comfortable, sanguine family circle Nicholas projected the most disturbing news that Mr. Lillyvick, the fairy-uncle, had married Henrietta Petowker. The rapidity with which Mr. Lillyvick's character crumbled at the touch of Mr. Kenwigs was remarkable.

XXXVII In his new office Nicholas showed himself so proficient a pupil of Tim Linkinwater that that exacting gentleman called the Brothers Cheeryble to witness as he displayed the ledger, and triumphantly compared Nicholas's work with his own. It was on the birthday of Tim, and the Brothers, Tim, Tim's sister, and Nicholas dined together in honor of the event. On his return from the dinner to his own cottage late in the evening, Nicholas was astounded to hear from his mother a tale, which to her ears meant that their next neighbor had fallen in love with her, and to his that there must be some lunatic on the other side of the wall who used cucumbers as other lovers used roses.

XXXVIII Miss La Creevy, who had been an energetic visitor at the cottage, took it into her head to take Smike to town with her on her return, and a sorrowful day it was for him; for as he was on his way back after leaving her, he was suddenly pounced upon by Mr. Squeers and Wackford, who came upon him unexpectedly, but none the less joyfully. They hustled him into a hackney coach, thrashed him there, and bore him off to their lodgings, which

XXXIX were in Somers Town. Squeers had taken lodgings there with Mr. Snawley as less expensive than the Saracen's Head, but that inn was his rendezvous, and thither he resorted the next day to meet his daughter Fanny, who had come up to London with John Browdie and Mrs. Browdie, née 'Tilda Price. Squeers was so delighted with his capture that he burst out with the news, and told further how he intended to return to Yorkshire the next day with Wackford and his victim. He had them all at his lodgings that night, and John Browdie, who had a level head, a warm heart, and a close mouth, managed to set Smike loose and put him out of the house on his way home to Nicholas.

XL Smike went to the first harbor of refuge, Newman Noggs's quarters, and by him was taken home to Nicholas, who had

been hunting in vain for him. Nicholas at first had been disposed to charge this abduction of Smike on his uncle, but at last made up his mind that Squeers was alone at the bottom of it. He was somewhat distracted, however, from these matters by a little affair of his own, for it chanced that about this time there was an apparition of a lovely girl in the counting-room of the Cheeryble Brothers, a girl whom he had once caught sight of on the occasion of his first visit to the agency office. Tim Linkinwater apparently knew who she was, but he was provokingly non-committal, and in default of other means Nicholas laid upon Newman Noggs the duty of watching her servant, with the result that Newman not only found name and residence, but brought about an interview for Nicholas with —
XLI the wrong person. Indeed, the love affairs of the family seemed to be in a sad way, for the old gentleman next door, pursuing his attentions in the most marked manner toward Mrs. Nickleby, went so far as to look over the garden wall and deliver himself of most sentimental utterances, and after all was carried off from the scene by his keeper, who explained to Mrs. Nickleby and Kate his unhappy lunacy.

XLII Nicholas for a moment thought, even feared, that he might be on the track of the girl whose name and home still baffled him, for, going to take supper with the Browdies at the Saracen's Head, where Squeers, Fanny, and Wackford unexpectedly appeared, though not as guests, he was witness to a sudden row in the bar-
XLIII room, which proved to be a punishment inflicted by a young man on an objectionable fellow who had been taking a certain young lady's name in vain. As Nicholas recognized in the culprit an offensive clerk at the Agency office, he put two and two together with the instinct of a lover, and was not a little dismayed at finding the young gentleman to be Mr. Frank Cheeryble, a nephew of the Brothers, just returned from Germany. The next Sunday the Cheerybles came to Mrs. Nickleby's to tea, and before the evening was over Nicholas, observing Frank and Kate, might readily have put one and one together.

XLIV Mr. Ralph Nickleby, stealthily pursuing his evil designs and consumed with a passionate hatred of Nicholas, did not disregard his own interests. It chanced that one day, as he was seting out on some of his errands of mercilessness toward poor debtors, he was accosted by a man, one Brooker, who had been his tool and dupe. He shook him off coldly and kept on his way to the Mantalinis, where he found Madame Mantalini coolly surveying her husband prostrated with one of his attacks of narrowly escaped suicide, and came back to his house to find waiting for him Mr. Squeers and Mr. Snawley. They were waiting for him in pursuance of a plan he had concocted for the furtherance of his own ends.

XLV At once he took them off in a coach and proceeded to Mrs. Nickleby's, where it chanced that John Browdie and his wife were taking supper. Here he proceeded to demand Smike as the son of Mr. Snawley by a former wife, in proof of which he produced papers that seemed to Nicholas incontrovertible. But Smike, terrified and revolting from the new relationship, clung to his real friends, who stood by him to the extent of ejecting Mr. Squeers from the house, and allowing Snawley and Ralph to follow, the last named breathing out vengeance in the form of law-suits.

XLVI Nicholas had no question as to his course in the matter, but he deemed it prudent to confide in his employers, and was rejoiced to find that they entirely agreed with him and with each other. At the end of the interview they stated that they had a delicate mission for him to perform. There was a certain young lady, the daughter of one whom they had both fondly loved and whom one of them gladly would have married. The mother had died, and the daughter, Madeline Bray, was living with her selfish, broken-down, spendthrift father, within the Rules of the King's Bench Prison. The Cheeryble Brothers were really maintaining them, but by the pretence of purchasing small drawings and other works of art produced by the young lady, and now Nicholas was to serve as a go-between. At last he stood face to face with the beautiful girl he had been pursuing ineffectually.

XLVII He was not the only one, however, who had looked on Madeline Bray and desired her. There was an old money-lender, Arthur Gride, who with Ralph Nickleby had been the means of detaining Mr. Bray for debt. He called on Ralph and disclosed to him the secret, Newman Noggs listening from behind a door, of his purpose to buy Madeline for a wife by releasing and pensioning Mr. Bray, and with this in view he asked Ralph's counsel and help. He intimated moreover that there was a piece of property which would fall into the hands of the husband of the girl. The two hoary plotters paid a visit to Mr. Bray, and Arthur Gride asked him formally for the hand of his daughter. Nicholas,
XLVIII so far from aspiring to Madeline's hand, was filled with a sense of immeasurable distance from her as he surveyed her charms and her noble self-sacrifice. It was a diversion thus of his melancholy when he came accidentally upon Mr. Vincent Crummles, and, finding that he was about to take leave of his native land for a theatrical season in America, assisted at a farewell dinner.

XLIX Nicholas could not fail to see that all this time poor Smike grew feebler and feebler. His wasting away was unaccountable. Could it be, the reader begins to surmise, that he was consumed by a hopeless passion for Kate? If so, his trouble certainly was increased by the frequent visits of Frank Cheeryble. It was on one of these occasions, when Frank came with Tim Linkinwater and found Miss La Creevy also at the house, that the party was suddenly disconcerted by a noise in the adjoining room which resolved itself into some disturbance in the chimney. The whole party, save Miss La Creevy, who did not at first enter, proceeded with improvised weapons to the next room. There was a pair of legs struggling out of the fireplace. They were the legs of Mrs. Nickleby's eccentric admirer, and when he was extracted in full, he was proceeding with his extraordinary love-making when Miss La Creevy suddenly entered. Instantly all his attention was given to her, and by thus attaching himself to a new object he detached Mrs. Nickleby.

L Since Nicholas had dealt Sir Mulberry Hawk a blow which retired that rascal from active life for a season, he and Lord Frederick Verisopht had been living in Belgium. But on Sir Mulberry's recovery they returned to England in time for the Hampton races. There Sir Mulberry avowed his intention of revenging himself on Nicholas. His companion had a spasm of better feeling, but in the orgies which followed, a quarrel sprang up between them, followed by a duel in which the younger roué fell by the hands of his preceptor in vice.

LI The affairs of the other villains seemed to be prospering. Arthur Gride went so far as to consult his old housekeeper, Peg Sliderskew, as to what suit he should wear at his wedding. While they were talking, Newman Noggs came with a letter from Ralph Nickleby, and, with his customary good luck at getting hold of Ralph's secrets, managed to read the letter when Gride was out of the room. It put him in possession of a piece of information which he communicated to Nicholas that evening, little suspecting how much it meant to his young friend. It meant so much that
LII Newman Noggs could hardly restrain Nicholas from rushing off upon some wild venture; but by degrees he calmed him, and Nicholas went home resolved at once to see what he could do by seeing Madeline. Newman returned home, and by good fortune could at once be of service to the Kenwigs family, for it chanced that Morleena, who was to go on a picnic on the morrow, needed to have her hair dressed, and Newman alone was available to escort her to the barber's. There whom should they encounter but Mr. Lillyvick, a much changed man, sadly in need of soap and other comforts. The cast-off uncle returned with them to the family, and

there disclosed the momentous fact that Mrs. Lillyvick had eloped with a half-pay captain. Sudden reversal of the engine, and return to the friendly relations of Mr. Lillyvick and the Kenwigs family.

LIII Nicholas, the next day, kept his purpose and went to see Madeline Bray and her father. He found the old man nervously anticipating the marriage which was to restore him to luxury, and the girl tearfully yet proudly resolved on sacrificing herself to her father's need. It seemed as if he could do no more. Yet he determined to make one more effort, and that night he visited Gride with threats, warnings, and expostulations. Nicholas showed so much knowledge of affairs that for a moment Gride was baffled, but he recovered himself and at last got rid of his very unwelcome visitor. Nothing now seemed to remain but the sacrifice of the victim. Gride and Ralph proceeded to the house
LIV in due season, but to their amazement and to the furious wrath of the latter they were confronted by Nicholas and Kate. A scene ensued of indignant words and bitter recriminations, in the midst of which old Mr. Bray suddenly died, and Nicholas and Kate bore off the prostrate Madeline from her baffled
LV persecutors. At the home of the Nicklebys Madeline slowly recovered from the shock occasioned by the death of her father, and time was given for Frank Cheeryble to make love to Kate so openly that the astute Mrs. Nickleby saw it all and Nicholas did not. But poor Smike failed rapidly, and in hopes of yet saving his life, Nicholas carried him away to Devonshire, breathing benedictions on Kate Nickleby.

LVI Ralph Nickleby and Arthur Gride had left the presence of the Brays with a humiliating sense of defeat, but to the latter an even worse catastrophe showed itself, when on their return to his house he found that Peg Sliderskew had meanwhile robbed him of his papers, among them one concerning Madeline Bray, the discovery of which would send him to Newgate. Ralph Nickleby had his own misfortune to bewail upon reaching his quarters, when he learned the failure of a house to which he had intrusted ten thousand pounds, but he had deeper feelings, feelings of intense resentment, against Nicholas, and in obedience to these he formed a subtle plan.

He sent for Squeers, and reminding him of the perjury which he and Snawley had committed in swearing to the relationship between Snawley and Smike, set him at the task of recovering the paper which Peg Sliderskew had stolen from Gride. He himself tracked Peg to her hiding-place, and Squeers, using all his art to
LVII possess himself of the paper, had just succeeded in secreting it in his pocket when Newman Noggs, who, with Frank

Cheeryble, had been an unseen witness of the act, felled him to the earth with a pair of bellows.

LVIII The journey which Nicholas took with Smike could not save the boy's life, and he was buried where he died, but not before he had seen suddenly, with great alarm, the man whom he remembered as the one who took him to Yorkshire to school. It was no other than the tramp Brooker, who had been moving about in a shadowy fashion, and consorting with Newman Noggs. It was he who held a dread secret, that was sure to come out. For Squeers was now in prison, and Ralph Nickleby seeking for him at

LIX Snawley's was repulsed by Snawley's wife, and again by Gride. He went to see the Brothers Cheeryble, for Mr. Charles had been to see him in the morning and had darkly hinted that he knew something of his affairs. At the office of the Cheeryble Brothers he encountered Newman Noggs and learned, as he had suspected, that his clerk had turned upon him. But he was still undaunted. He went now to see Squeers, and returned heavy-hearted

LX at the failure of his plot, which Squeers related in detail. Once more at home, at night, he was waited upon by Tim Linkinwater, who by a mysterious summons persuaded him to go once more to the Cheerybles. At first his wicked old heart flamed up in hope, as he thought from what he first heard that Nicholas was dead. Instead, he was confronted with Brooker and the disclosure was made that all present now knew Smike to be the child of Ralph Nickleby.

LXI Nicholas returned the next day and reported all particulars of Smike's end to his family, the Cheeryble Brothers, and Tim Linkinwater, but he had something else to report to the Brothers, for before going thither he and Kate had made mutual confessions, she that Frank Cheeryble had offered himself to her, and she had refused him, he, that he loved Madeline, but never, never would ask her to marry him, both resolutions being taken in consequence of the relations which these young people held to Cheeryble Brothers. These gentlemen received the news imperturbably, seemed to accept the situation, but told Nicholas he was to go with them by appointment to see his uncle. Thither they went, for

LXII Ralph had indeed agreed to meet them. They went and found him hanging by the neck, dead, dead, dead.

LXIII All unpleasantness was now over. At a dinner-party given by the Cheeryble Brothers, the story of Madeline's inheritance was told, and also that Madeline herself had something better than riches in the love of Nicholas Nickleby. Frank Cheeryble paired off with Kate, and bless us! Tim Linkinwater and Miss La Creevy were found of the same mind and heart.

XLIV And now the adventures of Nicholas Nickleby were near an end, yet since all this good fortune had come to him, he must needs revisit the scene of his wretched experience. Before he went to Yorkshire, however, he and Kate in one of their walks came unexpectedly on an old acquaintance of hers, Mantalini, engaged in mangling, under supervision of a vixenish substitute for Madame Mantalini. There was a moment of recognition, and then a wild flight of the disgraced dandy. In Yorkshire Nicholas visited the Browdies, and told them that Squeers had been sentenced to transportation for seven years. John Browdie rode over to Dotheboys Hall, but the news had outrun him, and when he reached the place he found a rebellion and riot which ended in a dispersion of the unhappy youngsters. What remains to be told but that the three
LXV happy couples were married, the firm became Cheeryble and Nickleby, and good and bad got their respective deserts.

---

## INDEX TO CHARACTERS.

**Adams, Captain.** One of the seconds in the duel between Sir Mulberry Hawk and Lord Verisopht.

**African Knife-Swallower, The.** A member of Mr. Crummles's theatrical company. xlviii.

**Alice.** *See* YORK, THE FIVE SISTERS OF.

**Alphonse.** Mrs. Wititterly's page; so diminutive, "that his body would not hold, in ordinary array, the number of small buttons which are indispensable to a page's costume; and they were consequently obliged to be stuck on four abreast." xxi, xxviii, xxxii.

**Belling, Master.** One of Mr. Squeers's pupils at Dotheboys Hall. iv.

**Belvawney, Miss.** A lady in Mr. Vincent Crummles's theatrical company. xxiii–xxv, xxix.

**Blockson, Mrs.** A charwoman employed by Miss Knag. xviii.

**Bobster, Mr.** A ferocious old fellow into whose house Nicholas Nickleby is introduced one evening by Newman Noggs, whom he has commissioned to find out where Madeline Bray lives, and who makes the ludicrous mistake of discovering the wrong party. xl.

**Bobster, Miss Cecilia.** His daughter; mistaken by Newman Noggs for Miss Madeline Bray, and persuaded by him to see Nicholas, and to hear him speak for himself. xl.

**Bolder.** A pupil at Mr. Squeers's educational establishment, called Dotheboys Hall. viii.

**Bonney, Mr.** A friend of Ralph Nickleby's, and the prime organizer of the "United Metropolitan Improved Hot Muffin and Crumpet Baking and Punctual Delivery Company." ii.

**Borum, Mr.** A gentleman at whose house Nicholas Nickleby and Miss Snevellicci call (accompanied by Miss Ninetta Crummles, the "Infant Phenomenon") to induce him to put his name to Miss Snevellicci's "bespeak." xxiv.

**Borum, Mrs.** His wife; mother of six interesting children. xxiv.

**Borum, Augustus.** Their son; a young gentleman who pinches the "Phenomenon" behind, to ascertain whether she is real. xxiv.

**Borum, Charlotte.** One of their daughters, who filches the "Phenomenon's" parasol, and carries it off. xxiv.

**Borum, Emma.** Another daughter. xxiv.

**Bravassa, Miss.** One of the members of Mr. Crummles's theatrical company. xxiii–xxv, xxix.

**Bray, Madeline.** Daughter of a gentleman who married a very particular friend of the Cheeryble Brothers. Her mother dies while she is a mere child; and her selfish and profligate father, at a somewhat later date, is reduced, between sickness and poverty, to the verge of death. Although she braves privation, degradation, and affliction, for the sake of supporting him, he is on the point of forcing her to marry a rich old miser named Gride, when death suddenly carries off the unnatural parent, and Madeline is removed to Mrs. Nickleby's house. She afterwards marries Nicholas. xvi, xl, xlvi, xlvii, li, lii, liv–lvi, lxiii, lxv.

**Bray, Walter.** Father to Madeline, a broken-down, irritable, and selfish debauchee. xlvi, xlvii, lii–liv.

**Brooker.** A felon and an outcast; a former clerk to Ralph Nickleby. Being ill-treated by his master, and hating him, he takes advantage of favoring circumstances to make him think his only son has died and been buried during his temporary absence from home; though, in reality, the boy has been left at a Yorkshire school, with the design of one day making the secret a means of getting money from the father. But the plan fails; and Mr. Nickleby, in the hot pursuit of bad ends, persecutes and hunts down his own child to death. xliv, lx, lxv.

**Browdie, John.** A stout, kind-hearted Yorkshire man, drawn from life. He is betrothed to Miss Matilda Price, whom he afterwards marries. At his first meeting with Nicholas Nickleby, he becomes furiously jealous of him. Finding, however, that Nicholas has no intention of making trouble between him and his intended, he conceives a more favorable opinion of the young gentleman, and they become good friends. ix, xiii, xxxix, xlii, xliii, xlv, lxiv.

**Bulph, Mr.** A pilot, who keeps a lodging house at which Mr. Crummles lives. xxiii.

**Cheeryble Brothers, The (Charles and Edwin).** Twin brothers, partners in business, and the benefactors and employers of Nicholas Nickleby. Having been encouraged to tell his story to one of the brothers whom he has accidentally met on the street, Nicholas is hurried into an omnibus, and taken straight to the warehouse, where he is introduced to the other brother, and, after some inquiries and private conference, is taken into their counting-room. xxxv, xxxvii, xl, xliii, xlvi, xlix, lv, lix, lx, lxi, lxiii, lxv.

**Cheeryble, Frank.** Nephew of the Cheeryble Brothers. He finally marries Kate Nickleby. xliii, xlix, lv, lvii, lix, lxi, lxiii, lxv.

**Chowser, Colonel.** One of the guests at a dinner-party given by Ralph Nickleby. xix, l.

**Cobbey.** A pupil at Squeers's school. viii.

**Crowl, Mr.** A fellow-lodger of Newman Noggs. xiv, xv, xxxii.

**Crummles, Mr. Vincent.** The manager of an itinerant theatrical company. Meeting Nicholas Nickleby and Smike at an inn not far from Portsmouth, he advises them to adopt the stage for a profession, and offers to bring them out. "There's a genteel comedy," he tells Nicholas, "in your walk and manner, juvenile tragedy in your eye, and touch-and-go farce in your laugh." Of Smike he says: —

"Without a pad upon his body, and hardly a touch of paint upon his face, he'd make such an actor for the starved business as was never seen in this country. Only let him be tolerably well up in the apothecary in 'Romeo and Juliet,' with the slightest possible dab of red on the tip of his nose, and he'd be certain of three rounds the moment he put his head out of the practicable door in the front grooves O. P."

The result is, that Nicholas, after a little deliberation, declares it a bargain; and he and Smike become a part of Mr. Crummles's company. He treats them very kindly, and pays them well; and when he finally separates from them, — on the occasion of his departure with his family for America, — he puts out his hand, with "not a jot of his theatrical manner" remaining, and says with great warmth, "We were a very happy little company. You and I never had a word. I shall be very glad to-morrow morning to think that I saw you again; but now I almost wish you had n't come." xxii–xxv, xxix, xxx, xlviii.

**Crummles, Mrs.** Wife of Mr. Vincent Crummles. xxiii–xxv, xxix, xxx, xlviii.

**Crummles, Master.** One of their sons, and a member of the theatrical company. xxii, xxiii, xxx, xlviii.

**Crummles, Master Percy.** Another son. xxii, xxiii, xxx, xlviii.

**Crummles, Miss Ninetta.** Their daughter, known and advertised as the "Infant Phenomenon." This character was drawn from life; and the original is now the wife of a distinguished American general. xxiii, xxiv, xxv, xxix, xlviii.

**Curdle, Mr.** A Portsmouth gentleman, whom Miss Snevellicci calls upon to request that he would put his name to her "bespeak;" he being a great critic, and having quite the London taste in matters relating to literature and the drama. He is the author of a pamphlet of sixty-four pages, post octavo, on the character of the nurse's deceased husband, in "Romeo and Juliet." xxiv.

**Curdle, Mrs.** His wife. xxiv.

**Cutler, Mr. and Mrs.** Friends of the Kenwigses. xiv.

**David.** Butler to the Cheeryble Brothers. xxxvii, lxiii.

**Digby.** Smike's theatrical name. *See* SMIKE.

**Folair, Mr.** A dancer and pantomimic actor belonging to Mr. Crummles's company. xxiii–xxv, xxix, xxx.

**Gazingi, Miss.** An actress in the theatrical company of Mr. Vincent Crummles. xxiii.

**Gentleman, The, in small-clothes.** *See* NICKLEBY, MRS.

**George.** A friend of the Kenwigses. He is a young man who had known Mr. Kenwigs when he was a bachelor, and is much esteemed by the ladies, as bearing the reputation of a rake. xiv.

**Graymarsh.** A pupil at Dotheboys Hall, Squeers's school. viii.

**Green, Miss.** A friend of the Kenwigses. xiv.

**Gregsbury, Mr.** A member of parliament, to whom Nicholas Nickleby applies for a situation as private secretary. The requirements, however, are so many, and so difficult to meet, that the situation is declined. Says Mr. Gregsbury: —

"My secretary would have to make himself master of the foreign policy of the world, as it is mirrored in the newspapers; to run his eye over all accounts of public meetings, all leading articles, and accounts of the proceedings of public bodies; and to make notes of anything which it appeared to him might be made a point of in any little speech upon the question of some petition lying on the table, or anything of that kind. Do you understand?"

"I think I do, sir," replied Nicholas.

"Then," said Mr. Gregsbury, "it would be necessary for him to make himself acquainted from day to day with newspaper paragraphs on passing events, such as 'Mysterious disappearance and supposed suicide of a pot-boy,' or anything of that sort, upon which I might found a question to the Secretary of State

CHEERYBLE BROTHERS AND TIM LINKINWATER.

for the Home Department. Then he would have to copy the question and as much as I remembered of the answer (including a little compliment about my independence and good sense), and to send the manuscript in a frank to the local paper, with perhaps half a dozen lines of leader, to the effect that I was always to be found in my place in parliament, and never shrunk from the discharge of my responsible and arduous duties, and so forth. You see?"

Nicholas bowed.

"Besides which," continued Mr. Gregsbury, "I should expect him now and then to go through a few figures in the printed tables, and to pick out a few results, so that I might come out pretty well on timber-duty questions, and finance questions, and so on; and I should like him to get up a few little arguments about the disastrous effects of a return to cash-payments and a metallic currency, with a touch now and then about the exportation of bullion, and the Emperor of Russia, and bank-notes, and all that kind of thing, which it 's only necessary to talk fluently about, because nobody understands it. Do you take me?"

"I think I understand," said Nicholas.

"With regard to such questions as are not political," continued Mr. Gregsbury, warming, "and which one can't be expected to care a damn about, beyond the natural care of not allowing inferior people to be as well off as ourselves (else where are our privileges?), I should wish my secretary to get together a few little flourishing speeches of a patriotic cast. . . . This is a hasty outline of the chief things you 'd have to do, except waiting in the lobby every night (in case I forgot anything, and should want fresh cramming), and now and then, during great debates, sitting in the front row of the gallery, and saying to the people about, 'You see that gentleman with his hand to his face, and his arm twisted round the pillar? That 's Mr. Gregsbury, the celebrated Mr. Gregsbury,'—with any other little eulogium that might strike you at the moment." xvi.

**Gride, Arthur.** An old miser. xlvii, li, liii, liv, lvi, lix, lxv.

**Grogzwig, Baron of.** *See* KOËLDWETHOUT, BARON VON.

**Grudden, Mrs.** An actress attached to Mr. Crummles's theatrical company, and an assistant to Mrs. Crummles in her domestic affairs. xxiii, xxiv, xxix, xxx, xlix.

**Hannah.** Servant to Miss La Creevy. iii.

**Hawk, Sir Mulberry.** A fashionable gambler, *roué*, and knave, remarkable for his tact in ruining young gentlemen of fortune. He endeavors to lead Kate Nickleby astray, but fails, and is punished by her brother. He afterwards fights a duel with his pupil and dupe, Lord Frederick Verisopht, in which the latter is killed. xix, xxvi–xxviii, xxxii, xxxviii, l, lxv.

**Johnson, Mr.** The stage name given by Mr. Crummles to Nicholas Nickleby.

**Kenwigs, Mr.** A turner in ivory, and a lodger in the same house with Newman Noggs; "looked upon as a person of some consideration on the premises, inasmuch as he occupied the whole of the first floor, comprising a suite of two rooms." xiv–xvi, xxxvi, lii.

**Kenwigs, Mrs.** His wife; "quite a lady in her manners, and of a very genteel family, having an uncle [Mr. Lillyvick] who collected a water-rate; besides which distinction, the two eldest of her little girls went twice a week to a dancing-school in the neighborhood, and had flaxen hair tied with blue ribbons hanging in luxuriant pigtails down their backs, and wore little white trousers with frills round the ankles,—for all of which reasons, and many more, equally valid, but too numerous to mention, she was considered a very desirable person to know." xiv–xvi, xxxvi, lii.

**Kenwigs, Morleena.** Her eldest daughter, "regarding whose uncommon Christian name it may be stated, that it was invented and composed by Mrs. Kenwigs previous to her first lying-in, for the special distinction of her eldest child, in case it should prove a daughter." xiv–xvi, xxxvi, lii.

**Knag, Miss.** Forewoman in Madame Mantalini's millinery establishment, and her successor in the business. xvii, xviii, xx, xxi, xliv.

**Knag, Mr. Mortimer.** Her brother; a young man whom unrequited affection has made miserable. xviii.

**Koëldwethout, Baron von,** of Grogzwig, Germany. Hero of one of the tales told at a roadside inn when Nicholas Nickleby and Squeers, with other passengers, were detained there by an accident to the stage-coach in which they were travelling. vi.

**Koëldwethout, Baroness von.** His wife. vi.

**La Creevy, Miss.** A mincing young lady of fifty; a miniature-painter, who becomes a fast friend of the Nicklebys, and finally marries Tim Linkinwater, the old clerk of the Cheeryble Brothers. iii, v, x, xi, xx, xxxi, xxxiii, xxxv, xxxviii, xlix, lxi, lxiii, lxv.

**Lane, Miss.** Governess in Mr. Borum's family. xxiv.

**Ledrook, Miss.** A member of Mr. Crummles's dramatic company. xxiii, xxv, xxx.

**Lenville, Thomas.** A tragic actor in Mr. Crummles's theatre. xxiii, xxiv, xxix.

**Lenville, Mrs.** His wife; a member of the same profession. xxiii, xxix.

**Lillyvick, Mr.** A collector of water-rates. He is uncle to Mrs. Kenwigs, at one of whose anniversary wedding-parties he meets Miss Henrietta Petowker, an amateur actress, and is smitten with her charms. He finally follows her to Portsmouth, — where she has engaged to appear in Mr. Crummles's theatre, — and marries her, much to the disgust of the Kenwigses, who have considered themselves his heirs. But Miss Petowker soon proves false, and runs away with another man, leaving the collector disconsolate. He returns to London, where he meets Newman Noggs, and is prevailed upon to go to the house of his relatives, where a ludicrously affecting scene ensues. A boy has been born to them during his absence. Mr. Lillyvick informs them that he never shall expect them to receive his wife, as she has deserted him.

"Eloped with a half-pay captain," repeated Mr. Lillyvick, — "basely and falsely eloped with a half-pay captain, with a bottle-nosed captain that any man might have considered himself safe from. It was in this room," said Mr. Lillyvick, looking sternly round, "that I first see Henrietta Petowker: it is in this room that I turn her off for ever."

This declaration completely changed the whole posture of affairs. Mrs. Kenwigs threw herself upon the old gentleman's neck, bitterly reproaching herself for her late harshness, and exclaiming, if she had suffered, what must his sufferings have been! Mr. Kenwigs grasped his hand, and vowed eternal friendship and remorse. . . . And Mr. and Mrs. Kenwigs both said, with strong feeling and tears of sympathy, that everything happened for the best, and conjured the good collector not to give way to unavailing grief, but to seek consolation in the society of those affectionate relations whose arms and hearts were ever open to him.

"Out of affection and regard for you, Susan and Kenwigs," said Mr. Lillyvick, "and not out of revenge and spite against her (for she is below it), I shall tomorrow morning settle upon your children, and make payable to the survivors of them, when they come of age or marry, that money that I once meant to leave 'em in my will. The deed shall be executed to-morrow, and Mr. Noggs shall be one of the witnesses. He hears me promise this, and he shall see it done." xiv–xvi, xxv, xxx, xxxvi, xlviii.

**Linkinwater, Miss.** Sister to Tim Linkinwater. xxxvii, lxiii.

**Linkinwater, Tim.** Chief clerk of the Cheeryble Brothers.

"It 's forty-four year," said Tim, making a calculation in the air with his pen, and drawing an imaginary line before he cast it up, — "forty-four year next May, since I first kept the books of

Cheeryble Brothers. I 've opened the safe every morning all that time (Sundays excepted), as the clock struck nine, and gone over the house every night at half-past ten (except on Foreign Post nights, and then twenty minutes before twelve) to see the doors fastened, and the fires out. I 've never slept out of the back attic one single night. There 's the same mignonette-box in the middle of the window, and the same four flower-pots, two on each side, that I brought with me when I first came. There ain't, — I 've said it again and again, and I 'll maintain it, — there ain't such a square as this in the world. I *know* there ain't," said Tim with sudden energy, and looking sternly about him, — "not one. For business or pleasure, in summer time or winter, — I don't care which, — there 's nothing like it. There 's not such a spring in England as the pump under the archway. There 's not such a view in England as the view out of my window. I 've seen it every morning before I shaved, and I ought to know something about it. I have slept in that room," added Tim, sinking his voice a little, "for four and forty year; and if it was n't inconvenient, and did n't interfere with business, I should request leave to die there." xxxv, xxxvii, xl, xliii, xlix, lv, lix–lxi, lxiii, lxv.

**Lumbey, Doctor.** A physician who attends on Mrs. Kenwigs in her last confinement. xxxv.

**Mantalini, Madame.** A fashionable milliner and dressmaker. x, xvii, xviii, xxi, xxxiv, xliv.

**Mantalini, Mr. Alfred.** Her husband.

His name was originally Muntle; but it had been converted, by an easy transition, into Mantalini, the lady rightly considering that an English appellation would be of serious injury to the business. He had married on his whiskers, upon which property he had previously subsisted, in a genteel manner, for some years; and which he had recently improved, after patient cultivation, by the addition of a mustache, which promised to secure him an easy independence; his share in the labors of the business being . . . confined to spending the money.

When Madame refuses to supply his demands, he at first resorts to flattery and honeyed words, then declares, that, being a burden, he will put an end to his existence; which generally has the effect of softening her heart, and bringing her to terms. She is at last, however, driven into bankruptcy by his reckless extravagance, and, the suicide dodge having been tried once too often, insists on a separation, and declares her firm determination to have nothing more to do with such a man. The elegant and dashing fop's butterfly-life is soon ended, and he goes "to the demnition bow-wows." He gets into prison, and is taken out by a vixenish washerwoman, who is at first captivated by his handsome person and graceful manners, but, becoming disenchanted, keeps him constantly turning a mangle in the cellar in which she lives, "like a demd old horse in a demnition mill;" making his life, as he says, "one demd horrid grind." x, xvii, xxii, xxxiv, xliv, lxiv.

**Mobbs.** A pupil at Squeers's school. viii.

**Nickleby, Mr. Godfrey.** Father of Ralph and the elder Nicholas, to the former of whom he left three thousand pounds in cash, and to the latter "one thousand and the farm, which was as small a landed estate as one would desire to see." i.

**Nickleby, Nicholas,** *the elder.* Son of Mr. Godfrey Nickleby, brother of Ralph, and father of Nicholas and Kate. By his wife's advice he undertook to speculate with what little capital he had, and, losing it all, lost heart too, took to his bed, and died. i.

**Nickleby, Nicholas,** *the younger.* The character from whom the story takes its name; a young man who finds himself, at the age of nineteen, reduced to poverty by the unfortunate speculations and death of his father, but possessed, notwithstanding, of a good education, and with abounding energy, honesty, and industry. His mother being determined to make an appeal for assistance to her deceased husband's brother, Mr. Ralph Nickleby, he accompanies her, with his sister, to London. On their first interview their relative receives them very roughly, and takes a dislike to his nephew, amounting to positive hatred; but he procures him a situation as assistant tutor at Dotheboys Hall, — a school kept by Mr. Wackford Squeers, in Yorkshire. Nicholas proceeds thither to assume his new duties; but such is the meanness, rapacity, and brutality of Mr. Squeers, that he soon forcibly interferes on behalf of the "pupils;" gives the master a sound drubbing; and then turns his back upon the place, taking with him a poor, half-starved, and shamefully-abused lad, named Smike. He returns to London only to find that the story of his adventure, highly magnified and distorted, has preceded him. Learning that his sister will lose a situation she has obtained, if he remains at home, he quits London again, and goes to Portsmouth, where he joins a theatrical company, and becomes a "star" actor. He is, however, suddenly summoned back to London to protect his sister from the insults and persecutions of two aristocratic *roués*, one of whom he chastises severely under circumstances of great provocation. He then takes his mother and sister under his own protection, and soon after makes the acquaintance of two benevolent merchants, — the Cheeryble Brothers; gains their respect and confidence; is, after a while, admitted into the firm; and finally marries a friend and *protégée* of his benefactors. iii–ix, xii, xiii, xv, xvi, xx, xxii–xxv, xxix, xxxii, xxxiii, xxxv, xxxvii, xl, xlii, xliii, xlv, xlvi, xlviii, xlix, li–lv, lviii, lxi, lxiii–lxv.

**Nickleby, Ralph.** A miser and usurer; uncle to the younger, and brother to the elder, Nicholas Nickleby.

These two brothers had been brought up together in a school at Exeter, and, being accustomed to go home once a week, had often heard from their mother's lips long accounts of their father's sufferings in his days of poverty, and of their deceased uncle's importance in his days of affluence, — which recitals produced a very different impression on the two; for while the younger, who was of a timid and retiring disposition, gleaned from thence nothing but forewarnings to shun the great world, and attach himself to the quiet routine of a country life, Ralph the elder deduced from the often-repeated tale the two great morals, — that riches are the only true source of happiness and power, and that it is lawful and just to compass their acquisition by all means short of felony. "And," reasoned Ralph with himself, "if no good came of my uncle's money when he was alive, a great deal of good came of it after he was dead; inasmuch as my father has got it now, and is saving it up for me, which is a highly virtuous purpose. And, going back to the old gentleman, good *did* come of it to him too; for he had the pleasure of thinking of it all his life long, and of being envied and courted by all his family besides." And Ralph always wound up these mental soliloquies by arriving at the conclusion, that there was nothing like money.

Not confining himself to theory, or permitting his faculties to rust, even at that early age, in mere abstract speculations, this promising lad commenced usurer on a limited scale at school, putting out at good interest a small capital of slate-pencil and marbles, and gradually extending his operations until they aspired to the copper coinage of this realm, in which he speculated to considerable advantage. Nor did he trouble his borrowers with abstract calculations of figures, or references to ready-reckoners; his simple rule of interest being all comprised in the one golden sentence, "twopence for every half-penny," which greatly simplified the accounts, and which, as a familiar precept, — more easily acquired, and retained in the memory, than any known rule of arithmetic, — cannot be too strongly recommended to the notice of capitalists, both large and small, and more especially of money-brokers and bill-discounters. Indeed, to do these gentlemen justice, many of them are to this day in the frequent habit of adopting it with eminent success.

On the death of his father, he is placed in a mercantile house in London; applies himself passionately to his old pursuit of money-getting; soon has a spacious house of his own in Golden Square; and enjoys the reputation of being immensely rich. When his brother's widow presents herself in London, with her two children, seeking his assistance, he gives her to understand that he is not to be looked to "as the support of a great hearty woman and a grown boy and girl." He makes them work, therefore, for their bread, and, taking an intense dislike to his nephew, tries in every way to humble and ruin him; but his machinations are all defeated, his illegal operations detected, his evil deeds discovered; and he finally hangs himself in a fit of mingled frenzy, hatred, and despair. i–iv, x, xix, xx, xxviii, xxxi, xxxiii, xxxv, xliv, xlv, xlvii, li, liv, lvi, lix, lx, lxii.

**Nickleby, Kate.** Sister of Nicholas. She marries Frank Cheeryble. iii, v, x, xi, xvii–xxi, xxvii, xxviii, xxxiii, xxxv, xxxviii, xli, xliii, xlv, xlix, lv, lxi, lxiii–lxv.

**Nickleby, Mrs.** Widow of the elder, and mother of the younger, Nicholas Nickleby; a well-meaning woman, but weak withal; very fond and proud of her children; very loquacious; very desirous of being considered genteel; and remarkable for the inaccuracy of her memory, the irrelevancy of her remarks, and the general discursiveness and inconsequence of her conversation,—traits which are said to have been characteristic, to some extent, of Mr. Dickens's mother.

When she leaves her quarters in London, and goes with Nicholas to live at Bow, her attention is attracted by the singular deportment of an elderly gentleman who lives in the next house. He is so plainly struck with Mrs. Nickleby's appearance, and becomes so very demonstrative, that, although she feels flattered by his homage, she determines, nevertheless, to acquaint her son with the facts.

"There can be no doubt," said Mrs. Nickleby, "that he *is* a gentleman, and has the manners of a gentleman, and the appearance of a gentleman; although he does wear smalls and gray worsted stockings. That may be eccentricity, or he may be proud of his legs. I don't see why he should n't be. The prince regent was proud of his legs, and so was Daniel Lambert, who was also a fat man; *he* was proud of his legs: so was Miss Biffin; she was — no," added Mrs. Nickleby, correcting herself, "I think she had only toes; but the principle is the same."

Nicholas looked on quite amazed at the introduction of this new theme, which seemed just what Mrs. Nickleby had expected him to be.

"You may well be surprised, Nicholas, my dear," she said: "I am sure *I* was. It came upon me like a flash of fire, and almost froze my blood. The bottom of his garden joins the bottom of ours, and, of course, I had several times seen him sitting among the scarlet-beans in his little arbor, or working at his little hot-beds. I used to think he stared rather; but I did n't take any particular notice of that, as we were new-comers, and he might be curious to see what we were like. But when he began to throw his cucumbers over our wall" —

"To throw his cucumbers over our wall!" repeated Nicholas in great astonishment.

"Yes, Nicholas, my dear," replied Mrs. Nickleby in a very serious tone, "his cucumbers over our wall, and vegetable-marrows likewise."

"Confound his impudence!" said Nicholas, firing immediately. "What does he mean by that?"

"I don't think he means it impertinently at all," replied Mrs. Nickleby.

'What!" said Nicholas, — "cucumbers and vegetable-marrows flying at the heads of the family as they walk in their own garden, and not meant impertinently! Why, mother" —

Nicholas stopped short; for there was an indescribable expression of placid triumph, mingled with a modest confusion, lingering between the borders of Mrs. Nickleby's night-cap, which arrested his attention suddenly.

"He must be a very weak and foolish and inconsiderate man," said Mrs. Nickleby, — "blamable, indeed; at least, I suppose other people would consider him so: of course, I can't be expected to express any opinion on that point, especially after always defending your poor dear papa, when other people blamed him, for making proposals to me. And, to be sure, there can be no doubt that he has taken a very singular way of showing it; still, at the same time, his attentions are — that is, as far as it goes, and to a certain extent, of course — a flattering sort of thing; and although I should never dream of marrying again, with a dear girl like Kate still unsettled in life" —

"Surely, mother, such an idea never entered your brain for an instant!" said Nicholas. . . . "You know there is no language of vegetables which converts a cucumber into a formal declaration of attachment."

"My dear," replied Mrs. Nickleby, tossing her head, and looking at the ashes in the grate, "he has done and said all sorts of things."

"Is there no mistake on your part?" asked Nicholas.

"Mistake!" cried Mrs. Nickleby. "Lord, Nicholas, my dear! do you suppose I don't know when a man 's in earnest?"

"Well, well," muttered Nicholas.

"Every time I go to the window," said Mrs. Nickleby, "he kisses one hand, and lays the other upon his heart: of course, it's very foolish of him to do so, and I dare say you'll say it's very wrong; but he does it very respectfully, — very respectfully indeed, and very tenderly, — extremely tenderly. So far he deserves the greatest credit: there can be no doubt about that. Then there are the presents, which come pouring over the wall every day; and very fine they certainly are — very fine: we had one of the cucumbers at dinner yesterday, and think of pickling the rest for next winter. And last evening," added Mrs. Nickleby with increased confusion, "he called gently over the wall, as I was walking in the garden, and proposed marriage and an elopement. His voice is as clear as a bell or a musical glass, — very like a musical glass indeed, — but, of course, I did n't listen to it. Then the question is, Nicholas, my dear, what am I to do?"

"Does Kate know of this?" asked Nicholas.

"I have not said a word about it yet," answered his mother.

"Then for Heaven's sake!" rejoined Nicholas, rising, "do not; for it would make her very unhappy. And with regard to what you should do, my dear mother, do what your better sense and feeling, and respect for my father's memory, would prompt. There are a thousand ways in which you can show your dislike of these preposterous and doting attentions. If you act as decidedly as you ought, and they are still continued, and to your annoyance, I can speedily put a stop to them." . . .

So saying, Nicholas kissed his mother, and bade her good night; and they retired to their respective chambers.

Mrs. Nickleby is finally convinced that her admirer is insane, which nobody else is slow to perceive; but she will not admit it until the old gentleman has transferred his admiration to another lady, when she suddenly becomes satisfied that such is the case; though she persists in thinking that her rejection of his addresses is the unhappy cause of his madness. iii, v, x, xi, xviii–xx, xxi, xxvi–xxviii, xxxiii, xxxv, xxxviii, xli, xliii, xlv, lv, lxi, lxiii, lxv.

**Noggs, Newman.** Mr. Ralph Nickleby's clerk and drudge.

He was a tall man, of middle age, with two goggle-eyes, — of which one was a fixture, — a rubicund nose, a cadaverous face, and a suit of clothes — if the term be allowable when they suited him not at all — much the worse for wear, very much too small, and placed upon such a short allowance of buttons, that it was quite marvellous how he contrived to keep them on. . . . He rarely spoke to anybody unless somebody spoke to him, . . . and [was in the habit of rubbing] his hands slowly over each other, crack ing the joints of his fingers, and squeezing them into all possible distortions. The incessant performance of this routine on every occasion, and the communication of a fixed and rigid look to his unaffected eye, so as to make it uniform with the other, and render it impossible for anybody to determine where or at what he was looking, were two among the numerous peculiarities of Mr. Noggs, which struck an inexperienced observer at first sight.

This man was once a gentleman; but, being of an open and unsuspicious nature, he falls into the hands of Ralph Nickleby and other knaves, who ruin him. Reduced to poverty, he enters Nickleby's service as clerk and fag, both because he is proud and there are no other drudges there to see his degradation, and because he is resolved to find Nickleby out, and hunt him down. He befriends and assists Nicholas, aids in unravelling his master's wicked plots, and at last has the satisfaction of telling him what he has done, "face to face, man to man, and like a man." ii–vi, xi, xiv–xvi, xxii, xxviii, xxxi, xxxiii, xxxiv, xl, xliv, xlvii, li, lii, lvii, lix, lxiii, lxv.

**Petowker, Miss Henrietta.** An actress who marries Mr. Lillyvick, and then elopes with a "half-pay captain." xiv, xv, xxv, xxx, xxxvi, xlviii.

**Phœbe,** *or* **Phib.** Miss Squeers's maid. xii.

**Pluck, Mr.** A creature of Sir Mulberry Hawk's. xix, xxvii, xxviii, xxxviii, l.

**Price, Matilda.** A friend of Miss Fanny Squeers's, engaged to John Browdie, whom she afterwards marries. ix, xii, xxxix, xlii, xliii, xlv, lxiv.

**Pugstyles, Mr.** One of Mr. Gregsbury's constituents, and the spokesman of a delegation that wait on that gentleman, to request him to resign his seat in parliament. xvi.

**Pupker, Sir Matthew.** A member of parliament, and chairman of a meeting called to organize "The United Metropolitan Improved Hot Muffin and Crumpet Baking and Punctual Delivery Company." ii.

**Pyke, Mr.** Toad-eater in ordinary to Sir Mulberry Hawk. xix, xxvii, xxviii, xxxviii, l.

**Scaley, Mr.** A sheriff's officer. xxi.

**Simmonds, Miss.** A workwoman of Madame Mantalini's. xvii.

**Sliderskew, Peg.** Arthur Gride's housekeeper; a short, thin, weazen, blear-eyed old woman, palsy-stricken, hideously ugly, and very deaf. li, liii, liv, lvii, lxv.

**Smike.** An inmate of Squeers's house. Left with Mr. Squeers at an early age, and no one appearing, after the first year, to claim him, or to pay for his board and tuition, he is made use of as a drudge for the whole family. Starved and beaten, he becomes broken-spirited, and nearly half-witted. When Nicholas Nickleby arrives at Dotheboys Hall as Squeers's assistant, his heart is filled with pity for the poor lad, and he treats him with great gentleness and kindness; and when Squeers undertakes to flog the boy within an inch of his life, for attempting to run away, Nicholas interferes, compels the ruffian to desist, and gives him as severe a beating as Smike himself was to have had. The two then leave the school and the village together, and, after various wanderings, fall in with Mr. Crummles, who is much struck with Smike's haggard countenance, and secures him for his theatrical company as "an actor for the starved business," bringing him out as the apothecary in "Romeo and Juliet," under the stage-name of Digby. Smike is subsequently captured by Squeers, who meets him on the street in London, and takes him to Snawley's house; but he is aided to escape by John Browdie, and succeeds in finding his way back to Nicholas, who refuses to give him up. Introduced to Mrs. Nickleby and Kate and Miss La Creevy, and surrounded by all the comforts and pleasures of a home, Smike gradually becomes accustomed to the new life upon which he has entered, and recovers much of his natural intelligence; but it is not long before he begins to droop, and, though he rallies once or twice, grows weaker and weaker till he dies. It is afterwards ascertained that he was the son of Ralph Nickleby. vii, viii, xii, xiii, xv, xx, xxii, xxiii, xxv, xxix, xxx, xxxii, xxxv, xxxvii–xl, xlv, xlix, lv, lviii.

**Snawley, Mr.** A sanctimonious, hypocritical rascal, who places his two little step-sons in the care of Squeers, at Dotheboys Hall, with the tacit understanding that they are to have no vacations, and are to "rough it a little." Acting as the tool of Ralph Nickleby, he afterwards claims Smike as his son, for the purpose of separating him from Nicholas, and restoring him to the custody of Squeers; but his villainy is discovered, and, to secure his own safety, he divulges the whole scheme, naming Ralph Nickleby as his employer, and implicating Squeers as a confederate. iv, xxxviii, xlv, lix.

**Snawley, Mrs.** His wife. xxxviii, lix.

**Snevellicci, Miss.** A member of Mr. Crummles's dramatic company. xxiii–xxv, xxix, xxx, xlviii.

**Snevellicci, Mr.** Her father; an actor belonging to the same company. xxx.

**Snevellicci, Mrs.** Her mother. xxx.

**Snewkes, Mr.** A friend of the Kenwigses. xiv.

**Snobb, The Honorable Mr.** A guest at the dinner-party given by Ralph Nickleby. xix.

**Squeers, Wackford.** A brutal, rapacious, and ignorant Yorkshire schoolmaster. To this person Nicholas Nickleby engages himself as a scholastic assistant on the faith of the following advertisement in the London papers: —

"EDUCATION. — At Mr. Wackford Squeers's Academy, Dotheboys Hall, at the delightful village of Dotheboys, near Greta Bridge, in Yorkshire, youth are boarded, clothed, booked, furnished with pocket-money, provided with all necessaries, instructed in all languages, living and dead, mathematics, orthography, geometry, astronomy, trigonometry, the use of the globes, algebra, single stick (if required), writing, arithmetic, fortification, and every other branch of classical literature. Terms, twenty guineas per annum. No extras, no vacations, and diet unparallelled. Mr. Squeers is in town, and attends daily, from one till four, at the Saracen's Head, Snow Hill. N. B. — An able assistant wanted. Annual salary, £5. A Master of Arts would be preferred."

Mr. Squeers was standing by one of the coffee-room fireplaces; and his appearance was not prepossessing. He had but one eye; and the popular prejudice runs in favor of two. The blank side of his face was much puckered up, which gave him a sinister appearance, especially when he smiled, at which times his expression bordered on the villainous. He wore a white neckerchief with long ends, and a scholastic suit of black; but his coat-sleeves being a great deal too long, and his trousers a great deal too short, he appeared ill at ease in his clothes, and as if he were in a perpetual state of astonishment at finding himself so respectable.

The learned gentleman had before him a small measure of coffee, a plate of hot toast, and a cold round of beef; but he was at that moment intent on preparing another breakfast for the little boys.

"This is twopenn'orth of milk; is it, waiter?" said Mr. Squeers, looking down into a large blue mug.

"That's twopenn'orth, sir," replied the waiter.

"What a rare article milk is, to be sure, in London! Just fill that mug up with lukewarm water, William; will you?"

"To the wery top, sir?" inquired the waiter. "Why, the milk will be drownded!"

"Serve it right for being so dear. You ordered that thick bread and butter for three; did you?"

"Coming directly, sir."

MR. AND MRS. SQUEERS AND WACKFORD.

"You need n't hurry yourself," said Squeers: "there's plenty of time. Conquer your passions, boys, and don't be eager after vittles." As he uttered this moral precept, Mr. Squeers took a large bite out of the cold beef, and recognized Nicholas.

"Sit down, Mr. Nickleby," said Squeers. "Here we are a breakfasting, you see."

Nicholas did not see that anybody was breakfasting except Mr. Squeers.

"Oh! that's the milk and water; is it, William? Here's richness! Think of the many beggars and orphans in the streets that would be glad of this, little boys. When I say number one, the boy on the left hand nearest the window may take a drink; and when I say number two, the boy next him will go in; and so till we come to number five. Are you ready?"

"Yes, sir."

"Keep ready till I tell you to begin. Subdue your appetites, and you 've conquered human natur. — This is the way we inculcate strength of mind, Mr. Nickleby."

Nicholas murmured something in reply; and the little boys remained in torments of expectation.

"Thank God for a good breakfast! Number one may take a drink."

Number one seized the mug ravenously, and had just drunk enough to make him wish for more, when Mr. Squeers gave the signal for number two, who gave up at the same interesting moment to number three; and the process was repeated till the milk and water terminated with number five.

"And now," said the schoolmaster, dividing the bread and butter for three into five portions, "you had better look sharp with your breakfast; for the horn will blow in a minute or two, and then every boy leaves off."

The boys began to eat voraciously, while the schoolmaster (who was in high good humor after his meal) picked his teeth with a fork, and looked on. In a very short time the horn was heard.

"I thought it would n't be long," said Squeers, jumping up, and producing a little basket. "Put what you have n't had time to eat, in here, boys! You'll want it on the road."

Mr. Squeers meets his just deserts at last, being sentenced to transportation for seven years for being in the unlawful possession of a stolen will; the result of which is, that Dotheboys Hall is broken up for ever. iv–ix, xiii, xxxiv, xxxviii, xxxix, xlii, xlv, lvi, lvii, lix, lx, lxv.

**Squeers, Mrs.** Wife of Mr. Wackford Squeers. viii, ix, xiii, lxiv.

**Squeers, Miss Fanny.** Daughter of Mr. and Mrs. Wackford

Squeers; a young lady in her three-and-twentieth year, resembling her mother in the harshness of her voice and the shrewishness of her disposition, and her father in the remarkable expression of her right eye, something akin to having none at all. ix, xii, xiii, xv, xxxix, xli, lxiv.

**Squeers, Master Wackford, junior.** Son of Mr. and Mrs. Wackford Squeers. viii, ix, xiii, xxix, xxxiv, xxxviii, xlii, lxiv.

**Swillenhausen, Baron von.** Neighbor and father-in-law to the Baron of Grogzwig. vi.

**Swillenhausen, Baroness von.** His wife. vi.

**Timberry, Mr. Snittle.** An actor belonging to Mr. Crummles's theatre. xxi.

**Tix, Mr. Tom.** A broker who makes an inventory of the stock in Madame Mantalini's millinery establishment on the occasion of her sudden failure. xlviii.

**Tom.** Clerk at the General Agency office. xvi, xliii.

**Tomkins.** One of Squeers's pupils. xiii.

**Trimmers, Mr.** A friend of the Cheeryble Brothers. xxxv.

**Verisopht, Lord Frederick.** A silly young nobleman, the tool of Sir Mulberry Hawk. He becomes enamored of Kate Nickleby, and has an angry altercation concerning her with Sir Mulberry. The quarrel leads to a duel, in which Lord Frederick is killed. xix, xxvi–xxviii, xxxviii, l.

**Westwood, Mr.** One of the seconds in the duel between Sir Mulberry Hawk and Lord Verisopht. l.

**William.** A waiter at the Saracen's Head Inn. v.

**Wititterly, Mrs. Julia.** A lady of the middle class, who apes the airs and style of the aristocracy, and with whom Kate Nickleby lives for a while as companion. xxi, xxvii, xxviii.

**Wititterly, Mr. Henry.** Husband of Mrs. Wititterly. Being informed that Kate has applied for a situation as companion to his wife, he discusses the matter for some time with Mrs. Wititterly in whispers. At last he notices Kate.

"Oh!" he said, turning round, "yes. This is a most important matter. Mrs. Wititterly is of a very excitable nature, very delicate, very fragile, a hot-house plant, an exotic."

"O Henry! my dear," interposed Mrs. Wititterly.

"You are, my love; you know you are. One breath"—said Mr. W., blowing an imaginary feather away. "Pho! you're gone."

The lady sighed.

"Your soul is too large for your body," said Mr. Wititterly. "Your intellect wears you out: all the medical men say so. You know that there is not a physician who is not proud of being called in to you. What is their unanimous declaration? 'My dear doctor,' said I to Sir Tumley Snuffim, in this very room, the very last time he came, — 'my dear doctor, what is my wife's complaint? Tell me all. I can bear it. Is it nerves?' — 'My dear fellow,' he said, 'be proud of that woman; make much of her: she is an ornament to the fashionable world, and to you. Her complaint is soul: it swells, expands, dilates — the blood fires, the pulse quickens, the excitement increases — whew!'" Here Mr. Wititterly, who, in the ardor of his description, had flourished his right hand to within something less than an inch of Mrs. Nickleby's bonnet, drew it hastily back again, and blew his nose as fiercely as if it had been done by some violent machinery.

"You make me out worse than I am, Henry," said Mrs. Wititterly with a faint smile.

"I do not, Julia; I do not," said Mr. W. "The society in which you move — necessarily move, from your station, connection, and endowments — is one vortex and whirlpool of the most frightful excitement. . . . And for that very reason you must have a companion in whom there is great gentleness, great sweetness, excessive sympathy, and perfect repose."

Here both Mr. and Mrs. Wititterly, who had talked rather at the Nicklebys than to each other, left off speaking, and looked at their two hearers with an expression of countenance which seemed to say, "What do you think of all that?"

"Mrs. Wititterly," said her husband, addressing himself to Mrs. Nickleby, "is sought after and courted by glittering crowds and brilliant circles. She is excited by the opera, the drama, the fine arts, the — the — the" —

"The nobility, my love," interposed Mrs. Wititterly.

"The nobility, of course," said Mr. Wititterly, "and the military. She forms and expresses an immense variety of opinions, on an immense variety of subjects. If some people in public life were acquainted with Mrs. Wititterly's real opinion of them, they would not hold their heads perhaps quite as high as they do." xxi, xxvii, xxviii, xxxiii.

**York, The Five Sisters of.** The title of a story told by a gray-haired gentleman at a roadside inn between Grantham and Newark, for the amusement of his fellow-passengers, who have been detained there by the breaking-down of a stage-coach. The five sisters are represented as living in York in the early part of the sixteenth century, in an old house belonging to the black monks of St. Benedict. While engaged in embroidering a complicated and intricate pattern, they are visited by one of the monks, who urges them to take the veil; but, under the influence of the youngest sister (named Alice), they refuse to do so, believing that peace and virtue can be found beyond as well as within a convent's walls. Years pass by, bringing change and separation and sorrow; but at last the four elder sisters meet again in the old home: and again the same black monk urges them by all the sad memories of the past to seek consolation and peace within the sheltering arms of the Church. Remembering how the young heart of their lost sister had sickened at the thought of cloistered walls, they again refuse. As a work of piety, however, as well as a memorial of affection, they cause to be executed in five compartments of stained glass fitted into a large window in York Cathedral (which is still shown there under the name of the Five Sisters), a faithful copy of their old embroidery-work through which the sun may shine brightly on a flat stone in the nave, which bears the name of Alice. vi.

# THE OLD CURIOSITY SHOP

## OUTLINE

Chapter A child, lost in London streets at night, fell into the hands
I of a gentleman, who led her back to her home and found on
entering a singular household, for this little Nell Trent lived with
her grandfather, the keeper of an old curiosity shop, and Kit Nubbles, an awkward but faithful errand boy. When the gentleman
left, the old grandfather took his stick and set forth, too, on some
mysterious errand. The whole scene affected the gentleman so
II much that he made a visit a week later to the old curiosity
shop, and entering, found an unwelcome visitor, who proved
to be a scapegrace brother of Nell's, bent on browbeating the old
grandfather into helping him with money. With Fred Trent was
a companion in idleness, one Dick Swiveller, who made up for
Fred's loss of virtue by an excess of good-natured vagabondism, and
a power of drawing at pleasure upon a solvent bank of poetical
quotations and images. As the three were together, Nell herself
III entered, followed by an old dwarf, Daniel Quilp, who appeared to have some secret dealings with the keeper of the
old curiosity shop. One by one they left, leaving the visitor
alone with Nell and her grandfather, the place enlivened by a pet
bird in a well-dressed cage. The old man opened his trembling
heart a little to the stranger, as he spoke of his hopes and fears for
his dependent granddaughter, who was engaged presently in giving
a writing lesson to the not very receptive Kit.

IV To know Daniel Quilp better, one needed to see him in his
own home on Tower Hill, not far from the Thames. His
place of business was Quilp's wharf, on the other side of the river.
Mrs. Quilp was a gentle, mild-mannered woman, who had somehow
been fascinated by this outlandish dwarf. Even Mrs. Jiniwin,
Mrs. Quilp's mother, who lived near by, though bold as a lion in
Quilp's absence, somehow became abject under his masterful presence. This was notable enough one afternoon when Quilp, coming
home, found the two women and some neighbors at tea, and overheard a little of their conversation not meant for his ears. He took
his revenge on his wife by sitting up all night smoking and keeping

her awake on the floor. Apparently he made up for lack of sleep
V when, the next morning, he went to his dingy office, and, after tyrannizing over his boy, who found a certain relief in standing on his own head, stretched himself out on his table. He was interrupted by the advent of little Nell.

VI Nell, accompanied by Kit, had come with a note from her grandfather, and Quilp, making horrible show of affection for the child, pretended he must needs go home to write the answer. So, taking the two with him, having first separated Kit and his wharf boy, who had been fighting over the reputation of their respective employers, he went to Tower Hill and gave Nell into Mrs. Quilp's charge, commanding that poor woman to worm all she could out of the child, while he listened on the other side of the door. Apparently, he was satisfied with what he heard, for soon he appeared with the note, which was to say he would see the grandfather in a day or two, and sent Nell and Kit back to their home.

VII Mr. Quilp, in his leering pleasantry, had suggested to Nell that when Mrs. Quilp died, in say four or five years, he would be happy to make her his second wife. She was terrified enough, but she would have been shocked in another way, had she known that her dissolute brother Fred had proposed to his boon companion, Dick Swiveller, that he should lay siege to the child's heart, — she was now fourteen, — and so secure for both the grandfather's money, which he himself had been baffled in attempting to secure. Dick saw the scheme in a rosy light, but presently remembered that really he was somewhat in the chains of Miss Sophy Wackles, who, at this moment, herself brought a note of invitation
VIII to a dance. In truth, Miss Wackles, in company with her mother and sisters, had grown somewhat distrustful of Dick's attentions, and, having secured a more promising claimant in the person of Mr. Cheggs, resorted to the expedient of a party, at which they could play off this enamored butcher against the shady Dick; and thus the plans of both jumped; for Dick, becoming at once jealous of Mr. Cheggs, made an excuse of his objectionable courtesies, and threw off the entire Wackles family, thus leaving himself clear for the more promising connection offered by Fred Trent.

IX Meantime, Nelly, living alone with her grandfather, grew more sorrowful over his mysterious suffering, and implored him one evening, as he waited, disconsolately, for Quilp's appearance, past the promised time, to take her away with him into the country, even if they were but beggars, so they might escape their present misery. As they talked, Quilp entered unnoticed, and overheard some of their talk. Then, when he was discovered, he sent

Nelly out of the room, and plainly told the old man that he knew now what became of the money he lent him; it was spent at the gambling table. The old man confessed it, but declared it was all for the sake of his granddaughter, and besought Quilp to let him once again have some money. But Quilp was obdurate, and took his leave, after giving the old man to believe that he had discovered his gambling habits through Kit.

X He did not go unobserved. Hanging about the entrance and watching his movements was Kit Nubbles, the faithful attendant of Nelly. Kit did not live at the old curiosity shop, and now went home to his mother, where he was complacent in the family circle, when, of a sudden, Nelly appeared, tearful and dishevelled, to say that her grandfather had been taken in a violent fit, and upon Kit's eagerly desiring to help her, to tell him that her grandfather raved about him as the cause of all his woes, though she did not know why, and he must never, never come near them again. At which word poor Kit's house of cards tumbled with a crash.

XI The keeper of the old curiosity shop was, indeed, very ill, and remained so. And no sooner was his illness known than Quilp was on hand, attended by a learned lawyer, of his own way of thinking and feeling, one Sampson Brass. The two worthies took possession of the house and all it contained by some process of law, and, for the better security of their possession, occupied the premises, along with Quilp's tumbling boy. Not so hermetically, however, did they seal the place, but that Kit Nubbles, coming again and again, made out to have a whispered conference with Nelly, in which he offered her and her grandfather a home in his mother's house, and begged to be restored to a confidence which he had unwittingly appeared to forfeit.

XII The sickness which befell the old man slowly passed away, leaving him weak and half-childish. His sole thought, now, seemed to be of Nell, and when Quilp informed him that he had sold all the effects in the house, he consented without difficulty to their removal in a few days. At sunrise of that day, while Quilp and Brass lay asleep, the old man and child left the house, their only home, and set out on their wanderings. It was clear now that the child was to lead and direct the old man.

XIII A few hours after they left, and while Quilp and Brass were still asleep, knockings sounded on the outer door, and Quilp, when fairly awake, opened the door cautiously and then flung himself violently upon a person whom he supposed to be his wife, but who proved to be Dick Swiveller, a very different recipient of his attentions, who had come up to aid Mrs. Quilp in her timid attempt at rousing her husband. It was quickly discovered, to the

surprise of all, that Nell and her grandfather had vanished. Soon the vans came for removing the goods and with them came Kit, as much taken aback as the rest at the disappearance of the pair. Now happened what Nell had secretly hoped; the bird which she had been forced to leave behind fell into the hands of Kit, who bore it off triumphantly after a scrimmage with Quilp, and deposited it at his own home. Kit, much perplexed at the loss of his friends,
XIV strolled the streets, seeking for a chance to hold horses' heads, and had the good luck to fall in with Mr. and Mrs. Garland in their pony chaise, driving up to the door of Mr. Witherden, the Notary, to complete the articling to that gentleman of their son Abel Garland, who with Mr. Chuckster was a clerk of Witherden's. The liberal payment which the boy received was a happy omen of later good fortune. For want of a sixpence Mr. Garland had given Kit a shilling, and Kit had seriously agreed to bring the change back at a later day.

XV Meanwhile the two poor pilgrims made their way through the streets of London and issued in the open country beyond. They found rest for a little while in a friendly cottage, but the old man was feverishly impatient to get farther and farther away. The driver of a cart took pity on them and gave them a lift, leaving them at last near the entrance of a town. Here, as they stopped to rest, they found themselves in the company of some
XVI itinerant showmen. They were engaged in putting their Punch show in order, and Nelly proving expert with her needle, quickly made herself of use, and so when the showmen set out for the public-house, the two travellers joined themselves to the company, and were readily admitted on the strength of Nelly's sweet face. She, with the instinct of a careful provider, took care, when they were alone, to make sure of her small store of money, sewing her one gold piece into her dress. Their new friends were bound for
XVII the races, and the next day, after some parley, it was agreed that Codlin and Short, the two proprietors of the show, should take the pilgrims with them. As they went, occasionally giving a Punch and Judy performance to groups by the way, they came upon a similar party, "Grinder's lot," bound on a similar errand, the lot consisting of a young gentleman and a young lady on stilts, who found this professional occupation an agreeable mode of getting over the ground. The whole party kept together and came to the
XVIII Jolly Sandboys inn, where Codlin and Short, after private consultation, agreed with each other to take a sort of protecting proprietorship of the gentle girl and her decaying grandfather.
XIX Hither also came another stroller, Jerry, with his four performing dogs, and before supper was over, the company was

reënforced by Mr. Vuffin, the proprietor of a giant and a little lady without legs or arms who had gone on in a van, and Sweet William, as he was called, a silent gentleman who earned his living by showing tricks at cards. In this motley assemblage Nelly began to shrink from unknown perils, and all the more that Codlin and Short separately and secretly charged her each to beware of the other. In the turmoil of the fair, which attended the races, she tried in vain to escape from both, but at last, seizing a favorable moment, she and her grandfather, slipping away from observation, crept out of the precincts of the fair and made for the open fields.

XX It was a sore trial to poor Kit that his friends, whom he supposed all this time to be in London, did not accept his and his mother's invitation to take refuge in their humble home. He sought them in vain, and suddenly remembering his appointment with old Mr. Garland, presented himself at the Notary's door at the right hour, and sure enough, there were the old gentleman and old lady, with Whiskers, the little pony that drew them. Mr. Garland was surprised, but pleased, to see the boy, and, asking him many questions about his home, drove off after he had attended to his business. But he drove straight to Kit's own door, and there
XXI the boy found the old couple when he returned home. In fact, they had taken a fancy to the boy, and it was not long before they had engaged Kit for an attendant at Abel Cottage, Finchley, on a salary of six pounds a year. Scarcely had the Garlands gone, before Quilp and Dick Swiveller arrived on the scene, having come in hopes of discovering the whereabouts of Nell and her grandfather, each for his own purpose. They could neither learn anything nor tell anything, and when they went away, after nearly frightening the Nubbles family into fits, Quilp, having designs of his own, easily coaxed Dick into a drinking place where he wormed that gentleman's secrets out of his oozy brain, and immediately cherished the notion of aiding and abetting him for his own
XXII profit. A happier scene was that which awaited Kit when he went to his new place and was introduced to his duties by the pretty little servant girl, Barbara. Daniel Quilp followed up
XXIII his advances with Dick Swiveller. He drew him back to his house with Nell's brother, Frederick Trent, and managed to strike a bargain with this profligate, by which, between them, they were to marry Dick to Nell.

XXIV Meanwhile Nell and her grandfather, all unconscious of these machinations, had escaped from their uncomfortable companions and were moving across the country. They came to a village school, and Nell quickly made friends with the schoolmaster, who was very anxious over the illness of a favorite little scholar

Indeed he had good reason, and the next day he was fain to give
XXV the school a half-holiday, as he watched the ebbing hours
of Dame West's grandson, to whom Nell — for the schoolmaster had begged the child and her grandfather to stay awhile with
him, — had already brought a soothing influence. Alas! it was a
XXVI sorrowful scene to which Nell was witness, and the next day
she and her grandfather parted from their bereft friend
and pushed on, coming at nightfall upon a gipsy-like caravan
drawn up to rest. Mrs. Jarley, the proprietor of the famous Jarley's
Waxworks, was in command of the caravan, and recognized Nell
and her grandfather as the pair she had seen with the disreputable
Punch show at the races; much at first to Nell's alarm, but presently to her relief, as it appeared that Mrs. Jarley highly disap-
proved of her late companions. So hospitable was the good woman,
that she insisted on the old gentleman and his granddaughter entering her covered wagon and jogging along with her, for the next
town was eight miles away.

XXVII Really, it was not at all an unpleasant mode of conveyance, and Mrs. Jarley, eying the child critically, saw how
excellent an addition she would make to her management. She
would have dispensed with the grandfather, but the two utterly
refused to be separated; so Mrs. Jarley made an offer including
them both, — the grandfather to dust the figures, and make himself
generally useful, and Nell to act as show-girl in pointing out the
wax-works, — an offer which, in their extremity, they were not unwilling to accept. When they drew up within the precincts of the
town, Nell made a bed for her grandfather in one of the old wagons
of the caravan, and herself shared Mrs. Jarley's quarters; but, as
she was passing from one to the other, whom should she descry
suddenly but Quilp, with his boy carrying a trunk. To be sure,
she gathered from what she heard that they were on their way to
London, but the sight brought a numbing terror to her heart.

XXVIII When morning came, the caravan proceeded to discharge
its contents in the hall of exhibition. Here appeared to them
Mr. Slum, the poet, ready to execute orders for poetical advertisements, and here Mrs. Jarley gave Nell her first lesson in exhibiting
XXIX the figures, — a lesson which the child quickly learned and
applied, to the edification of the admiring visitors. Mrs.
Jarley was kind to her, and, though visions of Quilp flitted across
her mind, she was in comparative peace. But one evening, when
she was out walking with her grandfather, they were caught in a
storm, and found refuge in a wayside house, the Valiant Soldier,
kept by Jem Groves. Here, as they rested, they heard voices, and
suddenly the old grandfather was transformed. The men within

were playing at cards. He eagerly begged Nell's purse of her, and
XXX tremblingly insisted on playing, his one thought being to win some money for his Nell. On and on he played, till midnight, when they all rose from the table, and every penny from Nell's purse had gone into the hands of the sharpers. It was now so late that they must perforce stay in the inn the rest of the night. Nell now told her grandfather that she still had a little money to pay for their lodging, and then, fearing the effect upon him if he discovered the secret of her gold piece, she went stealthily to the landlord and begged him to give her change for it, taking out what they needed to pay for their night's lodging; not so stealthily, however, but that her grandfather knew of it, and what was her horror in the middle of the night, when she discovered him greedily counting over the money which he had stolen from her. Sorrowfully, in
XXXI the morning, she led her grandfather back, and tried indirectly to win him from his return to old ways. She found plenty to do at the show, for Miss Monflathers and all her school had come to see the wax-works. So flourishing was the show that
XXXII Mrs. Jarley, with the art of the scientific exhibitor, ordered the caravan to move on, only to display her consideration for the public by reconsidering, and allowing the exhibition to be open a week longer.

XXXIII What Mr. Quilp was doing in the neighborhood of the caravan does not yet appear; but in his own haunts he was busily promoting his interests; for he made it clear to Mr. Sampson Brass that it would be a good thing for him to take Dick Swiveller
XXXIV as a clerk; and so Dick was introduced to the household consisting, as he quickly saw, of Sampson and his very masculine sister Sally. He was to learn of one other member of the household, for, upon being left alone by Sally Brass, there appeared presently a small, slipshod girl, very old-fashioned indeed in appearance, who represented herself as maid of all work, and now called on him to show the lodgings above to a single gentleman, who had presented himself, and who proceeded forthwith to take
XXXV possession of a room and go to bed. Sleep he did so profoundly and so long that Sampson and Sally Brass became a little uneasy, and at last, with the aid of the small servant and Dick, made a prodigious racket, which resulted in the admission of Dick into the irascible gentleman's room, where he was treated to the interesting spectacle of the gentleman making his own breakfast out of materials and with apparatus fetched from a mysterious
XXXVI trunk, but learned neither the gentleman's name nor his business. This was of small account, however, so long as he paid punctually and in advance for all he had. His only acquain-

tance in the household was Dick Swiveller, who, to be sure, invented the chief part of the acquaintance. Dick, for lack of better companionship, was forced to make the most of Sally Brass, and his lively behavior gradually transformed the gaunt spinster into something very like a boon companion. But what he could not make out was the condition of the small maid of all work, whom he had dubbed the Marchioness. What became of her, how she lived, what pleasure she got out of life, were all a mystery to him. One day, consumed with curiosity, he followed Sally Brass, unknown to her, into a dark, forbidding kichen, and there had what satisfaction could be got from seeing her administering a diminutive meal to the starved little Marchioness, with blows for dessert.

XXXVII The most extraordinary thing about the lodger was that he seemed to have a consuming passion for Punch shows, and succeeded in drawing innumerable showmen into the precincts of Mr. Brass's house. He made friends with them, moreover, but some inkling of what he was after appeared when, one day, he en-
XXXVIII tertained in his apartment the very Codlin and Short who had escorted Nell and her grandfather, and proceeded to question them most assiduously, but with precious little result, about the two wanderers. Yet, some clue he seemed to have, for it was not long after that Kit, driving Mr. Abel to the Notary's office, was bidden come in by Mr. Chuckster, as he was wanted; and, going in, he was questioned regarding Nell by a stranger, who was no other than Mr. Brass's lodger; for, on coming out of the office, they were seen by Dick Swiveller, who was there himself to meet his good friend, Mr. Chuckster. Dick was exceedingly astonished, but all his probing of Kit afterward could extract nothing of value regarding this mysterious man.

XXXIX All this was nothing to Kit beside the great glory of his first quarter day, when he was paid his first instalment of salary, along with Barbara, Barbara's mother and Kit's mother both being on hand, and all of them, together with Kit's small brother Jacob and the baby, going to Astley's to see the pantomime and having an oyster supper afterward. On his return to Abel
XL Cottage the next day Kit was rather disconcerted at being told by Mr. Garland that this strange gentleman whom he had seen was desirous of receiving him into his service. He stoutly refused to leave his benefactor, but was made more reasonable when it appeared that he would perhaps only be borrowed now and then. While they were yet talking, Mr. Chuckster arrived on the scene for the express purpose of carrying Kit off to a meeting with the strange gentleman at the Notary's, and going thither Kit learned great news. The gentleman had got track of Nell and her grand-

father through a hint which Codlin and Short had given him of Jerry and his dogs, and was impatient to go in search of them. He wanted Kit's aid, but more especially he needed Kit's mother to
XLI go with him on his quest. There was no time to lose, and off went Kit to his mother's house, only to find that she was absent with Jacob at Little Bethel.

It was not very easy to procure direction to the fold in question, as none of the neighbors were of the flock that resorted thither, and few knew anything more of it than the name. At last, a gossip of Mrs. Nubbles's, who had accompanied her to chapel on one or two occasions, when a comfortable cup of tea had preceded her devotions, furnished the needful information; which Kit had no sooner obtained than he started off again.

Little Bethel might have been nearer, and might have been in a straighter road, though, in that case, the reverend gentleman who presided over its congregation would have lost his favorite allusion to the crooked ways by which it was approached, and which enabled him to liken it to paradise itself, in contradistinction to the parish church, and the broad thoroughfare leading thereunto. Kit found it at last, after some trouble, and pausing at the door to take breath, that he might enter with becoming decency, passed into the chapel.

It was not badly named in one respect, being, in truth, a particularly little Bethel, — a Bethel of the smallest dimensions, — with a small number of small pews, and a small pulpit in which a small gentleman (by trade a shoemaker, and by calling a divine) was delivering in a by no means small voice a by no means small sermon, judging of its dimensions by the condition of his audience, which, if their gross amount were but small, comprised a still smaller number of hearers, as the majority were slumbering.

Among these was Kit's mother, who, finding it matter of extreme difficulty to keep her eyes open after the fatigues of last night, and feeling their inclination to doze strongly backed and seconded by the arguments of the preacher, had yielded to the drowsiness that overpowered her, and fallen asleep; though not so soundly but that she could from time to time utter a slight and almost inaudible groan, as if in recognition of the orator's doctrines. The baby in her arms was as fast asleep as she; and little Jacob, whose youth prevented him from recognizing in this prolonged spiritual nourishment anything half as interesting as oysters, was alternately very fast asleep and very wide awake, as his inclination to slumber, or his terror of being personally alluded to in the discourse, gained the mastery over him.

"And now I'm here," thought Kit, gliding into the nearest pew, which was opposite his mother's, and on the other side of the little aisle, "how am I ever to get at her, or persuade her to come out? I might as well be twenty miles off. She'll never wake till it's all over; and there goes the clock again! If he would but leave off for a minute, or if they'd only sing!"—

But there was little encouragement to believe that either event would happen for a couple of hours to come. The preacher went on telling them what he meant to convince them of before he had done; and it was clear, that if he only kept to one half of his promises, and forgot the other, he was good for that time, at least.

In his desperation and restlessness Kit cast his eyes about the chapel, and, happening to let them fall upon a little seat in front of the clerk's desk, could scarcely believe them when they showed him—Quilp!

He rubbed them twice or thrice; but still they insisted that Quilp was there: and there, indeed, he was, sitting with his hands upon his knees, and his hat between them on a little wooden bracket, with the accustomed grin on his dirty face, and his eyes fixed upon the ceiling. He certainly did not glance at Kit or at his mother, and appeared utterly unconscious of their presence; still Kit could not help feeling, directly, that the attention of the sly little fiend was fastened upon them, and upon nothing else.

But astounded as he was by the apparition of the dwarf among the Little Bethelites, and not free from a misgiving that it was the forerunner of some trouble or annoyance, he was compelled to subdue his wonder, and to take active measures for the withdrawal of his parent, as the evening was now creeping on, and the matter grew serious. Therefore, the next time little Jacob woke, Kit set himself to attract his wandering attention; and, this not being a very difficult task (one sneeze effected it), he signed to him to rouse his mother.

Ill-luck would have it, however, that, just then, the preacher, in a forcible exposition of one head of his discourse, leaned over upon the pulpit-desk, so that very little more of him than his legs remained inside, and while he made vehement gestures with his right hand, and held on with his left, stared, or seemed to stare, straight into little Jacob's eyes, threatening him by his strained look and attitude (so it appeared to the child), that, if he so much as moved a muscle, he, the preacher, would be literally, and not figuratively, "down upon him" that instant. In this fearful state of things, distracted by the sudden appearance of Kit, and fascinated by the eyes of the preacher, the miserable Jacob sat bolt upright, wholly incapable of motion, strongly disposed to cry, but afraid to do so, and returning his pastor's gaze until his infant eyes seemed starting from their sockets.

"If I must do it openly, I must," thought Kit. With that he walked softly out of his pew, and into his mother's, and, as Mr. Swiveller would have observed if he had been present, "collared" the baby without speaking a word.

"Hush, mother!" whispered Kit. "Come along with me: I 've got something to tell you."

"Where am I?" said Mrs. Nubbles.

"In this blessed Little Bethel," returned her son peevishly.

"Blessed indeed!" cried Mrs. Nubbles, catching at the word. "O Christopher, how have I been edified this night!"

"Yes, yes, I know," said Kit hastily. "But come along, mother: everybody 's looking at us. Don't make a noise; bring Jacob; that 's right!"

"Stay, Satan, stay!" cried the preacher as Kit was moving off.

"The gentleman says you 're to stay, Christopher," whispered his mother.

"Stay, Satan, stay!" roared the preacher again. "Tempt not the woman that doth incline her ear to thee, but hearken to the voice of him that calleth. He hath a lamb from the fold!" cried the preacher, raising his voice still higher, and pointing to the baby. "He beareth off a lamb, a precious lamb! He goeth about like a wolf in the night-season, and inveigleth the tender lambs!"

Kit was the best-tempered fellow in the world, but considering this strong language, and being somewhat excited by the circumstances in which he was placed, he faced round on the pulpit with the baby in his arms, and replied aloud: —

"No; I don't. He 's my brother!"

"He 's *my* brother!" cried the preacher.

"He is n't," said Kit indignantly. "How can you say such a thing? And don't call me names, if you please: what harm have I done? I should n't have come to take 'em away unless I was obliged: you may depend upon that. I wanted to do it very quiet; but you would n't let me. Now, you have the goodness to abuse Satan and them as much as you like, sir, and to let me alone, if you please."

So saying, Kit marched out of the chapel, followed by his mother and little Jacob, and found himself in the open air, with an indistinct recollection of having seen the people wake up, and look surprised, and of Quilp having remained throughout the interruption, in his old attitude, without moving his eyes from the ceiling, or appearing to take the smallest notice of anything that passed.

And Kit had the satisfaction of seeing his mother drive off finally with the strange gentleman in a post-chaise.

XLII But where was Nell all this time? She was still with Mrs. Jarley, but the experience she had had with her grandfather was but the beginning of her trouble and anxiety on his score. One evening she was alone in the fields, coming home from a walk, when she heard voices at what she thought was a gipsy encampment. Suddenly she discovered that her grandfather was in the camp, and drawing near she found the same men who had won her grandfather's money; listening, she heard to her horror how they egged on the poor old man to rob Mrs. Jarley, that he might win back the money he had lost and more too. When all was still and her grandfather had left, she too crept away, but her mind was frenzied at the thought of what was before them. The crime was to be committed the next night, and this night, in the darkness, she went to the old man's room, and with a power of will wrought up to a pitch of agony she compelled the old man to dress, and with her to escape from the terror which lay before them.

XLIII Out into the darkness they went, but at least they had been saved. In the early morning, they found themselves on the bank of a canal, where they rested, but were awaked from sleep by the noise of the men. A colloquy followed, and Nell and her grandfather were invited to board the boat and be carried to the neighboring town. It was a dubious relief, for though they were carried farther and farther from the scene of the possible crime, they were in very rude company; yet, boisterous and maudlin as the men were, Nell's gentleness and purity were her safeguard. Arrived at a town,
XLIV they pushed through it again into the open country, and might have perished of cold and exposure, had not a laboring man come to their rescue and given them shelter in the warmth of a great iron furnace. Their aimless course took them through
XLV scenes of misery, especially in a great manufacturing town; they could get barely enough to eat, and must needs sleep under the stars; poor Nell was on the verge of despair, when she saw before her a figure walking and reading at the same time. She moved toward him; he turned; it was the poor schoolmaster who had been good to them at the beginning of their wanderings. He
XLVI was a friend sent in an hour of need. It seems that he was on his way to a village where he had been appointed schoolmaster and would be passing rich on thirty-five pounds a year. He took the exhausted child to an inn near by. Here, with care, sleep,

and food she was restored, and seeing in the schoolmaster a true friend she told him all her story, and he, moved by her gentle attraction, warmly offered a home and shelter for her and her grandfather in his new place.

XLVII If the strange gentleman could but have known of the refuge! He had set off with Kit's mother at a furious rate, scarce able to restrain his impatience, and after driving all night came to a town where he bade the post-boy seek for the wax-works, for so far he had traced Nell. They drove up to find a small crowd at the door, and to learn that the redoubtable Mrs. Jarley had just been married to George, her man. She was full of interest in the matter, but could give them no real information, and so the strange gentleman and Kit's mother went to the inn. To their amazement, the
XLVIII first person they encountered there was Quilp, and the strange gentleman at once sought an interview with him, to learn if he could, in his impetuous fashion, something about Nell and her grandfather, but he was baffled at every point. It seems that Quilp, coming upon Dick Swiveller, had learned from him that Kit was in communication with the stranger; accordingly he had called on Kit's mother and learning that she was in chapel went thither, after which it was easy to dog her and Kit and to come down on the night coach. But he learned no more from the strange gentleman than he could tell him, and back he went to London atop of the coach with Kit's mother inside. Kit was on hand to receive his mother, and he gave Quilp likewise a somewhat warm reception for a boy of his size.

XLIX Quilp went to his own house, where he heard voices, both men's and women's, and with his keen scent for mischief he did not make entrance till he had collared his prankish boy and learned from him that the family thought him drowned, and were engaged now in getting ready to administer on him. He listened and peeped with ghoulish glee, while Sampson Brass prepared an advertisement of his personal appearance between copious draughts of rum punch, aided by Mrs. Jiniwin who was unsparing of the best adjectives, while Mrs. Quilp sat by in decorous grief, and two watermen who had been dragging the river completed the group.

"Ah!" said Mr. Brass, breaking the silence, and raising his eyes to the ceiling with a sigh, "who knows but he may be looking down upon us now! Who knows but he may be surveying us from — from somewheres or another, and contemplating us with a watchful eye! O Lor!"

Here Mr. Brass stopped to drink half his punch, and then resumed, looking at the other half, as he spoke, with a dejected smile.

"I can almost fancy," said the lawyer, shaking his head, "that I see his eye glistening down at the very bottom of my liquor. When shall we look upon his like again? Never, never! One minute we are here," — holding his tumbler before his eyes, — "the next we are there" — gulping down its contents, and striking himself emphatically a little below the chest — "in the silent tomb. To think that I should be drinking his very rum! It seems like a dream."

With the view, no doubt, of testing the reality of his position, Mr. Brass pushed his tumbler, as he spoke, towards Mrs. Jiniwin, for the purpose of being replenished, and turned towards the attendant mariners.

"The search has been quite unsuccessful, then?"

"Quite, master. But I should say, that, if he turns up anywhere, he'll come ashore somewhere about Grinidge to-morrow, at ebb tide; eh, mate?"

The other gentleman assented, observing that he was expected at the Hospital, and that several pensioners would be ready to receive him whenever he arrived.

"Then we have nothing for it but resignation," said Mr. Brass, — "nothing but resignation and expectation. It would be a comfort to have his body: it would be a dreary comfort."

"Oh, beyond a doubt!" assented Mrs. Jiniwin hastily. "If we once had that, we should be quite sure."

"With regard to the descriptive advertisement," said Sampson Brass, taking up his pen. "It is a melancholy pleasure to recall his traits. Respecting his legs now?" —

"Crooked, certainly," said Mrs. Jiniwin.

"Do you think they *were* crooked?" said Brass in an insinuating tone. "I think I see them now, coming up the street, very wide apart, in nankeen pantaloons, a little shrunk, and without straps. Ah! what a vale of tears we live in! Do we say crooked?"

"I think they were a little so," observed Mrs. Quilp with a sob.

"Legs crooked," said Brass, writing as he spoke. "Large head. short body, legs crooked" —

"Very crooked," suggested Mrs. Jiniwin.

"We'll not say very crooked, ma'am," said Brass piously. "Let us not bear hard upon the weaknesses of the deceased. He is gone, ma'am, to where his legs will never come in question. We will content ourselves with crooked, Mrs. Jiniwin."

"I thought you wanted the truth," said the old lady. "That's all."

"Bless your eyes, how I love you!" muttered Quilp. "There she goes again! Nothing but punch!"

"This is an occupation," said the lawyer, laying down his pen, and emptying his glass, "which seems to bring him before my eyes like the ghost of Hamlet's father, in the very clothes that he wore on work-a-days. His coat, his waistcoat, his shoes and stockings, his trousers, his hat, his wit and humor, his pathos and his umbrella, — all come before me like visions of my youth. His linen!" said Mr. Brass, smiling fondly at the wall, — "his linen, which was always of a particular color, for such was his whim and fancy, — how plain I see his linen now!"

"You had better go on, sir," said Mrs. Jiniwin impatiently.

"True, ma'am, true," cried Mr. Brass. "Our faculties must not freeze with grief. I'll trouble you for a little more of that, ma'am. A question now arises with relation to his nose."

"Flat," said Mrs. Jiniwin.

"Aquiline!" cried Quilp, thrusting in his head, and striking the feature with his fist, — "aquiline, you hag! Do you see it? Do you call this flat? Do you? Eh?"

"Oh, capital, capital!" shouted Brass, from the mere force of habit. "Excellent! How very good he is! He's a most remarkable man, — so extremely whimsical! Such an amazing power of taking people by surprise!"

Quilp paid no regard whatever to these compliments, nor to the dubious and frightened look into which the lawyer gradually subsided, nor to the shrieks of his wife and mother-in-law, nor to the latter's running from the room, nor to the former's fainting away. Keeping his eye fixed on Sampson Brass, he walked up to the table, and, beginning with his glass, drank off the contents, and went regularly round until he had emptied the other two; when he seized the case-bottle, and, hugging it under his arm, surveyed him with a most extraordinary leer.

"Not yet, Sampson!" said Quilp, — "not just yet!"

"Oh, very good indeed!" cried Brass, recovering his spirits a little. "Ha, ha, ha! Oh, exceedingly good! There's not another man alive who could carry it off like that. A most difficult position to carry off. But he has such a flow of good humor, such an amazing flow!"

"Good-night!" said the dwarf, nodding expressively.

"Good-night, sir, good-night!" cried the lawyer, retreating backwards towards the door. "This is a joyful occasion, indeed; extremely joyful. Ha, ha, ha! Oh, very rich, very rich indeed, remarkably so!"

Waiting until Mr. Brass's ejaculations died away in the distance (for he continued to pour them out all the way down stairs), Quilp advanced towards the two men, who yet lingered in a kind of stupid amazement.

"Have you been dragging the river all day, gentlemen?" said the dwarf, holding the door open with great politeness.

"And yesterday, too, master."

"Dear me! you 've had a deal of trouble. Pray consider everything yours that you find upon the — upon the body. Good-night!"

The men looked at each other, but had evidently no inclination to argue the point just then, and shuffled out of the room. The speedy clearance effected, Quilp locked the doors, and, still embracing the case-bottle with shrugged-up shoulders and folded arms, stood looking at his insensible wife like a dismounted nightmare.

When she came to, Quilp announced his intention of set-
L ting up a bachelor's establishment at Quilp's wharf, and bidding his wife and her mother get his things together, he set off
with Tom Scott, his boy, and made himself quite comfortable with
a hammock for bed and his own cooking things. Then he looked
up Dick Swiveller, to find him in a maudlin condition of emotion
over the recent marriage of Sophy Wackles to his rival Cheggs.
Quilp, pumping Dick as usual, learned that the mysterious stranger
had made the acquaintance of Fred Trent, who at this time was off
on a gambling jaunt. He went back to his wharf, where he was
waited on by his tearful wife, who vainly sought to coax him to the
LI house again. The next day he went to see Sampson and Sally
Brass, but encountered the Marchioness only. However, he
left a note with her inviting the worthy pair to take tea with him
that afternoon in the summer house of a water-side inn, and there
he let them know that he hated Kit and depended on them to get
him in some fashion out of his way.

LII While all this plotting was going on, Nell and her grandfather really seemed at last to have found a resting-place;
for in the village to which the schoolmaster had brought them was
an old church, and in a house next to the schoolmaster's the old
man and little girl were given a home, with the light duty on her
part of being keeper to the old church. Her special guardian beside the schoolmaster was a kindly old bachelor, who lived in the
village and was the good genius of the place. Nell soon made her-
LIII self at home in the house and in the church indeed, which
was to her a most peaceful place, next door to heaven. The
LIV old bachelor was, as it were, her tutor, telling her the stories
of tombs and inscriptions. She talked with the sexton and

grave-digger, and was filled with a nameless sorrow for the children who had died and lay buried here, so that with her grandfather's help she began to make a garden of the old graveyard, caring, as some frail little Old Mortality, for the neglected graves of forgotten
LV children. Yet it was apparent soon, even to the half awake old grandfather, that little Nell herself was wasting away, and the children who came to love her were filled with a bitter fear that she would not stay long with them.

LVI A day or two after the tea-party Dick Swiveller received a visit from his friend, Mr. Chuckster, and while they were both talking of the mysterious stranger and had got as far even as to note his intimacy with Kit, in walked that young man himself with a letter for the lodger, which he refused to deliver except to the person himself. No sooner had Kit gone up than Sampson and Sally Brass came in. Chuckster went out, and Sampson gave Dick a letter to carry to Peckham Rye. Then leaving the office door ajar, the old spider watched for the coming down of Kit, and calling him in, he made friends with him in a cheerful way, and with much mystery gave him to understand that a couple of half crowns on the desk came from the stranger above, and were to be taken by
LVII Kit, which Kit proceeded to do. This was the beginning of a series of performances, all calculated to inspire Kit with a better feeling toward Sampson Brass, who regularly, when he came alone, saw that Kit took the two half crowns, though Kit often drove the pony chaise, with Mr. Garland in it, to the strange gentleman's door. Whenever Kit was alone, Sampson Brass took occasion to send Dick Swiveller off on some errand. Dick, left much to himself, was fain to entertain his lonely hours with cribbage, setting up a dummy and jeopardizing his fortune at tremendous games of hazard with himself. He thought he heard a sort of snorting sound outside at such times, and suspecting the small servant, he softly opened the door one evening and pounced upon her. The poor little Marchioness confessed to watching at the keyhole out of pure loneliness, and Dick, with instantaneous compassion, made friends
LVIII with her, and for better security visited her in her subterranean abode, where he gave her copious draughts of ale and engaged in a game of cards with her.

Dick was, to be sure, in a melancholy mood after losing Sophy Cheggs, *née* Wackles; he even took to playing the flute. But he seemed now to be getting into other people's troubles, for Sally Brass, coming into the office one morning, complained to Dick that she had missed various articles, including some half crowns. Dick instantly thought of the Marchioness, and mentally fixed the crime on her. As they were talking, Sampson came in, and Sally

suddenly thought of Kit as the possible thief, to the terrible indignation of Sampson, who had, at the moment, a five pound note in his hand which he laid down on the desk. At this moment in came Kit himself with a letter for the lodger. When he came down stairs, the others being away, Sampson again engaged him in
LIX friendly talk, but managed to transfer the five pound note to Kit's hat. Then, apparently vexed at the prolonged absence of Dick, Sampson asked Kit to mind the office for a moment. When he came back he entered at the same moment with Dick and Sally, whereupon Kit left. He had not been gone long when Mr. Brass discovered his loss, and in great agitation ran after Kit. After him also ran Dick. Sampson, almost with tears in his eyes, told Kit of the misadventure, and the boy willingly went back, secure in his innocence, to the office. There he was searched, and of course it was Dick who found the five pound note in the lining of the boy's hat.

LX The constable whom Dick Swiveller was sent for appeared presently, and the whole party set out in a hackney coach to conduct this innocent little criminal to a magistrate. They passed Quilp on the way, and the dwarf was overcome with hilarity at discovering Kit in custody; they drove up to the notary's and exhibited Kit to Mr. Witherden, the Garlands, and Mr. Chuckster, and then went to the justice room, where the strange gentleman did his very best to save poor Kit, but in vain. The boy was com-
LXI mitted for trial, and wept in his cell, but presently was summoned to see visitors. They were his mother, the baby, little Jacob, and Barbara's mother, and it was a comfort at least to be assured by his mother that never for a moment did she suspect him. As he was returning to his cell under conduct of the turnkey, an officer stepped up with a pint pot of porter and a note. A friend had sent it, and the note was signed by the initials of Richard Swiveller.

LXII Mr. Brass, having accomplished the task set him, proceeded to report in person to his employer, and found that gentleman in his office, where he had set up a wooden figure of an admiral, and was engaged in driving sharp things into it and otherwise tormenting it, under the pretence that it was an effigy of Kit. Quilp made Brass drink a lot of infernal liquor, and bade him discharge Dick Swiveller as soon as the trial was over and he was no longer of any use. The lodger, Brass informed Quilp, had already abandoned his room and was at the Garlands'.

LXIII The trial came off with great promptness. Not a shred of evidence appearing to rebut the testimony put in by the counsel for the prosecution, Kit was declared guilty by the jury and sent back to prison. The chief comforter of his mother and little Jacob was Dick Swiveller, and when he returned to Mr. Brass's late one Saturday night, he was met with the notice that he need no longer waste his time at the office. He went off to his lodging, but LXIV what with all he had gone through, and all that had gone through him of late, he was taken violently ill with a delirious fever, and woke after three weeks to find himself in bed and the Marchioness playing cards by his bedside.

Yes; playing cribbage with herself at the table. There she sat, intent upon her game, coughing now and then in a subdued manner as if she feared to disturb him, — shuffling the cards, cutting, dealing, playing, counting, pegging, — going through all the mysteries of cribbage as if she had been in full practice from her cradle!

Mr. Swiveller raised the curtain again, determined to take the first favorable opportunity of addressing his companion. An occasion soon presented itself. The Marchioness dealt, turned up a knave, and omitted to take the usual advantage; upon which Mr. Swiveller called out as loud as he could, "Two for his heels!"

The Marchioness jumped up quickly, and clapped her hands . . . for joy, . . . declaring . . . that she was "so glad she did n't know what to do."

"Marchioness," said Mr. Swiveller thoughtfully, "be pleased to draw nearer. First of all, will you have the goodness to inform me where I shall find my voice, and, secondly, what has become of my flesh?"

The Marchioness only shook her head mournfully, and cried again; whereupon Mr. Swiveller (being very weak) felt his own eyes affected likewise.

"I begin to infer from your manner and these appearances, Marchioness," said Richard after a pause, and smiling with a trembling lip, "that I have been ill."

"You just have!" replied the small servant, wiping her eyes. "And have n't you been a talking nonsense!"

"Oh!" said Dick. "Very ill, Marchioness, have I been?"

"Dead, all but," replied the small servant. "I never thought you'd get better. Thank Heaven you have!"

Mr. Swiveller was silent for a long while. By and by he began to talk again, inquiring how long he had been there.

"Three weeks to-morrow," replied the small servant.

"Three what?" said Dick.

"Weeks," returned the Marchioness emphatically, — "three long, slow weeks."

The bare thought of having been in such extremity caused

Richard to fall into another silence, and to lie flat down again at his full length. The Marchioness, having arranged the bedclothes more comfortably, and felt that his hands and forehead were quite cool, — a discovery that filled her with delight, — cried a little more, and then applied herself to getting tea ready, and making some thin dry toast.

While she was thus engaged, Mr. Swiveller looked on with a grateful heart, very much astonished to see how thoroughly at home she made herself, and attributing this attention, in its origin, to Sally Brass, whom, in his own mind, he could not thank enough. When the Marchioness had finished her toasting, she spread a clean cloth on a tray, and brought him some crisp slices and a great basin of weak tea, with which (she said) the doctor had left word he might refresh himself when he awoke. She propped him up with pillows, if not as skilfully as if she had been a professional nurse all her life, at least as tenderly, and looked on with unutterable satisfaction while the patient — stopping every now and then to shake her by the hand — took his poor meal with an appetite and relish which the greatest dainties of the earth, under any other circumstances, would have failed to provoke. Having cleared away, and disposed everything comfortably about him again, she sat down at the table to take her own tea.

"Marchioness," said Mr. Swiveller, "how's Sally?"

The small servant screwed her face into an expression of the very uttermost entanglement of slyness, and shook her head.

"What! have n't you seen her lately?" said Dick.

"Seen her!" cried the small servant. "Bless you, I've run away!"

Mr. Swiveller immediately laid himself down again quite flat, and so remained for about five minutes. By slow degrees he resumed his sitting posture after that lapse of time, and inquired: —

"And where do you live, Marchioness?"

"Live!" cried the small servant. "Here!"

"Oh!" said Mr. Swiveller.

And with that he fell down flat again as suddenly as if he had been shot. Thus he remained, motionless, and bereft of speech, until she had finished her meal, put everything in its place, and swept the hearth; when he motioned her to bring a chair to the bedside, and, being propped up again, opened a further conversation.

"And so," said Dick, "you have run away?"

"Yes," said the Marchioness; "and they've been a tising of me."

"Been — I beg your pardon," said Dick, — "what have they been doing?"

"Been a tising of me — tising, you know, in the newspapers," rejoined the Marchioness.

"Ay, ay," said Dick, — "advertising?"

The small servant nodded and winked. Her eyes were so red with waking and crying, that the Tragic Muse might have winked with greater consistency. And so Dick felt.

"Tell me," said he, "how it was that you thought of coming here."

"Why, you see," returned the Marchioness, "when you was gone, I had n't any friend at all, because the lodger he never come back, and I did n't know where either him or you was to be found, you know. But one morning, when I was" —

"Was near a keyhole," suggested Mr. Swiveller, observing that she faltered.

"Well, then," said the small servant, nodding, — "when I was near the office keyhole, — as you see me through, you know, — I heard somebody saying that she lived here, and was the lady whose house you lodged at; and that you was took very bad; and would n't nobody come and take care of you? Mr. Brass he says, 'It 's no business of mine,' he says; and Miss Sally she says, 'He 's a funny chap; but it 's no business of mine.' And the lady went away, and slammed the door to when she went out, I can tell you. So I run away that night, and come here, and told 'em you was my brother; and they believed me; and I 've been here ever since."

LXV She went on to tell him how she had overheard Sampson and Sally laying the plot for entrapping Kit, and Dick, now in a state of great excitement, sent her off to the notary's office. Arrived there, she found the pony chaise and Mr. Abel about to drive off. She avoided Mr. Chuckster, and cutting on behind, surprised Mr. Abel, when at a safe distance, by her presence. She panted out her message and urged him to drive fast, which he did, stopping at last at the door of Dick's lodgings. Here the Marchioness by the sick man's bed told her story over again, and at Dick's feverish request Mr. Abel drove off as fast as possible to report affairs at headquarters.

LXVI As a consequence, when Dick woke the next morning it was to find Mr. Garland, Mr. Abel, Mr. Witherden, and the strange gentleman all in his room, talking in whispers. They assured him that it was not too late to arrest the course of injustice, and after the Marchioness had given him his breakfast and washed his face and hands, they proceeded to set forth the plan upon which they were to work, which was to confront Sally Brass with the knowledge they had and force a confession from her. Dick was somewhat skeptical of the result, but he left them to their devices, and they left him to a large hamper of good things which came as they departed. They took up their post at an inn near the place where the Brasses lived, and by a mysterious note brought Sally Brass before them. After they had propounded the matter to her and had let her know through whose instrumentality the discovery had been made, she deliberated what answer to make, when the door opened and Sampson Brass entered. He had followed his sister, being of a suspicious turn, had overheard the conversation, and now volunteered his services. In a word, he was so afraid of consequences, and so infuriated by the scurvy treatment he had received at the hands of Quilp, that he turned state's evidence for the purpose of bringing the dwarf's head under the law. Upon the demand of the gentlemen he reduced his testimony to writing. Sally meanwhile, pretending to sleep, slipped off.

The company of conspirators against the peace of Daniel Quilp returned to Dick's lodgings to report progress, and when all had gone but the notary, that gentleman gave a piece of news to Dick. Dick's aunt had died, and left him an annuity of a hundred and fifty pounds a year. Dick's first thought was for the Marchioness. The notary congratulated him on the small property he had come into.

> "Sir," said Dick, sobbing and laughing together, "you may. For, please God, we'll make a scholar of the poor Marchioness yet! And she shall walk in silk attire, and siller have to spare, or may I never rise from this bed again."

LXVII Sally Brass had slipped away from her brother and the company about him with a pretty clear sense of what was to be done. She took measures for her own safety, and then sent a note by Mrs. Quilp to that meek lady's husband apprising him of her brother's infidelity and advising him to clear out. Quilp, mad with rage over Sampson Brass, barred his place stoutly, and was ready to escape under cover of the darkness when his enemy appeared. Night came on; it was pitchy dark, and Quilp, hearing a knock at the outer door, made his way out of the place, but he lost his bearings, and as he climbed about among the slippery wharves he lost his footing and fell into the swift river. He uttered one despairing cry, and then the river bore his corpse along.

> It toyed and sported with its ghastly freight, now bruising it against the slimy piles, now hiding it in mud or long, rank grass,

now dragging it heavily over rough stones and gravel, now feigning to yield it to its own element, and in the same action luring it away, until, tired of the ugly plaything, it flung it on a swamp — a dismal place where pirates had swung in chains, through many a wintry night — and left it there to bleach.

LXVIII With the death of Quilp, fire struck his wharf and office also. Kit, meanwhile, had been visited by his friends, released from prison, and brought to the Garlands', where all made merry over the return of the innocent, the pony sharing in the common joy, and Barbara having her special share. Then it was that the best comfort of all came to the boy, when he learned that Miss Nell and her grandfather had been found, and by the most singular coincidence. Mr. Garland had a brother of remarkably quiet and retiring disposition, who rarely wrote about the people in the village where he lived, but of late he had written, because of his great interest, of an old man and child, whom he had befriended. He was, indeed, the "Bachelor" of the village, and thus the hiding-place of the pair had been discovered.

LXIX And now, Mr. Garland, the strange gentleman, and Kit set off on their journey to recover, in very truth, the lost pair, Kit on the rumble behind, the two gentlemen within. It was night, and the strange gentleman took this opportunity to divulge to Mr. Garland the story of Nell's grandfather. He was the elder of two brothers by some twelve years. Both had loved the same woman, and the younger had sacrificed himself and his love. He left the country, and his elder brother married their common love, who died soon, leaving an infant daughter. When the child grew, she married a man unworthy of her, who died at last, after making her wretched and despoiling her father. Then she died also, and her two children, the boy and girl, fell into their grandfather's hands. The boy took after his father, and led a wayward life. The girl, little Nell, was his cherished companion. And so, at last, the younger brother came home to seek his brother, and found him and the child gone. It had been his business since to find them, as he was now doing.

LXX It was night again, of the second day, before they reached the village. It was midnight, but they came upon the old sexton, who directed them. As they drew near the spot where Nell and her grandfather lived, Kit went on ahead. He found the house;

LXXI he heard strange voices within, and pushed the door open. He discovered the old man crouching over the fire and moaning. He did not seem to recognize Kit, but spoke constantly of Nell as cold in the inner room. Then came in the younger brother, Mr. Garland, the schoolmaster, and the bachelor. They tried in vain to bring the old man to a knowledge of his brother; he had but one thought, and that was for Nell.

"Where is she?" demanded Kit. "Oh, tell me but that, but that, dear master!"

"She is asleep — yonder — in there."

"Thank God!"

"Ay! Thank God!" returned the old man. "I have prayed to him many and many and many a livelong night, when she has been asleep. He knows. Hark! Did she call?"

"I heard no voice."

"You did. You hear her now. Do you tell me that you don't hear *that?*"

He started up, and listened again.

"Nor that?" he cried with a triumphant smile. "Can anybody know that voice so well as I? Hush, hush!"

Motioning to him to be silent, he stole away into another chamber. After a short absence (during which he could be heard to speak in a softened, soothing tone) he returned, bearing in his hand a lamp.

"She is still asleep," he whispered. "You were right. She did not call, unless she did so in her slumber. She has called to me in her sleep before now, sir. As I have sat by, watching, I have seen her lips move, and have known, though no sound came from them, that she spoke of me. I feared the light might dazzle her eyes, and wake her; so I brought it here."

He spoke rather to himself than to the visitor; but, when he had put the lamp upon the table, he took it up, as if impelled by some momentary recollection or curiosity, and held it near his face. Then, as if forgetting his motive in the very action, he turned away, and put it down again.

"She is sleeping soundly," he said; "but no wonder. Angel-hands have strewn the ground deep with snow, that the lightest footstep may be lighter yet; and the very birds are dead, that they may not wake her. She used to feed them, sir. Though never so cold and hungry, the timid things would fly from us; they never flew from her!"

Again he stopped to listen, and, scarcely drawing breath, listened for a long, long time. That fancy past, he opened an old chest, took out some clothes as fondly as if they had been living things, and began to smooth and brush them with his hand.

"Why dost thou lie so idle there, dear Nell," he murmured, "when there are bright red berries out of doors, waiting for thee to pluck them? Why dost thou lie so idle there, when thy little friends come creeping to the door, crying, 'Where is Nell, sweet

Nell?' and sob and weep because they do not see thee. She was always gentle with children. The wildest would do her bidding: she had a tender way with them; indeed she had."

Kit had no power to speak. His eyes were filled with tears.

"Her little homely dress, her favorite!" cried the old man, pressing it to his breast, and patting it with his shrivelled hand. "She will miss it when she wakes. They have hid it here in sport. But she shall have it; she shall have it! I would not vex my darling for the wide world's riches. See here, these shoes — how worn they are! She kept them to remind her of our last long journey. You see where the little feet went bare upon the ground. They told me afterwards that the stones had cut and bruised them. *She* never told me that. No, no, God bless her! And I have remembered since, she walked behind me, sir, that I might not see how lame she was; but yet she had my hand in hers, and seemed to lead me still."

. . . . . . . .

By little and little the old man had drawn back towards the inner chamber while these words were spoken. He pointed there, as he replied with trembling lips: —

"You plot among you to wean my heart from her. You never will do that! never, while I have life! I have no relative or friend but her; I never had: I never will have! She is all in all to me. It is too late to part us now!"

Waving them off with his hand, and calling softly to her as he went, he stole into the room. They who were left behind drew close together, and after a few whispered words, not unbroken by emotion, or easily uttered, followed him. They moved so gently, that their footsteps made no noise; but there were sobs from among the group, and sounds of grief and mourning.

For she was dead. There upon her little bed she lay at rest. The solemn stillness was no marvel now.

She was dead. No sleep so beautiful and calm, so free from trace of pain, so fair to look upon. She seemed a creature fresh from the hand of God, and waiting for the breath of life; not one who had lived, and suffered death.

Her couch was dressed with here and there some winter-berries and green leaves, gathered in a spot she had been used to favor. "When I die, put near me something that has loved the light, and had the sky above it always." Those were her words.

She was dead. Dear, gentle, patient, noble Nell was dead. Her little bird, a poor slight thing the pressure of a finger would have crushed, was stirring nimbly in its cage; and the strong heart of its child-mistress was mute and motionless forever.

Where were the traces of her early cares, her sufferings, and fatigues? All gone. Sorrow was dead indeed in her; but peace and perfect happiness were born, imaged in her tranquil beauty and profound repose.

And still her former self lay there, unaltered in this change. Yes. The old fireside had smiled upon that same sweet face: it had passed, like a dream, through haunts of misery and care. At the door of the poor schoolmaster on the summer evening, before the furnace-fire upon the cold wet night, at the still bedside of the dying boy, there had been the same mild, lovely look. So shall we know the angels in their majesty after death.

The old man held one languid arm in his, and had the small hand tight folded to his breast for warmth. It was the hand she had stretched out to him with her last smile; the hand that led him on through all their wanderings. Ever and anon he pressed it to his lips; then hugged it to his breast again, murmuring that it was warmer now; and as he said it he looked in agony to those who stood around, as if imploring them to help her.

She was dead, and past all help, or need of it. The ancient rooms she had seemed to fill with life, even while her own was waning fast, the garden she had tended, the eyes she had gladdened, the noiseless haunts of many a thoughtful hour, the paths she had trodden as it were but yesterday, could know her nevermore.

"It is not," said the schoolmaster as he bent down to kiss her on the cheek, and gave his tears free vent, — "it is not on earth that Heaven's justice ends. Think what earth is compared with the world to which her young spirit has winged its early flight; and say, if one deliberate wish expressed in solemn terms above this bed could call her back to life, which of us would utter it?"

LXXII Two days had she been dead, and the next day they buried her in the churchyard, while all the village mourned. The old grandfather continued still to think and speak only of her, and at last his wandering was over and he lay by her side.

LXXIII Little remains to be told save the exit of the several personages. Sampson Brass went to jail for a term of years. Sally Brass disappeared; various rumors were on foot about her, but finally it was said that she rejoined her brother, and they became night prowlers. Mrs. Quilp, made rich unintentionally by her dead husband, married again, and the second husband made it a condition that Mrs. Jiniwin should not live with them. Abel Garland went into partnership with the notary. Dick Swiveller, renaming the Marchioness Sophronia Sphynx, sent her to school, and when she appeared to be about nineteen, married her. He was much perplexed over her parentage, but though there were dark hints of a most unflattering origin, he accepted her cordially for what she was. Kit married Barbara. The younger brother, or strange gentleman, lived on, a benefactor to all whom he could help.

---

## INDEX TO CHARACTERS

**Bachelor, The.** A kind old gentleman at a village where Little Nell and her grandfather stay in the course of their wanderings.

None of the villagers had cared to ask his name, or, when they knew it, to store it in their memories; perhaps because he was unmarried he had been called the Bachelor. The name pleased him, or suited him as well as any other; and so the Bachelor he had ever since remained. lii, liv, lv, lxi, lxviii, lxix, lxxiii.

**Barbara.** A housemaid at Mrs. Garland's; afterwards the wife of Kit Nubbles. xxii, xxxviii–xl, lxviii, lxix, lxxiii.

**Barbara's Mother.** xxxix, xl, lxi, lxviii, lxix, lxxiii.

**Brass, Sally.** Sister and partner of Sampson Brass.

In face she bore a striking resemblance to her brother Sampson. So exact, indeed, was the likeness between them, that had it consorted with Miss Brass's maiden modesty and gentle womanhood to have assumed her brother's clothes in a frolic, and sat down beside him, it would have been difficult for the oldest friend of the family to determine which was Sampson, and which Sally; especially as the lady carried upon her upper lip certain reddish demonstrations, which, if the imagination had been assisted by her attire, might have been mistaken for a beard. These were, however, in all probability, nothing more than eyelashes in a wrong place, as the eyes of Miss Brass were free, quite, from any such natural impertinences. In complexion Miss Brass was sallow (rather a dirty sallow, so to speak); but this hue was agreeably relieved by the healthy glow which mantled in the extreme tip of her laughing nose. Her voice was exceedingly impressive, deep and rich in quality, and, once heard, not easily forgotten. . . . In mind she was of a strong and vigorous turn, having from her earliest youth devoted herself with uncommon ardor to the study of the law; not wasting her speculations upon its eagle flights, which are rare, but tracing it attentively through all the slippery and eel-like crawlings in which it commonly pursues its way. . . . Whether she had steeled her heart against mankind, or whether those who might have wooed and won her were deterred by fears that, being learned in the law, she might have too near her fingers' ends those particular statutes which regulate what are familiarly termed actions for breach, certain it is that she was still in a state of celibacy, and still in daily occupation of her old stool, opposite to that of her brother Sampson. And equally certain it is, by the way, that, between these two stools, a great many people had come to the ground. xxxiii–xxxviii, li, lvi, lviii–lx, lxiii–lxvii, lxxiii.

**Brass, Sampson.** A villainous attorney of Bevis Marks, with a cringing manner and a very harsh voice; Quilp's legal adviser. He is a tall, meagre man, with a nose like a wen, a protruding forehead, retreating eyes, and hair of a deep red. xi–xiii, xxxiii, xxxv, xxxvii, xxxviii, xlix, li, lvi–lx, lxii–lxiv, lxvi, lxvii, lxxiii.

**Cheggs, Mr.** A market-gardener; a rival of Mr. Swiveller's for the hand of Sophy Wackles, whom he finally marries. viii.

**Cheggs, Miss.** His sister. viii.

**Chuckster, Mr.** Clerk in the office of Witherden the notary; a member of the Lodge of Glorious Apollos, and a mortal enemy of Kit Nubbles. xiv, xx, xxxviii, xl, lvi, lx, lxv, lxix, lxxiii.

**Clergyman, The.** A very kind pastor at the village where Nell and her grandfather stay for a time. lii, lxxiii.

**Codlin, Tom.** One of the Punch and Judy showmen with whom Little Nell and her grandfather travel for a few days. xvi–xix, xxvii, lxxiii.

**David, Old.** Assistant to the old sexton in the village where Little Nell dies. liv.

**Edwards, Miss.** A pupil at Miss Monflather's educational establishment. xxxi, xxxii.

**Evans, Richard.** One of Mr. Marton's pupils. lii.

**Garland, Mr.** A little, fat, placid-faced, and very kind-hearted old gentleman, with whom Kit Nubbles lives after he leaves Little Nell. xiv, xx, xxii, xxxviii–xl, lx, lxvii–lxx, lxxii.

**Garland, Mrs.** His wife; a little old lady, plump and placid, like himself. xiv, xx, xxii, xxxviii–xl, lxvii–lxix, lxxiii.

**Garland, Mr. Abel.** Their son, articled to Mr. Witherden the notary, whose partner he afterwards becomes. xiv, xx, xxxviii–xli, lx, lxv, lxvii–lxix, lxxiii.

**George.** Driver of Mrs. Jarley's caravan; afterwards her husband. xxvi, xxviii, xlvii.

**George, Mrs.** A neighbor and friend of Mrs Quilp. iv.

**Grandfather, Little Nell's.** Proprietor of the Old Curiosity Shop. Possessed by an overmastering desire to provide for his granddaughter, he is drawn to the gaming-table, and tries his luck again and again, until at last he becomes — for her sake — a confirmed gambler. Losing heavily and constantly, but confident that fortune will finally favor him, he borrows money from Quilp, a rich dwarf, pledging his little stock as security for the debt. His resources, however, are soon all exhausted, his shop and its contents taken on execution, and he himself is thrown upon the world, a beggar, shattered in intellect, and tottering on the verge of the grave. Little Nell leads him away from London; and they wander together through the country. But the passion for play only slumbers in him, and is ready to awake with the first opportunity that offers. But in the seclusion of a quiet village, where they at last find a home, such temptation no longer comes; and his hopes and fears, and all his thoughts, are turned to the gentle object of his love, who soon begins to sink under the effects of her past trials and sufferings. Her death leaves him wholly oblivious to all else, and it is not long before he follows her to her grave. i–iii, ix, xi, xii, xv–xix, xxiv–xxxii, xlii–xlvi, lii, liv, lv, lxxi, lxxii.

**Grinder, Mr.** A showman. xvii.

**Groves, James.** Landlord of The Valiant Soldier inn. xxix, lxxiii.

**Harris, Mr.**, *alias* SHORT TROTTERS, *but commonly called either* SHORT *or* TROTTERS. One of the showmen with whom Little Nell and her grandfather travel for a few days. xvi–xix, xxvii, lxxiii.

**Harry.** A schoolboy; Mr. Marton's favorite pupil. xxiv, xxv.

**Jarley, Mrs.** Proprietor of "Jarley's Wax-Work." Little Nell is engaged by this lady to point out the figures to visitors. xxvi–xxix, xxxi, xxxii, xlvii, lxxiii.

**Jerry.** Proprietor of a troop of dancing-dogs. xvii, xix, xxxvii.

**Jiniwin, Mrs.** The mother of Mrs. Quilp, with whom she lives, and with whose husband she wages perpetual war, though she stands in no slight dread of him. iv–vi, xxiii, xlix, l, lxxiii.

**Jowl, Joe.** A gambler, who tempts Little Nell's grandfather to rob Mrs. Jarley. xxix, xlii, lxxiii.

**List, Isaac.** A gambler and knave. xxix, xxx, xlii, lxxiii.

**Marchioness, The.** A name given to the small servant at Sampson Brass's, by Dick Swiveller, who marries her. xxxiv–xxxvi, li, lvii, lviii, lxiv–lxvi, lxxiii.

**Marton, Mr.** An old schoolmaster who befriends Little Nell and her grandfather. xxiv–xxvi, xlv, xlvi, lii–liv, lxxi, lxxiii.

**Monflathers, Miss.** Principal of a select boarding-school for young ladies. xxxi.

**Nubbles, Christopher *or* Kit.** A shock-headed, shambling, awkward lad, with an uncommonly wide mouth, very red cheeks, a turned-up nose, and a peculiarly comical expression of face. He is very much attached to Little Nell, whose grandfather employs him as an errand-boy. After a while, however, the old man takes it into his head that Kit has told of his gambling habits, and that this is the reason why he cannot succeed in borrowing any more money. He therefore forbids his ever coming into his presence again. After the disappearance of his old master, Kit gets employment in the family of a kind old gentleman named Garland. At length he falls into trouble, being falsely accused of larceny, and is arrested, and thrown into prison; but his innocence is soon established, and he is set at liberty. He afterwards marries Barbara, Mrs. Garland's servant. i, iii, vi, x, xi, xiii, xiv, xx–xxii, xxxviii–xli, xlviii, lvi–lxi, lxiii, lxiv, lxviii–lxxii.

**Nubbles, Jacob.** Brother to Kit. x, xiii, xxi, xxii, xxxix, xli, lxi, lxix, lxxii.

**Nubbles, Mrs.** Mother to Kit Nubbles; a poor but industrious widow, very pious and very constant in her attendance at a dissenting chapel called Little Bethel. x, xiii, xxi, xxii, xxxix, xli, xlvii, xlviii, lxi, lxiii, lxix, lxxii.

**Owen, John.** A schoolboy; one of Mr. Marton's pupils. lii.

**Quilp, Daniel.** A hideous creature, full of ferocity and cunning. He is described as,—

An elderly man, of remarkably hard features and forbidding aspect, and so low in stature as to be quite a dwarf; though his head and face were large enough for the body of a giant. His black eyes were restless, sly, and cunning; his mouth and chin bristly with the stubble of a coarse, hard beard; and his complexion was one of that kind which never looks clean or wholesome. But what added most to the grotesque expression of his face was a ghastly smile, which, appearing to be the mere result of habit, and to have no connection with any mirthful or complacent feeling, constantly revealed the few discolored fangs that were yet scattered in his mouth, and gave him the aspect of a panting dog. His dress consisted of a large high-crowned hat, a worn dark suit, a pair of capacious shoes, and a dirty white neckerchief, sufficiently limp and crumpled to disclose the greater portion of his wiry throat. Such hair as he had was of a grizzled black, cut short and straight upon his temples, and hanging in a frowzy fringe about his ears. His hands, which were of a rough, coarse grain, were very dirty; his finger-nails were crooked, long, and yellow.

Mr. Quilp could scarcely be said to be of any particular trade or calling, though his pursuits were diversified, and his occupations numerous. He collected the rents of whole colonies of filthy streets and alleys by the water-side, advanced money to the seamen and petty officers of merchant-vessels, had a share in the ven-

QUILP, MRS. QUILP, AND MRS. JINIWIN.

tures of divers mates of East-Indiamen, smoked his smuggled cigars under the very nose of the custom-house, and made appointments on 'change with men in glazed hats and round jackets pretty well every day.

Quilp comes to his end by falling into the Thames, and drowning, on a dark night, in an attempt to escape from some officers who are on the point of arresting him for various crimes. His property falls to his wife, who bears her bereavement with exemplary resignation, and marries again, choosing the exact opposite of the dear departed. iii–vi, ix, xi–xiii, xxiii, xxvii, xxx, xli, xlviii–li, lx, lxii, lxiv, lxvii, lxxiii.

**Quilp, Mrs. Betsey.** His wife; "a pretty little, mild-spoken, blue-eyed woman, who, having allied herself in wedlock to the dwarf, in one of those strange infatuations of which examples are by no means scarce, performed a sound practical penance for her folly every day of her life." iv–vi, xiii, xxi, xxiii, xlix, l, lxvii, lxxiii.

**Scott, Tom.** Quilp's boy. Although he is habitually beaten and abused by Quilp, Tom retains a queer sort of affection and admiration for his master. His favorite amusement is to stand on his head; and he also adopts this attitude when he wishes to show his defiance of Mr. Quilp's instructions, or to revenge himself upon him. Being cast upon the world by his master's death, he determines to go through it upon his head and hands, and accordingly becomes a professional "tumbler," adopting the name of an Italian image-lad of his acquaintance, and meeting with extraordinary success. iv–vi, xi, xiii, xxvii, xlix–li, lxvii, lxxiii.

**Sexton, The Old.** An old man at the village where Little Nell and her grandfather find a home. liii–lv, lxx, lxxii.

**Short.** *See* Harris, Mr.

**Simmons, Mrs. Henrietta.** A neighbor of Mrs. Quilp. ix.

**Single Gentleman, The.** Brother to Little Nell's grandfather. He proves to be Master Humphrey, the narrator of the story. xxxiv–xxxviii, xl, xli, xlvii, xlviii, lv, lvi, lxvi, lxix–lxxiii.

**Slum, Mr.** A writer of poetical advertisements. xxviii.

**Sphynx, Sophronia.** *See* Marchioness, The, and page 168.

**Sweet William.** A silent man, who earns his living by showing tricks upon cards, and who has rather deranged the natural expression of his countenance by putting small leaden lozenges into his eyes, and bringing them out at his mouth. xix.

**Swiveller, Dick.** Friend to Fred Trent, and clerk to Sampson Brass. He is first introduced on the occasion of a visit which young Trent makes to his grandfather for the purpose of demanding to see his sister.

At length there sauntered up on the opposite side of the way, with a bad pretence of passing by accident, a figure conspicuous for its dirty smartness, which, after a great many frowns and jerks of the head, in resistance of the invitation, ultimately crossed the road, and was brought into the shop.

"There! It's Dick Swiveller," said the young fellow, pushing him in. "Sit down, Swiveller."

"But is the old min agreeable?" said Mr. Swiveller, in an undertone.

"Sit down!" repeated his companion.

Mr. Swiveller complied, and, looking about him with a propitiatory smile, observed that last week was a fine week for the ducks, and this week was a fine week for the dust: he also observed, that, whilst standing by the post at the street-corner, he had observed a pig with a straw in his mouth issuing out of the tobacco-shop, from which appearance he argued that another fine week for the ducks was approaching, and that rain would certainly ensue. He furthermore took occasion to apologize for any negligence that might be perceptible in his dress, on the ground that last night he had had "the sun very strong in his eyes," by which expression he was understood to convey to his hearers, in the most delicate manner possible, the information that he had been extremely drunk.

'But what," said Mr. Swiveller, with a sigh,—"what is the odds so long as the fire of soul is kindled at the taper of conwiviality, and the wing of friendship never moults a feather? What is the odds so long as the spirit is expanded by means of rosy wine, and the present moment is the least happiest of our existence?" . . .

It was, perhaps, not very unreasonable to suspect, from what had already passed, that Mr. Swiveller was not quite recovered from the effects of the powerful sunlight to which he had made allusion; but, if no such suspicion had been awakened by his speech, his wiry hair, dull eyes, and sallow face would still have been strong witnesses against him. His attire was not, as he had himself hinted, remarkable for the nicest arrangement, but was in a state of disorder, which strongly induced the idea that he had gone to bed in it. It consisted of a brown body-coat with a great many brass buttons up the front, and only one behind, a bright check neckerchief, a plaid waistcoat, soiled white trousers, and a very limp hat, worn with the wrong side foremost, to hide a hole in the brim. The breast of his coat was ornamented with an outside pocket, from which there peeped forth the cleanest end of a very large and very ill-favored handkerchief; his dirty wristbands were pulled down as far as possible, and ostentatiously folded back over his cuffs; he displayed no gloves, and carried a yellow cane having at the top a bone hand with the semblance of a ring on its little finger, and a black ball in its grasp. With all these personal advantages (to which may be added a strong savor of tobacco-smoke and a prevailing greasiness of appearance) Mr. Swiveller leaned back in his chair, with his eyes fixed on the ceiling, and, occasionally pitching his voice to the needful key, obliged the company with a few bars of an intensely dismal air, and then, in the middle of a note, relapsed into his former silence.

Mr. Swiveller and Fred enter into a sort of conspiracy to marry the former to Little Nell, and thus get possession of the enormous wealth which, it is supposed, the old man is hoarding up for her. After the disappearance of Little Nell and her grandfather, Dick makes a friend of Quilp, who obtains for him a situation as clerk in the law-office of Sampson Brass.

A coach stopped near the door, and presently afterwards there was a loud double-knock. As this was no business of Mr. Swiveller's, the person not ringing the office-bell, he pursued his diversion with perfect composure, notwithstanding that he rather thought there was nobody else in the house.

In this, however, he was mistaken; for, after the knock had been repeated with increased impatience, the door was opened, and somebody with a very heavy tread went up the stairs, and into the room above. Mr. Swiveller was wondering whether this might be another Miss Brass, twin-sister to the Dragon, when there came a rapping of knuckles at the office door.

"Come in!" said Dick. "Don't stand upon ceremony. The business will get rather complicated if I 've many more customers. Come in!"

"Oh! please," said a little voice very low down in the doorway, "will you come and show the lodgings?"

Dick leaned over the table, and descried a small, slipshod girl in a dirty coarse apron and bib, which left nothing of her visible but her face and feet. She might as well have been dressed in a violin-case.

"Why, who are you?" said Dick.

To which the only reply was, "Oh! please, will you come and show the lodgings?"

There never was such an old-fashioned child in her looks and manner. She must have been at work from her cradle. She seemed as much afraid of Dick as Dick was amazed at her.

"I have n't got anything to do with the lodgings," said Dick. "Tell 'em to call again."

"Oh! but please, will you come and show the lodgings?" returned the girl. "It 's eighteen shillings a week, and us finding plate and linen. Boots and clothes is extra, and fires in winter-time is eightpence a day."

"Why don't you show 'em yourself? You seem to know all about 'em," said Dick.

"Miss Sally said I was n't to, because people would n't believe the attendance was good, if they saw how small I was first."

"Well; but they 'll see how small you are afterwards; won't they?" said Dick.

"Ah! But then they 'll have taken 'em for a fortnight certain," replied the child with a shrewd look; "and people don't like moving when they 're once settled."

"This is a queer sort of thing," muttered Dick, rising. "What do you mean to say you are; the cook?"

"Yes, I do plain cooking," replied the child. "I 'm housemaid, too; I do all the work of the house."

"I suppose Brass and the Dragon and I do the dirtiest part of it," thought Dick. And he might have thought much more, being in a doubtful and hesitating mood, but that the girl again urged her request, and certain mysterious bumping sounds on the passage and staircase seemed to give note of the applicant's impatience. Richard Swiveller, therefore, sticking a pen behind each ear, and carrying another in his mouth as a token of his great importance and devotion to business, hurried out to meet and treat with the single gentleman.

After the arrest of Kit Nubbles, in consequence of the false testimony of Sampson Brass, Dick, who has sided with the poor boy, is discharged. He takes his little bundle under his arm, intending to go to Kit's mother, and comfort and assist her.

In the end, Kit is released, and returned to his friends. Dick falls into an annuity of one hundred and fifty pounds a year, and being very grateful to the Marchioness, his first thought is of her. "Please God," he says, "we 'll make a scholar of the poor Marchioness yet! And she shall walk in silk attire, and siller have to spare, or may I never rise from this bed again!"

After casting about for some time for a name which should be worthy of her, he decided in favor of Sophronia Sphynx, as being euphonious and genteel, and, furthermore, indicative of mystery. Under this title, the Marchioness repaired, in tears, to a school of his selection, from which, as she soon distanced all competitors, she was removed before the lapse of many quarters to one of a higher grade. It is but bare justice to Mr. Swiveller to say, that, although the expenses of her education kept him in straitened

DICK SWIVELLER AND THE MARCHIONESS.

circumstances for half a dozen years, he never slackened in his zeal, and always held himself sufficiently repaid by the accounts he heard (with great gravity) of her advancement, on his monthly visits to the governess, who looked upon him as a literary gentleman of eccentric habits, and of a most prodigious talent in quotation.

In a word, Mr. Swiveller kept the Marchioness at this establishment until she was, at a moderate guess, full nineteen years of age, good-looking, clever, and good-humored, when he began to consider seriously what was to be done next. On one of his periodical visits, while he was revolving this question in his mind, the Marchioness came down to him alone, looking more smiling and more fresh than ever. Then it occurred to him (but not for the first time) that, if she would marry him, how comfortable they might be! So Richard asked her. Whatever she said, it was n't No; and they were married in good earnest that day week, which gave Mr. Swiveller frequent occasion to remark at divers subsequent periods that there had been a young lady saving up for him after all. ii, iii, vii, viii, xiii, xxi, xxiii, xxxiv–xxxviii, xlviii, l, lvi–lxvi, lxxiii.

**Trent, Frederick.** Brother to Little Nell. ii, iii, vii, viii, xxiii, l, lxxiii.

**Trent, Little Nell.** A small and delicate child of angelic purity of character, and sweetness of disposition, who lives alone with her grandfather, an old man possessed by a mania for gambling; his object being to make her rich and happy. The account of their wanderings, after the old man loses the last of his property, and is turned into the streets a beggar and an imbecile, forms the thread of the story.

"Which way?" said the child.

The old man looked irresolutely and helplessly, first at her, then to the right and left, then at her again, and shook his head. It was plain that she was thenceforth his guide and leader. The child felt it, but had no doubts or misgiving, and, putting her hand in his, led him gently away.

It was the beginning of a day in June, the deep blue sky unsullied by a cloud, and teeming with brilliant light. The streets were as yet nearly free from passengers; the houses and shops were closed; and the healthy air of morning fell like breath from angels on the sleeping town.

The old man and the child passed on through the glad silence, elate with hope and pleasure. They were alone together once again. Every object was bright and fresh: nothing reminded them, otherwise than by contrast, of the monotony and constraint they had left behind. Church towers and steeples, frowning and dark at other times, now shone in the sun; each humble nook and corner rejoiced in light; and the sky, dimmed only by excessive distance, shed its placid smile on everything beneath.

Forth from the city, while it yet slumbered, went the two poor adventurers, wandering they knew not whither.

Nell and her grandfather fall into the company of many strange people during their wanderings, among whom are Messrs. Codlin and Short, a couple of itinerant showmen, who take it into their heads that the old man has stolen the child, and is endeavoring to elude pursuit, and that there will surely be a reward offered for their apprehension; whereupon they resolve to keep them in their company until the right time comes for surrendering them. Little Nell divines the object of these men; and, fearing that her grandfather, in case they should be handed over to the authorities, may be confined in some asylum, she escapes from the showmen, and shortly afterwards falls in with Mrs. Jarley, the proprietress of "Jarley's Wax-Work," who engages her to point out the figures to visitors. While walking, one evening, near the town where Mrs. Jarley is exhibiting her works, Nell and her grandfather are overtaken by a severe storm, and are forced to seek shelter for the night at a roadside inn called the Valiant Soldier. Behind a screen some men are playing at cards, and, with the sight of this, all the slumbering passion of the old man is aroused.

The old man plays until their little purse is exhausted, and nothing is left with which to pay for their entertainment. In this strait, Nell, after much hesitation, and fearful that her grandfather will observe her, takes from her dress a small gold piece which she has kept concealed there, in anticipation of some great emergency, and pays the reckoning, hiding the change which she receives, before rejoining her grandfather. Shortly afterwards she retires for the night, but is awaked by a sound and discovers a figure in the room, which eludes her and moves away. Fearful of some disaster to her grandfather, she steals into his room.

The door was partly open. Not knowing what she meant to do, but meaning to preserve him, or be killed herself, she staggered forward and looked in.

What sight was that which met her view!

The bed had not been lain on, but was smooth and empty; and at a table sat the old man himself, the only living creature there, — his white face pinched and sharpened by the greediness which made his eyes unnaturally bright, — counting the money of which his hands had robbed her.

Shocked beyond measure by the sight, the child returns to her room; but, during the night, she steals again to her grandfather's side, and finds him asleep.

She had no fear as she looked upon his slumbering features; but she had a deep and weighty sorrow, and it found its relief in tears.

"God bless him!" said the child, stooping softly to kiss his placid cheek. "I see too well now, that they would indeed part us if they found us out, and shut him up from the light of the sun and sky. He has only me to help him. God bless us both!"

Lighting her candle, she retreated as silently as she had come, and, gaining her own room once more, sat up during the remainder of that long, long, miserable night.

At last the day turned her waning candle pale; and she fell asleep. She was quickly roused by the girl who had shown her up to bed, and, as soon as she was dressed, prepared to go down to her grandfather. But first she searched her pocket, and found that her money was all gone: not a sixpence remained.

The old man was ready, and in a few seconds they were on their road. The child thought he rather avoided her eye, and appeared to expect that she would tell him of her loss. She felt she must do that, or he might suspect the truth.

"Grandfather," she said in a tremulous voice, after they had walked about a mile in silence, "do you think they are honest people at the house yonder?"

"Why?" returned the old man trembling. "Do I think them honest?—yes, they played honestly."

"I'll tell you why I ask," rejoined Nell. "I lost some money last night, out of my bedroom, I am sure. Unless it was taken by somebody in jest,—only in jest, dear grandfather, which would make me laugh heartily if I could but know it"—

"Who would take money in jest?" returned the old man in a hurried manner. "Those who take money take it to keep. Don't talk of jest."

"Then it was stolen out of my room, dear," said the child, whose last hope was destroyed by the manner of this reply.

By tears and entreaties, Nell succeeds in leading her grandfather away from the old temptation, which has again beset him, and forms fresh hopes of saving him; but these are soon dissipated. Unseen, herself, she discovers him in company with the same gamblers, and witnesses their cunning endeavors to induce him to rob Mrs. Jarley in order to obtain the means of winning back all he had lost, and perhaps of securing still greater gains.

She went back to her own room, and tried to prepare herself for bed. But who could sleep—sleep! who could lie passively down — distracted by such terrors? They came upon her more and more strongly yet. Half-undressed, and with her hair in wild disorder, she flew to the old man's bedside, clasped him by the wrist, and roused him from his sleep.

"What's this!" he cried, starting up in bed, and fixing his eyes upon her spectral face.

"I have had a dreadful dream," said the child, with an energy that nothing but such terrors could have inspired, — "a dreadful, horrible dream! I have had it once before. It is a dream of gray-haired men, like you, in darkened rooms, by night, robbing sleepers of their gold. Up, up!" The old man shook in every joint, and folded his hands like one who prays.

"Not to me," said the child, — "not to me; to Heaven, to save us from such deeds! This dream is too real. I cannot sleep; I cannot stay here; I cannot leave you alone under the roof where such dreams come. Up! We must fly."

He looked at her as if she were a spirit, — she might have been for all the look of earth she had, — and trembled more and more.

"There is no time to lose; I will not lose one minute," said the child. "Up! and away with me."

"To-night?" murmured the old man.

"Yes, to-night," replied the child. "To-morrow night will be too late. The dream will have come again. Nothing but flight can save us. Up!"

The old man rose from his bed, his forehead bedewed with the cold sweat of fear, and, bending before the child as if she had been an angel messenger sent to lead him where she would, made ready to follow her. She took him by the hand, and led him on. As they passed the door of the room he had proposed to rob, she shuddered, and looked up into his face. What a white face was that! and with what a look did he meet hers!

She took him to her own chamber, and still holding him by the hand, as if she feared to lose him for an instant, gathered together the little stock she had, and hung her basket on her arm. The old man took his wallet from her hands, and strapped it on his shoulders, — his staff, too, she had brought away, — and then she led him forth.

They suffer much privation after this, and the old man complains piteously of hunger and fatigue; but the child trudges on, with less and less of hope and strength, indeed, but with an undiminished resolution to lead her sacred charge somewhere — anywhere, indeed — away from guilt and shame. At last they encounter Mr. Marton, a poor but kind-hearted schoolmaster, whom they had met once before. He is travelling on foot to a distant village, where he has been appointed clerk and teacher; and, on learning from Little Nell the full story of her trials and sufferings and wanderings, asks her and her grandfather to accompany him, promising to use his best endeavors to find them some humble occupation by which they can subsist. Little Nell gladly embraces his offer; and they journey on together. Arrived at the village, their kind friend exerts himself successfully in their behalf, procures them a pleasant home and a light employment in connection with the parish church, which brings them money enough to live on. But the quiet and happy life they begin to lead is destined to be of short duration. Long exposure and suffering have been too much for the child's delicate organization, and her health fails. Slowly, but surely, the end draws on, and at last she dies.

They had read and talked to her in the earlier portion of the night; but, as the hours crept on, she sunk to sleep. They could tell, by what she faintly uttered in her dreams, that they were of her journeyings with the old man; they were of no painful scenes, but of people who had helped and used them kindly; for she often said, "God bless you!" with great fervor. Waking, she never wandered in her mind but once; and that was of beautiful music which she said was in the air. God knows. It may have been.

Opening her eyes, at last, from a very quiet sleep, she begged that they would kiss her once again. That done, she turned to the old man with a lovely smile upon her face, — such, they said, as they had never seen, and never could forget, — and clung with both her arms about his neck. They did not know that she was dead at first.

She had spoken very often of the two sisters, who, she said, were like dear friends to her. She wished they could be told how much she thought about them, and how she had watched them as they walked together by the river-side at night. She would like to see poor Kit, she had often said of late. She wished there was somebody to take her love to Kit. And even then she never thought or spoke about him, but with something of her old, clear, merry laugh.

For the rest, she had never murmured or complained, but with a quiet mind, and manner quite unaltered, — save that she every day became more earnest and more grateful to them, — faded like the light upon a summer's evening. i–vi, ix–xii, xv–xix, xxiv–xxxii, xlii–xlvi, lii–lv, lxxi, lxxii.

**Trotters.** *See* HARRIS, MR.

**Vuffin.** A showman; proprietor of a giant, and of a little lady without legs or arms. xix.

**Wackles, Miss Jane.** Youngest daughter of Mrs. Wackles, and instructor in the art of needlework, marking, and samplery, in the "Ladies' Seminary" presided over by her mother. viii.

**Wackles, Miss Melissa.** Teacher of English grammar, composition, geography, and the use of the dumb-bells, in her mother's seminary for young ladies. She is the eldest daughter, and verges on the autumnal, having seen thirty-five summers, or thereabouts. viii.

**Wackles, Miss Sophy.** A fresh, good-humored, buxom girl of twenty; Mrs. Wackles's second daughter, and teacher of writing, arithmetic, dancing, and general fascination in the "Ladies' Seminary." An unsuccessful attempt is made to inveigle Swiveller into a match with Miss Sophy. viii.

**Wackles, Mrs.** Proprietor of a very small day-school for young ladies, at Chelsea; an excellent but rather venomous old lady of threescore, who takes special charge of the corporal punishment, fasting, and other tortures and terrors of the establishment. viii.

**West, Dame.** The grandmother of a favorite pupil of Mr. Marton's, the schoolmaster. xxv.

**Whisker.** A pony belonging to Mr. Garland, obstinate, independent, and freakish, but "a very good fellow, if you know how to manage him." xiv, xx, xxii, xxxviii, xl, lvii, lxi, lxv, lxviii, lxxiii.

**William, Sweet.** *See* SWEET WILLIAM.

**Witherden, Mr.** A notary; short, chubby, fresh-colored, brisk, and pompous. xiv, xx, xxxviii, xl, xli, lxi, lxiii, lxv, lxvi, lxxiii.

# BARNABY RUDGE

## OUTLINE

Chapter I On the 19th of March, 1775, it being a cold and stormy night, a little group of people were gathered in the Maypole Inn, on the borders of Epping Forest, about twelve miles from London. There were old John Willet, the innkeeper, Solomon Daisy, the sexton, a few other cronies, Joe Willet, old John's son, and two guests. Of the latter, one was Mr. Edward Chester, a handsome young man, who, having ridden down from London to see Miss Haredale, the niece of a country gentleman in the vicinity, was sadly disappointed to find that the young lady was away, and presently set off for London. The other was a morose, shabby, ill-looking man, who sat apart from the others, with a big slouch hat drawn over his eyes. The fire burned cheerfully; the highly polished boiler reflected the blaze, and every member of the company was accommodated with a pipe and a glass of grog. Under these favoring circumstances Solomon Daisy related how, on that very day of the month, two and twenty years before, a double murder had occurred, at dead of night, in Mr. Haredale's house, called the Warren. His only brother, Reuben Haredale, was found dead in his room. The steward and gardener were both missing; but months afterward a body, supposed to be that of Rudge, the steward, was found at the bottom of a piece of water near by, with a deep gash in the breast where he had been stabbed with a knife. It was concluded, therefore, that the gardener was the guilty person.

II This story being finished, the ill-looking stranger hastily rose, mounted his horse, struck Joe Willet roughly on the head with the butt end of his whip, and galloped away, through the mud and darkness, with such recklessness that he ran into the chaise of stout Gabriel Varden, the locksmith from London. But finding that his horse had not been hurt, he remounted and, with an oath, galloped away as furiously as before.

After this encounter Gabriel Varden thought it necessary to call at the Maypole to replace his lantern, which had become broken· and once there he could not resist the temptation to partake of the

good cheer. When at last the convivial company broke up, Joe
III Willet brought round the locksmith's horse, and confided to him his intention of running away to seek his fortune, rather than to endure any longer the humiliation of being treated like a child, as his father still considered him. "I am a by-word all over Chigwell," cried the unfortunate lad. Giving him some kindly advice, Gabriel, in a rather muzzy condition, set out for London. But hearing loud outcries as he neared the city, he turned aside from the road and found Barnaby Rudge waving a torch over his head, while at his feet lay the figure of a man who proved to be young Mr. Chester, — stabbed and robbed by a highwayman. Barnaby was the son of the widow Rudge, as she was called, her husband having been Rudge, the steward, whose dead body — at least it was believed to be his — was found under the circumstances already related. Barnaby, born after that terrible event, was of a disordered intellect. His hair, of which he had a great profusion, was red, and hanging in disorder about his face and shoulders, gave to his restless looks an expression quite unearthly. With Barnaby's assistance, though he was mortally afraid of blood, Varden carried Mr. Chester, who proved to be not seriously wounded, to the house of Barnaby's mother, congratulating himself upon having had an adventure which would silence Mrs. Varden on the subject of the Maypole for that night, or there was no faith in woman.

IV The locksmith's family consisted of his wife, his beautiful and bewitching daughter, Dolly, Miss Miggs, a cantankerous maid-servant, and Simon Tappertit, his apprentice. Sim was an old-fashioned, thin-faced, sleek-haired, sharp-nosed, small-eyed little fellow, not much more than five feet high, but fully convinced in his own mind that he was above the common height. He also had a majestic idea of the power of his eye, and he was accustomed to boast that he could subdue the haughtiest beauty by a simple process which he termed "eyeing her over." Such was Simon Tappertit, and it is needless to say that he was in love with his master's daughter.

V The following night Gabriel Varden called at the widow Rudge's house, and found that her patient was in a fair way to recover. While Varden was in the house, a strange thing happened. There came a muffled knock at the door, and a voice close to the window — a voice which the locksmith seemed to recollect, and with which he seemed to have some disagreeable association — whispered, "Make haste." The locksmith rushed to the door, but the widow followed, clung to him, and kept him from pursuit. "What does this mean?" cried the locksmith. "Don't ask," said the woman, in agitation. "He is not to be followed,

checked, or stopped." Perplexed by this action, Varden remained
VI within, and when Barnaby Rudge entered he went with
him to the chamber where Edward Chester lay, and heard
from the injured man the story of the attack he had suffered. He
felt sure that the fellow who had felled Chester and the visitor of the
evening were one and the same man, and was startled enough when
a hoarse voice right beside him cried, "What 's the matter here?
Keep up your spirits! Never say die! I 'm a devil, I 'm a devil!"
but this was only Grip, Barnaby's tame raven.

VII There were other men abroad on that night besides the
mysterious caller at the house of the widow Rudge. When
all was quiet, Simon Tappertit stole downstairs and out of the
VIII house, and repaired to a dingy cellar, where a secret club of
'prentices, headed by Simon himself, held their meetings,
and plotted insurrection and rebellion, and death to their masters.

IX But Miggs heard Simon go out. She plugged the keyhole
of the front door, and sat up all night till he came back, and
was forced to call upon his "Angelic Miggs" (she was then looking out of an upper window) to let him in. This done, "Simmun
is safe," she cried, and fainted away.

X Not long after that windy, rainy night on which this
story opened, the Maypole Inn had another notable guest.
This was Mr. Chester, senior, the father of Edward, who was soon
installed in the best room of the inn, with a good dinner ordered,
and Barnaby despatched as a messenger to Mr. Haredale at the
XI Warren, requesting an interview. This aroused great excitement among the cronies below, for it was well known
that Mr. Chester and Mr. Haredale had been for many years bitter
enemies. "Willet," said Solomon Daisy, "when Mr. Chester
come, did he order the large room?" "He signified, sir," said
John, "that he wanted a large apartment. Yes, certainly."
"Why, then, I 'll tell you what," said Solomon. "He and Mr.
XII Haredale are going to fight a duel in it." And the little
party below, Mr. Haredale having now arrived, and having
been ushered upstairs, listened with bated breath for the sound
of falling bodies. The gentlemen did not fight, however, though
their interview was a stormy one. For the first time in their lives
they came to an agreement, Mr. Chester through self-interest, Mr.
Haredale from pride and resentment. The agreement was that, by
hook or by crook, by fair means or foul, the engagement between
Mr. Chester's son and Mr. Haredale's niece, whom he dearly loved,
XIII should be broken. It was unfortunate for the lovers that
Joe Willet was away from home, for he might have discovered the intrigue. It happened that he had gone to London on

that very day, as he did twice every year, to pay the vintner's bill.
Joe had also a little errand of his own, which was to see the charming
Dolly. But alas! when he arrived at the locksmith's house,
Dolly was just setting out for an evening party. Joe soon mounted,
XIV and rode despondently home, meeting on the way Mr.
Edward Chester, who was bound for the Warren. Joe held
his horse, while Mr. Chester alighted. A maid-servant admitted
him; and after waiting a few minutes in the old and gloomy hall,
a lovely girl appeared whose dark hair, next moment, rested on his
breast. Almost at the same instant Mr. Haredale stepped between
them, thrust Edward away, and forbade him the house. So Edward
and Joe, thus hampered in their loves, betook themselves to
XV the Maypole; and the next day Edward, having returned to
London, was informed by his selfish father that he was expected
to retrieve the family fortunes by marrying an heiress; and
when he indignantly declined to make this sacrifice of his honor
and his inclinations, Mr. Chester, senior, coolly and politely cast
him off and disowned him.

XVI Among the worst and poorest vagrants and criminals who
haunted the dark places of London at this time was one
whose constant restlessness gave rise to strange stories. He was
always in motion, always alone. He had a pale, wild face, and
was never seen without a slouch hat pulled over his brows. This
man forced his way into the widow Rudge's house early one evening.
XVII "The very marrow in my bones," he said, "is cold
with wet and hunger. I must have warmth and food, and
I will have them here." The widow gave him food, and after he
had eaten like a wild animal he sat crouching before the low-burning
fire. A voice and a knock were heard at the door. The man
seized a knife from the table, hid it in his coat-sleeve, and slunk
into the closet, just as Barnaby opened the window and stepped
into the room with Grip on his back. An hour later, when Barnaby
had fallen asleep, the fellow crept out of his hiding-place,
gazed intently at the face of the sleeper, and said in a hoarse
whisper to the widow, "Observe. In him of whose existence I was
ignorant until to-night, I have you in my power. Be careful how
you use me. I am destitute and starving, and a wanderer upon
XVIII the earth. I may take a sure and slow revenge." Then he
went out into the darkness, and after wandering about the
streets till it was nearly morning, bargained his last shilling for
permission to lie down and sleep in that very cellar where Simon
Tappertit and his companions at an earlier hour held their revels.

XIX As soon as Edward Chester was able to go out, he came
to the locksmith's with a note for Miss Haredale, thinking

that Dolly, who was a sort of companion for the young lady, might be going to the Warren. And so it proved; and as the day was fine, Mrs. Varden was prevailed upon to join with her husband and her daughter in an excursion to the Maypole Inn. Great was old John Willet's astonishment at seeing her, but the whole party were soon ensconced within the bar, — the snuggest, cosiest bar in Christendom, full of all manner of good things: cheeses, tankards, lemons, Dutch pipes, bottles of old gin, and savory condiments. After dinner Dolly tripped over the fields to deliver her letter to Miss Haredale; and in return she received a reply for Mr. Chester and
XX a bracelet for herself. But on the way back to the inn she had a sad adventure. Maypole Hugh, a tall, rough, handsome fellow in a savage way, the hostler of the inn, met her in the
XXI path, snatched away the letter, the bracelet, and a kiss withal, and left poor Dolly almost fainting just as Joe Willet, in answer to her shriek, came to the rescue. But Hugh had disappeared before Joe arrived; and terrified by the threats he had made, Dolly did not dare to say who had robbed her, but pretended that it was a stranger. Joe, on horseback, accompanied the Varden
XXII family part way home, his hand resting occasionally on the little, white hand of Dolly at such times as Dolly quite unconsciously laid it upon the arm of the chaise.

XXIII Now Hugh's misdeed, so far, at least, as the letter was concerned, was directly incited by Mr. Chester, senior, to whom the letter intended for his son was very soon conveyed by Maypole Hugh. The theft of the bracelet was a little affair of his own; and Mr. Chester, learning of it, held it over Hugh as a whip, for in those days men were hanged for crimes no greater.
XXIV Mr. Chester had another visitor the same day, in the person of Simon Tappertit, who came to suggest that Mr. Chester should call upon Mrs. Varden, "flatter her up a bit," and through her intervention have a stop put to Dolly's acting as a messenger between Edward Chester and Miss Haredale. Mr. Tappertit also had a word to say about Joe Willet. "Sir," he said, "there is a villain at that Maypole, a monster in human shape, a vagabond of the deepest dye, that unless you get rid of will marry your son to that young woman as certainly and surely, as if he was the Archbishop of Canterbury himself. Put Joseph Willet down, sir. Destroy him. Crush him. And be happy."

XXV Meanwhile Mrs. Rudge, without giving any explanation of her conduct, renounced the pension or yearly sum which Mr. Haredale had paid her since the double murder at the Warren,
XXVI and disappeared from the house where she had been living, so that no trace of her could be discovered. Mr. Chester had

a hand in this, for reasons of his own, possibly to remove Barnaby,
who had acted as a messenger between the lovers; and when they
were gone, he called on Mrs. Varden, represented his son as an insin-
XXVII cere trifler, and plied the locksmith's wife with such seduc-
tive flattery that she was quite won over to his side in the af-
XXVIII fair of Miss Haredale. Hugh, having learned his lesson, not
only brought the next letter to Mr. Chester, but gave him
information which led him on the following day to make another ex-
XXIX cursion to the Maypole, whence he sought Miss Haredale, and
told her a false story of his son's inconstancy to her. As he
was about to leave the Maypole the next morning, Mr. Willet not be-
XXX ing on hand, Joe came out to hold his stirrup. Seeing this,
old John came diving out of the porch, and collared him.
"None of that, sir," said John. "None of that, sir. No breaking of
patroles" (for poor Joe was at that time in durance on account of
his mixing with the affair of the lovers). "How dare you come out
of the door, sir, without leave! You're trying to get away, sir, are
you? What do you mean, sir?" This crowning humiliation was
too much for poor Joe. That night he administered a thrashing
XXXI in the bar to Tom Cobb, one of his father's cronies, who
was particularly insolent to him, and before morning he
stole out of the house, walked up to London, and after a farewell
XXXII visit to Dolly, who pretended not to care, but burst into tears
as soon as he was gone, took the king's shilling, and enlisted
for foreign parts. Edward Chester, too, had a final parting with his
father, and, like Joe, disappeared from England for five long years.

XXXIII The 19th of March came around again, the year being
1780. The usual group was gathered at the Maypole,—
all except one, Solomon Daisy, the sexton, who was very late, notwithstanding that it was a night of cold, and bluster, and rain.
At last, after midnight, the little man tumbled in at the door, the
very image of fright and horror. The fact was that when he left
the church (after winding the clock) he had seen in the churchyard
a ghost,—or at least the bareheaded figure of a man, which he took
to be a ghost,—in the likeness of Rudge, the former steward. This
XXXIV intelligence was so startling that old John carried it that
very night to Mr. Haredale at the Warren, taking Hugh as
an escort. As they approached the house they saw a light in that
upper room where Mr. Haredale's brother had been murdered.

"It's snug enough, ain't it?" said Hugh.

"Snug!" said John indignantly. "You have a comfortable idea of snugness, you have, sir. Do you know what was done in that room, you ruffian?"

"Why, what is it the worse for that!" cried Hugh, looking into

John's fat face. "Does it keep out the rain, and snow, and wind, the less for that? Is it less warm or dry, because a man was killed there? Ha, ha, ha! Never believe it, master. One man 's no such matter as that comes to."

Mr. Willet fixed his dull eyes on his follower, and began, by a species of inspiration, to think it just barely possible that he was something of a dangerous character. On their way home,
XXXV three horsemen very nearly ran over them; but stopping to inquire the road, and finding that there was an inn in the neighborhood, the three persons, who were Lord George
XXXVI Gordon, his secretary, and his servant, put up at the Maypole. That night Gashford, the secretary, carefully dropped in the inn yard a printed handbill, addressed on the back, "To every Protestant into whose hands this shall come." On the other side was inscribed, "Whoever shall find this letter, will take it as a warning
XXXVII to join, without delay, the friends of Lord George Gordon." This paper was found by Hugh, who, within a few days, followed the party to London, and joined the mob of "No Popery"
XXXVIII rioters whom Lord George Gordon had stirred up. At London Hugh made two friends, one Dennis, a mysterious person, whose calling was not known to his associates, but who was
XXXIX really the common hangman, and our old friend Simon Tappertit, Captain of the Bull-Dogs, both ardent "No Popery" men. Hugh was greatly tickled with the notion of submitting himself to the little captain. The bare fact of being patronized by a great man whom he could have crushed with one hand appeared in his eyes so eccentric and humorous that a kind of ferocious
XL merriment took possession of him. He roared and roared again. Sir John Chester — for Edward Chester's father had now become Sir John — had a hand in Hugh's conversion to "No
XLI Popery," his motive being one of revenge upon his old enemy, Mr. Haredale, who was a Catholic; and it was due to the knight's fascinations that Mrs. Varden also became an enthusiast for
XLII the faith, keeping a little bank in her parlor, where sundry pence and shillings were accumulated for the cause, greatly to the disgust of Gabriel, who was a militiaman and wore a red
XLIII coat, and was a staunch upholder of law and order. There was another person, also, who hated Mr. Haredale, and had determined to use Hugh and the "No Popery" mob to injure him:
XLIV that was Gashford, the renegade Catholic, who served Lord George Gordon as secretary. It was just as these events were happening that Mrs. Rudge, seeking to escape that terrible visitor
XLV who had invaded her house in London, and by whom she had been tracked to the country, fled back to London, hoping

to hide herself and Barnaby there. On Westminster bridge they
XLVI met the "No Popery" mob, and Barnaby, recognizing in the
crowd his old friend Hugh of the Maypole, and pleased with
the idea of wearing a cockade in his hat, was drawn along with the
XLVII rest, leaving his poor mother, almost distracted, behind.
Hugh gave Barnaby the banner to carry, — an honor which
pleased and elated him immensely. His face flushed and his eyes
XLVIII sparkled with delight, — he was in fact the only light-hearted, undesigning creature in the whole assembly.
But it troubled him that his mother was absent. "Would n't it
XLIX make her glad," he said to Hugh, "to see me at the head of
this large show! Where *can* she be? She never sees me at
my best, and what do I care to be gay and fine if *she*'s not by?"
Hugh assured him that his mother should be well taken care of, and charged him to preserve the banner at all costs. "I warrant you," said Barnaby. "You have put it in good hands. You know me, Hugh. Nobody shall wrest this flag away."

"Well said!" cried Hugh. "Ha ha! Nobly said. That 's the old stout Barnaby that I have climbed and leaped with many a day." And on they went. Before the day was over Barnaby had a chance to show his prowess. When a troop of cavalry charged the mob, Barnaby stood his ground, and unhorsed the soldier who bore down upon him. After that, the mob flying, Hugh and he escaped to the Boot Inn.

L Simon Tappertit, captain of the Bull-Dogs, was engaged in
the same affair, and returned late at night to his master's
house, very much worse for liquor and fighting. He handed a dirty
LI piece of paper to Mrs. Varden, assuring her that she would
need it on the morrow for protection. On this paper, in the handwriting, as the locksmith perceived, of Lord George Gordon himself, was written a protection for the house, on the ground that it belonged to a Protestant and friend of the cause.

Having delivered this, Mr. Tappertit slipped from his master's grasp and escaped. Varden, to his wife's dismay, tore the paper into fragments, and declared: "I would n't beg or buy them off, if instead of every pound of iron in the house there was a hundred weight of gold. Get you to bed, Martha. I shall take down the shutters, and go to work."

LII For the next two days the rioters had their way in the
streets of London: the Catholic chapels were pillaged and
burned; the houses of Catholics were plundered and pulled down,
LIII and many who were, or were supposed to be, of that faith
were cruelly beaten and misused. Hugh had posted Barnaby as a sentry at the Boot Inn, while he and the rest were off

marauding; and when they came back, Hugh shook hands with him with a kind of ferocious friendship, strange enough to see. "How are you, boy?" "Hearty!" cried Barnaby, waving his hat.

On the following night, Barnaby was left alone again, Hugh and his companions having more work on hand. Some hours after they had departed, Gashford came out on the roof of his house, and sat there alone gazing westward till the darkness deepened. "Dog," he muttered, "where is the redness in the sky that you promised me?"

LIV But the mob was on the road. Old John Willet, who happened to be alone in the bar that evening, heard them coming, and went to the door, dazed and stupid. Shouting and whooping like savages, the mob rushed at the Maypole, pell-mell, and in a few seconds he was bandied from hand to hand in the heart of a crowd of men.

"Holloa!" cried a voice that he knew. "Where is he? Don't hurt him. How now, old Jack! Ha, ha, ha!"

Mr. Willet looked at him, and saw that it was Hugh; but he said nothing, and thought nothing.

"These lads are thirsty, and must drink!" cried Hugh, thrusting him back towards the house. "Bustle, Jack, bustle. Show us the best — the very best — the over-proof that you keep for your own drinking, Jack!"

John faintly articulated the words, "Who 's to pay?"

"He says, 'who 's to pay!'" cried Hugh, with a roar of laughter which was loudly echoed by the crowd. Then turning to John he added, "Pay! Why, nobody."

Then the crowd helped themselves; the neat and cheerful bar was wrecked and gutted in a trice; and everything in the house that was breakable destroyed. After this diversion the mob proposed to knock old John in the head. But Hugh would not consent. Instead, the landlord was bound fast to his chair, and the mob departed for the

LV Warren. They had been gone but a short time when Mr. Willet had a strange caller. A man wearing a slouch hat pulled low on his forehead, and with a pale, worn face and glittering eyes, looked in at the window. Finding that old John was alone, he entered the room, fell voraciously upon such fragments of bread and meat as had been left, drank the dregs from a wine cask, and demanded to know which way the rioters had taken. Old John replied with a nod of his head, and the man was hurrying to the door, when suddenly there came towards them on the wind the loud and rapid tolling of an alarm bell, and then a bright glare of fire streamed up, which illumined not only the whole chamber, but all the country. At the sound of that bell the man stopped in horror; his face was convulsed; his eyes started from his head. Then

with his right hand held aloft, and with a dreadful cry, he rushed away. The glare that shot up into the sky was that of the burning Warren. The rioters, maddened by drink and excitement, after breaking down the gates and beating in the doors, set fire to the whole building; but first they broke open the casks in the wine cellar; and many of them, falling dead drunk, were devoured by the flames. Others ran to and fro, stark mad, setting fire to themselves and to one another. On the skull of one drunken lad — not twenty by his looks — who lay upon the ground with a bottle to his mouth, the lead from the roof came streaming down in a shower of liquid fire, white hot, melting his head like wax. At last the flames died down; the rioters struggled homeward; Miss Haredale and Dolly were carried off as prisoners by Hugh and Simon Tappertit, and the dreadful scene was left to silence and to solitude. But
LVI presently the gallop of a horse approaching at a furious pace
might have been heard; and Mr. Haredale, fresh from London and the Maypole, and with little Solomon Daisy clinging behind him, reached the spot. He dismounted, searched the ruins, called loudly, but no one answered. They were about to go away when some of the ashes in the high tower, which was still intact, slipped and rolled down. Mr. Haredale started, in a whisper bade his companion to be silent, and looked and listened; then, with drawn sword, he stole into the turret and disappeared. Solomon Daisy stood rooted to the spot in mortal terror. Again the ashes slipped and rolled, — very softly, — and then again, as though they crumbled under the tread of a stealthy foot. And now a figure was dimly visible, climbing very softly, but it quickly disappeared. Again the figure was coming on, for its shadow was already thrown upon the wall. Now it appeared, — and now looked round at him, — and now the horror-stricken sexton uttered a scream that pierced the air, and cried, "The ghost! The ghost!"

At the same moment, another form rushed out into the light, flung itself upon the foremost one, knelt down upon its breast, and clutched its throat with both hands.

"Villain!" cried Mr. Haredale, in a terrible voice, — for it was he. "You, Rudge, double murderer and monster, I arrest you in the name of God!"

Meanwhile, Barnaby, though he made a stout resistance,
LVII was captured at his post by a company of soldiers, and
LVIII lodged in Newgate, as Hugh was informed when he re-
LIX turned to the Boot Inn after depositing Miss Haredale and
Dolly in an obscure house in London, where they were
LX guarded by a party of his followers. Rudge the murderer
LXI was also placed in the same prison, Mr. Haredale having

LXII brought him bound to London. And in that place Barnaby and his father met for the first time in their lives.

The mob were now bent upon releasing the prisoners in Newgate,
LXIII Hugh, especially, having sworn a mighty oath that Barnaby should be set free. It was known that Gabriel Varden had made the great lock of the prison, and the first move of the rioters was to his house, Hugh and Simon Tappertit being as usual in the van. Finding all the doors and windows shut and barred, they were about to set fire to the house, when the locksmith appeared at an upper window, gun in hand, determined to resist to the death.

"Burn the door," commanded Hugh. "Stop!" cried the locksmith, in a voice that made them falter, presenting his gun as he spoke. "Let an old man do that, you can spare him better." The young fellow who held the light, and who was stooping before the door, rose hastily and fell back, and the whole mob paused irresolute. But at that moment Miggs appeared at another window. "Don't mind his gun," she screamed. "Simmun and gentlemen, I poured a mug of table beer right down the barrel." The mob roared and laughed, burst in the doors, and captured the locksmith, but not until he had wounded two men. Some were for hanging
LXIV him in short order, but the leaders, taking a basket of his tools also, bore him off to Newgate. Then ensued a terrible scene. The rioters demanded that he should pick the lock, but Gabriel bravely refused. From threats they came to blows. Dennis struck him in the face, and knocked him down, but Varden was up in a moment, and caught the hangman by the throat. They struggled together. Some cried, "Kill him!" Some strove to kick and trample him to death. Suddenly a tall fellow, fresh from a slaughter-house, whose dress and great thigh boots smoked hot with grease and blood, raised a pole-axe, and, swearing a horrible oath, aimed it at the old man's uncovered head. But at that very instant he fell himself, as if struck by lightning, and over his body a one-armed man came darting to the locksmith's side. Another man was with him, and both caught the locksmith in their grasp. "Leave him to us," they cried to Hugh. "Remember the prisoners, remember Barnaby." Then the two men fought their way back, as if they were among enemies, and carried the locksmith with
LXV them. And now the mob attacked the prison in good earnest. Finding that the doors, which were very massive, resisted their efforts, they set fire to the building, and soon the whole mass was in flames. The mob poured in and freed the prisoners, Barnaby and his father among the rest.

LXVI Quite unconscious of the fact that the murderer whom he had sought for so many years was at liberty again, Mr. Hare-

dale found himself houseless and homeless in London, for even the
tavern-keepers dared not take in a Catholic. But in this predicament
he was rescued by that same vintner, a Catholic himself, who sup-
LXVII plied the ample cellars of the Maypole Inn. It was night
again, and the streets were now a dreadful spectacle. The
soldiers had been called out, chains had been drawn across the main
thoroughfares, and there was bloody fighting in a hundred places.
One object of attack was the vintner's house. The leader at this
point was a man mounted upon a brewer's horse of immense size
and strength, about whose neck, like a collar, was a string of mana-
cles and fetters, taken from Newgate prisoners, which clashed and
jingled as he went. Hugh, for Hugh it was, mad with liquor and
excitement, led the mob upon the vintner's house; and seeing Mr.
Haredale by the light of the burning buildings, he called to him
by name and swore to have his life. But just as the mob poured
in at the front of the vintner's house, the same one-armed man, with
his companion, who had rescued the locksmith, entered the house
LXVIII from the rear, and took the vintner and Mr. Haredale to a
place of safety. These two men were Joe Willet, returned
from the wars with the loss of an arm, and Edward Chester.

LXIX Hugh, wounded at last, fell from his horse; and though
already frantic with drinking and with the wound in his
head, he crawled to a stream of burning spirit which ran from the
vintner's cellar, and began to drink from it as if it were a brook of
LXX water. Barnaby, however, was at hand, and carried Hugh
off to the Boot Inn, where he had already taken his father,
the murderer. Here they lay till the soldiers came (guided by
Dennis, who had turned traitor), and carried all three to prison.

LXXI The mob was, by this time, thoroughly put down. Miss
Haredale and Dolly were found in the wretched house where
they had been kept prisoners, Mr. Haredale, the locksmith, Joe, and
LXXII Edward bursting in, and knocking down all who stood in
their way, so that there was such a meeting of friends, relatives, and lovers as never took place before.

LXXIII Very different was the meeting of poor Mrs. Rudge with
her son, for their reunion was in the prison, where Barnaby lay under a sentence of death, as did his father, as did Hugh,
LXXIV as did Dennis the hangman, whose treachery had not availed
to save his life. The locksmith made one effort for Hugh.
He had been told by Dennis, what was the truth, that Hugh's fa-
LXXV ther was no other than Sir John Chester, his mother having
been a gipsy girl who was hanged at Tyburn. This information Varden communicated to Sir John, but he, affecting to dis-
believe it, left Hugh to his fate. Great efforts were made to save

poor Barnaby, but they came to nothing; and the day of the exe-
LXXVI cution arrived. The scaffold was up, the condemned men
were brought out, there was an immense throng of silent
spectators. Dennis, the hangman, howled upon his knees for
LXXVII mercy, a pitiable object. Hugh and Barnaby were brave
and calm. Barnaby was to be hanged an hour later in
Bloomsbury Square,—the others in the prison yard. They asked
Hugh if he had anything to say.

"To say!" he cried. "Not I. I'm ready.—Yes," he added, as his eye fell upon Barnaby, "I have a word to say, too. Come hither, lad."

There was, for the moment, something kind, and even tender, struggling in his fierce aspect, as he wrung his poor companion by the hand. "I'll say this," he cried, looking firmly round, "that if I had ten lives to lose, and the loss of each would give me ten times the agony of the hardest death, I'd lay them all down—ay, I would, though you gentlemen may not believe it—to save this one. This one," he added, wringing Barnaby's hand again, "that will be lost through me."

"Not through you," said the idiot mildly. "Don't say that. You were not to blame. You have been always very good to me.—Hugh, we shall know what makes the stars shine, *now!*"

"I took him from her in a reckless mood, and didn't think what harm would come of it," said Hugh, laying his hand upon Barnaby's head, and speaking in a lower voice; "I ask her pardon, and his."

Then were hanged Hugh of the Maypole, Dennis the hangman,
Rudge the murderer. But Barnaby was reprieved at the last mo-
LXXVIII ment; and for the rest of his life he and his mother lived
peacefully and happily at the Maypole, where Joe, having
married Dolly, revived the former glories of that fine old inn. Mr.
LXXIX Haredale killed Sir John Chester in a duel with swords,
and flying to the continent, passed the short remainder of
his life in a monastery. Edward Chester married Miss Haredale,
LXXX and rebuilt the Warren. Old John, whose intellect never
quite recovered from the shock of the riot, was installed in
a little cottage near the Maypole, where a miniature bar, exactly
LXXXI like that of the inn, the boiler included, was fitted up for
him; and where he entertained, as before, Solomon Daisy
and his other old cronies. The scores which he added up against
LXXXII them for pipes of tobacco and glasses of grog were of
enormous size; and great was the satisfaction which old
John derived from secretly contemplating these fictitious accounts
inscribed upon a blackboard behind the bar.

# INDEX TO CHARACTERS

**Akerman, Mr.** Head jailer at Newgate. lxiv, lxxvi.

**Black Lion, The.** Landlord of a London inn of the same name; so called because he had instructed the artist who painted his sign to convey into the features of the lordly brute whose effigy it bore as near a counterpart of his own face as his skill could compass and devise. He is such a swigger of beer that most of his faculties have been utterly drowned and washed away, except the one great faculty of sleep, which he retains in surprising perfection. xxxi.

**Chester, Mr.,** afterwards **Sir John.** An elegant and punctiliously polite, but thoroughly heartless and unprincipled gentleman; intended as a portrait of Lord Chesterfield (Philip Dormer Stanhope), who was equally celebrated for his polished grace of manner, his loose morality, and his love of intrigue. Mr. Chester attempts, but unsuccessfully, to break off the match between his son Edward and Miss Emma Haredale, both because the girl is poor, and because he is bent on an alliance which will add to his own wealth and importance. x–xii, xiv, xv, xxiii, xxiv, xxvi–xxx, xxxii, xl, xliii, liii, lxxv, lxxxi.

**Chester, Edward.** His son; in love with and finally married to Miss Emma Haredale. i, ii, v, vi, xiv, xv, xix, xxix, xxxii, lxvii, lxxi, lxxii, lxxix, lxxxii.

**Cobb, Tom.** General chandler and post-office keeper; a crony of old Willet's, and a frequent visitor at the Maypole Inn. i, xxx, xxxiii, liv.

**Conway, General.** A member of Parliament, and an opponent of Lord George Gordon. xlix.

**Daisy, Solomon.** Parish clerk and bell-ringer of Chigwell; a little man, with little round, black, shining eyes like beads, and studded all down his rusty black coat, and his long flapped waistcoat, with queer little buttons, like nothing except his eyes, but so like them that he seems all eyes from head to foot. i–iii, xi, xxx, xxxiii, liv, lvi.

**Dennis, Ned.** Ringleader of the Gordon rioters. Having formerly been a hangman, and therefore entertaining a profound respect for the law, he desires that everything should be done in a constitutional way. Yet, as an adept in the art of "working people off," he thinks it the better and neater method to hang everybody who stands in the way of the rioters; and he is frequently disgusted by the refusal of his fellow-insurgents to adopt his suggestions. When the riot is at last suppressed, and Dennis is arrested, and condemned to death, he suddenly discovers that the satisfaction which he has experienced for so many years in executing the capital sentence upon his fellow-mortals was, in all probability, not shared by the subjects of his skill; and he shrinks in the most abject fear from his fate.

"No reprieve, no reprieve! Nobody comes near us. There's only the night left now!" moaned Dennis faintly, as he wrung his hands. "Do you think they'll reprieve me in the night, brother? I've known reprieves come in the night, afore now. I've known 'em come as late as five, six, and seven o'clock in the morning. Don't you think there's a good chance yet; don't you? Say you do. Say *you* do, young man," whined the miserable creature, with an imploring gesture towards Barnaby, "or I shall go mad!"

"Better be mad than sane here," said Hugh. "*Go* mad!"

"But tell me what you think. Somebody tell me what he thinks!" cried the wretched object, — so mean and wretched and despicable, that even Pity's self might have turned away at sight of such a being in the likeness of a man. "Is n't there a chance for me? is n't there a good chance for me? Is n't it likely they may be doing this to frighten me? Don't you think it is? Oh!" he almost shrieked as he wrung his hands, "won't anybody give me comfort?"

"You ought to be the best, instead of the worst," said Hugh, stopping before him. "Ha, ha, ha! See the hangman when it comes home to him!"

"You don't know what it is," cried Dennis, actually writhing as he spoke: "I do. That I should come to be worked off! — I, I, — that *I* should come!"

"And why not?" said Hugh, as he thrust back his matted hair to get a better view of his late associate. "How often, before I knew your trade, did I hear you talking of this as if it was a treat!"

"I ain't unconsistent!" screamed the miserable creature. "I'd talk so again, if I was hangman. Some other man has got my old opinions at this minute. That makes it worse. Somebody's longing to work me off. I know by myself that somebody must be."

"He'll soon have his longing," said Hugh, resuming his walk. "Think of that, and be quiet." xxxvi–xl, xliv, xlix, l, lii–liv, lix, lx, lxiii–lxv, lxix–lxxi, lxxiv–lxxvii.

**Gashford, Mr.** Lord George Gordon's secretary; a tall, bony, high-shouldered, and angular man.

His dress, in imitation of his superior, was demure and staid in the extreme; his manner formal and constrained. This gentleman had an overhanging brow, great hands and feet and ears, and a pair of eyes that seemed to have made an unnatural retreat into his head, and to have dug themselves a cave to hide in. His manner was smooth and humble, but very sly and slinking. He wore the aspect of a man that was always lying in wait for something that *would n't* come to pass; but he looked patient (very patient), and fawned like a spaniel dog. xxxv–xxxviii, xliii, xliv, xlviii–l, lii, liii, lxxi, lxxxii.

**Gilbert, Mark.** One of the "'Prentice Knights, or United Bull-Dogs," a secret society formed by the apprentices of London for the purpose of resisting the tyranny of their masters. On the occasion of Mark's admission to this organization, he is thus described:—

"Age nineteen. Bound to Thomas Curzon, hosier, Golden Fleece, Aldgate. Loves Curzon's daughter. Cannot say that Curzon's daughter loves him. Should think it probable. Curzon pulled his ears last Tuesday week." viii, xxxix.

**Gordon, Colonel.** Member of Parliament, and an opponent of his kinsman Lord George Gordon. xlix.

**Gordon, Lord George.** Third son of Cosmo George, third duke of Gordon; born Sept. 19, 1750; noted as the chief instigator of the Protestant or "No Popery" riots, which took place in London in 1780, and were a result of the passage of a bill by Parliament relieving Roman Catholics from certain disabilities and penalties. In these riots (which lasted for several days) many Roman Catholic churches were destroyed, as were also Newgate Prison, the residence of Lord Chief Justice Mansfield, and numerous other private dwellings. Lord George was arrested on a charge of high treason, and was committed to the Tower; but, the offence not having been proved, he was acquitted. He died Nov. 1, 1793. Dickens's descriptions of this misguided man, and of the dreadful scenes in which he was the chief actor, are not only graphic and vigorous, but faithful to the facts of history. xxxv–xxxvii, xliii, xlviii–l, lvii, lxxiii, lxxxii.

**Green, Tom.** A soldier. lviii.

**Grip.** A raven; the constant companion of Barnaby Rudge; a very knowing bird, supposed to be a hundred and twenty years old, or thereabouts.

The widow tried to make light of Barnaby's remark, and endeavored to divert his attention to some new subject,—too easy a task at all times, as she knew. His supper done, Barnaby, regardless of her entreaties, stretched himself on the mat before the fire (Grip perched upon his leg), and divided his time between dozing in the grateful warmth, and endeavoring (as it presently appeared) to recall a new accomplishment he had been studying all day.

A long and profound silence ensued, broken only by some change of position on the part of Barnaby, whose eyes were still wide open, and intently fixed upon the fire, or by an effort of recollection on the part of Grip, who would cry in a low voice from time to time, "Polly, put the ket" — and there stop short, forgetting the remainder, and go off in a doze again.

After a long interval, Barnaby's breathing grew more deep and regular, and his eyes were closed. But even then the unquiet spirit of the raven interposed. "Polly, put the ket," — cried Grip; and his master was broad awake again.

At length he slept soundly; and the bird, with his bill sunk upon his breast, his breast itself puffed out into a comfortable alderman-like form, and his bright eye growing smaller and smaller, really seemed to be subsiding into a state of repose. Now and then he muttered in a sepulchral voice, "Polly, put the ket," — but very drowsily, and more like a drunken man than a reflecting raven.

The widow, scarcely venturing to breathe, rose from her seat. The man glided from the closet, and extinguished the candle.

"— tle on," cried Grip, suddenly struck with an idea, and very much excited. "— tle on. Hurrah! Polly, put the ket-tle on: we'll all have tea. Polly, put the ket-tle on: we'll all have tea. Hurrah, hurrah, hurrah! I'm a devil, I'm a devil, I'm a ket-tle on. Keep up your spirits. Never say die. Bow wow wow! I'm a devil, I'm a ket-tle, I'm a, — Polly, put the ket-tle on: we'll all have tea."

They stood rooted to the ground, as though it had been a voice from the grave.

But even this failed to awaken the sleeper. He turned over towards the fire; his arm fell to the ground; and his head drooped heavily upon it. v, vi, x, xvii, xxv, xlv–xlvii, lvii, lviii, lxviii, lxxiii, lxxv–lxxvii, lxxix, lxxxii.

**Grueby, John.** Servant to Lord George Gordon; a square-built, strong-made, bull-necked fellow, of the true English breed, self-possessed, hard-headed, and imperturbable. xxxv, xxxvii, xxxviii, lvii, lxvi, lxxxii.

**Haredale, Mr. Geoffrey.** A country gentleman, burly in person, stern in disposition, rough and abrupt in manner, but thoroughly honest and unselfish. He resides at a mansion called "The Warren," on the borders of Epping Forest, and not far from the Maypole Inn. Being a rigid Roman Catholic, he is made a special object of vengeance by the Lord Gordon mob. He kills Sir John Chester in a duel, and thereupon quits England forever, ending his days in the seclusion of an Italian convent. i, x–xii, xiv, xx, xxv–xxvii, xxix, xxxiv, xlii, xliii, lvi, lxi, lxvi, lxvii, lxxi, lxxvi, lxxix, lxxxi, lxxxii.

**Haredale, Miss Emma.** His niece; daughter of Mr. Reuben Haredale, who is mysteriously murdered. She is finally married to Edward Chester. i, iv, xii–xv, xx, xxv, xxvii–xxix, xxxii, lix, lxx, lxxi, lxxix, lxxxi.

**Hugh.** A wild, athletic, gipsy-like young fellow, with something fierce and sullen in his features. He is at first a hostler at the Maypole Inn, and afterwards a leader in the Gordon riots. He turns out to be a natural son of Sir John Chester, who, when urged to save him from the gallows, treats the appeal with the utmost *sang froid,* and permits him to be executed without making the least effort in his behalf. x–xii, xx, xxii, xxiii, xxviii, xxix, xxxiv, xxxv, xxxvii–xl, xliv, xlviii–l, lii–liv, lix, lx, lxiii–lxv, lxvii–lxix, lxxiv, lxxvi–lxxviii.

**Langdale, Mr.** A vintner and distiller; a portly, purple-faced, and choleric old gentleman. xiii, lxi, lxvi, lxvii, lxxxi.

**Miggs, Miss.** The single domestic servant of Mrs. Varden.

> This Miggs was a tall young lady, very much addicted to pattens in private life; slender and shrewish, of a rather uncomfortable figure, and, though not absolutely ill-looking, of a sharp and acid visage. As a general principle and abstract proposition, Miggs held the male sex to be utterly contemptible and unworthy of notice; to be fickle, false, base, sottish, inclined to perjury, and wholly undeserving. When particularly exasperated against them (which, scandal said, was when Sim Tappertit slighted her most), she was accustomed to wish, with great emphasis, that the whole race of women could but die off in order that the men might be brought to know the real value of the blessings by which they set so little store: nay, her feeling for her order ran so high, that she sometimes declared, if she could only have good security for a fair round number — say ten thousand — of young virgins following her example, she would, to spite mankind, hang, drown, stab, or poison herself with a joy past all expression.

When the Gordon riot breaks out, she forsakes her old master and mistress to follow and watch over Mr. Sim Tappertit. After the dispersion of the rioters, Miss Miggs returns to Mr. Varden's house, quite as a matter of course, expecting to be reinstated in her old situation. But Mrs. Varden, who is at first amazed at her audacity, orders her to leave the house instanter; whereupon the young lady relieves her mind after this wise: —

"I 'm quite delighted, I 'm sure, to find sich independency; feeling sorry, though, at the same time, mim, that you should have been forced into submissions when you could n't help yourself. He, he, he! It must be great vexations, 'specially considering how ill you always spoke of Mr. Joe, to have him for a son-in-law at last; and I wonder Miss Dolly can put up with him, either, after being off and on so many years with a coachmaker. But I *have* heerd say that the coachmaker thought twice about it, — he, he, he! — and that he told a young man as was a friend of his, that he hoped he knowed better than to be drawed into that, though she and all the family *did* pull uncommon strong."

Here she paused for a reply, and, receiving none, went on as before: —

"I *have* heerd say, mim, that the illnesses of some ladies was all pretensions, and that they could faint away stone-dead whenever they had the inclinations so to do. Of course, I never see sich cases with my own eyes: ho, no! — he, he, he! — nor master, neither: ho, no! He, he, he! I *have* heerd the neighbors make remark as some one as they was acquainted with was a poor good-natur'd, mean-spirited creetur as went out fishing for a wife one day, and caught a Tartar. Of course, I never, to my knowledge, see the poor person himself; nor did you, neither, mim: ho, no! I wonder who it can be; don't you, mim? No doubt you do, mim. Ho, yes! He, he, he!"

Cast upon a thankless, undeserving world, and baffled in all her schemes, matrimonial and otherwise, Miss Miggs turns sharper and sourer than ever. It happens, however, that, just at this time, a female turnkey is wanted for the county Bridewell, and a day and hour is appointed for the inspection of candidates. Miss Miggs attends, and is instantly chosen from a hundred and twenty-four competitors, and installed in office, which she holds till her decease, more than thirty years afterwards. vii, ix, xiii, xviii, xix, xxii, xxvii, xxxi, xxxvi, xxxix, xli, li, lxiii, lxx, lxxi, lxxx, lxxxii.

**Parkes, Phil.** A ranger who frequents the Maypole Inn; a tall man, very taciturn, and a profound smoker. i, xi, xxx, xxxiii, liv.

**Peak.** Sir John Chester's valet. xxiii, xxiv, xxxii, lxxv, lxxxii.

**Recruiting Sergeant, The.** A military officer in whose regiment Joe Willet enlists. xxxi.

**Rudge, Barnaby.** A fantastic youth, half-crazed, half-idiotic. Wandering listlessly about at the time of the Gordon riot, he is overtaken by the mob, and eagerly joins them in their work of destruction. His strength and agility make him a valuable auxiliary; and he continues fighting, until he is at last overpowered, arrested, and condemned to death. "Aha, Hugh!" says he to his companion on the eve of their execution, "we shall know what makes the stars shine *now*." A pardon is finally procured for him by Mr. Varden. iii–vi, x–xii, xvii, xxv, xxvi, xlv–l, lii, liii, lvii, lviii, lx, lxii, lxv, lxviii, lxix, lxxiii, lxxv–lxxvii, lxxix, lxxxii.

**Rudge, Mrs.** Mother of Barnaby. iv–vi, xvi, xvii, xxv, xxvi, xlii, xlv–l, lvii, lxii, lxix, lxxiii, lxxvi, lxxix, lxxxii.

**Rudge, Mr.** Father of Barnaby, and a former steward of Reuben Haredale's. One morning in the year 1733, Mr. Haredale is found murdered, and the steward is missing. Afterwards a body is discovered, which is supposed to be that of Rudge; but it is so disfigured as not to be recognizable. After the lapse of many years, it is proved that Rudge was the real murderer, and that the body which was taken to be his was really that of another of his victims. He is finally captured and executed. i–iii, v, vi, xvi–xviii, xxxiii, xlv, xlvi, lv, lvi, lxi, lxii, lxv, lxviii, lxix, lxxiii, lxxvi.

**Stagg.** A blind man; proprietor of a drinking-cellar and skittle-ground. viii, xviii, xlv, xlvi, lxii, lxix.

**Tappertit, Simon.** Apprentice to Mr. Gabriel Varden, and a sworn enemy to Joe Willet, who has rivalled him in the affections of his master's daughter Dolly.

Sim . . . was an old-fashioned, thin-faced, sleek-haired, sharp-nosed, small-eyed little fellow, very little more than five feet high, and thoroughly convinced in his own mind that he was above the middle size, — rather tall, in fact, than otherwise. Of his figure, which was well enough formed, though somewhat of the leanest, he entertained the highest admiration; and with his legs, which, in knee-breeches, were perfect curiosities of littleness, he was enraptured to a degree amounting to enthusiasm. . . . Add to this that he was in years just twenty, in his looks much older, and in conceit at least two hundred; that he had no objection to be jested with touching his admiration of his master's daughter; and had even, when called upon at a certain obscure tavern to pledge the lady whom he had honored with his love, toasted with many winks and leers a fair creature, whose Christian name, he said, began with a D [Dolly Varden].

Mr. Tappertit is captain of the "'Prentice Knights" (afterwards called the "United Bull-Dogs"), whose objects were vengeance on their tyrant masters (of whose grievous and insupportable oppression no 'prentice could entertain a moment's doubt), and the restoration of their ancient rights and holidays. He takes a leading part in the Lord George Gordon riots, but finally receives a gun-shot wound in his body, and has his precious legs crushed into shapeless ugliness. After being removed from a hospital to prison, and thence to his place of trial, he is discharged, by proclamation, on two wooden legs. By the advice and aid of his old master, to whom he applies for assistance, he is established in business as a shoe-black, and quickly secures a great run of custom: so that he thinks himself justified in taking to wife the widow of an eminent bone and rag collector. iv, vii–ix, xviii, xix, xxii, xxiv, xxvii, xxxi, xxxvi, xxxix, xlviii–lii, lix, lx, lxii, lxx, lxxi, lxxxii.

**Varden, Dolly.** A bright, fresh, coquettish girl, the very impersonation of good-humor and blooming beauty. She is finally married to Joe Willet. iv, xiii, xix–xxii, xxvii, xxxi, lix, lxx, lxxi.

**Varden, Gabriel.** A frank, hearty, honest old locksmith, at charity with all mankind; father to Dolly Varden. ii–vii, xiii, xiv, xix, xxi, xxii, xxvi, xxvii, xli, xlii, li, lxiii, lxiv, lxxi, lxxii, lxxiv–lxxvi, lxxix, lxxx, lxxxii.

**Varden, Mrs. Martha.** His wife.

Mrs. Varden was a lady of what is commonly called an uncertain temper, — a phrase, which, being interpreted, signifies a temper tolerably certain to make everybody more or less uncomfortable. Thus it generally happened, that, when other people were merry, Mrs. Varden was dull; and that, when other people were dull, Mrs. Varden was disposed to be amazingly cheerful. Indeed, the worthy housewife was of such a capricious nature, that she not only attained a higher pitch of genius than Macbeth, in respect of her ability to be wise, amazed, temperate and furious, loyal and neutral, in an instant, but would sometimes ring the changes backwards and forwards on all possible moods and flights in one short quarter of an hour; performing, as it were, a kind of triple bob major on the peal of instruments in the female belfry, with a skilfulness and rapidity of execution that astonished all who heard her.

It had been observed in this good lady (who did not want for personal attractions, being plump and buxom to look at, though, like her fair daughter, somewhat short in stature), that this uncertainty of disposition strengthened and increased with her temporal prosperity; and divers wise men and matrons on friendly terms with the locksmith and his family even went so far as to assert, that a tumble down some half-dozen rounds in the world's ladder — such as the breaking of the bank in which her husband kept his money, or some little fall of that kind — would be the making of her, and could hardly fail to render her one of the most agreeable companions in existence. iv, vii, xiii, xix, xxi, xxii, xxvii, xxxvi, xli, xlii, li, lxxi, lxxii, lxxx, lxxxii.

**Willet, John.** Landlord of the Maypole Inn at Chigwell; a burly, large-headed man, with a fat face, which betokened profound obstinacy and slowness of apprehension, combined with a very strong reliance upon his own merits.

The Maypole was an old building with more gable-ends than a lazy man would care to count on a sunny day; huge zigzag chimneys, out of which it seemed as if smoke could not choose but come in more than naturally fantastic shapes imparted to it in its tortuous progress; and vast stables, gloomy, ruinous, and empty. The place was said to have been built in the days of King Henry the Eighth. . . . Its windows were old diamond-pane lattices; its floors were sunken and uneven; its ceiling blackened by the hand of time, and heavy with massive beams. Over the doorway was an ancient porch quaintly and grotesquely carved; and here, on summer evenings, the more favored customers smoked and drank, — ay, and sung many a good song too, sometimes, — reposing on two grim-looking, high-backed settles, which, like the twin dragons of some fairy-tale, guarded the entrance to the mansion. . . . All bars are snug places; but the Maypole's was the very snuggest, cosiest, and completest bar that ever the wit of man devised. Such amazing bottles in old oaken pigeon-holes! such sturdy little Dutch kegs, ranged in rows on shelves! so many lemons, hanging in separate nets, and forming the fragrant grove already mentioned in this chronicle, suggestive, with goodly cans and snowy sugar stowed away hard by, of punch idealized beyond all mortal knowledge! such closets! such presses! such places for putting things away in hollow window-seats! — all crammed to the throat with eatables, drinkables, or savory condiments; lastly, and to crown all, as typical of the immense resources of the establishment, and its defiance to all visitors to cut and come again, such a stupendous cheese! i–iii, x–xiv, xix, xx, xxiv, xxix, xxx, xxxiii–xxxv, liv–lvi, lxxii, lxxviii, lxxxii.

**Willet, Joe.** Son of John Willet; a broad-shouldered, strapping young fellow, whom it pleases his father still to consider a little boy, and to treat accordingly. After being bullied, badgered, worried, fretted, and brow-beaten, until he can endure it no longer, Joe runs away and joins the army. At the time of the London riots, however, he turns up, and renders good service to his friends, notwithstanding the loss of an arm at the siege of Savannah. The father is only too glad to welcome him back; never speaks of him to a stranger afterwards, without saying proudly, "My son's arm was took off at the defence of the — Salwanners — in America, where the war is." Joe finally marries Dolly Varden, whom he has long loved. i–iii, xiii, xiv, xix, xxi, xxii, xxx, xxxi, xli, lviii, lxvii, lxxi, lxxii, lxxviii, lxxx, lxxxii.

# MASTER HUMPHREY'S CLOCK

## INDEX TO CHARACTERS

**Alice, Mistress.** Heroine of the tale told by Magog, the Guildhall giant, to his companion, Gog; the beautiful and only daughter of a wealthy London bowyer of the sixteenth century. She elopes with a gay young cavalier, by whom she is conveyed abroad, where shame and remorse overtake her, and wring her heart. Her father, dying, leaves all his property and trade to a trusted 'prentice, named Hugh Graham, charging him with his latest breath to revenge his child upon the author of her misery, if ever he has the opportunity. Twenty years afterwards, Alice suddenly returns; and Master Graham (who was formerly an aspirant for her hand, and who still loves her) gives her lodging in his house, — once hers, — taking up his own abode in a dwelling near by. Soon after, he encounters the man who wrought her ruin. The two exchange a few high, hot words, and then close in deadly contest. After a brief struggle, the noble falls, pierced through the heart with his own sword by the citizen. A riot ensues; and at last Graham is shot dead on his own doorstep. On carrying him up stairs, an unknown woman is discovered lying lifeless beneath the window.

**Belinda.** A distracted damsel, who writes a letter to Master Humphrey about her faithless lover.

**Benton, Miss.** Master Humphrey's housekeeper. Mr. Weller, senior, in a moment of weakness, falls in love with her: but she prefers Mr. Slithers the barber; and the old gentleman, recovering his "native hue of resolution," conjures his son Samivel to put him in a strait waistcoat until the fit is passed, in the event of his ever becoming amorous again.

**Deaf Gentleman, The.** An intimate friend of Master Humphrey's, and a cheerful, placid, happy old man. It is his humor to conceal his name, or he has a reason and purpose for doing so. Master Humphrey and the other members of the club respect his secret, therefore; and he is known among them only as the Deaf Gentleman.

**Gog.** One of the Guildhall giants.

**Graham, Hugh.** A bowyer's 'prentice, in love with his master's daughter.

**Jinkinson.** The subject of an anecdote related by Sam Weller.

**Magog.** One of the Guildhall giants. *See* TODDYHIGH, JOE.

**Marks, Will.** The hero of a tale which Mr. Pickwick submits to Master Humphrey and his friends as a "qualification" for admission to their club. Will is a wild, roving young fellow, living at Windsor in the time of James I. He volunteers to keep watch by night at a gibbet near Kingston, for the purpose of identifying some witches who have been holding hideous nocturnal revels there; but he finds, instead of witches, two gentlewomen, weeping and wailing for an executed husband and brother. He suffers himself to be conducted to Putney, where he is introduced to a masked cavalier, who induces him to take the body of the dead man by night for burial to St. Dunstan's Church in London. This task, though a difficult and dangerous one, he performs; and on his return home, finding the whole neighborhood worked up to a high pitch of mystery and horror over his disappearance, he adds to the excitement by telling them a most extraordinary story of his adventures, describing the witches' dance to the minutest motion of their legs, and performing it in character on the table with the assistance of a broomstick.

**Master Humphrey.** A kind-hearted, deformed old gentleman, living in an ancient house in a venerable suburb of London. He is the founder of a sort of club, which meets in his room one night in every week, at the hour of ten. In this room are six chairs, four of which are filled by Master Humphrey and his friends,—Jack Redburn, Mr. Owen Miles, and the "Deaf Gentleman." The two empty seats are reserved until they can fill them with two men to their mind; and Mr. Pickwick eventually becomes the occupant of one of them, while Mr. Jack Bamber is proposed as a candidate for the other. In a snug corner stands a quaint old clock in a huge oaken case curiously and richly carved; and in the bottom of this case the members of the club, from time to time, deposit manuscript tales of their own composition, which are taken out and read at their weekly meetings. Among these are the two well-known stories called "The Old Curiosity Shop" (the secondary title of which, as at first published, was "Personal Adventures of Master Humphrey") and "Barnaby Rudge." Master Humphrey thus describes himself and his friends:—

"We are men of secluded habits, with something of a cloud upon our early fortunes, whose enthusiasm, nevertheless, has not cooled with age; whose spirit of romance is not yet quenched;

who are content to ramble through the world in a pleasant dream, rather than waken again to its harsh realities. We are alchemists, who would extract the essence of perpetual youth from dust and ashes, tempt coy Truth in many light and airy forms from the bottom of her well, and discover one crumb of comfort or one grain of good in the commonest and least-regarded matter that passes through our crucible."

**Miles, Mr. Owen.** A wealthy retired merchant of sterling character; a great friend and admirer of Jack Redburn.

**Pickwick, Mr. Samuel.** The hero of "The Pickwick Papers." Reading Master Humphrey's account of himself, his clock, and his club, he is seized with a strong desire to become a candidate for one of the two vacant chairs in the club, and accordingly furnishes a witch-story of the time of James I as his qualification, which procures him the honor.

Mr. Pickwick's face, while his tale was being read, would have attracted the attention of the dullest man alive. The complacent motion of his head and forefinger as he gently beat time, and corrected the air with imaginary punctuation; the smile that mantled on his features at every jocose passage, and the sly look he stole around to observe its effect; the calm manner in which he shut his eyes and listened when there was some little piece of description; the changing expression with which he acted the dialogue to himself; his agony that the Deaf Gentleman should know what it was all about; and his extraordinary anxiety to correct the reader when he hesitated at a word in the manuscript, or substituted a wrong one, — were alike worthy of remark. And when at last, endeavoring to communicate with the Deaf Gentleman by means of the finger-alphabet, with which he constructed such words as are unknown in any civilized or savage language, he took up a slate, and wrote in large text, one word in a line, the question, How-do-you-like-it?— when he did this, and, handing it over the table, awaited the reply, with a countenance only brightened and improved by his great excitement, even Mr. Miles relaxed, and could not forbear looking at him for the moment with interest and favor.

**Podgers, John.** A character in Mr. Pickwick's tale; a stout, drowsy, fat-witted old fellow, held by his neighbors to be a man of strong sound sense; uncle to Will Marks.

**Redburn, Jack.** One of Master Humphrey's friends, and his factotum. Mr. Miles is his inseparable companion, and regards him with great admiration, believing not only that "no man ever lived who could do so many things as Jack, but that no man ever lived who could do anything so well."

**Slithers, Mr.** Mr. Pickwick's barber; a very bustling, active little man, with a red nose and a round bright face. He falls in love with Miss Benton, Master Humphrey's housekeeper, and finally marries her.

**Toddyhigh, Joe.** An old playmate of the lord-mayor elect of London. The two had been poor boys together at Hull; and when they separated, and went out into the world in different directions to seek their fortunes, they agreed always to remain fast friends. But time works many changes; and so it happens that the lord-mayor elect receives his old companion very coldly when he suddenly appears in his counting-room, and claims acquaintance, at a late hour on the very night before the grand inauguration. Ashamed and distrustful of his old friend, he gets rid of him as quickly as possible, giving him, however, a ticket to the grand dinner on the morrow. Joe takes it without a word, and instantly departs. The next day he goes to Guildhall, but, knowing nobody there, lounges about, and at last comes into an empty little music-gallery, which commands the whole hall. Sitting down, he soon falls asleep; and when he wakes, as the clock strikes three, he is astonished to find the guests departed, and to see the statues of the great giants Gog and Magog (the guardian genii of the city) endowed with life and motion, and to hear them speak in grave and solemn voices, agreeing to while away the dreary nights with legends of old London and with other tales; Magog making a beginning by relating the first of the "Giant Chronicles."

**Weller, Samuel.** Mr. Pickwick's body-servant; "the same true, faithful fellow" that he used to be in the days of the Pickwick Club, retaining all his native humor too, and all his old easy confidence, address, and knowledge of the world. *See* WELLER, TONY, *the elder.*

**Weller, Tony,** *the elder.* The old plethoric coachman of "The Pickwick Papers;" father to Sam Weller. When Mr. Pickwick, attended by Sam, visits Master Humphrey on club-nights, old Mr. Weller accompanies them as part of Mr. Pickwick's body-guard. While the members of Master Humphrey's Clock are holding their meeting in the study up stairs, Miss Benton the housekeeper, and her friend, Mr. Slithers the barber, entertain the two Wellers in the kitchen.

"I don't think," said Sam, who was smoking with great composure and enjoyment, "that, if the lady wos agreeable, it 'ud be wery far out o' the vay for us four to make up a club of our own, like the governors does up stairs, and let him" — Sam pointed with the stem of his pipe towards his parent — "be the president."

The housekeeper affably declared that it was the very thing she had been thinking of. The barber said the same. Mr. Weller said nothing; but he laid down his pipe as if in a fit of inspiration, and performed the following manœuvres: —

Unbuttoning the three lower buttons of his waistcoat, and pausing, for a moment, to enjoy the easy flow of breath consequent upon this process, he laid violent hands upon his watch-chain, and slowly, and with extreme difficulty, drew from his fob an immense double-cased silver watch, which brought the lining of the pocket with it, and was not to be disentangled but by great exertions and an amazing redness of face. Having fairly got it out at last, he detached the outer case, and wound it up with a key of corresponding magnitude; then put the case on again, and, having applied the watch to his ear to ascertain that it was still going, gave it some half-dozen hard knocks on the table to improve its performance.

"That," said Mr. Weller, laying it on the table, with its face upwards, "is the title and emblem o' this here society. Sammy, reach them two stools this vay for the wacant cheers. Ladies and gen'lmen, Mr. Weller's Watch is vound up, and now a goin'. Order!"

By way of enforcing this proclamation, Mr. Weller, using the watch after the manner of a president's hammer, and remarking with great pride that nothing hurt it, and that falls and concussions of all kinds materially enhanced the excellence of the works, and assisted the regulator, knocked the table a great many times, and declared the association formally constituted.

The old "whip" presides with great dignity, and observes the strictest rules of parliamentary law; thus, when Sam, in the course of some remarks, refers to a class of gentlemen as "barbers," and Mr. Slithers rises, and suggests that "hair-dressers" would be more "soothing" to his feelings, Mr. Weller rules that "hair-dressers" is the only designation proper to be used in the debate, and that all others are out of order.

"Well, but suppose he was n't a hair-dresser," suggested Sam.

"Wy then, sir, be parliamentary, and call him vun all the more," returned his father. "In the same vay as ev'ry gen'lman in another place is a *h*onorable, ev'ry barber in this place is a hair-dresser. Ven you read the speeches in the papers, and see as vun gen'lman says of another, 'the *h*onorable member, if he vill allow me to call him so,' you vill understand, sir, that that means, 'if he vill allow me to keep up that 'ere pleasant and uniwersal fiction.'"

Having taken a decided fancy to Miss Benton, but being afraid that she is a "widder," Mr. Weller gets Sam to inquire as to the fact. He is told that she is a spinster.

"A wot?" said his father with deep scorn.

"A spinster," replied Sam.

Mr. Weller looked very hard at his son for a minute or two, and then said:—

"Never mind vether she makes jokes, or not: that 's no matter. Wot I say is, Is that ere female a widder, or is she not?"

"Wot do you mean by her making jokes?" demanded Sam, quite aghast at the obscurity of his parent's speech.

"Never you mind, Samivel," returned Mr. Weller gravely. "Puns may be wery good things, or they may be wery bad 'uns, and a female may be none the better, or she may be none the vurse, for making of 'em: that 's got nothing to do vith widders."

"Wy, now!" said Sam, looking round, "would anybody believe as a man at his time o' life could be running his head agin spinsters and punsters being the same thing?"

"There ain't a straw's difference between 'em," said Mr. Weller. "Your father did n't drive a coach for so many years, not to be ekal to his own langvidge, as far as *that* goes, Sammy."

Mr. Weller insists upon the two words being synonymous, but is finally assured that Miss Benton is not a widow, which gives him great satisfaction.

**Weller, Tony,** *the younger.* A son of Sam Weller; named for his grandfather. He is a very small boy, about two feet six from the ground, having a very round face strongly resembling Mr. Weller's, and a stout little body of exactly his build, firmly set upon a couple of very sturdy legs. When Mr. Weller is first introduced to Master Humphrey, he immediately goes off, as he always does, into praises of his namesake.

"Samivel Weller, sir," said the old gentleman, "has con-ferred upon me the ancient title o' grandfather, vich had long laid dormouse, and wos s'posed to be nearly hex-tinct in our family. Sammy, relate a anecdote o' vun o' them boys,—that 'ere little anecdote about young Tony sayin' as he *vould* smoke a pipe unbeknown to his mother."

"Be quiet! can't you?" said Sam. "I never see such a old magpie,—never!"

"That 'ere Tony is the blessedest boy," said Mr. Weller, heedless of this rebuff,—"the blessedest boy as ever *I* see in *my* days! Of all the charmin'est as ever I heerd tell on, includin' them as wos kivered over by the robin redbreasts, arter they 'd committed sooicide, with blackberries, there never wos any like that 'ere little Tony. He 's always a playin' with a quart pot—

that boy is. To see him a settin' down on the doorstep, pretending to drink out of it, and fetching a long breath artervards, and smoking a bit of fire-vood, and sayin', 'Now I 'm grandfather,' — to see him a doin' that at two year old is better than any play as wos ever wrote. 'Now I 'm grandfather!' He would n't take a pint pot if you was to make him a present on it; but he gets his quart; and then he says, 'Now I 'm grandfather!'"

Mr. Weller was so overpowered by this picture, that he straightway fell into a most alarming fit of coughing, which must certainly have been attended with some fatal result but for the dexterity and promptitude of Sam, who, taking a firm grasp of the shawl, just under his father's chin, shook him to and fro with great violence, at the same time administering some smart blows between his shoulders. By this curious mode of treatment, Mr. Weller was finally recovered, but with a very crimson face, and in a state of great exhaustion.

## THE MYSTERY OF EDWIN DROOD

### OUTLINE

Chapter In a wretched opium den, early one morning, John Jasper
I slowly shook off his stupor and lay listening to the mutterings of his companions. He wanted to know how much of what they said in their sleep could be understood, and it was with evident satisfaction that he found their words unintelligible.

II John Jasper, music master, was Lay Precentor at the Cathedral of Cloisterham, and to all the Cloisterham world a thoroughly respectable man much wrapped up in the welfare of his nephew, Edwin Drood. Edwin, an orphan and his uncle's ward, was engaged to be married to Rosa Bud, who was also an orphan.
III The fathers of the young people had arranged the affair, which Rosa and Edwin, with youthful dislike for constraint, found rather irksome to live up to.

IV The Cloisterham world, for Mr. Jasper's purposes (which now began to develop), included even so humble a citizen as Durdles, stone-mason, habitual drunkard, and keeper of the key to
V the cathedral crypt. Jasper began making his way with Durdles by showing a friendly interest in the latter's hobby, — the finding of forgotten tombs.

VI On the evening of the arrival in Cloisterham of Helena Landless and her brother Neville, Mr. Crisparkle, with whom Neville was to read, gave a small dinner in their honor, at which they met Jasper, Edwin, and Rosa Bud. By the end of the evening
VII the two young ladies had become good friends, and Rosa had confided to Helena the fear she had of Jasper because of his love for her.

VIII Edwin and Neville, on their part, failed to hit it off so well together; for Neville's attempt to congratulate Edwin upon his engagement was met with a rebuff, and a quarrel ensued. Jasper appeared on the scene in time to act, to all appearances, as
IX peacemaker, but in reality to foment the trouble; rumor of which was abroad by the next morning in Cloisterham.

Now Rosa thought a great deal about this quarrel, with the feeling that she was involved in it, in some way, through being in a false position as to her marriage engagement. It was with great relief, therefore, that she learned from her guardian, Mr. Grewgious, that her betrothal was not binding unless she and Edwin voluntarily made it so. Unfortunately she told no one of her state of mind, as she wished Edwin to know it first.

X Mr. Crisparkle, too, thought a great deal about the quarrel, and set his mind upon bringing a complete reconciliation between the persons concerned in it. This determination was strengthened by the discovery, from Neville himself, that the latter was in love with Rosa, and that part of his anger against Edwin was due to that fact. Having obtained Neville's promise to forgive and forget, Mr. Crisparkle won Jasper to try to effect the same end with Edwin, and the meeting between the young men was arranged for Christmas Eve, at Jasper's lodgings.

XI Christmas was drawing nigh, and Edwin, on his way to Cloisterham, called on Mr. Grewgious in London by way of courteous attention to the guardian of his *fiancée*. Mr. Grewgious, though an angular man and unimaginative, had his ward's happiness very much at heart, and took this opportunity to talk with Edwin against the wicked folly of entering lightly into an engagement of marriage. In conclusion, he gave into Edwin's keeping a jewelled ring that had been the engagement ring of Rosa's mother, and that was now destined for Rosa herself. And he so impressed upon Edwin that the ring was rightly to be a symbol of love, that Edwin began at last to question seriously his motives for binding himself to Rosa.

XII In the mean while Jasper was quietly pursuing his ends, and making use of Durdles as guide for a moonlight ramble through the crypt of the cathedral, — an innocent journey enough had not Durdles fallen into a drunken sleep in the crypt, thus allowing Jasper to make what use of the keys he wished.

XIII Mr. Grewgious's words about their engagement to Edwin and Rosa, at different times, had so wrought upon the young people that they readily agreed to remain mere friends and to break any closer tie. On the plea that the news would pain Jasper, they decided to ask Mr. Grewgious to tell him, — an unwise course as events proved. Edwin, of course, retained the jewelled ring, in order to deliver it over again into Mr. Grewgious's safe-keeping.

XIV Christmas Eve came. Neville spent the day in setting his room in order and preparing for a journey afoot to be begun the next day; Edwin spent it in taking sauntering leave of ancient Cloisterham, in which he ran across a haggard old woman who, in return for money to buy opium, warned him that some one named Ned was in great danger of his life; Jasper spent it in preparing for his two guests. In the evening the three came together. The next morning Edwin was missing, and Neville had started on his journey.

XV Jasper raised so hideous a cry of foul play over the disappearance of his nephew, that the first thing done was to arrest and detain Neville on suspicion of murder. While search for Edwin was going on, Jasper learned from Mr. Grewgious of the arrangement arrived at between Rosa and Edwin, a bit of news which affected him so strangely that he swooned away when he heard it.

XVI The search for Edwin was well-nigh fruitless, revealing
nothing but a watch and shirt-pin which were identified as
his; but nothing was proven against Neville, who was, nevertheless,
XVII obliged to leave Cloisterham. He took lodgings in London
very near Mr. Grewgious, who also discovered that Jasper
sometimes occupied rooms in his neighborhood.

XVIII At about this time a Mr. Datchery — a single briefer, living on his means — appeared in Cloisterham, secured lodgings of Jasper's landlady, and rapidly enlarged his acquaintance with the townspeople. He seemed to have some curious interest in the mystery of Edwin Drood's disappearance.

XIX It was in consequence of a proposal of marriage from Jasper that Rosa fled to her guardian in London, in whose mind
XX various circumstances were serving to rouse suspicion of Jasper. For the latter, in his declaration to Rosa, had used
XXI threats scarcely consonant with purity of motives and up-
rightness of conduct. Accordingly Mr. Grewgious set about
circumventing Jasper, settling Rosa in London.

XXII Having concluded the bargain for rooms, he wrote and signed a few lines of agreement, and requested Mrs. Billickin to put her signature to the document also, "Christian and surname" in full.

"Mr. Grewgious," said Mrs. Billickin in a new burst of candor, "no, sir. You must excuse the Christian name."

Mr. Grewgious stared at her.

"The door-plate is used as a protection," said Mrs. Billickin, "and acts as such; and go from it I will not."

Mr. Grewgious stared at Rosa.

"No, Mr. Grewgious, you must excuse me. So long as this 'ouse is known indefinite as Billickin's, and so long as it is a doubt with the riff-raff where Billickin may be hidin' near the street-door or down the airy, and what his weight and size, so long I feel safe. But commit myself to a solitary female statement — no, miss! Nor would you for a moment wish," said Mrs. Billickin, with a strong sense of injury, "to take that advantage of your sex, if you was not brought to it by inconsiderate example."

Rosa, reddening as if she had made some disgraceful attempt to overreach the good lady, besought Mr. Grewgious to rest content with any signature; and accordingly, in a baronial way, the sign-manual BILLICKIN got appended to the document.

XXIII Once more the scene opens in the opium den. This time, however, the haggard keeper of the place watched and listened; nor did she find Jasper's mutterings unintelligible. This time, moreover, she traced him, when he left her den, to Cloisterham, where she fell in with Mr. Datchery, who discovered her hatred for the Lay Precentor, and laid up the discovery as important among some others he had made.

. . . . . . . . . . . . .

---

## INDEX TO CHARACTERS

**Bazzard, Mr.** Clerk to Mr. Grewgious, over whom he possesses a strange power. He is a pale, puffy-faced, dark-haired person of thirty, with big, dark eyes wholly wanting in lustre, and with a dissatisfied, doughy complexion, that seems to ask to be sent to the baker's. The secret of his influence over Mr. Grewgious is thus explained by that gentleman in a conversation he has with Miss Rosa Bud: —

"We were speaking of Mr. Bazzard. . . . What do you think Mr. Bazzard has done?"

"Oh, dear!" cried Rosa, drawing her chair a little nearer, and her mind reverting to Jasper, — "nothing dreadful, I hope?"

"He has written a play," said Mr. Grewgious in a solemn whisper, — "a tragedy."

Rosa seemed much relieved.

"And nobody," pursued Mr. Grewgious in the same tone, "will hear, on any account whatever, of bringing it out."

Rosa looked reflective, and nodded her head slowly, as who should say, "Such things are, and why are they!"

"Now, you know," said Mr. Grewgious, "*I* could n't write a play."

"Not a bad one, sir?" asked Rosa innocently, with her eyebrows again in action.

"No. If I was under sentence of decapitation, and was about to be instantly decapitated, and an express arrived with a pardon for the condemned convict Grewgious, if he wrote a play, I should be under the necessity of resuming the block, and begging the executioner to proceed to extremities, meaning," said Mr. Grewgious, passing his hand under his chin, "the singular number, and this extremity."

Rosa appeared to consider what she would do if the awkward supposititious case were hers.

"Consequently," said Mr. Grewgious, "Mr. Bazzard would have a sense of my inferiority to himself under any circumstances; but when I am his master, you know, the case is greatly aggravated."

Mr. Grewgious shook his head seriously, as if he felt the offence to be a little too much, though of his own committing.

"How came you to be his master, sir?" asked Rosa.

"A question that naturally follows," said Mr. Grewgious. "Let 's talk. Mr. Bazzard's father, being a Norfolk farmer, would have furiously laid about him with a flail, a pitchfork, and every agricultural implement available for assaulting purposes, on the slightest hint of his son's having written a play. So the son, bringing to me the father's rent (which I receive), imparted his secret, and pointed out that he was determined to pursue his genius, and that it would put him in peril of starvation, and that he was not formed for it."

"For pursuing his genius, sir?"

"No, my dear," said Mr. Grewgious,—"for starvation. It was impossible to deny the position that Mr. Bazzard was not formed to be starved; and Mr. Bazzard then pointed out that it was desirable that I should stand between him and a fate so perfectly unsuited to his formation. In that way, Mr. Bazzard became my clerk, and he feels it very much."

"I am glad he is grateful," said Rosa.

"I did n't quite mean that, my dear. I mean that he feels the degradation. There are some other geniuses that Mr. Bazzard has become acquainted with, who have also written tragedies, which, likewise, nobody will, on any account whatever, hear of bringing out; and these choice spirits dedicate their plays to one another in a highly panegyrical manner. Mr. Bazzard has been the subject of one of these dedications. Now, you know, *I* never had a play dedicated to *me!*"

Rosa looked at him as if she would have liked him to be the recipient of a thousand dedications.

"Which again, naturally, rubs against the grain of Mr. Bazzard," said Mr. Grewgious. "He is very short with me sometimes, and then I feel that he is meditating, 'This blockhead is my master!—a fellow who could n't write a tragedy on pain of death, and who will never have one dedicated to him with the most complimentary congratulations on the high position he has taken in the eyes of posterity.' Very trying, very trying. However, in giving him directions, I reflect beforehand, 'Perhaps he may not like this,' or, 'He might take it ill if I asked that;' and so we get on very well,—indeed, better than I could have expected."

"Is the tragedy named, sir?" asked Rosa.

"Strictly between ourselves," answered Mr. Grewgious, "it has a dreadfully appropriate name. It is called 'The Thorn of Anxiety.' But Mr. Bazzard hopes, and I hope, that it will come out at last." xi, xx.

**Billickin, Mrs.** A widowed cousin of Mr. Bazzard's, who lets furnished lodgings in Southampton Street, Bloomsbury Square. Personal faintness and an overpowering personal candor are the distinguishing features of her organization. xxii.

**Bud, Miss Rosa,** *called* ROSEBUD. A wonderfully pretty, childish, and whimsical young lady, who is an orphan, and the ward of Mr. Grewgious. While yet a mere child, she is betrothed to Edwin Drood; her father and his having been very dear and firm and fast friends, and desiring that their only children should be to one another even more than they themselves had been to one another. But, as Rosa and Edwin grow up, they find that they are not truly happy in their engagement, and that each resents being thus married by anticipation. They accordingly agree to break off the engagement, and to "change to brother and sister" thenceforth. Shortly after this event Edwin Drood disappears, and is supposed to have been murdered. iii, vii, ix, xiii, xix–xxii.

**China Shepherdess, The.** *See* CRISPARKLE, MRS.

**Crisparkle, The Reverend Septimus.** One of the minor canons of Cloisterham Cathedral; a model clergyman, and a true Christian gentleman.

Mr. Crisparkle, minor canon, fair and rosy, and perpetually pitching himself head foremost into all the deep running water in the surrounding country; Mr. Crisparkle, minor canon, early riser, musical, classical, cheerful, kind, good-natured, social, contented, and boy-like; Mr. Crisparkle, minor canon and good man, lately "Coach" upon the chief Pagan high-roads, but since promoted by a patron (grateful for a well-taught son) to his present Christian beat. ii, vi–viii, x, xii, xiv–xvii, xxi–xxiii.

**Crisparkle, Mrs.,** *called* THE CHINA SHEPHERDESS. His mother; a pretty old lady, with bright eyes, a calm and cheerful face, and a trim and compact figure. vi, vii, x.

**Datchery, Dick.** A mysterious white-haired man, with black eyebrows, who presents himself in Cloisterham shortly after the death of Edwin Drood, and who takes lodging overlooking the rooms of Mr. Jasper.

Being buttoned up in a tightish blue surtout, with a buff waistcoat and gray trousers, he had something of a military air; but he announced himself at the Crozier (the orthodox hotel, where he put up with a portmanteau) as an idle dog who lived upon his means; and he further announced that he had a mind to take a lodging in the picturesque old city for a month or two, with a view of settling down there altogether.

Who or what he is does not appear; but it is plain that he takes up his abode in Cloisterham for the sole purpose of watching Jasper. xviii, xxiii.

**Deputy.** A hideous small boy, hired by Durdles to pelt him home, if he catches him out too late. He explains to Jasper that he is a "man-servant up at the Travellers Twopenny," a crazy wooden inn near the cathedral. As a caution to Durdles to stand clear if he can, or to betake himself home, the young imp always chants the following note of preparation before beginning to fling stones: —

"Widdy widdy wen!
I — ket — ches — Im — out — ar — ter — ten,
Widdy widdy wy!
Then — E — don't — go — then — I — shy —
Widdy widdy Wake-cock warning!"

— with a comprehensive sweep on the last word. v, xii, xviii, xxiii.

**Drood, Edwin.** The character from whom the story takes its name; a young man left an orphan at an early age, and betrothed, in accordance with his father's dying wish, to Miss Rosa Bud, the daughter of an old and very dear friend. ii, vii, viii, xi, xiii, xiv.

**Durdles.** A stone-mason; chiefly in the grave-stone, tomb, and monument way, and wholly of their color from head to foot.

No man is better known in Cloisterham. He is the chartered libertine of the place. Fame trumpets him a wonderful workman — which, for aught that anybody knows, he may be (as he never works) — and a wonderful sot, which everybody knows he is. With the cathedral crypt he is better acquainted than any living authority: it may even be than any dead one. It is said that the intimacy of this acquaintance began in his habitually resorting to that secret place to lock out the Cloisterham boy-populace, and sleep off the fumes of liquor; he having ready access to the cathedral as contractor for rough repairs. Be this as it may, he does know much about it, and in the demolition of impedimental fragments of wall, buttress, and pavement, has seen strange sights.

He often speaks of himself in the third person; perhaps being a little misty as to his own identity when he narrates, perhaps impartially adopting the Cloisterham nomenclature in reference to a character of acknowledged distinction. Thus he will say, touching his strange sights, "Durdles come upon the old chap," in reference to a buried magnate of ancient time and high degree, "by striking right into the coffin with his pick. The old chap gave Durdles a look with his open eyes, as much as to say, 'Is your name Durdles? Why, my man, I've been waiting for you a devil of a time!' and then he turned to powder." With a two-foot rule always in his pocket, and a mason's hammer all but always in his hand, Durdles goes continually sounding and tapping all about and about the cathedral; and whenever he says to Tope, "Tope, here 's another old 'un in here," Tope announces it to the dean as an established discovery. iv, xii, xiv.

**Ferdinand, Miss.** A pupil at Miss Twinkleton's school. ix, xiii.

**Giggles, Miss.** Another pupil at the same school. ix, xiii.

**Grewgious, Hiram, Esquire.** Miss Rosa Bud's guardian, and "a particularly angular man." ix, xi, xv–xvii, xx–xxii.

**Honeythunder, Mr. Luke.** Chairman of the Convened Chief Composite Committee of Central and District Philanthropists, and guardian of Neville and Helena Landless. He is a large man, with a tremendous voice, and an appearance of being constantly engaged in crowding everybody to the wall.

Though it was not literally true, as was facetiously charged against him by public unbelievers, that he called aloud to his fellow-creatures, "Curse your souls and bodies! come here and be blessed!" still his philanthropy was of that gunpowderous sort, that the difference between it and animosity was hard to determine. You were to abolish military force; but you were first to bring all commanding officers who had done their duty to trial by court-martial for that offence, and shoot them. You were to abolish war, but were to make converts by making war upon them, and charging them with loving war as the apple of their eye. You were to have no capital punishment, but were first to sweep off the face of the earth all legislators, jurists, and judges who were of the contrary opinion. You were to have universal concord, and were to get it by eliminating all the people who would n't, or conscientiously could n't, be concordant. You were to love your brother as yourself, but after an indefinite interval of maligning him (very much as if you hated him), and calling him all manner of names. Above all things, you were to do nothing in private or on your own account. You were to go to the offices of the Haven of Philanthropy, and put your name down as a member and a professing philanthropist; then you were to pay up your subscription, get your card of membership, and your ribbon and medal, and were evermore to live upon a platform, and evermore to say what Mr. Honeythunder said, and what the treasurer said, and what the sub-treasurer said, and what the committee said, and what the sub-committee said, and what the secretary said, and what the vice-secretary said. And this was usually said in the unanimously-carried resolution under hand and seal, to the effect, "That this assembled body of professing philanthropists views with indignant scorn and contempt, not unmixed with utter detestation and loathing abhorrence,"—in short, the baseness of all those who do not belong to it, and pledges itself to make as many obnoxious statements as possible about them, without being at all particular as to facts. vi, xvii.

**Jasper, John.** A music-master who is employed as choir-master in Cloisterham Cathedral; uncle to Edwin Drood, for whom he professes the strongest affection.

Mr. Jasper is a dark man of some six and twenty, with thick, lustrous, well-arranged black hair and whisker. He looks older than he is, as dark men often do. His voice is deep and good, his face and figure are good, his manner is a little sombre.

Jasper is addicted to the use of opium, and resorts every now and then to a miserable hole in London, where the drug is prepared in a peculiar form by an old hag, and where he smokes himself into the wildest dreams. He goes to this place after the disappearance of Edwin Drood, and is followed, when he leaves, by the old woman, who thus ascertains who and what he is. The two are, in turn, watched by Mr. Datchery, who appears well satisfied on discovering the connection between them. i, ii, iv, v, vii–x, xii, xiv–xvi, xviii, xix, xxii, xxiii.

**Jennings, Miss.** A pupil at Miss Twinkleton's Seminary for Young Ladies. ix.

**Joe.** Driver of an omnibus, which is the daily service between Cloisterham and external mankind. vi, xv, xx.

**Landless, Helena.** A native of Ceylon, but the child of English parents; a ward of Mr. Honeythunder's, who sends her to Miss Twinkleton's School for Young Ladies in Cloisterham, where she becomes the friend and *confidante* of Rosa Bud. She is an unusually handsome, lithe girl, very dark and rich in color,—almost of the gipsy type,—with something untamed about her, as there is, also, about her twin-brother Neville.

A certain air upon them of hunter and huntress; yet, withal, a certain air of being the objects of the chase, rather than the followers. Slender, supple, quick of eye and limb, half-shy, half-defiant, fierce of look; an indefinable kind of pause coming and going on their whole expression both of face and form, which might be equally likened to the pause before a crouch or a bound. vi, vii, x, xiii, xiv, xxii.

**Landless, Neville.** Her brother, studying with the Reverend Mr. Crisparkle, and suspected of the murder of Edwin Drood. vi–viii, x, xii, xiv–xvii.

**Lobley, Mr.** A boatman in the service of Mr. Tartar, — "the dead image of the sun in old woodcuts," his hair and whisker answering for rays all around him. xxii.

**Reynolds, Miss.** A pupil at the Nuns' House, Miss Twinkleton's Seminary for Young Ladies. ix.

**Rickitts, Miss.** Another pupil at the same establishment.

**Sapsea, Mr. Thomas.** An auctioneer, afterwards mayor of Cloisterham.

Accepting the jackass as the type of self-sufficient stupidity and conceit, — a custom, perhaps, like some few other customs, more conventional than fair, — then the purest jackass in Cloisterham is Mr. Thomas Sapsea, auctioneer.

Mr. Sapsea "dresses at" the dean; has been bowed to for the dean, in mistake; has even been spoken to in the street as My Lord, under the impression that he was the bishop come down unexpectedly, without his chaplain. Mr. Sapsea is very proud of this, and of his voice and of his style. He has even (in selling landed property) tried the experiment of slightly intoning in his pulpit, to make himself more like what he takes to be the genuine ecclesiastical article: so, in ending a sale by public auction, Mr. Sapsea finishes off with an air of bestowing a benediction on the assembled brokers, which leaves the real dean — a modest and worthy gentleman — far behind.

Mr. Sapsea has many admirers: indeed, the proposition is carried by a large local majority, even including non-believers in his wisdom, that he is a credit to Cloisterham. He possesses the great qualities of being portentous and dull, and of having a roll in his speech and another roll in his gait; not to mention a certain gravely-flowing action with his hands, as if he were presently going to confirm the individual with whom he holds discourse. Much nearer sixty years of age than fifty; with a flowing outline of stomach, and horizontal creases in his waistcoat; reputed to be rich; voting at elections in the strictly respectable interest; morally satisfied that nothing but he himself has grown since he was a baby, — how can dunder-headed Mr. Sapsea be otherwise than a credit to Cloisterham and society? iv, xii, xiv–xvi, xviii.

**Tartar, Lieutenant.** An ex-officer of the Royal Navy, who has come into possession of a fortune, and has retired from the service.

A handsome gentleman, with a young face, but an older figure in its robustness and its breadth of shoulder, — say a man of eight and twenty, or, at the utmost, thirty, — so extremely sunburnt, that the contrast between his brown visage and the white forehead, shaded out of doors by his hat, and the glimpses of white throat below the neckerchief, would have been almost ludicrous, but for his broad temples, bright blue eyes, clustering brown hair, and laughing teeth. xvii, xxi, xxii.

**Tisher, Mrs.** A deferential widow, with a weak back, a chronic sigh, and a suppressed voice, who looks after the young ladies' wardrobes at the Nuns' House, Miss Twinkleton's seminary at Cloisterham. ii, vii, ix, xiii.

**Tope, Mr.** Chief verger of Cloisterham Cathedral. ii, vi, xii, xiv, xvi, xviii, xxiii.

**Tope, Mrs.** His wife. ii, xii, xiv, xvi, xviii, xxiii.

**Twinkleton, Miss.** Mistress of a boarding-school for young ladies in Cloisterham, attended by Rosa Bud and Helena Landless.

In the midst of Cloisterham stands the Nuns' House, a venerable brick edifice, whose present appellation is doubtless derived from the legend of its conventual uses. On the trim gate inclosing its old courtyard is a resplendent brass plate, flashing forth the legend, "Seminary for Young Ladies. Miss Twinkleton." The house-front is so old and worn, and the brass plate is so shining and staring, that the general result has reminded imaginative strangers of a battered old beau with a large modern eye-glass stuck in his blind eye.

Miss Twinkleton has two distinct and separate phases of being. Every night, the moment the young ladies have retired to rest, does Miss Twinkleton smarten up her curls a little, brighten up her eyes a little, and become a sprightlier Miss Twinkleton than the young ladies have ever seen. Every night, at the same hour, does Miss Twinkleton resume the topics of the previous night, comprehending the tenderer scandal of Cloisterham, of which she has no knowledge whatever by day, and references to a certain season at Tunbridge Wells (airily called by Miss Twinkleton, in this state of her existence, "The Wells"), notably the season wherein a certain finished gentleman (compassionately called by Miss Twinkleton, in this state of her existence, "Foolish Mr. Porters") revealed a homage of the heart, whereof Miss Twinkleton, in her scholastic state of existence, is as ignorant as a granite pillar. iii, vi, vii, ix, xiii, xxii.

# THE LIFE AND ADVENTURES OF MARTIN CHUZZLEWIT

## OUTLINE

Chapter I To record the life and adventures of one Chuzzlewit, it is expedient first to trace the Chuzzlewit race itself from Adam downward, and then, having got them upon their feet, to bring to

II notice one or two persons who lived in the same world with Martin; as, for example, Mr. Pecksniff, architect and land surveyor, coming home on a gusty night and knocked off his own doorstep by the slamming of his own door in his face. Mr. Pecksniff was rescued from his sudden plight by his two daughters, Charity and Mercy, named, apparently, on the general principle which dubbed Ptolemy Philadelphus, and as the three sat before the fire, and Mr. Pecksniff notified his daughters that a young gentleman was coming as a student in the place of John Westlock, who was going, Westlock himself appeared, preceded by the faithful Tom Pinch, Pecksniff's one constant student and drudge, who tried in vain to make his master recognize with friendliness his dear friend, and his friend to confess the virtues of his master, — virtues which Mr. Pecksniff wore conspicuously, nay, even flaunted.

III Now, at the very time when this was going on, there lay at the Blue Dragon in the village an old man, apparently very low. His attendant was a young girl not more than seventeen, and his landlady, Mrs. Lupin, being at her wits' end, and having tried in vain to get the village apothecary, sent a messenger to summon Mr. Pecksniff, as being a man of learning and of vast morality. Mr. Pecksniff came, and recognized shortly the countenance of a cousin of his, Martin Chuzzlewit, the elder, who proceeded, in the bitterness of his soul, to pour out a general execration on the world, having already, before the entrance of Pecksniff, destroyed what appeared to be his last will and testament. The discovery of the presence of

IV the old gentleman in the village was, however, sufficient to put Mr. Pecksniff very much on the alert. Thenceforth he haunted the Blue Dragon, and in his anxiety not to fail his ancient relative at any moment, he went as far as the keyhole to the door repeatedly. On one of these excursions in the dark he came unexpectedly in contact with another head, and, on both owners of these heads coming to the light, the one which belonged to the intruder proved to be that of one Montague Tigg, a hanger-on and confidential friend of Chevy Slyme, an impecunious kinsman of Martin Chuzzlewit. Then it transpired that the village was, so to speak, full of the kinsfolk of the dying man. They laid siege to the Blue Dragon, and failing to capture the citadel, they all met at Mr. Pecksniff's house with a view to conferring upon the measures to pursue, especially with reference to the designing young creature who appeared to be the only one in the confidence of old Martin Chuzzlewit. As they sat in conference, held back from tearing each other's hair only by their common greed, a messenger burst in with the news that the old man and the girl had escaped them altogether by actually leaving the Blue Dragon and the village itself for parts unknown.

V If one Martin Chuzzlewit disappeared, another took his place, for Tom Pinch was sent in a chaise to Salisbury to bring back the new pupil, for whom he was to ask at the inn by the name of Mr. Martin. Tom drove cheerily along, picking up by the way his acquaintance, Mark Tapley, quondam man-of-all-work at the Blue Dragon, — a man of great contrariety, inasmuch as, being a man of great good humor, he was depressed by the consciousness of the want of merit in being good humored when everything favored the virtue, and so studied the art of being jolly under adverse circumstances. At the inn Tom encountered Mr. Martin, who proved to be grandson to the old Martin Chuzzlewit, and bearing the same name. He was a comfortably selfish fellow, and Tom Pinch, in the innocence of his heart, beguiled the journey home by an account of his own adventures as volunteer organist in a little church, where he had had a vision of loveliness in a listener whose name and home he had, in his delicacy, never sought to learn. Arrived at the Pecksniffs', they found that worthy family engaged artlessly in occupations which betrayed their wise and beautiful natures. Mr. Pecksniff initiated Martin into the sanctities of his new home, and Tom Pinch was graciously permitted to share in the frugal festivities.

VI The next day Mr. Pecksniff took his two daughters with him to London for a week, leaving Tom Pinch and Martin Chuzzlewit by themselves. Tom made himself extremely useful in getting the party ready to go, and Martin had a private conference with Mr. Pecksniff on personal business, but when the two young men were left to themselves in the evening, Martin, who was in low spirits, was driven to making a confidant of Tom, and disclosed to him the fact that he had been brought up by his grandfather, that he had reasonable expectations of inheriting his grandfather's property, and was in love with the young girl who was his grandfather's constant companion, but that the obstinate old gentleman was so selfish, and the young woman so unreasonably governed by a mistaken sense of duty, that he was practically left out in the cold. The young woman, it appears, he had identified as the object of Tom Pinch's silent admiration.

VII As the two were at work the next morning, for Mr. Pecksniff had set Martin to work designing a grammar school, they were interrupted by the apparition of a most out-at-the-elbows man, who was none other than Montague Tigg, on an errand to see if he could insinuate out of Tom Pinch's pocket enough to pay the score which he and Chevy Slyme had run up at the Blue Dragon, on account of which they were miserably detained by the landlady. At the mention of Chevy Slyme's name Martin was uncomfortably stirred, for he recognized that disreputable man of unacknowledged genius as a kinsman; so he persuaded Tom to stand as a sort of surety for the two men, and the three set off for the Blue Dragon, accompanied by Mark Tapley, who had indeed escorted Mr. Tigg to Mr. Pecksniff's, being unwilling to lose sight of so valuable a piece of portable property as a walking debt. At the Blue Dragon, the landlady, Mrs. Lupin, cheerfully accepted Tom Pinch as security, and Mr. Tigg bound Tom still faster to him by borrowing a sovereign of him in the most elaborate and punctilious fashion. It was after they had all left that Mark Tapley announced his resolution to leave the Blue Dragon in search of his fortunes, after making the parting as difficult as possible by avowing his love for Mrs. Lupin.

VIII Mr. Pecksniff and his daughters had, as we have seen, got the start of him, and they found when fairly off in the coach for London that they had companions on the journey, old Anthony Chuzzlewit, one of the disappointed kinsfolk, and his sharp-set son Jonas, who had been lingering in the neighborhood looking out for business chances. Jonas devoted himself to the girls, with a keen eye for Mercy, the younger, who had giggled herself into his good graces at an early hour. The two parties separated when they reached London, and Mr. Pecksniff and his daughters made their way in the foggy morning of their arrival to the boarding-house of M. Todgers. M. Todgers, who was a woman, kept a house for men only, but Mr. Pecksniff, who had formerly resorted to the place, decided on prudential grounds that Todgers would take them all in, and so Todgers did. The conveniences were not great, but it
IX was much to be at Todgers's, which was inscrutably hidden in a very perplexed neighborhood. Here, under the eye of Mrs. Todgers, the young ladies could be secure, and that excellent

landlady treated them with all the indulgence of a prospective step-mother. One day the whole party sallied forth to look up Ruth Pinch, Tom's sister, to whom Mr. Pecksniff bore a letter from Tom. Ruth was governess in the family of a wealthy and haughty brass and copper founder at Camberwell, and there they found her instructing the very knowing young daughter of the establishment. With unspeakable condescension Mr. Pecksniff greeted the grateful sister of his grateful pupil, and kept his eye, as did his daughters and Mrs. Todgers, on the daughter of the house. As they retired at a very decided hint conveyed by the footman, Mr. Pecksniff, in the character of architect, uttered large and discriminating flattery on the mansion; he continued his observations in an audible tone when they were outside, and though he was ordered off the premises by the owner, he managed to retreat in dignified style, reserving his wrath for use a little farther away. The disagreeable incident was wiped out of memory, however, by an affair the next day, Sunday, when at the united request of the boarders at Todgers's, headed by Jinkins the Father of Todgers, the young ladies received the hospitality of the house and were guests at the dinner table. The evening closed with such draughts of gayety that Mr. Pecksniff finally had to be borne off to his chamber, whence he issued time and again with scraps of morality saved from his long-hoarded store, and he was finally reduced to peace only by having his door locked and young Bailey, the vivacious servant boy of the establishment, stationed as sentinel outside.

X The business which had brought Mr. Pecksniff to town appeared when, after a prolonged stay at Todgers's, old Martin Chuzzlewit one day paid a visit. For some reason known to himself he made friends with his kinsfolk and apparently took them into favor, mysteriously hinting that they should be the gainers by doing his bidding, and then insisted upon the dismissal of his grandson from their house.

Scarcely had he left them before sounds in the next room caught their notice. It was the voice of the youngest gentleman of the house, who was bitterly jealous of Mr. Jinkins, and was now engaged in a stormy interview with Mrs. Todgers, who succeeded at last in pacifying him and retaining his allegiance as a boarder. She could scarcely afford to affront eighteen shillings a week, or even to be very particular about the truthfulness of her discourse to him. But the Pecksniff sisters had indeed introduced a new atmosphere at Todgers's. It was shortly before they were to leave that young

XI Bailey one day at noon announced a visitor for Miss Pecksniff. On going to the parlor she found Jonas Chuzzlewit, who reproached her for giving him so much trouble in finding his cousins, and now proposed to show her and her sister the town, after which they were to dine with him and his father, all of which was in agreement with an understanding with their father, whom he had just met, fortunately, in the neighborhood. The invitation was accepted, and Jonas accompanied the sisters, always devoting himself to Charity, and always talking across her at Mercy. At supper in the bachelor establishment of Anthony Chuzzlewit and his son appeared the only other member of their household, an old clerk, Chuffey by name, who seemed to live and have his being only at the word of Anthony Chuzzlewit.

When the Pecksniff family made ready to leave London, Jinkins and other of the boarders gave a doleful serenade to the young ladies, and on the morning of their departure Jonas was also on hand to say good-by. Anthony, in a private interview with Mr. Pecksniff, had intimated that it might be as well for them to take no notice of the young people. Thus they set out on their return,
XII having sent word to Tom Pinch to meet the stage in the early morning of their arrival with a gig and cart. Tom meanwhile had been in luck, for not only had Martin, lazily building castles in Spain, told him that he would look after him when he was married and had his fortune, but he had received a letter from John Westlock, who had come into property, inviting him and the new pupil to dine with him at Salisbury; a right good dinner they had, and much conversation ensued, which showed the innocent character of Tom, the oblivious selfishness of Martin, and the penetrating sense and generosity of John, who, by the way, managed to pay Tigg's debt without awakening any suspicion in Tom's breast.

When the two young men went to meet the Pecksniff family in the early morning, to the amazement of both Mr. Pecksniff appeared not to see Martin and to see Tom with magnifying glasses. The attitude which he took toward the two continued, and at last Martin brought him to book, whereupon Mr. Pecksniff, with bold front but trembling rear, professed to have discovered Martin's perfidy, and Martin, with rage and scorn, flung himself out of the house and announced his purpose to go to America, there to seek his for-
XIII tune. He had small capital on which to start his enterprise, — a good suit of clothes, a gold watch, and a half sovereign which Tom Pinch had secretly conveyed to him as he set out. With a silk handkerchief he paid for a lift part way to London; he walked the rest of the way, and pawned his gold watch in the city at David Crimp, the pawnbroker's, where he encountered Montague Tigg, and then he sought in vain for some way of working his passage like a gentleman to the United States. Suddenly, when he

was in the lowest straits, a letter was brought him. It had his address on the envelope; there was no writing within, but there was something quite as serviceable, a Bank of England note for twenty pounds. As he was pondering this over a good meal, who should appear but Mark Tapley. It was not long before Martin had made so much of his story known as he cared to tell, and no longer before Mark had offered his services as a sort of companion valet. He be-
XIV gan his duties by carrying a letter from Martin to the young lady with old Martin, for Mark had come upon the pair and knew whereabouts in London they were. Through this means, an appointment was made in the park, and with Mark for guard, Martin and Mary had a farewell meeting, in which Martin confided to her that Tom Pinch, the organist whom she had heard, would act as go-between in conveying his letters to her. When they parted Mark escorted her home, and returning brought a diamond ring to her lover. Martin murmured that she was worthy of all the sacrifices he was making for her, and Mark, with his eyes open to the situation, hugged himself with the consciousness that now he could be jolly under most adverse circumstances.

XV Martin and Mark set out on the voyage to the United States, and a most miserable passage they had, rendered more miserable by the discomforts of their fellow passengers, among whom was a woman with three children going out to meet a husband from whom she had been separated for two years, and whom in her faith she hoped to find on the wharf upon their arrival. Before they
XVI could land, the steamer was boarded by a horde of youngsters crying the papers, the New York Sewer, Family Spy, Stabber, Peeper, Rowdy Journal, and the like, and a representative citizen of the new country, Colonel Diver, editor of the last named sheet, accosted Martin and did the honors of a free and enlightened country, inviting him finally to the office of his journal to partake of champagne, which he had just levied on the captain of the steamer by virtue of his important journalistic friendship. There Martin met the war correspondent of the Rowdy Journal, Mr. Jefferson Brick, and the two conducted him to their boarding-house, kept by Major Pawkins, where Martin had an opportunity to learn something of American manners.

XVII But where was Mark Tapley all this time? Sitting calmly on the landing at the Rowdy Journal office, where Martin, who had forgotten him, found him on his return, conversing with a black man who had been a slave and was therefore an exclamation point after the word Liberty! The black took their luggage to Major Pawkins's, and in the evening Martin's new friend, Mr. Bevan, took him to call on the Norris family, where Martin met a new variety of Americans, and was confronted also by one of his fellow passengers, General Fladdock, who to be sure came over in the cabin and Martin in the steerage. Martin went to bed somewhat disheartened at the prospect before him, and Mark had, by the same token, still greater cause for jollity.

XVIII Martin was but one of the Chuzzlewits, the only one who had undertaken to make his abode on the other side of the Atlantic. In London still dwelt Anthony Chuzzlewit and his son Jonas, with the clerk, old Chuffey. The money-loving son looked askance at this useless father clinging to the world he had done with. Already Jonas was enjoying his wealth in anticipation, and one evening stealthily drew out Anthony's will which he was guarding, that he might have a foretaste of pleasure. Suddenly he was aware of some one looking at him as he read. It was Pecksniff, who had unexpectedly come to town, and Jonas had a momentary panic as if he had been caught executing the man who made the will. He went out presently on a matter of business, leaving Pecksniff with his father. Then it transpired that Anthony had sent for Pecksniff, though it was hard to tell just what he wanted of him, now he had come, except to talk over Jonas's probable intention of marrying Pecksniff's daughter. After Jonas returned, Anthony, as they were talking, fell in a fit, and the next morning was dead, but not before he had, as it were, appeared as a ghost in the flesh shaking his head at Jonas. That young man and heir seemed struck with an awful fear, and as if to appease the ghost gave himself up
XIX to the luxury of a most expensive funeral. Mr. Pecksniff set off in a coach to get a professional nurse, Mrs. Sairey Gamp, a baggy woman of great experience, who came to help Mr. Mould the undertaker, and Mr. Mould, with a retinue of professional mourners, escorted the late Anthony to the grave, his only real mourner apparently being the sorrowful Chuffey, who seemed in some way to connect the dead Anthony with the living Jonas as
XX effect and cause. But the funeral over, Jonas went down into the country with Mr. Pecksniff, for change of air, and with purpose, apparently, of offering himself to Mr. Pecksniff's elder daughter, for in his conversation he as good as asked Mr. Pecksniff at what rate he would buy him for a son-in-law. What he really did was to ask Mercy to marry him, thereby greatly angering Charity. But the confusion of the scene was rendered worse confounded by the unexpected appearance of old Martin Chuzzlewit and Mary, announced by Tom Pinch.

XXI Yet the affairs of old Martin must needs be suspended till the fortunes of young Martin have been made clear. He left New York with Mark on his way to Eden, to which place he had

been recommended as one of the most promising spots in America
in which to make an investment. On their way thither by rail they
fell in with Mr. Lafayette Kettle, General Choke, and other very
free and enlightened Americans of the period, and finally at the
railway terminus were introduced to the agent of Eden, Mr. Zephaniah Scadder. As the result of Mr. Scadder's representations, they
sank pretty much all their savings in a choice lot in Eden. But
XXII before they went Martin gave a reception on compulsion, to
the townspeople, and lest he should lack for company, Major
Hominy confided to him Mrs. Hominy, a large, loquacious woman,
whom he was to escort to New Thermopylae, three days this side of
XXIII Eden. And now, having made necessary purchases, they
set out for Eden itself, which they reached at last, to find
it a swamp, breeding malaria and miasma, with the one solitary inhabitant more dead than alive. It was a bitter end to Martin's
hopes, and offered Mark the most substantial foundation he had yet
seen for the building up of a jolly temperament.

XXIV It was, indeed, old Martin and Mary Graham who presented themselves to Pecksniff, and that gentleman was for
a time in great confusion of mind over the difficulties involved in
bringing together the two branches of the family under his roof.
Yet to his surprise, old Martin proved not irreconcilable, and Jonas
presently was brought face to face with him. When Martin Chuzzlewit went back to the Blue Dragon with Mary Graham, Tom Pinch
accompanied them, and when Tom Pinch came back by himself, he
discovered that he had been followed by Jonas. Tom showed spirit
on the way back and even damaged Jonas's head, thereby gaining
the rather undesirable affection of Charity Pecksniff. Mercy, meanwhile, announced her intention of marrying Jonas chiefly for the
sake of teasing him, and though old Martin tried to induce her to
look seriously upon the approaching marriage, she did not heed him
any more than she did the signs of malignity which showed them-
XXV selves in Jonas himself. The name of that man was most
mysteriously on the lips of a delirious stranger whom Mrs.
Gamp was attending at night, upon the charge of John Westlock,
her days being spent in the care of Chuffey.

XXVI But Mrs. Gamp's days' business was to close, for Poll
Sweedlepipe, her landlord, came to fetch her home, young
Bailey accompanying, — young Bailey, who was a smart young Buttons now in another place. Jonas Chuzzlewit had come home, bring-
XXVII ing his bride with him, and Mrs. Gamp would not be needed
longer. The new place which young Bailey had was that
of boy to Mr. Tigg Montague, that name representing the whirligig
of fortune for Montague Tigg, who was chairman of the Anglo-Ben-

galee Disinterested Loan and Life Insurance Company, with David
Crimple, once Crimp the pawnbroker, as secretary of the same,
Jobling, the doctor who attended old Anthony Chuzzlewit, the medical officer, and Nadgett, the close-mouthed, open-eyed man, who at a
pound a week made inquiries for the office. Into this select company Jonas Chuzzlewit was introduced as a possible policy buyer, but,
being left alone with Tigg Montague, that gentleman conceived the
notion of making Jonas a director, instead, and for that purpose
XXVIII proceeded to disclose the methods of the company. He
did more. He had him at his rooms for dinner, and there
introduced him to a choice company, and fuddled him with wine so
that young Bailey had to see him home at three o'clock in the morning, and there caught sight of his old friend, now alas! less merry in
nature than in name; he stayed long enough to guess at the brutal
XXIX way in which Jonas met his patient wife. He was cautious,
however, in his conversation with Poll Sweedlepipe, when
he put his innocent smooth face into that barber's hands the next
day, and with Mrs. Gamp who came in to tell her landlord that she
was going down into the country to attend her patient, who had so
far recovered that he could be moved from the hospital. Mr. Lewsome, for that was his name, was in a very feeble way. He tried
hard to communicate something to John Westlock, but only confirmed his friend's apprehension that he was still delirious. It may
be added that Mr. Lewsome was an object of some curiosity to Mr.
Mould, who came along just then, for Mrs. Gamp had been quite
confident that she should turn her patient over to him shortly.

XXX The removal of Mercy from her father's house had not left
that home any more united, for Charity, still sore over the
deceit which had led her on and then turned its back on her,
vented her anger on her father, and finally proposed that she should
leave him, for a time at any rate, and take up her abode with M.
Todgers. Mr. Pecksniff was not at all reluctant, since he had already
begun to harbor certain deep designs. He had secured apparently
an influence over old Martin Chuzzlewit, who showed increasing
signs of physical decay, and he thought to clinch his success by
marrying Mary Graham. He approached her therefore with a
greasy offer of marriage, which she repelled indeed with loathing,
and yet was forced to endure from her anxiety not to estrange old
XXXI Martin and his grandson. In the midst of her perplexities,
she turned to the one person whom she could trust, Tom
Pinch, and in church where she had been listening to him at the
organ, she told him all, thereby causing the fictitious Pecksniff of
Tom's careful construction to crumble suddenly, and a hideous
image of the real Pecksniff to take its place. Now it chanced that

Pecksniff himself was present at this transformation scene, for he
had stolen into the church and heard the whole conversation. He
waited till Tom had left, then he let himself out of the window and
went back to his house. Mr. Chuzzlewit was reading, for he and
Mary Graham had taken up their abode with him. With an air of
grief, Pecksniff told the old man that he had been cruelly deceived
by one who should have been grateful to him, and calling Tom
Pinch he declared that, waking from a doze in the church, he had
overheard Tom making love to Mary. Tom did not deny it, seeing
that, if he told the truth, he was in danger of incensing old Martin
against young Martin as well as Mary. So he submitted. Mr. Pecksniff thereupon discharged him from his service, and Tom Pinch
went off, sent on his way with the blessings of all in the neighbor-
XXXII hood. Cherry meanwhile had made herself at home at M.
Todgers's, where she soon succeeded in capturing the Forlorn Hope of Mr. Augustus Moddle's affections, Mr. Moddle being the
young gentleman who had been made so unhappy by his blighted
affection for Mercy.

XXXIII The dismal swamp of an Eden was all this time telling
on young Martin Chuzzlewit, and he became distressingly
ill of chills and fever. Mark tended him, and when looking for
help came upon the family whom he had befriended on shipboard.
Another old acquaintance also turned up, Mr. Hannibal Chollop, who
had the indomitable confidence in the glory of the United States
which even Eden could not dim, and delivered it as his opinion that
the people of the United States reasonably required to be "cracked
up." Then Mark fell victim to the fever, and Martin in nursing
him slowly acquired some due conception not only of Mark's fidelity, but of his own selfishness and of Mary's sacrifices. On Mark's
recovery it was determined that they should make a retreat from the
place, and Martin threw himself upon the generosity of his friend Mr.
XXXIV Bevan, who promptly responded. Thereupon they made
their way back to New York, encountering by the way Major Pogram and his satellites, and seeing Mrs. Hominy once more.
Mr. Bevan would have sent them home in the cabin, but Mark ingeniously thwarted his generous intentions by succeeding promptly to
the position of a retiring cook, and thereby paying the passage money
XXXV of both of them. Arrived in England, and pondering in the
tavern what next to do, they were amazed at discovering
Mr. Pecksniff in a dignified man who passed by. It turned out that
the corner-stone of a new school was to be laid, and Mr. Pecksniff
had come to attend the ceremony. Martin and Mark also went, and
Martin had an opportunity of being indignant at the discovery that
the school was actually to be built from his plans, with the addition
of four windows put in by Mr. Pecksniff.

Tom Pinch, after parting with both the mock and the real Peck-
XXXVI sniff, bade good-by to Mrs. Lupin and went up to London. Arriving early in the day, he made his way to John Westlock's lodgings, and was most enthusiastically received by that gentleman, who at once insisted on his making his home there. But Tom would first see Ruth, and he set out for the house where she was governess. There he found such vulgar treatment both of Ruth and of himself that, after giving the family a piece of his mind, he withdrew Ruth. After a weary search the brother and sister found lodgings in Islington, though very doubtful Tom was
XXXVII how he was to maintain himself. On his way back to John Westlock's lodgings at Furnival's Inn, he stumbled on Charity Pecksniff, who, after some conversation with him, invited him to M. Todgers's, where he found Mercy also and learned from her something of her forlorn state. Augustus Moddle, who never seemed to have recovered from his blight, saw him on his way to Furnival's, and John Westlock went with him to Islington again, catching a glimpse there of the pretty Ruth Pinch.

XXXVIII It chanced that Tom, without knowing it, had that day passed in the street a man who had a good deal to do secretly with the fortunes of one and another of the persons who made up Tom Pinch's world. This was Mr. Nadgett, a man so in love with a mystery that his only regret was when he had to share it with some one else. He had been set to work by Tigg Montague to shadow Jonas Chuzzlewit, and by dint of persistent watching and note-taking, he had accumulated a fund of information which he proceeded to lay before Tigg Montague just before Jonas himself made a call. Just what the information was might be judged from its effect on Jonas, whom it turned from a swaggerer, ready to push Tigg hard, to a subservient tool, ready to do his part in bringing geese to the company to be plucked.

XXXIX To get back to pleasanter people. In the little establishment at Islington Ruth Pinch began her experiments in housekeeping with a beefsteak pudding, and Tom on the other side of the table fell to preparing a careful inventory of his qualifications, getting as far as the fact that he was a respectable man of thirty-five, when John Westlock walked in with the announcement that a certain Mr. Fips had called upon him to offer in the name of some unknown person the post of secretary and librarian to Tom Pinch, with the salary of a hundred pounds a year. The two men at once went to the city and saw Mr. Fips; they went also to the Temple and saw the library, now in great confusion, but they learned nothing whatever of the mysterious but very timely benefactor. Then back they went to dinner with Ruth. Tom went to work, but still without knowing who was employing him. He XL and Ruth were wont to take morning strolls before he went to his work, and one day they were down among the steamboats, when they encountered Mrs. Gamp, who was looking for the "Ankwerks package;" she was much concerned over a couple of people apparently about to start for Antwerp. As they were all looking, suddenly Tom's landlord appeared at his side with a packet which he begged him to deliver at once to the retreating couple. When Tom obligingly did so, what was his amazement to discover that the two were Jonas and Mercy. More than that, the missive had extraordinary power over Jonas. It brought him back, XLI sent Mercy home in charge of Mrs. Gamp, and showed him driving off with Tigg Montague, who seemed not quite ready to part with his brother director.

Mr. Montague, when he had driven Jonas to his rooms, had it out with him. Jonas had tried to run away, — that was plain; but the chairman of the Anglo-Bengalee had further use for him, and he held the secret he possessed as a threat over his head. Jonas apparently yielded, and agreed at once to go into the country to hook Pecksniff, and insisted on Montague's going with him. Montague, XLII rather ill at ease, added young Bailey to the party, and off they set. It was a wild night; more than once Montague was sure that Jonas was on the point of murdering him, and in an overturn of the coach young Bailey was left for dead.

XLIII Meanwhile a more harmonious party had gone to the same neighborhood, for Mrs. Lupin was surprised by the reappearance of Mark Tapley, and with him came young Martin Chuzzlewit. It was a rather disquieting picture which she drew of the situation at Mr. Pecksniff's, and Martin made one or two ineffectual attempts at seeing his grandfather apart from the baleful Pecksniffian influence; failing that, he took a bolder course and presented himself to old Martin in the very presence of Pecksniff. Yet he seemed to make no impression on the old man, who appeared to receive everything through the medium of Pecksniff. Only, after old Martin had left the room with Pecksniff, young Martin had a few cheering words with Mary, when he went back to the Blue Dragon, apparently baffled, to find that Jonas and Montague were there. XLIV Their errand was accomplished with little difficulty, for Pecksniff was no match for the two, and succeeded in placing pretty much all his property in their hands before parting with them.

XLV One of the mysteries attached to the return of Jonas and Mercy from their attempted journey was in the fact that it was Tom Pinch's landlord who gave the packet to Tom to deliver,

and the mystery was not made much clearer when Tom, who with his sister had puzzled over the affair, told the story to John Westlock one night when the three were dining together in John's chambers. Still, in hopes of being of some service to poor Mercy,
XLVI Tom, taking Ruth with him, went to visit that hapless wife. On the way thither, the pair fell in with Miss Charity Pecksniff and the melancholy Moddle, so all four went to the house, where they found Mercy, Mrs. Todgers, Mrs. Gamp, and old Chuffey. It was rather a dismal assemblage with old Chuffey continually talking about the dead and Moddle apparently wishing himself dead, and it was not rendered more cheerful by the unexpected advent of Jonas. As they were leaving Tom in vain attempted to tell Jonas who it was who had entrusted the letter to him, a fact which might have let in some light, for Tom's landlord was no other than Nadgett. After they all had left, Jonas announced to his wife and Mrs. Gamp that he wanted to sleep, it may be for thirty-six hours, and he was not to be disturbed in his room. Once left
XLVII to himself, he changed his clothing, stole out of the house, and, a different looking man, travelled secretly into the country, first by coach, then by foot. Concealing himself in a wood, he waited. Into the wood came Mr. Pecksniff and Tigg Montague. They parted from each other, and Mr. Pecksniff returned to his home. Later Jonas also returned to his home. No, he had not been disturbed, Mercy told him; only one man had come to see him, that early morning, — only one man, Nadgett.

XLVIII Nadgett's lodgers could not fathom the mystery of their landlord at once, and as they were at breakfast one morning they were surprised by a call, which brought a new wonder, for Martin and Mark were the visitors. Tom went with them to the city to see John Westlock and found him closeted with a stranger, who was Lewsome just recovering from his nearly fatal illness. Then it transpired that Lewsome, being a companion of Jonas Chuzzlewit, had supplied him with a drug which had doubtless been the means of old Anthony Chuzzlewit's death. It was a terrible revelation. Yet the secret must be made known in some way. Great was the perplexity of all, when Tom remembered hearing such words from old Chuffey's lips as confirmed the suspicion that Lewsome's tale was genuine. Accordingly it was determined to get at Chuffey through Mrs. Gamp, and as a minor settlement of accounts Martin also, at John's instigation, wrote to the trustees of the Grammar school boldly claiming the plans which Mr. Pecksniff had put forward as his own.

XLIX Mrs. Gamp was to be found at her own rooms, and thither Martin and John went, but not before Poll Sweedlepipe had burst in on her and Betsey Prig with the news that young Bailey had been killed, Crimple had made off with the funds of the Anglo-Bengalee, Montague was nowhere to be found and had probably gone off to join the other precious scoundrel, and that Jonas Chuzzlewit had appeared to charge the Anglo-Bengalee with having swindled him; all which narrative so far postponed the tea that Betsey Prig was in a very irritable state of mind, and indeed ready to quarrel; and though the quarrel was averted for the moment, it was renewed over the delicate contention of the existence of Mrs. Harris.

"Now, Sairah," said Mrs. Prig, "joining business with pleasure, wot is this case in which you wants me?"

Mrs. Gamp betraying in her face some intention of returning an evasive answer, Betsey added: —

"*Is* it Mrs. Harris?"

"No, Betsey Prig: it ain't," was Mrs. Gamp's reply.

"Well," said Mrs. Prig with a short laugh, "I 'm glad of that, at any rate!"

"Why should you be glad of that, Betsey?" Mrs. Gamp retorted warmly. "She is unbeknown to you, except by hearsay: why should you be glad? If you have anythink to say contrairy to the character of Mrs. Harris, which well I knows behind her back, afore her face, or anywheres, is not to be impeaged, out with it, Betsey. I have know'd that sweetest and best of women," said Mrs. Gamp, shaking her head, and shedding tears, "ever since afore her first, which Mr. Harris, who was dreadful timid, went and stopped his ears in a empty dog-kennel, and never took his hands away or come out once till he was showed the baby, wen, bein' took with fits, the doctor collared him, and laid him on his back upon the airy stones, and she was told to ease her mind, his 'owls was organs. And I have know'd her, Betsey Prig, wen he has hurt her feelin' 'art by sayin' of his ninth, that it was one too many, if not two; while that dear innocent was cooin' in his face, which thrive it did, though bandy: but I have never know'd as you had occagion to be glad, Betsey, on account of Mrs. Harris not requiring you. Require she never will, depend upon it; for her constant word in sickness is, and will be, 'Send for Sairey!'"

During this touching address, Mrs. Prig, adroitly feigning to be the victim of that absence of mind which has its origin in excessive attention to one topic, helped herself from the teapot without appearing to observe it. Mrs. Gamp observed it, however, and came to a premature close in consequence.

"Well, it ain't her, it seems," said Mrs. Prig coldly. "Who is it, then?"

"You have heerd me mention, Betsey," Mrs. Gamp replied, after glancing in an expressive and marked manner at the teapot, "a person as I took care on at the time as you and I was pardners, off and on, in that there fever at the Bull?"

"Old Snuffey," Mrs. Prig observed.

Sarah Gamp looked at her with an eye of fire; for she saw in this mistake of Mrs. Prig another wilful and malignant stab at that same weakness or custom of hers, an ungenerous allusion to which, on the part of Betsey, had first disturbed their harmony that evening. And she saw it still more clearly, when, politely but firmly correcting that lady by the distinct enunciation of the word "Chuffey," Mrs. Prig received the correction with a diabolical laugh. . . . Her countenance became about this time derisive and defiant; and she sat with her arms folded, and one eye shut up, in a somewhat offensive, because obtrusively intelligent manner.

Mrs. Gamp, observing this, felt it the more necessary that Mrs. Prig should know her place, and be made sensible of her exact station in society, as well as of her obligations to herself. She therefore assumed an air of greater patronage and importance as she went on to answer Mrs. Prig a little more in detail.

"Mr. Chuffey, Betsey," said Mrs. Gamp, "is weak in his mind. Excuge me if I makes remark, that he may neither be so weak as people thinks, nor people may not think he is so weak as they pretends; and what I knows I knows, and what you don't you don't: so do not ask me, Betsey. But Mr. Chuffey's friends has made propojals for his bein' took care on, and has said to me, 'Mrs. Gamp, *will* you undertake it? We could n't think,' they says, 'of trusting him to nobody but you; for, Sairey, you are gold as has passed the furnage. Will you undertake it at your own price, day and night, and by your own self?'—'No,' I says, 'I will not. Do not reckon on it. There is,' I says, 'but one creetur in the world as I would undertake on sech terms; and her name is Harris. But,' I says, 'I am acquainted with a friend, whose name is Betsey Prig, that I can recommend, and will assist me. Betsey,' I says, 'is always to be trusted, under me, and will be guided as I could desire.'"

Here Mrs. Prig, without any abatement of her offensive manner, again counterfeited abstraction of mind, and stretched out her hand to the teapot. It was more than Mrs. Gamp could bear. She stopped the hand of Mrs. Prig with her own, and said with great feeling,—

"No, Betsey! Drink fair, wotever you do!"

Mrs. Prig, thus baffled, threw herself back in her chair, and closing the same eye more emphatically, and folding her arms tighter, suffered her head to roll slowly from side to side, while she surveyed her friend with a contemptuous smile.

Mrs Gamp resumed, —

"Mrs. Harris, Betsey" —

"Bother Mrs. Harris!" said Betsey Prig.

Mrs. Gamp looked at her with amazement, incredulity, and indignation; when Mrs. Prig, shutting her eye still closer, and folding her arms still tighter, uttered these memorable and tremendous words: —

"I don't believe there 's no sich a person!"

After the utterance of which expressions, she leaned forward, and snapped her fingers once, twice, thrice, each time nearer to the face of Mrs. Gamp; and then rose to put on her bonnet, as one who felt that there was now a gulf between them which nothing could ever bridge across.

The shock of this blow was so violent and sudden, that Mrs. Gamp sat staring at nothing with uplifted eyes, and her mouth open as if she were gasping for breath, until Betsey Prig had put on her bonnet and her shawl, and was gathering the latter about her throat. Then Mrs. Gamp rose, — morally and physically rose, — and denounced her.

"What!" said Mrs. Gamp, "you bage creetur! Have I know'd Mrs. Harris five and thirty year, to be told at last that there ain't no sech a person livin'? Have I stood her friend in all her troubles, great and small, for it to come at last to sech a end as this, which her own sweet picter hanging up afore you all the time to shame your bragian words? But well you may n't believe there 's no sech a creetur; for she would n't demean herself to look at you. And often has she said, when I have made mention of your name, which to my sinful sorrow I have done, — 'What, Sairey Gamp! debage yourself to *her!*' Go along with you!"

"I'm a goin', ma'am; ain't I?" said Mrs. Prig, stopping as she said it.

"You had better, ma'am," said Mrs. Gamp.

"Do you know who you 're talking to, ma'am?" inquired her visitor.

"Aperiently," said Mrs. Gamp, surveying her with scorn from head to foot, "to Betsey Prig, — aperiently so. *I* know her. No one better. Go along with you!"

"And *you* was a going to take me under you!" cried Mrs. Prig, surveying Mrs. Gamp from head to foot, in her turn, — "*you* was; was you! Oh, how kind! Why, deuse take your imperence!" said Mrs. Prig, with a rapid change from banter to ferocity, "what do you mean?"

"Go along with you!" said Mrs. Gamp. "I blush for you."

"You had better blush a little for yourself while you *are* about it!" said Mrs. Prig. "You and your Chuffeys! What, the poor old creetur is n't mad enough; is n't he? Aha!"

"He 'd very soon be mad enough if you had anything to do with him," said Mrs. Gamp.

"And that 's what I was wanted for; is it?" cried Mrs. Prig triumphantly. "Yes. But you 'll find yourself deceived. I won't go near him. We shall see how you get on without me. I won't have nothink to do with him."

"You never spoke a truer word than that!" said Mrs. Gamp. "Go along with you!"

L One mystery seemed to give way before another. Martin came to see Tom and his sister with bitter reproaches for the deceit he had practised on him. He left without disclosing what this was, but Ruth, with her womanly instinct, made it clear to him, as to herself, that Martin suspected him of winning Mary's love. Tom himself was easier in his mind now that Ruth had made him confess his great secret; and the brother and sister were happier for sharing this confidence. Ruth walked with him to the city the next day, and Tom took up his work with a momentary thought as to who his mysterious employer could be, when in walked Martin Chuzzlewit the elder, who, in a few words, made it clear to him that he had been playing a part, and that now the time was come when he could throw off his disguise and reveal the depravity of Pecksniff.

LI Jonas Chuzzlewit had made his plans to put old Chuffey under close guard of the nurse, lest he should betray the secret which he knew him to possess; and he meant himself, as soon as all was effected, to slip off out of the country. He had one more interview with Chuffey, and in his rage was about to put him out of life when Mrs. Gamp appeared. He gave Chuffey into her hands, and she undertook to quiet the old man in his chamber. Jonas was eager to see his other attendant, and Mrs. Gamp was at her wits' end to produce Mrs. Harris, who was the other, when the door opened and in came a number of persons, all engaged in closing about Jonas, — old Martin, young Martin, Lewsome, Mark Tapley, Chevy Slyme, Nadgett. Chuffey reappeared, and a hope sprang up in Jonas's mind, as the old man made it clear that he and Anthony knew of Jonas's design, but that Anthony's death was not by Jonas's poison. But the reprieve was a short one, for Nadgett told how, step by step, he had traced the murder of Montague. The end had come; but Jonas, handcuffed and waiting only for the coach to take him to prison, bribed Chevy Slyme to let him go into another room for five minutes. There he killed himself with poison.

LII It was now time for a general settlement, and by the instrumentality of Mark Tapley, the several persons who had been dealing with each other came together in Mr. Martin Chuzzlewit's apartment. Last of all came Mr. Pecksniff; and now old Martin, with his kinsfolk about him, let out all his dammed-up wrath in a blow with his walking-stick upon the hypocrite Pecksniff, and then told the tale of his own dissembling, and of how he had secretly
LIII helped young Martin. He so disposed of all the entanglements of fortune that Martin and Mary, Mark and Mrs. Lupin, paired off, and it was not long before John Westlock and Ruth made another couple. Last of all was to come the dragging to the
LIV altar of the sacrificial Moddle by Charity Pecksniff, who held the cords, but oh, marvel to relate! at the last moment, Moddle, taking his courage in both hands, fled precipitately, and Charity was left with a wrecked Hope.

---

## INDEX TO CHARACTERS

**Bailey, junior.** The "boots" at Mrs. Todgers's "Commercial Boarding-house;" a small boy with a large red head, and no nose to speak of. He afterwards becomes "Tiger" to Tigg Montague, and finally engages with Mr. Sweedlepipe in the barber business. viii, x, xi, xxvi–xxix, xxxviii, xli, xlii, xlix, lii.

**Bevan, Mr.** A sensible, warm-hearted Massachusetts man, whom Martin Chuzzlewit meets at his boarding-house in New York, and who afterwards advances him money to enable him to return to England. xvi, xvii, xxi, xxxiii, xxxiv, xliii.

**Bib, Julius Washington Merryweather.** An American gentleman in the lumber line; one of a committee that waits upon the Honorable Elijah Pogram. xxxiv.

**Brick, Jefferson.** The war correspondent of the New York Rowdy Journal. He is introduced by Colonel Diver, the editor of the newspaper, to Martin Chuzzlewit, who had at first supposed him to be the colonel's son.

"My war correspondent, sir, Mr. Jefferson Brick!"

Martin could not help starting at this unexpected announcement and the consciousness of the irretrievable mistake he had nearly made.

Mr. Brick seemed pleased with the sensation he produced upon the stranger, and shook hands with him with an air of patronage designed to reassure him, and to let him know that there was no occasion to be frightened; for he (Brick) would n't hurt him.

"You have heard of Jefferson Brick, I see, sir," quoth the colonel with a smile. "England has heard of Jefferson Brick. Europe has heard of Jefferson Brick. Let me see. When did you leave England, sir?"

"Five weeks ago," said Martin.

"Five weeks ago," repeated the colonel thoughtfully, as he took his seat upon the table, and swung his legs. "Now, let me ask you, sir, which of Mr. Brick's articles had become at that time the most obnoxious to the British Parliament and the court of St. James."

"Upon my word," said Martin, "I" —

"I have reason to know, sir," interrupted the colonel, "that the aristocratic circles of your country quail before the name of Jefferson Brick. I should like to be informed, sir, from your lips, which of his sentiments has struck the deadliest blow" —

"At the hundred heads of the Hydra of Corruption now grovelling in the dust beneath the lance of Reason, and spouting up to the universal arch above us its sanguinary gore," said Mr. Brick, putting on a little blue cloth cap with a glazed front, and quoting his last article.

"The libation of freedom, Brick," hinted the colonel.

"Must sometimes be quaffed in blood, colonel," cried Brick. And when he said "blood," he gave the great pair of scissors a sharp snap, as if *they* said blood too, and were quite of his opinion.

This done, they both looked at Martin, pausing for a reply.

"Upon my life," said Martin, who had by this time quite recovered his usual coolness, "I can't give you any satisfactory information about it; for the truth is, that I" —

"Stop!" cried the colonel, glancing sternly at his war correspondent, and giving his head one shake after every sentence. "That you never heard of Jefferson Brick, sir; that you never read Jefferson Brick, sir; that you never saw the Rowdy Journal, sir; that you never knew, sir, of its mighty influence upon the cabinets of Eu–rope. Yes!"

"That 's what I was about to observe, certainly," said Martin.

"Keep cool, Jefferson," said the colonel gravely. "Don't bust! O you Europeans! Arter that let 's have a glass of wine!" xvi.

**Brick, Mrs. Jefferson.** His wife, and the mother of "two young

Bricks." She is taken by Martin Chuzzlewit for a "little girl;" but he is put right by Colonel Diver, who informs him that she is a "matron." xvi, xvii.

**Buffum, Mr. Oscar.** A member of a committee that waits upon the Honorable Elijah Pogram for the purpose of requesting the honor of his company "at a little le-Vee" in the ladies' ordinary at the National Hotel. xxxiv.

**Bullamy.** A porter in the service of the Anglo-Bengalee Disinterested Loan and Life Insurance Company.

When he sat upon a seat erected for him in a corner of the office, with his glazed hat hanging on a peg over his head, it was impossible to doubt the respectability of the concern. It went on doubling itself with every square inch of his red waistcoat, until, like the problem of the nails in the horse's shoes, the total became enormous. People had been known to apply to effect an insurance on their lives for a thousand pounds, and, looking at him, to beg, before the form of proposal was filled up, that it might be made two. And yet he was not a giant. His coat was rather small than otherwise. The whole charm was in his waistcoat. Respectability, competence, property in Bengal, or anywhere else; responsibility to any amount on the part of the company that employed him, — were all expressed in that one garment. xxvii, li.

**Choke, General Cyrus.** An American militia general, whose acquaintance Martin Chuzzlewit makes in a railway car. He is a member of the Eden Land Corporation, belongs to the Watertoast Association of United Sympathizers, and, taken all in all, is "one of the most remarkable men in the country." xxi.

**Chollop, Major Hannibal.** A man who calls upon Martin Chuzzlewit at Eden.

He was usually described by his friends in the South and West as "a splendid sample of our na-tive raw material, sir," and was much esteemed for his devotion to rational liberty, for the better propagation whereof he usually carried a brace of revolving pistols in his coat-pocket, with seven barrels apiece. He also carried amongst other trinkets a sword-stick, which he called his "Tickler," and a great knife, which (for he was a man of a pleasant turn of humor) he called "Ripper," in allusion to its usefulness as a means of ventilating the stomach of any adversary in a close contest. He had used these weapons with distinguished effect in several instances (all duly chronicled in the newspapers), and was greatly beloved for the gallant manner in which he had "jobbed out" the eye of one gentleman as he was in the act of knocking at his own street-door.

. . . Preferring, with a view to the gratification of his tickling and ripping fancies, to dwell upon the outskirts of society, and in the more remote towns and cities, he was in the habit of emigrating from place to place, and establishing in each some business, — usually a newspaper, — which he presently sold; for the most part closing the bargain by challenging, stabbing, pistolling, or gouging the new editor, before he had quite taken possession of the property.

He had come to Eden on a speculation of this kind, but had abandoned it, and was about to leave. He always introduced himself to strangers as a worshipper of freedom; was the consistent advocate of Lynch law and slavery; and invariably recommended, both in print and speech, the "tarring and feathering" of any unpopular person who differed from himself. He called this "planting the standard of civilization in the wilder gardens of My country."

The Honorable Elijah Pogram thus eulogizes him to Martin: —

Our fellow-countryman is a model of a man, quite fresh from Natur's mould! . . . He is a true-born child of this free hemisphere! Verdant as the mountains of our country, bright and flowing as our mineral licks, unspiled by withering conventionalities as air our broad and boundless perearers! Rough he may be: so air our barrs. Wild he may be: so air our buffalers. But he is a child of Natur' and a child of Freedom; and his boastful answer to the despot and the tyrant is, that his bright home is in the settin' sun. xxiii, xxiv.

**Chuffey, Mr.** Clerk to Anthony Chuzzlewit; a little, blear-eyed, weazen-faced old man, looking as if he had been put away and forgotten half a century before, and had just been found in a lumber closet. He hardly understands any one except his master, but always understands him, and wakes up quite wonderfully when Mr. Chuzzlewit speaks to him. xi, xviii, xix, xxv, xxvi, xlvi, xlviii, xlix, li, liv.

**Chuzzlewit, Anthony.** Father of Jonas, and brother of Martin Chuzzlewit the elder; an old man with a face wonderfully sharpened by the wariness and cunning of his life. iv, viii, xii, xviii, xix.

**Chuzzlewit, George.** A gay bachelor, who claims to be young, but has been younger. He is inclined to corpulency, over-feeds himself, and has such an obvious disposition to pimples, that the bright spots on his cravat, and the rich pattern on his waistcoat, and even his glittering trinkets, seem to have broken out upon him, and not to have come into existence comfortably. iv, liv.

**Chuzzlewit, Jonas.** Son of Anthony, and nephew of old Martin

Chuzzlewit; a sly, cunning, ignorant young man, who is in pecuniary matters a miser, and in instinct and disposition a brute. His rule for bargains is, "Do other men; for they would do you." "That 's the true business-precept," he says. "All others are counterfeit." Tired of the prolonged life of his father, and eager to come into possession of his property, he attempts to poison him, and believes that he has succeeded, as the old man dies shortly afterwards. The truth is, however, that his attempt has been discovered by his intended victim and an old clerk named Chuffey, who privately remove the poison. But the thought of his son's ingratitude and unnatural wickedness breaks old Anthony's heart; and in a few days he dies, having first made Chuffey promise not to reveal the dreadful secret. Jonas now marries Mercy, the youngest daughter of Mr. Pecksniff, and treats her very cruelly. Believing that he has murdered his father, and that the secret has in some way become known to Montague Tigg, a swindling director of the Anglo-Bengalee Disinterested Loan and Life Insurance Company, Jonas is forced, as a condition of his secrecy, not only to come into the company himself, but to pay large sums to Tigg as hush-money. At last, goaded to desperation, he follows Tigg into the country, where he waylays and murders him. The deed, though very cunningly devised and executed, is soon traced to him, and he is arrested, but poisons himself on his way to prison. iv, viii, xi, xviii–xx, xxiv, xxvi–xxviii, xxxviii, xl–xlii, xliv, xlvi–xlviii, li.

**Chuzzlewit, Martin, senior.** A very rich and eccentric old gentleman; brother of Anthony, and grandfather of young Martin. He is nearly driven mad by the fawning servility and hollow professions of his covetous relatives, and even quarrels with and disinherits his grandson, the only one among them all for whom he has ever cared. Receiving a visit from his cousin, Mr. Pecksniff, under whose assumption of honest independence he instantly detects the selfishness, deceit, and low design of his true character, he takes occasion to say: —

"Judge what profit you are like to gain from any repetition of this visit, and leave me. I have so corrupted and changed the nature of all those who have ever attended on me, by breeding avaricious plots and hopes within them; I have engendered such domestic strife and discord by tarrying even with members of my own family; I have been such a lighted torch in peaceable homes, kindling up all the inflammable gases and vapors in their moral atmosphere, which, but for me, might have proved harmless to the end, — that I have, I may say, fled from all who knew me, and, taking refuge in secret places, have lived, of late, the life of one who is hunted. The young girl whom you just now saw . . . is an orphan-child, whom, with one steady purpose, I have bred and educated, or, if you prefer the word, adopted. For a year or more she has been my constant companion, and she is my only one. I have taken, as she knows, a solemn oath never to leave her sixpence when I die; but, while I live, I make her an annual allowance, not extravagant in its amount, and yet not stinted. There is a compact between us that no term of affectionate cajolery shall ever be addressed by either to the other, but that she shall call me always by my Christian name, I her by hers. She is bound to me in life by ties of interest, and losing by my death, and having no expectation disappointed, will mourn it, perhaps; though for that I care little. This is the only kind of friend I have or will have. Judge from such premises what a profitable hour you have spent in coming here, and leave me, to return no more."

Notwithstanding this plain speaking, the old man, for purposes of his own, goes to reside with Mr. Pecksniff, and pretends to be entirely governed by his wishes. When young Martin returns from America, rendered humble and penitent by his hard experience, he sees Pecksniff drive him from the door, and yet does not interpose a word. But the time soon comes when, having thoroughly tested both, and proved his grandson true, and Pecksniff false, he makes ample amends to the former, and awards the latter his just deserts. iii, iv, x, xxiv, xxx, xxxi, xliii, l–liv.

**Chuzzlewit, Martin, the younger.** The hero of the story; a rather wild and selfish young man. He has been brought up by a rich grandfather, who has intended making him his heir. But the young man presumes to fall in love with a young lady (Mary Graham) of whom the old man does not approve, and he is therefore disinherited, and thrown upon his own resources. He goes to study with Mr. Pecksniff, with a vague intention of becoming an architect. His grandfather, upon ascertaining this fact, intimates to Mr. Pecksniff (who is his cousin), that he would find it to be for his own advantage, if he should turn young Martin out of the house. This Mr. Pecksniff immediately proceeds to do; and Martin again finds himself without money, or the means of obtaining it. He determines to go to America, and accordingly makes his way to London, where he meets Mark Tapley, who has saved a little from his wages at the Blue Dragon, and who wishes to accompany him. They take passage on the packet-ship Screw, going over as steerage passengers, but with sanguine expectations of amassing sudden wealth in the New World. Soon after their arrival at New York, Martin is led into investing the little money remaining to himself and Mark in a lot of fifty acres in the thriving city of Eden, in a distant part of the country; and they set out for it immediately. They find the city — which on paper had looked so fair, with its parks and fountains, its banks, factories, churches, and public buildings of all kinds — a dreary and malarious marsh, with a dozen log cabins comprising the whole settlement. Worse than all, Martin is seized with fever and ague, and barely escapes with his life; and, before he is fairly convalescent, Mark is also stricken down. When they are at last able to move about a little, they turn their faces toward England, and after some time arrive at home. Martin seeks an interview with his grandfather, but finds that Mr. Pecksniff's influence over him is paramount, and that not even a frank and manly avowal of error, coupled with a request for forgiveness, avails to revive the old love, or to save him from the indignity of being ordered out of the house. Miss Graham, however, has remained faithful to him; and with this one comfort he again turns his face towards London, to make his way in the great world as best he can. In the sequel he finds, much to his surprise, that his grandfather, distracted by suspicions, doubts, and fears, has only been probing Pecksniff, and accumulating proofs of his duplicity, and that, all through their separation, he himself has remained the old man's favorite. v–vii, xii–xvii, xxi, xxii, xxxiii–xxxv, xliii, xlviii–l, lii–liv.

**Cicero.** A negro truckman in New York, formerly a slave. xvii.

**Codger, Miss.** A Western literary celebrity. xxxiv.

**Crimple, David.** A pawnbroker, afterwards tapster at the Lombards' Arms, and then secretary of the Anglo-Bengalee Disinterested Loan and Life Insurance Company. His name was originally Crimp; but as this was susceptible of an awkward construction, and might be misrepresented, he altered it to Crimple. xiii, xxvii, xxviii, xlix, li.

**Diver, Colonel.** Editor of the New York Rowdy Journal; a sallow man, with sunken cheeks, black hair, small twinkling eyes, and an expression compounded of vulgar cunning and conceit. xv.

**Dunkle, Doctor Ginery.** One of a committee of citizens that waits upon the Honorable Elijah Pogram to request the honor of his company at a little le-Vee at the National Hotel. Although he has the appearance of a mere boy with a very shrill voice, he passes for "a gentleman of great poetical elements." xxxiv.

**Fips, Mr.** A lawyer, who, as the agent of an unknown person (old Martin Chuzzlewit), employs Tom Pinch as a kind of librarian and secretary. xxxix, xl, liii.

SAIREY GAMP AND BETSEY PRIG.

**Fladdock, General.** A corpulent American militia officer, starched and punctilious, to whom Martin Chuzzlewit is introduced at the Norrises in New York, as having come over from England in the same vessel with himself. The general does not recognize him; and Martin is obliged to explain, that, for the sake of economy, he had been obliged to take passage in the steerage, — a confession which at once stamps him as a fellow of no respectability, who has gained an entrance into good society under false pretences, and whose acquaintance must forthwith be disavowed. xv, xvii.

**Gamp, Sairey.** A professional nurse.

She was a fat old woman, this Mrs. Gamp, with a husky voice and a moist eye, which she had a remarkable power of turning up, and only showing the white of it. Having very little neck, it cost her some trouble to look over herself, if one may say so, at those to whom she talked. She wore a very rusty black gown, rather the worse for snuff, and a shawl and bonnet to correspond. In these dilapidated articles of dress she had, on principle, arrayed herself, time out of mind, on such occasions as the present; for this at once expressed a decent amount of veneration for the deceased, and invited the next of kin to present her with a fresher suit of weeds, — an appeal so frequently successful, that the very fetch and ghost of Mrs. Gamp, bonnet and all, might be seen hanging up, any hour in the day, in at least a dozen of the second-hand-clothes shops about Holborn. The face of Mrs. Gamp — the nose in particular — was somewhat red and swollen; and it was difficult to enjoy her society without becoming conscious of a smell of spirits. Like most persons who have attained to great eminence in their profession, she took to hers very kindly; insomuch, that, setting aside her natural predilections as a woman, she went to a lying-in or a laying-out with equal zest and relish.

Mrs. Gamp is represented as constantly quoting or referring to a certain Mrs. Harris — a purely imaginary person — as an authority for her own fancies and fabrications. Thus, when Mr. Pecksniff says to her, that he supposes she has become indifferent to the distress of surviving friends around the bed of the dying and of the dead, and that "use is second nature," —

"You may well say second nater, sir," returned that lady. "One's first ways is to find sich things a trial to the feelings, and so is one's lasting custom. If it was n't for the nerve a little sip of liquor gives me (I never was able to do more than taste it), I never could go through with what I sometimes has to do. 'Mrs. Harris,' I says at the very last case as ever I acted in, which it was but a young person, — 'Mrs. Harris,' I says, 'leave the bottle on the chimley-piece, and don't ask me to take none, but let me put my lips to it when I am so dispoged, and then I will do what I 'm engaged to do, according to the best of my ability.' — 'Mrs. Gamp,' she says in answer, 'if ever there was a sober creetur to be got at eighteen-pence a day for working-people, and three and six for gentlefolks' ('night-watching,'" said Mrs. Gamp, with emphasis, "'being a extra charge'), 'you are that inwallable person.' — 'Mrs. Harris,' I says to her, 'don't name the charge; for, if I could afford to lay all my feller-creeturs out for nothink, I would gladly do it; sich is the love I bears 'em. But what I always says to them as has the management of matters, Mrs. Harris'" (here she kept her eye on Mr. Pecksniff), "'be they gents or be they ladies, is, don't ask me whether I won't take none, or whether I will, but leave the bottle on the chimley-piece, and let me put my lips to it when I am so dispoged.'" xix, xxv, xxvi, xxix, xl, xlvi, xlix, li, lii.

**Gander, Mr.** A boarder at Mrs. Todgers's. ix.

**Graham, Mary.** Companion of old Martin Chuzzlewit, and betrothed to young Martin, whom she finally marries.

She was very young (apparently not more than seventeen), timid and shrinking in her manner, and yet with a greater share of self-possession and control over her emotions than usually belongs to a far more advanced period of female life. . . . She was short in stature, and her figure was slight, as became her years; but all the charms of youth and maidenhood set it off, and clustered on her gentle brow. iii, v, vi, xxiv, xxx, xxxi, xxxiii, xliii, lii, liii.

**Groper, Colonel.** One of a committee who wait upon the Honorable Elijah Pogram to request his attendance at a le-Vee at the National Hotel, given to him by the citizens. xxxiv.

**Hominy, Mrs.** A literary celebrity introduced to Martin Chuzzlewit. She is "one of our chicest spirits, and belongs toe one of our most aristocratic families." xxii, xxiii, xxxiv.

**Izzard, Mr.** One of the deputation of citizens who beg the attendance of the Honorable Elijah Pogram at a little le-Vee at eight o'clock in the evening at the National Hotel. xxxiv.

**Jack.** Driver of a stage-coach plying between London and Salisbury. xxxvi.

**Jane.** Mr. Pecksniff's female servant. xxxi.

**Jinkins, Mr.** The oldest boarder at Mrs. Todgers's; a gentleman of a fashionable turn, who frequents the parks on Sundays, and knows a great many carriages by sight. ix–xi, liv.

**Jobling, Doctor John.** Medical officer of the Anglo-Bengalee Disinterested Loan and Life Insurance Company. xxvii, xxviii, xxxviii, xli.

**Jodd, Mr.** A member of the committee of citizens that waits upon the Honorable Elijah Pogram to solicit the favor of his company at a le-Vee at the National Hotel. xxxiv.

**Kedgick, Captain.** Landlord of the National Hotel, at which Martin Chuzzlewit stays on his way to Eden, and also on his return to New York. xxii, xxxiv.

**Kettle, Lafayette.** An inquisitive, bombastic American, whom Martin Chuzzlewit meets while travelling; secretary of the Watertoast Association of United Sympathizers. xxi, xxii.

**Lewsome, Mr.** A young man bred a surgeon, and employed by a general practitioner in London as an assistant. Being indebted to Jonas Chuzzlewit, he sells him the drugs with which old Anthony Chuzzlewit is poisoned, though he has reason to suspect the use which will be made of them. After the death of the old man, he makes a voluntary confession of his agency in the matter; being impelled to do so by the torture of his mind and the dread of death caused by a severe sickness. xxv, xxix, xlviii, li.

**Lupin, Mrs.** Landlady of the Blue Dragon Inn at Salisbury; afterwards the wife of Mark Tapley.

The mistress of the Blue Dragon was in outward appearance just what a landlady should be,—broad, buxom, comfortable, and good-looking, with a face of clear red and white, which by its jovial aspect at once bore testimony to her hearty participation in the good things of the larder and cellar, and to their thriving and healthful influences. She was a widow, but years ago had passed through her state of weeds, and burst into flower again; and in full bloom she was now, with roses on her ample skirts, and roses on her bodice, roses in her cap, roses in her cheeks,—ay, and roses, worth the gathering too, on her lips, for that matter. She had still a bright black eye and jet black hair; was comely, dimpled, plump, and tight as a gooseberry; and, though she was not exactly what the world calls young, you may make an affidavit, on trust, before any mayor or magistrate in Christendom, that there are a great many young ladies in the world (blessings on them, one and all!) whom you would n't like half as well, or admire half as much, as the beaming hostess of the Blue Dragon. iii, iv, vii, xxxi, xxxvi, xxxvii, xliii, xliv, lii.

**Moddle, Mr. Augustus.** The "youngest gentleman" at Mrs. Todgers's Commercial Boarding-house. He falls desperately in love with Miss Mercy Pecksniff, and, becoming very low-spirited after her marriage to Jonas Chuzzlewit, is entrapped into an engagement with her sister Charity; but loses his courage, and breaks his word at the last moment, sending the injured fair one a letter to inform her that he is on his way to Van Diemen's

Land, and that it will be useless for her to send in pursuit, as he is determined never to be taken alive. ix–xi, xxxii, xxxvii, xlvi, liv.

**Montague, Tigg.** *See* TIGG, MONTAGUE.

**Mould, Mr.** An undertaker; a little bald elderly man, with a face in which a queer attempt at melancholy was at odds with a smirk of satisfaction. xix, xxv, xxix, xxxviii.

**Mould, Mrs.** His wife. xxv, xxix.

**Mould, The two Misses.** Their daughters; fair, round, and chubby damsels, with their peachy cheeks distended as though they ought of right to be performing on celestial trumpets. xxv.

**Mullit, Professor.** A very short gentleman, with a red nose, whom Martin Chuzzlewit meets at Mrs. Pawkins's boarding-house in New York. He is a professor "of education," a man of "fine moral elements," and author of some powerful pamphlets, written under the signature of Suturb, or Brutus reversed. xvi.

**Nadgett, Mr.** Tom Pinch's landlord, employed by Montague Tigg as a detective.

He was a short, dried-up, withered old man, who seemed to have secreted his very blood; for nobody would have given him credit for the possession of six ounces of it in his whole body. How he lived was a secret; where he lived was a secret; and even what he was was a secret. In his musty old pocket-book he carried contradictory cards, in some of which he called himself a coal-merchant, in others a wine-merchant, in others a commission-agent, in others a collector, in others an accountant; as if he really did n't know the secret himself. He was always keeping appointments in the city, and the other man never seemed to come. xxvii, xxviii, xxxviii, xl, xli, xlvii, li.

**Norris, Mr.** A New York gentleman, wealthy, aristocratic, and fashionable; a sentimental abolitionist, and "a very good fellow in his way," but inclined "to set up on false pretences," and ridiculously afraid of being disgraced by moneyless acquaintances. xvii.

**Norris, Mrs.** His wife; much older and more faded than she ought to have looked. xvii.

**Norris, The two Misses.** Their daughters; one eighteen, the other twenty, both very slender, but very pretty. xvii.

**Pawkins, Major.** A New York politician; a bold speculator (or swindler), an orator and a man of the people, and a general loafer. xvi.

**Pawkins, Mrs.** His wife; keeper of a boarding-house. xvi.

**Pecksniff, Seth.** A resident of Salisbury; ostensibly an architect and land-surveyor, though he had never designed or built anything, and his surveying was limited to the extensive prospect from the windows of his house.

Mr. Pecksniff was a moral man. . . . Perhaps there never was a more moral man than Mr. Pecksniff, especially in his conversation and correspondence. It was once said of him by a homely admirer, that he had a Fortunatus's purse of good sentiments in his inside. In this particular he was like the girl in the fairy-tale, except that, if they were not actual diamonds which fell from his lips, they were the very brightest paste, and shone prodigiously. He was a most exemplary man, — fuller of virtuous precept than a copy-book. Some people likened him to a direction-post, which is always telling the way to a place, and never goes there; but these were his enemies, the shadows cast by his brightness: that was all. His very throat was moral. You saw a good deal of it. You looked over a very low fence of white cravat (whereof no man had ever beheld the tie, for he fastened it behind), and there it lay, a valley between two jutting heights of collar, serene and whiskerless before you. It seemed to say, on the part of Mr. Pecksniff, "There is no deception, ladies and gentlemen; all is peace; a holy calm pervades me." So did his hair, just grizzled with an iron-gray, which was all brushed off his forehead, and stood bolt upright, or slightly drooped in kindred action with his heavy eyelids. So did his person, which was sleek, though free from corpulency. So did his manner, which was soft and oily. In a word, even his plain black suit, and state of widower, and dangling double eye-glass, — all tended to the same purpose, and cried aloud, "Behold the moral Pecksniff!"

Mr. Pecksniff's professional engagements were almost, if not entirely, confined to the reception of pupils; for the collection of rents, with which pursuit he occasionally varied and relieved his graver toils, can hardly be said to be a strictly architectural employment. His genius lay in insnaring parents and guardians, and pocketing premiums. A young gentleman's premium being paid, and the young gentleman come to Mr. Pecksniff's house, Mr. Pecksniff borrowed his case of mathematical instruments (if silver mounted, or otherwise valuable); entreated him from that moment to consider himself one of the family; complimented him highly on his parents or guardians, as the case might be; and turned him loose in a spacious room on the two-pair front; where, in the company of certain drawing-boards, parallel rulers, very stiff-legged compasses, and two, or, perhaps, three, other young gentlemen, he improved himself for three or five years, according to his articles, in making elevations of Salisbury Cathedral from every possible point of sight, and in constructing in the air a vast quantity of castles, houses of parliament, and other public buildings.

Mr. Pecksniff is a cousin of old Martin Chuzzlewit's, who being very ill, a general council and conference of his relatives is held at Mr. Pecksniff's house in order to devise means of inducing him to listen to the promptings of nature in the disposal of his large property. The meeting is far from being harmonious; and Mr. Pecksniff is compelled to listen to some very plain truths, Mr. Anthony Chuzzlewit telling him bluntly not to be a hypocrite.

"A what, my good sir?" demanded Mr. Pecksniff.

"A hypocrite."

"Charity, my dear," said Mr. Pecksniff, "when I take my chamber candle-stick to-night, remind me to be more than usually particular in praying for Mr. Anthony Chuzzlewit, who has done me an injustice."

Meeting Mr. Chuzzlewit in a stage-coach, some time afterwards, Mr. Pecksniff takes occasion to remark, incidentally, but cuttingly, "I may be a hypocrite; but I am not a brute."

"Pooh, pooh!" said the old man. "What signifies that word, Pecksniff? Hypocrite! Why, we are all hypocrites. We were all hypocrites t' other day. I am sure I felt that to be agreed upon among us, or I should n't have called you one. We should not have been there at all if we had not been hypocrites. The only difference between you and the rest was — Shall I tell you the difference between you and the rest now, Pecksniff?"

"If you please, my good sir; if you please."

"Why, the annoying quality in *you* is," said the old man, "that you never have a confederate or partner in *your* juggling. You would deceive everybody, even those who practise the same art; and have a way with you, as if you — he, he, he! — as if you really believed yourself. I'd lay a handsome wager now," said the old man, "if I laid wagers (which I don't, and never did), that you keep up appearances by a tacit understanding, even before your own daughters here."

During the journey, Pecksniff imbibes copious refreshment from a brandy-bottle, and is thereafter moved to give utterance to various moral precepts and weighty sentiments.

"What are we," said Mr. Pecksniff, "but coaches? Some of us are slow coaches" —

"Goodness, pa!" cried Charity.

"Some of us, I say," resumed her parent, with increased emphasis, "are slow coaches; some of us are fast coaches. Our Passions are the horses, and rampant animals too!" —

MR. PECKSNIFF AND HIS DAUGHTERS.

"Really, pa!" cried both the daughters at once. "How very unpleasant!"

"And rampant animals, too!" repeated Mr. Pecksniff, with so much determination, that he may be said to have exhibited, at the moment, a sort of moral rampancy himself; "and Virtue is the drag. We start from The Mother's Arms, and we run to The Dust Shovel."

When he had said this, Mr. Pecksniff, being exhausted, took some further refreshment. When he had done that, he corked the bottle tight, with the air of a man who had effectually corked the subject also, and went to sleep for three stages.

Mr. Pecksniff receives young Martin Chuzzlewit into his family as a student, and manifests a very strong interest in him; but, on a hint from the elder Mr. Chuzzlewit, he contumeliously turns him out of his house, and renounces him forever. This he does because Martin's grandfather has expressed his desire for a better understanding between himself and Mr. Pecksniff than has hitherto existed, and has declared his intention to attach him to himself by ties of interest and expectation. Systematic self-server that he is, in order to secure the old man's great wealth, Mr. Pecksniff sedulously studies his likings and dislikings, falls in with all his prejudices, lies, fawns, and worms himself (as he thinks) into his favor, through concessions and crooked deeds innumerable, through meannesses and vile endurance, and through all manner of dirty ways; but in the end he finds that, after all, his labor has been for naught, that his duplicity has been fathomed to the bottom, and his servile character thoroughly unmasked. Yet he remains the same canting hypocrite even in shame and discovery, and in the drunkenness and beggary in which he ends his days. ii–vi, viii–xii, xviii–xx, xxiv, xxx, xxxi, xxxv, xliii, xliv, xlvii, lii, liv.

**Pecksniff, Charity,** *called* CHERRY. Mr. Pecksniff's elder daughter, betrothed to Mr. Augustus Moddle, but deserted by him on the very day appointed for the wedding. ii, iv–vi, viii–xi, xviii, xx, xxiv, xxx, xxxii, xxxvii, xliv, xlvi, liv.

**Pecksniff, Mercy,** *called* MERRY. His younger daughter; a giddy, vain, and heartless girl, and a hypocrite like her father.

Her simplicity and innocence . . . were great,—very great. . . . She was all girlishness and playfulness and wildness and kittenish buoyancy. She was the most arch, and at the same time the most artless creature, was the youngest Miss Pecksniff, that you can possibly imagine. It was her great charm. She was too fresh and guileless to wear combs in her hair, or to turn it up, or to frizzle it, or to braid it. She wore it in a crop,—a loosely flowing crop, which had so many rows of curls in it, that the top row was only one curl.

Mr. Jonas Chuzzlewit, a thoroughly sordid and despicable villain, after making love to her sister, abruptly proposes to herself. She accepts and marries him, — partly to spite her sister, and partly because he has money. She soon finds out that he is a brute as well as a rascal, and she suffers much from his cruelty; yet — wonderful to relate! — "throwing aside at once the ingrained selfishness and meanness of nearly thirty years," she "becomes in less than two months a model of uncomplaining endurance and self-denying affection." ii, iv–vi, viii, x, xi, xx, xxii, xxiv, xxvi, xxviii, xxxvi, xl, xlvi, xlvii, li, liv.

**Pinch, Ruth.** Governess in a wealthy brass and copper founder's family at Camberwell; sister to Tom Pinch; afterwards the wife of John Westlock. ix, xxxvi, xxxvii, xxxix, xl, xlvi, xlviii, l, lii–liv.

**Pinch, Tom.** An ungainly, awkward-looking man, extremely short-sighted, and prematurely bald. He is an assistant to Mr. Pecksniff, for whom he has an unbounded respect, and in whose pretensions he has a wonderful faith; his nature being such, that he is timid and distrustful of himself, and trustful of all other men, — even the least deserving.

He was far from handsome, certainly; and was dressed in a snuff-colored suit, of an uncouth make at the best, which, being shrunken with long wear, was twisted and tortured into all kinds of odd shapes. But notwithstanding his attire and his clumsy figure, which a great stoop in his shoulders, and a ludicrous habit he had of thrusting his head forward, by no means redeemed, one would not have been disposed (unless Mr. Pecksniff said so) to consider him a bad fellow by any means. He was, perhaps, about thirty; but he might have been almost any age between sixteen and sixty, being one of those strange creatures who never decline into an ancient appearance, but look their oldest when they are very young, and get over it at once.

Tom's faith in his master remains unshaken for a long time; but his eyes are opened at last, and he sees him to be a consummate hypocrite and villain. Pecksniff, knowing himself to have been found out, discharges Tom, who goes to London to try his fortune, and is befriended by old Martin Chuzzlewit secretly, at first, but afterwards openly. ii, v–vii, ix, xii, xiv, xx, xxiv, xxx, xxxi, xxxvi–xl, xlv, xlvi, xlviii, l, lii–liv.

**Pip, Mr.** A theatrical character, and a "capital man to know;" a friend of Montague Tigg's. xxxviii.

**Piper, Professor.** One of a deputation chosen to wait upon the Honorable Elijah Pogram, to request the honor of his company at a little le-Vee, at eight o'clock in the evening, in the ladies' ordinary of the National Hotel. xxxiv.

**Pogram, The Honorable Elijah.** A member of Congress, and "one of the master minds of our country," whose acquaintance Martin Chuzzlewit makes on his return from Eden to New York. He is especially noted as the author of the "Pogram Defiance," "which rose so much con-test and preju-dice in Europe." Mr. Pogram is waited on at the National Hotel by a committee of the citizens, and tendered a public reception, or "levee," the same evening.

Each man took one slide forward as he was named, butted at the Honorable Elijah Pogram with his head, shook hands, and slid back again. The introductions being completed, the spokesman resumed.

"Sir!"

"Mr. Pogram!" cried the shrill boy.

"Perhaps," said the spokesman with a hopeless look, "you will be so good, Doctor Ginery Dunkle, as to charge yourself with the execution of our little office, sir?"

As there was nothing the shrill boy desired more, he immediately stepped forward.

"Mr. Pogram! Sir! A handful Of your fellow-citizens, sir, hearing Of your arrival at the National Hotel, and feeling the patriotic character Of your public services, wish, sir, to have the gratification Of beholding you, and mixing with you, sir, and unbending with you, sir, in those moments which"—

"Air," suggested Buffum.

"Which air so peculiarly the lot, sir, Of our great and happy country."

"Hear!" cried Colonel Groper in a loud voice. "Good! Hear him! Good!"

"And therefore, sir," pursued the doctor, "they request, as A mark Of their respect, the honor of your company at a little le-Vee, sir, in the ladies' ordinary, at eight o'clock."

Mr. Pogram bowed, and said:—

"Fellow countrymen!"

"Good!" cried the colonel. "Hear him! Good!"

Mr. Pogram bowed to the colonel individually, and then resumed:—

"Your approbation of My labors in the common cause goes to My heart. At all times and in all places, in the ladies' ordinary, My friends, and in the Battle Field"—

"Good, very good! Hear him! Hear him!" said the colonel.

"The name of Pogram will be proud to jine you. And may it, My friends, be written on My tomb, 'He was a member of the Con-gress of our common country, and was ac-Tive in his trust.'"

"The Com-mittee, sir," said the shrill boy, "will wait upon you at five minutes afore eight. I take My leave, sir."

Mr. Pogram shook hands with him, and everybody else, once more; and, when they came back again at five minutes before eight, they said, one by one, in a melancholy voice, "How do you do, sir?" and shook hands with Mr. Pogram all over again, as if he had been abroad for a twelvemonth in the mean time, and they met now at a funeral.

But by this time Mr. Pogram had freshened himself up, and had composed his hair and features after the Pogram statue: so that any one with half an eye might cry out, "There he is! as he delivered the Defiance!" The committee were embellished also; and, when they entered the ladies' ordinary in a body, there was much clapping of hands from ladies and gentlemen, accompanied by cries of "Pogram! Pogram!" and some standing up on chairs to see him.

The object of the popular caress looked round the room as he walked up it, and smiled, at the same time observing to the shrill boy, that he knew something of the beauty of the daughters of their common country, but had never seen it in such lustre and perfection as at that moment. Which the shrill boy put in the paper next day, to Elijah Pogram's great surprise.

"We will re-quest you, sir, if you please," said Buffum, laying hands on Mr. Pogram as if he were taking a measure for his coat, "to stand up with your back agin the wall right in the furthest corner, that there may be more room for our fellow cit-izens. If you could set your back right slap agin that curtain-peg, sir, keeping your leg everlastingly behind the stove, we should be fixed quite slick."

Mr. Pogram did as he was told, and wedged himself into such a little corner, that the Pogram statue would n't have known him.

The entertainments of the evening then began. Gentlemen brought ladies up, and brought themselves up, and brought each other up, and asked Elijah Pogram what he thought of this political question, and what he thought of that, and looked at him, and looked at one another, and seemed very unhappy indeed. The ladies on the chairs looked at Elijah Pogram through their glasses, and said audibly, "I wish he'd speak! Why don't he speak? Oh, do ask him to speak!" And Elijah Pogram looked sometimes at the ladies, and sometimes elsewhere, delivering senatorial opinions as he was asked for them. But the great end and object of the meeting seemed to be not to let Elijah Pogram out of the corner on any account: so there they kept him hard and fast. xxxiv.

ELIJAH POGRAM AND MRS. HOMINY.

**Prig, Betsey.** A day-nurse; a bosom-friend of Mrs. Gamp's.

Mrs. Prig was of the Gamp build, but not so fat; and her voice was deeper and more like a man's. She had also a beard.

These two ladies often "nuss together, turn and turn about, one off, one on." They are both engaged by John Westlock to take care of an acquaintance of his who lies dangerously ill at a public house in London; and, when Mrs. Gamp relieves Mrs. Prig, the following conversation occurs: —

"Anythin' to tell afore you goes, my dear?" asked Mrs. Gamp, setting her bundle down inside the door, and looking affectionately at her partner.

"The pickled salmon," Mrs. Prig replied, "is quite delicious. I can partick'ler recommend it. Don't have nothink to say to the cold meat; for it tastes of the stable. The drinks is all good."

Mrs. Gamp expressed herself much gratified.

"The physic and them things is on the drawers and mankle-shelf," said Mrs. Prig cursorily. "He took his last slime draught at seven. The easy-chair ain't soft enough. You'll want his piller."

Mrs. Gamp thanked her for these hints, and, giving her a friendly good-night, held the door open until she had disappeared at the other end of the gallery.

The patient at last recovers sufficiently to admit of his being removed to the country; and Mrs. Gamp and Mrs. Prig superintend the arrangements for the journey.

He was so wasted that it seemed as if his bones would rattle when they moved him. His cheeks were sunken, and his eyes unnaturally large. He lay back in the easy-chair like one more dead than living, and rolled his languid eyes towards the door when Mrs. Gamp appeared, as painfully as if their weight alone were burdensome to move.

"And how are we by this time?" Mrs. Gamp observed. "We looks charming."

"We looks a deal charminger than we are, then," returned Mrs. Prig, a little chafed in her temper. "We got out of bed back'ards, I think; for we're as cross as two sticks. I never see sich a man! He would n't have been washed if he'd had his own way."

"She put the soap in my mouth," said the unfortunate patient feebly.

"Could n't you keep it shut, then?" retorted Mrs. Prig. "Who do you think's to wash one feater, and miss another, and wear one's eyes out with all manner of fine work of that description, for half a crown a day? If you wants to be tittivated, you must pay accordin'."

"Oh, dear me!" cried the patient. "Oh, dear, dear!"

"There!" said Mrs. Prig, "that 's the way he 's been a-conducting of himself, Sairah, ever since I got him out of bed, if you 'll believe it."

"Instead of being grateful," Mrs. Gamp observed, "for all our little ways. Oh, fie for shame, sir! fie for shame!"

Here Mrs. Prig seized the patient by the chin, and began to rasp his unhappy head with a hair-brush.

"I suppose you don't like that, neither," she observed, stopping to look at him.

It was just possible that he did n't; for the brush was a specimen of the hardest kind of instrument producible by modern art, and his very eyelids were red with the friction. Mrs. Prig was gratified to observe the correctness of her supposition, and said triumphantly, she "know'd as much."

When his hair was smoothed down comfortably into his eyes, Mrs. Prig and Mrs. Gamp put on his neckerchief, adjusting his shirt-collar with great nicety, so that the starched points should also invade those organs, and afflict them with an artificial ophthalmia. His waistcoat and coat were next arranged; and as every button was wrenched into a wrong button-hole, and the order of his boots was reversed, he presented, on the whole, rather a melancholy appearance.

"I don't think it 's right," said the poor weak invalid. "I feel as if I was in somebody else's clothes. I 'm all on one side; and you 've made one of my legs shorter than the other. There 's a bottle in my pocket, too. What do you make me sit upon a bottle for?"

"Deuse take the man!" cried Mrs. Gamp, drawing it forth. "If he ain't been and got my night-bottle here! I made a little cupboard of his coat when it hung behind the door, and quite forgot it, Betsey. You 'll find an ingun or two, and a little tea and sugar, in his t'other pocket, my dear, if you 'll just be good enough to take 'em out."

Betsey produced the property in question, together with some other articles of general chandlery; and Mrs. Gamp transferred them to her own pocket, which was a species of nankeen pannier. Refreshment then arrived in the form of chops and strong ale for the ladies, and a basin of beef-tea for the patient; which refection was barely at an end when John Westlock appeared.

The arrangements are finally completed; and, as Mrs. Gamp is to accompany the invalid, she bids farewell to Mrs. Prig.

"Wishin' you lots of sickness, my darling creetur," Mrs. Gamp observed, "and good places. It won't be long, I hope, afore we works together, off and on, again, Betsey; and may our next meetin' be at a large family's, where they all takes it reg'lar, one from another, turn and turn about, and has it business-like!"

"I don't care how soon it is," said Mrs. Prig; "nor how many weeks it lasts."

The two friends have a falling out at last, however. Mrs. Prig has been invited to take tea with Mrs. Gamp, on which occasion the latter informs her of another prospective job of nursing in partnership, and Betsey has the temerity to doubt the existence of Mrs. Harris. xxv, xxix, xlix.

**Scadder, Zephaniah.** Agent of the Eden Land Corporation. He dupes Martin Chuzzlewit into buying, for the ridiculously small sum of a hundred and fifty dollars, a little lot of fifty acres in the city from which the company takes its name, and which looks wonderfully thriving on paper, but proves to consist of a few log-houses in the midst of a hideous and pestilential morass.

He was a gaunt man in a huge straw hat and a coat of green stuff. The weather being hot, he had no cravat, and wore his shirt-collar wide open, so that every time he spoke something was seen to twitch and jerk up in his throat, like the little hammers in a harpsichord when the notes are struck. Perhaps it was the truth feebly endeavoring to leap to his lips. If so, it never reached them.

Two gray eyes lurked deep within this agent's head; but one of them had no sight in it, and stood stock still. With that side of his face he seemed to listen to what the other side was doing. Thus each profile had a distinct expression; and, when the movable side was most in action, the rigid one was in its coldest state of watchfulness. It was like turning the man inside out, to pass to that view of his features in his liveliest mood, and see how calculating and intent they were.

Each long black hair upon his head hung down as straight as any plummet-line; but rumpled tufts were on the arches of his eyes, as if the crow whose foot was deeply printed in the corners had pecked and torn them in a savage recognition of his kindred nature as a bird of prey. xxi.

**Simmons, William.** Driver of a van, who carries Martin Chuzzlewit from near Salisbury to Hounslow, after his dismissal by Mr. Pecksniff. xiii.

**Slyme, Chevy.** A very poor and shiftless relative of old Martin Chuzzlewit, and anxious to come into a share of his property. He is a friend of Montague Tigg's, who thus describes his character to Mr. Pecksniff:—

"Every man of true genius has his peculiarity. Sir, the peculiarity of my friend Slyme is, that he is always waiting round the corner. He is perpetually round the corner, sir. He is round the corner at this instant. Now," said the gentleman, shaking his forefinger before his nose, and planting his legs wider apart as he looked attentively in Mr. Pecksniff's face, "that is a remarkably curious and interesting trait in Mr. Slyme's character; and, whenever Slyme's life comes to be written, that trait must be thoroughly worked out by his biographer, or society will not be satisfied. Observe me, society will not be satisfied."

. . . . . . . . . . . . .

With this announcement he hurried away to the outer door of the Blue Dragon, and almost immediately returned with a companion shorter than himself, who was wrapped in an old blue camlet cloak with a lining of faded scarlet. His sharp features being much pinched and nipped by long waiting in the cold, and his straggling red whiskers and frowzy hair being more than usually dishevelled from the same cause, he certainly looked rather unwholesome and uncomfortable than Shakspearian or Miltonic.

"Now," said Mr. Tigg, clapping one hand on the shoulder of his prepossessing friend, and calling Mr. Pecksniff's attention to him with the other, "you two are related; and relations never did agree, and never will, which is a wise dispensation and an inevitable thing, or there would be none but family parties, and everybody in the world would bore everybody else to death. If you were on good terms, I should consider you a most confoundedly unnatural pair; but, standing towards each other as you do, I look upon you as a couple of devilish deep-thoughted fellows, who may be reasoned with to any extent." iv, vii, li.

**Smif, Putnam.** A young and ardent clerk in a dry-goods store, who "aspirates" for fame, and applies to Martin Chuzzlewit for assistance. xxii.

**Sophia.** A pupil of Ruth Pinch's, called by Mrs. Todgers "a syrup" (meaning a seraph or a sylph); a premature little woman of thirteen years old, who had already arrived at such a pitch of whalebone and education, that she had nothing girlish about her. ix, xxxvi.

**Spottletoe, Mr.** A relative of old Martin Chuzzlewit, with testamentary designs upon his property. He is so bald, and has such big whiskers, that he seems "to have stopped his hair, by the sudden application of some powerful remedy, in the very act of falling off his head, and to have fastened it irrevocably on his face." iv, liv.

**Spottletoe, Mrs.** His wife; a woman "much too slim for her years, and of a poetical constitution." iv, liv.

**Sweedlepipe, Paul,** *called* POLL. A bird-fancier, who is an easy shaver and a fashionable hair-dresser also; Mrs. Gamp's landlord.

He was a little elderly man, with a clammy cold right hand, from which even rabbits and birds could not remove the smell of shaving-soap. Poll had something of the bird in his nature; not of the hawk or eagle, but of the sparrow, that builds in chimney-stacks, and inclines to human company. He was not quarrelsome, though, like the sparrow; but peaceful, like the dove. In his walk he strutted; and in this respect he bore a faint resemblance to the pigeon, as well as in a certain prosiness of speech, which might, in its monotony, be likened to the cooing of that bird. He was very inquisitive; and when he stood at his shop-door in the evening-tide, watching the neighbors, with his head on one side, and his eye cocked knowingly, there was a dash of the raven in him. Yet there was no more wickedness in Poll than in a robin. Happily, too, when any of his ornithological properties were on the verge of going too far, they were quenched, dissolved, melted down, and neutralized in the barber; just as his bald head — otherwise as the head of a shaved magpie — lost itself in a wig of curly black ringlets, parted on one side, and cut away almost to the crown, to indicate immense capacity of intellect. xix, xxvi, xxix, xlix, lii.

**Tacker.** Foreman, and chief mourner of Mr. Mould the undertaker.

An obese person, with his waistcoat in closer connection with his legs than is quite reconcilable with the established ideas of grace, with that cast of feature which is figuratively called a bottle-nose, and with a face covered all over with pimples. He had been a tender plant once upon a time, but, from constant blowing in the fat air of funerals, had run to seed. xix, xxv.

**Tamaroo.** An old woman in the service of Mrs. Todgers; successor to Bailey.

It appeared, in the fulness of time, that the jocular boarders had appropriated the word [Tamaroo] from an English ballad, in which it is supposed to express the bold and fiery nature of a certain hackney-coachman; and that it was bestowed upon Mr. Bailey's successor by reason of her having nothing fiery about her, except an occasional attack of that fire which is called St. Anthony's. This ancient female . . . was chiefly remarkable for a total absence of all comprehension upon any subject whatever. She was a perfect tomb for messages and small parcels; and, when despatched to the post-office with letters, had been frequently seen endeavoring to insinuate them into casual chinks in private doors, under the delusion that any door with a hole in it would answer the purpose. She was a very little old woman, and always wore a very coarse apron with a bib before, and a loop behind, together with bandages on her wrist, which appeared to be afflicted with an everlasting sprain. She was on all occasions chary of opening the street-door, and ardent to shut it again; and she waited at table in a bonnet. xxxii, liv.

**Tapley, Mark.** Hostler at the Blue Dragon Inn, kept by Mrs. Lupin; a young fellow of some five or six and twenty, with a whimsical face and a very merry pair of blue eyes, and usually dressed in a remarkably free and fly-away fashion. He believes that there never "was a man as could come out so strong under circumstances that would make other men miserable" as himself, if he could "only get a chance." But that he finds it difficult to do. He takes the situation at the Dragon in consequence of having made up his mind that it is the dullest little out-of-the-way corner in England, and that there would be some credit in being jolly in such a place. But he leaves it because there is no dulness there whatever; skittles, cricket, quoits, ninepins, comic songs, choruses, company round the chimney-corner every winter evening, making the little inn as merry as merry can be. Going to London, he meets Martin Chuzzlewit, and finding him moneyless, and resolved to go to America, he begs permission to accompany him as his man-servant. After some opposition, Martin consents; and they take passage in the steerage of the packet-ship Screw.

It is due to Mark Tapley to state, that he suffered at least as much from sea-sickness as any man, woman, or child on board; and that he had a peculiar faculty of knocking himself about on the smallest provocation, and losing his legs at every lurch of the ship. But resolved, in his usual phrase, to "come out strong" under disadvantageous circumstances, he was the life and soul of the steerage, and made no more of stopping in the middle of a facetious conversation to go away and be excessively ill by himself, and afterwards come back in the very best and gayest of temper to resume it, than if such a course of proceeding had been the commonest in the world.

It cannot be said that, as his illness wore off, his cheerfulness and good nature increased, because they would hardly admit of augmentation; but his usefulness among the weaker members of the party was much enlarged; and at all times and seasons there he was, exerting it. If a gleam of sunshine shone out of the dark sky, down Mark tumbled into the cabin; and presently up he came again with a woman in his arms, or half a dozen children, or a man, or a bed, or a saucepan, or a basket, or something, animate or inanimate, that he thought would be the better for the air. If an hour or two of fine weather in the middle of the day tempted those who seldom or never came on deck at other times to crawl into the long-boat, or lie down upon the spare spars, and try to eat, there, in the centre of the group, was Mr. Tapley, handing about salt beef and biscuit, or dispensing tastes of grog, or cutting up the children's provisions with his pocket-knife, for their greater ease and comfort, or reading aloud from a venerable newspaper, or singing some roaring old song to a select party, or writing the beginnings of letters to their friends at home for people who could n't write, or cracking jokes with the crew, or nearly getting blown over the side, or emerging half-drowned from a shower of spray, or lending a hand somewhere or other; but always doing something for the general entertainment. At night, when the cooking-fire was lighted on the deck, and the driving sparks that flew among the rigging and the cloud of sails seemed to menace the ship with certain annihilation by fire, in case the elements of air and water failed to compass her destruction, there again was Mr. Tapley, with his coat off, and his shirt-sleeves turned up to his elbows, doing all kinds of culinary offices; compounding the strangest dishes; recognized by every one as an established authority; and helping all parties to achieve something, which, left to themselves, they never could have done, and never would have dreamed of. In short, there never was a more popular character than Mark Tapley became on board that noble and fast-sailing line-of-packet ship the Screw; and he attained at last to such a pitch of universal admiration, that he began to have grave doubts within himself, whether a man might reasonably claim any credit for being jolly under such exciting circumstances.

Arrived at New York, Martin invests all his own means and Mark's, in the purchase of a fifty-acre lot in the distant "city" of Eden, which is represented to them as a flourishing town with banks, churches, markets, wharves, and the like. It is Martin's intention to establish himself here as an architect; and he takes Mark into partnership, in consideration of his having furnished much the larger share of their joint stock. On reaching the place, however, after a long and fatiguing journey of many days, they find it to be a hideous swamp, exhaling deadly miasms, and containing only a few scattered log-cabins. Martin is terribly disheartened on discovering the outrageous swindle that has been practised upon him, and soon sinks under an attack of the fever that prevails throughout the settlement.

"Now, Mr. Tapley," said Mark, giving himself a tremendous blow in the chest by way of reviver, "just you attend to what I've got to say. Things is looking about as bad as they *can* look, young man. You'll not have such another opportunity for showing your jolly disposition, my fine fellow, as long as you live. And therefore, Tapley, now's your time to come out strong, or never!"

Martin no sooner recovers than Mark is prostrated. For many weary days and nights he lies burning up with fever; but as long as he can speak, he assures Martin that he is still "jolly," and when, at last, he is too far gone to speak, he feebly writes "jolly" on a slate. After a long and lingering illness, he slowly recovers; and when able to get about once more, they both set their faces towards Old England, where they arrive in due time. Mark turns his steps towards the Blue Dragon, and he finds his old friend Mrs. Lupin alone in the bar. Wrapped up as he is in a great-coat, she does not know him at first, but soon utters a glad cry of recognition, and he catches her in his arms.

"Yes, I will!" cried Mark, "another — one more — twenty more! You did n't know me in that hat and coat? I thought you would have known me anywheres. Ten more!"

"So I should have known you if I could have seen you; but I could n't, and you spoke so gruff! I did n't think you could speak gruff to me, Mark, at first coming back."

"Fifteen more!" said Mr. Tapley. "How handsome and how young you look! Six more! The last half-dozen war n't a fair one, and must be done over again. Lord bless you, what a treat it is to see you! One more! Well, I never was so jolly! Just a few more on account of there not being any credit in it."

When Mr. Tapley stopped in these calculations in simple addition, he did it, not because he was at all tired of the exercise, but because he was out of breath. The pause reminded him of other duties.

"Mr. Martin Chuzzlewit's outside," he said. "I left him under the cart-shed while I came on to see if there was anybody here. We want to keep quiet to-night, till we know the news from you, and what it's best for us to do."

"There's not a soul in the house, except the kitchen company," returned the hostess. "If they were to know you had come back, Mark, they'd have a bonfire in the street, late as it is."

"But they must n't know it to-night, my precious soul," said Mark: "so have the house shut, and the kitchen-fire made up; and, when it's all ready, put a light in the winder, and we'll come in. One more! I long to hear about old friends. You'll tell me all about 'em; won't you, — Mr. Pinch, and the butcher's dog down the street, and the terrier over the way, and the wheelwright's, and every one of 'em. When I first caught sight of the church to-night, I thought the steeple would have choked me, I did. One more! Won't you? Not a very little one to finish off with?"

"You have had plenty, I am sure," said the hostess. "Go along with your foreign manners!"

"That ain't foreign, bless you!" cried Mark. "Native as oysters, that is! One more, because it's native; as a mark of respect for the land we live in! This don't count as between you and me, you understand," said Mr. Tapley. "I ain't a kissing you now, you'll observe. I have been among the patriots! I'm a kissin' my country!"

This love-passage ends in the marriage of Mark to the fair widow, and the conversion of the Blue Dragon into Jolly Tapley. "A sign of my own invention," said Mark; "wery new, conwivial, and expressive." v, vii, xiii–xv, xvii, xxi–xxiii, xxxiii–xxxv, xliii, xlviii, li–liii.

**Tigg, Montague,** *alias* Tigg Montague. A needy sharper, and a friend of Chevy Slyme's.

The gentleman was of that order of appearance which is currently termed shabby-genteel, though, in respect of his dress, he can hardly be said to have been in any extremities, as his fingers were a long way out of his gloves, and the soles of his feet were at an inconvenient distance from the upper-leather of his boots. His nether garments were of a bluish-gray, — violent in its colors once, but sobered now by age and dinginess, — and were so stretched and strained in a tough conflict between his braces and his straps, that they appeared every moment in danger of flying asunder at the knees. His coat, in color blue, and of a military cut, was buttoned and frogged up to his chin. His cravat was, in hue and pattern, like one of those mantles which hair-dressers are accustomed to wrap about their clients during the progress of the professional mysteries. His hat had arrived at such a pass, that it would have been hard to determine whether it was originally white or black. But he wore a mustache, — a shaggy mustache, too; nothing in the meek and merciful way, but quite in the fierce and scornful style, — the regular satanic sort of thing; and he wore, besides, a vast quantity of unbrushed hair. He was very dirty and very jaunty, very bold and very mean, very swaggering and very slinking, very much like a man who might have been something better, and unspeakably like a man who deserved to be something worse.

At a later period, having come into the possession of a few pounds, he unites with David Crimple, a tapster who has saved a few pounds (*see* CRIMPLE, DAVID), and, reversing his name and making it Tigg Montague, Esquire, organizes a swindling concern called the Anglo-Bengalee Disinterested Loan and Life Insurance Company, and, peculating on a grander scale than formerly, becomes a grander man altogether.

He had a world of jet black shining hair upon his head, upon his cheeks, upon his chin, upon his upper lip. His clothes, symmetrically made, were of the newest fashion and the costliest kind. Flowers of gold and blue, and green, and blushing red, were on his waistcoat; precious chains and jewels sparkled on his breast; his fingers, clogged with brilliant rings, were as unwieldy as summer flies but newly rescued from a honey-pot; the daylight mantled in his gleaming hat and boots as in a polished glass: and yet, though changed his name, and changed his outward surface, it was Tigg. Though turned and twisted upside down and inside out, as great men have been sometimes known to be; though no longer Montague Tigg, but Tigg Montague: still it was Tigg,—the same satanic, gallant, military Tigg. The brass was burnished, lacquered, newly stamped, yet it was the true Tigg metal notwithstanding.

Obtaining private information of Jonas Chuzzlewit's attempt to poison his father, Tigg makes use of his knowledge of the fact to compel him not only to invest largely in the stock of the Anglo-Bengalee out of his own wealth, but to persuade his father-in-law, Mr. Pecksniff, to do so likewise. Jonas, finding his secret known and himself baffled, hunted, and beset, watches his opportunity, and murders Tigg; but his crime is discovered, and he is arrested, and put into a coach to be carried to prison, but poisons himself on the way. iv, vii, xii, xiii, xxii, xxviii, xxxviii, xl–xlii, xliv, xlvii.

**Todgers, Mrs. M.** Keeper of a Commercial Boarding-house in London; a bony and hard-featured lady, with a row of curls in front of her head, shaped like little barrels of beer.

"Presiding over an establishment like this makes sad havoc with the features, my dear Miss Pecksniffs," said Mrs. Todgers. "The gravy alone is enough to add twenty years to one's age, I do assure you."

"Lor!" cried the two Miss Pecksniffs.

"The anxiety of that one item, my dears," said Mrs. Todgers, "keeps the mind continually upon the stretch. There is no such passion in human nature as the passion for gravy among commercial gentlemen. It's nothing to say a joint won't yield—a whole animal would n't yield—the amount of gravy they expect each day at dinner; and what I have undergone, in consequence," cried Mrs. Todgers, raising her eyes, and shaking her head, "no one would believe."

Though not a handsome woman, Mrs. Todgers is a very kind-hearted one; and when Mrs. Jonas Chuzzlewit (Mercy Pecksniff), heart-broken and destitute, applies to her for sympathy and assistance, she extends both ready hand and heart.

Commercial gentlemen and gravy had tried Mrs. Todgers's temper: the main chance—it was such a very small one, in her case, that she might have been excused for looking sharp after it, lest it should entirely vanish from her sight—had taken a firm hold on Mrs. Todgers's attention. But in some odd nook in Mrs. Todgers's breast, up a great many steps, and in a corner easy to be overlooked, there was a secret door, with "Woman" written on the spring, which, at a touch from Mercy's hand, had flown wide open, and admitted her for shelter.

When boarding-house accounts are balanced with all other ledgers, and the books of the Recording Angel are made up forever, perhaps there may be seen an entry to thy credit, lean Mrs. Todgers, which shall make thee beautiful. viii–xi, xxxii, xxxvii, xlvi, liv.

**Toppit, Miss.** A literary lady whom Mrs. Hominy introduces to the Honorable Elijah Pogram. xxxiv.

**Westlock, John.** A young man who has been a pupil of Pecksniff's, but has a difference with him, and leaves him. He is a warm friend of Tom Pinch's, whose sister Ruth he finally marries. ii, xii, xxv, xxix, xxxvi, xxxvii, xxxix, xl, xlv, xlviii, xlix, li–liii.

**Wolf, Mr.** A friend and confederate of Montague Tigg's; introduced to Jonas Chuzzlewit as a literary character connected with a remarkably clever weekly paper. xxviii.

## DOMBEY AND SON

### OUTLINE

Chapter I Paul Dombey was eight and forty years old when the hope of his ten years of married life was realized in the birth of a son. A daughter, Florence, had been born six years before, but what was a daughter to the head of the firm of Dombey and Son? Even the death of his wife — for Mrs. Dombey died in giving birth to little Paul — was chiefly important to him as it deprived his

II son of the natural source of nourishment. In consequence of the deprivation, Mrs. Toodle, under the name of Richards, became little Paul's nurse. She was selected, with much care, from among a great many applicants, by Mr. Dombey's sister, Mrs.

III Chick, aided by her friend, Lucretia Tox. It was not long before Richards found out the neglect that Florence was suffering from her father. In every way she could Richards tried to remedy the fault, but to no avail. Little Florence had no attraction for her father's eyes, so full were they of the future of the Son of the House.

IV Soon after little Paul's birth, young Walter Gay became a clerk in the house of Dombey and Son. His employment by that noted city firm was a great event to him and to his uncle, old Solomon Gills, maker of nautical instruments. They celebrated it duly with the aid of Captain Cuttle.

His face, remarkable for a brown solidity, brightened as he shook hands with uncle and nephew; but he seemed to be of a laconic disposition, and merely said, —

"How goes it?"

"All well," said Mr. Gills, pushing the bottle towards him.

He took it up, and, having surveyed and smelt it, said with extraordinary expression: —

"*The?*"

"*The,*" returned the instrument-maker.

Upon that he whistled as he filled his glass, and seemed to think they were making holiday indeed.

"Wal'r!" he said, arranging his hair (which was thin) with his hook, and then pointing it at the instrument-maker, "look at him! Love! Honor! And Obey! Overhaul your catechism till you find that passage, and when found turn the leaf down. Success, my boy!"

He was so perfectly satisfied both with his quotation and his reference to it, that he could not help repeating the words again in a low voice, and saying he had forgotten 'em these forty year.

"But I never wanted two or three words in my life that I did n't know where to lay my hand upon 'em, Gills," he observed. "It comes of not wasting language as some do."

The reflection, perhaps, reminded him that he had better, like young Norval's father, "increase his store." At any rate, he became silent.

There could be no doubt, however, that the two old men, at least, entertained the most Whittingtonian hopes as to the outcome of Walter's employment.

V When little Paul was christened, Mr. Dombey, in his self-centred way, made some acknowledgment of the kindnesses that had been done for little Paul. He gave Miss Tox a bracelet, — she had been assiduous in helping Mrs. Chick look after the motherless boy, — thereby setting her susceptible heart in a flutter. To Mrs. Richards he announced that he had procured a place for her oldest boy, Rob, in a charity school. The thought of Rob in

VI the uniform of a charity grinder so wrought upon Mrs. Richards's motherly feelings that she determined to see him the next day. As it was against Mr. Dombey's rules for her to see any of her family while she was nursing Paul, she had to make her visit home as secret as possible. All would have gone well had not Florence, who, with her nurse, accompanied Mrs. Richards, been lost on the way back. Very luckily she was found and taken home by Walter Gay, — a circumstance which enhanced the Whittingtonian hopes of his uncle and Captain Cuttle. But the accident resulted in the discharge of Mrs. Richards.

VII Upon the departure of the warm-hearted Richards, Mrs. Chick and Miss Tox increased their watchfulness over the care of little Paul. Apparently Miss Tox had an end in view, for about this time Major Bagstock, — "Joey B., sir!" — who had lodgings in Princess's Place, where the susceptible Lucretia dwelt, began to find her growing neglectful of his neighborliness, and to suspect in consequence that her thoughts were centring elsewhere.

"Joey B., sir," the major would say, with a flourish of his walking-stick, "is worth a dozen of you! If you had a few more of the Bagstock breed among you, sir, you 'd be none the worse for it. Old Joe, sir, need n't look far for a wife, even now, if he was on the lookout: but he 's hard-hearted, sir, is Joe; he 's tough, sir, — tough, and de-vilish sly!" After such a declaration, wheezing sounds would be heard; and the major's blue would deepen into purple, while his eyes strained and started convulsively. . . .

And yet Miss Tox, as it appeared, forgot him, — gradually forgot him. She began to forget him soon after her discovery of the Toodle family; she continued to forget him up to the time of the christening; she went on forgetting him with compound interest after that. Something or somebody had superseded him as a source of interest.

"Good-morning, ma'am!" said the major, meeting Miss Tox in Princess's Place, some weeks after the changes chronicled in the last chapter.

"Good-morning, sir," said Miss Tox very coldly.

"Joe Bagstock, ma'am," observed the major with his usual gallantry, "has not had the happiness of bowing to you at your window for a considerable period. Joe has been hardly used, ma'am. His sun has been behind a cloud."

Miss Tox inclined her head, but very coldly indeed.

"Joe's luminary has been out of town, ma'am, perhaps," inquired the major.

"I out of town? Oh, no! I have not been out of town," said Miss Tox. "I have been much engaged lately. My time is nearly all devoted to some very intimate friends. I am afraid I have none to spare even now. Good-morning, sir!"

As Miss Tox, with her most fascinating step and carriage, disappeared from Princess's Place, the major stood looking after her with a bluer face than ever, muttering and growling some not at all complimentary remarks.

"Why, damme, sir!" said the major, rolling his lobster-eyes round and round Princess's Place, and apostrophizing its fragrant air, "six months ago, the woman loved the ground Josh Bagstock walked on. What 's the meaning of it?"

The major decided, after some consideration, that it meant man-traps; that it meant plotting and snaring; that Miss Tox was digging pitfalls. "But you won't catch Joe, ma'am," said the major. "He 's tough, ma'am; tough is J. B., — tough and de-vilish sly!" Over which reflection he chuckled for the rest of the day.

VIII With all the care of his aunt and his aunt's friends, however, little Paul failed to grow strong or like other boys; so, when he was nearly five years old, he was ordered to the seashore for a change of air. He and Florence were placed, therefore, under the charge of Mrs. Pipchin, a notable trainer of children, who lived at Brighton.

IX Walter's uncle Sol falling into financial difficulties, Walter, by the advice of Captain Cuttle, sought aid of Mr.
Dombey, who granted it in the name of little Paul. The generosity
X of Mr. Dombey confirmed in the minds of the captain and
the instrument-maker the idea that Walter was another
Whittington.

XI Under Mrs. Pipchin's restraining influence Paul grew more and more "old-fashioned," more and more apart from normal boyhood. His great pleasure was in Florence, and the two children clung to each other with rare affection. They had been with Mrs. Pipchin a year when Mr. Dombey decided to place Paul under Dr. Blimber, who kept a sort of intellectual forcing-house at Brighton. To Dr. Blimber's, accordingly, Paul was escorted by his
father and sister (to whom he clung). And there they left him to
XII endure the forcing process that had produced the brainless
(but amiable) Toots, Dr. Blimber's head boy. His only comfort was the nearness of Florence, to whom he went every Saturday at Mrs. Pipchin's, and from whom he got the help and loving kindness and sympathy that sustained him through his unnatural, loveless life at Dr. Blimber's.

XIII Now Walter Gay had inadvertently incurred the displeasure of Mr. Dombey, so that, opportunity affording, the latter determined to send him to a distant office of the firm, and gave his manager instructions accordingly. There were two brothers in the office of Dombey and Son, of whom one was the manager and the other a mere clerk. The latter, John Carker, because of a theft committed, and forgiven him, in the early years of his employment with the firm, had remained a mere clerk and an object of hatred to his brother. By showing kindness to John Carker, Walter had incurred the dislike of James Carker, the manager, so that he, too, had an object in getting rid of the boy.

XIV It was just before the end of his first half-year at Dr. Blimber's school that little Paul, never strong, began to fail seriously in health. He stayed on, nevertheless, until the end of the term in order to give Florence the pleasure of the Blimbers' closing party.

XV In the mean while Walter, who fully realized that his appointment to the Barbadoes was not an advancement, was greatly puzzled to know how to break the news of it to his uncle Sol without dashing the latter's hopes of him to the ground. He decided finally to consult Captain Cuttle, and to leave the matter
with him. He had done so when he was summoned to the bedside
XVI of little Paul, who was very ill. And little Paul died leaving
kind words for all those who had been kind to him. But at

the end his love and his thought were all for Florence; and death came while his arms were about her neck.

"Don't be so sorry for me, dear papa. Indeed, I am quite happy!"

His father coming and bending down to him, he held him round the neck, and repeated those words to him several times, and very earnestly; and he never saw his father in his room again at any time, whether it were day or night, but he called out, "Don't be so sorry for me! Indeed, I am quite happy!" This was the beginning of his always saying in the morning that he was a great deal better, and that they were to tell his father so.

How many times the golden water danced upon the wall, how many nights the dark river rolled towards the sea in spite of him, Paul never sought to know. If their kindness, or his sense of it, could have increased, they were more kind, and he more grateful, every day; but whether there were many days or few appeared of little moment now to the gentle boy.

One night he had been thinking of his mother, and her picture in the drawing-room down stairs. The train of thought suggested to him to inquire if he had ever seen his mother; for he could not remember whether they had told him yes or no; the river running very fast, and confusing his mind.

"Floy, did I ever see mamma?"

"No, darling: why?"

"Did I never see any kind face, like a mamma's, looking at me when I was a baby, Floy?"

"Oh, yes, dear!"

"Whose, Floy?"

"Your old nurse's. Often."

"And where is my old nurse? Show me that old nurse, Floy, if you please."

"She is not here, darling. She shall come to-morrow."

"Thank you, Floy!"

Little Dombey closed his eyes with those words, and fell asleep. When he awoke, the sun was high, and the broad day was clear and warm. Then he awoke, — woke mind and body, — and sat upright in his bed. He saw them now about him. There was no gray mist before them, as there had been sometimes in the night. He knew them every one, and called them by their names.

"And who is this? Is this my old nurse?" asked the child, regarding with a radiant smile a figure coming in.

Yes, yes. No other stranger would have shed those tears at sight of him, and called him her dear boy, her pretty boy, her own poor blighted child. No other woman would have stooped down by his bed, and taken up his wasted hand, and put it to her lips and breast as one who had some right to fondle it. No other woman would have so forgotten everybody there but him and Floy, and been so full of tenderness and pity.

"Floy, this is a kind, good face! I am glad to see it again. Don't go away, old nurse. Stay here! Good-by!"

"Good-by, my child?" cried Mrs. Pipchin, hurrying to his bed's head. "Not good-by?"

"Ah, yes! Good-by! — Where is papa?"

His father's breath was on his cheek before the words had parted from his lips. The feeble hand waved in the air, as if it cried, "Good-by!" again.

"Now lay me down; and, Floy, come close to me, and let me see you."

Sister and brother wound their arms around each other, and the golden light came streaming in, and fell upon them locked together.

"How fast the river runs between its green banks and the rushes, Floy. But it's very near the sea now. I hear the waves! They always said so!"

Presently he told her that the motion of the boat upon the stream was lulling him to rest. Now the boat was out at sea; and now there was a shore before him. Who stood on the bank?

He put his hands together as he had been used to do at his prayers. He did not remove his arms to do it; but they saw him fold them so behind his sister's neck.

"Mamma is like you, Floy. I know her by the face! But tell them that the picture on the stairs at school is not divine enough. The light about the head is shining on me as I go."

The golden ripple on the wall came back again, and nothing else stirred in the room. The old, old fashion! — the fashion that came in with our first garments, and will last unchanged until our race has run its course, and the wide firmament is rolled up like a scroll; the old, old fashion, — Death!

Oh, thank God, all who see it, for that older fashion yet of Immortality! And look upon us, angels of young children, with regards not quite estranged, when the swift river bears us to the ocean!

XVII It was part of Captain Cuttle's idea concerning Walter's future that he was to marry Florence. To further this consummation, he called upon Mr. Carker, the manager, who, for some purpose of his own, allowed the captain to infer that the sending of Walter away was the first step toward raising him to fortune and ultimately to the hand of Florence.

Throughout her brother's short life, Florence had been sadly un-
XVIII noticed by any of her relatives excepting him, and now that
Paul was dead she longed more than ever to comfort, and to be comforted by, her father. But the loss of his hopes in Paul had so embittered Mr. Dombey against "the rival of his son in health and life" — for thus he thought of Florence — that he kept her at a distance. In spite of this, however, Florence resolved to try the harder to win her place in her father's heart.

When the time came for Walter to set sail for the Barba-
XIX does, it was very sad for him and for his uncle. It was sad for Florence, too, although she helped to ease his going away, for now she added to her own liking for him her remembrance of Paul's fondness. Walter had a send-off by Cap'n Cuttle and Sol Gills.

"Wal'r," said the captain, when they took their seats at table, "if your uncle 's the man I think him, he 'll bring out the last bottle of *the* Madeira on the present occasion."

"No, no, Ned!" returned the old man. "No! That shall be opened when Walter comes home again."

"Well said!" cried the captain. "Hear him!"

"There it lies," said Sol Gills, "down in the little cellar, covered with dirt and cobwebs. There may be dirt and cobwebs over you and me, perhaps, Ned, before it sees the light."

"Hear him!" cried the captain. "Good morality! Wal'r, my lad. Train up a fig-tree in the way it should go, and when you are old sit under the shade on it. Overhaul the— Well," said the captain, on second thoughts, "I ain't quite certain where that 's to be found; but, when found, make a note of. Sol Gills, heave ahead again!"

Old Sol and the captain accompanied the lad on board the ship to see him off, the former with moist eyes, the latter with a very grave face.

The captain. . . drew Walter into a corner, and, with a great effort that made his face very red, pulled up the silver watch, which was so big, and so tight in his pocket, that it came out like a bung.

"Wal'r," said the captain, handing it over, and shaking him heartily by the hand, "a parting gift, my lad. Put it back a half an hour every morning, and about a quarter towards the arternoon, and it 's a watch that 'll do you credit."

To get rest and to recuperate after little Paul's death,
XX Mr. Dombey with Major Bagstock went to Leamington,
where they met Mrs. Skewton — a woman of Heart — and
XXI her daughter, the beautiful and disdainful Edith.

Mr. Carker, the manager, in the mean while, was in the
XXII city pursuing his own plans, of which a part was to discover

what friendly relation existed between Florence and old Solomon Gills. For that purpose he obtained for Rob Toodle — formerly a charity grinder and now an idle vagabond entirely subject to Mr. Carker — nominal work in Mr. Gills's shop.

XXIII While her father was away Florence lived alone with her maid, schooling herself to patience. Besides her father's neglect there was new cause for grief in the absence of news from Walter, and in the anxiety the lack of news caused his uncle Sol. What relief she and Sol could get was in calling on Cap'n Cuttle and allowing him to conduct them to the oracle Bunsby.

"With regard to old Sol Gills," here the captain became solemn, "who I 'll stand by, and not desert until death doe us part, and when the stormy winds do blow, do blow, do blow, — overhaul the catechism," said the captain, parenthetically, "and there you 'll find them expressions, — if it would console Sol Gills to have the opinion of a seafaring man as has got a mind equal to any undertaking that he puts it alongside of, and as was all but smashed in his 'prentice ship, and of which the name is Bunsby, that 'ere man shall give him such an opinion in his own parlor as 'll stun him. Ah!" said Captain Cuttle vauntingly, "as much as if he 'd gone and knocked his head again a door!"

They accordingly go to see Captain Bunsby, and, under the pilotage of Captain Cuttle, board The Cautious Clara.

Immediately there appeared, coming slowly up above the bulkhead of the cabin, another bulkhead, — human and very large, — with one stationary eye in the mahogany face, and one revolving one, on the principle of some lighthouses. This head was decorated with shaggy hair, like oakum, which had no governing inclination towards the north, east, west, or south, but inclined to all four quarters of the compass, and to every point upon it. The head was followed by a perfect desert of chin, and by a shirt-collar and neckerchief, and by a dread-nought pilot-coat, and by a pair of dread-nought pilot-trousers, whereof the waistband was so very broad and high, that it became a succedaneum for a waistcoat, being ornamented near the wearer's breastbone with some massive wooden buttons like backgammon-men. As the lower portions of these pantaloons became revealed, Bunsby stood confessed; his hands in their pockets (which were of vast size), and his gaze directed not to Captain Cuttle or the ladies, but the mast-head.

. . . Whispering to Florence that Bunsby had never in his life expressed surprise, and was considered not to know what it meant, the captain watched him as he eyed his mast-head, and afterwards swept the horizon; and, when the revolving eye seemed to be coming round in his direction, said: —

"Bunsby, my lad, how fares it?"

A deep, gruff, husky utterance, which seemed to have no connection with Bunsby, and certainly had not the least effect upon his face, replied, "Ay, ay, shipmet, how goes it?" At the same time, Bunsby's right hand and arm, emerging from a pocket, shook the captain's, and went back again.

"Bunsby," said the captain, striking home at once, "here you are, — a man of mind, and a man as can give an opinion. Here's a young lady as wants to take that opinion in regard of my friend Wal'r; likewise my t'other friend, Sol Gills, which is a character for you to come within hail of, being a man of science, which is the mother of inwention, and knows no law. Bunsby, will you ware, to oblige me, and come along with us?"

The great commander, who seemed by the expression of his visage to be always on the lookout for something in the extremest distance, and to have no ocular knowledge of anything within ten miles, made no reply whatever.

He finally consents to go with them, however, and at last delivers the following "opinion:" —

"My name 's Jack Bunsby!"

"He was christened John," cried the delighted Captain Cuttle. "Hear him!"

"And what I says," pursued the voice, after some deliberation, "I stands to."

The captain, with Florence on his arm, nodded at the auditory, and seemed to say, "Now he 's coming out! This is what I meant when I brought him."

"Whereby," proceeded the voice, "why not? If so, what odds? Can any man say otherwise? No. Awast then!"

When it had pursued its train of argument to this point, the voice stopped and rested. It then proceeded very slowly, thus: —

"Do I believe this here Son and Heir 's gone down, my lads? Mayhap. Do I say so? Which? If a skipper stands out by Sen' George's Channel, making for the Downs, what 's right ahead of him? The Goodwins. He is n't forced to run upon the Goodwins; but he may. The bearings of this observation lays in the application on it. That ain't no part of my duty. Awast then, keep a bright lookout for'ard, and good luck to you!"

The voice here went out of the back-parlor and into the street, taking the commander of The Cautious Clara with it, and accompanying him on board again with all convenient expedition, where he immediately turned in, and refreshed his mind with a nap.

XXIV But distraction came to her in the form of a visit to Lady Skettles, with whom she met Mr. Carker, the manager, and felt something of his cat-like nature.

XXV It was while she was away that Mr. Gills suddenly disappeared, and that Captain Cuttle assumed the direction of his shop, though this involved a secret flight from the MacStinger tyranny.

In the silence of night, the captain packed up his heavier property in a chest, which he locked, intending to leave it there, in all probability forever, but on the forlorn chance of one day finding a man sufficiently bold and desperate to come and ask for it. Of his lighter necessaries the captain made a bundle, and disposed his plate about his person, ready for flight. At the hour of midnight, when Brig Place was buried in slumber, and Mrs. MacStinger was lulled in sweet oblivion, with her infants around her, the guilty captain, stealing down on tiptoe, in the dark, opened the door, closed it slowly after him, and took to his heels.

Pursued by the image of Mrs. MacStinger springing out of bed, and, regardless of costume, following and bringing him back, pursued also by a consciousness of his enormous crime, Captain Cuttle held on at a great pace, and allowed no grass to grow under his feet between Brig Place and the instrument-maker's door. It opened when he knocked (for Rob was on the watch); and when it was bolted and locked behind him, Captain Cuttle felt comparatively safe.

"Whew!" cried the captain, looking round him, "it 's a breather!"

"Nothing the matter; is there, captain?" cried the gaping Rob.

"No, no," said Captain Cuttle, after changing color, and listening to a passing footstep in the street. "But mind ye, my lad, if any lady, except either of them two as you see t'other day, ever comes and asks for Cap'en Cuttle, be sure to report no person of that name known, nor never heard of here. Observe them orders; will you?"

"I 'll take care, captain," returned Rob.

"You might say, if you liked," hesitated the captain, "that you 'd read in the paper, that a cap'en of that name was gone to Australia, emigrating along with a whole ship's complement of people as had all swore never to come back no more."

XXVI When Mr. Carker, the manager, visited his chief at Leamington — he had been called there on business of the firm — he began to carry out the plan he had of widening the estrangement of Mr. Dombey from Florence. To help him, though unwittingly,

XXVII in his plans he found there another figure coming into Mr. Dombey's life; for Edith — the disdainful beauty — by a process of sale, as she felt it to be, was to become the second Mrs. Dombey.

XXVIII While Florence was visiting Lady Skettles, Toots — formerly Dr. Blimber's head boy — called regularly upon her and her hostess, in his queer embarrassed way, to the great amusement of Florence's maid, Susan Nipper. When Florence returned home, she was greatly surprised to learn of her father's intended marriage. Between Edith and Florence, however, a bond of sympathy was formed at their first meeting, — a bond of which Mr. Carker was later to make fatal use.

XXIX Mr. Dombey's engagement to Edith had the effect of blighting Miss Tox's hopes, and of revealing to Mrs. Chick the undesirability of having friends of the sincerely susceptible Lucretia's station in life.

XXX Edith and Florence, in the interval between their first meeting and the approaching marriage, drew closer and closer together, although the degradation she was undergoing op-
XXXI pressed Edith's proud soul. Moreover, the sense of degradation was increased by the fact, made clear to her on her wedding day, that Mr. Carker read her thoroughly — that he knew that she realized that she was selling herself.

XXXII At this time, those who took an interest in Walter Gay gave him up for lost; for the report was published that the Son and Heir, in which he had sailed, had been found totally wrecked. Mr. Toots carried the news to Captain Cuttle.

XXXIII In the house of Mr. Carker, the manager, — it was richly furnished and comfortable, — hung a portrait that bore a strange resemblance to Edith. To the house of Mr. Carker, the junior clerk, came a poor travel-stained woman who also bore some strange resemblance to Edith, and received alms from the hands of the junior clerk's sister. From the junior clerk's house the poor
XXXIV woman went to seek out a wretched dwelling in the heart of London where her mother was. For she had just returned from a period of penal servitude, having been betrayed into crime years before by Mr. Carker, the manager.

XXXV With the return of Mr. and Mrs. Dombey from their wedding journey, the real separation between them became more and more manifest. Nor did the sympathy between Edith and Florence tend to mend matters any. So the breach
XXXVI grew, until Mr. Dombey resolved to assert himself in subduing his wife's proud, disdainful spirit. The occasion came after a house-warming at which Mrs. Dombey had failed in

her duty as hostess to her husband's guests, and Mr. Dombey took her to task for it in the presence of his manager. The latter circumstance gave Mr. Carker an opportunity to begin his machinations upon Edith and against Florence, whom he used as a goad upon Edith's proud opposition to Mr. Dombey.

XXXVII

XXXVIII Miss Tox, forlorn, and abandoned by Mrs. Chick, cultivated the Toodles in the hope of hearing through them of the Dombeys.

XXXIX A year had passed, and there was still no news of the old instrument-maker, Solomon Gills. Captain Cuttle, who had kept the shop (having deserted his lodgings) ever since Mr. Gills's disappearance, now undertook, with the advice of his friend, Captain Bunsby, to open the letter and packet that Mr. Gills had left behind him. No sooner had they done so than they were descended upon by Captain Cuttle's former landlady, Mrs. MacStinger, and her family.

"O Cap'en Cuttle, Cap'en Cuttle!" said Mrs. MacStinger, making her chin rigid, and shaking it in unison with what, but for the weakness of her sex, might be described as her fist,— "O Cap'en Cuttle, Cap'en Cuttle! do you dare to look me in the face, and not be struck down in the herth?"

The captain, who looked anything but daring, feebly muttered, "Stand by!"

"Oh! I was a weak and trusting fool when I took you under *my* roof, Cap'en Cuttle,—I was!" cried Mrs. MacStinger. "To think of the benefits I've showered on that man, and the way in which I brought my children up to love and honor him as if he was a father to 'em; when there ain't a 'ousekeeper, no nor a lodger, in our street, don't know that I lost money by that man, and by his guzzlings and his muzzlings" (Mrs. MacStinger used the last word for the joint sake of alliteration and aggravation, rather than for the expression of any idea); "and when they cried out one and all, shame upon him for putting upon an industrious woman, up early and late for the good of her young family, and keeping her poor place so clean, that a individual might have ate his dinner, yes, and his tea, too, if he was so disposed, off any one of the floors or stairs, in spite of all his guzzlings *and* his muzzlings, such was the care and pains bestowed upon him!"

Mrs. MacStinger stopped to fetch her breath; and her face flushed with triumph in this second happy introduction of Captain Cuttle's muzzlings.

"And he runs awa-a-a-ay!" cried Mrs. MacStinger, with a lengthening-out of the last syllable that made the unfortunate captain regard himself as the meanest of men, "and keeps away a twelvemonth! From a woman! Sitch is his conscience! He has n't the courage to meet her hi-i-i-igh" (long syllable again), "but steals away like a felion. . . . A pretty sort of a man is Cap'en Cuttle," said Mrs. MacStinger, with a sharp stress on the first syllable of the captain's name, "to take on for, and to lose sleep for, and to faint along of, and to think dead, forsooth, and to go up and down the blessed town like a mad woman, asking questions after! Oh, a pretty sort of a man! Ha, ha, ha, ha! He's worth all that trouble and distress of mind, and much more. *That's* nothing, bless you! Ha, ha, ha, ha! Cap'en Cuttle," said Mrs. MacStinger, with severe reaction in her voice and manner, "I wish to know if you're a coming home."

The frightened captain looked into his hat, as if he saw nothing for it but to put it on, and give himself up.

"Cap'en Cuttle," repeated Mrs. MacStinger in the same determined manner, "I wish to know if you're a coming home, sir."

The captain seemed quite ready to go, but faintly suggested something to the effect of "not making so much noise about it." And home he would have gone but for the saving action of Jack Bunsby, who with his arm about her waist "convoyed" Mrs. MacStinger away.

XL As time went on, the relations between Mr. Dombey and his wife grew more and more strained, and more and more suited to the purposes of Mr. Carker, the manager. Edith's opposition only served to strengthen Mr. Dombey in his self-centred determination to assert his supremacy.

XLI At Brighton, where Florence had gone with Edith and Mrs. Skewton for the latter's health, Mr. Toots plucked up heart to propose to Florence, who, however, put him off with gentleness.

XLII Mr. Dombey, in his folly, determined to assert his supremacy over his wife by commissioning his manager to bear to her his commands. It was an idea that played directly into Mr. Carker's hands, as it gave him the means not only of approaching her, but of widening the breach between her husband and herself.

XLIII Florence, in the mean while, was growing to feel further than ever removed from her father by the realization that in some way she was an innocent cause in the difference between her father and his wife.

XLIV The growing unhappiness of her young mistress finally urged Susan Nipper to tell Mr. Dombey what his duty toward Florence was. The result, of course, was to infuriate Mr. Dombey, and to lead him to discharge Susan from his service.

XLV Immediately upon Susan's outburst came Mr. Carker to Edith with the command from Mr. Dombey that she show less affection for Florence. Mr. Carker so contrived the delivery of this message that Edith was compelled to acknowledge his personal service to her, and to yield to his claim upon her attention.

XLVI Some time before this, Rob Toodle had taken service under Mr. Carker, the manager. It was an unlucky thing for the manager's plans; for Rob, in the days of his vagabondage, had given a certain Mrs. Brown a hold upon him which he could not shake off, and Mrs. Brown and her daughter (who strangely resembled Edith) hated Mr. Carker beyond all men.

XLVII Still the breach between Mr. Dombey and his wife grew, made worse by the separation from Florence that Edith forced herself to make in obedience to Mr. Dombey's threat and Mr. Carker's warning. Matters culminated on the second anniversary of her marriage, when Edith fled from her husband with his manager, and Florence was driven from home by her father.

XLVIII Florence took refuge in the instrument-maker's shop,
where she was given kindly welcome by cheery old Captain
XLIX Cuttle, and where a day or two later Walter returned, safe
and sound.

L To Captain Cuttle's great delight, it was not long before Florence and Walter discovered that they loved each other.

LI Mr. Dombey and the world agreed as to the pursuit of
his runaway wife and treacherous manager, and as soon as
he learned where they were he set off in a frenzy after them. He
LII obtained the information from Rob, the grinder, through
Mrs. Brown, who hated Carker. But Mrs. Brown's daughter,
who resembled Edith and who had been so cruelly wronged by Mr.
LIII Carker, the manager, tried to save him by sending him warning through his sister.

LIV In good time the fugitives, by different ways, arrived at
Dijon and met there, and there Edith unmasked Carker,—
showed him for the vile thing he was and for the dupe she had made
of him. For she had run away with him to satisfy her hatred of
her husband; that accomplished, she left him to Mr. Dombey's rage.
No sooner had she gone than her husband appeared, and there was
LV nothing but flight left for the treacherous Carker. And so
he fled ignominiously, and died by accident just as his pursuer caught up with him.

LVI In the mean while Florence was joined in her refuge at Captain Cuttle's by her former maid, Susan, and all were made

happy by the return of Walter's uncle. And then Walter and
LVII Florence were married amid the rejoicings of their friends.
A year passed, and the great house of Dombey and Son failed.
LVIII Its crafty manager had enriched himself in the pursuance of
his plan, and had impoverished the house. Mr. Dombey, a man with high sense of honor, made himself penniless to pay his creditors, and things must have been hard for him but for the aid of John Carker and his sister. From the abundance which came to them at the death of their brother, they settled an annuity upon Mr. Dombey, the source of which was kept secret from him. Mr.
LIX Dombey, terribly reduced in every way, felt himself humbled in the dust, when Florence returned to him to forgive and be forgiven.

LX Toots, apparently inconsolable when Florence was married, had found solace in the mean while in Susan, who was now Mrs. Toots. And Captain Cuttle was forever relieved of his fear of Mrs. MacStinger by his being witness of her marriage to his imperturbable friend Bunsby.

LXI One day, during her father's convalescence, — he had fallen very ill in consequence of his misfortunes — Florence was called upon by a cousin of Edith's, who had faithfully befriended her since she left her husband. His object was to get Florence to see Edith and to receive from her the explanation of her flight. And Florence did so, and thus learned that there was peace in the separation of her father and his wife.

LXII And so the story ends in love and forgiveness and joy. Mr. Dombey himself helped to drink the last bottle of Solomon Gills's Madeira, and so did Mr. Toots, who rejoiced exceedingly in "that extraordinary woman," his wife. But Mr. Dombey, having learned to love Florence, found his deepest joy in her and her children.

---

## INDEX TO CHARACTERS

Although Major Bagstock had arrived at what is called in polite literature the grand meridian of life, and was proceeding on his journey down hill with hardly any throat, and a very rigid pair of jaw-bones, and long-flapped elephantine ears, and his eyes and complexion in the state of artificial excitement already mentioned, he was mightily proud of awakening an interest in Miss Tox, and tickled his vanity with the fiction that she was a splendid woman, who had her eye on him. This he had several times hinted at the club, in connection with little jocularities of which old Joe Bagstock, old Joey Bagstock, old J. Bagstock, old Josh. Bagstock, or so forth, was the perpetual theme; it being, as it were, the major's stronghold and donjon-keep of light humor to be on the most familiar terms with his own name.

The major becomes a friend and companion of Mr. Dombey, introduces him to Edith Granger and Mrs. Skewton, and plays the agreeable to the mother, while Mr. Dombey makes love to the daughter. vii, x, xx, xxi, xxvi, xxvii, xxxi, xxxvi, xl, li, lix, lx.

**Baps, Mr.** Dancing-master at Doctor Blimber's; a very grave gentleman with a slow and measured manner of speaking. xiv.

**Baps, Mrs.** His wife. xiv.

**Berinthia,** *called* BERRY. Niece and drudge to Mrs. Pipchin, whom she regards as one of the most meritorious persons in the world. She is a good-natured spinster of middle age, but possessing a gaunt and iron-bound aspect, and much afflicted with boils on her nose. viii, xi.

**Biler.** *See* TOODLE, ROBIN.

**Bitherston, Master.** A child boarding at Mrs. Pipchin's; a boy of mysterious and terrible experiences. viii, x, xli, lx.

**Blimber, Doctor.** Proprietor of an expensive private boarding-school for boys, at Brighton, to which Paul Dombey is sent to be educated.

The doctor was a portly gentleman, in a suit of black, with strings at his knees, and stockings below them. He had a bald head highly polished, a deep voice, and a chin so very double that it was a wonder how he ever managed to shave into the creases. He had likewise a pair of little eyes that were always half shut up, and a mouth that was always half expanded into a grin, as if he had that moment posed a boy, and were waiting to convict him from his own lips. . . . The doctor's walk was stately, and calculated to impress the juvenile mind with solemn feelings. It was a sort of march; but, when the doctor put out his right foot, he gravely turned upon his axis, with a semicircular sweep towards the left; and, when he put out his left foot, he turned in the same manner towards the right: so that he seemed, at every stride he took, to look about him, as though he were saying, "Can anybody have the goodness to indicate any subject, in any direction, on which I am uninformed? I rather think not."

Whenever a young gentleman was taken in hand by Doctor Blimber, he might consider himself sure of a pretty tight squeeze. The doctor only undertook the charge of ten young gentlemen; but he had always ready a supply of learning for a hundred, on the lowest estimate; and it was at once the business and delight of his life to gorge the unhappy ten with it.

In fact, Doctor Blimber's establishment was a great hot-house, in which there was a forcing apparatus incessantly at work. All the boys blew before their time. Mental green-peas were produced at Christmas, and intellectual asparagus all the year round. Mathematical gooseberries (very sour ones too) were common at untimely seasons, and from mere sprouts of bushes, under Doctor Blimber's cultivation. Every description of Greek and Latin vegetable was got off the dryest twigs of boys, under the frostiest circumstances. Nature was of no consequence at all. No matter what a young gentleman was intended to bear, Doctor Blimber made him bear to pattern, somehow or other. xi, xii, xix, xxiv, xli, lx.

**Blimber, Mrs.** His wife.

Mrs. Blimber . . . was not learned herself; but she pretended to be: and that did quite as well. She said at evening parties, that, if she could have known Cicero, she thought she could have died contented. It was the steady joy of her life to see the doctor's young gentlemen go out walking, unlike all other young gentlemen, in the largest possible shirt-collars and the stiffest possible cravats. It was so classical, she said. xi, xii, xix, xxiv, xli, lx.

**Blimber, Miss Cornelia.** The daughter; a slim and graceful maid.

There was no light nonsense about Miss Blimber. She kept her hair short and crisp, and wore spectacles. She was dry and sandy with working in the graves of deceased languages. None of your live languages for Miss Blimber. They must be dead,—stone dead; and then Miss Blimber dug them up like a ghoul. xi, xii, xiv, xli, lx.

**Blockitt, Mrs.** Mrs. Dombey's nurse; a simpering piece of faded gentility. i.

**Bokum, Mrs.** A friend of Mrs. MacStinger's, and her bridesmaid on the occasion of her marriage to Jack Bunsby. lx.

**Briggs.** A pupil of Dr. Blimber's, and the room-mate of Paul Dombey. xii, xiv, xli, lx.

**Brogley, Mr.** A sworn broker and appraiser, and second-hand furniture-dealer ; a friend of Sol. Gills. ix.

**Brown, Alice,** *alias* Alice Marwood. A handsome woman of about thirty years of age ; a former mistress of James Carker. After suffering transportation for crime, she comes back to England filled with scorn, hate, defiance, and recklessness. xxxiii, xxxiv, xl, xlvi, lii, liii, lviii.

**Brown, Mrs.,** *called (by herself)* Good Mrs. Brown. Her mother ; a very ugly old woman, with red rims round her eyes, and a mouth that mumbled and chattered of itself when she was not speaking. vi, xxvii, xxxiv, xl, xlvi, lii, lviii.

**Bunsby, Captain Jack.** Master of a vessel called The Cautious Clara, and a warm friend of Captain Cuttle, who looks up to him as an oracle. Notwithstanding his sagacity and independence, Captain Bunsby is finally captured and married, perforce, by his landlady, Mrs. MacStinger. xxiii, xxxix, lx.

**Carker, Harriet.** Sister of John and James Carker; afterwards the wife of Mr. Morfin. xxii, xxxiiii, xxxiv, liii, lxii.

**Carker, James.** Mr. Dombey's head clerk or manager.

Mr. Carker was a gentleman thirty-eight or forty years old, of a florid complexion, and with two unbroken rows of glistening teeth, whose regularity and whiteness were quite distressing. It was impossible to escape the observation of them ; for he showed them whenever he spoke, and bore so wide a smile upon his countenance (a smile, however, very rarely indeed, extending beyond his mouth), that there was something in it like the snarl of a cat. He affected a stiff white cravat, after the example of his principal, and was always closely buttoned up and tightly dressed. His manner towards Mr. Dombey was deeply conceived, and perfectly expressed. He was familiar with him in the very extremity of his sense of the distance between them. "Mr. Dombey, to a man in your position, from a man in mine, there is no show of subservience compatible with the transaction of business between us that I should think sufficient. I frankly tell you, sir, I give it up altogether. I feel that I could not satisfy my own mind ; and Heaven knows, Mr. Dombey, you can afford to dispense with the endeavor." If he had carried these words about with him printed on a placard, and had constantly offered it to Mr. Dombey's perusal on the breast of his coat, he could not have been more explicit than he was.

Enjoying the confidence of his employer, Mr. Carker speculates on his own account, and amasses a fortune. When Mr. Dombey marries a second time, Carker observes that there is no love or sympathy in the case, and that both parties are of a proud and unyield-

ing disposition; and he secretly takes advantage of the confidence reposed in him by Mr. Dombey to increase the constantly widening breach between husband and wife. Goaded to desperation by the conduct of Mr. Dombey in making his clerk the medium of communicating his directions to her, but equally despising both man and master, Mrs. Dombey revenges herself on her husband by eloping with his clerk, and on the clerk by taunting him with his supposed victory, and leaving him, in the very hour of his anticipated triumph, to the vengeance of her husband, who has pursued them. In trying to avoid Mr. Dombey, whom he accidentally encounters at a railway-station, he staggers, slips on to the track, and is killed by a passing train. xiii, xvii, xxii, xxiv, xxvi, xxvii, xxxi, xxxiii, xxxvi, xxxvii, xl, xlii, xlv, xlvi, xlvii, lii–lv.

**Carker, Mr. John.** Brother of James and Harriet Carker, and under-clerk at Dombey and Son's. When a young man, he had been led astray by evil companions, and had robbed his employers, who had reposed great confidence in him. His guilt was soon discovered; but the house was merciful, and, instead of dismissing him, retained him in a subordinate capacity, in which he made expiation for his crime by long years of patient, faithful service. After the elopement of his brother James with Edith Dombey, he is discharged; but, by the sudden death of his brother, he comes into possession of a fortune, the interest of which, when Mr. Dombey becomes a bankrupt, he secretly makes over to him year by year as if it were the repayment of an old lost debt. vi, xix, xxii, xxxiii, xxxiv, liii, lviii, lxii.

**Chick, Mr. John.** Brother-in-law to Mr. Dombey; a stout, bald gentleman with a very large face, and his hands continually in his pockets, and with a tendency to whistle and hum tunes on every sort of occasion. ii, v, xxix, xxxvi.

**Chick, Mrs. Louisa.** His wife; sister to Mr. Dombey; a weak, good-natured, self-satisfied woman, very proud of her family and of having always tried, as she puts it, to "make an effort." i, ii, v–viii, x, xviii, xxix, xxxvi, li, lix.

**Chicken, The Game.** *See* GAME CHICKEN, THE.

**Chowley.** *See* MACSTINGER, CHARLES.

**Clark, Mr.** A clerk of Mr. Dombey's. vi.

**Cleopatra.** *See* SKEWTON, MRS.

**Cuttle, Captain Edward.** Protector of Florence Dombey, friend of Walter Gay, and friend and afterwards partner of Walter's uncle, Sol Gills. His first advent in the story is at the house of the latter at dinner-time.

An addition to the little party now made its appearance in the shape of a gentleman in a wide suit of blue, with a hook instead

CAPTAIN CUTTLE.

of a hand attached to his right wrist, very bushy black eyebrows, and a thick stick in his left hand, covered all over (like his nose) with knobs. He wore a loose black silk handkerchief round his neck, and such a very large coarse shirt-collar, that it looked like a small sail. He was evidently the person for whom the spare wineglass was intended, and evidently knew it; for having taken off his rough outer coat, and hung up on a particular peg behind the door such a hard glazed hat as a sympathetic person's head might ache at the sight of, and which left a red rim round his own forehead, as if he had been wearing a tight basin, he brought a chair to where the clean glass was, and sat himself down behind it. He was usually addressed as captain, this visitor; and had been a pilot, or a skipper, or a privateersman, or all three, perhaps; and was a very salt-looking man indeed. iv, ix, x, xv, xvii, xix, xxiii, xxv, xxxii, xxxix, xlviii–l, lvi, lvii, lx, lxii. *See* MACSTINGER, MRS.

**Daws, Mary.** A young kitchen-maid in Mr. Dombey's service. lix.

**Diogenes.** A dog given by Mr. Toots to Florence Dombey, "as a sort of keepsake," he having been a favorite with her brother, little Paul.

Though Diogenes was as ridiculous a dog as one would meet with on a summer's day, — a blundering, ill-favored, clumsy, bullet-headed dog, continually acting on a wrong idea that there was an enemy in the neighborhood whom it was meritorious to bark at, — and though he was far from good-tempered, and certainly was not clever, and had hair all over his eyes, and a comic nose, and an inconsistent tail, and a gruff voice, he was dearer to Florence . . . than the most beautiful of his kind. xiv, xviii, xxii, xxiii, xxviii, xxx, xxxi, xxxv, xli, xliv, xlviii, xlix, l, lvi, lxii.

**Dombey, Mrs. Edith.** Mr. Dombey's second wife; daughter of Mrs. Skewton, and widow of Colonel Granger. She is a woman under thirty, very handsome, very haughty, and very wilful; pure at heart, but defiant of criticism. Though she feels neither love nor esteem for Mr. Dombey, and does not tempt him to seek her hand, yet she suffers him to marry her, content to be made rich so long as the transaction is understood to be a mere matter of traffic, in which beauty, grace, and varied accomplishments are exchanged for wealth and social position. As might be expected, the alliance proves to be a very unfortunate one. No friendship, no fitness for each other, no mutual forbearance, springs up between the unhappy pair: but indifference gives place to aversion and contempt; arrogance is repaid in kind; opposition arouses opposition. At last, Edith elopes with Mr. Carker, a confidential clerk of Mr. Dombey's; and this she does with the double motive of revenging herself on her husband, and of befooling and punishing the clerk, who has pursued her from her wedding day with humiliating solicitations and the meanest stratagems. But she leaves him in the very hour of their meeting, and he is killed by a passing train in trying to escape pursuit. xxi, xxvi–xxviii, xxx, xxxi, xxxv–xxxvii, xl–xliii, xlv, xlvii, liv, lxi. *See* Skewton, Mrs.

**Dombey, Mrs. Fanny.** Mr. Dombey's first wife; mother of Florence and of little Paul. i.

**Dombey, Florence.** Daughter of Mr. Dombey, and sister of little Paul. She is a loving and lovable child, but, not having had the good fortune to be born a boy, is of no account in her father's eyes. At first she is merely an object of indifference to him, but by degrees he comes to conceive a positive dislike for her, and at last drives her from his house. She finally marries Walter Gay, a junior clerk in Mr. Dombey's bank. i, iii, v, vi, viii–xii, xiv, xvi, xviii, xix, xxii–xxiv, xxviii, xxx, xxxv–xxxvii, xl, xli, xliii–xlv, xlvii–l, lvi, lvii, lix, lxi, lxii.

**Dombey, Little Paul.** Mr. Dombey's son and heir. His advent into the world is thus described:—

Rich Mr. Dombey sat in the corner of his wife's darkened bedchamber, in the great arm-chair by the bedside; and rich Mr. Dombey's son lay tucked up warm in a little basket carefully placed on a low settee in front of the fire, and close to it, as if his constitution were analogous to that of a muffin, and it was essential to toast him brown while he was very new.

Rich Mr. Dombey was about eight and forty years of age; rich Mr. Dombey's son, about eight and forty minutes. Mr. Dombey was rather bald, rather red, and rather stern and pompous; Mr. Dombey's son was very bald, and very red, and rather crushed and spotty in his general effect, as yet.

Mr. Dombey, exulting in the long-looked-for event,—the birth of a son,—jingled his heavy gold watch-chain as he sat in his blue coat and bright buttons by the side of the bed, and said:—

"Our house of business will once again be not only in name, but in fact, Dombey and Son; Dombey and Son! He will be christened Paul, of course,—his father's name, Mrs. Dombey, and his grandfather's. I wish his grandfather were alive this day!" And again he said, "Dom-bey and Son!"

Those three words conveyed the one idea of Mr. Dombey's life. The earth was made for Dombey and Son to trade in, and the sun and moon were made to give them light. Common abbreviations took new meanings in his eyes, and had sole reference to them.

A. D. had no concern with Anno Domini, but stood for Anno Dombei — and Son.

He had been married ten years, and, until this present day on which he sat jingling his gold watch-chain in the great arm-chair by the side of the bed, had had no issue.

— To speak of. There had been a girl some six years before; and she, who had stolen into the chamber unobserved, was now crouching in a corner whence she could see her mother's face. But what was a girl to Dombey and Son!

Mr. Dombey's cup of satisfaction was so full, however, that he said, "Florence, you may go and look at your pretty brother, if you like. Don't touch him!" i–iii, v–viii, x–xii, xiv, xvi.

**Dombey, Mr. Paul.** A London merchant, very wealthy, very starched and pompous, intensely obstinate, and possessed by a conviction that the old banking-house of Dombey and Son is the central fact of the universe. He has a daughter Florence, who is of no consequence in his eyes; and a son Paul, on whom all his hopes and affections centre, but who dies in childhood. He marries for his second wife a woman whose pride is equal to his own, and who not only has no love to give him, but refuses to render him the deference and submission which he exacts as his due. Goaded to desperation, at last, by his arrogance, and by the slights and affronts he puts upon her, she elopes, upon the anniversary of her marriage, with a confidential clerk whom he had chosen as an instrument of her humiliation, content to wear the appearance of an adulteress (though not such in reality), if she can only avenge herself upon her husband. But Mr. Dombey, though keenly sensitive to the disgrace she has inflicted upon him, and haunted by the dread of public ridicule, abates no jot of his pride or obstinacy. He drives his daughter from his house, believing her to be an accomplice of his wife, forbids the name of either to be mentioned in his presence, and preserves the same calm, cold, impenetrable exterior as ever. His trouble preys upon his mind, however; his prudence in matters of business deserts him; and the great house of which he is the head soon goes down in utter bankruptcy. But this crowning retribution proves a blessing after all; for it undermines his pride, melts his obstinacy, and sets his injustice plainly before him. His daughter seeks him out, and in her home he passes the evening of his days, a wiser and a better man. i–iii, v, vi, viii, x, xi, xiii, xvi, xviii, xx, xxi, xxvi–xxviii, xxx, xxxi, xxxv, xxxvi, xl–xliv, xlvii, li, lii, lv, lviii, lix, lxi, lxii.

**Feeder, Reverend Alfred, M. A.** A brother of Mr. Feeder, B. A. lx.

**Feeder, Mr., B. A.** An assistant in the establishment of Blimber; afterwards his son-in-law and successor. xi, xii, xiv, xli, lx.

**Feenix, Cousin.** A superannuated nobleman, nephew to the Honorable Mrs. Skewton, and cousin to Edith Dombey.

Cousin Feenix was a man about town forty years ago; but he is still so juvenile in figure and manner, and so well got up, that strangers are amazed when they discover latent wrinkles in his lordship's face, and crow's-feet in his eyes, and first observe him not exactly certain, when he walks across a room, of going quite straight to where he wants to go. But Cousin Feenix getting up at half-past seven o'clock, or so, is quite another thing from Cousin Feenix got up; and very dim indeed he looks while being shaved at Long's Hotel, in Bond Street. xxxi, xxxvi, xli, li, lxi.

**Flowers.** Mrs. Skewton's maid. xxvii, xxx, xxxv–xxxvii, xl.

**Game Chicken, The.** A professional boxer and prize-fighter, with very short hair, a broken nose, and a considerable tract of bare and sterile country behind each ear. He is a friend of Mr. Toots, whom he knocks about the head three times a week for the small consideration of ten and six per visit. xxii, xxviii, xxxii, xli, liv, lvi.

**Gay, Walter.** A young man in the employ of Mr. Dombey; nephew to Sol Gills. He makes the acquaintance of Florence Dombey, and falls in love with her, but is soon afterward sent to Barbadoes to fill a junior situation in the counting-house there. The ship in which he sails is lost at sea, and it is long thought that he went down with her; but he finally returns, and marries Florence. iv, vi, ix, x, xiii, xv–xvii, xix, xlix, l, lvi, lvii, lxi, lxii.

**Gills, Solomon.** A nautical instrument-maker; uncle to Walter Gay. When he hears of the loss of the ship in which his nephew has sailed, he goes abroad in quest of him, leaving his shop in the hands of Captain Cuttle.

To say nothing of his Welsh wig, which was as plain and stubborn a Welsh wig as ever was worn, and in which he looked like anything but a rover, he was a slow, quiet-spoken, thoughtful old fellow, with eyes as red as if they had been small suns looking at you through a fog; and a newly-awakened manner, such as he might have acquired by having stared for three or four days successively through every optical instrument in his shop, and suddenly come back to the world again to find it green. iv, vi, ix, x, xv, xvii, xix, xxii, xxiii, xxv, lvi, lvii, lxii.

**Glubb, Old.** An old man employed to draw little Paul Dombey's couch. xii.

**Granger, Mrs. Edith.** *See* DOMBEY, MRS. EDITH.

**Howler, The Reverend Melchisedech.** A minister "of the ranting persuasion," who predicts the speedy destruction of the world. He was formerly employed in the West India Docks, but was "discharged on suspicion of screwing gimlets into puncheons, and applying his lips to the orifice." xv, lx.

**Jemima.** Mrs. Toodle's unmarried sister, who lives with her, and helps her take care of the children. ii, vi.

**Joe.** A laborer. vi.

**John.** A poor man with no regular employment; father of Martha, a deformed and sickly girl. xxiv.

**Johnson.** A pupil of Doctor Blimber's. xii, xiv.

**Kate.** An orphan child, visiting Sir Barnet and Lady Skettles, at Fulham, with her aunt, during Florence Dombey's stay there. xxv.

**MacStinger, Alexander.** Son of Mrs. MacStinger, aged two years and three months. His mother never enters upon any action of importance, without previously inverting him to bring him within range of a brisk battery of slaps, and then setting him down on the street pavement; a cool paving-stone being usually found to act as a powerful restorative. xxiii, xxv, xxix, lx.

**MacStinger, Charles,** *called* CHOWLEY by his playmates. Another son of Mrs. MacStinger. xxxix, lx.

**MacStinger, Juliana.** Mrs. MacStinger's daughter; the very picture of her mother. "Another year or two, the captain [Captain Cuttle] thought, and to lodge where that child was would be destruction." xxv, xxix, lx.

**MacStinger, Mrs.** Captain Cuttle's landlady; a vixenish widow-woman, living at No. 9 Brig Place, near the India Docks. She exhibits a disposition to retain her lodgers by physical force, if necessary. The captain stands in mortal fear of her; though, as he says, he "never owed her a penny," and has "done her a world of good turns too." Mrs. MacStinger subsequently marries Captain Bunsby. ix, xvii, xxiii, xxv, xxxix, lvi, lx.

**Martha.** The daughter of a poor laboring-man, who finds it very difficult to get work to do. She is ugly, misshapen, peevish, ill-conditioned, ragged, and dirty, but dearly loved by her father, who robs himself, and makes his own life miserable, to add to her comfort. xxiv.

**Marwood, Alice.** *See* BROWN, ALICE.

**'Melia.** A servant-girl at Doctor Blimber's. xii, xiv, xli.

**Miff, Mrs.** A wheezy little pew-opener; a mighty dry old lady, with a vinegary face, an air of mystery, and a thirsty soul for six-pences and shillings. xxxi, lvii.

**Morfin, Mr.** Head clerk at Dombey and Son's; a cheerful-looking, hazel-eyed, elderly bachelor, who befriends John Carker, and marries his sister Harriet. xiii, xxxiii, liii, lviii, lxii.

**Native, The.** A dark servant of Major Bagstock's, so called by Miss Tox, though without connecting him with any geographical idea whatever. He has no particular name, but answers to any vituperative epithet. vii, x, xx, xxi, xxvi, xxvii, xxix, lviii, lix.

**Nipper, Susan.** Florence Dombey's maid; a short, brown, womanly girl, with a little snub nose, and black eyes like jet beads. Notwithstanding a peculiarly sharp and biting manner that she has, she is, in the main, a good-natured little body, and is wholly devoted to her mistress. She has the audacity to tell Mr. Dombey what she thinks of his treatment of his daughter, and is immediately discharged from that gentleman's service. She afterwards marries Mr. Toots, who considers her "a most extraordinary woman." iii, v, vi, xiii, xv, xvi, xviii, xix, xxii, xxiii, xxviii, xxxii, xliii, xliv, lvi, lvii, lx–lxii.

**Pankey, Miss.** A boarder at Mrs. Pipchin's "select infantine boarding-house," worth "a good eighty pounds a year" to her. viii, xi.

**Peps, Doctor Parker.** One of the court physicians, and a man of immense reputation for assisting at the increase of great families, on which account his services are secured by Mr. Dombey when little Paul is born. i, xvi.

**Perch, Mr.** Messenger in Mr. Dombey's office, living (when at home) at Balls Pond. xiii, xvii, xxii, xxiv, xxxi, xlvi, li, liii, lviii, lix.

**Perch, Mrs.** His wife, always in an interesting condition. xiii, xxii, xxxi, xxxv, li, liii, lviii, lix.

**Pilkins, Mr.** Mr. Dombey's family physician. i, viii.

**Pipchin, Mrs.** An old lady living at Brighton, with whom little Paul Dombey, accompanied by his sister Florence and a nurse, is sent to board. She afterwards becomes Mr. Dombey's housekeeper.

Mrs. Pipchin . . . had acquired an immense reputation as "a great manager" of children; and the secret of [her] management was to give them everything that they did n't like, and nothing that they did. Mrs. Pipchin had also founded great fame on being a widow-lady whose husband had broken his heart in pumping water out of some Peruvian mines. This was a great recommendation to Mr. Dombey; for it had a rich sound. "Broke his heart of the Peruvian mines," mused Mr. Dombey. "Well! — a very respectable way of doing it."

This celebrated Mrs. Pipchin was a marvellous ill-favored, ill-conditioned old lady, of a stooping figure, with a mottled face like bad marble, a hook nose, and a hard gray eye, that looked as if it might have been hammered at on an anvil. Forty years, at least, had elapsed since the Peruvian mines had been the death of Mr. Pipchin; but his relict still wore black bombazine. And she was such a bitter old lady, that one was tempted to believe there had been some mistake in the application of the Peruvian machinery, and that all her waters of gladness, and milk of human kindness, had been pumped out dry, instead of the mines. viii, xi, xii, xiv, xvi, xlii–xliv, xlvii, li, lix.

**Richards.** *See* Toodle, Polly.

**Rob the Grinder.** *See* Toodle, Robin.

**Skettles, Lady.** The wife of Sir Barnet Skettles. xiv, xxiii, xxiv, xxviii, lx.

**Skettles, Sir Barnet.** A member of the House of Commons living in a pretty villa at Fulham, on the banks of the Thames. It was anticipated, that, when he did catch the speaker's eyes (which he had been expected to do for three or four years), he would rather touch up the radicals. His object in life is constantly to extend the range of his acquaintance. xiv, xxiii, xxiv, xxviii, lx.

**Skettles, Barnet, junior.** His son; a pupil of Doctor Blimber's. xiv, xxiv, xxviii.

**Skewton, The Hon. Mrs.**, *called* Cleopatra, from the name appended to a sketch of her published in her youth. Aunt to Lord Feenix, and mother to Edith Dombey. An old lady, who was once a belle, and who still retains, at the age of seventy, the juvenility of dress, the coquettishness of manner, and the affectation of speech, which distinguished her fifty years before. She parades her fair daughter through all the fashionable resorts in England in order to sell her to the highest bidder. She succeeds in making a very "advantageous match" for her, but dies soon after, a hideous paralytic, demanding rose-colored curtains for her bed, to improve her complexion. xxi, xxvi–xxviii, xxx, xxxv–xxxvii, xl, xli.

**Sownds.** A portentous beadle, orthodox and corpulent, who spends the greater part of his time sitting in the sun, on the church-steps, or, in cold weather, sitting by the fire. v, xxxi, lvii.

**Toodle, Mr.** Husband to Polly Toodle, and father to "Rob the Grinder." He is at first a stoker, but afterwards becomes an engine-driver. ii, xv, xx, lix.

**Toodle, Mrs. Polly**, *called* Richards by Mr. Dombey and his family. His wife; foster-mother of little Paul Dombey; a plump, rosy-cheeked, wholesome, apple-faced young woman with five children of her own, one of them being a nursing infant. ii, iii, v–vii, xv, xvi, xxii, xxxviii, lvi, lix.

**Toodle, Robin**, *called by the family* Biler (in remembrance of the steam-engine), *otherwise styled* Rob the Grinder. Their son, nominated by Mr. Dombey to a vacancy in the ancient establishment of "The Charitable Grinders;" but the child meets with so much badgering from the boys in the street, and so much abuse from the master of the school, that he runs away. He afterwards becomes the spy and instrument of Mr. Carker, and finally enters the service of Miss Tox with a view to his "restoration to respectability." ii, v, vi, xx, xxii, xxiii, xxv, xxxi, xxxii, xxxviii, xxxix, xlii, xlvi, lii, lix.

**Toots, Mr. P.** The eldest of Doctor Blimber's pupils; a wealthy young gentleman, with swollen nose and excessively large head, of whom people did say that the doctor had rather overdone it with young Toots, and that, when he began to have whiskers, he left off having brains. Having license to pursue his own course of study, he occupies his time chiefly in writing long letters to himself from persons of distinction, addressed "P. Toots, Esq., Brighton, Sussex," which he preserves in his desk with great care. His personal appearance takes a great deal of his attention, and he prides himself especially upon his tailors, Burgess and Co., as being "fash'nable, but very dear." His conversational ability is not remarkable; but his deep voice, his sheepish manner, and his stock phrases,—of which "It 's of no consequence" is the most usual—are particularly noteworthy. Of his intellectual and social deficiencies he is by no means ignorant, however. "I am not what is considered a quick sort of a person," he says: "I am perfectly aware of that. I don't think anybody could be better acquainted with his own,—if it was not too strong an expression, I should say with the thickness of his own head than myself." Mr. Toots conceives so strong a passion for Miss Florence Dombey, that he is—to use his own words—"perfectly sore with loving her." His attentions, however, are not encouraged, and he becomes very down-hearted. "I KNOW I'm wasting away," he says to Captain Cuttle. "Burgess and Co. have altered my measure, I 'm in that state of thinness. If you could see my legs when I take my boots off, you 'd form some idea what unrequited affection is." He recovers his health and spirits, however, after no long time, and consoles himself for the loss of Miss Dombey by marrying her maid, Miss Susan Nipper. The result of this union is a large family of children. After the birth of the third, Mr. Toots betakes himself to the "Wooden Midshipman" to give information of the happy event to his friend Captain Cuttle, whom he always misnames Captain Gills.

"I knew that you 'd be glad to hear, and so I came down myself. We 're positively getting on, you know. There 's Florence and Susan, and now here 's another little stranger."

"A female stranger?" inquires the captain.

"Yes, Captain Gills," says Mr. Toots; "and I 'm glad of it: the oftener we can repeat that most extraordinary woman, my opinion is, the better."

"Stand by!" says the captain, turning to the old case-bottle with no throat; for it is evening, and the Midshipman's usual moderate provision of pipes and glasses is on the board. "Here 's to her; and may she have ever so many more!"

"Thank 'ee, Captain Gills!" says the delighted Mr. Toots. "I echo the sentiment." xi, xii, xiv, xviii, xxii, xxviii, xxxi, xxxii, xxxix, xli, xlv, xlviii, l, lvi, lvii, lx, lxii.

**Toots, Mrs.** *See* NIPPER, SUSAN.

**Towlinson, Thomas.** Mr. Dombey's footman. v, xviii, xx, xxviii, xxxi, xxxv, xliv, li, lix.

**Tox, Miss Lucretia.** A friend of Mrs. Chick's, greatly admired by Major Bagstock.

The lady . . . was a long, lean figure, wearing such a faded air, that she seemed not to have been made in what linen-drapers call "fast colors" originally, and to have, by little and little, washed out. But for this, she might have been described as the very pink of general propitiation and politeness. From a long habit of listening admiringly to everything that was said in her presence, and looking at the speakers as if she were mentally engaged in taking off impressions of their images upon her soul, never to part with the same but with life, her head had quite settled on one side. Her hands had contracted a spasmodic habit of raising themselves of their own accord as in involuntary admiration. Her eyes were liable to a similar affection. She had the softest voice that ever was heard; and her nose, stupendously aquiline, had a little knob in the very centre or keystone of the bridge, whence it tended downwards towards her face, as in an invincible determination never to turn up at anything.

After the death of the first Mrs. Dombey, Miss Tox has a modest ambition to succeed her, but, failing of doing so, her regard for Mr. Dombey becomes severely platonic. i, ii, v–viii, x, xviii, xx, xxix, xxxi, xxxvi, xxxviii, li, lix, lxii.

**Tozer.** A room-mate of Paul Dombey's at Dr. Blimber's; a solemn young gentleman whose shirt-collar curls up the lobes of his ears. xii, xiv, xli, lx.

**Wickam, Mrs.** A waiter's wife (which would seem equivalent to being any other man's widow), and little Paul Dombey's nurse. viii, xi, xii, xviii, lviii.

Mrs. Wickam was a meek woman, of a fair complexion, with her eyebrows always elevated, and her head always drooping:

who was always ready to pity herself, or to be pitied, or to pity anybody else; and who had a surprising natural gift of viewing all subjects in an utterly forlorn and pitiable light, and bringing dreadful precedents to bear upon them, and deriving the greatest consolation from the exercise of that talent.

**Withers.** Page to Mrs. Skewton, tall, wan, and thin. **xxi, xxvi, xxvii, xxx, xxxvii, xl.**

## THE PERSONAL HISTORY OF DAVID COPPERFIELD

### OUTLINE

Chapter I was born on a Friday night, six months after the death
I of my father; and, though it was no fault of mine, the fact that I proved to be a boy was so exasperating to my father's aunt, Betsey Trotwood (who had gone so far as to adopt, and even to name me, upon the assumption of my being a girl), that, when the news was announced to her, she left the house in a fury, and never entered it more. My earliest recollections are of my poor
II widowed mother, with her pretty hair and youthful shape, and Peggotty (her first name was Clara, which was also my mother's), our maid-servant, with jet black eyes and red cheeks. Both my mother and I were a little afraid of Peggotty, but she was very good to us, being, in fact, the most affectionate, devoted, and single-hearted woman that ever lived.

We were very happy until a shadow fell across us, — the shadow of Mr. Murdstone, with his black whiskers, black eyebrows, and black hair. I hated him instinctively from the first, and so did Peggotty; but my mother used to blush and smile when he complimented her, and he began to be often at our house. It was at this time that Peggotty and I went to Yarmouth, to spend a fortnight
III with her brother, by whom we were warmly greeted. Mr. Peggotty's house — it was really not a house, but a superannuated schooner which formerly had sailed the seas, but now was snugly anchored in the sand, high and dry — formed the most cosy and fascinating abode imaginable. Mr. Peggotty's family consisted of himself, — he being a "bacheldore," to use his own expression, — Mrs. Gummidge, the widow of his former partner (since drowned), his nephew, Ham Peggotty, and his niece, "Little Em'ly," a beautiful child, with whom I used to wander on the shore, and with whom I fell in love. The two weeks sped quickly by, and then we were at home again, but alas! it was the old home no longer. Mr. Murdstone was installed there, for he and my mother had been married
IV in the interval. I went up to my room — not the one I used to have — and threw myself upon the bed weeping and sobbing. My mother followed to comfort me, but very soon

Mr. Murdstone came in and sent her away. Then, having given me to understand that if I proved obstinate he would beat me as if I were a dog, he took me by the arm and led me down stairs. That was the beginning. Mr. Murdstone's sister, who also was to live with us, arrived the next morning. She greatly resembled her brother, being tall, dark, gloomy, with very heavy eyebrows nearly meeting over her big nose. Miss Murdstone disliked me from the start, and was at no pains to conceal the fact. The Murdstones set about to form my mother's character, and to correct my faults. I had lessons with my mother, but the Murdstones were always in the room, ready to pounce upon me when I made a mistake, or upon my mother when she secretly attempted to give me a hint of the answer; and one day, when I had been unusually stupid (Mr. Murdstone having ostentatiously exhibited a cane during the lessons), he took me up stairs, and, despite my mother's cries and tears, beat me. Half mad with terror and pain, I bit him through the
V hand. This was the climax, and I was forthwith sent, as being incorrigibly bad, to a boarding-school near London, but the journey was not so bad. On the way to Yarmouth I had a conversation with the carrier, Mr. Barkis. I asked him if we were going no farther together than Yarmouth.

"That 's about it," said the carrier. "And there I shall take you to the stage-cutch; and the stage-cutch, that 'll take you to — wherever it is."

As this was a great deal for the carrier to say, — he being of a phlegmatic temperament, and not at all conversational, — I offered him a cake as a mark of attention, which he ate at one gulp, exactly like an elephant; and which made no more impression on his big face than it would have done on an elephant's.

"Did *she* make 'em, now?" said Mr. Barkis, always leaning forward in his slouching way, on the footboard of the cart, with an arm on each knee.

"Peggotty, do you mean, sir?"

"Ah!" said Mr. Barkis, — "her."

"Yes. She makes all our pastry, and does all our cooking."

"Do she, though?" said Mr. Barkis.

He made up his mouth as if to whistle; but he did n't whistle. He sat looking at the horse's ears as if he saw something new there, and sat so for a considerable time. By and by, he said: —

"No sweethearts, I b'lieve?"

"Sweetmeats, did you say, Mr. Barkis?" For I thought he wanted something else to eat, and had pointedly alluded to that description of refreshment.

"Hearts," said Mr. Barkis, — "sweethearts: no person walks with her?"

"With Peggotty?"

"Ah!" he said, — "her."

"Oh, no! She never had a sweetheart."

"Did n't she, though?" said Mr. Barkis.

Again he made up his mouth to whistle, and again he did n't whistle, but sat looking at the horse's ears.

"So she makes," said Mr. Barkis, after a long interval of reflection, "all the apple-parsties, and does all the cooking; do she?"

I replied that such was the fact.

"Well, I'll tell you what," said Mr. Barkis. "P'raps you might be writin' to her?"

"I shall certainly write to her," I rejoined.

"Ah!" he said, slowly turning his eyes towards me. "Well! If you was writin' to her, p'raps you 'd recollect to say that Barkis was willin'; would you?"

"That Barkis was willing," I repeated innocently. "Is that all the message?"

"Ye–es," he said, considering. "Ye–es: Barkis is willin'."

"But you will be at Blunderstone again to-morrow, Mr. Barkis," I said, faltering a little at the idea of my being far away from it then, "and could give your own message so much better."

As he repudiated this suggestion, however, with a jerk of his head, and once more confirmed his previous request by saying with profound gravity, "Barkis is willin'; that 's the message," I readily undertook its transmission. While I was waiting for the coach in the hotel at Yarmouth, that very afternoon, I procured a sheet of paper and an inkstand, and wrote a note to Peggotty, which ran thus: "My dear Peggotty, I have come here safe. Barkis is willing. My love to mamma. Yours affectionately. P. S. — He says he particularly wants you to know — *Barkis is willing.*"

VI When I first entered the school to which I had been sent, I was compelled to carry on my back a placard, inscribed "Take care! he bites!" Seeing this the boys could not help pretending that I was a dog, patting and smoothing me lest I should bite, and saying, "Lie down, sir!" and calling me "Towzer." The master, Mr. Creakle, was so cruel, and flogged us so ferociously, that often half the school would be writhing and crying in their seats. The only boy whom he did not beat was Steerforth, the head of the school, a handsome, extremely clever, curly-headed, dashing lad, who took me under his especial wing, though, by the way, he never interceded with Creakle for me or anybody else; and I could not understand the arrogant way in which he treated poor shabby Mr Mell, the usher.

Another boy that I particularly liked, without venerating him,
VII as I did Steerforth, was Traddles, a chubby, jolly, but very
unlucky fellow — perpetually being caned for other fellows' faults.

VIII At last the term was over, and Barkis, the carrier, brought
me home for the holidays. After asking many questions about Peggotty, who seemed to have struck his fancy, he gave me the same enigmatic message to her as before, strongly urging me not to forget or miscarry it, — "Barkis is willin'." By great good fortune the Murdstones were out when I arrived, and I found my dear mother alone, — very pale and anxious-looking, with a new baby at her breast. She was overjoyed to see me, and so, I need not say, was Peggotty. When I gave the carrier's message to Peggotty, she threw her apron over her head, and laughed till the tears rolled down her face. My mother, who seemed to fear that she was going to be married, took her hand and said tenderly, "Don't leave me, Peggotty, stay with me. It will not be for long, perhaps. What should I ever do without you?" "Me leave you, my precious!" cried Peggotty. "Not for all the world." That was the last time that I saw my mother, except in the presence of the Murdstones, who made life so miserable for me and for her (she was always in fear of my incurring Mr. Murdstone's anger), that it was a great relief to us both when, the month being over, I went back to school.

IX Three weeks later she died, and the baby dying the next
day, was buried, as she had requested, in her arms.

X After her death I went with Peggotty (whom the Murd-
stones had dismissed the day after the funeral) to Yarmouth, and fell more in love than ever with Little Em'ly, who was getting to be a beautiful young girl. Peggotty married Barkis, the carrier, and I was sent by Mr. Murdstone to London, to earn my living by washing bottles in a wine store which he partly owned. Thus, at
XI the age of ten, I was launched upon the world, and a very
hard world I found it. A lodging was provided for me in the house of a bankrupt gentleman, one Wilkins Micawber, whose family consisted of himself, his wife (she came of a very good family, as she informed me the first day that I saw her, and on numerous days thereafter), and their young children. The Micawbers were very kind to me, and I became much attached to them. They had no visitors except creditors, but these came at all hours of the day and night. At such times Mr. Micawber would be transported with grief and mortification, even to the length (as I was once made aware by a scream from his wife) of making motions at himself with a razor; but within half an hour afterward he would polish his shoes with extraordinary pains, and go out humming a tune

with a greater air of gentility than ever. Mrs. Micawber was equally elastic. I have known her to be thrown into fainting fits by the king's taxes at three o'clock, and to eat lamb chops breaded and drink warm ale (paid for with two teaspoons that had gone to
XII the pawnbroker's) at four. The Micawbers were my only friends, and they left London for Plymouth. Before leaving Mr. Micawber gave me some parting counsel.

"My dear young friend," said Mr. Micawber, "I am older than you; a man of some experience in life, and — and — of some experience, in short, in difficulties, generally speaking. At present, and until something turns up (which I am, I may say, hourly expecting), I have nothing to bestow but advice. Still my advice is so far worth taking, that — in short, that I have never taken it myself, and am the" — here Mr. Micawber, who had been beaming and smiling all over his head and face, up to the present moment, checked himself, and frowned, — "the miserable wretch you behold."

"My dear Micawber!" urged his wife.

"I say," returned Mr. Micawber, quite forgetting himself, and smiling again, — "the miserable wretch you behold. My advice is, never do to-morrow what you can do to-day. Procrastination is the thief of time. Collar him!"

"My poor papa's maxim," Mrs. Micawber observed.

"My dear," said Mr. Micawber, "your papa was very well in his way, and Heaven forbid that I should disparage him! Take him for all in all, we ne'er shall — in short, make the acquaintance, probably, of anybody else possessing, at his time of life, the same legs for gaiters, and able to read the same description of print without spectacles. But he applied that maxim to our marriage, my dear, and that was so far prematurely entered into, in consequence, that I never recovered the expense."

Mr. Micawber looked aside at Mrs. Micawber, and added, "Not that I am sorry for it: quite the contrary, my love." After which he was grave for a minute or so.

"My other piece of advice, Copperfield," said Mr. Micawber, "you know. Annual income twenty pounds; annual expenditure nineteen, nineteen, six — result happiness. Annual income twenty pounds; annual expenditure twenty pounds nought and six, — result misery. The blossom is blighted, the leaf is withered, the god of day goes down upon the dreary scene, and — and, in short, you are forever floored. As I am!"

To make his example the more impressive, Mr. Micawber drank a glass of punch with an air of great enjoyment and satisfaction, and whistled the College Hornpipe.

I was so disheartened at parting with the Micawbers that I made
XIII a desperate resolve, travelled down to Dover on foot, and
presented myself, ragged, dirty, and tired, to my aunt, already
mentioned, Miss Betsey Trotwood. Miss Trotwood was a tall,
rather hard-featured, but handsome woman. She was of a stern,
resolute character, very high-handed and hot-tempered, but kind
and generous. There were two other occupants of her house, —
Janet, a pretty, neat maid-servant, and Mr. Dick, a gray-headed,
half-mad gentleman, good-natured and smiling, and perpetually rattling
the loose change in the pockets of his trousers. He had been
engaged for ten years or more in drawing up a memorial to the
Lord Chancellor, relating to Mr. Dick's affairs; but his inability
to keep out of it the name of Charles I. had, as yet, prevented
its completion. My aunt received me kindly, washed and fed and
XIV clothed me; and when, at her request, Mr. Murdstone and
his sister called upon her, she routed them most gallantly
and effectually, making even Mr. Murdstone wince; and constituted
XV herself and Mr. Dick my guardians. In a short time my
aunt sent me to Canterbury, where I went to school, but I
lived with Mr. Wickfield, a lawyer, and a friend of my aunt's, who
had a beautiful daughter, Agnes, of about my own age. Mr. Wickfield's
clerk was one Uriah Heep, a pale, bloodless fellow, with no
eyebrows or eyelashes to speak of, and cold, clammy hands, which
it was very unpleasant to shake. Uriah Heep was, so at least he
frequently said, a very "'umble" person; but he had a sly way of
peering about, and of turning up in unexpected places at unexpected
times, which was not quite pleasant.

XVI The master of the school was Dr. Strong, an absent-minded,
learned, and very kindly man, of nearly sixty years
of age, with a young and lovely wife. (People wondered, by the
way, why the doctor was not jealous of Mr. Jack Maldon, his wife's
handsome young cousin, for whom the doctor generously found
a remunerative employment.)

XVII Once I condescended, as Uriah Heep expressed it, to take
tea with his mother and himself in their "'umble" abode;
and I must confess that they wormed out of me much information
about myself, and more especially about Mr. Wickfield, which I
never intended to reveal. While I was with Uriah on this occasion,
who should meet us but Mr. Micawber, then on a flying visit to
Canterbury in an (unsuccessful) search for employment. I was
obliged to introduce them to each other.

XVIII At Canterbury I spent five peaceful, happy years; I rose
to the head of the school, thrashed the strongest butcher-boy
in town, and then, at my dear aunt's suggestion, I started off

first for London, and then to visit Peggotty at Yarmouth. In
XIX London I met my old friend and schoolmate, Steerforth,
who proposed to accompany me to Yarmouth, but first I
XX stayed with him for a few days at his mother's house in
Highgate. There were two persons there besides Steerforth
himself, of whom I shall have something to say later. These were
Rosa Dartle, a dark woman of thirty years or thereabout, with
great restless black eyes, and a clever way of insinuating things
which she wished not to say outright. She was disfigured somewhat by a red scar on her upper lip, the effect, as Steerforth told
me, of a wound from a hammer which he had thrown at her in a
fit of anger, when he was a boy. The other person was Littimer,
Steerforth's valet, an intensely respectable, cat-like sort of man,
who always gave me an uncomfortable impression that he considered me extremely young and unsophisticated, — as indeed I
was.

XXI We reached Mr. Peggotty's cottage at an interesting time,
— just after Little Em'ly had given her word to marry Ham,
who had been her faithful suitor for many years. The whole
family were in an excited frame of mind, and even Mrs. Gummidge
was cheerful for once. Steerforth took his place in the family
circle so easily and naturally, and with so much tact, that he
charmed them all. As we were going home, I said to him, "I
never saw people so happy. How delightful to have shared in their
honest joy, as we have done!" "That's rather a chuckle-headed
fellow for the girl, isn't he?" said Steerforth.

XXII We stayed there for two weeks, Steerforth mingling with
the sailors and going off on fishing trips with them, and becoming intimate with the Peggottys, while I visited my old home
near by, and spent many hours with Mrs. Barkis and her husband,
the latter being now incapacitated by rheumatism, and keeping his
XXIII money in a chest under his bed, which he pretended, even
to his wife, contained nothing but old clothes. Just as we
were going away, Steerforth informed me that he had bought a
lugger, had christened it the "Little Em'ly," placed it under the
command of Mr. Peggotty, and that Littimer was to oversee the
repairing and outfitting of it. And Mr. Littimer, as respectable and
self-contained as ever, arrived just before our departure.

XXIV Going up to London, I met my aunt there, and became an articled clerk to Messrs. Spenlow and Jorkins, Proctors, my aunt
generously agreeing to pay the one thousand pounds premium which
was required, in order that I might eventually become a proctor myself. I was installed in very comfortable little chambers in the Adelphi, and there, soon afterward, I entertained Steerforth and two of

his friends at dinner, and — I blush to write it even now — for the
first and last time in my life I got drunk. After dinner it was proposed that we should go to the theatre; and there, as fate would have
XXV it, I met the woman whom of all women, I liked and respected most, — Agnes Wickfield. The next day, having had
a note from her telling me where she was, I called upon her, and
explained, and was forgiven for, my beastly conduct of the previous
day. She warned me, very unjustly as I thought, against Steerforth and his influence over me; and she told me certain bad news,
namely, that Uriah Heep had wormed himself into her father's
confidence, was about to become his partner, and had established
XXVI some mysterious power over him. Soon afterward both
Agnes and Uriah returned to Canterbury, and I was invited
by Mr. Spenlow to spend a Sunday at his country-place, his only
daughter, Dora, having lately returned from Paris, where she had
been at school. Dora Spenlow was a slight, blonde girl, with the
most delightful little voice, the gayest little laugh, the pleasantest
and most fascinating little ways, that ever led a lost youth into hopeless slavery. I fell madly in love with her at first sight.
XXVII Having at this time a vague craving for sympathy, I sought
out my school friend, Traddles, who lived at Camden town in the
upper story of a house which wore an aspect of faded gentility. The
house reminded me of my old friends, the Micawbers, and I can
hardly say that I was surprised to find that they were actually living there, Traddles being a sub-tenant of Mr. Micawber's. My old
school friend gave me an account of his prospects.

"I had never been brought up to any profession, and at first I was at a loss what to do for myself. However, I began, with the assistance of the son of a professional man, who had been to Salem House, — Yawler, with his nose on one side. Do you recollect him?"

No. He had not been there with me. All the noses were straight, in my day.

"It don't matter," said Traddles. "I began, by means of his assistance, to copy law-writings. That did n't answer very well; and then I began to state cases for them, and make abstracts, and do that sort of work; for I am a plodding kind of fellow, Copperfield, and had learned the way of doing such things pithily. Well. That put it into my head to enter myself as a law-student; and that ran away with all that was left of the fifty pounds. Yawler recommended me to one or two other offices, however, — Mr. Waterbrook's for one, — and I got a good many jobs. I was fortunate enough, too, to become acquainted with a person in the publishing way, who was getting up an encyclopædia, and he set me to work; and, indeed" (glancing at his table), "I am at work for him at this minute. I am not a bad compiler, Copperfield," said Traddles, preserving the same air of cheerful confidence in all he said; "but I have no invention at all; not a particle. I suppose there never was a young man with less originality than I have."

As Traddles seemed to expect that I should assent to this as a matter of course, I nodded; and he went on with the same sprightly patience — I can find no better expression — as before.

"So, by little and little, and not living high, I managed to scrape up the hundred pounds at last," said Traddles: "and, thank Heaven! that 's paid; though it was — though it certainly was" — said Traddles, wincing again as if he had had another tooth out, "a pull. I am living by the sort of work I have mentioned, still, and I hope, one of these days, to get connected with some newspaper; which would almost be the making of my fortune. Now, Copperfield, you are so exactly what you used to be, with that agreeable face, and it 's so pleasant to see you, that I sha'n't conceal anything. Therefore you must know that I am engaged."

Engaged! O Dora!

"She is a curate's daughter," said Traddles, "one of ten down in Devonshire. Yes." For he saw me glance, involuntarily, at the prospect on the inkstand. "That 's the church! You come round here, to the left, out of this gate," tracing his finger along the inkstand; "and exactly where I hold this pen there stands the house, facing, you understand, towards the church. . . . She is such a dear girl! . . . a little older than me, but the dearest girl! I told you I was going out of town? I have been down there. I walked there, and I walked back, and I had the most delightful time! I dare say ours is likely to be a rather long engagement; but our motto is, 'Wait and hope.' We always say that. 'Wait and hope,' we always say. And she would wait, Copperfield, till she was sixty — any age you can mention — for me."

Traddles rose from his chair, and, with a triumphant smile, put his hand upon the white cloth I had observed.

"However," he said, "it 's not that we have n't made a beginning towards housekeeping. No, no: we have begun. We must get on by degrees; but we have begun. Here," drawing the cloth off with great pride and care, "are two pieces of furniture to commence with. This flower-pot and stand she bought herself. You put that in a parlor window," said Traddles, falling a little back from it to survey it with the greater admiration, "with a plant in it, and — and there you are! This little round table with the marble top (it 's two feet ten in circumference) *I* bought. You want to lay a book down, you know, or somebody comes to see you or your wife, and wants a place to stand a cup of tea upon, and — and there you are again!" said Traddles. "It 's an admirable piece of workmanship, firm as a rock!"

I praised them both highly, and Traddles replaced the covering as carefully as he had removed it.

"It 's not a great deal towards the furnishing," said Traddles; "but it 's something. The table-cloths and pillow-cases, and articles of that kind, are what discourage me most, Copperfield. So does the ironmongery, candle-boxes, and gridirons, and that sort of necessaries; because those things tell, and mount up. However, 'wait and hope!' And I assure you she 's the dearest girl!"

"I am quite certain of it," said I.

"In the mean time," said Traddles, coming back to his chair, "and this is the end of my prosing about myself, I get on as well as I can. I don't make much; but I don't spend much."

XXVIII I invited Traddles and the Micawbers to a little dinner at my rooms, and a very jolly time we had of it, although Mr. Micawber was much depressed at first, and referred to his "wounded spirit, made sensitive by a recent collision with the Minion of Power, — in other words, with a ribald Turncock attached to the water-works." He meant that his domestic supply of water had been cut off for non-payment of rates.

XXIX The next day, in response to an invitation from Steerforth, I paid another visit at his home in Highgate. Rosa Dartle asked me privately, and in her own peculiar, indirect way, what it was that engrossed Steerforth so completely of late. I replied, as was the truth, that I did not know. That night there was a strange scene in the drawing-room. Steerforth, with much difficulty, induced Rosa Dartle to sing to the music of her harp. The song was most unearthly, most thrilling; it seemed to spring from the very depths of her passionate nature. When she stopped Steerforth left his seat, put his arm laughingly around her, and said, "Come, Rosa, for the future we will love each other very much." She struck him, threw him off with the fury of a wild cat, and burst out of the room.

XXX Steerforth, who, it seemed, had been making a visit to Yarmouth on his own account, brought me a message from Peggotty to the effect that her husband was ill and not expected to recover; and so I went down to Yarmouth to be of what use I could. I found poor Barkis very ill indeed.

"Barkis, my dear," said Peggotty, . . . bending over him, . . .

"here 's my dear boy, — my dear boy, Master Davy, who brought us together, Barkis; that you sent messages by, you know! Won't you speak to Master Davy?"

He was as mute and senseless as the box, from which his form derived the only expression it had.

"He's a going out with the tide," said Mr. Peggotty to me, behind his hand.

My eyes were dim, and so were Mr. Peggotty's; but I repeated in a whisper, "With the tide?"

"People can't die along the coast," said Mr. Peggotty, "except when the tide's pretty nigh out. They can't be born unless it 's pretty nigh in, — not properly born, till flood. He 's a going out with the tide. It 's ebb at half-arter three, slack water half an hour. If he lives till it turns, he 'll hold his own till past the flood, and go out with the next tide."

We remained there, watching him, a long time, — hours. What mysterious influence my presence had upon him in that state of his senses, I shall not pretend to say; but when he at last began to wander feebly, it is certain he was muttering about driving me to school.

"He 's coming to himself," said Peggotty.

Mr. Peggotty touched me, and whispered with much awe and reverence, "They are both a going out fast."

"Barkis, my dear!" said Peggotty.

"C. P. Barkis," he cried faintly. "No better woman anywhere!"

"Look! Here 's Master Davy!" said Peggotty. For he now opened his eyes.

I was on the point of asking him if he knew me, when he tried to stretch out his arm, and said to me distinctly, with a pleasant smile, —

"Barkis is willin'!"

And, it being low water, he went out with the tide.

XXXI Mr. Barkis left a little fortune of several thousand pounds, which he gave by will to Peggotty his wife, excepting a legacy to Mr. Peggotty, and another to Little Em'ly. I stayed at Yarmouth for the funeral, on the evening after which we were all to meet at Mr. Peggotty's house. When I got there I found Peggotty in her old place, looking as if she had never left it, and Mr. Peggotty standing before the fire, rubbing his hands, in a state of great hilarity. Ham and Little Em'ly were to be married the next day, and we were expecting them to come in every moment. Presently there was a knock at the door, I opened it, and there stood Ham, alone, pale as a sheet, with wild eyes. "She 's gone," he groaned, "she 's gone." He gave me a letter.

I remember a great wail and cry, and the women hanging about him, and we all standing in the room, — I with an open letter in my hand; which Ham had given me; Mr. Peggotty with his vest torn open, his hair wild, his face and lips white, and blood trickling down his bosom (it had sprung from his mouth, I think).

"Read it, sir; slow, please. I doen't know as I can understand."

In the midst of the silence of death I read thus from the blotted letter Ham had given me, in Em'ly's hand, addressed to himself:

"'When you, who love me so much better than I ever have deserved, even when my mind was innocent, see this, I shall be far away. When I leave my dear home — my dear home — oh, my dear home! — in the morning'" (the letter bore date on the previous night), "'it will be never to come back, unless he brings me back a lady. This will be found at night, many hours after, instead of me. For mercy's sake tell uncle that I never loved him half so dear as now. Oh! don't remember you and I were ever to be married, but try to think as if I died when I was very little, and was buried somewhere. Pray Heaven that I am going away from, have compassion on my uncle! Be his comfort. Love some good girl, that will be what I was once to uncle, and that will be true to you, and worthy of you, and know no shame but me. God bless all! If he don't bring me back a lady and I don't pray for my own self, I'll pray for all. My parting love to uncle! My last tears, and my last thanks, for uncle!'" That was all.

He stood, long after I had ceased to read, still looking at me. Slowly, at last, he moved his eyes from my face, and cast them round the room.

"Who's the man? I want to know his name." Ham glanced at me, and suddenly I felt a shock. "Mas'r Davy, go out a bit, and let me tell him what I must. You doen't ought to hear it, sir."

I sank down in a chair, and tried to utter some reply: but my tongue was fettered, and my sight was weak; for I felt that the man was my friend, the friend I had unhappily introduced there, — Steerforth, my old schoolfellow and my friend.

"I want to know his name!"

"Mas'r Davy," exclaimed Ham in a broken voice, "it ain't no fault of yourn; and I am far from laying of it to you: but it is your friend Steerforth, and he's a damned villain!"

Mr. Peggotty moved no more, until he seemed to wake all at once, and pulled down his rough coat from its peg in a corner.

"Bear a hand with this! I'm struck of a heap, and can't do

it. Bear a hand and help me. Well! Now give me that theer hat!"

Ham asked him whither he was going.

"I'm a going to seek my niece. I'm a going to seek my Em'ly. I'm a going, first, to stave in that theer boat as he gave me, and sink it where I would have drownded *him*, as I'm a livin' soul, if I had had one thought of what was in him! As he sat afore me in that boat, face to face, strike me down dead, but I'd have drownded him, and thought it right! I'm a going fur to seek my niece."

"Where?"

"Anywhere! I'm a going to seek my niece through the wureld. I'm a going to find my poor niece in her shame, and bring her back wi' my comfort and forgiveness. No one stop me! I tell you I'm a going to seek my niece! I'm a going to seek her fur and wide!"

XXXII I cannot describe how desolate the household was by this dreadful news. Mr. Peggotty, taking his stick, a small bag of clothes, and what little money he had, set out in search of his niece, — though he knew not where she was gone, — determined never to come back till he had found her. Ham stayed at home, heartbroken but manful, while Mrs. Gummidge, who rose to the occasion in a wonderful manner, kept house for him. Peggotty and I went up to London to settle her affairs. During all these trials
XXXIII I had gone on loving Dora Spenlow harder than ever, and altogether I was becoming quite mad and feverish. At last Mr. Spenlow invited me to a little picnic in honor of his daughter's birthday. I rode down on a gallant gray horse, and carried an enormous bouquet. To see Dora lay the flowers against her little dimpled chin was to lose all presence of mind. Then Dora held my flowers for Jip, her diminutive dog, to smell. Then Jip growled and would n't smell them. Then Dora laughed, and held them a little closer to Jip to wake him. Then Jip laid hold of a bit of geranium with his teeth, and worried imaginary cats in it. Then Dora beat him, and pouted, and said, "My poor beautiful flowers!" as compassionately, I thought, as if Jip had laid hold of me. I wished he had! Well, well, it was not long, that is, it was not many days, before I declared my passion, on my knees — while Jip barked. The more I raved, the more Jip barked. Each of us, in his own way, got more mad every moment. But by and by Dora and I were sitting on the sofa quietly enough, and Jip was lying in her lap, peacefully winking at me. We were engaged.

XXXIV One night, shortly after this momentous occurrence, and while Peggotty was still in London, I went home to my chambers, and found my aunt and Mr. Dick encamped there. The fact was, as my aunt told me calmly and courageously, after supper, she had lost all her property, and was a ruined woman.

XXXV Agnes Wickfield with her father and Uriah Heep were in London at this time, and Agnes came to see my aunt. When she laid her bonnet on the table, and sat down, I could not but think, looking in her mild eyes and her radiant forehead, how natural it seemed to have her there; how trustfully, although she was so young and inexperienced, my aunt confided in her; how strong she was in simple love and truth. Agnes evidently had some fears that my aunt's property had been lost while in her father's hands for investment, — though she did not say so. But my aunt declared — and who should know better than she? — that she had taken charge of it herself, and had made disastrous invest-
XXXVI ments. The firm was now Wickfield and Heep, and a new clerk had been engaged, — no other than my old friend Micawber. With Traddles I passed an evening with the family before they left for Canterbury, and Mr. Micawber made a farewell speech, ending: —

"Under the temporary pressure of pecuniary liabilities, contracted with a view to their immediate liquidation, but remaining unliquidated through a combination of circumstances, I have been under the necessity of assuming a garb from which my natural instincts recoil, — I allude to spectacles, — and possessing myself of a cognomen to which I can establish no legitimate pretensions. All I have to say on that score is, that the cloud has passed from the dreary scene, and the god of day is once more high upon the mountain-tops. On Monday next, on the arrival of the four o'clock afternoon coach at Canterbury, my foot will be on my native heath — my name, Micawber!"

Mr. Micawber resumed his seat on the close of these remarks, and drank two glasses of punch in grave succession. He then said with much solemnity: —

"One thing more I have to do before this separation is complete; and that is to perform an act of justice. My friend Mr. Thomas Traddles has, on two several occasions, 'put his name,' if I may use a common expression, to bills of exchange for my accommodation. On the first occasion Mr. Thomas Traddles was left — let me say, in short, in the lurch. The fulfilment of the second has not yet arrived. The amount of the first obligation," here Mr. Micawber carefully referred to papers, "was, I believe, twenty-three, four, nine and a half; of the second, according to my entry of that transaction, eighteen, six, two. These sums, united, make a total, if my calculation is correct, amounting to forty-one, ten, eleven and a half. My friend Mr. Copperfield will perhaps do me the favor to check that total?"

I did so and found it correct.

"To leave this metropolis," said Mr. Micawber, "and my friend Mr. Thomas Traddles, without acquitting myself of the pecuniary part of this obligation, would weigh upon my mind to an insupportable extent. I have therefore prepared for my friend Mr. Thomas Traddles, and I now hold in my hand, a document which accomplishes the desired object. I beg to hand to my friend Mr. Thomas Traddles my I. O. U. forty-one, ten, eleven and a half; and I am happy to recover my moral dignity, and to know that I can once more walk erect before my fellow-man."

With this introduction (which greatly affected him), Mr. Micawber placed his I. O. U. in the hands of Traddles, and said he wished him well in every relation of life. I am persuaded, not only that this was quite the same to Mr. Micawber as paying the money, but that Traddles himself hardly knew the difference until he had had time to think about it.

XXXVII My aunt having lost her fortune, I bestirred myself to earn what money I could, and was engaged by my old Canterbury school-teacher, Dr. Strong, to assist in the production of his long-deferred dictionary. Of course I told Dora of my altered prospects, and quite alarmed her by calling myself a beggar. "Don't talk about being poor," said Dora, nestling close to me, "oh, don't." "My dearest love," said I, "the crust well earned" — "Oh, yes, but I don't want to hear any more about crusts!" said Dora. "And Jip must have a mutton chop every day at twelve, or
XXXVIII he'll die!" As for Spenlow, whether or not my loss of fortune had anything to do with it, he sternly forbade me the house when he learned of the love affair in progress; but a few days after our interview, Mr. Spenlow fell from his carriage and died in a fit, and Dora was taken in charge by her two maiden aunts at Putney. Mr. Spenlow left his affairs in great confusion, and it was found that his debts very nearly equalled his assets.

XXXIX Going down to Canterbury at this time, on some business for my aunt, I found Mr. Micawber very dark and mysterious in regard to the affairs of the firm; Agnes very unhappy about her father, who seemed to be getting more and more under Uriah Heep's thumb; and Uriah himself beginning to display in the midst of his "'umbleness" a sort of triumphant insolence.

XL All these things troubled my aunt very much when I related them to her on my return to London; and, to add to the general gloom of my life at this time, poor Mr. Peggotty met me in London, still on his fruitless search for Little Em'ly. He

had sought her in France and Italy, had missed her by a few days in Switzerland; and was now, after a visit to his home at Yarmouth, just setting out for a town on the upper Rhine, where he had
XLI learned that she was. But brighter days were in store for me. Dora's maiden aunts consented to receive me as an acknowledged suitor. Besides attending to my duties at the office, I was practising shorthand, with the hope of fitting myself to be
XLII a parliamentary reporter. I continued also to assist Dr. Strong with his dictionary; and Mr. Dick, who had a subtle sympathy with the old gentleman which sprang from the heart, and was really better than any intellectual fellowship, used almost always to accompany me to the doctor's house. I even added a third industry,—that of writing short stories, and be-
XLIII tween them all I acquired an income sufficient to be married upon; and, though I could hardly believe it, Dora and I were really installed as husband and wife in a miniature house,
XLIV where Jip had a pagoda to sleep in, almost as big as the house itself. We had our little troubles, with the cook and otherwise; and possibly it would have been better if Jip had never been encouraged to walk about the table-cloth during dinner. I began to think (when we had company) that there was something disorderly in his being there at all, even if he had not been in the habit of putting his foot in the salt or in the melted butter. But Dora was the prettiest, most affectionate, most lovable child in the world.

XLV I have mentioned, I think, that Mr. Dick had, through me, become intimate with Dr. Strong and his young and lovely wife; and I ought to add that he did them a signal service. The doctor loved his wife, but feared that she found him dull and unattractive. She loved him, but feared that he considered her mercenary,—as indeed, her mother was. Mr. Dick divined the trouble by sheer force of sympathy, and brought husband and wife most happily together.

XLVI I had been married about a year, when one day I was summoned to Mrs. Steerforth's house. There I saw Littimer, and heard from him that Steerforth had left Little Em'ly, meaning to have her marry Littimer himself; that Little Em'ly, learning this, had fled from the house, and had not been heard of
XLVII since. I communicated this intelligence to Mr. Peggotty, and we arranged with an unfortunate woman, whom Little Em'ly had once befriended, to be on the lookout for her in London.

XLVIII Dora and I encountered, as I have hinted, a good many difficulties in housekeeping, so many in fact that we finally gave up the task, and let the house keep itself, with the assistance of a page, who finally stole Dora's watch, for which he was tried, and transported. The truth was, that tradespeople and servants had all been battening upon us; and I thought it my duty to have a serious talk with Dora about it. "My dear," I began, "we should be more careful: I fear that these people turn out ill because we do not turn out very well ourselves." "Oh, what an accusation," exclaimed Dora, opening her eyes wide, "to say that you ever saw me take gold watches! Oh!"

"My dearest," I remonstrated, "who has made the least allusion to gold watches?" "You did," returned Dora. "You know you did. You said I had n't turned out well, and compared me to him."

"To whom?" I asked. "To the page," sobbed Dora. "Oh, you cruel fellow, to compare your affectionate wife to a transported page!" In short, Dora was so afflicted that I gave up this effort at reform, — and we were happy.

But as the year wore on, the second year of our marriage, Dora seemed to lose her strength, and finally she became ill. One Sunday she was well enough to come down to dinner, and we thought that in a few days she would be running about again. But they said, wait a few days more; and then, wait a few days more; and still she neither ran nor walked. She looked very pretty, and was very merry; but she and Jip danced together no longer.

XLIX It was on account of Dora's illness that I took Mr. Micawber to my aunt's house, instead of to my own, when that gentleman came up to London — in a state of mysterious agitation. His mind was so preoccupied that even when materials for a punch were set before him, he could not attend to them; and finally, after making an appointment to meet my aunt, Traddles, and me at Canterbury a week afterward, he hurried from the house; and half an hour later I received a letter from him which concluded with the statement that in a short time he should certainly be reposing in a grave upon which rested a plain stone bearing (as he trusted) no words except those of "Wilkins Micawber."

L At last Mr. Peggotty's long search was rewarded. He found Little Em'ly in London. She had come back to England, but was afraid to go home. Mr. Peggotty now proposed
LI that he and she should emigrate to Australia. But first he went down to Yarmouth, and I accompanied him. I saw Ham, and walked with him on the beach. I asked him if there was any message that I could deliver for him. "Yes," he said. "'T ain't that I forgive her. 'T is more as I beg of her to forgive me, for having pressed my affections upon her." "Is that all?" "Theer 's yet a something else," he replied, "if I can say it, Mas'r Davy. I loved her — and I love the mem'ry of her — too deep — to

be able to lead her to believe of my own self, as I'm a happy man. But if you could say anything as would ease her sorrowful mind, and yet not make her think as I could ever marry, — I should ask you to say that."

LII The week came round, and we met Mr. Micawber at Canterbury. He led us all solemnly into Uriah Heep's office, and then came an explosion. Mr. Micawber drew from his breast pocket a bundle of MS., and read a long indictment against his employer, showing how Mr. Wickfield had been deluded and cheated; how, by taking advantage of Mr. Micawber's pecuniary difficulties, Heep had endeavored to make a tool of him in that nefarious business; and finally Mr. Micawber charged and proved that Uriah had actually forged Mr. Wickfield's name. Seeing this, Uriah Heep surrendered to Traddles (who produced a power of attorney from Mr. Wickfield), and disgorged money (including my aunt's fortune), books, and papers. My aunt proposed to Mr. Micawber that he should emigrate to Australia, and offered to advance to him the necessary capital; and Mr. Micawber declared that to emigrate had been the dream of his youth and the fallacious aspiration of his riper years, — though I am sure that he had never thought of it in his life.

LIII When I got back to London I found that my poor little wife was worse. Day by day she became weaker. One night, when she seemed very ill, she told me, with her arms about my neck, speaking of herself as past, that perhaps it was better that she should die; that she was too young and inexperienced to have been my wife; that, as time went on, I might have found her wanting, and have ceased to love her. "It is much better as it is!" Then she asked me to send Agnes to her; and I sat down stairs alone with Jip. Jip crawled out of his house, wandered to the door, and whined to go up stairs. "Not to-night, Jip!" I said. "Not to-night." He licked my hand, and lifted his dim eyes to my face. "O Jip! It may be, never again!" He lay down at my feet, stretched himself out as if to sleep, and with a plaintive cry, was dead. Almost at the same moment his little mistress, his old companion, passed away in sleep, with her head resting upon the bosom of Agnes.

LIV It was not at first that I felt the despair which overwhelmed me later. There was so much to be done that my mind was confused and overwrought. My aunt and I went down to Canterbury again, where Traddles had remained, and the affairs of Mr. Wickfield and the Micawbers were settled. My aunt and I had just returned to London, when she received a letter from Mr. Micawber, stating that he had been arrested in another cause of

Heep *v.* Micawber, and was then languishing in the debtors' prison, where some future traveller might trace with sympathy, on the wall, inscribed with a rusty nail, the obscure initials "W. M." But there was a postscript stating that the bill had been paid by Mr. Traddles, "in the noble name of Miss Trotwood."

LV The Micawbers and Mr. Peggotty, with Little Em'ly, were to sail on the same ship; and I had a note of farewell from little Em'ly to Ham to deliver, in answer to his message to her. I concluded to deliver this in person, and went down to Yarmouth. The night before I arrived there had been a terrible gale, and before I was up in the morning I heard that a ship had come ashore, and was fast breaking up, almost within a stone's throw of dry land. I hurried to the beach. One mast was standing, and to that there clung four men. Even as I watched them, three — one after another — were swept away, and there remained only one. He wore a singular red cap, not like a sailor's cap, which he waved to the people on the beach. Suddenly Ham appeared upon the scene. "Mas'r Davy," he said, cheerily grasping me with both hands, "if my time is come, 't is come. If 't ain't, I 'll bide it. Lord above bless you. Mates, make me ready! I 'm a going off." With a rope around his waist he plunged into the sea. Then, failing to reach the ship, he was drawn back. Again he plunged in, and buffetted the waves. But there came a great, green hillside of water, which swept away the wreck, and cast ashore the dead body of Ham, and the dead body of the man in the red cap, — who was Steerforth.

LVI I had the dreadful task of telling Mrs. Steerforth of her son's death. The intelligence made Rosa Dartle frantic with grief and passion. "I loved him," she cried to his mother, "better than you ever did." Mrs. Steerforth moaned and stared, and lay back in her chair like a statue, bereft of reason. And so, calling in the servants and bidding them send for a doctor, I left them.

LVII One thing more I had to do, which was to conceal what had happened from Mr. Peggotty and Little Em'ly, so that they might hear of it first in far-off Australia; and in this Mr. Micawber promised me his willing assistance. I saw them off. On deck I took leave of poor Mrs. Micawber. She was looking distractedly about for her family even then; and her last words to me were that she never would desert Mr. Micawber.

LVIII I went abroad, and roamed about for a year, distracted, restless, and desolate. Then, stirred to action by a letter from Agnes, I resolved to resume my work. I worked early and late, patiently and hard. I wrote a story which Traddles disposed of for me, and which brought me some fame. After an absence of

three years I came back to England. The first person that I saw was Traddles. I found him established with his wife —
LIX for the "dearest girl" had become his at last — in his chambers at Gray's Inn, where they lived most happily and cosily and even found room for three or four sisters, who happened to be on a visit there when I arrived in London, and who made the place a perfect nest of roses. From London I hastened to Dover,
LX where I found my dear aunt and Mr. Dick well and happy. The next day I saw Agnes and her father at Canterbury. She was the same sweet, noble, sympathetic girl as ever, but it seemed to me that her smile was more sad than it used to be.

Until my book should be finished, I lived with my aunt
LXI at Dover; and one day Traddles and I, at the invitation of our old schoolmaster and tyrant, Creakle, paid a visit to a model prison in which Creakle was much interested. Creakle had developed a great tenderness for criminals, and it appeared that in this prison all the inmates were good and religious men. The very best and most religious were, it was said, No. 27 and No. 28. At last we came to their cells, and who should step out but Uriah Heep and Littimer, — Uriah with a hymn book in his hand, and Littimer with an air of pious resignation.

Christmas Day I spent with Agnes; and now at last we
LXII came to understand each other. We walked that winter evening in the fields together, and the blessed calm within us seemed to be partaken by the frosty air. When, on the next day, I told my aunt that Agnes and I were to be married, she went into hysterics for the first and only time in her life, and when she recovered she embraced Mr. Dick, and Peggotty, and me.

Ten years after we were married, there came one night
LXIII to our house Mr. Peggotty, — an old man now, but ruddy and vigorous. He had come back to England for a short visit only. He reported that all our friends in Australia were doing well; that Mr. Micawber was a magistrate and a prominent, flourishing man, — and I may add that he had long since paid his debts in England. As to his niece, he said, looking at the fire, "A slight figure, kiender worn, a quiet voice and way — timid a'most. That's Em'ly."

It remains only to take a last retrospect. I see my aunt
LXIV and Peggotty, both in spectacles, but still upright and sturdy; and between them a Betsey Trotwood Copperfield, whose tottering steps they guide, as Peggotty guided mine when I was a child. I see Mrs. Steerforth, a querulous, imbecile woman, with fitful gleams of former pride and beauty, and Rosa Dartle, a worn and withered figure with a white scar upon her lip. I see Traddles,

busy with a large and growing practice; the same simple, unaffected fellow; and Sophy, still the "dearest of girls," presiding over the ample table where her sisters and her sisters' husbands are gathered on numerous occasions. Above all, I see one beautiful face, shining on me like a heavenly light. I turn my head, and see it in its noble serenity. O Agnes, when realities are melting from me like the shadows which I now dismiss, may I still see thee beside me!

---

## INDEX TO CHARACTERS

**Adams.** Head boy at Doctor Strong's; affable and good-humored, and with a turn for mathematics. xvi, xviii.

**Babley, Richard,** *called* Mr. Dick. A mild lunatic, and a *protégé* of Miss Betsey Trotwood's, who insists that he is not mad.

"He had a favorite sister," said my aunt, — "a good creature, and very kind to him: but she did what they all do, — took a husband; and *he* did what they all do, — made her wretched. It had such an effect upon the mind of Mr. Dick (*that 's* not madness, I hope!) that, combined with his fear of his brother and his sense of his unkindness, it threw him into a fever. That was before he came to me; but the recollection of it is oppressive to him even now. Did he say anything to you about King Charles the First, child?"

"Yes, aunt."

"Ah!" said my aunt, rubbing her nose as if she were a little vexed. "That 's his allegorical way of expressing it. He connects his illness with great disturbance and agitation, naturally; and that 's the figure, or the simile, or whatever it 's called, which he chooses to use. And why should n't he, if he thinks proper?"

I said, "Certainly, aunt."

"It 's not a business-like way of speaking," said my aunt, "nor a worldly way. I am aware of that; and that 's the reason why I insist upon it that there sha'n't be a word about it in his memorial."

"Is it a memorial about his own history that he is writing, aunt?"

"Yes, child," said my aunt, rubbing her nose again. "He is memorializing the Lord Chancellor, or the Lord Somebody or other, — one of those people, at all events, who are paid to *be* memorialized, — about his affairs. I suppose it will go in one of these days. He has n't been able to draw it up yet, without introducing that mode of expressing himself; but it don't signify; it keeps him employed."

In fact, I found out afterwards that Mr. Dick had been for upwards of ten years endeavoring to keep King Charles the First out of the memorial; but he had been constantly getting into it, and was there now. xiii–xv, xvii, xix, xxxiv, xxxvi, xxxviii, xlii, xliii, xlv, xlix, lii, liv, lx, lxii, lxiv.

**Bailey, Captain.** An admirer of the eldest Miss Larkins. xviii.

**Barkis, Mr.** A carrier, who takes David Copperfield from Blunderstone to Yarmouth, on his first being sent away to school, and afterwards marries Peggotty. ii–v, vii, viii, x, xxix, xxxi.

**Barkis, Mrs.** *See* PEGGOTTY, CLARA.

**Charley.** A drunken, ugly old dealer in second-hand sailor's clothes and marine stores, to whom David Copperfield sells his jacket for fourpence when travelling on foot to his aunt's. xiii.

**Chestle, Mr.** A hop-grower; a plain, elderly gentleman who marries the eldest Miss Larkins. xviii.

**Chillip, Mr.** The doctor who officiates at the birth of David Copperfield.

He was the meekest of his sex, the mildest of little men. He sidled in and out of a room to take up the less space. He walked as softly as the Ghost in "Hamlet," and more slowly. He carried his head on one side, — partly in modest depreciation of himself, partly in modest propitiation of everybody else. It is nothing to say that he had n't a word to throw at a dog. He could n't have *thrown* a word at a mad dog. i, ii, ix, x, xxii, xxx, lix.

**Clickett.** An "orfling" girl from St. Luke's Workhouse; servant to the Micawbers. She is a dark complexioned young woman with a habit of snorting. xi, xii.

**Copperfield, Mrs. Clara.** The mother of David; an artless, affectionate little woman, whom Miss Betsey Trotwood insists upon calling a mere baby. She marries Mr. Murdstone, a stern man, who, in conjunction with his sister, attempts to teach her "firmness," but breaks her heart in the experiment. i–iv, viii, ix.

**Copperfield, David.** The character from whom the story takes its name, and by whom it is supposed to be told. He is a posthumous child, having been born six months after his father's death. His mother, young, beautiful, inexperienced, loving, and lovable, not long afterwards marries a handsome and plausible, but hard and stern man, — Mr. Murdstone by name, — who soon crushes her gentle spirit by his exacting tyranny and by his cruel treatment of her boy. After being for some time instructed at home by his mother, and reduced to a state of dulness and sullen desperation by his stepfather, David is sent from home. He is sent to a villainous school, near London, kept by one Creakle, where he receives more stripes than lessons. Here he is kept until the death of his mother, when his stepfather sends him (he being now ten years old) to London, to be employed in Murdstone and Grinby's warehouse in washing out empty wine-bottles, pasting labels on them when filled, and the like, at a salary of six shillings a week. But such is the secret agony of his soul at sinking into companionship with Mick Walker, "Mealy Potatoes," and other boys with whom he is forced to associate, that he at length resolves to run away, and throw himself upon the kindness of a great-aunt (Miss Betsey Trotwood), whom he has never seen, but of whose eccentric habits and singular manner he has often heard. She receives him much better than he has expected, and soon adopts him, and sends him to school in the neighboring town of Canterbury. He does well here, and finally graduates with high honors. Having made up his mind to become a proctor, he enters the office of Mr. Spenlow, in London. Soon after this, his aunt loses the greater part of her property; and David, being compelled to look about him for the means of subsistence, learns the art of stenography, and supports himself comfortably by reporting the debates in Parliament. In the mean time he has fallen desperately in love with Dora, the daughter of Mr. Spenlow, but has been discouraged in his suit by the young lady's father. Mr. Spenlow dying, however, he becomes her accepted suitor. Turning his attention soon after to authorship, he acquires a reputation, and obtains constant employment on magazines and periodicals. He now marries Dora, a pretty, captivating, affectionate girl, but utterly ignorant of everything practical. It is not long before David discovers that it will be altogether useless to expect that his wife will develop any stability of character, and he resolves to estimate her by the good qualities she has, and not by those which she has not. One night she says to him in a very thoughtful manner that she wishes him to call her his "child-wife."

"It's a stupid name," she said, shaking her curls for a moment, — "child-wife."

I laughingly asked my child-wife what her fancy was in desiring to be so called. She answered without moving, otherwise than as the arm I twined about her may have brought her blue eyes nearer to me, —

"I don't mean, you silly fellow, that you should use the name instead of Dora: I only mean that you should think of me that way. When you are going to be angry with me, say to yourself, It's only my child-wife.' When I am very disappointing, say, 'I knew, a long time ago, that she would make but a child-wife.'

When you miss what I should like to be, and I think can never be, say, 'Still my foolish child-wife loves me.' For indeed I do."

I had not been serious with her, having no idea, until now, that she was serious herself. But her affectionate nature was so happy in what I now said to her with my whole heart, that her face became a laughing one before her glittering eyes were dry. She was soon my child-wife indeed, sitting down on the floor outside the Chinese House, ringing all the little bells one after another, to punish Jip for his recent bad behavior; while Jip lay blinking in the doorway with his head out, even too lazy to be teased.

This appeal of Dora's made a strong impression on me. I look back on the time I write of; I invoke the innocent figure that I dearly loved, to come out from the mists and shadows of the past, and turn its gentle head towards me once again; and I can still declare that this one little speech was constantly in my memory.

At length Dora falls into a decline, and grows weaker and weaker, day by day.

It is night, and I am with her still. Agnes has arrived; has been among us for a whole day and an evening. She, my aunt, and I have sat with Dora since the morning, all together. We have not talked much; but Dora has been perfectly contented and cheerful. We are now alone.

Do I know now that my child-wife will soon leave me? They have told me so; they have told me nothing new to my thoughts; but I am far from sure that I have taken that truth to heart. I cannot master it. . . . I cannot shut out a pale lingering shadow of belief that she will be spared.

"I am going to speak to you, Doady. I am going to say something I have often thought of saying lately. You won't mind?" with a gentle look.

"Mind, my darling?"

"Because I don't know what you will think, or what you may have thought sometimes. Perhaps you have often thought the same. Doady, dear, I am afraid I was too young."

I lay my face upon the pillow by her, and she looks into my eyes, and speaks very softly. Gradually, as she goes on, I feel with a stricken heart that she is speaking of herself as past.

"I am afraid, dear, I was too young: I don't mean in years only, but in experience and thoughts and everything. I was such a silly little creature! I am afraid it would have been better if we had only loved each other as a boy and girl, and forgotten it. I have begun to think I was not fit to be a wife."

I try to stay my tears, and to reply, "O Dora, love! — as fit as I to be a husband."

"I don't know," with the old shake of her curls. "Perhaps. But, if I had been more fit to be married, I might have made you more so too. Besides, you are very clever, and I never was."

"We have been very happy, my sweet Dora."

"I was very happy, very. But as years went on my dear boy would have wearied of his child-wife. She would have been less and less a companion for him. He would have been more and more sensible of what was wanting in his home. She would n't have improved. It is better as it is."

"O Dora, dearest, dearest, do not speak to me so! Every word seems a reproach."

"No, not a syllable!" she answers, kissing me. . . . "O Doady! after more years, you never could have loved your child-wife better than you do; and after more years she would so have tried and disappointed you, that you might not have been able to love her half so well. I know I was too young and foolish. It is much better as it is."

After the death of his wife, David goes abroad, passing through many weary phases of mental distress. During his absence, Agnes Wickfield, a dear friend of Dora's and of himself, writes to him.

She gave me no advice; she urged no duty on me; she only told me in her own fervent manner what her trust in me was. She knew (she said) how such a nature as mine would turn affliction to good. She knew how trial and emotion would exalt and strengthen it. She was sure that, in my every purpose, I should gain a firmer and a higher tendency through the grief I had undergone. She who so gloried in my fame, and so looked forward to its augmentation, well knew that I would labor on. She knew that in me sorrow could not be weakness, but must be strength. As the endurance of my childish days had done its part to make me what I was, so greater calamities would nerve me on to be yet better than I was; and so, as they had taught me, would I teach others. She commended me to God, who had taken my innocent darling to his rest; and in her sisterly affection cherished me always, and was always at my side, go where I would, proud of what I had done, but infinitely prouder yet of what I was reserved to do.

When three years have passed, David returns to England, where his few works have already made him famous. But more than all else he values the praise and encouragement he receives from Agnes, whom he has come to think the better angel of his life, and whom he would gladly make his wife, did he not believe that her feeling towards him was merely one of sisterly affection, and that she has formed a deeper attachment for another. He discovers at last, however, that she loves him only, and that she has loved him all her life; though she unselfishly subdued the feelings of her heart so far as to rejoice sincerely in his marriage to Dora. They are soon united, and she then tells him that Dora, on the last night of her life, expressed the earnest wish that she, and she alone, should succeed to her place.

And now, as I close my task, subduing my desire to linger yet, these faces fade away. But one face, shining on me like a heavenly light, by which I see all other objects, is above them and beyond them all. And that remains.

I turn my head, and see it in its beautiful serenity beside me. My lamp burns low, and I have written far into the night; but the dear presence, without which I were nothing, bears me company.

O Agnes, oh, my soul, so may thy face be by me when I close my life indeed! so may I, when realities are melting from me like the shadows which I now dismiss, still find thee near me, pointing upward!

**Copperfield, Mrs. Dora.** *See* SPENLOW, DORA.

**Creakle, Mr.** Master of Salem House, the school to which David Copperfield is sent by Mr. Murdstone; an ignorant and ferocious brute, who prides himself on being a "Tartar." v,–vii, ix, lxi.

**Creakle, Mrs.** His wife; a thin and quiet woman, ill-treated by her husband. vi, ix.

**Creakle, Miss.** Their daughter; supposed to be in love with Steerforth. vi, vii, ix.

**Crewler, Mrs.** Wife of the Reverend Horace Crewler; a very superior woman, who has lost the use of her limbs. She becomes the mother-in-law of Traddles. Whatever occurs to harass her (as the engagement and prospective loss of her daughters) usually settles in her legs, but sometimes mounts to her chest and head, and pervades her whole system in a most alarming manner. xxxiv, xli, lx.

**Crewler, Miss Caroline.** Eldest daughter of Mrs. Crewler; a very handsome girl, who marries a dashing vagabond, but soon separates from him. xli, lx, lxiv.

**Crewler, Miss Lousia.** Mrs. Crewler's third daughter. xli, lx, lxiv.

**Crewler, Miss Lucy.** One of Mrs. Crewler's two youngest daughters, educated by her sister Sophy. xli, lx, lxvi.

**Crewler, Miss Margaret.** One of Mrs. Crewler's two youngest daughters, educated by her sister Sophy. xli, lx, lxvi.

**Crewler, Miss Sarah.** Mrs. Crewler's second daughter. xxxiv, xli, lx, lxiv.

**Crewler, Miss Sophy.** Fourth daughter of Mrs. Crewler; always forgetful of herself, always cheerful and amiable, and as much a mother to her mother (who is a confirmed invalid) as she is to her sisters. She becomes the wife of Tommy Traddles, who regards her both before and after marriage as "the dearest girl in the world." xxvii, xxviii, xxxiv, xli, xliii, lix, lxi, lxii, lxiv.

**Crewler, The Reverend Horace.** A poor Devonshire clergyman, with a large family and a sick wife. xxxiv, xli, lx, lxiv.

**Crupp, Mrs.** A stout woman living in Buckingham Street, in the Adelphi, who lets a set of furnished chambers to David Copperfield when he becomes an articled clerk in the office of Spenlow and Jorkins. She is a martyr to a curious disorder called "the spazzums," which is generally accompanied with inflammation of the nose, and requires to be constantly treated with peppermint. xxiii–xxvi, xxviii, xxxiv, xxxv, xxxvii.

**Dartle, Rosa.** A lady some thirty years old, living with Mrs. Steerforth as a companion, and passionately in love with her son, who does not return her affection. She is of a slight, short figure, and a dark complexion; has black hair, and large black eyes, and a remarkable scar on her lip, caused by a wound from a hammer thrown at her by Steerforth, when a boy, in a moment of exasperation. She is very clever, bringing everything to a grindstone, and even wearing herself away by constant sharpening, till she is all edge. xx, xxi, xxiv, xxix, xxxii, xxxvi, xlvi, l, lvi, lxiv.

**Demple, George.** A schoolmate of David Copperfield's at Salem House. v, vii.

**Dolloby, Mr.** A dealer in second-hand clothes, rags, bones, and kitchen-stuff, to whom David Copperfield sells his waistcoat for ninepence when he runs away from "Murdstone and Grinby's" to seek his aunt. xiii.

**Dora.** *See* SPENLOW, DORA.

**Em'ly, Little.** Niece and adopted daughter of Mr. Peggotty, and the object of David Copperfield's first love. She is afterwards betrothed to her cousin Ham, but is seduced by Steerforth. iii, vii, x, xvii, xxi–xxiii, xxx.

**Endell, Martha.** An unfortunate young woman, without money or reputation, who finally discovers "Little Em'ly," and restores her to her uncle. She is reclaimed, and emigrates to Australia, where she marries happily. xxii, xl, xlvi, xlvii, l, li, lvii, lxiii.

**Fibbetson, Mrs.** An old woman, inmate of an almshouse. v.

**George.** Guard of the Yarmouth mail. v.

**Grainger.** A friend of Steerforth's, and a very gay and lively fellow. xxiv.

**Grayper, Mr.** A neighbor of Mrs. Copperfield. ix, xxii.

**Grayper, Mrs.** His wife. ii, xxii.

**Gulpidge, Mr.** A guest of the Waterbrooks, who has something to do at second-hand with the law business of the Bank. xxv.

**Gulpidge, Mrs.** His wife. xxv.

**Gummidge, Mrs.** The widow of Mr. Peggotty's partner. Her husband dying poor, Mr. Peggotty offers her a home, and supports her for years; and this kindness she acknowledges by sitting in the most comfortable corner, by the fireside, and complaining that she is "a lone, lorn creetur, and everythink goes contrairy with her." iii, vii, x, xxi, xxii, xxxi, xxxii, xl, li, lvii, lxiii.

**Hamlet's Aunt.** *See* SPIKER, MRS. HENRY.

**Heep, Mrs.** A very 'umble widow woman, mother of Uriah Heep, and his "dead image, only short." xvii, xxix, xlii, lii, lxi.

**Heep, Uriah.** A clerk in the law-office of Mr. Wickfield, whose partner he afterwards becomes. David Copperfield's first meeting with him is thus described:—

When the pony-chaise stopped at the door, and my eyes were intent upon the house, I saw a cadaverous face appear at a small window on the ground-floor (in a little round tower that formed one side of the house), and quickly disappear. The low-arched door then opened, and the face came out. It was quite as cadaverous as it had looked in the window; though, in the grain of it, there was that tinge of red which is sometimes to be observed in the skins of red-haired people. It belonged to a red-haired person,—a youth of fifteen, as I take it now, but looking much older,—whose hair was cropped as close as the closest stubble; who had hardly any eyebrows, and no eyelashes, and eyes of a red-brown, so unsheltered and unshaded, that I remember wondering how he went to sleep. He was high-shouldered and bony; dressed in decent black with a white wisp of a neck-cloth; buttoned up to the throat; and had a long, lank, skeleton hand, which particularly attracted my attention as he stood at the pony's head, rubbing his chin with it, and looking up at us in the chaise.

As time runs on, David finds that Uriah is obtaining an unbounded influence over Mr. Wickfield, whom he deludes in every possible way, and whose business he designedly perplexes and complicates in order to get it wholly into his own hands; and, furthermore, that he looks with greedy eyes upon Mr. Wickfield's daughter Agnes, to whom David himself is warmly attached. He even goes so far as to boast of this, and to declare his intention of making her his wife.

Uriah goes on weaving his meshes around Agnes and her father

URIAH HEEP AND HIS MOTHER

until he has them completely in his power. But his rascality is at last unravelled and exposed by Mr. Micawber; and Mr. Wickfield not only recovers all the property of which he has been defrauded, but is absolved from all suspicion of any criminal act or intent. Uriah pursues his calling in another part of the country, but is finally arrested for fraud, forgery, and conspiracy, and is sentenced to solitary imprisonment. xv–xvii, xix, xxv, xxxv, xxxvi, xxxix, xlii, xlix, lii, liv, lxi.

**Hopkins, Captain.** A prisoner for debt, in the King's Bench Prison, at the time that Mr. Micawber is also confined there. xi.

**Janet.** Miss Betsey Trotwood's handmaid. xiii–xv, xxiii, xxxix, xliii, lx.

**Jip** (*a contraction of* GIPSY). Dora's pet dog. xxvi, xxxiii, xxxvi–xxxviii, xli–xliv, xlviii, lii, liii.

**Joram, Mr.** The partner and son-in-law of Mr. Omer the undertaker. ix, xxi, xxiii, xxx, li, lvi.

**Joram, Mrs.** *See* OMER, MISS MINNIE.

**Jorkins, Mr.** A proctor, partner of Mr. Spenlow.

He was a mild man of a heavy temperament, whose place in the business was to keep himself in the background, and be constantly exhibited, by name, as the most obdurate and ruthless of men. If a clerk wanted his salary raised, Mr. Jorkins would n't listen to such a proposition; if a client were slow to settle his bill of costs, Mr. Jorkins was resolved to have it paid; and, however painful these things might be (and always were) to the feelings of Mr. Spenlow, Mr. Jorkins would have his bond. The heart and hand of the good angel Spenlow would have been always open, but for the restraining demon Jorkins. As I have grown older, I think I have had experience of some other houses doing business on the principle of Spenlow and Jorkins. xxiii, xxix, xxxv, xxxviii, xxxix.

**Larkins, Miss.** A tall, dark, black-eyed, fine figure of a woman, of about thirty, with whom David Copperfield falls desperately in love when about seventeen. His passion for her is beyond all bounds; but she crushes his hopes by marrying a hop-grower. xviii.

**Larkins, Mr.** Her father; a gruff old gentleman with a double chin, and one of his eyes immovable in his head. xviii.

**Littimer.** Confidential servant of Steerforth.

I believe there never existed in his station a more respectable-looking man. He was taciturn, soft-footed, very quiet in his manner, deferential, observant, always at hand when wanted, and never near when not wanted; but his great claim to consideration was his respectability. He had not a pliant face; he had rather a stiff neck, rather a tight smooth head with short hair clinging to it at the sides, a soft way of speaking, with a peculiar habit of whispering the letter S so distinctly, that he seemed to use it oftener than any other man: but every peculiarity that he had he made respectable. . . . He surrounded himself with an atmosphere of respectability, and walked secure in it. It would have been next to impossible to suspect him of anything wrong, he was so thoroughly respectable. Nobody could have thought of putting him in a livery, he was so highly respectable. To have imposed any derogatory work upon him would have been to inflict a wanton insult on the feelings of a most respectable man. xxi–xxiii, xxviii, xxix, xxxi, xxxii, xlvi, lxi.

**Maldon, Jack.** Cousin to Mrs. Dr. Strong; an idle, needy libertine with a handsome face, a rapid utterance, and a confident, bold air. xvi, xix, xxxvi, xli, xlv, lxiv.

**Markham.** A gay and lively fellow of not more than twenty; a friend of Steerforth's. xxiv, xxv.

**Markleham, Mrs.** Mother of Mrs. Dr. Strong.

Our boys used to call her the Old Soldier, on account of her generalship and the skill with which she marshalled great forces of relations against the doctor. She was a little, sharp-eyed woman, who used to wear, when she was dressed, one unchangeable cap, ornamented with some artificial flowers, and two artificial butterflies supposed to be hovering about the flowers. xvi, xix, xxxvi, xlii, xlv, lxiv.

**Mealy Potatoes.** (So called on account of his pale complexion.) A boy employed at Murdstone and Grinby's wine-store, with David Copperfield and others, to examine bottles, wash them out, label and cork them, and the like. xi.

**Mell, Mr. Charles.** An under master at Salem House, Mr. Creakle's school. He is a gaunt, sallow young man, with hollow cheeks, and dry and rusty hair. Mr. Creakle discharges him because it is ascertained that his mother lives on charity in an almshouse. He emigrates to Australia, and finally becomes Doctor Mell of Colonial Salem-House Grammar-School. v–vii, lxiii.

**Mell, Mrs.** His mother. v, vii.

**Micawber, Master Wilkins.** Son of Mr. Wilkins Micawber. He has a remarkable head voice, and becomes a chorister-boy in the cathedral at Canterbury. At a later date he acquires a high reputation as an amateur singer. xi, xii, xvii, xxvii, xxxvi, xlii, xlix, lii, liv, lvii, lxiv.

**Micawber, Miss Emma.** Daughter of Mr. Wilkins Micawber; afterwards Mrs. Ridger Begs of Port Middlebay, Australia. xi, xii, xvii, xxvii, xxxvi, xlii, xlix, lii, liv, lvii, lxiv.

**Micawber, Mr. Wilkins.** A gentleman — remarkable for his reckless improvidence, his pecuniary involvements, his alternate elevation and depression of spirits, his love of letter-writing and speech-making, his grandiloquent rhetoric, his shabby devices for eking out a genteel living, and his constantly "waiting for something to turn up" — with whom David Copperfield lodges while drudging in the warehouse of Murdstone and Grinby. Mr. Micawber is thus introduced upon the scene: —

The counting-house clock was at half-past twelve, and there was general preparation for going to dinner, when Mr. Quinion tapped at the counting-house window, and beckoned me to go in. I went in, and found there a stoutish, middle-aged person, in a brown surtout and black tights and shoes, with no more hair upon his head (which was a large one, and very shining) than there is upon an egg, and with a very extensive face, which he turned full upon me. His clothes were shabby; but he had an imposing shirt-collar on. He carried a jaunty sort of a stick with a large pair of rusty tassels to it; and a quizzing-glass hung outside his coat, — for ornament, I afterwards found, as he very seldom looked through it, and could n't see anything when he did.

"This," said Mr. Quinion, in allusion to myself, "is he."

"This," said the stranger, with a certain condescending roll in his voice, and a certain indescribable air of doing something genteel, which impressed me very much, "is Master Copperfield. I hope I see you well, sir?"

I said I was very well, and hoped he was. I was sufficiently ill at ease, Heaven knows; but it was not in my nature to complain much at that time of my life: so I said I was very well, and hoped he was.

"I am," said the stranger, "thank Heaven! quite well. I have received a letter from Mr. Murdstone, in which he mentions that he would desire me to receive into an apartment in the rear of my house, which is at present unoccupied, and is, in short, to be let as a — in short," said the stranger, with a smile, and in a burst of confidence, — "as a bedroom, the young beginner whom I have now the pleasure to" — and the stranger waved his hand, and settled his chin in his shirt-collar.

"This is Mr. Micawber," said Mr. Quinion to me.

"Ahem!" said the stranger: "that is my name."

"Mr. Micawber," said Mr. Quinion, "is known to Mr. Murdstone. He takes orders for us on commission, when he can get any. He has been written to by Mr. Murdstone on the subject of your lodgings, and he will receive you as a lodger." xi, xii, xvii, xxvii, xxviii, xxxvi, xxxix, xlii, xlix, lii, liv, lvii, lxiii.

**Micawber, Mrs. Emma.** Wife of Wilkins Micawber.

Arrived at his [Mr. Micawber's] house in Windsor Terrace (which I noticed was shabby, like himself, but also, like himself, made all the show it could), he presented me to Mrs. Micawber, a thin and faded lady, not at all young, who was sitting in the parlor (the first floor was altogether unfurnished, and the blinds were kept down to delude the neighbors) with a baby at her breast. This baby was one of twins; and I may remark here, that I hardly ever, in all my experience of the family, saw both the twins detached from Mrs. Micawber at the same time. One of them was always taking refreshment.

When her husband's resources are at the lowest ebb, she determines to come to his rescue if she can.

Poor Mrs. Micawber! She said she had tried to exert herself; and so I have no doubt she had. The centre of the street-door was perfectly covered with a great brass plate, on which was engraved, "Mrs. Micawber's Boarding Establishment for Young Ladies:" but I never found that any young lady had ever been to school there; or that any young lady ever came, or proposed to come; or that the least preparation was ever made to receive any young lady.

In the ease of her temper and the elasticity of her spirits, Mrs. Micawber is scarcely surpassed by her husband.

I have known her to be thrown into fainting-fits by the king's taxes at three o'clock, and to eat lamb chops breaded, and to drink warm ale (paid for with two teaspoons that had gone to the pawnbroker's), at four. On one occasion, when an execution had just been put in, coming home, through some chance, as early as six o'clock, I saw her lying (of course with a twin) under the grate in a swoon, with her hair all torn about her face; but I never knew her more cheerful than she was that very same night, over a veal cutlet before the kitchen fire, telling me stories about her papa and mamma, and the company they used to keep.

Among the striking and praiseworthy characteristics of this remarkable lady, her devoted attachment to her husband is deserving of special mention. On one occasion, she tells David Copperfield: —

"I never will desert Mr. Micawber! Mr. Micawber may have concealed his difficulties from me in the first instance; but his sanguine temper may have led him to expect that he would overcome them. The pearl necklace and bracelets which I inherited from mamma have been disposed of for less than half their value; and the set of coral which was the wedding-gift of my papa has been actually thrown away for nothing. But I never

MR. MICAWBER AND HIS FAMILY.

will desert Mr. Micawber. No!" cried Mrs. Micawber, more affected than before, "I never will do it! It 's of no use asking me."

I felt quite uncomfortable, — as if Mrs. Micawber supposed I had asked her to do anything of the sort, — and sat looking at her in alarm.

"Mr. Micawber has his faults. I do not deny that he is improvident. I do not deny that he has kept me in the dark as to his resources and his liabilities both," she went on, looking at the wall; "but I never will desert Mr. Micawber!"

Mrs. Micawber having now raised her voice into a perfect scream, I was so frightened that I ran off to the club-room, and disturbed Mr. Micawber, in the act of presiding at a long table, and leading the chorus of

Gee up, Dobbin,
Gee ho, Dobbin,
Gee up, Dobbin,
Gee up, and Gee ho — o — o!

with the tidings that Mrs. Micawber was in an alarming state; upon which he immediately burst into tears, and came away with me with his waistcoat full of the heads and tails of shrimps of which he had been partaking.

"Emma, my angel!" cried Mr. Micawber, running into the room, "what is the matter?"

"I never will desert you, Micawber!" she exclaimed.

"My life!" said Mr. Micawber, taking her in his arms. "I am perfectly aware of it!"

"He is the parent of my children! He is the father of my twins! He is the husband of my affections!" cried Mrs. Micawber, struggling; "and I ne — ver — will — desert Mr. Micawber!"

Mr. Micawber was so deeply affected by this proof of her devotion (as to me, I was dissolved in tears), that he hung over her in a passionate manner, imploring her to look up and to be calm. But the more he asked Mrs. Micawber to look up, the more she fixed her eyes on nothing; and the more he asked her to compose herself, the more she would n't. Consequently Mr. Micawber was soon so overcome, that he mingled his tears with hers and mine, until he begged me to do him the favor of taking a chair on the staircase while he got her into bed. xi, xii, xvii, xxvii, xxviii, xxxvi, xlii, xlix, lii, liv, lvii, lxiii.

**Mills, Miss Julia.** The bosom friend of Dora Spenlow.

I learned . . . that Miss Mills had had her trials in the course of a checkered existence, and that to these, perhaps, I might refer that wise benignity of manner which I had already noticed. I found, in the course of the day, that this was the case; Miss Mills having been unhappy in a misplaced affection, and being understood to have retired from the world on her awful stock of experience, but still to take a calm interest in the unblighted hopes and loves of youth.

For the more exact discharge of the duties of friendship, Miss Mills keeps a journal, of which the following is a sample:—

"MONDAY.—My sweet D. still much depressed. Headache. Called attention to J. as being beautifully sleek. D. fondled J. Associations thus awakened opened flood-gates of sorrow. Rush of grief admitted. (Are tears the dew-drops of the heart?—J. M.)" xxxiii, xxxvii, xxxviii, xli, lxiv.

**Mills, Mr.** Her father; a terrible fellow to fall asleep after dinner. xxxiii, xxxvii, xxxviii, xli.

**Mowcher, Miss.** A dealer in cosmetics, a fashionable hair-dresser, etc., who makes herself useful to a variety of people in a variety of ways. She is very talkative, and plumes herself on being "volatile," but is thoroughly kind-hearted and honest.

I was still looking at the doorway, thinking that Miss Mowcher was a long while making her appearance, when, to my infinite astonishment, there came waddling round a sofa which stood between me and it, a pursy dwarf of about forty or forty-five, with a very large head and face, a pair of roguish gray eyes, and such extremely little arms, that, to enable herself to lay a finger archly against her snub nose as she ogled Steerforth, she was obliged to meet the finger half-way, and lay her nose against it. Her chin, which was what is called a double chin, was so fat, that it entirely swallowed up the strings of her bonnet,—bow and all. Throat she had none; waist she had none; legs she had none, worth mentioning; for though she was more than full sized down to where her waist would have been (if she had had any), and though she terminated, as human beings generally do, in a pair of feet, she was so short, that she stood at a common sized chair as at a table, resting a bag she carried on the seat. This lady,—dressed in an offhand, easy style; bringing her nose and her fore-finger together with the difficulty I have described; standing with her head necessarily on one side, and, with one of her sharp eyes shut up, making an uncommonly knowing face,—after ogling Steerforth for a few moments, broke into a torrent of words. xxii, xxxii, lxi.

**Murdstone, Mr. Edward.** Stepfather of David Copperfield. ii–iv, viii–x, xiv, xxxiii, lix.

**Murdstone, Miss Jane.** Sister to Edward Murdstone; a gloomy-looking, severe, metallic lady, dark, like her brother, whom she greatly resembles in face and voice; and with very heavy eyebrows, nearly meeting over her large nose, as if, being disabled by the wrongs of her sex from wearing whiskers, she had carried them to that account. She is constantly haunted by a suspicion that the servants have a man secreted somewhere on the premises; and, under the influence of this delusion, she dives into the coal-cellar at the most untimely hours, and scarcely ever opens the door of a dark cupboard without clapping it to again, in the belief that she has got him. iv, viii–x, xii, xiv, xxvi, xxxiii, xxxviii, lix.

**Nettingall, The Misses.** Principals of a boarding-school for young ladies. xviii.

**Old Soldier, The.** *See* MARKLEHAM, MRS.

**Omer, Minnie.** Daughter of Mr. Omer; a pretty, good-natured girl, engaged to Mr. Joram. ix, xxi, xxx, xxxii, li.

**Omer, Mr.** A draper, tailor, haberdasher, undertaker, etc., at Yarmouth; a fat, short-winded, merry-looking little old man in black, with rusty little bunches of ribbons at the knees of his breeches, black stockings, and a broad-brimmed hat. ix, xxi, xxx, xxxii, li.

**Paragon, Mary Anne.** A servant who keeps house for David Copperfield and Dora. xliv.

**Passnidge, Mr.** A friend of Mr. Murdstone's. ii.

**Peggotty, Clara.** Servant to Mrs. Copperfield, and nurse and friend to her son David; a girl with no shape at all, and eyes so dark, that they seem to darken their whole neighborhood in her face, and with cheeks and arms so hard and red that the birds might peck them in preference to apples. Being very plump, whenever she makes any little exertion after she is dressed, some of the buttons on the back of her gown fly off. After the death of her mistress, Peggotty marries Mr. Barkis, a carrier, who has long admired her; but she never forgets her old love for David, whose housekeeper she finally becomes. i–v, viii–x, xii, xiii, xvii, xix–xxiii, xxvii, xxx–xxxv, xxxvii, xliii, li, lv, lvii, lix, lxii, lxiv.

**Peggotty, Mr. Daniel.** A rough but kind-hearted and noble-souled fisherman; brother to Clara Peggotty.

I had known Mr. Peggotty's house very well in my childhood; and I am sure I could not have been more charmed with it if it had been Aladdin's palace, roc's egg, and all. It was an old black barge, or boat, high and dry on Yarmouth sands, with an iron funnel sticking out of it for a chimney. There was a delightful door cut in the side, and it was roofed in, and there were little windows in it. It was beautifully clean, and as tidy as possible. There were some lockers and boxes, and there was a table, and there was a Dutch clock, and there was a chest of drawers, and there was a tea-tray with a painting on it; and the tray was kept from tumbling down by a Bible; and the tray, if it *had* tumbled down, would have smashed a quantity of cups and saucers and a teapot that were grouped around the book. On the walls were colored pictures of Abraham in red going to sacrifice Isaac in blue, and of Daniel in yellow being cast into a den of green lions. Over the little mantel-shelf was a picture of the Sarah Jane, lugger, built at Sunderland, with a real little wooden stern stuck on it, — a work of art combining composition with carpentry, which I had regarded in my childhood as one of the most enviable possessions the world could afford. Mr. Peggotty, as honest a seafaring man as ever breathed, dealt in lobsters, crabs, and crawfish; and a heap of those creatures, in a state of wonderful conglomeration with one another, and never leaving off pinching whatever they laid hold of, were usually to be found in a little wooden outhouse, where the pots and kettles were kept. ii, iii, vii, x, xxi, xxii, xxx–xxxii, xl, xliii, xlvi, xlvii, l, li, lvii, lxiii.

**Peggotty, Ham.** Nephew of Daniel Peggotty. He is engaged to Little Em'ly; but on the eve of their marriage she elopes with Steerforth. Years afterwards he attempts, one night, to rescue some unfortunate passengers from a vessel wrecked in a great storm on Yarmouth beach. One of these passengers proves to be Steerforth, who is returning home from abroad. A mighty wave ingulfs them all; and the wronged and wrong-doer perish together on the very scene which had witnessed the triumph of the one and the blighted hopes of the other. ii, iii, vii, x, xxi, xxii, xxx–xxxii, xl, xlvi, li, lv. *See* PEGGOTTY (DANIEL), STEERFORTH (JAMES).

**Quinion, Mr.** A friend of Mr. Murdstone's, and chief manager at Murdstone and Grinby's warehouse in London. ii, x–xii.

**Sharp, Mr.** First master at Salem House, Mr. Creakle's school, near London; a limp, delicate-looking gentleman, with a good deal of nose, and a way of carrying his head on one side, as if it were a little too heavy for him. vi, vii, ix.

**Shepherd, Miss.** A boarder at the Misses Nettingall's Establishment for Young Ladies, with whom David Copperfield is for a time deeply in love. She is a little girl in a spencer, with a round face, and curly flaxen hair. xviii.

**Spenlow, Miss Clarissa.** The elder of two maiden sisters of Mr. Spenlow, with whom his daughter Dora resides after his death. They are both dry little ladies, upright in their carriage, formal, precise, composed, and quiet. xxxviii, xxxix, xli–xliii, liii.

**Spenlow, Miss Lavinia.** Aunt to Dora, and sister to Miss Clarissa and Mr. Francis Spenlow.

PEGGOTTY AND BARKIS.

Miss Lavinia was an authority in affairs of the heart, by reason of there having anciently existed a certain Mr. Pidger, who played short whist, and was supposed to have been enamored of her. My private opinion is, that this was entirely a gratuitous assumption, and that Pidger was altogether innocent of any such sentiments, to which he had never given any sort of expression, that I could ever hear of. Both Miss Lavinia and Miss Clarissa had a superstition, however, that he would have declared his passion, if he had not been cut short in his youth (at about sixty) by over-drinking his constitution, and overdoing an attempt to set it right again by swilling Bath water. They had a lurking suspicion even, that he died of secret love; though I must say there was a picture of him in the house, with a damask nose which concealment did not appear to have ever preyed upon. xxxviii, xxxix, xli–xliii, liii.

**Spenlow, Miss Dora.** Only daughter of Mr. Spenlow; afterwards the "child-wife" of David Copperfield; a timid, trustful, sensitive, artless little beauty, who is not much more than a plaything, and who dies young. xxvi, xxxiii, xxxv, xxxvii, xxxviii, xli–xliv, xlviii, l–liii.

**Spenlow, Mr. Francis.** One of the firm of Spenlow and Jorkins (proctors in Doctor's Commons), and the father of Dora, who is afterwards David Copperfield's wife.

He was a little light-haired gentleman, with undeniable boots, and the stiffest of white cravats and shirt-collars. He was buttoned up mighty trim and tight, and must have taken a great deal of pains with his whiskers, which were accurately curled. . . . He was got up with such care, and was so stiff, that he could hardly bend himself; being obliged, when he glanced at some papers on his desk, after sitting down in his chair, to move his whole body from the bottom of his spine, like Punch. xxiii, xxvi, xxix, xxxiii, xxxv, xxxviii.

**Spiker, Mr. Henry.** A guest at a party given by Mr. and Mrs. Waterbrook. He is solicitor to somebody or something remotely connected with the treasury, and is so cold a man, that his head, instead of being gray, seems to be sprinkled with hoar-frost. xxv.

**Spiker, Mrs. Henry.** His wife; a very awful lady, looking like a near relation of Hamlet's, — say his aunt. xxv.

**Steerforth, James.** A schoolfellow and friend of David Copperfield's; a young man of great personal attractions and the most easy and engaging manners. Always adapting himself readily to the society he happens to be in, he has no trouble in securing the regard and confidence of simple-hearted Mr. Peggotty, whose humble house he visits with David. Here he meets Mr. Peggotty's niece and adopted daughter, Emily, — a beautiful young woman, betrothed to her cousin Ham, — and deliberately sets to work to effect her ruin. In this he is successful; and, on the eve of her intended marriage, she consents to elope with him. They live abroad for some time; but he finally tires of her, and, after insultingly proposing that she should marry his valet, a detestable scoundrel, cruelly deserts her. vi, vii, ix, xix–xxv, xxviii, xxix, xxxi, lv.

**Steerforth, Mrs.** Mother of James Steerforth; an elderly lady, with a proud carriage and a handsome face, entirely devoted to her son, but estranged from him at last; both of them being imperious and obstinate. xx, xxi, xxiv, xxix, xxxii, xxxvi, xlvi, lvi, lxiv.

**Strong, Doctor.** Master of a school at Canterbury attended by David Copperfield; a quiet, amiable old gentleman, who has married a young lady many years his junior.

Some of the higher scholars boarded in the doctor's house, and, through them, I learned at second-hand some particulars of the doctor's history, — as how he had not been married twelve months to the beautiful young lady I had seen in the study, whom he had married for love, as she had not a sixpence, and had a world of poor relations (so our fellows said) ready to swarm the doctor out of house and home; also how the doctor's cogitating manner was attributable to his being always engaged in looking out for Greek roots . . . with a view to a new dictionary which he had in contemplation. Adams, our head boy, who had a turn for mathematics, had made a calculation, I was informed, of the time this dictionary would take in completing, on the doctor's plan and at the doctor's rate of going. He considered that it might be done in one thousand six hundred and forty-nine years, counting from the doctor's last or sixty-second birthday. xvi, xvii, xix, xxxvi, xxxix, xlii, xlv, lxii, lxiv.

**Strong, Mrs. Annie.** The wife of Doctor Strong, and daughter of Mrs. Markleham (the Old Soldier). She is a beautiful woman, much her husband's junior. xvi, xix, xxxvi, xlii, xlv, lxii, lxiv.

**Tiffey, Mr.** An old clerk in the office of Spenlow and Jorkins; a little dry man, wearing a stiff brown wig that looks as if it were made of gingerbread. xxiii, xxvi, xxxiii, xxxv, xxxviii.

**Tipp.** A carman employed in Murdstone and Grinby's warehouse. xi, xii.

**Traddles, Thomas.** A schoolmate of David Copperfield's at Salem House (Mr. Creakle's school).

Poor Traddles! In a tight sky-blue suit, that made his arms and legs like German sausages or roly-poly puddings, he was the merriest and most miserable of all the boys. He was always being caned,—I think he was caned every day that half-year, except one holiday Monday, when he was only rulered on both hands,—and was always going to write to his uncle about it, and never did. After laying his head on the desk for a little while, he would cheer up, somehow, begin to laugh again, and draw skeletons all over his slate before his eyes were dry. I used, at first, to wonder what comfort Traddles found in drawing skeletons, and for some time looked upon him as a sort of hermit, who reminded himself, by those symbols of mortality, that caning could n't last forever. But I believe he only did it because they were easy, and did n't want any features.

He was very honorable, Traddles was, and held it as a solemn duty in the boys to stand by one another. He suffered for this on several occasions, and particularly once, when Steerforth laughed in church, and the beadle thought it was Traddles, and took him out. I see him now, going away in custody, despised by the congregation. He never said who was the real offender, though he smarted for it next day, and was imprisoned so many hours that he came forth with a whole churchyardful of skeletons swarming all over his Latin dictionary. But he had his reward. Steerforth said there was nothing of the sneak in Traddles; and we all felt that to be the highest praise.

In due time Traddles is married, and, getting on by degrees in his profession, at last accumulates a competence, becomes a judge, and is honored and esteemed by all who know him. vi, vii, ix, xxv, xxvii, xxviii, xxxiv, xxxvi, xxxviii, xli, xliii, xliv, xlviii, xlix, li, liv, lvii–lix, lxi, lxii, lxiv.

**Trotwood, Miss Betsey.** The great-aunt of David Copperfield; an austere, hard-favored, and eccentric, but thoroughly kind-hearted woman. ii, xiii–xv, xvii, xix, xxii–xxv, xxxvii–xl, xliii–xlv, xlvii–xlix, li–lv, lvii, lix, lx, lxiv.

**Trotwood, Husband of Miss Betsey.** A handsome man, younger than Miss Betsey, whom he treats so falsely, ungratefully, and cruelly that she separates from him, and resumes her maiden name. He marries another woman; becomes an adventurer, a gambler, and a cheat; and finally sinks into the lowest depths of degradation. ii, xvii, xxiii, xlvii, lv.

**Tungay.** Lodge-keeper and tool of Mr. Creakle, at Salem House; a stout man with a bull-neck, a wooden leg, a surly face, overhanging temples, and his hair cut close all round his head. v–vii.

**Walker, Mick.** A boy employed at Murdstone and Grinby's, with three or four others (including David Copperfield), to rinse out bottles, cork and label them, etc. xi, xii.

**Waterbrook, Mr.** Mr. Wickfield's agent in London; a middle-aged gentleman with a short throat and a good deal of shirt-collar, who only wants a black nose to be the portrait of a pug-dog. xxv.

**Waterbrook, Mrs.** His wife; a woman who affects to be very genteel; likes to talk about the aristocracy; and maintains that, if she has a weakness, it is "blood." xxv.

**Wickfield, Agnes.** Daughter and housekeeper of Mr. Wickfield, and friend and counsellor of David Copperfield, whose second wife she becomes after the death of Dora. xv–xix, xxiv, xxxiv, xxxv, xxxix, xlii, xliii, lii–liv, lvii, lviii, lx, lxii–lxiv.

**Wickfield, Mr.** A lawyer at Canterbury, and the agent and friend of Miss Betsey Trotwood. He is nearly ruined by Uriah Heep (at first a clerk in his office, and afterwards his partner), who by adroit management, the falsification of facts, and various mal-practices, acquires a complete ascendency over him, and obtains control of all his property; but in the end Uriah's machinations are foiled, and his rascality exposed, by Mr. Micawber, whom he has endeavored to make use of as an instrument to assist in the accomplishment of his dishonest purposes. xv, xvii, xix, xxxv, xxxix, xlii, lii, liv, lx.

**William.** A waiter in an inn at Yarmouth, who wheedles little David Copperfield out of the greater part of his dinner. v.

**William.** Driver of the Canterbury coach. xix.

# BLEAK HOUSE

## OUTLINE

Chapter There was once a notable case in Chancery, the case of
I Jarndyce and Jarndyce, which stretched back through the fog
beyond the memory of man. It had more than one family
II involved in its procedure, and counted indeed such mighty personages as Sir Leicester Dedlock and Lady Dedlock, who had come up from Lincolnshire to their town house in London. It was to them that Mr. Tulkinghorn, the rusty Chancery lawyer, was reading in brief some of the latest documents in the case, when Lady Dedlock was overcome with sudden faintness, and the reading was interrupted.

III There were two others who were wards in Chancery in this case, Ada Clare and Richard Carstone, and Mr. Jarndyce of Bleak House, who was their guardian, had provided a companion for Ada in Esther Summerson, a girl of unknown parentage, who had been under the general charge of Mr. Kenge, called for his felicity of speech Conversation Kenge, of Kenge and Carboy, solicitors, who had much to do with the great case. Esther, since reaching years of discretion, had been a governess in Miss Donny's establishment, and had come thence to the court, where she had been made acquainted with Ada. As she was leaving the court with Ada and Richard, they all three encountered a singular apparition, Miss Flite, who had some dim and very remote connection with the case, so remote that her wits also had retired into some vacant antiquity.

IV The three young people were conducted by Mr. Guppy, a young man from Kenge and Carboy, to the house of Mrs. Jellyby in Thavies' Inn, where they were to pass the night before starting for Bleak House. They found themselves the guests of a singular pair, pronounced by Mr. Quale, an evening caller, as the union of mind and matter, though Mr. Jellyby was no great matter, and Mrs. Jellyby did not mind her children, but devoted herself all the evening to the distant woes of Africa, while Caddy, her eldest daughter, acted sullenly as her amanuensis, and in the depth of the night confided to Esther, while Ada slept, her detestation of the whole business of Borrioboola-Gha. She continued in the same

strain the next morning, including Mr. Quale in her animadver-
sions, as she took Esther and Ada as well as Richard to walk
V before breakfast. On this walk they fell in with Miss Flite,
who insisted on their paying her a visit at her rooms. She lived in
the upper part of an establishment where Krook, who was sometimes called the Chancellor in derision, kept a sort of junk shop in
which bottles, law-books, parchment, and what not were strangely
mixed up. He lived alone with his cat, Lady Jane, and entertained
the young people with grewsome accounts of persons who had been
engaged in the case of Jarndyce and Jarndyce, especially one Tom
Jarndyce, so that they came away from him and Miss Flite with a
most dismal sense of the misery which seemed to wait on every one
who was involved in the suit. But their young minds quickly recovered their wonted cheerfulness, and after breakfast they
VI set off for the country, and by nightfall had arrived at Bleak
House, where they were received by their guardian, John Jarndyce,
an impulsive, warm-hearted man, who when suddenly stirred to indignation, as he readily was, seemed to feel himself attacked by a
sharp flaw of east wind. His only companion was an idle dreamer,
a fantastic fellow, a mere child in worldly things, named Harold
Skimpole, who accepted cheerfully the world of Mr. John Jarndyce's
making from which all cares and anxieties were banished for
Harold Skimpole. How very childlike and bland he was appeared
later in the evening, when Esther was called out of the room to
learn that an officer had come to arrest Harold Skimpole for debt,
and was dismissed only by Esther and Richard paying the amount
out of their own pockets, a proceeding which somehow seemed to
put them in the wrong and Skimpole in the right.

The other country house in which Jarndyce and Jarndyce
VII appeared to be interested was Chesney Wold in Lincolnshire,
the home of the Dedlocks. In the absence of the family, the only
person in authority there was the housekeeper, Mrs. Rouncewell, who
for fifty years had been connected with the estate. Her companion
was Rosa, a pretty young girl from the village, but just at this time
the housekeeper had also for a visitor her grandson, Watt Rouncewell, the son of a well-to-do manufacturer, for Mrs. Rouncewell had
two sons, the father of this lad, and a wild vagrant who had gone
off as a soldier, carrying his mother's heart with him. It was during Watt's visit that two young men from law offices, Mr. Guppy
and a friend, Tony Jobling, being in this part of the country, obtained leave to see Chesney Wold and were shown the picture gallery, where Mr. Guppy, who had never seen Lady Dedlock, was
greatly astonished at the recognition of some familiar face in her
portrait, as it hung there.

At Bleak House, Esther Summerson was established as a sort of
VIII housekeeper. John Jarndyce had long been a real guardian to her, though just what the beginning of their connection had been she could not tell. However, he made now a confidante of her, and drew her to him by his kindness and thoughtfulness. Kind he certainly was, for as Esther and Ada had charge of his papers, they discovered that he was set upon by all sorts of claimants for help for all sorts of preposterous persons. One of these charitable beggars was Mrs. Pardiggle, who presented herself in person one day, accompanied by her young children who were bobs to her charitable kite. Mrs. Pardiggle insisted on taking Ada and Esther with her on one of her business of charity expeditions, and they saw how she invaded the home of a brickmaker and distributed cold comfort. They lingered behind with compassion for a poor mother and her ailing child, and found that the child had died. So Esther laid her handkerchief over the poor thing, and both did their best to console the unhappy women who were in the household. Richard,
IX in his impulsive way, was for giving five pounds at once to the brickmaker, for the young fellow was full of charming generosity, though he seemed not yet in the line of doing anything for himself, and to be occupied chiefly with falling in love with Ada Clare. The happy family was amused by the breaking in upon them of an uproarious Lawrence Boythorn, a man who delighted in the most extravagant and bloodthirsty language, especially about a quarrel with his neighbor, Sir Leicester Dedlock, and all the while kept for his pet and gently caressed a little canary. He was a man who had known disappointment in love, but whose volcanic nature had but a thin crust of hardening over it. While he was visiting at Bleak House, Kenge and Carboy sent him some legal documents at the hands of their young man named Guppy, who in his few and brief interviews had contracted a passion for Esther and proceeded on this occasion to enter his case, but was promptly denied suit by the young lady herself.

X The other legal concern that was deep in the case, Mr. Tulkinghorn, to wit, had noticed, on the evening when he read his documents to Sir Leicester and Lady Dedlock, that the faintness of my lady had followed upon noting the handwriting of one of the documents, and being a secretive man, that is, one who divines the secrets of others and never lets his own out, he took occasion to call on Mr. Snagsby, the law stationer who had procured the copying for him, to learn who was the copyist. Mr. and Mrs. Snagsby, or rather the reverse, with their maid-servant Guster, subject to fits, and therefore cheap, lived not far from Krook's, and it was to Krook's that Snagsby conducted Mr. Tulkinghorn, since

there lodged Nemo the copyist. Mr. Tulkinghorn, when he had made
XI his way to Nemo's room, found the man dead, and a coroner's
inquest being summoned, the verdict was that he died of an overdose of opium. No one seemed to know anything of him save a small street-sweeper named Jo, a waif, who had somehow struck up a friendship with Nemo, but his testimony scarcely resolved itself into anything more than that "he wos wery good to me." And poor Jo was the only mourner, apparently, creeping at night to the railing of the dismal churchyard within which had been laid away the body of the miserable copyist.

XII The information which Mr. Tulkinghorn obtained about
Nemo must have had some value to him, for he took pains to mention in a postscript in a letter to Sir Leicester that he could tell Lady Dedlock something about the copyist who had interested her. Sir Leicester read the postscript to Lady Dedlock when they were on their way to Chesney Wold, for my lady had been restless and fearfully bored with Paris. She had brought back with her as lady's maid a Frenchwoman of two and thirty, Hortense, who was thrown into a furious fit of jealousy by the favoritism which Lady Dedlock showed for little Rosa. Chesney Wold was now gay with company, and at last Mr. Tulkinghorn himself came as a guest and occupied his customary room in the tower. He had a few words with Sir Leicester respecting his suit against Boythorn, but the really important message which he had, though carelessly delivered, was his announcement to Lady Dedlock of the death of the law-writer, unattended and leaving no papers behind.

XIII It was quite desirable that Mr. Richard Carstone should
find some means of livelihood, and after various conferences with Mr. Kenge, among others, it was decided that he should take up the study of medicine with Mr. Bayham Badger, the third husband of Mrs. Bayham Badger. This took them all to town, where Miss Summerson was persecuted by the mute attentions of the young man named Guppy. Then Richard, being thus on the high road to fortune, became engaged to Ada, and a young surgeon, Mr.
XIV Woodcourt, edged into the circle in which Esther Summer-
son sat. Richard began his studies, but he had been drawn into the shadow of the upas-tree of Jarndyce and Jarndyce, for he was beginning to speculate on the chances of a fortune from it. While they were in the city, Caddy Jellyby came to see them with news of her engagement to a dancing-master, Prince Turveydrop, whose father was Deportment itself. She had been in the way of meeting him at Miss Flite's; and when Esther and Ada, with Mr. Jarndyce, went there, they met Mr. Woodcourt again, as well as old Krook, who was teaching himself to write. Other sights of the

great city came within their knowledge, poverty especially, which
XV they saw in the orphan children of the officer who had once
presented himself as the law in the presence of Skimpole.
Great was the miracle by which the little thirteen-year-old girl
Charley provided for her little brother and sister. With them, too,
XVI they saw a fierce Mr. Gridley, a man rendered nearly crazed
by the delays of the law. One sight they did not see, though
Mr. Tulkinghorn was aware of it, — a lady disguised as a servant
intercepting poor Jo at his crossing, and bidding him take her past
Krook's to the neglected churchyard where lay buried the starving
writer.

XVII Richard's application to the study of medicine was short-
lived. He began to waver toward the law, and always kept
one eye out on the Chancery chances. Mr. Woodcourt, on the other
hand, was so absorbed in his profession that he bade them all
good-by, that he might engage in his calling in the east, and all he
XVIII left behind, apparently, was a few flowers. Mr. Jarndyce,
meanwhile, and the girls, with Mr. Skimpole, paid a visit to
Lawrence Boythorn, and, quite by accident, met Lady Dedlock in
the park. She took little notice of Esther. Why should she? Yet
XIX Esther must have had a history; for when Mrs. Snagsby had
a little tea-party, at which the chief guests were Mr. Chadband, a volunteer minister, and his wife, it turned out that Mrs.
Chadband had once had the girl in her charge, delivered over to her
by Kenge and Carboy, a fact which was elicited by the cross-exam-
ination of Mr. Guppy, who had dropped in behind a constable who
had poor Jo in custody, Jo having got himself into trouble by not
moving on when he was told, and telling an extraordinary story
about a lady who gave him a sovereign, and so had named Mr.
XX Snagsby as a friend who could vouch for him. For Mr.
Guppy was determined to distinguish himself on his own
account, and he laid deep, very deep plots for the discovery of something or other. It was with this in view that he entertained at dinner his satellite, young Bart Smallweed, as well as his out-at-the-
elbows friend, Tony Jobling, whom he induced to take a room at
Krook's, and engage as a writer for Snagsby, apparently with the
XXI intention that he should find out something. As for Bart
Smallweed, he lived at home with his grandfather and grandmother, and his twin-sister, Judy, all of them being waited on by
little Charley. Old Smallweed, who was a screw, was equally mer-
ciless toward his half-imbecile wife and toward a certain trooper,
Mr. George, to whom he had lent money, and who dropped in to
pay the interest due. Mr. George's ostensible occupation was that
of the keeper of a shooting-gallery, which he kept with the aid of
lame Phil.

Mr. Tulkinghorn seemed strangely desirous of getting infor-
XXII mation, for he had Snagsby at his rooms in order to learn what he could of Jo's performances, and they were attended by Mr. Bucket, a detective officer, who pushed matters still further by conducting Snagsby to Tom-all-Alone's, and there finding Jo, who was not the only acquaintance there; for the brickmakers of St. Albans and their women were there also. Jo told his story again of the lady who used him as a guide to the graveyard, and went back with them to Tulkinghorn's chambers. There, in the passage, he met, to his surprise, the very person who had given him the sovereign. At least she wore the same veil and cloak, though her hands and rings were not the same. He could not be expected to know Hortense, Lady Dedlock's maid, now discharged by her.
XXIII Hortense applied to Esther Summerson to be her maid, but without success. Instead, little Charley was sent by Mr. Jarndyce to fill this position.

Caddy Jellyby took the important step of marrying Prince Turveydrop, and adopting old Deportment as a charge, and it was to Esther she turned for help in making her peace with that portentous fraud, and also telling the news to Mrs. Jellyby, who was really
XXIV too far away in Africa to be greatly disturbed. What was more disturbing was the renewed restlessness of Richard Carstone, who could not get away from the fascination of the Chancery case, but could and did escape from the confinement of Kenge and Carboy for a new experiment, — that of the army, devoting himself at once with great energy to learning some of the details of his new profession in Mr. George's shooting-gallery. Mr. Jarndyce insisted on declaring the engagement with Ada off, not in anger, but in painful doubt about Richard, as well he might be, when he saw one more tragic end to a victim of the law in the death of Gridley, just when Bucket had traced him to Mr. George's gallery.

XXV The lynx-eyed and very suspicious Mrs. Snagsby was quite sure she had got upon the track of some secret wickedness in her meek husband, and that Jo of Tom-all-Alone's was inscrutably connected with it. Else why her husband's kindness to him? And so she set that moral policeman, Mr. Chadband, on him, but with-
XXVI out extracting any information. Others were after other information, for Mr. George in his gallery was waited on by Grandfather Smallweed with Judy, the old gentleman being desirous of showing to a lawyer some bit of handwriting of a certain Captain Hawdon, whom Mr. George had befriended. Mr. George consented to take what he had with him and to accompany Judy
XXVII and her grandfather to Mr. Tulkinghorn's. But he was uncomfortable in all this mystery and would not show his

paper till he had first consulted a friend. The friend in question
was Mr. Bagnet, an ex-artillery man, who thought through his wife,
and now advised George to do nothing in the dark. So he politely
declined Mr. Tulkinghorn's invitation.

XXVIII At Chesney Wold a very little affair forced itself upon
the attention of the mighty people, for Mrs. Rouncewell's
son came to see Sir Leicester and Lady Dedlock about the marriage
of his son to Rosa, Lady Dedlock's pretty maid. More interesting
XXIX for Lady Dedlock was a visit which she received on her
return to town, a visit from the young man named Guppy,
who little by little let her know that he had discovered a likeness
between her and Esther Summerson, that Esther's real name was
Esther Hawdon, and that he, Guppy, would be in possession the
next day of a bundle of letters belonging to the late Captain Hawdon.

XXX Esther herself, comfortably at home with Mr. Jarndyce,
had such light concerns as a visit from Mr. Woodcourt's
mother, and an attendance at Caddy Jellyby's wedding. Yet
XXXI graver experience was to come. Charley, her maid,
brought her word of tramps, who were none other than
the brickmakers and their women with poor Jo, who had been
taken ill. They had Jo brought to a loft in one of the buildings
near Mr. Jarndyce's place. But after a short space he disappeared
mysteriously. Then all at once Charley fell ill, evidently of a disease caught from these poor people. Esther nursed her, and then
fell ill herself, so ill, that when she recovered her strength a little
she knew that she was blind.

XXXII When Tony Jobling went to live at Krook's he took
the name of Mr. Weevle. It was he who had ferreted out
the fact that Krook had a bundle of Captain Hawdon's letters, and
Guppy came to him on the night when Krook was to pass the
letters over. What was the consternation of both plotters when,
alarmed by a singular appearance in the air, they entered Krook's
room and found that the wretched sot had perished by spontaneous
XXXIII combustion. With him the letters perished, and Tony and
Guppy found to their astonishment the next morning, by
the arrival in the neighborhood of the Smallweeds, that Krook was
a disreputable brother of Mrs. Smallweed. On going to tell Lady
Dedlock of his inability to produce the letters, Guppy encountered
Mr. Tulkinghorn, who made an instantaneous note of his pres-
XXXIV ence as inculpating Lady Dedlock. There was another paper, however, of Captain Hawdon's, and Mr. Tulkinghorn
secured that. For old Smallweed suddenly came down on George
for the amount of his debt, and when George with his security,

Bagnet, went to the old man to try as usual to renew his note, the malignant miser sent him to Tulkinghorn, and the paper which George before refused to give up became the price he paid for the relief of himself and Bagnet.

XXXV The fever which struck Esther Summerson blind passed away and the blindness gradually disappeared, but her face was left marred with the disease. When she could once more bear light and talk, she learned that Richard, poisoned by the Jarndyce and Jarndyce malaria, had broken with his guardian; and from Miss Flite, who came to see her, she learned of the heroic deeds of Allan Woodcourt in a recent shipwreck. Then she confessed to herself that she loved him. A singular incident also came to her knowledge. An unknown lady had appeared in the neighborhood, and had taken the handkerchief which Esther had spread over the
XXXVI face of the dead child of the brickmaker. As soon as she was sufficiently recovered Esther went to pay a visit at Mr. Boythorn's, and as she was by herself in the park one day Lady Dedlock appeared. She had with her Esther's handkerchief, and then the unhappy woman disclosed the terrible secret of her life, — that she was Esther's mother.

XXXVII All this time Esther had not seen Ada, but now her dearest friend returned to her. She was keeping bravely her compact with her guardian, but it was plain that she had not ceased to love her erring cousin. Richard himself appeared in the neighborhood, and Esther was his confidante. But he had with him Skimpole, and Skimpole had introduced him to a lawyer, Mr. Vholes, who had three daughters and an aged father in the Vale of Taunton; and Mr. Vholes was the spider, and poor Richard was the
XXXVIII fascinated fly entangled more and more in the meshes of Jarndyce and Jarndyce. Esther herself, mindful of her poor mother, went to London shortly after, and accompanied by Caddy called upon Mr. Guppy at his mother's house and asked him not to pursue the inquiries which he had told her he was making into her parentage. It may be added that the price she paid for this silence was an explicit acknowledgment that Mr. Guppy never, never had made her any proposal of marriage; her lifted veil was
XXXIX the cause of this. And Guppy was as good as his word, when shortly afterward he and Tony went to Krook's to secure Tony's possessions and found there not only the Smallweed family looking over the effects, but Mr. Tulkinghorn, who meant plainly to get something out of Guppy about Lady Dedlock. If he
XL could not get anything out of Guppy, he had another string to his bow, for shortly after, when the Dedlocks were at Chesney Wold, he told in the presence of Lady Dedlock the

whole story of her shame, under the disguise of no names. Lady
XLI Dedlock, in consequence, visited him in his apartment and
announced her intention of leaving Chesney Wold secretly
that night. He restrained her by pointing out that the one effect of
XLII such a course would be absolutely to prostrate Sir Leicester. Tulkinghorn, on returning to London, encountered
Snagsby, who told him with great distress that his life was rendered
miserable by his wife's suspicion of Hortense, who, failing to find
Mr. Tulkinghorn in her repeated visits, was persecuting Tulkinghorn's subordinate, Snagsby. The lawyer reassured him, and
mounting to his chambers presently was confronted by Hortense
herself. She was in a rage against Lady Dedlock, but almost
equally against the imperturbable Tulkinghorn for using her and
then throwing her aside.

XLIII The secret of Esther's parentage became known to Mr.
Jarndyce through her confession, brought about through a
curious coincidence. Both Ada and Esther had been disturbed by
Harold Skimpole's intimacy with Richard, and they and Mr. Jarndyce paid a visit to that gentleman; while there, who should appear
but Sir Leicester Dedlock, and it turned out that Skimpole had been
treated somewhat impolitely at Chesney Wold in consequence of be-
XLIV ing connected with Boythorn. Esther now shared her secret
with her guardian; perhaps it was this which brought about
another disclosure, for Mr. Jarndyce asked her to marry him, and
she, in her grateful soul, burning the flowers she had kept, given
her by Allan Woodcourt, accepted him.

XLV Richard Carstone had now come to such a pass that he had
been forced to sell his commission, and was quite penniless
Mr. Vholes came to Bleak House to confer with Mr. Jarndyce, and
as a result, that gentleman sent Esther to see Richard. She found
him and by chance found Woodcourt also; she met him bravely and
received from him a promise that he would look after Richard.
XLVI He did keep a watch of him, and he met others connected
with him in a roundabout way, for he came upon the poor
woman, the wife of the brickmaker, who told him of Esther's goodness to her, and upon Jo, who had been all this while in a hospital.
XLVII Jo had an intense fear of Mr. Bucket, who had told him to
clear out of London, and Woodcourt was much perplexed
where to bestow him, for Jo evidently was in a bad way. Miss
Flite came to his rescue and suggested Mr. George's, and thither
the surgeon went. But poor Jo had come to his end, and died at
the shooting-gallery.

XLVIII Lady Dedlock determined to part with Rosa for Rosa's
good, and had an interview with Mr. Rouncewell, the father,

in regard to it. Mr. Tulkinghorn was present and, after the interview was over, had one with Lady Dedlock, in which he intimated
the power he held over her, a power which he could exercise to
make everything known to Sir Leicester. But Mr. Tulkinghorn
had gone as far as his power could carry him, for that night he was
found dead in his chambers, shot through the heart. Who fired that
XLIX shot? Mr. Bucket had his suspicions. At any rate, he did
his duty when he dropped in at Mr. Bagnet's, where they
were celebrating the old lady's birthday, and when he and Mr.
George came away, took the trooper into custody on charge of murdering Mr. Tulkinghorn.

Esther had a new interest at this time in the birth of a
L little Esther to Caddy. Allan Woodcourt was the doctor in
LI attendance. He was looking after Richard also, but one day
when Esther and Ada went to visit that young man, Ada did
not return. She had been married two months to Richard, and
LII elected now to remain with her poor deluded husband. When
Esther, now left alone with her guardian, learned from Mr.
Woodcourt of the murder of Mr. Tulkinghorn and the arrest of
George, they were filled with compassion for the trooper and were
confident that he was innocent. They went to visit him in prison,
and there met Mr. Bagnet and his wife. This energetic woman
had a sudden inspiration. She was sure George's mother was living, and putting this and that together set off for Lincolnshire to
LIII find her. Mr. Bucket on his part was resorting to all sorts
of ingenious devices for pursuing the mystery of the murder.
He was in receipt of letters, anonymous, which all pointed to Lady
Dedlock as the criminal. He had the *entrée*, by virtue of his office,
at Sir Leicester's, and learned from one of the servants of his lady's
habit of solitary nightly walking.

LIV The hour finally struck for him. He presented himself to
Sir Leicester and told him of his lady's former lover, Captain
Hawdon, and of the jeopardy in which she stood from Mr. Tulkinghorn's knowledge of her secret. Then, summoning some people
who were quarrelling below, he presented the Smallweeds and
finally Hortense. He explained the relation which George bore to
them, he bought the papers of Captain Hawdon which old Smallweed had, and then he explained with the enthusiasm of a triumphant detective how he had traced the murder to Hortense, who
had for some time past been his lodger. George, whom he had
LV arrested, not because he thought him guilty, but because suspicion rested on him, was still in prison, when Mrs. Bagnet
arrived, successful, for she brought with her Mrs. Rouncewell; and
Mrs. Rouncewell after she had been with her son went to the town

house and had an interview with Lady Dedlock. From her and from Guppy, who also called, Lady Dedlock believed that at last her story was known to the whole world, and thereupon, with a wailing letter to Sir Leicester, she fled into the darkness.

LVI Sir Leicester was struck down with paralysis, but Inspector
Bucket was master of the situation. He sprang like a hound
to the pursuit; found a handkerchief among her ladyship's belongings, marked Esther Summerson; was off to Mr. Jarndyce's; took
LVII Esther, with him in the carriage; asked her questions by the
way; drove furiously to St. Albans; had word with the brickmakers; turned back, dashing for London, where Sir Leicester, able
LVIII now to speak with difficulty, and under George's care, made
known his perfect confidence in Lady Dedlock; still the pair
in the carriage kept on; they went to Chancery Lane; Mr. Wood-
LIX court joined them; piece by piece new evidence came to
them, and at last Esther stood by the neglected graveyard
where her father lay buried, and there lay her mother, cold and
dead, on the ground.

LX When Esther recovered from the sickness that followed,
she visited Ada and found her bearing her great misfortune,
for Richard was rapidly sinking into Miss Flite's condition, though
Allan Woodcourt was everything that a friend could be. Friend
LXI he was to Esther also, and at last could restrain himself no
longer and confessed his love to her, and heard from her lips
LXII of her betrothal to Mr. Jarndyce. That gentleman appeared
to have nothing now to look forward to except his marriage,
when there came to him one morning Inspector Bucket, bringing
the fabric of Grandfather Smallweed, and disclosing the fact that
the old man, in rummaging through Krook's things, had come upon
a document of great interest in the affairs of Jarndyce and Jarndyce.

LXIII George Rouncewell made a journey to his brother's and
was received with open arms, but steadily refused to leave
the service of Sir Leicester. He wrote also a formal letter to
Esther, explaining his connection with her father, who had been
LXIV reported drowned at sea. As for Esther, she found her
guardian almost more than human, for before their wedding-
day he disclosed his own little plot. He gave her Bleak House, and
with it Allan Woodcourt for husband. Guppy the irresolute came
again with Jobling to offer his hand, just when another had
Esther's.

LXV And now the great case of Jarndyce and Jarndyce came to
an end, for the paper which Smallweed had found proved to
be a will which settled the whole case. But the costs had eaten up
the whole estate, and as the case disappeared, so poor Richard Car-

LXVI stone also disappeared out of this world. For a little longer Sir Leicester Dedlock held funereal state at Chesney Wold,
LXVII but Esther Woodcourt lived on her happy life at Bleak House.

---

## INDEX TO CHARACTERS

**Badger, Mr. Bayham.** A medical practitioner in London, to whom Richard Carstone is articled. Mr. Badger is noted principally for his enthusiastic admiration of his wife's former husbands; he being the third.

Mr. Bayham Badger . . . was a pink, fresh-faced, crisp-looking gentleman with a weak voice, white teeth, light hair, and surprised eyes, — some years younger, I should say, than Mrs. Bayham Badger. He admired her exceedingly, but principally, and to begin with, on the curious ground (as it seemed to us) of her having had three husbands. We had barely taken our seats, when he said to Mr. Jarndyce, quite triumphantly: —

"You would hardly suppose I was Mrs. Bayham Badger's third!"

"Indeed?" said Mr. Jarndyce.

"Her third," said Mr. Badger. "Mrs. Bayham Badger has not the appearance, Miss Summerson, of a lady who has had two former husbands?"

I said, "Not at all!"

"And most remarkable men!" said Mr. Badger in a tone of confidence. "Captain Swosser of the Royal Navy, who was Mrs. Badger's first husband, was a very distinguished officer indeed. The name of Professor Dingo, my immediate predecessor, is one of European reputation. . . . Perhaps you may be interested . . . in this portrait of Captain Swosser. . . . I feel when I look at it . . . that's a man I should like to have seen. . . . On the other side, Professor Dingo. I knew him well; attended him in his last illness. A speaking likeness. Over the piano, Mrs. Bayham Badger when Mrs. Swosser; over the sofa, Mrs. Bayham Badger when Mrs. Dingo. Of Mrs. Bayham Badger *in esse*, I possess the original, and have no copy." xiii, xvii, l.

**Badger, Mrs. Bayham.** A lady of about fifty, who dresses youthfully, and improves her fine complexion by the use of a little rouge. She is not only the wife of Mr. Badger, but the widow of Captain Swosser of the Royal Navy, and of Professor Dingo, to the loss of whom she has become inured by custom, combined with science, — particularly science. xiii, xvii.

**Bagnet, Matthew,** *called* LIGNUM VITÆ. An ex-artillery-man, "tall and upright, with shaggy eyebrows, and whiskers like the fibres of a cocoanut, not a hair upon his head, and a torrid complexion." On leaving the service, he goes into "the musical business," and becomes a bassoon-player. Of his wife's judgment he has a very exalted opinion; though he never forgets the apostolic maxim that "the head of the woman is the man." To an old companion-in-arms he says:—

"George! You know me. It 's my old girl that advises. She has the head; but I never own to it before her: discipline must be maintained. Wait till the greens is off her mind; then we 'll consult. Whatever the old girl says do, do it." xxvii, xxxiv, xlix, liii, lxvi.

**Bagnet, Mrs.** His wife; a soldierly-looking woman, usually engaged in washing greens.

Mrs. Bagnet is not an ill-looking woman; rather long-boned, a little coarse in the grain, and freckled by the sun and wind, which have tanned her hair upon the forehead, but healthy, wholesome, and bright-eyed. A strong, busy, active, honest-faced woman, of from forty-five to fifty. xxvii, xxxiv, xlix, liii, lv, lxvi.

**Bagnet, Malta.** Their elder daughter; so called in the family (though not so christened), from the place of her birth in barracks. xxvii, xxxiv, xlix, lxvi.

**Bagnet, Quebec.** Their younger daughter; so called in the family (though not so christened), from the place of her birth in barracks. xxvii, xxxiv, xlix, lxvi.

**Bagnet, Woolwich.** Their son; so called in the family (though not so christened), from the place of his birth in barracks. xxvii, xxxiv, xlix.

**Barbary, Miss.** Aunt and godmother to Esther Summerson.

She was a good, good woman. She went to church three times every Sunday, and to morning prayers on Wednesdays and Fridays, and to lectures whenever there were lectures; and never missed. She was handsome, and, if she had ever smiled, would have been (I used to think) like an angel; but she never smiled. She was always grave and strict. She was so very good herself, I thought that the badness of other people made her frown all her life. iii.

**Blinder, Mrs.** A good-natured old woman, with a dropsy, or an asthma, or perhaps both; a friend of the Necketts. xv, xxiii.

**Bogsby, James George.** Landlord of "The Sol's Arms" tavern. xxxiii.

**Boodle, Lord.** A friend of Sir Leicester Dedlock's; a man of considerable reputation with his party, and who has known what office is. xii.

**Boythorn, Lawrence.** A friend of Mr. Jarndyce's; intended as a portrait of Dickens's friend, Walter Savage Landor.

"I went to school with this fellow, Lawrence Boythorn," said Mr. Jarndyce, . . . "more than five and forty years ago. He was then the most impetuous boy in the world, and he is now the most impetuous man; he was then the loudest boy in the world, and he is now the loudest man; he was then the heartiest and sturdiest boy in the world, and he is now the heartiest and sturdiest man. He is a tremendous fellow."

"In stature, sir?" asked Richard.

"Pretty well, Rick, in that respect," said Mr. Jarndyce; "being some ten years older than I, and a couple of inches taller, with his head thrown back like an old soldier, his stalwart chest squared, his hands like a clean blacksmith's, and his lungs!— there 's no simile for his lungs. Talking, laughing, or snoring, they make the beams of the house shake. . . . But it 's the inside of the man, the warm heart of the man, the passion of the man, the fresh blood of the man, . . . that I speak of. . . . His language is as sounding as his voice. He is always in extremes; perpetually in the superlative degree. In his condemnation he is all ferocity. You might suppose him to be an ogre from what he says, and I believe he has the reputation of one with some people. There! I tell you no more of him beforehand."

We were sitting round the fire, with no light but the blaze, when the hall-door suddenly burst open, and the hall resounded with these words, uttered with the greatest vehemence, and in a stentorian tone:—

"We have been misdirected, Jarndyce, by a most abandoned ruffian, who told us to take the turning to the right, instead of to the left. He is the most intolerable scoundrel on the face of the earth. His father must have been a most consummate villain ever to have had such a son. I would have that fellow shot without the least remorse!"

"Did he do it on purpose?" Mr. Jarndyce inquired.

"I have not the slightest doubt that the scoundrel has passed his whole existence in misdirecting travellers!" returned the other. "By my soul, I thought him the worst looking dog I had ever beheld, when he was telling me to take the turning to the right. And yet I stood before that fellow face to face, and did n't knock his brains out!" . . .

We all conceived a prepossession in his [Boythorn's] favor; for there was a sterling quality in his laugh, and in his vigorous healthy voice, and in the roundness and fulness with which he uttered every word he spoke, and in the very fury of his superlatives, which seemed to go off like blank cannons, and hurt nothing. . . . He was not only a very handsome old gentleman, — upright and stalwart, as he had been described to us, — with a massive gray head, a fine composure of face when silent, a figure that might have become corpulent but for his being so continually in earnest that he gave it no rest, and a chin that might have subsided into a double chin but for the vehement emphasis in which it was constantly required to assist; but he was such a true gentleman in his manner, so chivalrously polite, his face was lighted by a smile of so much sweetness and tenderness, and it seemed so plain that he had nothing to hide, but showed himself exactly as he was, . . . that really I could not help looking at him with equal pleasure as he sat at dinner, whether he smilingly conversed with Ada and me, or was led by Mr. Jarndyce into some great volley of superlatives, or threw up his head like a bloodhound, and gave out that tremendous "Ha, ha, ha!" ix, xii, xiii, xv, xviii, xxiii, xliii, lxvi.

**Bucket, Mr. Inspector.** A detective officer, wonderfully patient, persevering, affable, alert, imperturbable, and sagacious; a stoutly-built, steady-looking, sharp-eyed man in black, of about the middle age. The original of this character is supposed to have been Inspector Field of the London police, with whom Mr. Dickens was well acquainted, and whom he has described in the article in "Reprinted Pieces," entitled "On Duty with Inspector Field."

Mr. Bucket and his fat forefinger are much in consultation. . . . He puts it to his ears, and it whispers information; he puts it to his lips, and it enjoins him to secrecy; he rubs it over his nose, and it sharpens his scent; he shakes it before a guilty man, and it charms him to his destruction. . . . Otherwise mildly studious in his observation of human nature, on the whole, a benignant philosopher not disposed to be severe upon the follies of mankind, Mr. Bucket pervades a vast number of houses, and strolls about an infinity of streets; to outward appearance rather languishing for want of an object. He is in the friendliest condition towards his species, and will drink with most of them. He is free with his money, affable in his manners, innocent in his conversation; but through the placid stream of his life there glides an undercurrent of forefinger. Time and place cannot bind Mr. Bucket. Like man in the abstract, he is here to-day, and gone to-morrow; but, very unlike man indeed, he is here again the next day. xxii, xxiv, xxv, xlix, liii, liv, lvi, lvii, lix, lxi, lxii.

**Bucket, Mrs.** Wife of Mr. Inspector Bucket; a lady of a natural detective genius, which, if it had been improved by professional exercise, might have done great things, but which has paused at the level of a clever amateur. liii, liv.

**Buffey, The Right Honorable William, M. P.** A friend of Sir Leicester Dedlock's. xii, xxviii, liii, lviii, lxvi.

**Carstone, Richard.** A ward of John Jarndyce, and a suitor in Chancery; a handsome young man with an ingenuous face and a most engaging laugh, afterwards married to Ada Clare. Though possessed of more than ordinary talent, and of excellent principles, he yet lacks tenacity of purpose, and becomes successively a student of law, a student of medicine, and a soldier. Ever haunted by the long-pending Chancery suit, and always basing his expenditures and plans on the expectation of a speedy and favorable decision of the case, he at last becomes very restless, leaves the army, and devotes all his energies to the suit. When the case is finally closed, and the whole estate is found to have been swallowed up in costs, the blow proves too much for him, and quickly results in his death. iii–vi, viii, ix, xii, xiv, xvii, xviii, xx, xxiii, xxiv, xxxv, xxxvii, xxxix, xliii, xlv, li, lx, lxi, lxiv, lxv.

**Chadband, The Reverend Mr.** A large yellow man, with a fat smile, and a general appearance of having a good deal of train-oil in his system.

He is very much embarrassed about the arms, as if they were inconvenient to him, and he wanted to grovel; is very much in a perspiration about the head; and never speaks without first putting up his great hand, as if delivering a token to his hearers that he is going to edify them.

From Mr. Chadband's being much given to describe himself, both verbally and in writing, as a vessel, he is occasionally mistaken by strangers for a gentleman connected with navigation; but he is, as he expresses it, "in the ministry." Mr. Chadband is attached to no particular denomination, and is considered by his persecutors to have nothing so very remarkable to say on the greatest of subjects, as to render his volunteering on his own account, at all incumbent on his conscience; but he has his followers, and Mrs. Snagsby is of the number.

Visiting Mrs. Snagsby's with his wife, one day, he salutes the lady of the house, and her husband, in the following manner, which may serve as a specimen of his usual style of delivering himself:—

"My friends, . . . peace be on this house!—on the master thereof, on the mistress thereof, on the young maidens, and on the young men. My friends, why do I wish for peace? What is peace? Is it war? No. Is it strife? No. Is it lovely and gentle and beautiful and pleasant and serene and joyful? Oh, yes! Therefore, my friends, I wish for peace on you and yours." xix, xxv, liv.

**Chadband, Mrs.**, *formerly* MRS. RACHAEL. Wife of the Reverend Mr. Chadband; a stern, severe-looking, silent woman. iii, xix, xxv, xxix, liv. *See* RACHAEL, MRS.

**Charley.** *See* NECKETT, CHARLOTTE.

**Chickweed.** *See* SMALLWEED, BARTHOLOMEW.

**Clare, Ada.** A ward of Mr. John Jarndyce, and a friend of Esther Summerson; afterwards wife of Richard Carstone. iii–vi, viii, ix, xiii–xv, xvii, xviii, xxiii, xxiv, xxx, xxxi, xxxv, xxxvii, xliii, xlv, l, li, lix, lx–lxii, lxiv, lxvii.

**Coavinses.** *See* NECKETT, MR.

**Darby.** A constable who accompanies Mr. Bucket to Tom-all-Alone's. xxii.

**Dedlock, Sir Leicester.** Representative of one of the great county families of England.

Sir Leicester Dedlock is only a baronet; but there is no mightier baronet than he. His family is as old as the hills, and infinitely more respectable. He has a general opinion that the world might get on without hills, but would be done up without Dedlocks. . . . He is a gentleman of strict conscience, disdainful of all littleness and meannesses, and ready, on the shortest notice, to die any death you please to mention rather than give occasion for the least impeachment of his integrity. He is an honorable, obstinate, truthful, high-spirited, intensely prejudiced, perfectly unreasonable man.

Sir Leicester is twenty years, full measure, older than my lady. He will never see sixty-five again, nor perhaps sixty-six, nor yet sixty-seven. He has a twist of the gout now and then, and walks a little stiffly. He is of a worthy presence, with his light gray hair and whiskers, his fine shirt-frill, his pure white waistcoat, and his blue coat with bright buttons always buttoned. He is ceremonious, stately, most polite on every occasion to my lady, and holds her personal attractions in the highest estimation. His gallantry to my lady, which has never changed since he courted her, is the one little touch of romantic fancy in him. ii, vii, ix, xii, xvi, xviii, xxviii, xxix, xl, xli, xliii, xlviii, liii–lvi, lviii, lxiii, lxvi.

**Dedlock, Lady Honoria.** Mother of Esther Summerson by Captain Hawdon, a gay rake, to whom she is engaged, but whom she never marries. She afterwards becomes the wife of Sir Leicester Dedlock, who knows nothing of this portion of her history, but, fascinated by her beauty and wit, marries her solely for love, for she has not even "family." Being a proud and ambitious woman, she assumes her new position with dignity, and holds it with cold composure, hiding in her heart, however, her disgraceful secret. She flies from home upon the eve of its discovery, and dies miserably, from the combined effects of shame, remorse, and exposure, at the gate of a wretched graveyard, in which the father of her child lies buried, in one of the worst and filthiest portions of London. ii, vii, ix, xii, xvi, xviii, xxviii, xxix, xxxiii, xxxvi, xxxix–xli, xlviii, liii–lviii.

**Dedlock, Volumnia.** A cousin of Sir Leicester Dedlock's, from whom she has an annual allowance, on which she lives slenderly at Bath, making occasional visits at the country house of her patron. She is a young lady of sixty, of high standing in the city in which she resides, but a little dreaded elsewhere, in consequence of an indiscreet profusion in the article of rouge, and persistency in an obsolete pearl necklace, like a rosary of little bird's-eggs. xxviii, xl, liii, liv, lvi, lviii, lxvi.

**Donny, Miss.** Proprietor of a boarding-school, called Greenleaf, at Reading, where Esther Summerson spends six years. iii.

**Flite, Miss.** A half-crazed little old woman, who is a suitor in Chancery, and attends every sitting of the court, expecting judgment in her favor. She tells Esther Summerson: —

"There 's a cruel attraction in the place: you can't leave it. And you must expect. . . . I have been there many years, and I have noticed. It 's the Mace and Seal upon the table."

What could they do, did she think? I mildly asked her.

"Draw," returned Miss Flite, — "draw people on, my dear; draw peace out of them, sense out of them, good looks out of them, good qualities out of them: I have felt them even drawing my rest away in the night. Cold and glittering devils! . . . Let me see," said she. "I'll tell you my own case. Before they ever drew me, before I had ever seen them, — what was it I used to do? Tambourine-playing? No; tambour-work. I and my sister worked at tambour-work. Our father and our brother had a builder's business. We all lived together; ve-ry respectably, my dear! First our father was drawn, — slowly: home was drawn with him. In a few years he was a fierce, sour, angry bankrupt, without a kind word or a kind look for any one. He had been so different, Fitz-Jarndyce! He was drawn to a debtor's prison: there he died. Then our brother was drawn, swiftly, to drunkenness and rags and death. Then my sister was drawn. Hush! Never ask to what! Then I was ill, and in misery, and heard, as I had often heard before, that this was all the work of Chancery. When I got better, I went to look at the monster; and

Everything set forth in these pages concerning the Court of Chancery is substantially true, and within the truth. The case of Gridley is in no essential altered from one of actual occurrence, made public by a disinterested person, who was professionally acquainted with the whole of the monstrous wrong from beginning to end. i, xv, xxiv.

**Grubble, W.** Landlord of "The Dedlock Arms," a pleasant-looking, stoutish, middle-aged man, who never seems to consider himself cosily dressed for his own fireside, without his hat and top-boots, but who never wears a coat except at church. xxxvii.

**Guppy, Mrs.** Mother of William Guppy; a wayward old lady, in a large cap, with rather a red nose and rather an unsteady eye, but always smiling all over. xxxviii, lxiv.

**Guppy, William.** A lawyer's clerk, in the employ of Kenge and Carboy, Mr. Jarndyce's solicitors; usually spoken of as "the young man of the name of Guppy." He conceives a passion for Esther Summerson, the heroine of the story, and declares his love ("files a declaration," as he phrases it) in a very amusing manner. Though refused, and greatly disappointed, he does not quite despair, and, on taking his leave, tells her:—

"In case you should think better—at any time, however distant, *that*'s no consequence, for my feelings can never alter—of anything I have said, particularly what might I not do,—Mr. William Guppy, eighty-seven Penton Place, or if removed or dead (of blighted hopes or anything of that sort), care of Mrs. Guppy, three hundred and two Old Street Road, will be sufficient."

At a later day, on receiving a business call from Miss Summerson, and discovering that, from the effects of a fever, she has lost her former beauty, he fancies that she has come to hold him to his proposal, and becomes, in consequence, very confused and apprehensive. Although she assures him that such is not the case, he nevertheless asks her to make a full and explicit statement, before a witness, whose name and address he carefully notes with legal precision, that there has never been any engagement, or promise of marriage, between them. iii, iv, vii, ix, xiii, xix, xx, xxiv, xxix, xxxii, xxxiii, xxxviii, xxxix, xliv, liv, lv, lx, lxiii, lxiv.

**Guster** (*by some supposed to have been christened* AUGUSTA). Maid-servant of the Snagsbys; a lean young woman of some three or four and twenty, subject to fits. Taken originally from the workhouse, she is so afraid of being sent back there, that, except when she is found with her head in the pail, or the sink, or the copper, or the dinner, or anything else that happens to be near at the time of her seizure, she is always at work. x, xi, xix, xxii, xxv, xlii, lix.

**Gusher, Mr.** A friend of Mrs. Pardiggle's; a flabby gentleman, with a moist surface, and eyes so much too small for his moon of a face, that they seem to have been originally made for somebody else. xv.

**Hawdon, Captain.** A law-writer who lodges at Mr. Krook's, and gives himself the name of Nemo; formerly a rakish military officer, and a lover of a young lady (afterwards Lady Dedlock), who gives birth to a child (Esther Summerson), of which he is the father. He dies in a garret, and is buried in the Potter's Field (set apart for strangers and paupers), at the gate of which Lady Dedlock is found lying lifeless, after her flight from her husband's house. v, x, xi.

**Hortense, Mademoiselle.** Lady Dedlock's waiting-woman, and the murderess of Mr. Tulkinghorn; intended as a portrait of a Mrs. Manning, a real murderess.

My lady's maid is a Frenchwoman of two and thirty, from somewhere in the southern country about Avignon and Marseilles,—a large-eyed brown woman with black hair, who would be handsome, but for a certain feline mouth, and general uncomfortable tightness of face, rendering the jaws too eager, and the skull too prominent. There is something indefinably keen and watchful about her anatomy; and she has a watchful way of looking out of the corners of her eyes, without turning her head, which could be pleasantly dispensed with,—especially when she is in an ill-humor, and near knives. xii, xviii, xxii, xxiii, xlii, xliv, liv.

**Jarndyce, John.** Guardian of Richard Carstone and Ada Clare, and friend and protector of Esther Summerson. He is an unmarried man of about sixty, upright, hearty, and robust, with silvered iron-gray hair; a handsome, lively, quick face, full of change and motion; pleasant eyes; a sudden, abrupt manner; and a very benevolent heart. He affects to be subject to fits of ill-humor, and has a habit of saying, when deceived or disappointed in any person or matter, that "the wind is in the east;" and of taking refuge in his library, which he calls "The Growlery." Mr. Jarndyce is one of the parties in the celebrated Chancery suit of "Jarndyce and Jarndyce." i, iii, vi, viii, ix, xiii–xv, xvii, xviii, xxiii, xxiv, xxx, xxxi, xxxv–xxxvii, xxxix, xliii–xlv, xlvii, l–lii, lvi, lx–lxii, lxiv, lxv, lxvii.

**Jellyby, Caroline,** *called* "CADDY." Mrs. Jellyby's eldest daughter, and her amanuensis; a pretty and industrious, but sadly neglected and overworked girl. Becoming heartily disgusted and tired with copying never-ending letters to innumerable correspondents, concerning the welfare of her species, she resolves that she won't be a slave all her life, and accordingly marries Prince

Turveydrop, who makes her very happy. iv, v, xiv, xviii, xxiii, xxx, xxxviii, l, lxv, lxvii.

**Jellyby, Mrs.** A very pretty, very diminutive, plump woman, of from forty to fifty, with handsome eyes, though they have a curious habit of seeming to look a long way off. She is a lady of remarkable strength of character, who has devoted herself to an extensive variety of public subjects, at various times, and especially to the subject of Africa, with a view to the general cultivation of the coffee-berry, *and* the natives, and the happy settlement of a portion of our superabundant home-population in Borrioboola-Gha, on the left bank of the Niger. Her energies are so entirely devoted to this philanthropic project, that she finds no time to consider the happiness or welfare of her own family; and the result is, that her children grow up dirty, ignorant, and uncared-for; her house is disgracefully cold, cheerless, and untidy; and her husband becomes a dejected and miserable bankrupt. iv, v, xix, xxiii, xxx, xxxviii, l, lxvii.

**Jellyby, Mr.** The husband of Mrs. Jellyby; a mild, bald, quiet gentleman in spectacles, who is completely merged in the more shining qualities of his wife. iv, xiv, xxiii, xxx, xxxviii, l, lvii.

**Jellyby, "Peepy"** (so self-named). A neglected and unfortunate son of Mr. and Mrs. Jellyby. iv, v, xiv, xxiii, xxx, xxxviii, lxvii.

**Jenny.** Wife of a drunken brickmaker. viii, xxii, xxxi, xxxv, xlvi, lvii.

**Jo**, *called* "TOUGHEY." A street-crossing sweeper. A stranger who has died very suddenly has been seen speaking to Jo, who is brought before the coroner's jury. xi, xvi, xix, xx, xxv, xxix, xxxii, xlvi, xlvii.

**Jobling, Tony**, *otherwise* WEEVLE. A friend of Mr. Guppy's, and a law-writer for Mr. Snagsby. "He has the faded appearance of a gentleman in embarrassed circumstances; even his light whiskers droop with something of a shabby air." vii, xx, xxxii, xxxiii, xxxix, liv, lv, lxiv.

**Kenge, Mr.**, *called* CONVERSATION KENGE. Senior member of the firm of Kenge and Carboy, solicitors; a portly, important-looking gentleman dressed all in black, with a white cravat, large gold watch seals, a pair of gold eye-glasses, and a large seal-ring upon his little finger.

He appeared to enjoy beyond everything the sound of his own voice. I could n't wonder at that; for it was mellow and full, and gave great importance to every word he uttered. He listened to himself with obvious satisfaction, and sometimes gently beat time to his own music with his head, or rounded a sentence with

make a great deal of noise. She is a School lady, a Visiting lady, a Reading lady, a Distributing lady, and on the Social Linen Box Committee, and many general committees. viii, xv, xxx.

**Pardiggle, Alfred.** Youngest son of Mr. and Mrs. Pardiggle, aged five years. He voluntarily enrolls himself in the "Infant Bonds of Joy," and is pledged never, through life, to use tobacco in any form. viii.

**Pardiggle, Egbert.** Eldest son of Mr. and Mrs. Pardiggle, aged twelve years. He sends out his pocket-money, to the amount of five and threepence, to the Tockahoopo Indians. viii.

**Pardiggle, Felix.** Fourth son of Mr. and Mrs. Pardiggle, aged seven years; contributor of eightpence to the "Superannuated Widows." viii.

**Pardiggle, Francis.** Third son of Mr. and Mrs. Pardiggle, aged nine years; a contributor of one and sixpence half-penny to the "Great National Smithers Testimonial." viii.

**Pardiggle, Oswald.** Second son of Mr. and Mrs. Pardiggle, aged ten and a half. He gives two and ninepence to the "Great National Smithers Testimonial." viii.

**Perkins, Mrs.** An inquisitive woman living near the Sol's Arms: neighbor to Mr. Krook. xi, xx, xxxii, xxxiii, xxxix.

**Piper, Mrs.** A woman who lives near Krook's rag-and-bottle shop, and who leads the court. xi, xx, xxxii, xxxiii, xxxix.

**Priscilla.** Mrs. Jellyby's servant girl; "always drinking." iv, xv.

**Quale, Mr.** A friend of Mrs. Jellyby's; a loquacious young man with large shining knobs for temples, and his hair all brushed to the back of his head. He is a philanthropist, and has a project for teaching the coffee colonists of Borrioboola-Gha to teach the natives to turn piano-forte legs, and establish an export trade. iv, v, xv, xxiii.

**Rachael, Mrs.** Servant to Miss Barbary; afterwards the wife of the Reverend Mr. Chadband.

**Rosa.** Lady Dedlock's maid; a dark-haired, shy village beauty, betrothed to Watt Rouncewell. vii, xii, xvi, xviii, xxviii, xl, xlviii, lxiii.

**Rouncewell, Mrs.** Sir Leicester Dedlock's housekeeper at Chesney Wold; a fine old lady, handsome, stately, and wonderfully neat. vii, xii, xvi, xxviii, xxxiv, xl, lii, lv, lvi, lviii.

**Rouncewell, Mr.** Her son; an ironmaster; father of Watt Rouncewell. vii, xxviii, xl, xlviii, lxiii.

**Rouncewell, George,** *called* MR. GEORGE. Another son; a wild young lad, who enlists as a soldier, and afterwards becomes keeper of a shooting-gallery in London. vii, xxi, xxiv, xxvi, xxvii, xxxiv, xlvii, xlix, lii, lv, lvi, lviii, lxiii, lxvi.

HAROLD SKIMPOLE.

**Rouncewell, Watt.** Her grandson, betrothed to Rosa. vii, xii, xviii, xxviii, xl, xlviii, lxiii.

**Shropshire, The Man from.** *See* GRIDLEY, MR.

**Skimpole, Arethusa.** Mr. Skimpole's blue-eyed "Beauty" daughter, who plays and sings odds and ends, like her father. xliii.

**Skimpole, Harold.** A *protégé* of Mr. John Jarndyce's; a sentimentalist, brilliant, vivacious, and engaging, but thoroughly selfish and unprincipled. iv, viii, ix, xv, xviii, xxxi, xxxvii, xliii, xlvi, lvii, lxi.

**Skimpole, Mrs.** Wife of Harold Skimpole; a delicate, high-nosed invalid, suffering under a complication of disorders. xliii.

**Skimpole, Kitty.** Mr. Skimpole's "Comedy" daughter, who sings a little, but don't play. xliii.

**Skimpole, Laura.** Mr. Skimpole's "Sentiment" daughter, who plays a little, but don't sing. xliii.

**Smallweed, Bartholomew,** *jocularly called* SMALL *and* CHICK WEED, to express a fledgling, as it were. Grandson of Mr. and Mrs. Smallweed, twin-brother of Judy, and a friend of Mr. William Guppy, from whom he sponges dinners as often as he can.

He is a town-made article, of small stature and weazen features, but may be perceived from a considerable distance by means of his very tall hat. To become a Guppy is the object of his ambition. He dresses at that gentleman (by whom he is patronized), talks at him, walks at him, founds himself entirely on him. . . . He is a weird changeling, to whom years are nothing. He stands precociously possessed by centuries of owlish wisdom. If he ever lay in a cradle, it seems as if he must have lain there in a tail-coat. He has an old, old eye; . . . and he drinks and smokes in a monkeyish way; and his neck is stiff in his collar; and he is never to be taken in; and he knows all about it, whatever it is. xx, xxi, xxxiii, xxxix, lv, lxiii.

**Smallweed, Grandfather.** An old man who has been in the "discounting profession," but has become superannuated, and nearly helpless. His mind, however, is unimpaired, and still holds, as well as it ever did, the first four rules of arithmetic, and a certain small collection of the hardest facts. His favorite amusement is to throw at the head of his venerable partner a spare cushion, with which he is provided, whenever she makes an allusion to money, — a subject on which he is particularly sensitive. The exertion this requires has the effect of always throwing him back into his chair like a broken puppet, and makes it necessary that he should undergo the two operations, at the hands of his granddaughter, of being shaken up like a great bottle, and poked and punched like a great bolster. xxi, xxvi, xxvii, xxxiii, xxxiv, liv, lv, lxiii.

**Smallweed, Grandmother.** His wife; so far fallen into a childish state as to have regained such infantine graces as a total want of observation, memory, understanding, and interest, and an eternal disposition to fall asleep over the fire, and into it. xxi, xxvi, xxvii, xxxiii, xxxiv, lxiii.

**Smallweed, Judy.** Granddaughter of Mr. and Mrs. Smallweed, and twin-sister of Bartholomew. She is so indubitably his sister, that the two kneaded into one would hardly make a young person of average proportions. xxi, xxvi, xxvii, xxxiii, xxxiv, lxiii.

**Snagsby, Mr.** A law-stationer in Cook's Court, Cursitor Street; a mild, bald, timid man, tending to meekness and obesity, with a shining head and a scrubby clump of black hair sticking out at the back. Being a timid man, he is accustomed to cough with a variety of expressions, and so to save words. x, xi, xix, xx, xxii, xxv, xxxiii, xlii, xlvii, liv, lix.

**Snagsby, Mrs.** His wife; a short shrewish woman, something too violently compressed about the waist, and with a sharp nose, like a sharp autumn evening, inclining to be frosty towards the end.

Mr. and Mrs. Snagsby are not only one bone and one flesh, but, to the neighbors' thinking, one voice too. That voice appearing to proceed from Mrs. Snagsby alone, is heard in Cook's Court very often. . . . Mr. Snagsby refers everything not in the practical mysteries of the business to Mrs. Snagsby. She manages the money, reproaches the tax-gatherers, appoints the times and places of devotion on Sundays, licenses Mr. Snagsby's entertainments, and acknowledges no responsibility as to what she thinks fit to provide for dinner. . . . Rumor, always flying, bat-like, about Cook's Court and skimming in and out at everybody's windows, does say that Mrs. Snagsby is jealous and inquisitive; and that Mr. Snagsby is sometimes worried out of house and home; and that, if he had the spirit of a mouse, he would n't stand it. x, xi, xix, xx, xxii, xxv, xxxiii, xlii, xlvii, liv, lix.

**Squod, Phil.** A man employed in Mr. George's shooting-gallery.

He is a little man, with a face all crushed together, who appears, from a certain blue and speckled appearance that one of his cheeks presents, to have been blown up, in the way of business, at some odd time or times. . . . On the speckled side of his face he has no eyebrow, and on the other side he has a bushy black one; which want of uniformity gives him a very singular and rather sinister appearance. Everything seems to have happened to his hands that could possibly take place, consistently with the retention of all the fingers; for they are notched and seamed, and crumpled all over. . . . He has a curious way of limping round the gallery with his shoulder against the wall, and tacking off at objects he wants to lay hold of, instead of going straight to them, which has left a smear all round the four walls, conventionally called "Phil's mark." xxi, xxiv, xxvi, xxxiv, xlvii, lvi, lxvi.

**Stables, The Honorable Bob.** Cousin to Sir Leicester Dedlock. ii, xxviii, xl, lviii.

**Summerson, Esther.** *Protégée* of Mr. Jarndyce; afterwards the wife of Allan Woodcourt. She is the narrator of a part of the story, and is represented as a prudent, wise little body, a notable housewife, a self-denying friend, and a universal favorite. She proves to be an illegitimate daughter of Lady Dedlock and Captain Hawdon. According to Doctor Shelton Mackenzie (Life of Dickens, p. 203), this character is supposed to have been drawn from real life, and to have been intended as a portrait of Miss Sophia Iselin, author of a volume of poems published in 1847. iii–vi, viii, ix, xiii–xv, xvii–xix, xxiii, xxiv, xxix–xxxi, xxxv–xxxviii, xliii–xlv, xlvii, l–lii, liv, lvi, lvii, lix–lxv, lxvii.

**Swills, Little.** A red-faced comic vocalist engaged at the Harmonic meetings at the Sol's Arms. xi, xix, xxxii, xxxiii, xxxix.

**Tangle, Mr.** A lawyer, who knows more about the case of Jarndyce and Jarndyce than anybody, and is supposed never to have read anything else since he left school. i.

**Thomas.** Sir Leicester Dedlock's groom. xl.

**Toughey.** *See* Jo.

**Tulkinghorn, Mr.** An attorney-at-law, and a solicitor of the Court of Chancery, who is the legal adviser of Sir Leicester Dedlock.

The old gentleman is rusty to look at, but is reputed to have made good thrift out of aristocratic marriage-settlements and aristocratic wills, and to be very rich. He is surrounded by a mysterious halo of family confidences, of which he is known to be the silent depositary. . . . He is of what is called the old school, — a phrase generally meaning any school that seems never to have been young, — and wears knee-breeches tied with ribbons, and gaiters or stockings. One peculiarity of his black clothes and of his black stockings, be they silk or worsted, is, that they never shine. Mute, close, irresponsive to any glancing light, his dress is like himself. He never converses when not professionally consulted. He is found sometimes, speechless, but quite at home, at corners of dinner-tables in great country-houses, and near doors of drawing-rooms, concerning which the fashionable intelligence is eloquent, where everybody knows him, and where half the peerage stops to say, "How do you do, Mr. Tulkinghorn?" He receives these salutations with gravity, and buries them along with the rest of his knowledge.

Becoming acquainted with the early history of Lady Dedlock, he quietly informs her of the fact, and of his intention to reveal it to her husband, which causes her to flee from home, and results in her death. Shortly after this disclosure, he is murdered in his room by a French waiting-maid, whom he has made use of to discover certain family secrets, and whom he refuses to reward to the amount she desires. ii, vii, x–xii, xv, xvi, xxii, xxiv, xxvii, xxix, xxxiii, xxxiv, xxxvi, xl–xlii, xliv, xlvii, xlviii.

**Turveydrop, Mr.** "A very gentlemanly man, celebrated almost everywhere for his deportment."

He was a fat old gentleman with a false complexion, false teeth, false whiskers, and a wig. He had a fur collar, and he had a padded breast to his coat, which only wanted a star, or a broad blue ribbon, to be complete. He was pinched in, and swelled out, and got up, and strapped down, as much as he could possibly bear. He had such a neckcloth on (puffing his very eyes out of their natural shape), and his chin and even his ears so sunk into it, that it seemed as though he must inevitably double up, if it were cast loose. He had under his arm a hat of great size and weight, shelving downward from the crown to the brim; and in his hand a pair of white gloves, with which he flapped it, as he stood poised on one leg, in a high-shouldered, round-elbowed state of elegance not to be surpassed. He had a cane, he had an eye-glass, he had rings, he had wristbands, he had everything but any touch of nature. He was not like youth, he was not like age: he was like nothing in the world but a model of deportment.

He had married a meek little dancing-mistress, with a tolerable connection (having never in his life before done anything but deport himself), and had worked her to death, or had, at the best, suffered her to work herself to death, to maintain him in those expenses which were indispensable to his position. At once to exhibit his Deportment to the best models, and to keep the best models constantly before himself, he had found it necessary to frequent all public places of fashionable and lounging resort, to be seen at Brighton and elsewhere at fashionable times, and to lead an idle life in the very best clothes. To enable him to do this, the affectionate little dancing-mistress had toiled and labored, and would have toiled and labored to that hour, if her strength had lasted so long. For, . . . in spite of the man's absorbing selfishness, his wife (overpowered by his Deportment) had, to the last, believed in him, and had, on her death-bed, in the most mov-

MR. TURVEYDROP AND HIS SON.

ing terms, confided him to their son as one who had an inextinguishable claim upon him, and whom he could never regard with too much pride and deference. The son, inheriting his mother's belief, and having the Deportment always before him, had lived and grown in the same faith, and now, at thirty years of age, worked for his father twelve hours a day, and looked up to him with veneration on the old imaginary pinnacle. xiv, xxiii, xxx, xxxviii, l, lvii.

**Turveydrop, Prince.** His son; so named in remembrance of the Prince Regent, whom Mr. Turveydrop the elder adored on account of his deportment. He is a little, blue-eyed, fair man, of youthful appearance, with flaxen hair parted in the middle, and curling at the ends all round his head. He marries Miss Caddy Jellyby. xiv, xvii, xxiii, xxx, xxxviii, l, lvii.

**Vholes, Mr.** Richard Carstone's solicitor; a man who is always "putting his shoulder to the wheel," without any visible results, and is continually referring to the fact that he is a widower, with three daughters and an aged father in the Vale of Taunton, who are dependent on him for their support. xxxvii, xxxix, xlv, li, lxi, lxii, lxv.

**Weevle, Mr.** *See* JOBLING, TONY.

**Wisk, Miss.** A friend of Mrs. Jellyby's, betrothed to Mr. Quale. Her "mission" is to show the world that woman's mission is man's mission, and that the only genuine mission of both man and woman is to be always moving declaratory resolutions about things in general at public meetings. xxx.

**Woodcourt, Allan.** A young surgeon, who afterwards marries Esther Summerson. xi, xiii, xiv, xvii, xxx, xxxv, xlvi, xlvii, l–lii, lix–lxi, lxiv, lxv, lxvii.

**Woodcourt, Mrs.** His mother; a handsome old lady, small, sharp, upright, and trim, with bright black eyes; very proud of her descent from an illustrious Welsh ancestor, named Morgan-ap-Kerrig. xvii, xxx, lx, lxii, lxiv.

# LITTLE DORRIT

## OUTLINE

### BOOK THE FIRST: POVERTY

Chapter I In a jail in Marseilles two prisoners were awaiting trial. One, short and thickset in person, and good-natured of face, was a smuggler, and shut up by the police because his papers were wrong; the other, tall, insolent, domineering, and calling himself M. Rigaud, was waiting to be tried for the murder of his wife.

II At the same time there were in quarantine at Marseilles some English travellers, notably Mr. Arthur Clennam, Mr. Meagles and his family, and a Miss Wade. The latter kept herself apart, and, except that she exercised a strange power over Miss Meagles's maid, Tattycoram, repulsed all intercourse with the other travellers. Mr. and Mrs. Meagles and their daughter were "practical people," as Mr. Meagles phrased it, and did what good in the world they could find to do. Tattycoram was an instance of their large-heartedness. She was a foundling, befriended and educated by Mr. Meagles, but who yet found the kindness of her benefactor wounding to her pride, wherein lay Miss Wade's baleful influence. The other member of the party, Arthur Clennam, was just returning from China, after being there twenty years in business with his father. The latter had recently died, and Arthur was returning to London, where his mother managed the home branch of the House of Clennam.

III Not many days after the travellers had been dismissed from quarantine at Marseilles, Arthur Clennam reached his old home in London. It was an ancient, musty house, so near ruin that it had had to be propped up by heavy beams, which in their turn were rotting. Yet Mrs. Clennam, who was a paralytic and confined to her room, lived there with two old servants, and there conducted business. For she was a woman of extraordinary force of character, and had always ruled her husband from the time of her marriage. All of this Arthur felt when he entered his mother's room with Jeremiah, his mother's right-hand man, and it was all forced upon him anew with Mrs. Clennam's coldly austere greeting. He felt again the lack of love that there had been between his father and mother; all the repressive influence that had shorn his life of its youth; all the vindictiveness, so mingled with piety that his mother boasted herself a special instrument in the hands of God for the punishment of her own and His enemies. Both of them felt that his home-coming could draw them no closer together than they had been; that their differing temperaments would continue to keep them apart.

IV The night of Arthur Clennam's arrival witnessed a strange scene. When Jeremiah thought every one asleep in the house, he gave into the charge of his brother an iron box containing papers that Mrs. Clennam wished destroyed. But Jeremiah's wife, Affery, saw the transaction and long remembered it.

V Next morning Arthur and his mother met for a business conference, in which Arthur incurred his mother's displeasure for two things, — for giving up his part in the business, and for telling her of his suspicions that his father had died unhappy in some great wrong committed. So wrathful did she become at his suspicions that she threatened to curse him from her sight if ever he alluded to them again. But she did not lull his doubts: they were confirmed from day to day by the sight of a shy little woman who visited his mother sometimes as seamstress, sometimes as friend, but always as dependent. He shrewdly guessed that in her own hard way his mother was endeavoring to make reparation for wrong done in some way to Little Dorrit — the name of the shy little seamstress.

VI Now the story of Little Dorrit was a pathetic one. Years
before Arthur Clennam's return from China, her father had
VII been imprisoned in the Marshalsea for debt. Soon after
this happened Little Dorrit was born within the prison walls. There was another daughter and a son in the Dorrit family, both older than the child of the Marshalsea, but as the years rolled on and she grew up, Little Dorrit gradually came to be the stay of them all. Her mother had died, so upon her devolved the planning and contriving for her irresolute father, her shallow sister, and her shiftless brother. Mr. Dorrit came to be the oldest inhabitant of the prison — the Father of the Marshalsea — and as such to receive gifts in money, taking them as his due; but his real support came from the planning and work of Little Dorrit.

VIII So strong had Arthur Clennam's interest grown, as he saw Little Dorrit from day to day at his mother's house, that he finally resolved to find out where she lived, that he might more effectually help her. Accordingly he followed her one day to the Marshalsea prison, where he gained admission, and where he was presented, as all visitors of a certain distinction were presented, to Mr.

Dorrit. That vain old gentleman received Arthur with all the pathetic dignity gained from long experience as the Father of the Marshalsea, and obtained from him the usual "Testimonial" left by visitors. Her father's manner of begging for the gift troubled Little Dorrit very much, chiefly because she feared that Arthur would misjudge her father by it. But the thought that Arthur Clennam carried away from the visit was not so much of Mr. Dorrit's vanity and lack of pride, as of Little Dorrit's unselfishness and modest care for her family; and above all, of the reparation for some unknown wrong done them that he was coming to believe in more and more as due from him.

IX The next day, accordingly, he saw Little Dorrit again and made proffer of his help. He learned nothing from her in confirmation of his suspicion that her father had suffered wrong at the hands of his father, but he learned further of her gentle
X strength of character. One clue she gave him to the cause of her father's imprisonment, and to follow that up he endeavored to meet Mr. Tite Barnacle of the Circumlocution Office. But although he saw Mr. Barnacle after many delays, his efforts in Mr. Dorrit's behalf with the Office for the Obstruction of Government proved unavailing. His visits at that office, however, led to one good thing at least, — an acquaintance with Mr. Daniel Doyce, inventor, and luckless suitor for the attention of the government.

XI It was some time after the smuggler and the murderer were awaiting trial in the Marseilles jail, when a solitary man, bedraggled and footsore, toiled along the road to Chalons. It was Rigaud, who had escaped conviction at Marseilles, and was fleeing now from the wrath of the people.

XII Mr. Doyce's manufactory was at one end of Bleeding Heart Yard, where the Plornishes, friends of the Dorrits, lived. In pursuance of his plan for helping the Dorrits and for discovering the reason for Little Dorrit's dependence upon his mother, Clennam went to see the Plornishes. They were poor people, as were all the tenants at Bleeding Heart Yard, but he found them ready to do all they could for Little Dorrit. They told him how Little Dorrit came to be employed by Mrs. Clennam through their landlord, Mr. Casby; and Plornish himself readily undertook to help Clennam settle secretly the debt for which Little Dorrit's brother was confined in the Marshalsea.

XIII Mr. Casby's name awakened a train of recollection in Clennam's mind. When hardly more than a boy he had fallen in love with Flora Casby, and would have married her if his mother had not interfered. In the years that had intervened, however, he had not forgotten his old ideal, so that it was with a good deal of curiosity and interest that he called at the Casbys'. He was ushered in to Mr. Casby, whom he found patriarchal and benevolent-looking as of old, but uncommunicative. He would say nothing definite about Little Dorrit. Flora, Arthur found, had become a fat, florid, and foolish widow, but good-hearted withal, who had hopes still that "the broken chain that once had bound them" might be repaired.

"Oh good gracious me I hope you never kept yourself a bachelor so long on my account!" tittered Flora; "but of course you never did why should you, pray don't answer, I don't know where I'm running to, oh do tell me something about the Chinese ladies whether their eyes are really so long and narrow always putting me in mind of mother-of-pearl fish at cards and do they really wear tails down their back, and plaited too or is it only the men, and when they pull their hair so very tight off their foreheads don't they hurt themselves, and why do they stick little bells all over their bridges and temples and hats and things or don't they really do it!" Flora gave him another of her old glances. Instantly she went on again, as if he had spoken in reply for some time:—

"Then it's all true and they really do! good gracious Arthur!—pray excuse me—old habit—Mr. Clennam far more proper—what a country to live in for so long a time, and with so many lanterns and umbrellas too how very dark and wet the climate ought to be and no doubt actually is, and the sums of money that must be made by those two trades where everybody carries them and hangs them everywhere, the little shoes too and the feet screwed back in infancy is quite surprising, what a traveller you are!"

In this ridiculous distress, Clennam received another of the old glances, without in the least knowing what to do with it.

"Dear dear," said Flora, "only to think of the changes at home Arthur—cannot overcome it, seems so natural, Mr. Clennam far more proper—since you became familiar with the Chinese customs and language which I am persuaded you speak like a native if not better for you were always quick and clever though immensely difficult no doubt, I am sure the tea-chests alone would kill *me* if I tried, such changes Arthur—I am doing it again, seems so natural, most improper—as no one could have believed, who could have ever imagined Mrs. Finching when I can't imagine it myself!"

"Is that your married name?" asked Arthur, struck, in the midst of all this, by a certain warmth of heart that expressed itself in her tone when she referred, however oddly, to the youthful relation in which they had stood to one another. "Finching?"

"Finching oh yes, is n't it a dreadful name, but as Mr. F. said when he proposed to me which he did seven times and handsomely consented I must say to be what he used to call on liking twelve months after all, he was n't answerable for it and could n't help it could he, excellent man, not at all like you but excellent man!"

His old ideal in her shattered, he found his interest in the call centring in Mr. Casby's agent, Mr. Pancks, whose hobby was "advertisements relative to next of kin."

XIV Late that night, after Clennam had returned to his lodgings, Little Dorrit knocked at his door. She had come to tell him that her brother was again at large through the kindness of some one whom it grieved her that she might never thank, as he withheld his name. But he comforted her as best he might, saying that whoever had done her brother the kindness would find his reward in the deed. Then she begged him not to encourage her father in his prideless asking for help by giving him money; for, as she sadly explained, she wished Clennam to think as well as he could of her father.

XV In the mean time, things were not going altogether smoothly between Mrs. Clennam and her trusted servant Jeremiah Flintwinch. For one evening the latter took his mistress to task for not clearing her husband of the doubts that Arthur had of him, and for taking refuge in Arthur's suspicion of the dead. The object Jeremiah had in his reproaches was chiefly to assert himself and to try his power over Mrs. Clennam. The result was to disclose a part of the secret they held between them, for Affery, Jeremiah's wife, overheard their quarrel.

XVI The time came for Arthur Clennam to fulfil a promise to visit Mr. Meagles at his home. Accordingly he paid the visit with Mr. Doyce, who was a common friend of Mr. Meagles and himself. The Meagles cottage was a very delightful one, and as charming as the Meagles family. With "Pet," the daughter of the house, Arthur began to fall in love, when he became aware of a rival in

XVII the field. This was Mr. Henry Gowan, relative of the Barnacles of the Circumlocution Office. Too poor to live on his means, he had turned half-heartedly to painting, for which he had some talent. He was, on the whole, a cynically disagreeable fellow, and Pet's liking for him grieved her parents deeply.

XVIII Little Dorrit had not attained her twenty-second birthday without finding a lover. He was young John Chivery, son of the turnkey of the Marshalsea prison. He had paid his

court for long before he spoke to her, though in a shy and not very hopeful way. Every Sunday he presented Mr. Dorrit with cigars and received patronage in turn. Little by little he felt encouraged, and at last tried to tell Little Dorrit of his love. But she, with kindly tact, made him understand that she could not love him
XIX in the way he wished. Poor John was so crushed by her refusal that his dejection caused his parents much anxiety. This had the effect of roughening the turnkey's manner towards Mr. Dorrit, and the latter in turn became querulous with Little Dorrit, to whom he owed so much. But she only felt his unkindness as the blight that the years of imprisonment had put upon him.

XX In the mean while Little Dorrit's sister Fanny was looking out, as she expressed it, for the interests of the family in Society. She was a professional dancer, and happened to attract the attention of Mr. Edward Sparkler, a gilded young fool. Now Fanny, in spite of her vanity, was clever, and so managed the affair as to bring Mr. Sparkler's mother, Mrs. Merdle, to beg her to send that foolish youth about his business, — a thing which Fanny was perfectly willing to do.

XXI Mrs. Merdle was a high priestess of Society, partly by virtue of her birth, partly by virtue of her presence, chiefly by virtue of her husband's wealth. For Mr. Merdle was a financial giant, and seemed in the eyes of Society to personify the business energy of the nation. Before his wealth, accordingly, Society bowed.

XXII Now Arthur Clennam's compliance with Little Dorrit's request that he should not encourage her father to beg "Testimonials" of him, brought him into disfavor with the Father of the Marshalsea. The latter still was not above asking by letter for a loan from Arthur, however, and gave his I. O. U. for it with as much dignity as if he expected to be able to repay the money. But all this was a great trial to Little Dorrit, who found cause in her heart to be peculiarly sensitive to Arthur's kindness.

XXIII Arthur Clennam, by this time, had entered into partnership with Mr. Doyce, the inventor. But in the midst of his new business cares, he thought much over the problem concerning his mother's patronage of Little Dorrit. To his surprise he found one day that Mr. Pancks was interested in the Dorrits, too, and the latter and he made a bargain to help each other in forwarding Little Dorrit's welfare.

XXIV Through Arthur Clennam, Little Dorrit gained another friend in Mrs. Finching, whom he had loved when she was Flora Casby. In the goodness of her heart Flora gave Little Dor rit work to do, and in her folly told the Child of the Marshalsea of Arthur's boyish love, intimating at the same time that it still continued. And by so doing she caused Little Dorrit great sorrow, for the latter had come to love Arthur herself.

Mr. Pancks, at this time, began to give Little Dorrit mysterious hints, of which she could make nothing but that he was friendly

XXV toward her. In reality, Mr. Pancks was on the track of something of great importance to the Dorrits — something that involved careful examination of certain family records, tombstones, and the like.

XXVI Arthur Clennam's state of mind in regard to Miss Meagles was not peaceful, especially as he learned from time to time of the progress of Mr. Henry Gowan's courtship. For Gowan had won Pet's love, to the grief of her parents, and the only thing in the way of their marriage was the objection of Mr. Meagles. In

XXVII the midst of all this, a new cause for distress came upon the Meagles household. Tattycoram ran away in a fit of rage at what she called their neglect of her. She had been in correspondence with the taciturn Miss Wade ever since meeting her at Marseilles, and the effect of the acquaintance was her running away from her benefactors. By dint of much seeking over London, Mr. Meagles and Clennam found her and Miss Wade together, but by no kind persuasion could they get Tattycoram to return.

XXVIII Soon after this occurrence Clennam went to visit at the Meagles's cottage, and there learned of the hopelessness of his case with Miss Meagles. It was Pet herself who told him of her engagement to Henry Gowan, and who begged him to help her father to bear the disappointment of her choice, — a thing which he readily promised, and tried to fulfil.

XXIX Once more Affery Flintwinch was eavesdropper to something unusual on the part of her mistress. This time she overheard Mrs. Clennam ask Little Dorrit some questions which afterwards proved to be very significant. They related to Little Dorrit's poverty, and the privations she suffered, and Mrs. Clennam seemed to find relief in Little Dorrit's uncomplaining answers.

Scarcely had Little Dorrit left Mrs. Clennam when a stranger appeared asking to see her. He was tall and foreign-looking, with a sinister smile and glittering eyes. It was M. Rigaud, under the

XXX name of Blandois, and he had important business to transact with the house of Clennam and Company. What his business was he did not state at his first call upon Mrs. Clennam, and, on the whole, he had the air of a man looking carefully over ground and probing characters with an end in view.

XXXI In spite of their misfortunes, the Dorrits were a proud family, with the exception of their main stay and support,

Little Dorrit, and had developed a tradition of gentility in spite of untoward circumstances. It was a sore affliction to the spirit of her father and brother and sister, for instance, to see Little Dorrit publicly care for an old pauper friend; while the vanities attendant upon Mr. Dorrit's assumption of dignity as Father of the Marshalsea were dear to their hearts. Even Arthur Clennam was disliked by Fanny and her brother, and would have been disliked by Mr. Dorrit, if the latter had not been so largely dependent upon him.

XXXII This made no difference to Clennam, however, for his kindness was altogether for the sake of Little Dorrit, though influenced by the suspicion that reparation was due them all from his family.

In the mean while, keeping his compact with Arthur in mind, Pancks had been at work following a clue through records of various sorts, with the result that he found the good fortune for Little Dorrit that she so richly deserved.

XXXIII It was not until Mr. Meagles gave his consent to his daughter's marriage with Henry Gowan that the latter's family, in the person of his mother, agreed upon its part. For it was a fiction pleasant to Mrs. Gowan's mind, that her son, while bettering himself in means by the marriage, was condescending socially, and that, for that reason, as she explained to Mrs. Merdle, Society's high priestess, she had given her consent reluctantly.

XXXIV Pleasing as the marriage was to her, however, it was the reverse to Mr. Meagles and his wife, in spite of the grandeur and ceremony lent the occasion by the presence of the Circumlocution Office Barnacles in force.

XXXV The good fortune that Mr. Pancks had discovered for Little Dorrit was that her father was heir at law to a great estate that had long lain unknown of, unclaimed, and accumulating. Mr. Pancks made Arthur the bearer of his news to Little Dorrit, whose sole thought upon receiving it was for her father. To the latter it came with pathetic effect, tending to increase his vanity and the feeling of false pride that had developed in him with his years of imprisonment.

XXXVI The exit of the Dorrit family from the Marshalsea was very characteristic of its members. Mr. Dorrit had greatly increased his dignity of carriage, and walked out at the gate with great show of state. Fanny and Edward were already impatient of their familiar surroundings, and burning to put time and space between themselves and the prison taint. All but Little Dorrit had reached the carriage that was to bear them away, before they missed her. Then she was carried to them in Arthur Clennam's arms. He had found her in a swoon in her old garret room.

## BOOK THE SECOND: RICHES

XXXVII Not long after the accession of the Dorrit family to its good fortune, some travellers came together upon the Great Saint Bernard in Switzerland. They were all on their way to Italy, and one party at least had climbed the mountain because it was one of the places that was talked about. That was Mr. Dorrit's party, consisting chiefly of his daughters, his son, a Mrs. General, and himself. Among the other travellers was an English lady, to whom Little Dorrit and her sister had the opportunity of being kind, and who proved to be Mrs. Henry Gowan. She was travelling with her husband to Italy, where the latter was to study and paint. With them was a new acquaintance of Mr. Gowan, who was no
XXXVIII other than Blandois. The Mrs. General who was registered with the Dorrit party was one of the advantages of their recently acquired wealth, gained for the purpose of "forming" the Misses Dorrit.

XXXIX Among the disadvantages brought into relief by their wealth was the fact that Little Dorrit was not so "presentable" as the others. To her their wealth and all it brought seemed unreal; and she did not fill, with her simple nature, her enlarged conditions to the satisfaction of her family. Her simple kindliness in helping others gave her father and sister great offence, as it had done in the old prison days. She was never consulted about the route or the family doings; and when they settled down in a Venetian palace for a period, she was left more than ever to herself. All this, as she wrote to Arthur Clennam, made her long sometimes for
XL old faces and old surroundings and her old work. Now, and she wrote this uncomplainingly, even her natural impulses toward little affectionate acts were repressed. In fact, none of the
XLI Dorrit family were happy in their altered circumstances. They were oppressed by their wealth and the position they sought to maintain, and hampered by shame of the old prison life.

XLII In Venice appeared Mr. Sparkler, the foolish youth who had made love to Fanny when she was a dancer, and who began immediately to show signs of renewing his attentions. Because of his knowledge of the Gowans, who had also come to Venice, the Dorrits decided to cultivate the artist and his wife, whom they found living in out-of-the-way lodgings, and still attended by Blandois.

XLIII And now new causes for discomfort began to harass members of the Dorrit family. Fanny began to think that her father was treating Mrs. General with more than ordinary consideration, and to draw conclusions from so doing that troubled her.

Little Dorrit, on her part, was pained by the insincere way in which Fanny treated Mr. Sparkler, who had become thoroughly enslaved.

In due course of time the family went on to Rome, where their social advancement was still greater than it had been in Venice, and when they renewed the acquaintance with Mrs. Merdle, — not upon the foundation laid in Fanny's dancing days, however.

XLIV Back in England, in the mean time, the Dowager Mrs. Gowan was asserting herself and her attitude toward her son's marriage so unpleasantly as to cause Mr. and Mrs. Meagles grave doubts as to their daughter's happiness. Accordingly they
XLV determined to go to her in Italy, leaving Clennam with the duty of occasionally visiting their house for the sake of putting life into it. Upon one such visit Arthur learned that Tattycoram had been seen near the house, but had vanished from the neighborhood when search was made for her.

Not long after, he came upon her himself in London, upon the arm of an evil-looking foreigner. Arthur immediately followed them until they met with Miss Wade, when he learned (without being seen himself) that the foreigner was employed in some service for that strange woman. When the foreigner went his way alone, Clennam followed Miss Wade and her companion, and saw them admitted, to his great surprise, at Mr. Casby's house. Entering there himself, he was detained so long by Flora's foolishness, that when he saw Mr. Casby, the latter's visitors had gone; nor could Arthur learn anything of them from Mr. Casby.

XLVI A few days later Arthur came upon the same foreigner at his mother's house whom he had seen with Miss Wade and Tattycoram. They entered together, and Arthur was surprised, not only at the foreigner's insolent manner, but at his mother's reception of Mr. Blandois, as she called him. It was with misgivings that he left the stranger, at his mother's request, alone with her and Flintwinch.

XLVII At this time a letter from Little Dorrit informed Arthur of the state of things with the Gowans, — how Mr. Gowan fell short of his duty to his wife, of his cynical, half-hearted way of pursuing his profession, and of the unpleasantness between Mr. Meagles and his son-in-law. But of herself, Little Dorrit could write that she was improving under Mrs. General's teaching.

XLVIII In response to his wife's request and by means of his wealth, Mr. Merdle obtained for his step-son a position in
XLIX the Circumlocution Office. Mr. Merdle's influence was not confined to that notable institution, however. In a very subtle way he was encouraging a spirit in business enterprise that was spreading like an epidemic. This was the spirit of speculation,

which was influencing rich and poor alike, and which was fostered by a general belief in the safety of the Merdle enterprises. Mr. Pancks had invested with Merdle, and tried to influence Arthur to do likewise.

In the mean time Mr. Sparkler was being promoted at
L Rome by being gradually advanced in the favor of Fanny,
until he occupied the position of her lover. Fanny did not accept
him until after a long period of trial, and then it was more for the
furthering of ends of her own than for love that she did so. To
every one, excepting Little Dorrit, whose loving heart had
LI received so much of Fanny's confidence that she feared the
results of the marriage, the engagement was entirely satisfactory.
Through a winter in Rome, then, it lasted, and in the spring the
marriage occurred.

Mr. Dorrit accompanied the newly married pair back to
LII England. His object was to consult with the great Mr.
Merdle upon the subject of placing his money. He found the great
man eager to advise him on the matter, and followed the advice by
investing his wealth in one of Mr. Merdle's "own things."

Just two days before the time set for his return to Rome,
LIII a hand-bill was brought to Mr. Dorrit's notice setting forth
the disappearance of Mr. Blandois, last seen at the house of Clennam
and Company. For some whimsical reason, Mr. Dorrit determined
to see Mrs. Clennam for the purpose of gaining what information
she could give him concerning the disappearance, in order that he
might carry some definite news of it to Henry Gowan. He found
that the disappearance had caused Mrs. Clennam considerable annoyance, and that her decaying house was under close surveillance,
but he learned nothing more than the hand-bill had told him.

The day of his departure from London, Mr. Dorrit re-
LIV ceived a great shock in the shape of a call from the Marshalsea turnkey's son, who violently recalled to mind the old prison
days. In fact, Mr. Dorrit did not breathe freely again until he had
crossed the Channel, so greatly did the visit of the turnkey's son
oppress him. Once in France, however, he began building an air-
castle of vast proportions, which only wanted realization until he
returned to Rome. Arriving there late at night, he became querulous at finding himself unexpected. The next day he was
LV not well, although he held a pointed conversation with Mrs.
General relative to his castle in the air, the plan of which was no
less than making her Mrs. Dorrit. That evening Little Dorrit and
he dined at Mrs. Merdle's, where a sad thing happened. He rose
suddenly at the end of the dinner, and made a speech after his old
prison fashion, believing himself to be once more the Father of

the Marshalsea. With difficulty his daughter got him home, where he died very shortly.

LVI Arthur Clennam was worried over the disappearance of Blandois in so inexplicable a manner from his mother's house. Obtaining from Pancks, who had found it accidentally among Mr. Casby's papers, the address of Miss Wade, he set out to learn from her, if he could, the missing man's whereabouts. In Calais he found that mysterious woman, and learned that aside from some employment she had given Blandois, she knew nothing of him. Incidentally, however, he learned from Miss Wade of her hatred of Henry Gowan and his wife, and had a chance to observe the unhappiness of Tattycoram with her mysterious friend. The latter, to show him how intense her hatred was, gave him an account of herself in which she had set down the story of her life. It
LVII told how she was a foundling like Tattycoram, and how from early childhood she had been of a jealous, exacting temper that continually misunderstood kindnesses done for her; how she had been loved and engaged to be married, and how the engagement was broken, partly through her unfortunate temper, partly through Henry Gowan; how she had grown to love Gowan until he turned from her to the girl he married, and how Pet then, as well as he, had incurred her hatred; and finally how she had won Tattycoram away from the Meagles household because she was of a temper and condition similar to her own.

LVIII By chance Clennam discovered that a workman of his had knowledge of Blandois through being imprisoned with him once in Marseilles, and that this workman, Cavaletto by name, was eager to search out the whereabouts of the missing man.

LIX Arthur's distress of mind was increased upon learning from Cavaletto that Blandois was a murderer, so that he determined to tell his mother what he knew, in the hope of gaining her confidence in turn. All his good intention was turned against him by Mrs. Clennam's perversity, however, although his conviction strengthened that something was very wrong, and that his mother was hiding it from him. Before he left the house he contrived to get speech with Affery, and to make her promise to tell what she knew of the wrong when he proved himself a match for her husband and her mistress.

LX For a long while Mr. Merdle had had a complaint, though his physician could not make anything out of it. He was suffering from it one day — it had been a long, long day for Fanny — when he called upon Mrs. Sparkler to borrow a penknife.

LXI Late that night his physician was called to some baths in his neighborhood, where it had happened that the great finan-

cier had bled himself to death. A note, addressed to the physician, was found which stated the nature of the complaint under which Mr. Merdle had labored so long. It was simply forgery and robbery, and with his death came a tremendous crash in the business
LXII world. The crash involved Mr. Pancks and Arthur Clennam, whom he had persuaded to invest in one of Merdle's "safe things." Unfortunately, Arthur had involved his partner, Mr. Doyce, in the ruin, but he honorably tried to assume all the consequences, as well as all the blame, himself. The result was that he had to go to prison, to the Marshalsea, where the turnkey, remembering him as a visitor of old, gave him Mr. Dorrit's old room.

LXIII With a good deal of emotion Clennam took up his quarters in the jail, — emotion due not only to old association, but to the kindness of the turnkey's son, John. Now John had a curious manner toward Arthur; it was half-belligerent, half-conciliatory, and turned out to be strangely compounded of a sense of his own unworthiness, of Arthur's obtuseness, and of Little Dorrit's transcendent worth. For John had perceived, with the sensitiveness of a lover, that the object of his love, Little Dorrit, was in love with Arthur. The knowledge came like a blow to the latter.

LXIV As time passed, Clennam began to feel the effects of imprisonment and of worry over the ruin he had brought upon his partner. His peace of mind was still further shattered by a visit one day from Pancks and Cavaletto, who brought the missing Blandois with them. Blandois came with all the insolent swagger of an acknowledged villain. Upon learning why Clennam wished him, he explained his disappearance, saying that he had hoped by means of it to compel Mrs. Clennam and her partner Jeremiah to come to his terms in purchasing something of him. As his plans had been interfered with, he proposed bringing his business to a conclusion immediately, and accordingly he wrote to Mrs. Clennam, appointing a day for conference, which she accepted.

LXV As the days dragged on toward the one appointed for the conference at which he might not be present, Arthur grew weaker and more despondent. One day he lay in a half stupor, when the door opened and Little Dorrit appeared in the worn dress of the prison days. She had come to make offer of help, to ask him to use what he needed of her wealth to satisfy his creditors. But he would not avail himself of her kindness, knowing the love she bore him and feeling love for her in his heart.

LXVI At last the appointed day came, and Blandois, Affery, Jeremiah, and Mrs. Clennam each told a portion of the disclosures made. Among them they told the story of the House of Clennam, and it ran in this wise. Arthur's father had been entirely subdued to the control of his uncle first, and afterwards to the wife his uncle chose for him, except in one respect: he loved another woman who became Arthur's mother. By accident, Mrs. Clennam learned of this son and mother, and so worked upon her husband's cowed spirit that he gave them over into her hands. Then Mrs. Clennam obtained the boy from his mother, to be reared as her own and to know nothing of his real mother, who in turn for giving up her son was to be allowed to bury her sin. So Arthur's mother was taken and cared for by Frederick Dorrit, Little Dorrit's uncle, and Arthur himself was brought up as Mrs. Clennam's son. But the old uncle was stirred to pity for the girl whose sin he did not know, but whose life he feared he had blighted by taking his nephew from her, and so before he died he provided in his will that a certain sum be paid her at his death and another equal sum be paid to her patron, Frederick Dorrit, on behalf of his youngest daughter: failing the latter, the second sum was to be paid to Little Dorrit. And then the uncle died, but the money was never paid, for Mrs. Clennam and Jeremiah suppressed that provision of the will.

Now the object of rehearsing this sad story of wrong was that Blandois might enforce his demand for silence-money. And to enforce it more strongly, he threatened to expose the wrong to Arthur and to Little Dorrit. Then Mrs. Clennam, upon whom the rehearsal of her wrong-doing had so strongly wrought, and who had been paralyzed for fifteen years, suddenly arose from her invalid's chair and hastened to the Marshalsea prison with Affery at her heels. Arrived there, she saw Little Dorrit and told her the whole

LXVII pitiful story, only stipulating that Arthur be kept in ignorance of it while she, his supposed mother, lived. Then she and Little Dorrit hastened back to deal with the villain Blandois together, and they arrived at the instant in which the old house tumbled into ruin and buried that evil foreigner beneath its crumbled walls.

LXVIII Now Arthur was very ill at the Marshalsea, and Mr. Pancks suffered wretchedly from the thought that he was the cause of his friend's trouble. This made him too restive to submit to the increasing pressure as a squeezing machine that his employer was putting upon him, so he discharged himself after wreaking whimsical vengeance upon Mr. Casby.

> Going close up to the most venerable of men, and halting in front of the bottle-green waistcoat, [he] made a trigger of his right thumb and forefinger, applied the same to the brim of the broad-brimmed hat, and, with singular smartness and precision, shot it off the polished head as if it had been a large marble.
>
> Having taken this little liberty with the patriarchal person,

Mr. Pancks further astounded and attracted the Bleeding Hearts by saying in an audible voice, "Now, you sugary swindler, I mean to have it out with you!"

Mr. Pancks and the patriarch were instantly the centre of a press, all eyes and ears; windows were thrown open, and door-steps were thronged.

"What do you pretend to be?" said Mr. Pancks. "What's your moral game? What do you go in for? Benevolence; ain't it? You benevolent!" Here Mr. Pancks, apparently without the intention of hitting him, but merely to relieve his mind, and expand his superfluous power in wholesome exercise, aimed a blow at the bumpy head, which the bumpy head ducked to avoid. This singular performance was repeated, to the ever-increasing admiration of the spectators, at the end of every succeeding article of Mr. Pancks's oration.

"I have discharged myself from your service," said Pancks, "that I may tell you what you are. You're one of a lot of impostors that are the worst lot of all the lots to be met with. . . . You're a driver in disguise, a screwer by deputy, a wringer and squeezer and shaver by substitute! You're a philanthropic sneak! You're a shabby deceiver!"

(The repetition of the performance at this point was received with a burst of laughter.)

"Ask these good people who's the hard man here. They'll tell you Pancks, I believe."

This was confirmed with cries of "Certainly!" and "Hear!"

"But I tell you, good people, — Casby! This mound of meekness, this lump of love, this bottle-green smiler, — this is your driver!" said Pancks. "If you want to see the man who would flay you alive, here he is! Don't look for him in me, at thirty shillings a week, but look for him in Casby, at I don't know how much a year."

"Good!" cried several voices. "Hear Mr. Pancks!"

"Hear Mr. Pancks?" cried that gentleman (after repeating the popular performance), "yes, I should think so! It's almost time to hear Mr. Pancks! Mr. Pancks has come down into the yard to-night on purpose that you should hear him. Pancks is only the works; but here's the winder!"

The audience would have gone over to Mr. Pancks as one man, woman, and child, but for the long, gray, silken locks, and the broad-brimmed hat.

"Here's the stop," said Pancks, "that sets the tune to be ground. And there is but one tune, and its name is Grind, Grind, Grind! Here's the proprietor, and here's his grubber. . . . He provides the pitch, and I handle it, and it sticks to me. Now," said Mr. Pancks, closing upon his late proprietor again, from whom he had withdrawn a little for the better display of him to the yard, "as I am not accustomed to speak in public, and as I have made a rather lengthy speech, all circumstances considered, I shall bring my observations to a close by requesting you to get out of this."

The Last of the Patriarchs had been so seized by assault, and required so much room to catch an idea in, and so much more room to turn it in, that he had not a word to offer in reply. He appeared to be meditating some patriarchal way out of his delicate position, when Mr. Pancks once more, suddenly applying the trigger to his hat, shot it off again with his former dexterity. On the preceding occasion, one or two of the Bleeding-Heart-Yarders had obsequiously picked it up, and handed it to its owner; but Mr. Pancks had so far impressed his audience, that the patriarch had to turn, and stoop for it himself.

Quick as lightning, Mr. Pancks, who for some moments had had his right hand in his coat-pocket, whipped out a pair of shears, swooped upon the patriarch behind, and snipped off short the sacred locks that flowed upon his shoulders. In a paroxysm of animosity and rapidity, Mr. Pancks then caught the broad-brimmed hat out of the astounded patriarch's hand, cut it down into a mere stewpan, and fixed it on the patriarch's head.

Before the frightful results of this desperate action Mr. Pancks himself recoiled in consternation. A bare-polled, goggle-eyed, big-headed, lumbering personage stood staring at him, not in the least impressive, not in the least venerable, who seemed to have started out of the earth to ask what was become of Casby. After staring at this phantom in return, in silent awe, Mr. Pancks threw down his shears, and fled for a place of hiding, where he might lie sheltered from the consequences of his crime. Mr. Pancks deemed it prudent to use all possible despatch in making off, though he was pursued by nothing but the sound of laughter in Bleeding Heart Yard, rippling through the air, and making it ring again.

LXIX With the knowledge that although Blandois's acquaintance with Mrs. Clennam's secret perished with him, the documents from which he had learned what he knew were in safe-keeping somewhere, Little Dorrit considered it best to take Mr. Meagles partially into her confidence, and to get him to do what he could toward recovering the papers. Accordingly Mr. Meagles undertook to follow in the track of Blandois, in the hope of finding what he wished. Finally the suggestion reached him that he see Miss Wade at

Calais. He did so, but to no avail, for Miss Wade denied all knowledge of such papers as he described. Despondently, then, he crossed the Channel, only to meet Tattycoram at his hotel in London with the wished-for documents. She had overheard Miss Wade's untruth, and, feeling her heart soften toward her old benefactor, she had returned to him with the things he sought as a peace-offering.

LXX Not many days later Arthur, who was on the road to recovery, listened to Little Dorrit as she told him how the whole Dorrit property had gone in the Merdle crash. And then he realized that he might in honor take her to wife, and so it was arranged. Very opportunely, Mr. Meagles appeared at this juncture with Daniel Doyce, who had made a great success of his work abroad, and who had returned to straighten out the tangled affairs of Doyce and Clennam, with the result that Arthur was again a free man. So Arthur and Little Dorrit walked together from the prison to the church, where they were married.

---

## INDEX TO CHARACTERS

**Aunt, Mr. F.'s.** *See* MR. F.'s AUNT.

**Bangham, Mrs.** A charwoman and messenger; nurse of Mrs. Dorrit in the Marshalsea Prison. vi, vii, lv.

**Barnacle, Clarence,** *called* BARNACLE, JUNIOR. Son of Mr. Tite Barnacle; an empty-headed young gentleman employed in the Circumlocution Office. I: x, xvii, xxxiv, xxxv.

[He] had a youthful aspect, and the fluffiest little whisker, perhaps, that ever was seen. Such a downy tip was on his callow chin, that he seemed half fledged like a young bird; . . . He had a superior eyeglass dangling round his neck, but unfortunately had such flat orbits to his eyes, and such limp little eyelids, that it would n't stick in when he put it up, but kept tumbling out against his waistcoat buttons with a click that discomposed him very much.

**Barnacle, Lord Decimus Tite.** Uncle of Mr. Tite Barnacle; a windy peer, high in the Circumlocution Office.

The Circumlocution Office was (as everybody knows without being told) the most important department under government. No public business of any kind could possibly be done at any time without the acquiescence of the Circumlocution Office. Its finger was in the largest public pie and in the smallest public tart. It was equally impossible to do the plainest right, and to undo the plainest wrong, without the express authority of the Circumlocution Office. If another gunpowder plot had been discovered half an hour before the lighting of the match, nobody would have been justified in saving the Parliament until there had been half a score of boards, half a bushel of minutes, several sacks of official memoranda, and a family vault full of ungrammatical correspondence, on the part of the Circumlocution Office.

This glorious establishment had been early in the field when the one sublime principle involving the difficult art of governing a country was first distinctly revealed to statesmen. It had been foremost to study that bright revelation, and to carry its shining influence through the whole of the official proceedings. Whatever was required to be done, the Circumlocution Office was beforehand with all the public departments in the art of perceiving — HOW NOT TO DO IT. xvii, xxv, xxxiv, xliii, lx, lxiv.

**Barnacle, Ferdinand.** Private secretary to Lord Decimus Tite Barnacle; a vivacious, well-looking, well-dressed, agreeable young fellow, on the more sprightly side of the family. Arthur Clennam, wishing to investigate Mr. Dorrit's affairs, with the view of releasing him, if possible, from the Marshalsea, inquires of Barnacle how he can obtain information as to the real state of the case.

"You'll find out what department the contract was in, and then you'll find out all about it there."

"I beg your pardon. How shall I find out?"

"Why, you'll — you'll ask till they tell you. Then you'll memorialize that department (according to regular forms which you'll find out) for leave to memorialize this department. If you get it (which you may, after a time), that memorial must be entered in that department, sent to be registered in this department, sent back to be signed by that department, sent back to be countersigned by this department, and then it will begin to be regularly before that department. You'll find out when the business passes through each of these stages by asking at both departments till they tell you."

"But surely this is not the way to do the business," Arthur Clennam could not help saying.

This airy young Barnacle was quite entertained by his simplicity in supposing for a moment that it was. This light-in-hand young Barnacle knew perfectly that it was not. This touch-and-go young Barnacle had "got up" the department in a private secretaryship, that he might be ready for any little bit of fat that came to hand; and he fully understood the department to be a politico-diplomatico-hocus-pocus piece of machinery for the assistance of the nobs in keeping off the snobs. The dashing young Barnacle, in a word, was likely to become a statesman, and to make a figure.

"When the business is regularly before that department, whatever it is," pursued this bright young Barnacle, "then you can watch it from time to time through that department. When it comes regularly before this department, then you must watch it from time to time through this department. We shall have to refer it right and left; and, when we refer it anywhere, then you 'll have to look it up. When it comes back to us at any time, then you had better look *us* up. When it sticks anywhere, you 'll have to try to give it a jog. When you write to another department about it, and then to this department about it, and don't hear anything satisfactory about it, why, then you had better — keep on writing." xxxiv, xlviii, lxiv.

**Barnacle, Mr. Tite.** A man of family, a man of place, and a man of a gentlemanly residence, who usually coaches or crams the statesman at the head of the Circumlocution Office. ix, x, xxxiv, xlviii.

**Beadle, Harriet,** *called* TATTYCORAM. A girl taken from the Foundling Hospital by Mr. Meagles to be a maid to his daughter Minnie. She is a handsome girl, but headstrong and passionate. Mr. Meagles takes great pains to improve her disposition and character, and always advises her, when she is not in a good temper, to "take a little time," and to "count five and twenty." She proves insensible, however, to all his goodness and kind consideration, runs away after a time, and places herself under the protection of a certain Miss Wade; but in the end she returns, humble and penitent, to her benefactor's house.

"She was called, in the institution, Harriet Beadle, — an arbitrary name, of course. Now Harriet we changed into Hatty, and then into Tatty, because, as practical people, we thought even a playful name might be a new thing to her, and might have a softening and affectionate kind of effect; don't you see? As to Beadle, that I need n't say was wholly out of the question. If there is anything that is not to be tolerated on any terms; anything that is a type of Jack-in-office insolence and absurdity; anything that represents in coats, waistcoats, and big sticks, our English holding-on by nonsense after every one has found it out — it is a Beadle. . . . The name of Beadle being out of the question, and the originator of the institution for these poor foundlings having been a blessed creature of the name of Coram, we gave that name to Pet's little maid. At one time she was Tatty, and at one time she was Coram, until we got into a way of mixing the two names together; and now she is always Tattycoram." ii, xvi, xxvii, xxviii, xlv, xlvi, lvi, lxix.

**Blandois.** *See* RIGAUD.

**Bob.** Turnkey of the Marshalsea Prison; godfather to Little Dorrit. vi, vii, lv.

**Casby, Christopher.** Landlord of Bleeding Heart Yard; a selfish, crafty impostor, who likes to be thought a benefactor to his species, and who grinds his tenants by proxy.

Patriarch was the name which many people delighted to give him. Various old ladies in the neighborhood spoke of him as The Last of the Patriarchs. So gray, so slow, so quiet, so impassionate, so very bumpy in the head, Patriarch was the word for him. . . . His smooth face had a bloom upon it like ripe wall-fruit. What with his blooming face, and that head, and his blue eyes, he seemed to be delivering sentiments of rare wisdom and virtue. In like manner, his physiognomical expression seemed to teem with benignity. Nobody could have said where the wisdom was, or where the virtue was, or where the benignity was; but they all seemed to be somewhere about him. xii, xiii, xxiii, xxiv, xxxv, xlv, lix, lxviii.

**Cavalletto, John Baptist.** A fellow-prisoner with Rigaud at Marseilles; afterwards in Arthur Clennam's employ, and of use to him in discovering that person.

A sunburnt, quick, lithe little man, though rather thick-set. Ear-rings in his brown ears, white teeth lighting up his grotesque brown face, intensely black hair clustering about his brown throat. i, xi, xxiii, xxv, xxix, xlviii, lviii, lix, lxiv, lxvi.

**Chivery, John.** A non-resident turnkey of the Marshalsea Prison. xviii, xix, xxii, xxv, xxxi, xxxv, xxxvi, liv, lxii, lxiii, lxv, lxvii, lxx.

**Chivery, Young John.** His son; a lover of Little Dorrit.

Young John was small of stature, with rather weak legs, and very weak light hair. One of his eyes was also weak, and looked larger than the other, as if it could n't collect itself. Young John was gentle likewise. But he was great of soul; poetical, expansive, faithful. xviii, xix, xxii, xxv, xxxi, xxxv, xxxvi, liv, lv, lxii, lxiii, lxv, lxvii, lxix, lxx.

**Chivery, Mrs.** Wife of John Chivery, and keeper of a small tobacco-shop round the corner of Horsemonger Lane. xviii, xxii, xxv.

**Clennam, Arthur.** Reputed son, but really the adopted son, of Mrs. Clennam. He gives this account of himself to Mr. Meagles: —

"I am the son of a hard father and mother. I am the only child of parents who weighed, measured, and priced everything;

for whom what could not be weighed, measured, and priced, had no existence. Strict people, as the phrase is, professors of a stern religion, their very religion was a gloomy sacrifice of tastes and sympathies that were never their own, offered up as a part of a bargain for the security of their possessions. Austere faces, inexorable discipline, penance in this world and terror in the next, nothing graceful or gentle anywhere, and the void in my cowed heart everywhere, — this was my childhood, if I may so misuse the word as to apply it to such a beginning of life."

At the age of twenty he had been sent to China to join his father, a merchant who had been living in that country for some years, taking care of the business there, while his mother managed the business at home. He stays there till he is forty, and, his father then dying, he returns to London to see his mother; but she receives him very coldly, as her old servant and confidential adviser Flintwinch also does. Finding a young woman in the house, who is called "Little Dorrit," and who is employed by his mother to do needle-work, and feeling a growing interest in her, he ascertains her history, and is the means of her father's release from the Marshalsea. Being afterwards unfortunate in business, he is arrested for debt, and is thrown into the same prison; but he finds a fast friend in Little Dorrit, and, when he at last gains his liberty, she marries him. ii, iii, v, vii–x, xii–xvii, xxii, xxiv–xxviii, xxxi, xxxii, xxxiv–xxxvi, xxxix, xl, xliv–xlvii, xlix, lvi, lviii, lix, lxii–lxx.

**Clennam, Mrs.** The supposed mother of Arthur Clennam, who turns out, however, to have been the child of another woman, whom his father had known before marrying Mrs. Clennam. She is a hard, stern woman, with cold gray eyes, cold gray hair, and an immovable face. Though an invalid, who has lost the use of her limbs, and is confined to a single room, she retains the full vigor of her mind, and is still, as she has always been, a thorough woman of business. An austere moralist, a religionist whose faith is in a system of gloom and darkness, of vengeance and destruction, she yet does not hesitate to suppress a will by virtue of which two thousand guineas were to go to Little Dorrit on her coming of age. Finding that her guilt has been discovered, and is certain to be made known, she throws herself on the mercy of the girl she has so grievously wronged, and is freely forgiven. iii–v, viii, xv, xxix, xxx, xlvi, liii, lix, lxiv, lxvi, lxvii.

**Cripples, Master.** A white-faced boy, son of Mr. Cripples. ix.

**Cripples, Mr.** Teacher of an academy for "evening tuition." ix.

**Dawes.** A rosy-faced, gay good-humored nurse, who is Miss Wade's special antipathy. lvii.

**Dorrit, Amy,** *called* LITTLE DORRIT. Daughter of Mr. William Dorrit. She becomes the wife of Arthur Clennam. iii, v–ix, xii–xvi, xviii–xxv, xxvii, xxix, xxxi, xxxii, xxxv, xxxvi, xxxvii–xliv, xlvii, l, li, lv, lx, lxii, lxiii, lxv–lxvii, lxix, lxx.

**Dorrit, Edward,** *called* TIP. The brother of Little Dorrit; a spendthrift and an idler, for whom his sister is always calculating and planning.

Tip tired of everything. . . . His small second mother [his sister Amy] got him into a warehouse, into a market-garden, into the hop-trade, into the law again, into an auctioneer's, into a brewery, into a stockbroker's, into the law again, into a coach-office, into a wagon-office, into the law again, into a general dealer's, into a distillery, into the law again, into a wool-house, into a dry-goods-house, into the Billingsgate trade, into the foreign fruit-trade, and into the docks. But whatever Tip went into, he came out of tired, announcing that he had cut it. vi–viii, xii, xviii, xx, xxii, xxxi, xxxv, xxxvi, xxxvii, xxxix, xli, xlvii, li, lv, lx, lxv, lxix, lxx.

**Dorrit, Fanny.** Daughter of Mr. William Dorrit, and elder sister of Amy, or "Little Dorrit." She is, for a time, a ballet-dancer, but finally marries Mr. Edmund Sparkler, and rules him with a rod of iron. vi–ix, xviii, xx, xxxi, xxxv, xxxvi, xxxvii–xxxix, xli–xliii, xlvii, l–lii, liv, lv, lx, lxix, lxx.

**Dorrit, Mr. Frederick.** Brother to Mr. William Dorrit.

There was a ruined uncle in the family group, — ruined by his brother, the Father of the Marshalsea, and knowing no more how than his ruiner did, but accepting the fact as an inevitable certainty. Naturally a retired and simple man, he had shown no particular sense of being ruined at the time when that calamity fell upon him, further than that he left off washing himself when the shock was announced, and never took to that luxury any more. He had been a very indifferent musical amateur in his better days, and, when he fell with his brother, resorted, for support, to playing a clarionet as dirty as himself in a small theatre orchestra. vii–ix, xix, xx, xxvi, xxxvii, xl, xli, lv.

**Dorrit, Mr. William.** A prisoner for debt in the Marshalsea; a shy, retiring man, well-looking, though in an effeminate style, with a mild voice, curling hair, and irresolute hands.

The affairs of this debtor were perplexed by a partnership of which he knew no more than that he had invested money in it; by legal matters of assignment and settlement, conveyance here and conveyance there, suspicion of unlawful preference of creditors in this direction, and of mysterious spiriting away of property in that: and as nobody on the face of the earth could be more incapable of explaining any single item in the heap of confusion than the debtor himself, nothing comprehensible could be made of his case. To question him in detail, and endeavor to reconcile his answers, to closet him with accountants and sharp practitioners learned in the wiles of insolvency and bankruptcy, was only to put the case out at compound interest of incomprehensibility. The irresolute fingers fluttered more and more ineffectually about the trembling lip on every such occasion, and the sharpest practitioners gave him up as a hopeless job.

His young wife joins him with their two children; and in a few months another child is born to them, a girl, from whom the story takes its name. When this child is eight years old, his wife dies. Years pass by, and he becomes gray-haired and venerable, and is known in the prison as the Father of the Marshalsea, — a title he grows to be very vain of. From an early period, his little daughter devotes herself to the task of being his support and protection, becoming, in all things but precedence, the head of the fallen family, and bearing in her own heart its anxieties and shames. After twenty-five years spent within the prison walls, Mr. Dorrit proves to be heir at law to a great estate that has long remained, unknown of, unclaimed and accumulating. He leaves the Marshalsea a rich man, but that quarter of a century behind its bars has done its work, and he leaves it with a failing intellect, and makes himself ridiculous by his pride, by the lofty airs he gives himself, and by his unwillingness to recall at any time the old days of his poverty and confinement. He declines slowly but surely, and at last dies in a palace at Rome, fancying it to be the Marshalsea. vi–ix, xviii, xix, xxii, xxiii, xxxi, xxxii, xxxv, xxxvi, xxxvii–xxxix, xli–xliii, xlviii, xlix, li–lv.

**Doyce, Daniel.** An engineer and inventor, who becomes the partner of Arthur Clennam. x, xii, xvi, xvii, xxiii, xxvi, xxviii, xxxiv, xliv, xlix, lviii, lxii, lxx.

**F.'s Aunt, Mr.** *See* Mr. F.'s Aunt.

**Finching, Mrs. Flora.** Daughter of Christopher Casby; a wealthy widow of some thirty-eight or forty years of age, sentimental and affected, but thoroughly good-hearted. She talks with the most disjointed volubility, pointing her conversation with nothing but commas, and very few of them. xiii, xxiii, xxiv, xxxv, xlv, liii, lix, lxx.

**Flintwinch, Affery.** An old servant of Mrs. Clennam's; wife of Jeremiah Flintwinch. She is apt to fall into a dreamy sleep-waking state, much to the displeasure of her husband, who tells her, "If you ever have a dream of this sort again, it 'll be a sign of your being in want of physic, and I 'll give you such a dose, old woman, — such a dose!" iii–v, xv, xxix, xxx, xlvi, liii, lix, lxvi, lxvii.

**Flintwinch, Ephraim.** A lunatic-keeper; Jeremiah's "double" and confederate. iv, lxvi.

**Flintwinch, Jeremiah.** Servant and afterwards partner of Mrs. Clennam. He is a short, bald old man, bent and dried, with a one-sided crab-like manner of locomotion.

His neck was so twisted, that the knotted ends of his white cravat usually dangled under one ear; his natural acerbity and energy, always contending with a second nature of habitual repression, gave his features a swollen and suffused look; and, altogether, he had a weird appearance of having hanged himself at one time or other, and of having gone about ever since, halter and all, exactly as some timely hand had cut him down. iii–v, xv, xxix, xxx, xlvi, liii, lix, lxiii, lxvi, lxvii.

**General, Mrs.** A widow-lady of forty-five, whom Mr. Dorrit engages to "form the mind" and manners of his daughters.

In person, Mrs. General, including her skirts, which had much to do with it, was of a dignified and imposing appearance; ample, rustling, gravely voluminous, always upright behind the proprieties. She might have been taken — had been taken — to the top of the Alps and the bottom of Herculaneum, without disarranging a fold in her dress, or displacing a pin. If her countenance and hair had rather a floury appearance, as though from living in some transcendently genteel mill, it was rather because she was a chalky creation altogether, than because she mended her complexion with violet-powder, or had turned gray. If her eyes had no expression, it was probably because they had nothing to express. If she had few wrinkles, it was because her mind had never traced its name or any other inscription on her face. A cool, waxy, blown-out woman, who had never lighted well. xxxvii–xli, xliii, xlviii, li, lv.

**Gowan, Henry.** An artist who marries Miss Minnie Meagles.

The Gowan family were a very distant ramification of the Barnacles; and . . . the paternal Gowan, originally attached to a legation abroad, had been pensioned off as a commissioner of nothing particular somewhere or other, and had died at his post with his drawn salary in his hand, nobly defending it to the last extremity. In consideration of this eminent public service, the Barnacle then in power had recommended the crown to bestow a pension of two or three hundred a year on his widow; to which the next Barnacle in power had added certain shady and sedate apartments in the palace at Hampton Court, where the old lady still lived, deploring the degeneracy of the times, in company with several other old ladies of both sexes. Her son Mr. Henry Gowan, inheriting from his father, the commissioner, that very questionable help in life, a very small independence, had been difficult to settle; the rather as public appointments chanced to be scarce, and his genius during his earlier manhood was of that exclusively agricultural character which applies itself to the cultivation of wild oats. At last he had declared that he would become a painter; partly because he had always had an idle knack that way, and partly to grieve the souls of the Barnacles in chief who had not provided for him. So it had come to pass successively, first, that several distinguished ladies had been frightfully shocked; then that portfolios of his performances had been handed about o' nights, and declared with ecstasy to be perfect Claudes, perfect Cuyps, perfect phenomena; then that Lord Decimus had bought his picture, and had asked the president and council to dinner at a blow, and had said with his own magnificent gravity, "Do you know, there appears to me to be really immense merit in that work?" and, in short, that people of condition had absolutely taken pains to bring him into fashion. But somehow it had all failed. The prejudiced public had stood out against it obstinately. They had determined not to admire Lord Decimus's picture. They had determined to believe, that in every service, except their own, a man must qualify himself, by striving, early and late, and by working heart and soul, might and main. xvii, xxvi, xxviii, xxxiii, xxxiv, xxxvii, xxxix–xliv, xlvii, l, liii, lvi, lvii, lxix

**Gowan, Mrs.** His mother; a courtly old lady, a little lofty in her manner. xvii, xxvi, xxxiii, xxxiv, xli, xliv.

**Gowan, Mrs. Henry.** *See* MEAGLES, MINNIE.

**Haggage, Doctor.** A poor debtor in the Marshalsea; a hoarse, puffy, red-faced, dirty, brandy-drinking, medical scarecrow, who assists Little Dorrit into the world. vi, vii.

**Jenkinson.** A messenger at the Circumlocution Office. x.

**Lagnier.** *See* RIGAUD.

**Maggy.** A grand-daughter of Mrs. Bangham's, and a *protégée* of Little Dorrit's; afterwards an assistant to Mrs. Plornish.

She was about eight and twenty, with large bones, large features, large feet and hands, large eyes, and no hair. Her large eyes were limpid and almost colorless: they seemed to be very little affected by light, and to stand unnaturally still. There was also that attentive, listening expression in her face, which is seen in the faces of the blind; but she was not blind, having one tolerably serviceable eye. Her face was not exceedingly ugly, though it was only redeemed from being so by a smile, — a good-humored smile, and pleasant in itself, but rendered pitiable by being constantly there. ix, xiv, xx, xxii, xxiv, xxxi, xxxii, xxxv, xxxvi, xxxix, xl, xlix, lxv, lxix, lxx.

**Maroon, Captain.** A horse-jockey; one of Mr. Edward Dorrit's creditors. xii.

**Marshalsea, Father of the.** *See* DORRIT, MR. WILLIAM.

**Meagles, Mr.** A retired banker, good-natured and benevolent, and always priding himself on being a practical man. ii, x, xii, xvi, xvii, xxiii, xxvi–xxix, xxxiii, xxxiv, xliv–xlvi, lxix, lxx.

**Meagles, Mrs.** His wife; a comely and healthy woman, with a pleasant English face, which, like her husband's, has been looking at homely things for five and fifty years or more, and shines with a bright reflection of them. ii, xvi, xvii, xxviii, xxxiii, xxxiv, xliv, xlv, lxix, lxx.

**Meagles, Minnie,** *called* PET. Their daughter; afterwards the wife of Mr. Henry Gowan.

Pet was about twenty, — a fair girl with rich brown hair hanging free in natural ringlets; a lovely girl, with a frank face and wonderful eyes, so large, so soft, so bright, set to such perfection in her kind, good head! She was round and fresh and dimpled and spoilt, and there was in Pet an air of timidity and dependence which was the best weakness in the world, and gave her the only crowning charm a girl so pretty and pleasant could have been without. ii, xvi, xvii, xxvi, xxviii, xxxiv, xxxvii, xxxix, xl–xliv, xlvii, lxiv, lxix.

**Merdle, Mr.** A London banker, who, after running a remarkably successful career, becomes a bankrupt and commits suicide.

Mr. Merdle was immensely rich; a man of prodigious enterprise; a Midas without the ears, who turned all he touched to gold. He was in everything good, from banking to building. He was in Parliament, of course. He was in the city necessarily. He was chairman of this, trustee of that, president of the other. The weightiest of men had said to projectors, "Now, what name have you got? Have you got Merdle?" And the reply being in the negative, had said, "Then I won't look at you." . . .

He was the most disinterested of men, — did everything for society, and got as little for himself, out of all his gain and care, as a man might.

That is to say, it may be supposed that he got all he wanted, otherwise, with unlimited wealth, he would have got it. But his desire was, to the utmost, to satisfy society (whatever that was), and take up all its drafts upon him for tribute. He did not shine in company; he had not very much to say for himself; he was a reserved man, with a broad, overhanging, watchful head, that particular kind of dull red color in his cheeks which is rather stale than fresh, and a somewhat uneasy expression about his coat-cuffs, as if they were in his confidence, and had reasons for being anxious to hide his hands. In the little he said, he was a pleasant man enough; plain, emphatic about public and private confidence, and tenacious of the utmost deference being shown by every one, in all things, to society. In this same society (if that were it which came to his dinners, and to Mrs. Merdle's receptions and concerts), he hardly seemed to enjoy himself much, and was mostly to be found against walls, and behind doors. Also when he went out to it instead of its coming home to him, he seemed a little fatigued, and, upon the whole, rather more disposed for bed; but he was always cultivating it, nevertheless, and always moving in it, and always laying out money on it with the greatest liberality. xxi, xxxiii, xli, xliii, xlviii–lii, liv, lv, lx, lxi, lxiv.

**Merdle, Mrs.** His wife, and the mother of Mr. Edmund Sparkler; a very fashionable lady.

The lady was not young and fresh from the hand of Nature, but was young and fresh from the hand of her maid. She had large, unfeeling, handsome eyes, and dark, unfeeling, handsome hair, and a broad, unfeeling, handsome bosom, and was made the most of in every particular. Either because she had a cold, or because it suited her face, she wore a rich white fillet tied over her head, and under her chin. And if ever there were an unfeeling, handsome chin, that looked as if, for certain, it had never been, in familiar parlance, "chucked" by the hand of man, it was the chin curbed up so tight and close by that laced bridle. xx, xxi, xxxiii, xxxix, xli, xliii, xlviii, l–lii, lv, lx, lxi, lxix.

**Mr. F.'s Aunt.** A singular old lady, who is a legacy left to Mrs. Flora Finching by her deceased husband.

This was an amazing little old woman, with a face like a staring wooden doll (too cheap for expression), and a stiff yellow wig perched unevenly on the top of her head, as if the child who owned the doll had driven a tack through it anywhere, so that it only got fastened on. Another remarkable thing in this little old woman was, that the same child seemed to have damaged her face in two or three places with some blunt instrument in the nature of a spoon; her countenance, and particularly the tip of her nose, presenting the phenomena of several dints, generally answering to the bowl of that article. A further remarkable thing in this little old woman was, that she had no name but Mr. F.'s Aunt.

The major characteristics discoverable by the stranger in Mr.

F.'s Aunt were extreme severity and grim taciturnity, sometimes interrupted by a propensity to offer remarks, in a deep warning voice, which, being totally uncalled for by anything said by anybody, and traceable to no association of ideas, confounded and terrified the mind. Mr. F.'s Aunt may have thrown in these observations on some system of her own, and it may have been ingenious, or even subtle; but the key to it was wanted. xiii, xxiii, xxiv, xxxv, xl, lxx.

**Nandy, John Edward.** Father to Mrs. Plornish; an old man with a weak, piping voice, though his daughter considers him "a sweet singer." xiii, xlix, lxii, lxiii.

**Pancks, Mr.** Mr. Casby's collector of rents.

He was [a short, dark man] dressed in black and rusty iron-gray; had jet black beads of eyes, a scrubby little black chin, wiry black hair, striking out from his head in prongs, like forks or hair-pins, and a complexion that was very dingy by nature, or very dirty by art, or a compound of nature and art. He had dirty hands and dirty broken nails, and looked as if he had been in the coal; he was in a perspiration, and snorted and sniffed and puffed and blew like a little laboring steam-engine.

Though the agent of a man who, despite his benevolent and patriarchal air, is a hard, avaricious old sinner, and though, in accordance with his instructions, he periodically squeezes and harasses his employer's tenants, he is by no means a cruel or ungenerous man. xii, xiii, xxiii–xxv, xxvii, xxix, xxxii, xxxiv, xxxv, xlv, xlvii, xlix, liii, lvi, lviii, lxii, lxiv–lxvi, lxviii, lxx.

**Patriarch, The.** *See* CASBY, CHRISTOPHER.

**Pet.** *See* MEAGLES, MINNIE.

**Plornish, Mr.** A plasterer living in Bleeding Heart Yard; one of Mr. Casby's tenants, and a friend of Little Dorrit's; a smooth-cheeked, fresh-colored, sandy-whiskered man of thirty; long in the legs, yielding at the knees, foolish in the face, flannel-jacketed, lime-whitened. vi, ix, xii, xxiii, xxiv, xxxi, xxxvi, xl, xlix, lxiii, lxv.

**Plornish, Mrs.** His wife; a young woman, made somewhat slatternly in herself and her belongings by poverty; and so dragged at by poverty and the children together, that their united forces have already dragged her face into wrinkles. vi, xii, xxiii, xxxi, xl, xlix, lxii, lxiii, lxv, lxvi.

**Rigaud,** *alias* BLANDOIS, *alias* LAGNIER. A *chevalier d'industrie,* with polished manners, but a scoundrel's heart. Having murdered his wife, and been lodged in a French jail, he contrives to effect his escape, and flees to England. Gaining a knowledge of Mrs. Clennam's frauds, he tries to wring from her a very large amount of hush-money, but is killed by the sudden falling of the house in which he is waiting for her.

His eyes, too close together, . . . were sharp rather than bright. . . . They had no depth or change: they glittered, and they opened and shut. So far, and waiving their use to himself, a clockmaker could have made a better pair. He had a hook nose, handsome after its kind, but too high between the eyes by probably just as much as his eyes were too near to one another. For the rest, he was large and tall in frame, had thin lips (where his thick mustache showed them at all), and a quantity of dry hair, of no definable color in its shaggy state, but shot with red. i, xi, xxix, xxx, xxxvii, xxxix, xlii, xliii, xlv, xlvi, liii, lvi, lviii, lix, lxiv, lxvi, lxvii, lxix.

**Rugg, Miss Anastasia.** Daughter of Mr. Rugg. She has little nankeen spots, like shirt-buttons, all over her face; and her yellow tresses are rather scrubby than luxuriant.

Miss Rugg was a lady of a little property, which she had acquired, together with much distinction in the neighborhood, by having her heart severely lacerated, and her feelings mangled, by a middle-aged baker [named Hawkins], resident in the vicinity, against whom she had, by the agency of Mr. Rugg, found it necessary to proceed at law to recover damages for a breach of promise of marriage. The baker having been, by the counsel for Miss Rugg, witheringly denounced on that occasion up to the full amount of twenty guineas, at the rate of about eighteenpence an epithet, and having been cast in corresponding damages, still suffered occasional prosecution from the youth of Pentonville; but Miss Rugg, environed by the majesty of the law, and having her damages invested in the public securities, was regarded with consideration. xxv, lxii, lxiv.

**Rugg, Mr.** A general agent, accountant, and collector of debts, who is Mr. Pancks's landlord. He has a round, white visage, — as if all his blushes had been drawn out of him long ago, — and a ragged yellow head like a worn-out hearth-broom. xxv, xxxii, xxxv, xxvi, lxii, lxiv, lxx.

**Sparkler, Mr. Edmund.** Son of Mrs. Merdle by her first husband. He marries Fanny Dorrit, considering her to be "a young lady with no nonsense about her."

Mrs. Merdle's first husband had been a colonel, under whose auspices the bosom had entered into competition with the snows of North America, and had come off at little disadvantage in point of whiteness, and at none in point of coldness. The colonel's son was Mrs. Merdle's only child. He was of a chuckle-headed, high-shouldered make, with a general appearance of being not so much a young man as a swelled boy. He had given so few signs of reason, that a byword went among his companions, that his brain had been frozen up in a mighty frost which prevailed at St. John, New Brunswick, at the period of his birth there, and had never thawed from that hour. Another byword represented him as having in his infancy, through the negligence of a nurse, fallen out of a high window on his head, which had been heard, by responsible witnesses, to crack. It is probable that both these representations were of *ex post facto* origin; the young gentleman (whose expressive name was Sparkler) being monomaniacal in offering marriage to all manner of undesirable young ladies, and in remarking of every successive young lady to whom he tendered a matrimonial proposal, that she was "a doosed fine gal, well educated too, with no biggodd nonsense about her." xx, xxi, xxxiii, xxxix, xlii, xliii, xlviii, l–lii, liv, lx, lxix.

**Sparkler, Mrs. Edmund.** *See* DORRIT, FANNY.

**Stiltstalking, Lord Lancaster.** A gray old gentleman of dignified and sullen appearance, whom the Circumlocution Office has maintained for many years as a representative of the Britannic majesty abroad.

This noble refrigerator had iced several European courts in his time, and had done it with such complete success, that the very name of Englishman yet struck cold to the stomachs of foreigners who had the distinguished honor of remembering him at a distance of a quarter of a century. xxvi.

**Tattycoram.** *See* BEADLE, HARRIET.

**Tickit, Mrs.** Mr. Meagles's cook and housekeeper. She makes Buchan's "Domestic Medicine" her constant *vade-mecum*, though she is believed never to have consulted it to the extent of a single word in her life. xvi, xxxiv, xlv, lxix.

**Tinkler.** Mr. William Dorrit's valet. xxxix, xli, li, lv.

**Tip.** *See* DORRIT, EDWARD.

**Wade, Miss.** A woman with a sullen and ungovernable temper, a self-tormentor, who fancies that wrongs and insults are heaped upon her on every side. Finding a kindred spirit in Tattycoram, the adopted child of Mr. Meagles, she entices the girl to leave that excellent couple, and live with her, and, when she has done so, makes and keeps her as miserable, suspicious, and tormenting as herself. But Tattycoram grows tired of such a life, and at length returns, repentant and grateful, to her old master and mistress.

One could hardly see the face, so still and scornful, set off by the arched dark eyebrows and the folds of dark hair, without wondering what its expression would be if a change came over it.

That it could soften or relent appeared next to impossible. That it could deepen into anger or any extreme of defiance, and that it must change in that direction, when it changed at all, would have been its peculiar impression upon most observers. It was dressed and trimmed into no ceremony of expression. Although not an open face, there was no pretence in it. I am self-contained and self-reliant; your opinion is nothing to me; I have no interest in you, care nothing for you, and see and hear you with indifference, — this it said plainly. It said so in the proud eyes, in the lifted nostril, in the handsome but compressed and even cruel mouth. Cover either two of those channels of expression, and the third would have said so still. Mask them all, and the mere turn of the head would have shown an unsubduable nature. ii, xvi, xxvii, xxviii, xlv, xlvi, lvi, lvii, lxix.

**Wobbler, Mr.** A functionary in the secretarial department of the Circumlocution Office. x.

# A TALE OF TWO CITIES

## OUTLINE

### BOOK THE FIRST: RECALLED TO LIFE

Chapter I It is likely enough that on the very day when this story opens, there were sheltered in the rough outhouses of some tillers of the heavy lands adjacent to Paris, rude carts bespattered with rustic mire and roosted in by poultry which the farmer, Death, had already set apart to be his tumbrils of the Revolution. For it
II was the year 1775. It was a cold, wet night in November, and the Dover mail had just surmounted a long, steep hill, when a horseman, galloping fast and furious, overtook it.

"So-ho!" roared the guard, as loud as he could, for it was a time when highwaymen were numerous and desperate, and he raised his blunderbuss. "Yo, there! Stand, or I shall fire!" The horseman pulled up suddenly, and cried out that he was Jerry Cruncher, and that he had a message from Tellson's Bank for Mr. Jarvis Lorry, one of the passengers. The message, read by the light of the coach lamp, was to the effect that Mr. Lorry would be joined at Dover by a young lady, who would accompany him to Paris; and the answer given verbally was this, "Recalled to life." "Recalled to life," muttered Jerry Cruncher, whose voice was uncommonly hoarse, and whose fingers seemed to be red with iron rust. "I say, Jerry. You 'd be in a blazing bad way if recalling to life was to come into fashion, Jerry."

III At Dover, divested of his shawls and wrappers, Mr. Lorry, as he sat in the coffee-room sipping his wine before a sea-coal fire, proved to be a middle-aged, kindly man, neatly dressed in a
IV brown suit, and wearing a small wig. Presently it was announced that Miss Manette, the young lady of Jerry Cruncher's message, was ready to receive him; and, entering her room, he saw a short, slight, pretty figure, a quantity of golden hair, a pair of blue eyes, and a forehead with a singular capacity of lifting and knitting itself into an expression that was not quite one of perplexity, or wonder, or alarm, or merely of a bright, fixed attention, though it included all four expressions. Miss Manette had been brought from Paris to London in Mr. Lorry's arms fifteen years

before; and ever since, her father, whom she supposed to be dead, had been a prisoner in the Bastille. Recently he had been released, and he was now in the hands of a former servant, until Mr. Lorry and his daughter should come for him. All this Mr. Lorry broke to the girl as gently as he could, but at the end she fainted. Thereupon appeared her companion, Miss Pross, always in a state of excitement, sometimes suppressed, and sometimes not.

"Why don't you go and fetch things?" cried Miss Pross to the inn-servants. "Smelling salts, cold water, vinegar, quick! And you in brown," she said indignantly, turning to Mr. Lorry, "do you call this being a banker?"

V However, Miss Manette soon recovered, and she, Miss Pross,
and Mr. Lorry crossed over to France; and there, in an upper room in the house of one Defarge, a wine-seller, they found Dr. Manette, a white-haired man, sitting on a low stool, very busy making shoes. That he was now free he could not realize; nor did he recognize those about him. But at last his daughter's voice, or the touch of her hand, or the sight of her rippling hair, seemed to awake in him some faint recollection; and then, recalled to life, Dr. Manette, with his shoemaker's tools, was brought to London.

### BOOK THE SECOND: THE GOLDEN THREAD

Chapter Five years later, — and the reader must remember that
I these were days of frequent hangings, of jail fevers, of drawing and quartering, of a populace to whom the execution of a fel-
II low-being was a source of amusement, — a young man was
on trial for his life at the Old Bailey. He was charged with carrying messages between the enemies of the king in London and in Paris; and among the witnesses summoned, most unwillingly, to give evidence against him were Dr. Manette, now restored to reason, and his daughter. They testified to having met Charles Darnay (so he was called, though his real name was Evrémonde) on the Dover packet upon a certain night in November; and two spies, John
III Barsad and Roger Cly, swore that at this time Darnay was
carrying treasonable papers, which they produced in court. Altogether, the shadow of death seemed to be descending upon the prisoner, a handsome young man of five and twenty, who stood, pale and composed, in the dock, while the great throng of people in the court-room gazed hungrily at him, when a strange diversion was made in his favor. Within the bar, among the other barristers, with his hands in his pockets and his eyes fixed upon the ceiling, sat one Sydney Carton, a man of about the prisoner's age, and astonishingly like him in face and figure, except that he had a rakish, careless air, which Darnay had not.

At a hint from Carton the prisoner's counsel, who was cross-examining the spy, said, "You are quite sure that it *was* the prisoner?" The witness was quite sure. "You never saw anybody closely resembling him?" No, the witness never had. "Look well upon that gentleman, my learned friend there," pointing to Sydney Carton, "and then answer my question again." Carton arose, doffed his wig, and, his expression being now more serious, the great resemblance between him and the prisoner was apparent to everybody in the court-room. Darnay's counsel followed up this advantage, compelling the spy to admit that what happened once might happen twice; that if he had seen the two men together before he could not have been so sure in his identification of the prisoner, and so forth. In short, this important witness for the prosecution was riddled, and Darnay was acquitted.

IV That night Darnay and Sydney Carton supped together, and Carton, as was his habit, drank heavily. As they were about to part, Carton said: "A last word, Mr. Darnay: you think I am drunk?" "I think you have been drinking, Mr. Carton." "'Think.' You know I have been drinking." "Since I must say so, I know it." "Then you shall likewise know why. I am a disappointed drudge, sir. I care for no man on earth, and no man on earth cares for me."

V Dr. Manette and his daughter, with the faithful Miss Pross, had established themselves in a quiet corner of London, and the doctor had resumed the practice of medicine. Mr. Lorry
VI was a frequent visitor at the house, and one night he, Charles Darnay, and Sydney Carton all met there, — for the last time.

On the morning after this little gathering of friends in London,
VII a certain Monsieur the Marquis, uncle of Charles Darnay, set out from Paris for his chateau. His carriage was driven at reckless speed through the city, — so the nobility always drove, — and presently there came a sickening little jolt; there was a loud cry; the carriage stopped. A tall man in a nightcap had caught up a bundle from among the feet of the horses, and was down in the mud and wet, howling over it like a wild animal. "Why does he make that abominable noise?" asked the Marquis. "Is it his child?" "Excuse me, Monsieur the Marquis," said a ragged and submissive laborer, who stood by, — "it is a pity — yes." The Marquis flung a gold piece at the father, and the carriage rolled quickly away. But there was now something attached to the vehicle that had not been there before, — a dark object that hung in the chains underneath, and looked not unlike the figure of a man. Mile after mile, over dusty roads, rolled the carriage, the Marquis reclining

luxuriously on the cushions, until, toward the close of a beautiful
summer's day, he approached his own estate. And now the carriage
slowly ascended a long hill, and Jacques, in a blue cap, a mender
of roads, gazed with open mouth at some object beneath it, as it
VIII passed him. "He was" — so Jacques related the next day to
his fellow-peasants — "he was whiter than the miller. All
covered with dust, white as a spectre, tall as a spectre." But there
was nothing there when the carriage passed through the village,
and certainly there was nothing there when it drew up in the quiet
courtyard of the chateau. By midnight the Marquis had gone to
IX sleep in his cool chamber; everybody was asleep; and there
was no sound in the courtyard except that of the fountain
plashing softly in the moonlight. But before morning a tall man,
pale, and covered with dust, stole into the house, and plunged a
knife in the heart of Monsieur the Marquis.

X Charles Darnay, the heir of the Marquis, renouncing his inheritance, remained in London, and taught French for his
support. But he was not the only suitor for the hand of Miss Ma-
XI nette. Stryver, his counsel in the trial, also had designs in
that quarter, and had it not been for Mr. Lorry, would have
XII incurred the ignominy of a refusal. "This is something
new to me, Mr. Lorry. You deliberately advise me not to
offer myself, *myself*, Stryver, of the King's Bench bar." But, unprepared as he was for the large pill that he had to swallow, Mr.
Stryver got it down, and retired from the field. Carton, too, was
sometimes at Dr. Manette's house, — the same moody and morose
lawyer as always. But often, late at night, when the lights were
out in the doctor's house, Sydney Carton wandered there, as if he
loved the very streets that environed it, and the senseless stones
that made their pavements.

On a day in August, . . . Sydney's feet . . . became animated by an intention; and, in the working-out of that intention, they took him to the doctor's door.

He was shown up stairs, and found Lucie at her work alone. She had never been quite at her ease with him, and received him with some little embarrassment as he seated himself near her table. But, looking up at his face in the interchange of the first few commonplaces, she observed a change in it.

"I fear you are not well, Mr. Carton."

"No. But the life I lead, Miss Manette, is not conducive to health. What is to be expected of or by such profligates?"

"Is it not — forgive me; I have begun the question on my lips — a pity to live no better life?"

"God knows it is a shame!"

"Then why not change it?"

Looking gently at him again, she was surprised and saddened to see that there were tears in his eyes. There were tears in his voice too, as he answered: —

"It is too late for that. I shall never be better than I am. I shall sink lower, and be worse."

He leaned his elbow on her table, and covered his eyes with his hand. The table trembled in the silence that followed.

She had never seen him softened, and was much distressed. He knew her to be so without looking at her, and said: —

"Pray, forgive me, Miss Manette. I break down before the knowledge of what I want to say to you. Will you hear me?"

"If it will do you any good. Mr. Carton, if it would make you happier, it would make me very glad."

"God bless you for your sweet compassion!"

He unshaded his face after a little while, and spoke steadily.

"Don't be afraid to hear me. Don't shrink from anything I say. I am like one who died young. All my life might have been."

"No, Mr. Carton. I am sure that the best part of it might still be; I am sure that you might be much, much worthier of yourself."

"Say of you, Miss Manette; and although I know better — although in the mystery of my own wretched heart, I know better — I shall never forget it."

She was pale and trembling. He came to her relief with a fixed despair of himself, which made the interview unlike any other that could have been holden.

"If it had been possible, Miss Manette, that you could have returned the love of the man you see before you — self-flung away, wasted, drunken, poor creature of misuse as you know him to be — he would have been conscious this day and hour, in spite of his happiness, that he would bring you to misery, bring you to sorrow and repentance, blight you, disgrace you, pull you down with him. I know very well that you can have no tenderness for me; I ask for none; I am even thankful that it cannot be."

"Without it, can I not save you, Mr. Carton? Can I not recall you — forgive me again! — to a better course? Can I in no way repay your confidence? I know this is a confidence," she modestly said after a little hesitation, and in earnest tears. "I know you would say this to no one else. Can I turn it to no good account for yourself, Mr. Carton?"

He shook his head.

"To none. No, Miss Manette, to none. If you will hear me through a very little more, all you can ever do for me is done.

I wish you to know that you have been the last dream of my soul. In my degradation I have not been so degraded, but that the sight of you with your father, and of this home (made such a home by you), has stirred old shadows that I thought had died out of me. Since I knew you I have been troubled by a remorse that I thought would never reproach me again, and have heard whispers from old voices impelling me upward, that I thought were silent forever. I have had unformed ideas of striving afresh, beginning anew, shaking off sloth and sensuality, and fighting out the abandoned fight. A dream, all a dream, that ends in nothing, and leaves the sleeper where he lay down; but I wish you to know that you inspired it."

"Will nothing of it remain? O Mr. Carton! think again, try again."

"No, Miss Manette: all through it I have known myself to be quite undeserving. And yet I have had the weakness, and have still the weakness, to wish you to know with what a sudden mastery you kindled me, heap of ashes that I am, into fire, — a fire, however, inseparable in its nature from myself, quickening nothing, lighting nothing, doing no service, idly burning away. . . . Let me carry through the rest of my misdirected life the remembrance that I opened my heart to you last of all the world; and that there was something left in me at this time which you could deplore and pity."

XIII Meanwhile Tellson's Bank still stood in London, and Jerry
Cruncher, the messenger, still sat on his stool in front of it.
One day there came by the bank the funeral procession of Roger
XIV Cly, one of the two spies who had sworn falsely at the trial
of Darnay. Jerry, who was always interested in funerals, was
particularly interested in this one, remembering Mr. Cly as "a young 'un and a straight made 'un." On his way home, Jerry stopped to see his medical adviser, a distinguished surgeon; and that night he went, as he said, a fishing. Mr. Cruncher started on this excursion at the peculiar hour of one A. M.; and his tackle also was peculiar, consisting of a rope, a crow-bar, and a sack. He was back at breakfast time, but without fish or anything else, and in a very bad humor.

XV The other of the two spies who had sworn against Darnay, John Barsad, appeared about this time at Paris, and
one morning he casually strolled into the wine-shop of Defarge,
XVI former servant of Dr. Manette. As he entered the shop
Madame Defarge, a large, dark-haired, handsome woman,
with a stern face, put down her knitting and, taking up a red rose which lay on the table beside her, pinned it in her hair. It was

curious, the moment Madame Defarge took up the rose, the customers ceased talking, and began gradually to drop out of the wine-shop. At last the spy and Madame Defarge were left alone. "John," thought Madame, as her fingers knitted and her eyes looked at the stranger. "Stay long enough, and I shall knit 'Barsad' before you go." "Business seems bad?" said the spy. "Business is very bad. The people are so poor." "Ah, the unfortunate, miserable people! So oppressed too, — as you say." "As *you* say," Madame retorted, correcting him, and deftly knitting an extra something into his name that boded him no good.

XVII Charles Darnay and Lucie Manette had been married
nearly two years, and a child had been born to them, when,
XVIII one hot night in mid-July, in the year 1789, Mr. Lorry came
in late from the bank. "I began to think," said he, pushing
XIX his brown wig back, "that I should have to pass the night at
Tellson's. There is such an uneasiness in Paris that our cus-
XX tomers there are all sending their property over to us." And
that very night the Bastille fell — with Defarge of the wine-
XXI shop heading the mob, which fought its way into his old
master's prison. The disturbance was not confined to Paris:
XXII on every highway leading out of the city, there was a thin
stream of fire; one such traversed the very road over which
the carriage of Monsieur the Marquis had passed two years before:
and the splendid chateau which Charles Darnay's ancestors had
XXIII built went up in flames. That same night the sky for a
hundred miles around was illuminated by similar bonfires.
Seeing these sights, the mender of roads (he of the blue cap), once so submissive to authority, remarked to M. Gabelle, the postmaster and general functionary of the village, that "carriages would burn well, and that post-horses would roast."

XXIV It was not long, indeed, before this same M. Gabelle was
taken a prisoner to Paris, where his life hung by a thread, and whence he addressed a piteous letter to Charles Darnay, the heir, begging him to come to the rescue. "My fault is," he wrote, "that I have been true to you." Darnay could not resist this appeal. Making his preparations secretly, so as not to alarm his wife and her father, he set out alone, leaving a letter to apprise them of his intention. Mr. Lorry, attended by Jerry Cruncher as body-guard, had already gone to Paris on business for Tellson's.

### BOOK THE THIRD: THE TRACK OF A STORM

Chapter Using M. Gabelle's letter as a passport, Darnay, with
I great difficulty and amid many dangers, made his way
through France toward Paris. One night he went to bed, tired

out, at a small village in the high road to the city, but still a long way from it. Soon after midnight he was rudely awakened from sleep by a timid local functionary and three armed patriots in rough red caps, and with pipes in their mouths, who sat down on the bed. "Emigrant," said the functionary, "you are an aristocrat, and must have an escort, — and must pay for it." And so Charles Darnay was taken as a prisoner to Paris, and when he reached the city, he was cast into the prison of La Force, and placed in solitary confinement, in a cell which (as he very soon discovered) measured exactly five paces by four and a half.

II Three days after Darnay's arrival at Paris, Mr. Lorry was sitting alone in his quarters at the French department of Tellson's Bank. The building stood in a sort of courtyard retired from the street. It was growing dark, and the roar of the mob in the adjacent street, the crash of buildings, the discharge of fire-arms, and the shrieks of the wounded were horrible to hear. "Thank God!" Mr. Lorry exclaimed, "that no one near and dear to me is in this dreadful town to-night." But scarcely had he said the words, when the door opened and two figures rushed in, Lucie and her father. Their errand was soon told; and in spite of Mr. Lorry's warnings, Dr. Manette was bent upon going to seek Darnay that very night. "I have a charmed life in this city," he said, "for I have been a Bastille prisoner." And so it proved, for shortly after he had passed out bareheaded among the mob, those in the house heard them cry, "Long live the Bastille prisoner! Help for the Bastille prisoner's kindred in La Force! Room for the Bastille prisoner in front there!" and a thousand answering shouts. Dr.

III Manette did not return for three days, but in the mean time Lucie received a note from her husband. This note was brought by Defarge, and with him came his wife, — knitting as ever; and Lucie, after thanking Defarge, turned to his wife and kissed one of the hands that knitted. It was a grateful, womanly action, but the hand made no response, — dropped cold and heavy, and took to its knitting again. There was something in its touch that gave Lucie a check. She stopped in the act of putting the note in her bosom, and looked terrified at Madame Defarge. Madame Defarge met the lifted eyebrows and forehead with a cold, impassive stare. "Is that his child?" said she, stopping in her work for the first time, and pointing her knitting-needle at little Lucie, as if it were the finger of Fate. "Yes, Madame," answered Mr. Lorry, — "his only child." "It is enough, my husband," said Madame Defarge. "I have seen them. We may go."

IV This life continued for one year and three months. Every day at a certain hour Lucie and her child used to go and

stand in a side street, which was in view of that part of La Force where Darnay was confined. Sometimes he could see them from a certain lofty grated window, to which occasionally he had access;
V sometimes he was locked in his cell; but they never saw him. At last, however, a day for his trial was fixed, and, as if he had been forewarned in some manner, Sydney Carton arrived in Paris, and joined the anxious group at Mr. Lorry's the night before.

VI The trial began. Charles Evrémonde, called Darnay, was charged with being an emigrant. "Off with his head," cried the audience. But when Darnay told how he had come back to save a citizen's life, and asked, "Was that criminal in the eyes of the republic?" the populace cried enthusiastically, "No!" In short, the prisoner was acquitted unanimously (each of the twelve jurors gave his vote *viva voce*), and the fickle people carried him home
VII in triumph. That evening the little family — reunited at last — were gathered before the fire. All was subdued and quiet, and Lucie's fears had begun to subside.

"What is that?" she cried all at once.

"My dear," said her father, "command yourself. What a disordered state you are in!"

"I thought," she said, "that I heard strange steps on the staircase."

"My love, the staircase is as still as death."

As he said the word, a blow was struck upon the door. Four men in red caps, and armed with sabres, entered the room. They came to arrest Darnay again.

"Who denounced him?" cried Dr. Manette.

"Citizen Defarge, his wife, and a third person whose name will remain unknown till the trial which takes place to-morrow."

VIII While this new horror was transacting, Sydney Carton met Barsad the spy, and very soon convinced him that he, Carton, knowing the spy's former history, could easily send him to the guillotine. Then there arose a question as to the other spy who also had sworn falsely against Darnay, — Roger Cly. Carton thought that he had seen him in Paris. Barsad declared that he was dead and buried in London. But hereupon Jerry Cruncher, who had been standing by unobserved, interposed, "He wan't in the coffin, — it was a take-in. Me and two more knows it?"

"How do you know it!" exclaimed the spy in astonishment.

"Never you mind," growled Mr. Cruncher. "You with your imposition on a honest tradesman!"

Thus cornered, Barsad said to Carton, "What do you want of me?"

"Come into this room alone with me," replied Carton gravely; "and I will tell you."

IX When they had gone, "Jerry," said Mr. Lorry, "come here."

Mr. Cruncher came forward sideways, with one shoulder considerably in advance of the other.

"What have you been besides a messenger?"

Jerry thought for a moment, and replied, "Agricultooral character."

"My mind misgives me much," said Mr. Lorry angrily, "that you have used the respectable and great house of Tellson's as a blind, and that you have had an unlawful occupation of an infamous character."

At this point in the conversation, Sydney Carton returned to the room, dismissing Barsad with a parting injunction whispered in his ear.

"What have you done?" asked Mr. Lorry.

"Nothing much," said Carton. "I have arranged with Barsad that, if it goes ill with the prisoner, I shall have access to him once before he dies."

Leaving Mr. Lorry, and stopping at a street lamp to write a few words on a scrap of paper, Carton sought out a small chemist's shop. He gave the scrap of paper to the chemist.

"You will be careful to keep them separate, citizen, you know the consequences of mixing them?"

"Perfectly."

Then two small packets were given to him, and he put them in his breast pocket. Sydney Carton walked the streets till morning, sober, grave, and yet not despondent, nor even sad. He thought of many things, of Lucie, of his childhood, of his father. His mother died while he was yet an infant; but as a boy, he had followed his father to the grave; and these words, read at his father's funeral, and fixed in his mind, were again and again on his lips, as he paced the dark and solitary streets. "I am the resurrection and the life, saith the Lord; he that believeth in me, though he were dead, yet shall he live; and whosoever liveth and believeth in me shall never die." When morning came, he washed and dressed himself, drank a cup of coffee, ate some bread, and was early at the scene of the trial.

"Charles Evrémonde, called Darnay. By whom is he denounced?" asked the President.

"By three persons. Ernest Defarge, wine-vender of St. Antoine."

"Good."

"Thérèse Defarge, his wife."

"Good."

"Alexander Manette, Physician."

"It is an infamous lie," cried Dr. Manette, starting to his feet, pale and trembling. The doctor was silenced and Defarge, being called as a witness, produced a paper which he had found hidden in Dr. Manette's cell in the Bastille, and which explained how he came to be imprisoned there. This paper Defarge read in the breathless silence of the court-room.

X

The paper related how, on the night of December 27, 1757, the Doctor had been taken (almost by force) by two young noblemen (whom he afterward discovered to be the Marquis of Evrémonde and his brother) to a half-furnished house in an obscure part of Paris. There he found two patients, a beautiful peasant girl dying of brain fever, and her brother, a boy of seventeen, dying from a wound inflicted by the younger Evrémonde. The boy had attempted to avenge his sister. Both perished, in spite of the doctor's attentions. He refused to accept the gold offered to him for his services; and in a letter to a minister of the crown he stated the circumstances of the case. Shortly afterward, one dark night, he was summoned to attend a patient. A coach, he was told, was in waiting. "It brought me here," so ran the paper, "it brought me to my grave. When I was clear of the house, a black muffler was drawn tightly over my mouth from behind, and my arms were pinioned. The two brothers crossed the road from a dark corner, and identified me with a single gesture."

This was the doctor's story, and it concluded as follows: "Them and their descendants, to the last of their race, I, Alexander Manette, unhappy prisoner, do this last night of the year 1767, in my unbearable agony, denounce to Heaven and to earth."

A terrible sound arose when the reading of this paper was finished, — an inarticulate cry for blood. At every juryman's vote there was a roar. Another and another. Roar and roar. Unanimously voted. At heart and by descent an Aristocrat, an oppressor of the People. Back to the Conciergerie, and Death within four and twenty hours!

XI

Lucie fell, as if she had received a mortal wound. Then, issuing from the obscure corner from which he had never moved, Sydney Carton came and took her up. His arm trembled as it raised her, and supported her head. Yet, there was an air about him that was not all of pity, that had a flash of pride in it. After he had left her, with her father and Mr. Lorry, in their lodgings, Carton paused in the street, not quite decided where to go. "It is best," he said to himself at last, "that these people should know there is such a man as I here." And he directed his steps to St.

XII

Antoine, to the wine-shop of Defarge. There, exaggerating his character as an Englishman, and pretending not to understand French, he overheard a conversation between Defarge and his wife (who noticed, by the way, his close resemblance to Darnay) in which Madame Defarge sternly demanded — and her husband weakly opposed — the destruction of Darnay's wife, of his child, and even of Dr. Manette himself. Spurred rather than terrified by this discovery, Carton went back to the house of his friends. Dr. Manette had not come in. He had been gone now more than five hours. Carton and Mr. Lorry sat in silence waiting for him. Ten o'clock struck, eleven, twelve, and still he had not come. At last they heard his step on the stairs. The instant that he came in they saw that all was lost. "I cannot find it," said he, "and I must have it." His head and throat were bare; he dropped his coat on the floor. "Where is my bench? Time presses, I must finish those shoes." And he sank into a chair, cowering, whimpering, with head and back bent, — the exact figure that Defarge had in his keeping when he was first released from the Bastille. Then Carton, explaining to Mr. Lorry the necessity for an immediate flight from Paris, arranged with him that, at two o'clock in the afternoon of the next day, Lucie, her father, her child, and Mr. Lorry should be seated in their carriage, with the horses harnessed, ready to start; and he gave Mr. Lorry his passport to keep till then. "Wait for nothing," said Carton, "but to have my place occupied, and then for England!"

XIII Very early the next morning Carton was at the prison, and Barsad — according to their agreement — admitted him to Darnay's cell. Then, partly by force, partly by persuasion, partly by his overmastering will, he induced Darnay to change clothes with him. Darnay protested that escape in that way was impossible; that Carton was only endangering his own life. But Carton made Darnay sit down and write at his dictation; he confused him with strange words and gestures; finally, he overpowered him with a vapor from a sponge which he took from his breast pocket. Darnay became insensible, and, dressed in Carton's clothes, he was carried out by the spy with the assistance of a turnkey who supposed him to be Carton.

Two hours later a jailer opened the door of the cell. "Follow me, Evrémonde," and Carton followed him, to a large, dimly lighted hall where the condemned were gathering. As he stood there in a dark corner, a young woman with a slight, girlish form, large eyes, and wan face, came up and touched him with her cold hand. "Citizen Evrémonde, I am a poor little seamstress who was with you in La Force. If I may ride with you,

SYDNEY CARTON AND THE SEAMSTRESS.

Citizen Evrémonde, will you let me hold your hand? I am not afraid, but I am little and weak, and it will give me more courage." As the patient eyes were lifted to his face, he saw a sudden doubt in them, and then astonishment. He pressed the work-worn, hunger-worn young fingers, and touched her lips.

"Are you dying for him?" she whispered.

"And for his wife and child. Hush! Yes."

"O you will let me hold your brave hand, stranger?"

"Hush! Yes! my poor sister, to the last."

XIV Meanwhile the scheme succeeds; Carton's friends escape in their coach, and Miss Pross and Jerry Cruncher are left to follow them in a light carriage. They were ready to start, and Jerry Cruncher had already gone to hasten the coming of their conveyance, when Madame Defarge, bent on some sinister errand, presented herself at the lodgings. She demanded admittance. Miss Pross, to gain time for the coach, refused, and bravely withstood her; there was a struggle, Madame Defarge's pistol went off, and she fell dead on the threshold. Miss Pross, disfigured and almost crazed, locked up the apartment, and rushed to the street; the faithful Jerry was there with the carriage, and off they went.

"Is there any noise in the streets?" she asked him.

"The usual noises," said Jerry, surprised.

"I hear nothing," said Miss Pross. "I feel as if there had been a flash and a crash, and that crash was the last thing I should ever hear in this life." And so indeed it was!

XV The coach containing Carton's friends, and the light chaise with Miss Pross and Jerry Cruncher, long since had passed in safety the barriers of Paris and were speeding toward the coast, when six tumbrils, rumbling hollow and harsh, passed out from the gates of the Conciergerie. They carried the prisoners who on that day were to be offered to the insatiable guillotine. They were twenty-three in number.

As the sombre wheels . . . go round, they seem to plough up a long crooked furrow among the populace in the streets. Ridges of faces are thrown to this side and to that, and the ploughs go steadily onward. So used are the regular inhabitants of the houses to the spectacle, that, in many windows, there are no people, and in some the occupation of the hands is not so much as suspended while the eyes survey the faces in the tumbrils. . . .

Of the riders in the tumbrils, some observe these things, and all things on their last roadside, with an impassive stare; others with a lingering interest in the ways of life and men. Some, seated with drooping heads, are sunk in silent despair; again, there are some so heedful of their looks, that they cast upon the multitude such glances as they have seen in theatres and in pictures. Several close their eyes, and think, or try to get their straying thoughts together. Only one, and he a miserable creature of a crazed aspect, is so shattered and made drunk by horror, that he sings, and tries to dance. Not one of the whole number appeals by look or gesture to the pity of the people.

There is a guard of sundry horsemen riding abreast of the tumbrils; and faces are often turned up to some of them, and they are asked some question. It would seem to be always the same question; for it is always followed by a press of people toward the third cart. The horsemen abreast of that cart frequently point out one man in it with their swords. The leading curiosity is to know which is he: he stands at the back of the tumbril with his head bent down. . . . He has no curiosity or care for the scene about him . . . . Here and there in the long street of St. Honoré, cries are raised against him. If they move him at all, it is only to a quiet smile, as he shakes his hair a little more loosely about his face. He cannot easily touch his face, his arms being bound.

On the steps of a church, awaiting the coming-up of the tumbrils, stands the spy and prison-sheep [Solomon Pross]. He looks into the first of them: not there. He looks into the second: not there. He already asks himself, "Has he sacrificed me?" when his face clears as he looks into the third.

"Which is Evrémonde?" says a man behind him.

"That. At the back there."

"With his hand in the girl's?"

"Yes."

The man cries, "Down, Evrémonde! To the guillotine all aristocrats! Down, Evrémonde!"

"Hush, hush!" the spy entreats him timidly.

"And why not, citizen?"

"He is going to pay the forfeit: it will be paid in five minutes more. Let him be at peace."

But the man continuing to exclaim, "Down, Evrémonde!" the face of Evrémonde is for a moment turned towards him. Evrémonde then sees the spy, and looks attentively at him, and goes his way. . . .

The murmuring of many voices, the upturning of many faces, the pressing-on of many footsteps in the outskirts of the crowd so that it swells forward in a mass, like one great heave of water, all flashes away. . . .

They said of him about the city, that night, that it was the peacefullest man's face ever beheld there. Many added that he looked sublime and prophetic.

---

## INDEX TO CHARACTERS

**Aggerawayter.** *See* CRUNCHER, MRS.

**Barsad, John.** *See* PROSS, SOLOMON.

**Carton, Sydney.** A dissipated, reckless drudge for Mr. Stryver; a man of good abilities and good emotions, incapable of their directed exercise, incapable of his own help and his own happiness, sensible of the blight on him, and resigning himself to let it eat him away; and yet in the end making a noble sacrifice. II: ii–vi, xi, xiii, xx, xxi; III: viii, ix, xi, xii, xiii, xv.

**Cly, Roger.** An Old Bailey spy, partner of Solomon Pross, and formerly servant to Charles Darnay. II: iii, xiv; III: viii, xv.

**Cruncher, Jerry.** An odd-job man at Tellson's Bank, in London, who is also a resurrection-man. His wife, a pious woman, is greatly distressed by her knowledge of the horrible nature of his nightly occupation; and, as her remonstrances prove to be unavailing, she resorts to prayers and supplications to Heaven to aid her in the reformation of her husband. This is very distasteful to Mr. Cruncher, — so much so, indeed, that he sometimes resorts to violence to prevent it.

Mr. Cruncher reposed under a patchwork counterpane, like a harlequin at home. At first he slept heavily, but by degrees began to roll and surge in bed, until he rose above the surface with his spiky hair looking as if it must tear the sheets to ribbons. At which juncture, he exclaimed in a voice of dire exasperation: —

"Bust me, if she ain't at it agin!"

A woman of orderly and industrious appearance rose from her knees in a corner, with sufficient haste and trepidation to show that she was the person referred to.

"What!" said Mr. Cruncher, looking out of bed for a boot. "You 're at it agin; are you?"

After hailing the morn with this second salutation, he threw a boot at the woman as a third. It was a very muddy boot, and may introduce the odd circumstance connected with Mr. Cruncher's domestic economy, that, whereas he often came home after banking-hours with clean boots, he often got up next morning to find the same boots covered with clay.

"What, said Mr. Cruncher, varying his apostrophe after missing his mark,—"what are you up to, aggerawayter?"

"I was only saying my prayers."

"Saying your prayers! You 're a nice woman! What do you mean by flopping yourself down, and praying agin me?"

"I was not praying against you: I was praying for you."

"You were n't; and, if you were, I won't be took the liberty with. Here, your mother 's a nice woman, young Jerry, going a praying agin your father's prosperity. You 've got a dutiful mother; you have, my son. You 've got a religious mother; you have, my boy: going and flopping herself down, and praying that the bread and butter may be snatched out of the mouth of her only child!"

Master Cruncher (who was in his shirt) took this very ill, and, turning to his mother, strongly deprecated any praying away of his personal board.

"And what do you suppose, you conceited female," said Mr. Cruncher with unconscious inconsistency, "that the worth of *your* prayers may be? Name the price that you put *your* prayers at."

"They only come from the heart, Jerry. They are worth no more than that."

"Worth no more than that," repeated Mr. Cruncher: "they ain't worth much, then. Whether or no, I won't be prayed agin, I tell you. I can't afford it. I 'm not a going to be made unlucky by *your* sneaking. If you must go flopping yourself down, flop in favor of your husband and child, and not in opposition to 'em. If I had had any but a unnat'ral wife, and this poor boy had had any but a unnat'ral mother, I might have made some money last week, instead of being counterprayed and countermined, and religiously circumwented into the worst of luck. Bu-u-ust me!" said Mr. Cruncher, who all this time had been putting on his clothes, "if I ain't, what with piety and one blowed thing and another, been choused this last week into as bad luck as ever a poor devil of a honest tradesman met with! Young Jerry, dress yourself, my boy, and, while I clean my boots, keep a eye upon your mother now and then, and, if you see any signs of more flopping, give me a call. For I tell you," here he addressed his wife once more, "I won't be gone agin in this manner. I am as rickety as a hackney-coach; I 'm as sleepy as laudanum; my lines is strained to that degree that I should n't know, if it was n't for the pain in 'em, which was me, and which somebody else: yet I 'm none the better for it in pocket; and it 's my suspicion that you 've been at it from morning to night to prevent me from being the better for it in pocket; and I won't put up with it, aggerawayter; and what do you say now?" . . . Mr. Cruncher betook himself to his boot-cleaning and his general preparations for business. In the mean time, his son . . . kept the required watch upon his mother. He greatly disturbed that poor woman, at intervals, by darting out of his sleeping-closet, where he made his toilet, with a suppressed cry of, "You are going to flop, mother! — Halloo, father!" and, after raising this ficticious alarm, darting in again with an undutiful grin.

Mr. Cruncher's temper was not at all improved when he came to his breakfast. He resented Mrs. Cruncher's saying grace with particular animosity.

"Now, aggerawayter, what are you up to? At it agin?"

His wife explained that she had merely "asked a blessing."

"Don't do it!" said Mr. Cruncher, looking about as if he rather expected to see the loaf disappear under the efficacy of his wife's petitions. "I ain't a going to be blest out of house and home. I won't have my wittles blest off my table. Keep still!" I: ii, iii; II: i–iii, vi, xiv, xxiv; III: vii–ix, xiv.

**Cruncher, Young Jerry.** His son and assistant.

Young Jerry, while yet a mere boy, and not in the secret of his father's night-excursions, masters the name of the business, and forms an idea of its nature. II: i, ii, xiv; III: ix.

**Cruncher, Mrs.** Wife of Jerry Cruncher; called by him "Aggerawayter." II: i, ii, xiv; III: ix, xiv.

**Darnay, Charles.** *See* St. Evrémonde, Charles.

**Darnay, Mrs. Lucie.** *See* Manette, Lucie.

**Defarge, Madame Thérèse.** Wife of Monsieur Defarge, and leader of the St. Antoine rabble of women in the Revolution. She is a stout woman, with a watchful eye that seldom seems to look at anything, a steady face, strong features, and great composure of manner. She is killed in an encounter with Miss Manette's maid, Miss Pross, who refuses to admit her into a room in which her mistress is supposed to be.

Of a strong and fearless character, of shrewd sense and readiness, of great determination, of that kind of beauty which not only seems to impart to its possessor firmness and animosity, but to strike into others an instinctive recognition of those qualities, the troubled time would have heaved her up under any circumstances; but, imbued from her childhood with a brooding sense of wrong and an inveterate hatred of a class, opportunity had developed her into a tigress. She was absolutely without pity. If she had ever had the virtue in her, it had quite gone out of her. I: v, vi; II: vii, xv, xvi, xxi, xxii; III: iii, v, vi, viii–x, xii, xiv, xv.

**Defarge, Monsieur Ernest.** Keeper of a wine-shop in the suburb of St. Antoine, in Paris, and ringleader of the revolutionists in that quarter of the city. At his house, Doctor Manette is temporarily placed after being released from the Bastille; and it is he who finds the record which the old man had written and secreted in the prison, and who produces it in court against Darnay.

This wine-shop keeper was a bull-necked, martial-looking man of thirty, and he should have been of a hot temperament; for, although it was a bitter day, he wore no coat, but carried one slung over his shoulder. His shirt-sleeves were rolled up, too, and his brown arms were bare to the elbows. Neither did he wear anything more on his head than his own crisply-curling, short dark hair. He was a dark man altogether, with good eyes, and a good bold breadth between them; good-humored-looking on the whole, but implacable-looking too; evidently a man of a strong resolution and a set purpose, — a man not desirable to be met rushing down a narrow pass with a gulf on either side; for nothing would turn the man. I: v, vi; II: vii, xv, xvi, xxi, xxii; III: i, iii, vi, ix, x, xii, xiv, xv.

**Evrémonde, Charles.** *See* ST. EVRÉMONDE, CHARLES.

**Gabelle, Monsieur Théophile.** A postmaster, and some other taxing functionary united. II: viii, ix, xxiii, xxiv; III: i, vi.

**Gaspard.** Assassin of the Marquis St. Evrémonde. I: v; II: vii, xv, xvi.

**Jacques One.** A prominent assistant of Defarge in the French Revolution. I: v; II: xv, xxi, xxiii.

**Jacques Two.** Another revolutionist, who is also an assistant of Defarge. I: v; II: xv, xxi, xxiii.

**Jacques Three.** An associate of Defarge, and a member of the revolutionary jury; a cannibal-looking, bloody-minded man. I: v; II: xv, xxi–xxiii; III: xii, xiv.

**Jacques Four.** A name given to himself by Monsieur Defarge as one of the St. Antoine revolutionists.

**Jacques Five.** An associate of Defarge; a mender of roads, afterwards a wood-sawyer. II: viii, ix, xv, xvi, xxiii; III: v, ix, xiv, xv.

**Joe.** A coachman. I: ii.

**Lorry, Mr. Jarvis.** A confidential clerk at the banking-house of Tellson and Company, in London. He is a friend of the Manettes, and their companion during the terrible scenes of the Revolution in Paris.

Very orderly and methodical he looked, with a hand on each knee, and a loud watch ticking a sonorous sermon under his flapped waistcoat, as though it pitted its gravity and longevity against the levity and evanescence of the brisk fire. He had a good leg, and was a little vain of it; for his brown stockings fitted sleek and close, and were of a fine texture: his shoes and buckles, too, though plain, were trim. He wore an odd little sleek, crisp, flaxen wig, setting very close to his head; which wig, it is to be presumed, was made of hair, but which looked far more as though it were spun from filaments of silk or glass. His linen, though not of a fineness in accordance with his stockings, was as white as the tops of the waves that broke upon the neighboring beach, or the specks of sail that glinted in the sunlight far at sea. A face habitually suppressed and quieted was still lighted up under the quaint wig by a pair of moist bright eyes, that it must have cost their owner in years gone by some pains to drill to the composed and reserved expression of Tellson's Bank. He had a healthy color in his cheeks; and his face, though lined, bore few traces of anxiety. But perhaps the confidential bachelor clerks in Tellson's Bank were principally occupied with the cares of other people; and perhaps second-hand cares, like second-hand clothes, come easily off and on. I: ii–vi; II: ii–iv, vi, xii, xvi–xxi, xxiv; III: ii–vi, viii, ix, xi–xiii, xv.

**Manette, Dr. Alexander.** A physician of Paris, confined for eighteen years in the Bastille, because, in his professional capacity, he had become acquainted with the secret crimes of a noble family. Released just before the outbreak of the Revolution, he goes to England, whither his wife and daughter had preceded him, and where the former had died. Restored to his child, who nurses him with tender solicitude, he gradually recovers the use of his faculties, which had become greatly impaired during his long imprisonment. About this time a young French nobleman, disgusted with the tyranny of the class to which he belongs, renounces his title and fortune, expatriates himself, and settles in England, where he passes under the name of Charles Darnay. He there becomes acquainted with and marries the daughter of Dr. Manette. Having been summoned back to Paris, at the outbreak of the Revolution, to release from prison, by his testimony, an old and faithful servant of his family, he is himself thrown into La Force, immediately upon his arrival, as a proscribed emigrant. His wife and her father follow him, however; and Dr. Manette, whose popularity is very high, succeeds in securing his acquittal. Yet in a few days he is re-accused and re-arrested; the charge against him being that he is an aristocrat, one of a family of tyrants, denounced enemies of the Republic; and the evidence against him is a paper written by Dr. Manette, when a prisoner in the Bastille, and secreted by him in a hole in the chimney of his cell. This document, which had been discovered at the capture of the prison, recites the story of the good doctor's sufferings, details the abominable iniquities of the St. Evrémonde family (to which Darnay belongs), and ends by denouncing them and their descendants, to the last of the race, to the times when all such things shall be answered for. Darnay is condemned to death; but, through the heroic self-devotion of Sydney Carton, he is saved from such a fate, and is taken to England by his wife and her father, where they all lead a peaceful, prosperous, and happy life, and pass at last to a tranquil death. I: ii–vi; II: ii–iv, vi, ix, x, xii, xiii, xvi–xxi, xxiv; III: ii–vii, ix–xii, xiv, xv.

**Manette, Lucie.** His daughter; afterwards the wife of Charles Darnay.

A young lady of . . . a short, slight, pretty figure, a quantity of golden hair, a pair of blue eyes . . . and a forehead with a singular capacity (remembering how young and smooth it was) of lifting and knitting itself into an expression that was not quite one of perplexity or wonder or alarm, or merely of a bright fixed attention; though it included all the four expressions. I: iv–vi; II: ii–vi, ix–xiii, xvi–xxi, xxiv; III: iii–vii, ix–xii, xiv, xv.

**Mender of Roads, The.** *See* Jacques Five.

**Monseigneur.** A personification of the French nobility. II: vii, xxiii, xxiv; III: ii.

**Prison-Sheep, The.** *See* Pross, Solomon.

**Pross, Miss.** Miss Lucie Manette's maid; sister of Solomon Pross. She is a grim, wild-looking woman, with red face and hair, brawny arms, abrupt manners, and singular habits; yet, —

Beneath the surface of her eccentricity, one of those unselfish creatures — found only among women — who will, for pure love and admiration, bind themselves willing slaves, to youth, when they have lost it, to beauty that they never had, to accomplishments that they were never fortunate enough to gain, to bright hopes that never shone upon their own sombre lives.

When the Manettes escape from Paris, Miss Pross remains behind to conceal their flight, and, in trying to do so, gets involved in a hand-to-hand conflict with Madame Defarge, a ruthless and desperate woman, who is on their track. In the struggle Madame Defarge draws a pistol, and attempts to shoot her antagonist; but Miss Pross strikes at it at the moment of firing, and the charge takes effect on the French woman, killing her instantly. Miss Pross hurries from the house, closely veiled; takes a carriage which has been in waiting for her; and succeeds in escaping safely to England. I: iv; II: vi, x, xvii–xix, xxi; III: ii, iii, vii, viii, xiv.

**Pross, Solomon,** *called also* JOHN BARSAD, *and nicknamed* "PRISON-SHEEP." A heartless scoundrel, who strips his sister of everything she possesses, as a stake to speculate with, and then abandons her in her poverty to support herself as she can. He becomes a spy and secret informer in the service of the English government, and afterwards a turnkey in the Conciergerie in Paris. I: iii, vi, xiv, xvi; III: viii, ix, xi, xiii–xv.

**St. Evrémonde, Marquis.** Uncle of Charles Darnay; twin-brother, joint inheritor, and next successor of the elder marquis.

He was a man of about sixty, handsomely dressed, haughty in manner, and with a face like a fine mask,—a face of a transparent paleness; every feature in it clearly defined; one set expression on it. The nose, beautifully formed otherwise, was very slightly pinched at the top of each nostril. In those two compressions, or dints, the only little change that the face ever showed resided. They persisted in changing color sometimes, and they would be occasionally dilated and contracted by something like a faint pulsation; then they gave a look of treachery and cruelty to the whole countenance. Examined with attention, its capacity of helping such a look was to be found in the line of the mouth and the lines of the orbits of the eyes being much too horizontal and thin; still, in the effect the face made, it was a handsome face, and a remarkable one. II: vii–ix; III: x.

**St. Evremonde, Marquis.** Twin-brother of the younger marquis, and father of Charles Darnay. III: x.

**St. Evrémonde Marquise.** His wife; a young lady, handsome, engaging, and good, but not happy in her marriage. III: x.

**St. Evrémonde, Charles,** *called* CHARLES DARNAY. His son; a French *émigré*, afterwards married to Lucie Manette. II: ii–vi, ix, x, xvi–xviii, xx, xxi, xxiv; III: i–vii, ix–xv.

**St. Evrémonde, Lucie.** His daughter. II: xxi; III: ii, iii, v–vii, xi, xiii, xiv.

**Stryver, Mr.** A London barrister; counsel of Charles Darnay, and patron of Sydney Carton.

A man of little more than thirty, but looking twenty years older than he was; stout, loud, red, bluff, and free from any drawback of delicacy; [with] a pushing way of shouldering himself (morally and physically) into companies and conversations, that argued well for his shouldering his way up in life. II: ii–v, xi, xxi, xxiv.

**Tellson and Company.** An old and eminent banking-firm in London. I: iii, iv; II: i, iii, vii, ix.

**Tom.** Coachman of the Dover mail. I: ii.

**Vengeance, The.** One of the leading revolutionists among the Saint Antoine women; lieutenant to Madame Defarge. II: xxii; III: ix, xii, xiv, xv.

# GREAT EXPECTATIONS

## OUTLINE

Chapter Philip Pirrip, an orphan, whose name had been boiled
I down to Pip, was in the churchyard near the marshes, beyond
which were the Hulks, or prison-ships, when he was accosted by a
fearful man, an escaped convict, who made him promise to bring
him something to eat, and a file to rid himself of his fetters, at the
II Battery early the next morning. The boy, who lived with
his sister, who had brought him up by hand, and her husband, the blacksmith, Joe Gargery, whom she had under her thumb,
stealthily secured some provisions and a file, and the next morning
III went down to the marshes to keep his word. He was startled to come upon another man, also an escaped convict,
whom he managed to avoid, however, carrying his load to the man
who had met him the night before. He told his acquaintance
of his chance meeting, which seemed to fill the fearful man with a
new fury.

IV As for Pip, he was in a state of panic all day, which was
Christmas, in his apprehension of his sister when she should
discover the theft he had committed. His uncle Pumblechook and
V other choice spirits were at the table, and Pip, at the fatal
moment, actually set out to run away, when the door opened,
and in came a file of soldiers under charge of a sergeant, who wished
to get a pair of handcuffs mended. This created a diversion; then
it turned out that a couple of convicts had escaped, and the party
was out after them. Pip and Joe joined them, and they came
upon them at last, Pip's acquaintance holding the other fellow in
his grip, apparently ready to be revenged on him for something,
VI even if trapped himself thereby. He managed to convey his
good will to Pip by declaring that he had stolen food and a
file from the blacksmith, a story which helped Pip out of his quandary, and left Mrs. Joe's guests busily discussing the manner in
which the convict had committed his theft.

VII It was about a year after this that Pip, who had been painfully beginning his education at a school kept by Mr. Wopsle's
great-aunt, where he was assisted by Biddy, her grand-daughter, fell
to talking with Joe Gargery about Joe's academic training.

"Did n't you ever go to school, Joe, when you were as little as me?"

"No, Pip."

"Why did n't you ever go to school, Joe, when you were as little as me?"

"Well, Pip," said Joe, taking up the poker, and settling himself to his usual occupation, when he was thoughtful, of slowly raking the fire between the lower bars, "I 'll tell you. My father, Pip, — he were given to drink; and, when he were overtook with drink, he hammered away at my mother most onmerciful. It were a'most the only hammering he did, indeed, 'xcepting at myself; and he hammered at me with a wigor only to be equalled by the wigor with which he did n't hammer at his anwil. You 're a listening and understanding, Pip?"

"Yes, Joe."

"Consequence: my mother and me, we ran away from my father several times; and then my mother, she 'd go out to work; and she 'd say, 'Joe,' she 'd say, 'now, please God, you shall have some schooling, child;' and she 'd put me to school. But my father were that good in his hart, that he could n't abear to be without us; so he 'd come with a most tremenjous crowd, and make such a row at the doors of the houses where we was, that they used to be obligated to have no more to do with us, and to give us up to him. And then he took us home, and hammered us; which you see, Pip," said Joe, pausing in his meditative raking of the fire, and looking at me, "were a drawback on my learning."

"Certainly, poor Joe!"

"Though mind you, Pip," said Joe, with a judicial touch or two of the poker on the top bar, "rendering unto all their doo, and maintaining equal justice betwixt man and man, my father were that good in his hart; don't you see?"

I did n't see; but I did n't say so.

"Well," Joe pursued, "somebody must keep the pot a biling, Pip, or the pot won't bile; don't you know?"

I saw that, and said so.

"Consequence: my father did n't make objections to my going to work: so I went to work at my present calling, which were his, too, if he would have followed it; and I worked tolerable hard, I assure *you*, Pip. In time, I were able to keep him; and I kep him till he went off in a purple leptic fit. And it were my intentions to have had put upon his tombstone that Whatsume'er the failings on his part, Remember, reader, he were that good in his hart."

Joe recited this couplet with such manifest pride and careful perspicuity, that I asked him if he had made it himself.

"I made it," said Joe, "my own self. I made it in a moment. It was like striking out a horse-shoe complete in a single blow. I never was so much surprised in all my life, — could n't credit my own ed; to tell you the truth, hardly believed it *was* my own ed. As I was saying, Pip, it were my intentions to have had it cut over him: but poetry costs money, cut it how you will, small or large; and it were not done. Not to mention bearers, all the money that could be spared were wanted for my mother. She were in poor elth, and quite broke. She were n't long of following, poor soul; and her share of peace come round at last."

Joe's blue eyes turned a little watery: he rubbed first one of them, and then the other, in a most uncongenial and uncomfortable manner, with the round knob on the top of the poker.

"It were but lonesome then," said Joe, "living here alone, and I got acquainted with your sister. Now, Pip," Joe looked firmly at me, as if he knew I was not going to agree with him, "your sister is a fine figure of a woman."

I could not help looking at the fire in an obvious state of doubt.

"Whatever family opinions, or whatever the world's opinions on that subject may be, Pip, your sister is" — Joe tapped the top bar with the poker after every word following — "a — fine — figure — of — a — woman!"

I could think of nothing better to say than "I am glad you think so, Joe."

"So am I," returned Joe, catching me up. "*I* am glad I think so, Pip. A little redness, or a little matter of bone here or there, — what does it signify to me?"

I sagaciously observed, if it did n't signify to him, to whom did it signify?

"Certainly!" assented Joe. "That 's it. You 're right, old chap! When I got acquainted with your sister, it were the talk how she was bringing you up by hand. Very kind of her, too, all the folks said, and I said along with all the folks. As to you," Joe pursued, with a countenance expressive of seeing something very nasty indeed, "if you could have been aware how small and flabby and mean you was, — dear me, you 'd have formed the most contemptible opinions of yourself!"

Not exactly relishing this, I said, "Never mind me, Joe."

"But I did mind you, Pip," he returned, with tender simplicity. "When I offered to your sister to keep company, and to be asked in church at such times as she was willing and ready to come to the forge, I said to her, 'And bring the poor little child. God bless the poor little child!' I said to your sister: 'there's room for *him* at the forge.'"

I broke out crying, and begging pardon, and hugged Joe round the neck, who dropped the poker to hug me, and to say, "Ever the best of friends; ain't us, Pip? Don't cry, old chap!"

The conversation was interrupted by the return of Mrs. Joe from market in great excitement, with the news that Miss Havisham, an eccentric and mysteriously isolated lady in town, had sent an invitation, instigated apparently by Uncle Pumblechook, to Pip to come
VIII to her house to play; and Uncle Pumblechook being in waiting, off Pip was packed at once. It was a singular part he was called on to play. He went to Satis House the next morning, was admitted by a proud, beautiful, and insolent girl of about his own age, named Estella, who took him to the room where sat Miss
IX Havisham, dressed as for a party, with candles about her, and bade him play at cards with Estella. When he was let out from this festive scene, he was bidden come again in six days: but when he went home and was pursued with questions by Mrs. Joe and Uncle Pumblechook, he told a string of stories as fast as he could make them up, only confessing the honest truth to honest Joe Gargery.

X Before he went back for his second visit, he had a curious adventure. He had gone to the Three Jolly Bargemen at Mrs. Joe's demand to bring Joe home, and there found Joe and Wopsle in company with a stranger who seemed to take a lively interest in them, and who stirred his rum with a file. This performance was intended, with success, to notify Pip that the stranger knew the convict. When they left, the convict's friend gave Pip a shilling,
XI and wrapped it, moreover, in two one-pound notes. Pip made his second visit to Miss Havisham. It was her birthday, and three or four of her relations came in a hypocritical spirit to remind her of themselves. Again Pip played with Estella, and on going out of the house into the garden he fell in with a pale young gentleman who persuaded him into a fight. Perhaps it was because he thrashed the pale young gentleman that Estella rewarded
XII him with a kiss. Miss Havisham, after a series of these ghostly entertainments, asked Pip if he would bring Joe Gargery with him with his indenture papers, for Pip was to be appren-
XIII ticed to Joe, and when the two appeared before her, she gave Joe twenty-five guineas as his premium, and with that Joe and Pip went before the magistrates and Pip was apprenticed; but
XIV that was the end of his visits at Satis House. It was the end also, in a way, of Pip's peace of mind, for the intercourse with Miss Havisham and Estella had made him very conscious of his own coarseness and lack of refinement.

Nevertheless Pip could not withstand the attraction of Estella,
XV and he begged a holiday of Joe, that he might go and pay his
respects to Miss Havisham. Dolge Orlick, a journeyman of
Joe's, demanded a like favor, and got it, but Mrs. Joe coming to the
forge, the ugly Orlick said uncomplimentary things about her which
led to his being knocked down by Joe. Pip made his visit, but
found that Estella had gone to the continent to perfect her education. Coming home with Orlick, who had fallen in with him, he
found his sister insensible on the floor, felled by a blow from some
XVI unknown hand. Although certain ponderous officials from
London came down, the wretch who had dealt the blow was
not found. Meanwhile for Joe's aid Biddy came into the household,
and very quick she proved to be, interpreting as others could not
the signs that Mrs. Joe made. She even translated a T which Mrs.
Joe drew, into Orlick's hammer, and Orlick accordingly was invited
in, and Mrs. Joe seemed very desirous of making all things comfort-
XVII able for him, who now was quite one of the household and
bearing an evident affection for Biddy, much to her discom-
posure, as she showed Pip who had made a confidante of her, not
perceiving in his blind devotion to the absent Estella that Biddy
was truer to him.

XVIII Pip had been to see Miss Havisham on his birthday each
year, and each year she had given him a guinea, but one day,
some four years after his apprenticeship, he and Joe were accosted
by a lawyer named Jaggers, whom Pip had seen at Miss Havisham's,
and told that a friend who did not wish to be known had expressed
the intention of calling Pip into a handsome property, and meanwhile desired him to break off from his present life and live as a
gentleman. Joe with his affectionate nature cheerfully relinquished,
XIX without compensation, his rights in Pip, but Pip himself,
wrapped up in his prospects, could see in his sister's great-
hearted husband only an uneducated, ill-mannered lout, not having
the eyes to see him that Biddy, for instance, had. He was not allowed to know who his benefactor was, but after arraying himself
in a fine suit of clothes, he presented himself to Miss Havisham and
bade her a significant good-by.

XX Pip went up to London and reported himself to Mr. Jaggers, who was a criminal lawyer much in demand, and Mr.
Jaggers turned him over to his clerk Wemmick, who took him to
XXI Barnard's Inn to give him in charge of Mr. Herbert Pocket,
the son of the Matthew Pocket who was to be his tutor. To
their mutual surprise, Mr. Pocket, Jr., turned out to be the pale
XXII young gentleman whom Pip had once fought. That did not
prevent their getting on very well together now, and Herbert

Pocket told Pip what he knew of Miss Havisham's story, and at the
end of the week took him to Hammersmith and delivered him over
to his father, a cousin of Miss Havisham's, and so very independent
XXIII that he had never got on with that eccentric dame. Here
Pip was established to read with Mr. Pocket, and a pretty
disorganized household he found it, with Mrs. Pocket ruling it like
XXIV an abdicated queen. The situation was so unpleasant that
Pip decided to make his quarters with Herbert Pocket, and
did so with Mr. Jaggers's consent. Mr. Wemmick was Mr. Jaggers's
XXV agent in all these matters, and Pip made his acquaintance
more thoroughly, when he went down to Walworth to dine
with him in his toy castle where he lived with his Aged Parent. He
XXVI dined also with Mr. Jaggers, and with him two of his fellow students, Bentley Drummle and Startop.

XXVII Joe Gargery, announced by a letter from Biddy, came up
to town to see Pip, who had the shame to be mortified at
having Herbert see his great friend, and the grace to repent of his
weakness afterwards. Joe's errand turned out to be a message from
Miss Havisham to the effect that Estella had come home, and Pip
XXVIII at once made up his mind to go back to his home and see
her. It so chanced that on the coach by which he went
down were two convicts, and in one of them he recognized the man
who had given him the shilling wrapped up in two one-pound notes.
XXIX Pip paid his respects to Miss Havisham, and saw Estella,
now grown a beautiful lady. He was surprised also at
finding Orlick there on duty as porter, and at seeing his guardian,
Mr. Jaggers, who suddenly appeared in Miss Havisham's room. Pip
XXX went back to London desperately in love with Estella, and
made a confidante of Herbert, who responded by informing
him that he was also in love with, in fact engaged to, a girl named
XXXI Clara, with a father who was apparently a somewhat objectionable sort of father. The two companions thereupon
went to the theatre to see Wopsle play Hamlet. It might almost
XXXII be said that it was the drama that Pip saw when he went
with Wemmick through Newgate prison. He saw it again
XXXIII on the outside shortly after, when he had the honor of
escorting Estella to Richmond, where she was to be introduced to the great world.

XXXIV All this time Pip and Herbert were getting sadly into
debt, and did a deal of figuring to make their affairs look
more business like.

"My dear Herbert," said I [Pip], "we are getting on badly."

"My dear Handel," Herbert would say to me in all sincerity, "if you will believe me, those very words were on my lips by a strange coincidence."

"Then, Herbert," I would respond, "let us look into our affairs."

We always derived profound satisfaction from making an appointment for this purpose. I always thought myself, this was business, this was the way to confront the thing, this was the way to take the foe by the throat. And I know Herbert thought so too.

We generally ordered something rather special for dinner, with a bottle of something similarly out of the common way, in order that our minds might be fortified for the occasion, and we might come well up to the mark. Dinner over, we produced a bundle of pens, a copious supply of ink, and a goodly show of writing and blotting paper; for there was something very comfortable in having plenty of stationery.

I would then take a sheet of paper, and write across the top of it, in a neat hand, the heading, "Memorandum of Pip's Debts," with Barnard's Inn and the date very carefully added. Herbert would also take a sheet of paper, and write across it, with similar formalities, "Memorandum of Herbert's Debts."

Each of us would then refer to a confused heap of papers at his side, which had been thrown into drawers, worn into holes in pockets, half-burned in lighting candles, stuck for weeks into the looking-glass, and otherwise damaged. The sound of our pens going refreshed us exceedingly, insomuch that I sometimes found it difficult to distinguish between this edifying business-proceeding and actually paying the money. In point of meritorious character, the two things seemed about equal. . . .

When I had got all my responsibilities down upon my list, I compared each with the bill, and ticked it off. My self-approval when I ticked an entry was almost a luxurious sensation. When I had no more ticks to make, I folded all my bills up uniformly, docketed each on the back, and tied the whole into a symmetrical bundle. Then I did the same for Herbert (who modestly said he had not my administrative genius), and felt that I had brought his affairs into a focus for him.

My business habits had one other bright feature, which I called "leaving a margin." For example: supposing Herbert's debts to be one hundred and sixty-four pounds four and twopence, I would say, "Leave a margin, and put them down at two hundred." Or, supposing my own to be four times as much, I would leave a margin, and put them down at seven hundred. I had the highest opinion of the wisdom and prudence of this same margin; but I am bound to acknowledge that, on looking back, I deem it to have been an expensive device; for we always ran into new debt immediately, to the full extent of the margin, and sometimes, in the sense of freedom and solvency it imparted, got pretty far into another margin.

XXXV Then suddenly came word to Pip of the death of his sister, Mrs. Joe Gargery. He went down to his old home and
paraded with the other mourners, and tried to place Joe and Biddy
in their right places, but succeeded only in putting himself in the
XXXVI wrong. Not long after his return to London both Herbert
and he came of age, and his guardian, Mr. Jaggers, still
withholding the name of his benefactor, now greatly increased his
allowance, whereupon Pip arranged for the transfer of a good portion of it as a loan to Herbert to advance his interests, though with-
XXXVII out Herbert's knowledge of the part he played. He was
able to do this through Wemmick, whom he visited at
his little toy castle, where he observed the intimacy springing up
XXXVIII between Wemmick and Miss Skiffin. The love-passages of
other people gave him a different feeling, for on taking
Estella back to Miss Havisham he found that Drummle was paying court to her, and that through some miserable fate she seemed
to be falling into his arms.

XXXIX Pip was now twenty-three years old, in the enjoyment of
a comfortable income, yet though he had no doubt that Miss Havisham was the source of it, he was debarred from having the knowledge direct from her or her lawyer, Jaggers. Then it was that a sudden revelation came to him. He was alone in his lodgings one stormy night, when he heard sounds below. On opening the door and calling, he heard his own name, and so lighted his visitor into his room. The new-comer was a roughly dressed, hard-worn man, who looked searchingly at Pip. Then he began to put questions to him, and it was not long before the terrible truth came to Pip that this was the convict he had helped, and that the money which he was enjoying was the gift of this strange man. He had come back with pride to see the gentleman he had made out of Pip, but it was at the risk of his life, for the penalty of discovery was death.

XL Herbert was away, and so Pip could guard his uncle, as he
elected to call him for safety, his uncle Provis. But the situation was a perilous one. Pip called on Mr. Jaggers, to find that
gentleman very cautious in dealing with the case. Herbert came
XLI back and was sworn to secrecy. He was most sympathetic
with Pip, and they both agreed that they must if possible
get Provis, or Abel Magwitch as he really was, out of England.
XLII But first they persuaded Magwitch to tell his story. It was
a dismal tale, but one or two points arrested their attention.

About twenty years before he had been the pal of one Compeyson, a gentlemanly swindler. This Compeyson used Magwitch, but finally both were committed for felony, and by this time Magwitch was bitter against Compeyson and swore to damage him. It was Compeyson who escaped at the same time with Magwitch, and who was seen by Pip when he went to feed Magwitch. Now Compeyson was the lover who had been false to Miss Havisham.

XLIII Before Pip could take Magwitch to the continent, he felt that he must once more see Estella and Miss Havisham. To add to his bitterness, he found Drummle in the neighborhood. He
XLIV had a conference with Miss Havisham, in which he begged her to do for Herbert now what he could no longer do, and he parted with Estella, knowing that she was to marry Drummle. That night, on returning to London, he was met before entering his lodgings by a messenger with a line from Wemmick, — "Don't go home." Pip obeyed, and in the morning went at once to Wemmick,
XLV who told him that some one was watching for Magwitch or for him; that he had conferred with Herbert, and between them they had managed to transfer Magwitch to a house by the
XLVI riverside where Clara, Herbert's betrothed, lived. Pip spent the day at Wemmick's, and at night went to Mrs. Whimple's, where he saw Herbert and Magwitch. It was agreed that Pip should set up a boat and disarm suspicion by rowing constantly on the river, against the time when he and Herbert could secretly row Magwitch away.

XLVII Things went on for some time without change, and Pip went one night to the play to see Mr. Wopsle, and in their talk afterward Mr. Wopsle declared that he saw behind Pip during the play, the other convict, who was no other than Compeyson.
XLVIII Not long after, Pip meeting Mr. Jaggers was taken home to dinner. Again Pip noticed Jaggers's housekeeper, and this time from certain movements was sure she was Estella's mother; a surmise which was strengthened by Wemmick's narrative of her story afterward. Pip paid another visit to Miss Havisham
XLIX and learned of Estella's marriage. He was present also when that night her poor bridal dress which she always wore caught fire, and the desolate woman was saved from death by burning by his exertions only.

L When Pip returned to London with his own hands badly burned, he learned from Herbert a further story which Magwitch had told him, showing clearly that he was Estella's father; a
LI story which was made all the more certain to Pip when afterward he saw both Jaggers and Wemmick.

LII It became possible now to move Magwitch, and Pip and Herbert, taking Startop into their counsels since Pip's hands

were burned, had made arrangements, when Pip received a mysterious note bidding him meet the writer on the old marshes to learn something about his uncle Provis; but he must tell no one, and he must go alone. He acted promptly as he needed to, by the terms
LIII of the note, and went at night to the lonely place. He went
as bidden to an old sluice house, and groping about in the dark was suddenly seized and bound. Then a light was struck, and he discovered in the man who had bound him, Orlick. Old Orlick was to take his revenge on him, and first he poured out all his accumulated rage. He told him he had killed his sister, and then drinking heavily to heat his rage, he took up his heavy stone hammer to fell him. Pip did all that he had left to do: he uttered a despairing cry. That cry brought instantaneous help, Herbert and Startop, whose coming gave him his liberty and life, as Orlick fled into the darkness. It transpired that Pip had left the anonymous letter in his room, and Herbert finding it had scented mischief. By a series of tracings they came upon Pip at the critical moment.
LIV It was still not too late for their errand, and carrying out
their plan they rowed down the river and took Magwitch aboard. They had a night of it, hoping to make the Hamburg steamer in the morning. Instead, they were watched by officers who had been directed by Compeyson, and Magwitch was captured, though not till he had struck Compeyson his death-blow. Mag-
LV witch was held for trial, and Pip secured Jaggers for his
defence. Wemmick about this time casually invited Pip to take a walk with him, and casually they entered a church, where Wemmick was married quite in an impromptu fashion to Miss Skiffins.

LVI Magwitch never came to his trial, for he lay in prison till
he died, but before he died he had from Pip the great gift he longed for, Pip's real affection, and from him he learned of his daughter Estella, and of Pip's love for her still. Pip himself had
LVII a long illness after this, but his recovery was made happy
by Joe Gargery's presence, and Joe told him of Miss Havisham's death, and of Orlick's breaking into Uncle Pumblechook's
LVIII and being arrested and shut up in the county jail. Pip
went once more to his old haunts, where Joe married Biddy. Eleven years after, he saw Estella once more. She was a
LIX widow now, but apparently was not long to remain so, if
Pip can be trusted.

# INDEX TO CHARACTERS

**Aged, The.** *See* WEMMICK, Mr., *senior*.

**Amelia.** One of Mr. Jaggers's clients. xx.

**Avenger, The.** *See* PEPPER.

**Barley, Clara.** Daughter of Old Bill Barley; a very pretty, slight, dark-eyed girl of twenty, or so, of natural and winning manners, and a confiding and amiable disposition. She is betrothed to Herbert Pocket, whom she afterward marries. xlvi, lv, lviii, lix.

**Barley, Old Bill.** A bedridden purser; a sad old rascal, always inebriated, and tormented by the gout in his right hand — and everywhere else. xlvi, lviii.

**Biddy.** An orphan; second cousin to Mr. Wopsle, being his "great-aunt's grand-daughter." She is a good, honest girl, poor in purse and condition, but with a wealth of true womanliness which makes Joe Gargery, whose second wife she becomes, very rich indeed. vii, xvi–xix, xxxv, lviii, lix.

**Brandley, Mrs.** A widow lady at Richmond, with whom Estella is placed by Miss Havisham. xxxviii.

**Camilla, Mr. John** *or* **Raymond.** A relative of Miss Havisham's; a toady and a humbug. xi, xxv.

**Camilla, Mrs.** His wife; sister to Mr. Pocket. She professes a great deal of love for Miss Havisham, and calls on her husband to testify that her solicitude for that lady is gradually undermining her to the extent of making one of her legs shorter than the other. xi, xxv.

**Clarriker.** A young merchant or shipping-broker. lii, lviii.

**Coiler, Mrs.** A toady neighbor of Mr. and Mrs. Pocket's; a widow lady of that highly sympathetic nature, that she agrees with everybody, blesses everybody, and sheds smiles or tears on everybody, according to circumstances. xxiii.

**Compeyson.** A convict, and "the worst of scoundrels." He proves to be the man who professed to be Miss Havisham's lover. Magwitch gives the following account of him to Pip: —

Compey took me on to be his man and pardner. And what was Compey's business in which we was to go pardners? Compey's business was the swindling, handwriting forging, stolen bank-note passing, and such like. All sorts of traps as Compey could set with his head, and keep his own legs out of, and get the profits from, and let another man in for, was Compey's business. He'd no more heart than a iron file; he was as cold as death, and had the head of the Devil. . . . Not to go into the

things that Compey planned, and I done, — which 'ud take a week, — I 'll simply say to you, dear boy, . . . that that man got me into such nets as made me his black slave. I was always in debt to him, always under his thumb, always a working, always a getting into danger. He was younger than me; but he 'd got craft; and he 'd got learning; and he overmatched me five hundred times told, and no mercy.

He is at length committed for felony, is sentenced to seven years' imprisonment; and is finally killed in a struggle with Magwitch. iii, v, xlii, xlv, xlvii, l, liii–lvi.

**Drummle, Bentley,** *called* THE SPIDER. A sulky, old-looking young man of a heavy order of architecture: idle, proud, niggardly, reserved, and suspicious. He is a fellow-boarder with Pip at Mr. Pocket's, and his rival for the hand of Estella, whom he marries, and treats with great cruelty. xxiii, xxv, xxxviii, xliii, xliv, xlviii.

**Estella.** The adopted daughter of Miss Havisham, and the heroine of the story. She proves to be the daughter of Abel Magwitch (or Provis), Pip's benefactor. Her foster-mother tells Pip that she had wished for a little girl to rear, and to save from her own fate; and that Mr. Jaggers had accordingly brought her such a child, — an orphan of about three years.

"When she first came to me, I meant to save her from misery like my own. At first, I meant no more."

"Well, well!" said I. "I hope so."

"But as she grew, and promised to be very beautiful, I gradually did worse, and with my praises, and with my jewels, and with my teachings, and with this figure of myself always before her, — a warning to back and point my lessons, — I stole her heart away, and put ice in its place."

Not content with moulding the impressionable child into the form that her own wild resentment, spurned affection, and wounded pride finds vengeance in, she marries her to an ill-tempered, clumsy, contemptible booby (Bentley Drummle), who has nothing to recommend him but money and a ridiculous roll of addle-headed predecessors. After leading a most unhappy life, she separates from her husband, who subsequently dies from an accident consequent on his ill-treatment of a horse. Some two years after this event, she happens to meet Pip (who has always loved her) on the very spot where their first meeting had been when they were children.

I took her hand in mine, and we went out of the ruined place; and as the morning mists had risen long ago, when I first left the forge, so the evening mists were rising now; and, in all the broad expanse of tranquil light they showed to me, I saw the shadow of no parting from her. vii, ix, xi–xvi, xviii, xxii, xxvii, xxix, xxx, xxxii, xxxiii, xxxviii, xxxix, xliii, xliv, xlviii–li, lvi, lvii, lix.

**Flopson.** A nurse in Mr. Pocket's family. xxii, xxiii.

**Gargery, Joe.** A blacksmith; married to Pip's sister, who is an out-and-out termagant.

Joe was a fair man, with curls of flaxen hair on each side of his smooth face, and eyes of such a very undecided blue, that they seemed to have somehow got mixed with their own whites. He was a mild, good-natured, sweet-tempered, easy-going, foolish, dear fellow, — a sort of Hercules in strength, and also in weakness.

When Pip is a small boy, he is harshly treated by his sister (with whom he lives, both of his parents being dead); but his kind-hearted brother-in-law befriends him as much as is possible, and makes quite a companion of him.

After the death of his wife, Joe marries Biddy, a sweet-tempered woman, who makes him an excellent wife, and with whom he lives happily for many years, ever doing the duty that lies before him with a strong hand, a quiet tongue, and a gentle heart. ii–vii, ix, x, xii–xx, xxvii, xxxv, lvii–lix.

**Gargery, Mrs. Georgiana Maria.** His wife; sister to Pip, and a thorough shrew.

My sister . . . was more than twenty years older than I, and had established a great reputation with herself and the neighbors because she had brought me up "by hand." Having at that time to find out for myself what the expression meant, and knowing her to have a hard and heavy hand, and to be much in the habit of laying it upon her husband, as well as upon me, I supposed that Joe Gargery and I were both brought up by hand.

She was not a good-looking woman, my sister; and I had a general impression that she must have made Joe Gargery marry her by hand. . . .

With black hair and eyes [she] had such a prevailing redness of skin, that I sometimes used to wonder whether it was possible she washed herself with a nutmeg-grater instead of soap. She was tall and bony, and almost always wore a coarse apron, fastened over her figure behind with two loops, and having a square, impregnable bib in front that was stuck full of pins and needles. She made it a powerful merit in herself, and a strong reproach against Joe, that she wore this apron so much. . . .

Joe's forge adjoined our house, which was a wooden house, as many of the dwellings in our country were — most of them — at that time. When I ran home from the churchyard, the forge was shut up, and Joe was sitting alone in the kitchen. Joe and I being fellow-sufferers, and having confidence as such, Joe imparted a confidence to me the moment I raised the latch of the door, and peeped in at him opposite to it, sitting in the chimney-corner.

"Mrs. Joe has been out a dozen times, looking for you, Pip; and she 's out now; making it a baker's dozen."

"Is she?"

"Yes, Pip," said Joe; "and, what 's worse, she 's got Tickler with her."

At this dismal intelligence, I twisted the only button on my waistcoat round and round, and looked in great depression at the fire. Tickler was a wax-ended piece of cane, worn smooth by collision with my tickled frame.

"She sat down," said Joe; "and she got up; and she made a grab at Tickler; and she ram-paged out. That 's what she did," said Joe, slowly clearing the fire between the bars with the poker: "she ram-paged out, Pip."

"Has she been gone long, Joe?" I always treated him as a larger species of child, and as no more than my equal.

"Well," said Joe, looking up at the Dutch clock, "she 's been on the ram-page, this last spell, about five minutes, Pip. She 's a coming! Get behind the door, old chap, and have the jack-towel betwixt you."

I took the advice. My sister, Mrs. Joe, throwing the door wide open, and finding an obstruction behind it, immediately divined the cause, and applied Tickler to further investigation. She concluded by throwing me — I often served her as a connubial missile — at Joe, who, glad to get hold of me on any terms, passed me on into the chimney, and quietly fenced me there with his great legs.

When Pip grows up, he goes out into the world, and his experiences of his sister's tender mercies come to an end; but poor Joe continues to bear his cross with exemplary patience, until death relieves him of it by opening a grave for Mrs. Gargery.

"She had been in one of her bad states — though they had got better, of late, rather than worse — for four days, when she came out of it in the evening, just at tea-time, and said quite plainly, 'Joe.' As she had never said any word for a long while, I [Biddy] ran and fetched in Mr. Gargery from the forge. She made signs to me that she wanted him to sit down close to her, and wanted me to put her arms around his neck. So I put them round his neck and she laid her head down on his shoulder quite content and satisfied. And so she presently said, 'Joe,' again,

JOE GARGERY AND MRS. JOE.

and once, 'pardon,' and once, 'Pip.' And so she never lifted her head up any more; and it was just an hour later when we laid it down on her own bed, because we found she was gone." ii, iv–vii, ix, x, xii–xviii, xxiv, xxv.

**Georgiana.** A cousin of Mr. Pocket's, and a relative of Miss Havisham's; an indigestive single woman, who calls her rigidity religion, and her liver love. xi, xxv, lvii.

**Havisham, Miss.** Estella's foster-mother. In her youth she had been a beautiful heiress, and looked after as a great match. She was pursued in particular by a certain showy man (Compeyson), who professed to be devoted to her.

She had not shown much susceptibility up to that time; but all she possessed certainly came out then, and she passionately loved him: there is no doubt that she perfectly idolized him. He practised on her affection in that systematic way, that he got great sums of money from her; and he induced her to buy her brother out of a share in the brewery (which had been weakly left him by his father), at an immense price, on the plea, that, when he was her husband, he must hold and manage it all. . . . The marriage-day was fixed, the wedding-dresses were bought, the wedding-tour was planned out, the wedding-guests were invited. The day came, but not the bridegroom.

She received a letter from him, however, when she was dressing for church, that most heartlessly broke the marriage off. When she recovered from a bad illness that she had, she laid waste the whole place where she resided (Satis House), stopped all the clocks at twenty minutes to nine, — the time of her receiving the letter, — and never afterwards looked upon the light of day. Pip, who was invited to her house when a small boy, thus describes it and its inmate: —

I entered . . . , and found myself in a pretty large room well lighted with wax-candles. No glimpse of daylight was to be seen in it. It was a dressing-room, as I supposed from the furniture; though much of it was of forms and uses then quite unknown to me. But prominent in it was a draped table with a gilded looking-glass; and that I made out, at first sight, to be a fine lady's dressing-table.

Whether I should have made out this object so soon, if there had been no fine lady sitting at it, I cannot say. In an arm-chair, with an elbow resting on the table, and her head leaning on that hand, sat the strangest lady I have ever seen or shall ever see.

She was dressed in rich materials, — satins and lace and silks, — all of white. Her shoes were white; and she had a long white veil dependent from her hair; and she had bridal flowers in her hair: but her hair was white. Some bright jewels sparkled on her neck and on her hands; and some other jewels lay sparkling on the table. Dresses less splendid than the dress she wore, and half-packed trunks, were scattered about. She had not quite finished dressing; for she had but one shoe on (the other was on the table near her hand); her veil was but half arranged, her watch and chain were not put on; and some lace for her bosom lay with those trinkets, and with her handkerchief and gloves, and some flowers, and a prayer-book, — all confusedly heaped about the looking-glass.

It was not in the first minute that I saw all these things; though I saw more of them in the first minute than might be supposed. But I saw that everything within my view which ought to be white had been white long ago, and had lost its lustre, and was faded and yellow. I saw that the bride within the bridal dress had withered like the dress, and like the flowers, and had no brightness left but the brightness of her sunken eyes. I saw that the dress had been put upon the rounded figure of a young woman, and that the figure upon which it now hung loose had shrunk to skin and bone.

Filled with bitterness towards all mankind, Miss Havisham adopts a beautiful orphan girl (Estella), and rears her in the midst of all this desolation, educating her to steel her heart against all tenderness, but to lead young men on to love her, that she may break their hearts. viii, ix, xi–xiv, xix, xxii, xxix, xxxviii, xliv, xlix, lvii.

**Hubble, Mr.** A wheelwright, who is a friend of Mrs. Joe Gargery's; a tough, high-shouldered, stooping old man, of a sawdusty fragrance, with his legs extraordinarily wide apart. iv, v, xxxv.

**Hubble, Mrs.** His wife; a little, sharp-eared person, who holds a conventionally juvenile position, because she married Mr. Hubble when she was much younger than he. iv, v, xxxv.

**Jack.** A grizzled, slimy man, with a slushy voice, who is employed on a little causeway on the Thames. liv.

**Jaggers, Mr.** A criminal lawyer of Little Britain, employed by Pip's unknown patron to inform him of his "great expectations," and to act as his guardian until he comes into full possession of his fortune.

He was a burly man of an exceedingly dark complexion, with an exceedingly large head and a correspondingly large hand. . . . He was prematurely bald on the top of his head, and had bushy, black eyebrows that would n't lie down, but stood up bristling. His eyes were set very deep in his head and were disagreeably sharp and suspicious. He had a very large watch-chain, and very strong black dots where his beard and whiskers would have been if he had let them.

Mr. Jaggers had an air of authority that is not to be disputed, and a manner expressive of knowing something secret about everybody that would effectually do for each individual, if he chose to disclose it. His clerk tells Pip that it always seems to him as if his master had set a man-trap, and was watching it. When he is not biting his large forefinger, he is in the habit of throwing it, in a half-bullying sort of way, at the person he is talking with. He never laughs; but he wears great, bright, creaking boots, and in poising himself on these, with his large head bent down, and his eyebrows joined together, awaiting an answer, he sometimes causes the boots to creak as if *they* laughed in a dry and suspicious way. xi, xviii, xx, xxi, xxiv, xxvi, xxix, xxxvi, xl, xlviii, xlix, li, lvi.

**Magwitch, Abel,** *alias* PROVIS. A convict who escapes from the Hulks, and, meeting Pip, terrifies the boy into supplying him with food, and a file to enable him to file off his fetters. Though very soon captured, and transported to New South Wales, he retains a grateful remembrance of Pip, and after some years, growing wealthy in the business of sheep-farming, sets him up as a gentleman, making Mr. Jaggers his guardian and banker. He does this privately, however; and Pip supposes himself to be indebted to Miss Havisham for his good fortune, — a mistake which that lady, for reasons of her own, does not trouble herself to correct. Magwitch at last returns to England under the assumed name of Provis, and makes himself known to Pip, who endeavors to save his benefactor from recapture, but in vain, In spite of every precaution, Magwitch is discovered and taken; but he dies in prison, and thus escapes execution. i, iii, v, xxxix–xlii, xlvi, liv–lvi.

**Mary Anne.** A neat little girl who is Wemmick's servant. xxv, xlv.

**Mike.** A one-eyed client of Mr. Jaggers. xx, li.

**Millers.** A nurse in Mr. Pocket's family. xxii, xxiii.

**Molly.** Mr. Jaggers's housekeeper, and a former mistress of Abel Magwitch, by whom she is the mother of Estella.

Rather tall, of a lithe, nimble figure, extremely pale, with large blue eyes and a quantity of streaming light hair. I cannot say whether any diseased affection of the heart caused her lips to be parted as if she were panting, and her face to bear a curious expression of suddenness and flutter; but I know that I had been to see Macbeth at the theatre a night or two before, and that her face looked to me as if it were all disturbed by fiery air, like the faces I had seen rise out of the caldron. xxiv, xxvi.

**Orlick, Dolge.** A journeyman employed by Joe Gargery. He

secretly strikes a blow, which results in the death of Mrs. Gargery; and he afterwards attempts the life of Pip.

He was a broad-shouldered, loose-limbed, swarthy fellow, of great strength, never in a hurry, and always slouching. He never even seemed to come to his work on purpose, but would slouch in as if by mere accident; and when he went to the Jolly Bargemen to eat his dinner, or went away at night, he would slouch out like Cain or the Wandering Jew,—as if he had no idea where he was going, and no intention of ever coming back. He lodged at a sluice-keeper's, out on the marshes, and on working-days would come slouching from his hermitage, with his hands in his pockets, and his dinner loosely tied in a bundle round his neck, and dangling on his back. On Sundays, he mostly lay all day on sluice-gates, or stood against ricks or barns. He always slouched, locomotively, with his eyes on the ground; and when accosted, or otherwise required to raise them, he looked up in a half-resentful, half-puzzled way, as though the only thought he ever had was, that it was rather an odd and injurious fact that he should never be thinking. xv–xvii, xxix, xxx, liii.

**Pepper,** *called* THE AVENGER. Pip's boy.

I got on so fast, of late, that I had even started a boy in boots,—top-boots,—in bondage and slavery to whom I might have been said to pass my days. For after I had made my monster (out of the refuse of my washerwoman's family), and had clothed him with a blue coat, canary waistcoat, white cravat, creamy breeches, and the boots already mentioned, I had to find him a little to do and a great deal to eat; and with both of those horrible requirements he haunted my existence. xxvii.

**Pip.** *See* PIRRIP, PHILIP.

**Pirrip, Philip,** *called* PIP. The narrator and the hero of the story; "a good fellow, with impetuosity and hesitation, boldness and diffidence, action and dreaming, curiously mixed in him."

**Pocket, Herbert.** A son of Matthew Pocket's, who becomes a warm friend of Pip's. He has "great expectations" as well as Pip, whom he quite astonishes with the grandeur of his ideas and his plans for making money.

Pip's lavish habits lead Herbert into expenses that he cannot afford, corrupt the simplicity of his life, and disturb his peace with anxieties and regrets.

At a later date Herbert becomes a partner in the house of Clarriker & Co., through the kind assistance of Pip, which is secretly rendered, and is not discovered for many a year. He marries Clara Barley. xi, xxi–xxviii, xxx, xxxi, xxxiv, xxxvi–xlii, xlv–xlvii, xlix, l, lii–lv, lviii.

**Pocket, Alick.** One of Mr. Pocket's children, who makes arrangements, while still wearing a frock, for being married to a suitable young person at Kew. xxii, xxiii.

**Pocket, Jane.** A little daughter of Mr. Pocket's; a mere mite, who has prematurely taken upon herself some charge of the others. Her desire to be matrimonially established is so strong, that she might be supposed to have passed her short existence in the perpetual contemplation of domestic bliss. xxii, xxiii.

**Pocket, Joe.** Another child. xxiii.

**Pocket, Fanny.** Another child. xxiii.

**Pocket, Mr. Matthew.** A relative of Miss Havisham's, living at Hammersmith, with whom Pip studies for a time. He is a gentleman with a rather perplexed expression of face, and with his hair disordered on his head, as if he did n't quite see his way to putting anything straight.

By degrees I learned, and chiefly from Herbert, that Mr. Pocket had been educated at Harrow and at Cambridge, where he had distinguished himself; but that, when he had had the happiness of marrying Mrs. Pocket very early in life, he had impaired his prospects, and taken up the calling of a grinder. After grinding a number of dull blades (of whom it was remarkable that their fathers, when influential, were always going to help him to preferment, but always forgot to do it when the blades had left the grindstone), he had wearied of that poor work, and come to London. Here, after gradually failing in loftier hopes, he had "read" with divers who had lacked opportunities, or neglected them, and had refurbished divers others for special occasions, and had turned his acquirements to the account of literary compilation and correction, and on such means, added to some very moderate private resources, still maintained the house I saw. xxii–xxiv, xxxiii, xxxix.

**Pocket, Mrs. Belinda.** His wife.

Mrs. Pocket was the only daughter of a certain quite accidental deceased knight, who had invented for himself a conviction that his deceased father would have been made a baronet, but for somebody's determined opposition, arising out of entirely personal motives (I forget whose, if I ever knew, — the sovereign's, the prime minister's, the lord chancellor's, the Archbishop of Canterbury's, anybody's), and had tacked himself on the nobles of the earth in right of this quite supposititious fact. I believe he had been knighted himself for storming the English grammar at the point of a pen in a desperate address, engrossed on vellum, on the occasion of the laying of the first stone of some building or other, and handing some royal personage either the trowel or the mortar. Be that as it may, he had directed Mrs. Pocket to be brought up from her cradle as one who, in the nature of things, must marry a title, and who was to be guarded from the acquisition of plebeian domestic knowledge. So successful a watch and ward had been established over the young lady by this judicious parent, that she had grown up highly ornamental, but perfectly helpless and useless. With her character thus happily formed, in the first bloom of her youth she had encountered Mr. Pocket, who was also in the first bloom of youth, and not quite decided whether to mount to the woolsack, or to roof himself in with a mitre. As his doing the one or the other was a mere question of time, he and Mrs. Pocket had taken time by the forelock (at a season when, to judge from its length, it would seem to have wanted cutting), and had married without the knowledge of the judicious parent. The judicious parent, having nothing to bestow or withhold but his blessing, had handsomely settled that dower upon them after a short struggle, and had informed Mr. Pocket that his wife was "a treasure for a prince." Mr. Pocket had invested the prince's treasure in the ways of the world ever since; and it was supposed to have brought him in but indifferent interest. Still, Mrs. Pocket was, in general, the object of a queer sort of respectful pity, because she had not married a title; while Mr. Pocket was the object of a queer sort of respectful reproach, because he had never got one. xxii, xxiii, xxxiii.

**Pocket, Sarah.** A relative of Miss Havisham; a little, dry, brown, corrugated old woman, with a blandly vicious manner, a small face that might have been made of walnut-shells, and a large mouth like a cat's, without the whiskers. xi, xv, xix, xxix.

**Potkins, William.** A waiter at the Blue Boar. lviii.

**Provis.** *See* MAGWITCH, ABEL.

**Pumblechook, Uncle.** A well-to-do corn-chandler and seedsman: uncle to Joe Gargery, but appropriated by Mrs. Joe. He is a large, hard-breathing, middle-aged, slow man, with a mouth like a fish, dull, staring eyes, and sandy hair standing upright on his head; so that he looks as if he had been choked, and had just come to. Pumblechook is the torment of Pip's life. While a mere boy, the bullying old fellow is in the habit of coming to Mrs. Gargery's house, where Pip lives, and discussing his character and prospects; but this he can never do without having the child before him to operate on.

He would drag me up from my stool (usually by the collar) when I was quiet in a corner, and putting me before the fire, as if I were going to be cooked, would begin by saying, "Now, mum, here is this boy,—here is this boy which you brought up by

PUMBLECHOOK AND WOPSLE.

hand. Hold up your head, boy, and be forever grateful unto them which so did do. Now, mum, with respections to this boy." And then he would rumple my hair the wrong way (which, from my earliest remembrance, . . . I have in my soul denied the right of any fellow-creature to do), and would hold me before him by the sleeve, a spectacle of imbecility only to be equalled by himself. iv–ix, xiii, xv, xix, xxxv, lviii.

**Skiffins, Miss.** A lady of an uncertain age and a wooden appearance, but "a very good sort of fellow." She stands possessed of "portable property," which is so strong a recommendation in the eyes of Mr. Wemmick that he makes her his wife. xxxvii, lv.

**Sophia.** A housemaid in Mr. Pocket's service. xxiii.

**Spider, The.** *See* DRUMMLE, BENTLEY.

**Startop, Mr.** A lively, bright young man, with a woman's delicacy of feature, who is a fellow-boarder with Pip at Mr. Pocket's. xxiii, xxv, xxvi, xxxiv, lii–liv.

**Trabb, Mr.** A prosperous old bachelor, who is a tailor and an undertaker in the quiet old town where Pip lives during his boyhood. xix, xxxv.

**Trabb's Boy.** One of the most audacious young fellows in all that country-side. When Pip comes into a handsome property, and people stare after him, and are excessively polite if he happens to speak to them, the only effect upon Trabb's boy is, to make him more independent and impudent than before. As Pip is returning, on one occasion, to the Blue Boar from Satis House, to take the coach back to London, fate throws him in the way of "that unlimited miscreant."

Casting my eyes along the street at a certain point of my progress, I beheld Trabb's boy approaching, lashing himself with an empty blue bag. Deeming that a serene and unconscious contemplation of him would best beseem me, and would be most likely to quell his evil mind, I advanced with that expression of countenance, and was rather congratulating myself on my success, when suddenly the knees of Trabb's boy smote together; his hair uprose; his cap fell off; he trembled violently in every limb, staggered out in the road, and crying to the populace, "Hold me! I'm so frightened!" feigned to be in a paroxysm of terror and contrition, occasioned by the dignity of my appearance. As I passed him, his teeth loudly chattered in his head; and, with every mark of extreme humiliation, he prostrated himself in the dust.

This was a hard thing to bear; but this was nothing. I had not advanced another two hundred yards, when to my inexpressible terror, amazement, and indignation, I again beheld

Trabb's boy approaching. He was coming round a narrow corner. His blue bag was slung over his shoulder; honest industry beamed in his eyes; a determination to proceed to Trabb's with cheerful briskness was indicated in his gait. With a shock he became aware of me and was severely visited as before; but this time his motion was rotatory, and he staggered round and round me with knees more afflicted, and with uplifted hands, as if beseeching for mercy. His sufferings were hailed with the greatest joy by a knot of spectators; and I felt utterly confounded.

I had not got as much farther down the street as the post-office, when I again beheld Trabb's boy shooting round by a back-way. This time, he was entirely changed. He wore the blue bag in the manner of my great-coat, and was strutting along the pavement toward me on the opposite side of the street, attended by a company of delighted young friends, to whom he from time to time exclaimed, with a wave of his hand, "Don't know yah!" Words cannot state the amount of aggravation and injury wreaked upon me by Trabb's boy, when, passing abreast of me, he pulled up his shirt-collar, twined his side hair, struck an arm akimbo, and smirked extravagantly by, wriggling his elbows and body, and drawling to his attendants, "Don't know yah; don't know yah; 'pon my soul, don't know yah!" The disgrace attendant on his immediately afterward taking to crowing, and pursuing me across the bridge with crows as from an exceedingly dejected fowl who had known me when I was a blacksmith, culminated the disgrace with which I left the town, and was, so to speak, ejected by it into the open country. XXX.

**Waldengarver, Mr.** *See* WOPSLE, MR.

**Wemmick, Mr. John.** Mr. Jaggers's confidential clerk. He is a dry man, rather short in stature, with a square wooden face, whose expression seems to have been imperfectly chipped out with a dull-edged chisel. He has glittering eyes, — small, keen, and black, — and thin, white mottled lips, and has had them, apparently, from forty to fifty years. His guiding principle, and his invariable advice to his friends, is, to take care of portable property, and never on any account to lose an opportunity of securing it. Although his business relations to Mr. Jaggers are of the most intimate nature, their acquaintance and fellowship goes no further, and each pretends to the other that he is made of the sternest and flintiest stuff. But notwithstanding their hard exterior and their fear of showing themselves to one another in a weak and unprofessional light, they are kindly men at heart, — Wemmick especially, who has a pleasant home at Walworth, where he devotes himself to the comfort of his venerable father, and refreshes his business life in many pleasant and playful ways, the latest and most important of them being the transformation of Miss Skiffins into Mrs. Wemmick.

The district of Walworth . . . appeared to be a collection of back lanes, ditches, and little gardens, and to present the aspect of a mighty dull retirement. Wemmick's house was a little wooden cottage in the midst of plots of garden; and the top of it was cut out and painted like a battery mounted with guns.

"My own doing," said Wemmick. "Looks pretty; don't it?"

I highly commended it. I think it was the smallest house I ever saw, with the queerest Gothic windows (by far the greater part of them sham), and a Gothic door, almost too small to get in at.

"There's a real flag-staff, you see," said Wemmick; "and on Sundays I run up a real flag. Then look here. After I have crossed this bridge, I hoist it up, — so, — and cut off the communication."

The bridge was a plank; and it crossed a chasm about four feet wide and two deep. But it was very pleasant to see the pride with which he hoisted it up, and made it fast; smiling, as he did so, with a relish, and not merely mechanically.

"At nine o'clock, every night, Greenwich time," said Wemmick, "the gun fires. There he is, you see; and, when you hear him go, I think you'll say he's a stinger."

The piece of ordnance referred to was mounted into a separate fortress lightly constructed of lattice-work. It was protected from the weather by an ingenious little tarpaulin contrivance in the nature of an umbrella.

"Then, at the back," said Wemmick, "out of sight, so as not to impede the idea of fortifications — for it's a principle with me, if you have an idea carry it out, and keep it up. I don't know whether that's your opinion" —

I said, "Decidedly."

"At the back there's a pig, and there are fowls and rabbits; then I knock together my own little farm, you see, and grow cucumbers; and you'll judge at supper what sort of a salad I can raise. So, sir," said Wemmick, smiling again, but rather seriously too, "if you can suppose the little place besieged, it would hold out a devil of a time in point of provisions."

Then he conducted me to a bower about a dozen yards off, but which was approached by such ingenious twists of path, that it took quite a long time to get at; and in this retreat our glasses were already set forth. Our punch was cooling in an ornamental lake, on whose margin the bower was raised. This piece of water (with an island in the middle, which might have been the salad for supper) was of a circular form; and he had constructed a fountain in it, which, when you set a little mill going, and took a cork out of a pipe, played to that powerful extent that it made the back of your hand quite wet.

"I am my own engineer, and my own carpenter, and my own plumber, and my own gardener, and my own 'Jack of all trades,'" said Wemmick in acknowledging my compliments. "Well, it's a good thing, you know. It brushes the Newgate cobwebs away, and pleases the Aged." xx, xxi, xxiv–xxvi, xxxii, xxxvi, xxxvii, xlv, xlviii, li, lv.

**Wemmick, Mr., senior,** *called* THE AGED. Mr. John Wemmick's father; a very old man, clean, cheerful, comfortable, and well cared for, but intensely deaf. xxv, xxxvii, xlv, xlviii, li, lv.

**Wemmick, Mrs.** *See* SKIFFINS, MISS.

**Whimple, Mrs.** A lodging-house keeper at Mill Pond Bank, Chinks's Basin; an elderly woman of a pleasant and thriving appearance, who is the best of housewives. xlvi.

**William.** *See* POTKINS, WILLIAM.

**Wopsle, Mr.** A friend of Mrs. Joe Gargery's; at first parish clerk, afterwards an actor in London under the stage-name of Mr. Waldengarver.

Mr. Wopsle, united to a Roman nose and a large bald forehead, had a deep sonorous voice, which he was proud of; indeed, it was understood among his acquaintance, that, if you could only give him his head, he would read the clergyman into fits. He himself confessed, that if the Church was "thrown open," meaning to competition, he would not despair of making his mark in it. The Church not being "thrown open," he was, as I have said, our clerk. But he finished the amens tremendously; and when he gave out the psalm,—always giving us the whole verse,—he looked all round the congregation first, as much as to say, "You have heard my friend overhead: oblige me with your opinion of this."

His success as an actor is not particularly brilliant or encouraging. Pip and Herbert go to the small theatre where he is engaged, to witness his impersonation of Hamlet.

Whenever that undecided prince had to ask a question or state a doubt, the public helped him out with it. As, for example, on the question, whether 't was nobler in the mind to suffer, some roared, Yes; and some, No; and some, inclining to both opinions, said, "Toss up for it;" and quite a debating society arose. When he asked what should such fellows as he do crawling between earth and heaven, he was encouraged with loud cries of, "Hear,

hear!" When he appeared with his stocking disordered (its disorder expressed, according to usage, by one very neat fold in the top, which I suppose to be always got up with a flat-iron), a conversation took place in the gallery respecting the paleness of his leg, and whether it was occasioned by the turn the ghost had given him. On his taking the recorders, — very like a little black flute that had just been played in the orchestra, and handed out at the door, — he was called upon, unanimously, for "Rule Britannia." When he recommended the player not to saw the air thus, the sulky man said, "And don't *you* do it, neither; you 're a deal worse than *him!*" And I grieve to add, that peals of laughter greeted Mr. Wopsle on every one of these occasions. iv–vii, x, xiii, xv, xviii, xxxi, xlvii.

# OUR MUTUAL FRIEND

## OUTLINE

### BOOK THE FIRST: THE CUP AND THE LIP.

Chapter It had been a chill autumn day, and night was just
I closing in, when Gaffer Hexam's shabby boat, rowed by his handsome, dark-haired daughter, with face averted, while he sat in the stern towing some object behind, touched the muddy bank of the Thames, not far from London Bridge. At almost the same hour Mr. and Mrs. Veneering — very new people in a new
II house, with everything new and costly about them — were receiving a party of new friends at dinner, including Twemlow, a rather feeble-minded old bachelor (second cousin to Lord Snigsworth), the puzzle of whose life it was whether he, or somebody else, was Veneering's oldest friend. He had known Veneering about two weeks.

III One of the guests at this party was Mortimer Lightwood, a young solicitor, who, before dinner was over, was summoned by Gaffer Hexam's boy to look at the object which Gaffer had towed ashore. Another of the guests, his friend Eugene Wrayburn, a briefless young barrister, went with him. The body was identified by Lightwood by the papers found upon it, as that of Mr. John Harmon, a young man who had lately returned from abroad with £700 in his pocket, and the same man — as Lightwood had just been relating — to whom a fortune had recently been left by his father, an old Dustman, on condition that he married a certain young woman. A mysterious stranger, one Julius Handford, viewed the body with much agitation, but failed to identify it.

IV The young woman in question was Bella Wilfer, a very handsome, spoiled child, the daughter of R. Wilfer, a cherubic, middle-aged clerk in Mr. Veneering's drug house. He was too modest to make use of his full name, which was the fine one Reginald; and he was known to his intimates as Rumty. At this juncture the Wilfers took in a lodger, Mr. John Rokesmith, a handsome young man, between whom and Miss Bella Wilfer, as the young lady declared after their first meeting, "there is a natural antipathy and a deep distrust." Young Harmon being dead, the
V property was inherited by Nick Boffin, of Boffin's Bower, an

old gentleman who had served the elder Harmon faithfully for many years; and who now took life easy. Being unable to read, he hired one Silas Wegg, a crafty rascal with a wooden leg, who kept an apple stand, to read to him, six nights a week, at a crown per week.

"Half a crown," said Wegg, meditating. "Yes. (It ain't much, sir.) Half a crown!"

"Per week, you know."

"Per week. Yes. As to the amount of strain upon the intellect now. Was you thinking at all of poetry?" Mr. Wegg inquired, musing.

"Would it come dearer?" Mr. Boffin asked.

"It would come dearer," Mr. Wegg returned; "for, when a person comes to grind off poetry night after night, it is but right he should expect to be paid for its weakening effect on his mind."

"To tell you the truth, Wegg," said Boffin, "I was n't thinking of poetry, except in so far as this: if you was to happen now and then to feel yourself in the mind to tip me and Mrs. Boffin one of your ballads, why, then, we should drop into poetry."

"I follow you, sir," said Wegg; "but, not being a regular musical professional, I should be loath to engage myself for that; and therefore, when I dropped into poetry, I should ask to be considered so fur in the light of a friend."

At this Mr. Boffin's eyes sparkled; and he shook Silas earnestly by the hand, protesting that it was more than he could have asked, and that he took it very kindly indeed.

"What do you think of the terms, Wegg?" Mr. Boffin then demanded with unconcealed anxiety.

Silas, who had stimulated this anxiety by his hard reserve of manner, and who had begun to understand his man very well, replied, with an air as if he was saying something extraordinarily generous and great: —

"Mr. Boffin, I never bargain."

"So I should have thought of you," said Mr. Boffin admiringly.

"No, sir, I never did 'aggle, and I never will 'aggle. Consequently I meet you at once, free and fair, with: Done for double the money!"

Mr. Boffin seemed a little unprepared for this conclusion, but assented, with the remark, "You know better what it ought to be than I do, Wegg," and again shook hands with him upon it.

"Could you begin to-night, Wegg?" he then demanded.

"Yes, sir," said Mr. Wegg, careful to leave all the eagerness to him. "I see no difficulty if you wish it. You are provided with the needful implement, — a book, sir?"

"Bought him at a sale," said Mr. Boffin. "Eight wollumes.

Red and gold. Purple ribbon in every wollume to keep the place where you leave off. Do you know him?"

"The book's name, sir?" inquired Silas.

"I thought you might have know'd him without it," said Mr. Boffin, slightly disappointed. "His name is 'Decline-and-Fall-Off-the-Rooshan-Empire.'" (Mr. Boffin went over these stones slowly and with much caution.)

"Ay, indeed!" said Mr. Wegg, nodding his head with an air of friendly recognition.

"You know him, Wegg?"

"I have n't been not to say right slap through him very lately," Mr. Wegg made answer, "having been otherways employed, Mr. Boffin. But know him? Old familiar declining and falling off the Rooshan! Rather, sir! Ever since I was not so high as your stick. Ever since my eldest brother left our cottage to enlist into the army. On which occasion, as the ballad that was made about it describes, —

"Beside that cottage-door, Mr. Boffin,
A girl was on her knees:
She held aloft a snowy scarf, sir,
Which (my eldest brother noticed) fluttered in the breeze.

"She breathed a prayer for him, Mr. Boffin;
A prayer he could not hear:
And my eldest brother lean'd upon his sword, Mr. Boffin,
And wiped away a tear."

Much impressed by this family circumstance, and also by the friendly disposition of Mr. Wegg, as exemplified in his so soon dropping into poetry, Mr. Boffin again shook hands with that ligneous sharper, and besought him to name his hour. Mr. Wegg named eight.

"I shall expect you, Wegg," said Mr. Boffin, clapping him on the shoulder with the greatest enthusiasm, "most joyfully. I shall have no peace or patience till you come. Print is now opening ahead of me. This night, a literary man, *with* a wooden leg," — he bestowed an admiring look upon that decoration, as if it greatly enhanced the relish of Mr. Wegg's attainments, — "will begin to lead me a new life. My fist again, Wegg: morning, morning, morning!"

VI The death of Harmon was commonly looked upon as a murder; and there was talk at the Six Jolly Fellowship Porters (Miss Potterson's waterside inn) of Gaffer Hexam's being the murderer.

The accuser was Rogue Riderhood, a former "pardner" of Hexam, lately out of "Quod" for robbing a sailor, between whom and Hexam there was now an enmity. Lizzie Hexam thought it time that her brother, for whose schooling she had secretly paid, should leave home and seek his fortune; and she sent him off with what money she had, resolved to stay herself with her father. She suspected that Rogue Riderhood was the murderer of Harmon.

VII The bones of Harmon, by the way, or some of them, came into the possession of Mr. Venus, a queer little man, who strung skeletons, stuffed birds and animals, and who also owned Mr. Wegg's missing leg, which he bought at the hospital where it was cut off. Wegg was in treaty with him to get it back. Wegg

VIII had a rival claimant for Mr. Boffin's employment. Mr. John Rokesmith, the Wilfers' lodger, offered himself as private secretary. Mr. Boffin was n't sure as yet that he needed

IX a private secretary; but he and Mrs. Boffin, a motherly soul, were resolved upon adopting an orphan, and also upon doing something for Bella Wilfer, who had so cruelly lost the possibility of a rich husband. It was settled that she should come to live with them. Mrs. Boffin had an ambition for society

X and fashion, but in a kindly, unsophisticated way. The Veneerings, on the other hand, were doing the thing in a different way; and they had already made an unfortunate match between two of their new old friends. Mr. and Mrs. Alfred Lammle had their wedding breakfast at Veneering's house; Twemlow, as an old friend of the Veneerings, gave away the bride, and Mortimer Lightwood, who barely knew Lammle, was his best man. Before their honeymoon was over, the Lammles discovered that they had been duped, — each supposing the other to be wealthy: they quarrelled, reviled each other, but finally came to an understanding, which was to keep their discomfiture to themselves, to be revenged upon the Veneerings, and to prey upon the world in general.

XI Another new old friend of the Veneerings was Mr. Podsnap, a highly respectable, well-to-do man, who had everything expensive and ugly about him, who had a big rocking-horse kind of woman for a wife, and a crushed "young person" for a daughter. Mrs. Lammle, at her husband's instigation, became confidential and intimate with Miss Podsnap, who needed a friend. Their intimacy began at a party given one night by the Podsnaps.

XII On the same night Mortimer Lightwood (with whom was Eugene Wrayburn) had a caller, an ill-looking fellow, with a squinting leer, who, as he spoke, fumbled at an old sodden fur cap, formless and mangy, that looked like a furry animal, dog or cat, drowned and decaying. This was Roger (or "Rogue") Riderhood, who had come to claim the reward offered for Harmon's murderer.

Riderhood declared that Hexam had done the deed and had confessed it to him. At his request, the statement was taken down in
XIII writing, and then the two young men followed him to the police station, which was near the river and also near the Six Jolly Fellowship Porters. The night was cold and stormy, with sleet and rain driving from the northeast. Gaffer Hexam was still out in his boat, though it was long past his usual hour for returning. The inspector in charge, with Riderhood, waited for him under the lee of an upturned boat, while Lightwood and Wrayburn sought the shelter of the inn.

About midnight, however, Eugene, with unwonted energy, went out to see the lay of the land, and before returning he crept up to the window of Hexam's rude home, and looked in. The fire was burning brightly; Gaffer's supper was laid out, ready to be cooked, when he should come home, and there sat Lizzie, her face resting on her hand, a flush upon her cheeks, the firelight bringing out the lustre of her dark hair, the tears springing in her eyes. While he stood there, she started up, opened the door, and cried, "Father, father! did you call me?" But there was no answer. Two hours
XIV later Gaffer Hexam's dead body was found in tow of his own drifting boat. He had fallen overboard, and the rope which he usually carried about his neck, in order to secure a dead body when he found it, had formed a noose in which his arms became entangled.

XV The Golden Dustman, as he was now called, and his secretary got on extremely well together. Silas Wegg was put in charge of Boffin's Bower, and the Boffins moved to a larger house
XVI in a more fashionable region, where Bella Wilfer and John Rokesmith, the secretary, were soon installed; and where beggars, in person and by letter, importuned the Golden Dustman
XVII for a share of that fortune which for some inscrutable and, as it appeared to them, insufficient, reason had been bestowed upon him.

## BOOK THE SECOND: BIRDS OF A FEATHER

Chapter I One autumn evening, six months after his father's death, Charley Hexam, accompanied by his friend, Bradley Headstone, the schoolmaster, paid a visit to his sister, Lizzie. She was now earning her living, and lodging with a queer little crippled girl, Jenny Wren, who supported herself as a dolls' dressmaker, and kept house for her father, — who was given to drink. Bradley Headstone was a young man, who, with infinite pains and difficulty, had worked himself up from the gutter. He was doggedly persevering, but not clever; and though excessively formal and decent,

there was enough of what was fiery (but smouldering) still visible
in him to suggest that if, when he was a pauper lad, he had been
told off for the sea, he would not have been the last man in a ship's
crew. Bradley Headstone was smitten, against his will, by Lizzie Hexam's handsome face and quiet manner; and it angered him,
though he did not know why, when he and Charley, as they
started homeward, met Eugene Wrayburn sauntering toward Lizzie
Hexam's house. Wrayburn's errand was to beg Lizzie to accept for
II herself and for the dolls' dressmaker the services of a teacher
whom he would supply. Lizzie was troubled, and strongly
averse to accepting this offer, but Wrayburn put it so ingeniously,
as if to refuse would be a slight upon the memory of her father,
perpetuating the fault by which he had kept her ignorant, that
III finally she consented. It was at this juncture that Veneering suddenly determined to run for Parliament, the offer of a
pocket borough having been made to him, with the trifling condition that he should "put down" five thousand pounds. Veneering
agreed to do so, provided his friends would "rally round him," and
accordingly Twemlow, Podsnap, and the others threw themselves
into cabs, and went about London in great haste, and in due course
Veneering was returned.

IV But while Podsnap was burying himself in this matter
and in others equally important, Mr. and Mrs. Lammle were
secretly getting up a love affair between Miss Podsnap and one
"Fascination" Fledgeby. Fledgeby was a tall, slim young man
V (with eyes too close together), the son of a money-lender (now
deceased), and secretly engaged in the same occupation,
though ostensibly he was a gentleman of leisure. He wanted to
marry Miss Podsnap, because she had money in her own right,
and Lammle wanted him to, because if he brought about the
match, Fledgeby was to pay him a round sum of money. Fledgeby
was very shy in the company of ladies, though sharp and shrewd
enough where his interest was concerned. It will be remembered
VI that Eugene Wrayburn had provided a teacher for Lizzie
Hexam. Her brother and Bradley Headstone had intended
to do this, and, furious at his interference, they came to his chambers to protest against it. Wrayburn received them with a cool insolence which provoked the schoolmaster almost beyond endurance.
When they were gone Lightwood asked his friend what was to
be the result of his relations with Lizzie Hexam, and Wrayburn
answered: "Upon my life, I don't know."

VII Silas Wegg having finally concluded a bargain with Mr.
Venus for his long-lost leg, the latter brought it one evening to Boffin's Bower, where Mr. Wegg, for interested reasons, re-

ceived him with Jamaica rum and tobacco and great friendliness. Wegg, having screwed as much money out of Mr. Boffin as he dared to ask for, and being envious of the Golden Dustman's property, and especially angry with John Rokesmith for having supplanted him, as he thought, was always scheming against his generous benefactor; and he now made an alliance with Mr. Venus to search the dust heaps at Boffin's Bower, with the hope of discovering some treasure buried there by the late Mr. Harmon.

VIII Mr. Boffin was much more fortunate in his secretary; there was a mystery about him; he would see no stranger — especially he would not meet Mortimer Lightwood; but he was invaluable to Mr. Boffin; and even Bella Wilfer, who really did not like him, found herself, much to her surprise, acting upon his suggestion that she should visit her family, whom, to tell the truth, she had a little neglected. "Well, and how do you do, Bella?" said her sister Lavinia. "And how are your Boffins?" "Peace!" exclaimed Mrs. Wilfer. "Hold! I will not suffer this tone of levity." "My goodness me! How are your Spoffins, then?" said Lavvy, "since ma so very much objects to your Boffins."

"Impertinent girl! Minx!" said Mrs. Wilfer, with dread severity. "I don't care whether I am a Minx or a Sphinx," returned Lavinia coolly, tossing her head. "It was to be expected," said Mrs. Wilfer, waving her gloved hands; "a child of mine deserts me for the proud and prosperous, and another child of mine despises me!" The truth was, that before long all three women were angry, and all three were in tears. But then Bella went off in Mr. Boffin's carriage for her father; he obtained a holiday; Bella fitted him out in a complete new suit of clothes, new hat, new boots, new gloves; and after that they dined at Greenwich; and Bella arranged his hair, as she used to do, and told him how mercenary she had become, and finally sent him home, after the happiest day of his life, with his waistcoat pockets crammed with bank notes.

IX Another object of Mr. Boffin's intended bounty was little Johnny Higden, the orphan whom he and Mrs. Boffin wished to adopt; but poor Johnny fell ill of scarlet fever, and was taken to a children's hospital. He had a wooden horse and some other toys, and in the cot next to him was a little boy with a broken leg who had no toys. It was late at night, and Rokesmith stood beside his bed. The child was very ill and gasping for breath, but he wanted to speak. Rokesmith gently lifted him up. "Him!" said he. "Those!" He meant that his toys should be given to the mite in the next bed. This was done, and with a sigh of content little Johnny breathed his last; and in his place, as a sort of pen-
X ance, Mrs. Boffin took a good but ungainly youth called

Sloppy. About the same time two calls were made. Bradley Head-
XI stône went to see Lizzie Hexam, to offer himself as a teacher in place of the one selected by Wrayburn; but he made no progress except that Lizzie agreed to see him, with her brother, again.
XII The other call was made by John Rokesmith, disguised with a wig, at the house of Rogue Riderhood. And now the mystery of the Harmon murder was cleared up: Rokesmith was, in fact, Harmon; the murdered man was a seaman, who had come ashore with Harmon, and tried to rob and murder him; but his accomplices, one of whom was Riderhood, threw both him and Harmon into the river. Harmon escaped; the other, George Radfoot, was drowned; and Gaffer Hexam, as has been related, found his body,
XIII with Harmon's coat and papers upon it. Harmon's object now was to make Rogue Riderhood retract his accusation of murder against Hexam's father. But things were going badly with Harmon. Bella Wilfer—perhaps she was mercenary, as she con-
XIV fessed—refused him. However, he obtained Rogue Riderhood's retraction, and, having learned Lizzie's address from Headstone, sent it to her. The unhappy Headstone had his second
XV interview with Lizzie; all the passion of a strong, long-suppressed nature was laid at her feet; but Lizzie did not even like the man, and as gently as she could, she refused him. "Then," said Bradley Headstone, striking his hand against the iron fence, till the blood ran from it, "I hope that I may never kill him." "Whom?" asked Lizzie. "Mr. Eugene Wrayburn," was his answer.

XVI That other love affair, between Fledgeby and Georgiana Podsnap, was progressing; but now Mrs. Lammle took a heroic step. At a party given by the Lammles she secretly begged Twemlow to warn Podsnap against herself, and to save his daughter. Poor Twemlow was stunned, but promised to do so; and apparently he did, for Mr. Lammle soon received a note from Podsnap requesting that there should be no further intercourse between the two families.

### BOOK THE THIRD: A LONG LANE

Chapter I Fledgeby proposed to Lammle that they should find out who had betrayed them and "mark" him; in the mean time he proposed to himself to be revenged on Lammle, who had bullied him without mercy, by buying up some of his over-due promissory notes. This he did through a kindly old Jew named Riah, whom he always put forward as a cover for the note-shaving business which he carried on in secret.

II This same Riah, by the way, was a friend to Lizzie Hexam and Jenny Wren, and, at this juncture, he had advised and

assisted Lizzie to find a new home, where she might hide from her two lovers, each of whom she feared, but from very different reasons. Riah accompanied Jenny Wren one night to the Six Jolly Fellowship Porters, in order to show Rogue Riderhood's retraction to Miss Potterson, the landlady. That very night the Rogue was run down in his boat by a steamer, and very nearly drowned. He was taken to the inn, and, after some hours of hard work, resusci-
III tated. "Where 's my fur cap?" he asked in a surly voice. "In the river," somebody answered. "And warn't there no honest man to pick it up? O' course there was, though, and to cut off with it arterwards. You are a rare lot, all on you!" Thus he rendered thanks for being restored to life.

IV Bella made another visit to her family, on the anniversary of R. W.'s wedding day. There was a family dinner party, with George Sampson (a former lover of Bella's, now transferred to Lavinia) as a guest. Mrs. Wilfer was very grand, and very melancholy, and entertained the company with reminiscences of how her mother had prophesied that she would marry a little man whose mind would be below the average, and how, within a month, she met R. W., and within a year married him,

V On her way back to the Boffins', Bella confessed to her father that prosperity seemed to be spoiling the Golden Dustman, and it is certain that in her presence he drove a hard bargain with Rokesmith in regard to the latter's salary; and Mr. Boffin was now always talking to Bella about the value of money, and the necessity of her making a good match. Mrs. Lammle, who had now become rather intimate with the Boffins, talked to her in the same strain; and Bella was foolish enough to tell her one day about
VI Rokesmith's offer of marriage, and her refusal of it. Since the change in his character, Mr. Boffin's taste in reading had turned to the history of misers, and going to Boffin's Bower one night (when Wegg and Venus were about to continue their search for hidden treasure), he made Wegg read to him from a book which he brought about various misers who had stowed away their gains in odd places. Then he went out and poked about the
VII mounds with a dark lantern, dug up a bottle, and carried it off. When he had gone, Wegg disclosed to his partner that he had found in one of the mounds a will made by Harmon, deceased (which was later than the will under which Mr. Boffin held the property), which gave one mound to Mr. Boffin, and all the rest of his property to the crown. Mr. Venus took charge of this will.

VIII An odd circumstance was the means of bringing Bella and John Rokesmith together. Little Johnny's grandmother, old

Betty Higden, who had gone afoot to the country with a basket of small wares to sell, fell sick near the factory where Lizzie Hexam was
IX working, and died in Lizzie Hexam's arms. A letter that she carried on her person gave the name and address of Mr. Boffin. Lizzie communicated with him, and, as the result, Rokesmith and Bella came down to give poor old Betty a decent burial. So Lizzie and Bella became friends: and Bella (who was beginning to think that after all there might be something better than money) cast off
X her haughtiness, and was really rather kind to John Rokesmith. Lizzie Hexam had confided to Bella that she feared one of her lovers would kill the other (without naming them), and Mortimer Lightwood had the same apprehension. Bradley Headstone believed that Eugene Wrayburn had spirited Lizzie away; and with the hope of tracking her, he used to follow Wrayburn night after night, — the latter maliciously taking him on long and furious jaunts. But the fact was, that Wrayburn was himself trying in every way to find out Lizzie's address. He could not get it out of Jenny Wren, the dolls' dressmaker, but there was a chance
XI of getting it from her drunken old father. One night, when Bradley Headstone had been following Wrayburn — Wrayburn well knowing it — on a long and fruitless trip, he met Rogue Riderhood, now a deputy lock-keeper on the Thames. Riderhood's errand had been, as he told Headstone, "to have the law of a busted B'low-Bridge steamer which drownded of me."

Bradley looked at him in astonishment.

"The steamer," said Mr. Riderhood obstinately, "run me down and drownded of me. Interference on the part of other parties brought me round; but I never asked 'em to bring me round, nor yet the steamer never asked 'em to it. I mean to be paid for the life as the steamer took."

XII The two men came to a kind of understanding that they both hated Wrayburn; and Headstone felt, vaguely, that Riderhood might in some way be made an instrument of revenge. Meanwhile the Lammles plotted to make trouble between Rokesmith and his employer, Lammle hoping to succeed the secretary. The fact was, that the Lammles had sunk deep into the
XIII toils of Riah the Jew, — who was but a name for the sly Fledgeby; and even poor Twemlow, who had once put his
XIV name to a bill for a friend, found himself in the same boat. Wegg's intrigue, however, seemed to be less prosperous. Mr. Venus, smitten by his conscience, revealed everything to Mr. Boffin, and then he hid Mr. Boffin behind a stuffed alligator when Wegg came into his shop, and inveighed against his benefactor, whom he styled "that minion of fortune and worm of the hour." But poor

Boffin was surrounded by enemies, for on his way home Mrs. Lam-
XV mle waylaid him (in pursuance of the plot). The next morning the Golden Dustman, having been told by Mrs. Lammle of John Rokesmith's proposal to Bella, made a terrible scene in the presence of his family. He discharged Rokesmith, with many abusive words, declaring that the secretary was an insolent, mercenary villain, who cared for nothing but Bella's money; whereas Bella would never marry any one who had n't money, and plenty of it. So the secretary left in a rage, and Bella, in a passion of tears and anger and indignation, mixed with gratitude for his past kindness, took an excited leave of the Golden Dustman, wept over his kind-hearted wife, and, clad in her old clothes, fled to the
XVI counting-house where her father was employed. There she found R. W. (it being after hours) enjoying a modest luncheon of bread and milk; and before she had been there many minutes in came John Rokesmith, exclaiming, "My love, my life! You ARE mine!" "Yes," said Bella, "I am yours, if you think me worth taking." Then they fell into each other's arms, to the infinite astonishment of R. W. But presently everything was explained; and Bella and her father went home to encounter Mrs. Wilfer and Lavvy. The encounter was a severe one; but after the family had separated for the night, Bella came downstairs with bare feet to hug poor R. Wilfer, and to assure him that in her future home there should always be a warm corner for him.

XVII Meanwhile the Lammles are "sold out," the Veneerings give a dinner of wonder at the event, at which the Lammles are not present, and Eugene discovers Lizzie Hexam's address.

### BOOK THE FOURTH: A TURNING

Chapter I Two or three days afterward, it being a fine summer evening, Rogue Riderhood, dozing at his lock, was awakened by the cry, "Lock ho!" The speaker was an amateur sculler in a light boat, well up to his work, but taking it easily, and on a second glance the Rogue recognized him as Eugene Wrayburn. Scarcely had he passed through when a bargeman, dressed with a curious similarity to Riderhood himself, crept by; and in this figure the Rogue detected Bradley Headstone. Three nights later, in a violent thunderstorm, Headstone returned to the lock, and after telling Riderhood that he had seen Wrayburn walking with Lizzie Hexam, threw himself exhausted on Riderhood's bed.

II Mr. Boffin's affairs were becoming more and more complicated. He paid off Mrs. Lammle for her services with a hundred pound note, and politely informed her and her husband that their intention (which the Golden Dustman acutely perceived) to

take the places of Bella and Rokesmith "would not do." Then poor
III Mr. Boffin had an encounter with Wegg, and was shown the
lately discovered will, and Wegg insolently triumphed over
him, and called him "Boffin," and demanded that his property should
be distributed into three parts, of which Mr. Boffin should retain one
only. The Golden Dustman bore all this and much more with strange
IV meekness. One morning, very early, not long after Bella's
return home, she and her father stole out of the house and
went off to Greenwich, where she was married to John Rokesmith.
After which the three dined together very cosily and happily in the
identical room where Bella and her father had dined once before.
Mrs. Rokesmith sent a note to her mother, informing her of the event,
V and requesting her to tell her father, for Mr. Wilfer's complicity in the affair was to be kept secret. Upon his return at
night he was tragically informed by Mrs. Wilfer that "his" daughter
Bella was married to a "mendicant." Lavvy thought that she ought
to have been present at the wedding. "Bella," she added, "might
have asked me to keep it a secret from ma and pa, as of course I
should have done." "'As of course you would have done?' In-
grate!" exclaimed Mrs. Wilfer. "Viper!" George Sampson protested at this, and there was a great quarrel, in the course of which
Lavinia thought it her duty to faint. But a week or so later Bella
and her husband came to tea, and the family were reconciled.

VI Eugene Wrayburn had a final meeting with Lizzie in a
quiet spot on the banks of the river. She begged him to
leave her and the town, and to pursue her no more, and he,
having wrung from her a confession that she loved him, half
promised to obey. Then she went home, and Eugene walked up
and down, thinking what he should do. He stopped, and looked
at the water. At that moment a man came behind him, and
struck him a terrible blow on the head. Eugene, almost paralyzed,
grappled with him, and clutched at a red silk handkerchief that he
wore; but more and more blows were rained upon him, and at last
he was flung into the river, and his assailant disappeared. Lizzie
Hexam, having heard a cry and the sounds of a struggle, rushed
back, saw a man's body floating in the river, put off in a boat, and
when he came to the surface again, rescued him, and carried Eugene,
unaided, to the nearest house. The next morning, just as day was
VII breaking, Bradley Headstone appeared at Riderhood's lock,
still in his bargeman's clothes, and wearing a red silk handkerchief about his neck, such as Riderhood had worn when Headstone saw him last. He threw himself on Riderhood's bed, and
slept, or feigned to sleep, for twelve hours. While he was asleep,
Riderhood examined his clothes — without awaking him — and

found that they were torn and bloody. Then, after eating something, Headstone started homeward; but Riderhood secretly followed him, and saw him stop in a wood near the river, take off his bargeman's suit, make it into a bundle, which he threw in the river, and then, after a plunge in the water, resume his customary decent suit of black.

VIII Another man who had been smitten by Lizzie Hexam's handsome face — though he saw it but once — was "Fascination" Fledgeby. He, too, called on Miss Jenny Wren, in order to ascertain, if possible, the address of "the handsome gal." Miss Wren put him off till the next morning, when she would call at his chambers. Having arrived there in due course, she found on the steps a lady, holding a man's hat in her hand, and with a strange smile on her face, while from above came a sound of spluttering and of blows, as if some one were taking a bath and beating a carpet at the same time. The fact was, that Mr. Lammle, having crammed Fledgeby's mouth with salt, was giving him a good thrashing, while Mrs. Lammle waited on the steps. Lammle coming out, Miss Wren went upstairs, and assisted Fledgeby by making some brown paper and vinegar plasters for him; but, inasmuch as she could n't resist the temptation surreptitiously to add a few grains of pepper, the plasters did not seem to do Mr. Fledgeby much good. Events were crowding thick upon the poor little dolls'
IX dressmaker. Her wretched father died of drink, and when, after industriously making dolls' dresses for several days, in order to get money enough, Jenny had given him a decent burial, she
X was summoned to the bedside of Eugene Wrayburn. There she was of great assistance, for no one could tell as well as she what Eugene wanted to say in his moments of consciousness. It was she who made out that he wanted to be married to Lizzie;
XI and Lightwood went to London for a minister and for Bella, who immediately consented to go, though her husband refused even to see Lightwood, — assuring Bella, however, that his reason would be explained in due time, and Bella was content, though curious. Headstone, hearing of the intended marriage, fell down in a fit; but Eugene, after the marriage, began very slowly to mend. He charged Lightwood to see that, if he should die, there should be no pursuit of Headstone for the murder, lest Lizzie's name should be tarnished.

XII Bella's baby was born, and was fast developing a wonderful intelligence, and dimples like its mother's, and a strange aversion from its grandmother, when at last John Rokesmith and Mortimer Lightwood met. Lightwood started back in astonishment, for he saw the mysterious Julius Handford, suspected of complicity in the Harmon murder. Lightwood had him arrested forthwith, but he explained matters to the inspector, and was identified by a steward of the ship upon which he returned as John Harmon, though Bella did not know it as yet. That night he told Bella that they would move the next day to a better house in London, which proved to be no other than the Boffin mansion, where they were received by the Boffins with open arms. And now

XIII Bella learned the whole story: how her husband was John Harmon; how Mrs. Boffin had discovered that Rokesmith was Harmon, and how, at his request, the secret was kept, in order that he might, if possible, win Bella for himself; how Mr. Boffin, by way of curing Bella's love of money, had pretended to be a miser, and, as he expressed it, "a reg'lar brown bear all round," and how "the old lady" had nearly upset matters by her grief that Bella should be misled, even for a time, by Mr. Boffin's assumption

XIV of a mean character. It remained only to dispose of Wegg, who thought that the hour had now arrived for coming down on Mr. Boffin with the will which he had found, and getting two thirds of his property. So he called at the house, and demanded to see "Boffin," and was very abusive, and kept his hat on till John Harmon threw it out of the window. Then it was explained to him that the will in his possession was not the last, — the last one gave everything to Mr. Boffin; and, out of pure generosity, Mr. Boffin had given up the property (reserving a small share) to John Harmon. Then Wegg was carried out by Sloppy and thrown into a garbage cart which happened to be passing at the moment. Brad-

XV ley Headstone's agony of mind, now that he had been the means of bringing Eugene and Lizzie together instead of separating them forever, as he had intended, was terrible. Rogue Riderhood demanded, as the price of his silence, that Bradley should give him his watch and his money, and even that he should sell his furniture and hand over the proceeds. This occurred at the lock. All night Headstone sat looking at the fire in Riderhood's hut. In the morning he started homeward, but the Rogue kept with him; then he turned about and walked three miles in the opposite direction, but Riderhood was still at his heels. When they returned to the lock Headstone caught Riderhood around the waist. "I'll hold you living," he cried, "and I'll hold you dead. Come down!" And down they went into the black pool of water; and there they were found afterward, with Bradley Headstone's arm still gripping tight the body of the Rogue.

XVI Mrs. Wilfer's first visit to her daughter's new house was a great and solemn event. She went in the Harmon carriage, accompanied by Lavinia and George Sampson, and she scornfully declined to "loll," though requested thereto by Lavvy. She carefully abstained from any signs of surprise or admiration at the glories of the new house, and treated Bella as if she were a young lady of good position whom she had met in society a few years before.

XVII R. Wilfer was appointed Secretary, and resigned from Mr. Veneering's drug house. Mr. Veneering, by the way, came to smash at last, and retired to Calais, where he and his wife lived comfortably upon the latter's diamonds. Eugene Wrayburn completely recovered, and though Podsnap sneered at his choice of a wife, Twemlow declared that Eugene had shown the spirit of a gentleman.

---

## INDEX TO CHARACTERS

**Akershem, Miss Sophronia.** An acquaintance of the Veneerings; a fast young lady of society, with raven locks, and a complexion that lights up well when well powdered. She marries Mr. Alfred Lammle. I: ii, x, xi; II: iv, v, xvi; III: v, xii, xiv, xvii; IV: ii, viii.

**Blight, Young.** A dismal boy, who is Mr. Mortimer Lightwood's clerk and office-boy. I: viii; III: xvii; IV: ix, xvi.

**Boffin, Mrs. Henrietta.** Wife of Mr. Boffin; a stout lady of a rubicund and cheerful aspect, described by her husband as "a high-flyer at fashion." I: v, ix, xv–xvii; II: viii–x, xiv; III: iv, v, xv; IV: ii. xii–xiv, xvi.

**Boffin, Nicodemus,** *called* NODDY, *also* THE GOLDEN DUSTMAN. A confidential servant of the elder Mr. Harmon, who at death leaves him all his property, in case his son refuses to marry a certain young lady named in his will.

With respect to his personal appearance, Mr. Boffin is described as —

> A broad, round-shouldered, one-sided old fellow . . . dressed in a pea overcoat, and carrying a large stick. He wore thick shoes, and thick leather gaiters, and thick gloves like a hedger's. Both as to his dress and to himself, he was of an overlapping, rhinoceros build, with folds in his cheeks, and his forehead, and his eyelids, and his lips, and his ears, but with bright, eager, childishly-inquiring gray eyes under his ragged eyebrows and broad-brimmed hat. A very odd-looking old fellow altogether.
>
> . . . . . . . . . . . . . .
>
> These two ignorant and unpolished people [Mr. and Mrs. Boffin] had guided themselves . . . so far in their journey of life by a religious sense of duty and desire to do right. Ten thousand weaknesses and absurdities might have been detected in the

breasts of both; ten thousand vanities additional, possibly, in the breast of the woman. But the hard, wrathful, and sordid nature that had wrung as much work out of them as could be got in their best days for as little money as could be paid to hurry on their worst had never been so warped but that it knew their moral straightness, and respected it. In its own despite, in a constant conflict with itself and them, it had done so. And this is the eternal law. For evil often stops short at itself, and dies with the doer of it; but good never. I: v, viii, ix, xv–xvii; II: vii, viii, x, xiv; III: iv–vii, xiv, xv; IV: ii, iii, xii–xiv, xvi.

**Boots, Mr.** } Fashionable toadies; friends of the Veneerings. I:
**Brewer, Mr.** } ii, x; II: iii, xvi; III: xvii; IV: xvi.

**Cherub, The.** *See* WILFER, REGINALD.

**Cleaver, Fanny,** *called* JENNY WREN. A dolls' dressmaker. Lizzie Hexam, after her father's death, has temporary lodgings with her. II: i, ii, v, xi, xv; III: ii, iii, x, xiii; IV: viii–xi, xv.

**Cleaver, Mr.,** *called* MR. DOLLS. Her father; a good workman at his trade, but a weak, wretched, trembling creature, falling to pieces, and never sober. II: ii; III: x, xvii; IV: viii, ix.

**Dolls, Mr.** *See* CLEAVER, MR.

**Fledgeby, Mr.,** *called* FASCINATION FLEDGEBY. A dandified young man, who is a dolt in most matters, but sharp and tight enough where money is concerned.

Young Fledgeby had a peachy cheek, or a cheek compounded of the peach and the red red red wall on which it grows, and was an awkward, sandy-haired, small-eyed youth, exceeding slim (his enemies would have said lanky), and prone to self-examination in the articles of whisker and mustache. While feeling for the whisker that he anxiously expected, Fledgeby underwent remarkable fluctuations of spirits, ranging along the whole scale from confidence to despair. There were times when he started, as exclaiming, "By Jupiter, here it is at last!" There were other times when, being equally depressed, he would be seen to shake his head, and give up hope. To see him at those periods, leaning on a chimney-piece, like as on an urn containing the ashes of his ambition, with the cheek that would not sprout upon the hand on which that cheek had forced conviction, was a distressing sight. . . .

In facetious homage to the smallness of his talk and the jerky nature of his manners, Fledgeby's familiars had agreed to confer upon him (behind his back) the honorary title of Fascination Fledgeby. II: iv, v, xvi; III: i, xii, xiii, xvii; IV: viii, ix, xvi.

**Glamour, Bob.** A customer at the Six Jolly Fellowship Porters. I: vi; III: iii.

**Gliddery, Bob.** Pot-boy at the Six Jolly Fellowship Porters. I: vi, xiii; III: iii.

**Golden Dustman, The.** *See* BOFFIN, NICODEMUS.

**Greenwich, Archbishop of.** Head waiter at a hotel in Greenwich; a solemn gentleman in black clothes and white cravat, looking much like a clergyman. IV: iv.

**Gruff and Glum.** An old wooden-leg pensioner at Greenwich. IV: iv.

**Handford, Julius.** *See* HARMON, JOHN.

**Harmon, John,** *alias* JULIUS HANDFORD, *alias* JOHN ROKESMITH. Heir of the Harmon estate. On the death of his father, he returns to England from South Africa, where he has been living for a good many years. On his arrival he is inveigled into a waterside inn by a pretended friend, named George Radfoot, with whom he has made the passage, and is drugged, robbed, and thrown into the Thames. This pretended friend had previously changed clothes with Harmon, at the request of the latter, who desired to avoid recognition until he had seen a certain young lady whom he is required by his father's will to marry. The would-be assassin falls into a quarrel with a confederate over the money obtained by the robbery, and is himself murdered, and thrown into the river. The cold water into which Harmon is plunged restores him to consciousness, and, swimming to the shore, he escapes. The body of his assailant is found by a boatman named Hexam, and is taken in charge by the authorities. The clothes and the papers on the body having been identified, it is supposed that the body itself is that of young Harmon, who, finding himself reported dead, resolves to take advantage of the circumstance to further his own plans, and assumes the name of JULIUS HANDFORD, which he afterwards changes to JOHN ROKESMITH. I: ii–iv, viii, ix, xv–xvii; II: vii–x, xii–xiv; III: iv, v, ix, xv, xvi; IV: iv, v, xi–xiv, xvi.

**Harmon, Mrs. John.** *See* WILFER, MISS BELLA.

**Headstone, Bradley.** A master in a school in that district of the flat country tending to the Thames, where Kent and Surrey meet.

Bradley Headstone, in his decent black coat and waistcoat, and decent white shirt, and decent, formal black tie, and decent pantaloons of pepper and salt, with his decent silver watch in his pocket, and its decent hair-guard round his neck, looked a thoroughly decent young man of six and twenty. He was never seen in any other dress; and yet there was a certain stiffness in his manner of wearing this, as if there were a want of adaptation between him and it, recalling some mechanics in their holiday clothes. He had acquired mechanically a great store of teacher's knowledge. He could do mental arithmetic mechanically, sing at sight mechanically, blow various wind-instruments mechanically, even play the great church-organ mechanically. From his early childhood up, his mind had been a place of mechanical stowage. The arrangement of his wholesale warehouse so that it might be always ready to meet the demands of retail dealers (history here, geography there, astronomy to the right, political economy to the left, natural history, the physical sciences, figures, music, the lower mathematics, and what not, all in their several places), — this care had imparted to his countenance a look of care; while the habit of questioning and being questioned had given him a suspicious manner, or a manner that would be better described as one of lying in wait. There was a kind of settled trouble in the face. It was the face belonging to a naturally slow or inattentive intellect that had toiled hard to get what it had won, and that had to hold it, now that it was gotten. He always seemed to be uneasy lest anything should be missing from his mental warehouse, and taking stock to assure himself. II: i, vi, xi, xiv, xv; III: x, xi; IV: i, vi, vii, xi.

**Hexam, Charley.** His son; a pupil of Bradley Headstone's, and a curious mixture of uncompleted savagery and completed civilization. He is tenderly loved and cared for by his sister, but renounces her because she refuses his friend Headstone. Always utterly selfish and empty-hearted, and always bent on rising in the social scale, and increasing his "respectability," he renounces Headstone with equal readiness, when he finds good reason to think him guilty of the murder of his sister's favored lover, Eugene Wrayburn, and that his own name is therefore likely to be dragged into injurious notoriety. I: iii, vi; II: i, vi, xv; IV: vii.

**Hexam, Jesse,** *called* Gaffer. A Thames "waterside character;" a strong man with ragged grizzled hair and a sun-browned face. He is falsely accused of the murder of John Harmon. I: i, iii, vi, xii–xiv, xvi.

**Hexam, Lizzie.** Daughter of Jesse or "Gaffer" Hexam. She is in the habit of rowing with her father on the Thames, and on one occasion, while thus engaged, they find the body of a man, afterwards identified as John Harmon. Through the jealousy of Rogue Riderhood, suspicion is cast upon her father; and the officers undertake to arrest him as being concerned in the murder, but they find him in the river drowned, and attached to his own boat by a cord, in which he had apparently become entangled when he fell overboard. A young lawyer, Eugene Wrayburn, who accompanies the officers, becomes interested in the daughter, manifests much sympathy with her in her affliction, and aids her in obtaining an education. Her brother's teacher, Bradley Headstone, falls deeply in love with her, and makes an offer of marriage. This she refuses, and to escape his importunities, and also to save Wrayburn from his vengeance (for Headstone believes him to be the cause of his rejection), she leaves London, and obtains employment in a paper-mill in the country. After much fruitless search for her, Wrayburn ascertains where she is, and follows, bent on having an interview with her. He is, in turn, followed by Headstone, who comes upon them while they are engaged in conversation. Waiting until they part, the schoolmaster stealthily follows his rival, and deals him a murderous blow as he stands for a moment looking into the river. Lizzie hears the blows, a faint groan, and a fall into the water. Brave by nature and by habit, she runs towards the spot from which the sound had come. Seeing a bloody face turned up to the moon, and drifting away with the current, she jumps into a boat near by, puts out into the stream, and, when she has rescued the sufferer, finds that it is her lover. She tenderly nurses him through the dangerous illness that follows. When consciousness returns, he asks to be married to his preserver without delay, though no hope of his recovery is entertained by any one. Lizzie becomes his wife, and he grows stronger and better by slow degrees, and is at last restored to perfect health. I: i, iii, vi, xiii, xiv; II: i, ii, v, xi, xiv–xvi; III: i, ii, viii, ix; IV: v, x, xi, xvi, xvii.

**Higden, Mrs. Betty.** A poor woman who keeps a "minding-school," and also a mangle, in one of the complicated back settlements of Brentford.

She was one of those old women, . . . who, by dint of an indomitable purpose and a strong constitution, fight out many years, though each year has come with its new knock-down blows fresh to the fight against her wearied by it; an active old woman, with a bright dark eye and a resolute face, yet quite a tender creature too; not a logically-reasoning woman. But God is good; and hearts may count in heaven as high as heads. I: xvi; II: ix, x, xiv; III: viii.

**Inspector, Mr.** A police-officer who examines into the Harmon murder. I: iii; IV: xii.

**Joey, Captain.** A bottle-nosed regular customer at the Six Jolly Fellowship Porters. I: vi; III: iii.

**Johnny.** An orphan, grandson of Betty Higden. The Boffins propose to adopt him; but he dies before the plan is carried into effect. I: xvi; II: viii, ix, xiv; III: ix.

**Jonathan.** A customer at the Six Jolly Fellowship Porters. I: vi; III: iii.

**Mullins, Jack.** A frequenter of the Six Jolly Fellowship Porters. I: vi.

**Peecher, Miss Emma.** A teacher in the female department of the school in which Bradley Headstone is a master.

Small, shining, neat, methodical, and buxom was Miss Peecher; cherry-cheeked and tuneful of voice. A little pincushion, a little housewife, a little book, a little work-box, a little set of tables and weights and measures, and a little woman, all in one. She could write a little essay on any subject, exactly a slate long, beginning at the left-hand top of one side, and ending at the right-hand bottom of the other; and the essay should be strictly according to rule. If Mr. Bradley Headstone had addressed a written proposal of marriage to her, she would probably have replied in a complete little essay on the theme exactly a slate long; but would certainly have replied, "Yes," for she loved him. The decent hair-guard that went round his neck, and took care of his decent silver watch, was an object of envy to her: so would Miss Peecher have gone round his neck, and taken care of him, — of him, insensible, because he did not love Miss Peecher. I: xi, xv; III: xi; IV: vii.

**Poddles.** The pet name of a little girl in Mrs. Betty Higden's "minding-school." I: xvi.

**Podsnap, Miss Georgiana.** A shy, foolish, affectionate girl, of nearly eighteen, in training for "society."

She was but an under-sized damsel, with high shoulders, low spirits, chilled elbows, and a rasped surface of nose, who seemed to take occasional frosty peeps out of childhood into womanhood, and to shrink back again, overcome by her mother's head-dress, and her father from head to foot, — crushed by the mere dead-weight of Podsnappery. I: xi, xvii; II: iv, v, xvi; III: i, xvii; IV: ii.

**Podsnap, Mr. John.** Her father; a member of "society," and a pompous, self-satisfied man, swelling with patronage of his friends and acquaintances.

Mr. Podsnap was well to do, and stood very high in Mr. Podsnap's opinion. Beginning with a good inheritance, he had married a good inheritance, and had thriven exceedingly in the marine insurance way, and was quite satisfied. He never could make out why everybody was not quite satisfied, and he felt conscious that he set a brilliant social example in being particularly well satisfied with most things, and, above all other things, with himself.

Thus happily acquainted with his own merit and importance, Mr. Podsnap settled, that, whatever he put behind him, he put

MR. PODSNAP.

out of existence. There was a dignified conclusiveness, not to add a grand convenience, in this way of getting rid of disagreeables, which had done much towards establishing Mr. Podsnap in his lofty place in Mr. Podsnap's satisfaction. "I don't want to know about it: I don't choose to discuss it; I don't admit it!" Mr. Podsnap had even acquired a peculiar flourish of his right arm in often clearing the world of its most difficult problems by sweeping them behind him (and consequently sheer away) with those words and a flushed face: for they affronted him. I: ii, x, xi, xvii; II: iii–v, xvi; III: i, xvii; IV: xvii.

**Podsnap, Mrs.** His wife; a "fine woman for Professor Owen, quantity of bone, neck and nostrils like a rocking-horse, hard features," and a majestic presence. I: ii, x, xi, xvii; II: iii, iv; III: i, xvii; IV: xvii.

**Potterson, Miss Abbey.** Sole proprietor and manager of a well-kept tavern called the Six Jolly Fellowship Porters; a woman of great dignity and firmness, tall, upright, and well-favored, though severe of countenance, and having more the air of a schoolmistress than mistress of a public house. I: vi, xiii; III: ii, iii; IV: xii.

**Potterson, Job.** Her brother; steward of the ship in which John Harmon is a passenger. I: iii; II: xiii; IV: xii.

**Pubsey and Co.** The name of a fictitious firm of money-brokers in Saint Mary-Axe, used by "Fascination" Fledgeby to conceal his sharp practice in "shaving" notes. II: v.

**Riah, Mr.** An aged Jew, of venerable aspect and a generous and noble nature, who befriends Lizzie Hexam, and obtains employment for her. He is the agent of "Fascination" Fledgeby, who directs all his proceedings, while keeping himself in the background. II: v, xv; III: i, ii, x, xii, xiii; IV: viii, ix, xvi.

**Riderhood, Pleasant.** Daughter of Roger Riderhood; finally married to Mr. Venus, after rejecting him more than once.

Upon the smallest of small scales, she was an unlicensed pawnbroker, keeping what was popularly called a leaving-shop, by lending insignificant sums on insignificant articles of property deposited with her as security. In her four and twentieth year of life, Pleasant was already in her fifth year of this way of trade.

Why christened Pleasant, the late Mrs. Riderhood might possibly have been at some time able to explain, and possibly not. Her daughter had no information on that point: Pleasant she found herself, and she could n't help it. She had not been consulted on the question, any more than on the question of her coming into these terrestrial parts to want a name. Similarly she found herself possessed of what is colloquially termed a swivel eye (derived from her father), which she might perhaps have declined if her sentiments on the subject had been taken. She was not otherwise positively ill-looking, though anxious, meagre, of a muddy complexion, and looking as old again as she really was.

As some dogs have it in the blood, or are trained, to worry certain creatures to a certain point, so — not to make the comparison disrespectfully — Pleasant Riderhood had it in the blood, or had been trained, to regard seamen, within certain limits, as her prey. Show her a man in a blue jacket, and, figuratively speaking, she pinned him instantly. Yet, all things considered, she was not of an evil mind or an unkindly disposition. II: xii, xiii; III: iv, vii; IV: xiv.

**Riderhood, Roger,** *called* Rogue. A desperate "waterside character," in whose house an attempt is made on John Harmon's life. Quarrelling with Gaffer Hexam, who had been his partner, and anxious to obtain the reward offered by Mr. Boffin for the arrest of the supposed murderer, he goes to Mortimer Lightwood's office, and accuses Hexam of having done the deed. Search being made for Hexam, he is discovered drowned; and the reward is consequently not paid. Riderhood finally becomes a deputy lock-keeper at Plashwater Weir Mill, and is cognizant of Bradley Headstone's attack on Eugene Wrayburn. He uses his knowledge as a means of extorting money from Headstone, and at last, by his continued demands, drives him to desperation. A quarrel ensues, which results in the death of both. I: i, vi, xii–xiv; II: xii–xiv; III: ii, iii, viii, xi; IV: i, vii, xv.

**Rokesmith, John.** *See* Harmon, John.

**Rokesmith, Mrs. John.** *See* Harmon, Mrs. John.

**Sampson, George.** A young man who is very intimate with the Wilfer family. At first he hovers around Miss Bella, but, on her betrothal to Mr. John Harmon, transfers his affections to her sister Lavinia, who keeps him — partly in remembrance of his bad taste in having overlooked her in the first instance — under a course of stinging discipline. I: iv, ix; II: xiv; III: iv, xvi; IV: v, xvi.

**Sloppy.** A love-child, found in the street, brought up in the poorhouse, and adopted by Betty Higden, who keeps him employed in turning a mangle. He is afterwards taken into Mr. Boffin's service.

Of an ungainly make was Sloppy, — too much of him longwise, too little of him broadwise, and too many sharp angles of him anglewise. One of those shambling male human creatures, born to be indiscreetly candid in the revelation of buttons; every button he had about him glaring at the public to a quite preternatural extent. A considerable capital of knee and elbow, and wrist and ankle, had Sloppy; and he did n't know how to dispose of it to the best advantage, but was always investing it in wrong securities, and so getting himself into embarrassed circumstances. Full-private Number One in the Awkward Squad of the rank and file of life was Sloppy, and yet had his glimmering notions of standing true to the colors. I: xvi; II: ix, x, xiv; III: ix; IV: iii, xiv, xvi.

**Snigsworth, Lord.** First cousin to Mr. Twemlow; a nobleman with gout in his temper. I: ii, x; II: iii, v, xvi; IV: xvi.

**Sprodgkin, Mrs.** A portentous old parishioner of the Reverend Frank Milvey, and the plague of his life. She is constantly wishing to know who begat whom, or wanting some information concerning the Amorites. IV: xi.

**Tapkins, Mrs.** A fashionable woman who calls at the door of the "eminently aristocratic" mansion to which the Boffins remove from the "Bower," and leaves a card for herself, Miss Tapkins, Miss Frederica Tapkins, Miss Antonina Tapkins, Miss Malvina Tapkins, and Miss Euphemia Tapkins; also the card of Mrs. Henry George Alfred Swoshle, *née* Tapkins; also a card, Mrs. Tapkins at home Wednesdays, Music, Portland Place. I: xvii.

**Tippins, Lady.** A friend of the Veneerings, and a member of "society:" relict of the late Sir Thomas Tippins, knighted, by mistake, for somebody else by his Majesty, King George the Third. She is a charming old woman, with an immense, obtuse, drab, oblong face, like a face in a tablespoon, and a dyed long walk up the top of her head, as a convenient public approach to the bunch of false hair behind. She affects perennial youth in her dress and manners, and exerts herself to fascinate the male sex, especially the unmarried portion of it.

A grisly little fiction concerning her lovers is Lady Tippins's point. She is always attended by a lover or two; and she keeps a little list of her lovers; and she is always booking a new lover, or striking out an old lover, or putting a lover in her black list, or promoting a lover to her blue list, or adding up her lovers, or otherwise posting her book. I: ii, x, xvii; II: iii, xvi: III: xvii; IV: xvii.

**Toddles.** The pet name of a little boy in Mrs. Betty Higden's "minding-school." I: xvi.

**Tootle, Tom.** A frequenter of the Six Jolly Fellowship Porters, who is on the point of being married. I: vi; III: ii, iii.

**Twemlow, Mr. Melvin.** A friend of the Veneerings, and a member of "society." He is poor, and lives over a livery-stable yard in Duke Street, St. James's; but being first cousin to Lord

Snigsworth, he is in frequent requisition, and at many houses may be said to represent the dining-table in its normal state. His noble relative allows him a small annuity, on which he lives; and takes it out of him, as the phrase goes, in extreme severity; putting him, when he visits at Snigsworthy Park, under a kind of martial law; ordaining that he shall hang his hat on a particular peg, sit on a particular chair, talk on particular subjects to particular people, and perform particular exercises, — such as sounding the praises of the family varnish (not to say pictures), and abstaining from the choicest of the family wines, unless expressly invited to partake. I: ii, x, xvii; II: iii, xvi; III: xiii; IV: xvi, xvii.

**Veneering, Mr. Hamilton.** A *parvenu*, tolerated by "society" on account of his wealth. Formerly traveller or commission agent of Chicksey and Stobbles, druggists, but afterwards admitted into the firm, of which he becomes the supreme head, absorbing both his partners. He is a man of forty, wavy-haired, dark, tending to corpulence, sly, mysterious, filmy, — a kind of sufficiently well-looking veiled prophet, not prophesying. By a liberal expenditure of money, he gets himself returned to the House of Commons from the borough of Pocket-Breaches.

Mr. and Mrs. Veneering were bran-new people in a bran-new house in a bran-new quarter of London. Everything about the Veneerings was spick-and-span-new. All their furniture was new; all their friends were new; all their servants were new; their plate was new; their carriage was new; their harness was new; their horses were new; their pictures were new; they themselves were new; they were as newly married as was lawfully compatible with their having a bran-new baby; and if they had set up a great-grandfather, he would have come home in matting from the Pantechnicon, without a scratch upon him, French polished to the crown of his head. For in the Veneering establishment, from the hall-chairs with the new coat of arms to the grand pianoforte with the new action, and up stairs again to the fire-escape, all things were in a state of high varnish and polish. And what was observable in the furniture was observable in the Veneerings, — the surface smelt a little too much of the workshop, and was a trifle sticky. I: ii, x, xi, xvii; II; iii, xvi; III: xvii; IV: xvii.

**Veneering, Mrs. Anastasia.** His wife; a fair woman, aquiline nosed and fingered, not so much light hair as she might have, gorgeous in raiment and jewels, enthusiastic, propitiatory, conscious that a corner of her husband's veil is over herself. I: ii, x, xi, xvii; II: iii, xvi; III: xvii; IV: xvii.

**Venus, Mr.** A preserver of animals and birds, and articulator of human bones. He becomes a confederate of Mr. Wegg's in his plan of blackmailing Mr. Boffin; but being, on the whole, a very honest man, and repenting of what he has done, he makes amends by confidentially disclosing the whole plot. I: vii; II: vii; III: vi, vii, xiv; IV: iii, xiv.

**Wegg, Silas.** A ballad-monger, who also keeps a fruit-stall, near Cavendish Square.

Assuredly this stall of Silas Wegg's was the hardest little stall of all the sterile little stalls in London. It gave you the face-ache to look at his apples, the stomach-ache to look at his oranges, the tooth-ache to look at his nuts. Of the latter commodity he had always a grim little heap, on which lay a little wooden measure, which had no discernible inside, and was considered to represent the penn'orth appointed by Magna Charta. Whether from too much east wind or no,—it was an easterly corner,—the stall, the stock, and the keeper were all as dry as the desert. Wegg was a knotty man, and a close-grained, with a face carved out of very hard material, that had just as much play of expression as a watchman's rattle. When he laughed, certain jerks occurred in it, and the rattle sprung. Sooth to say, he was so wooden a man, that he seemed to have taken his wooden leg naturally, and rather suggested to the fanciful observer that he might be expected—if his development received no untimely check—to be completely set up with a pair of wooden legs in about six months.

Mr. Boffin thinking himself too old "to begin shovelling and sifting at alphabeds and grammar-books," and wanting to engage some one to read to him, is attracted by Mr. Wegg's collection of ballads displayed on an unfolded clothes-horse. He enters into conversation with the proprietor, and, when he finds that "all print is open to him," is filled with admiration of him as being "a literary man *with* a wooden leg," and engages him at half a crown a week to read to him two hours every evening.

Mr. Wegg turns out to be a rascal. Not resting satisfied with the salary which he receives from Mr. Boffin, he tries to better his condition by knavery. Prying everywhere about the premises, he at last discovers a will in which the elder Mr. Harmon leaves all his property to the crown. Ascertaining that this will is of later date than the one in Mr. Boffin's favor, which has been admitted to probate, he conspires with an acquaintance (Mr. Venus), either to oust Mr. Boffin, or to compel him to buy them off. He finds, to his astonishment, however, that there is a still later will in the possession of Mr. Boffin, who has suppressed it because it leaves him all the property; while the one which has been proved leaves it to the testator's son on the condition of his marrying Miss Bella Wilfer. Discomfited and crestfallen, the avaricious Wegg returns, perforce, to his old trade of selling ballads, gingerbread, and the like. I: v. vii, xv, xvii; II: vii, x; III: vi, vii, xiv; IV: iii, xiv.

**Wilfer, Miss Bella.** Daughter of Reginald Wilfer, and *protégée* of the Boffins; afterwards the wife of John Harmon. I: iv, ix, xvi, xvii; II: viii–x, xiii,; III: iv, v, vii, ix, xv, xvi; IV: iv, v, xi–xiii, xvi.

**Wilfer, Miss Lavinia.** Youngest of Mr. Wilfer's children; a sharp saucy, and irrepressible girl. I: iv, ix; II: i, ix, xiii; III: iv, xvi; IV: v, xvi.

**Wilfer, Reginald,** *called* THE CHERUB. A poor henpecked clerk in the drug house of Chicksey, Veneering, and Stobbles.

So poor a clerk, though having a limited salary and an unlimited family, that he had never yet attained the modest object of his ambition, which was to wear a complete new suit of clothes, hat and boots included, at one time. His black hat was brown before he could afford a coat; his pantaloons were white at the seams and knees before he could buy a pair of boots; his boots had worn out before he could treat himself to new pantaloons; and, by the time he worked round to the hat again, that shining modern article roofed-in an ancient ruin of various periods.

If the conventional Cherub could ever grow up and be clothed, he might be photographed as a portrait of Wilfer. His chubby, smooth, innocent appearance was a reason for his being always treated with condescension when he was not put down. A stranger entering his own poor house at about ten o'clock, P. M., might have been surprised to find him sitting up to supper. So boyish was he in his curves and proportions, that his old schoolmaster, meeting him in Cheapside, might have been unable to withstand the temptation of caning him on the spot. I: iv; II: viii, xiii; III: iv, xvi; IV: iv, v, xvi.

**Wilfer, Mrs. Reginald.** His wife; a tall, angular woman, very stately and impressive.

Her lord being cherubic, she was necessarily majestic, according to the principle which matrimonially unites contrasts. She was much given to tying up her head in a pocket-handkerchief knotted under her chin. This head-gear, in conjunction with a pair of gloves worn within doors, she seemed to consider as at once a kind of armor against misfortune (invariably assuming it when in low spirits or difficulties), and as a species of full dress. I: iv, ix, xvi; II: i, ix, xiii; III: iv, xvi; IV: v, xvi.

**Williams, William.** A frequenter of the Six Jolly Fellowship Porters. I: vi, III: iii.

**Wrayburn, Eugene.** A briefless barrister, who hates his profession. He is a gloomy, indolent, unambitious, and reckless young man.

"Idiots talk," said Eugene, leaning back, folding his arms, smoking with his eyes shut, and speaking slightly through his nose, "of energy. If there is a word in the dictionary, under any letter from A to Z, that I abominate, it is 'energy.' It is such a conventional superstition! such parrot gabble! What the deuse! — Am I to rush out into the street, collar the first man of a wealthy appearance that I meet, shake him, and say, 'Go to law upon the spot, you dog, and retain me, or I'll be the death of you?' Yet that would be energy."

Becoming interested in Lizzie Hexam, he assists her to obtain an education; and though he seeks her society, he does so with no definite aim in view.

Lizzie saves Wrayburn's life with wonderful energy and address, nurses him tenderly through a long and dangerous sickness, is married to him, and finds that, transformed by the power of love, he has a mine of purpose and energy, which he turns to the best account. I: ii, iii, viii, x, xii–xiv; II: i, iii, vi, xi, xiv–xvi; III: x, xi, xvii; IV: i, vi, ix–xi, xvi, xvii.

**Wrayburn, Mrs. Eugene.** *See* HEXAM, LIZZIE.

**Wren, Jenny.** *See* CLEAVER, FANNY.

# CHRISTMAS BOOKS, TALES AND SKETCHES

## INDEX TO CHARACTERS

## A CHRISTMAS CAROL IN PROSE

**Belle.** A comely matron, whom the Ghost of Christmas Past shows to Scrooge, and in whom he recognizes an old sweetheart. ii.

**Caroline.** Wife of one of Scrooge's debtors, shown to him in a dream by the Ghost of Christmas Yet To Come. iv.

**Cratchit, Bob.** Clerk to Scrooge. He works in a dismal little cell, — a sort of tank leading out of Scrooge's counting-room. i, iii, iv, v.

**Cratchit, Mrs.** His wife. iii, iv.

**Cratchit, Belinda.** Their second daughter. iii, iv.

**Cratchit, Martha.** Their eldest daughter. iii, iv.

**Cratchit, Master Peter.** One of their sons. iii, iv.

**Cratchit, Tim,** *called* TINY TIM. Their youngest son, a cripple. iii.

**Dilber, Mrs.** A laundress whom the Ghost of Christmas Yet To Come shows to Scrooge. iv.

**Fan.** A little girl, Scrooge's sister (afterwards the mother of Fred, his nephew), whom the Ghost of Christmas Past shows to Scrooge in a dream. ii.

**Fezziwig, Mr.** A kind-hearted, jolly old merchant to whom Scrooge was a 'prentice when a young man, whom the Ghost of Christmas Past brings before him in a vision when he has become an old man and a miser. ii.

**Fezziwig, Mrs.** His wife, "worthy to be his partner in every sense of the term." At the ball which her husband gave to his work-people on Christmas Eve, and which the Ghost of Christmas Past shows to old Scrooge, "in came Mrs. Fezziwig, one vast, substantial smile." ii.

**Fezziwigs, The three Miss.** Their daughters, beaming and lovable, with six young followers, whose hearts they break. ii.

**Fred.** Scrooge's nephew. iii, v.

**Ghost of Christmas Past.** A phantom that shows Scrooge "shadows of things that have been" in his past life. ii.

BOB CRATCHIT AND TINY TIM.

**Ghost of Christmas Present.** A jolly spirit, glorious to see, of a kind, generous, hearty nature, who invisibly conducts old Scrooge through various scenes on Christmas Eve.

Much they saw, and far they went, and many homes they visited, but always with a happy end. The spirit stood beside sick-beds, and they were cheerful; on foreign lands, and they were close at home; by struggling men, and they were patient in their greater hope; by poverty, and it was rich. In almshouse, hospital, and jail, in misery's every refuge, where vain man, in his little brief authority, had not made fast the door, and barred the spirit out, he left his blessing, and taught Scrooge his precepts. iii.

**Ghost of Christmas Yet To Come.** An apparition which shows Scrooge "shadows of things that have not happened," but which may happen in the time before him. iv.

**Joe.** A junk-dealer, and a receiver of stolen goods, shown to old Scrooge by the Ghost of Christmas Yet To Come. iv.

**Marley, The Ghost of Jacob.** A spectre that visits Scrooge on Christmas Eve, and was in life his partner in business.

**Scrooge, Ebenezer.** The Hero of the "Carol;" surviving partner of the firm of Scrooge and Marley.

Oh! but he was a tight-fisted hand at the grindstone, Scrooge! — a squeezing, wrenching, grasping, scraping, clutching, covetous old sinner! Hard and sharp as flint, from which no steel had ever struck out generous fire; secret and self-contained and solitary as an oyster. The cold within him froze his old features, nipped his pointed nose, shrivelled his cheek, stiffened his gait, made his eyes red, his thin lips blue, and spoke out shrewdly in his grating voice. A frosty rime was on his head, and on his eyebrows and his wiry chin. He carried his own low temperature always about with him: he iced his office in the dog-days, and did n't thaw it one degree at Christmas.

One Christmas Eve, after having declined in a very surly manner to accept an invitation to dinner the next day from his nephew Fred, and having reluctantly given his clerk, Bob Cratchit, permission to be absent the whole day, Scrooge goes home to his lodgings, where, brooding over a low fire, he is visited by the ghost of Old Marley, who has been dead seven years.

Scrooge fell upon his knees, and clasped his hands before his face.

"Mercy!" he said. "Dreadful apparition, why do you trouble me?"

"Man of the worldly mind!" replied the ghost, "do you believe in me, or not?"

"I do," said Scrooge. "I must. But why do spirits walk the earth? and why do they come to me?"

"It is required of every man," the ghost returned, "that the spirit within him should walk abroad among his fellow-men, and travel far and wide; and, if that spirit goes not forth in life, it is condemned to do so after death. It is doomed to wander through the world, — oh, woe is me! — and witness what it cannot share, but might have shared on earth, and turned to happiness."

Again the spectre raised a cry, and shook its chain, and wrung its shadowy hands.

"You are fettered," said Scrooge, trembling. "Tell me why."

"I wear the chain I forged in life," replied the ghost. "I made it link by link, and yard by yard: I girded it on of my own free will, and of my own free will I wore it. Is its pattern strange to *you?*"

Scrooge trembled more and more.

. . . . . . . . . . . . . .

"Hear me!" cried the ghost. "My time is nearly gone. . . . I am here to-night to warn you that you have yet a chance and hope of escaping my fate, — a chance and hope of my procuring, Ebenezer."

"You were always a good friend to me," said Scrooge. "Thank'ee!"

"You will be haunted," resumed the ghost, "by three spirits. . . . Expect the first to-morrow, when the bell tolls one."

"Could n't I take 'em all at once, and have it over, Jacob?" hinted Scrooge.

"Expect the second on the next night at the same hour; the third upon the next night, when the last stroke of twelve has ceased to vibrate. Look to see me no more; and look, that, for your own sake, you remember what has passed between us!" . . .

Scrooge became sensible of confused noises in the air, incoherent sounds of lamentation and regret, wailings inexpressibly sorrowful and self-accusatory. The spectre, after listening a moment, joined in the mournful dirge, and floated out upon the bleak, dark night.

Being much in need of repose, whether from the emotion he had undergone, or the fatigues of the day, or his glimpse of the invisible world, or the lateness of the hour, or from all combined, Scrooge goes straight to bed, without undressing, and falls asleep upon the instant. When he awakes, it is nearly one. The hour soon strikes; and, as the notes die away, the curtains of the bed are drawn aside, and a child stands before him. It is the Ghost of Christmas Past. The spirit bids him follow, and takes him to scenes long past. His childhood comes back to him. His sister Fan is before him. His old master Fezziwig reappears, and Dick Wilkins, the companion of his boyish days. It is Christmas time; and he and Dick and many are made happy by their master's liberality. The scene changes, and Scrooge sees himself in the prime of life. "His face had not the harsh and rigid lines of later years, but it had begun to wear the signs of avarice;" and a young girl stands beside him, and tells him that another idol, a golden one, has displaced her, and that she releases him. "May you be happy in the life you have chosen!" she says sorrowfully, and disappears. "Spirit!" says Scrooge, "show me no more; conduct me home." But the ghost points again, and the wretched man sees a happy home, — husband and wife, and many children; and the matron is she whom he might have called his own. The spirit vanishes, and Scrooge, exhausted and drowsy, throws himself upon the bed, and sinks into a heavy sleep. He awakes as the bell is upon the stroke of one; and the Ghost of Christmas Present is before him. Again he goes forth.

And perhaps it was the pleasure the good spirit had in showing off this power of his, or else it was his own kind, generous, hearty nature, and his sympathy with all poor men, that led him straight to Scrooge's clerk's; for there he went, and took Scrooge with him, holding to his robe; and on the threshold of the door the spirit smiled, and stopped to bless Bob Cratchit's dwelling with the sprinklings of his torch. Think of that! Bob had but fifteen "Bob" a week himself; he pocketed on Saturdays but fifteen copies of his Christian name: and yet the Ghost of Christmas Present blessed his four-roomed house!

Then up rose Mrs. Cratchit, Cratchit's wife, dressed out but poorly in a twice-turned gown, but brave in ribbons, which are cheap, and make a goodly show for sixpence; and she laid the cloth, assisted by Belinda Cratchit, second of her daughters, also brave in ribbons; while Master Peter Cratchit plunged a fork into the saucepan of potatoes, and, getting the corners of his monstrous shirt-collar (Bob's private property, conferred upon his son and heir in honor of the day) into his mouth, rejoiced to find himself so gallantly attired, and yearned to show his linen in the fashionable parks. And now two smaller Cratchits, boy and girl, came tearing in, screaming that outside the baker's they had smelt the goose, and known it for their own; and, basking in luxurious thoughts of sage and onion, these young Cratchits danced about the table, and exalted Master Peter Cratchit to the skies; while he (not proud, although his collar near choked him) blew the fire until the slow potatoes, bubbling up, knocked loudly at the saucepan-lid to be let out, and peeled.

"What has ever got your precious father, then?" said Mrs. Cratchit. "And your brother Tiny Tim? And Martha warn't as late last Christmas Day by half an hour!"

"Here's Martha, mother!" said a girl, appearing as she spoke.

"Here's Martha, mother!" cried the two young Cratchits. "Hurrah! There's *such* a goose, Martha!"

"Why, bless your heart alive, my dear, how late you are!" said Mrs. Cratchit, kissing her a dozen times, and taking off her shawl and bonnet for her with officious zeal.

"We'd a deal of work to finish up last night," replied the girl, "and had to clear away this morning, mother!"

"Well, never mind, so long as you are come," said Mrs. Cratchit. "Sit ye down before the fire, my dear, and have a warm; Lord bless ye!"

"No, no! There's father coming," cried the two young Cratchits, who were everywhere at once. "Hide, Martha, hide!"

So Martha hid herself; and in came little Bob the father, with at least three feet of comforter, exclusive of the fringe, hanging down before him, and his threadbare clothes darned up and brushed to look seasonable; and Tiny Tim upon his shoulder. Alas for Tiny Tim! he bore a little crutch, and had his limbs supported by an iron frame.

"Why, where's our Martha?" cried Bob Cratchit, looking round.

"Not coming!" said Mrs. Cratchit.

"Not coming!" said Bob, with a sudden declension in his high spirits; for he had been Tim's blood-horse all the way from church, and had come home rampant. "Not coming upon Christmas Day!"

Martha didn't like to see him disappointed, if it were only a joke: so she came out prematurely from behind the closet-door, and ran into his arms; while the two young Cratchits hustled Tiny Tim, and bore him off into the wash-house, that he might hear the pudding singing in the copper.

"And how did little Tim behave?" asked Mrs. Cratchit, when she had rallied Bob on his credulity, and Bob had hugged his daughter to his heart's content.

"As good as gold," said Bob, "and better. Somehow he gets thoughtful, sitting by himself so much, and thinks the strangest things you ever heard. He told me, coming home, that he hoped the people saw him in the church, because he was a cripple, and it might be pleasant to them to remember upon Christmas Day who made lame beggars walk, and blind men see."

Bob's voice was tremulous when he told them this, and

trembled more when he said that Tiny Tim was growing strong and hearty.

His active little crutch was heard upon the floor; and back came Tiny Tim before another word was spoken, escorted by his brother and sister to his stool beside the fire. And while Bob, turning up his cuffs, — as if, poor fellow! they were capable of being made more shabby, — compounded some hot mixture in a jug with gin and lemons, and stirred it round and round, and put it on the hob to simmer, Master Peter and the two ubiquitous young Cratchits went to fetch the goose, with which they soon returned in high procession.

Such a bustle ensued, that you might have thought a goose the rarest of all birds, — a feathered phenomenon, to which a black swan was a matter of course, and, in truth, it was something very like it in that house. Mrs. Cratchit made the gravy (ready beforehand in a little saucepan) hissing hot; Master Peter mashed the potatoes with incredible vigor; Miss Belinda sweetened up the apple-sauce; Martha dusted the hot plates; Bob took Tiny Tim beside him in a tiny corner at the table; the two young Cratchits set chairs for everybody, not forgetting themselves, and, mounting guard upon their posts, crammed spoons into their mouths, lest they should shriek for goose before their turn came to be helped. At last the dishes were set on, and grace was said. It was succeeded by a breathless pause, as Mrs. Cratchit, looking slowly all along the carving-knife, prepared to plunge it in the breast; but when she did, and when the long-expected gush of stuffing issued forth, one murmur of delight arose all round the board; and even Tiny Tim, excited by the two young Cratchits, beat on the table with the handle of his knife, and feebly cried, "Hurrah!"

. . . . . . . . . . . . .

At last the dinner was all done, the cloth was cleared, the hearth swept, and the fire made up. The compound in the jug being tasted, and considered perfect, apples and oranges were put upon the table, and a shovelful of chestnuts on the fire. Then all the Cratchit family drew round the hearth, in what Bob Cratchit called a circle, meaning half a one; and at Bob Cratchit's elbow stood the family display of glass, — two tumblers and a custard-cup without a handle.

These held the hot stuff from the jug, however, as well as golden goblets would have done; and Bob served it out with beaming looks, while the chestnuts on the fire sputtered and cracked noisily. Then Bob proposed: —

"A merry Christmas to us all, my dears! God bless us!" Which all the family re-echoed.

"God bless us every one!" said Tiny Tim, the last of all.

Bob then proposes the health of Mr. Scrooge; and although his wife does not relish the toast, yet, at the solicitation of her husband, she consents to drink it for her husband's sake and the day's.

Again the scene changes, and Scrooge finds himself in the bright gleaming house of his nephew, where a merry company are enjoying themselves, and are laughing at his surly refusal to join in their Christmas festivities.

The third and last spirit comes at the same hour, and introduces itself as the Ghost of Christmas Yet To Come. It shows Scrooge a room in which a dead man is lying, and in which a motley crowd is joking and laughing, and casting lots for the very curtains surrounding the bed on which the body lies. The spirit points to the head, covered by the thin sheet; but Scrooge has no power to pull it aside, and view the features. As they leave the room, however, he beseeches the spirit to tell him what man it is who lies there so friendless and uncared for. The ghost does not answer, but conveys him hurriedly to a churchyard, neglected, overgrown with weeds, "choked up with too much burying, fat with repleted appetite. A worthy place!" The spirit stands among the graves, and points down to one; and Scrooge beholds upon the stone of the neglected grave his own name, — "Ebenezer Scrooge."

> "Am *I* that man who lay upon the bed?" he cried upon his knees.
>
> The spirit pointed from the grave to him, and back again.
>
> "No, spirit! Oh, no, no!"
>
> The finger still was there.

Scrooge asks if there is no hope; if these sights are the shadows of what *must*, or what *may* come to him? The kind hand trembles; and Scrooge sees room for hope.

> "I will honor Christmas in my heart, and try to keep it all the year. I will live in the Past, the Present, and the Future. The spirits of all three shall strive within me. I will not shut out the lessons they teach. Oh! tell me I may sponge away the writing on this stone!" . . .
>
> Holding up his hands in a last prayer to have his fate reversed, he saw an alteration in the phantom's hood and dress. It shrunk, collapsed, and dwindled down into a bed-post.
>
> Yes! and the bed-post was his own; the bed was his own; the room was his own, — best and happiest of all, the time before him was his own to make amends in!

And he does make amends most amply. The lesson of his dream is not forgotten. He instantly sends a prize turkey to the Cratchits, twice the size of Tiny Tim, and gives half a crown to the boy that goes and buys it for him. He surprises his nephew by dining with him, and the next day raises Bob Cratchit's salary. In short, "he became as good a friend, as good a master, and as good a man, as the good old city knew, or any other good old city, town, or borough in the good old world."

**Tiny Tim.** *See* CRATCHIT, TIM.

**Topper, Mr.** One of the guests at Fred's Christmas dinner-party; a bachelor, who thinks himself a wretched outcast because he has no wife, and consequently gets his eye upon one of Scrooge's niece's sisters. iii.

**Wilkins, Dick.** A fellow 'prentice of Scrooge's. ii.

## THE CHIMES

### A GOBLIN STORY OF SOME BELLS THAT RANG AN OLD YEAR OUT, AND A NEW YEAR IN

**Bowley, Lady.** Wife to Sir Joseph Bowley; a very stately lady. i.

**Bowley, Master.** Her son, a little gentleman aged twelve. iii.

**Bowley, Sir Joseph.** An old and very stately gentleman, who is a member of Parliament, and who prides himself upon being the "poor man's friend and father." The poor man in his district he considers his business. "I endeavor," he says, "to educate his mind by inculcating on all occasions the one great moral lesson which that class requires; that is, entire dependence on myself." ii, iii.

**Chickenstalker, Mrs. Anne.** A stout old lady, keeper of a shop "in the general line," who, Toby Veck dreams, is married to Tugby, Sir Joseph Bowley's porter. ii, iv.

**Cute, Alderman.** A plain man and a practical man; an easy, affable, joking, knowing fellow, up to everything, and not to be imposed on; one who understands the common people, and has not the least difficulty in dealing with them. Being a justice, he thinks he can "put down" anything among "this sort of people," and so sets about putting down the nonsense that is talked about want, and the cant in vogue about starvation; and declares his intention of putting down distressed wives, boys without shoes and stockings, wandering mothers, and indeed all young mothers of all sorts and kinds, all sick persons and young children; and, if there is one thing on which he can be said to have made up his mind more than on another, it is to put suicide down. Under this name Mr. Dickens scarified Sir Peter Laurie, a wealthy Scotch saddler residing in London, who was knighted in 1823 on being appointed sheriff of London and Middlesex, and who was chosen alderman from Aldersgate in 1826, and was elected lord-mayor in 1832. Sir Peter was a garrulous and officious magistrate, severe in his treatment of the poor, and in the habit of threatening to put down want, vagabondage, suicide, and the like, among them. i, iii.

**Fern, Lilian.** An orphan; niece to Will Fern. ii, iv.

**Fern, Will.** A poor but honest man, who only wants "to live like one of the Almighty's creeturs," but has a bad name, and can't. ii, iv.

**Filer, Mr.** A low-spirited gentleman of middle age, of a meagre habit and a disconsolate face, full of facts and figures, and ready to prove anything by tables; a friend of Alderman Cute's. i, iii.

**Fish, Mr.** Confidential secretary to Sir Joseph Bowley. ii, iii.

**Lilian.** *See* FERN, LILIAN.

**Richard.** A handsome, well-made, powerful young smith, engaged to Meg Veck. i, iii, iv.

**Tugby.** Porter to Sir Joseph Bowley; afterwards married, as Toby Veck dreams, to Mrs. Chickenstalker. ii, iv.

**Veck, Margaret** *or* **Meg.** Toby Veck's daughter.

**Veck, Toby,** *called* TROTTY from his pace, "which meant speed, if it did n't make it." A ticket-porter.

A weak, small, spare old man, he was a very Hercules, this Toby, in his good intentions. He loved to earn his money. He delighted to believe — Toby was very poor, and could n't well afford to part with a delight — that he was worth his salt. With a shilling or an eighteen-penny message or small parcel in hand, his courage, always high, rose higher. As he trotted on, he would call out to fast postmen ahead of him to get out of the way, devoutly believing that, in the natural course of things, he must inevitably overtake and run them down; and he had perfect faith — not often tested — in his being able to carry anything that man could lift.

Toby has a great liking for the bells in the church near his station.

Being but a simple man, he invested them with a strange and solemn character. They were so mysterious (often heard, and never seen), so high up, so far off, so full of such a deep, strong melody, that he regarded them with a species of awe; and sometimes, when he looked up at the dark arched windows in the tower, he half expected to be beckoned to by something which was not a bell, and yet was what he heard so often sounding in the chimes. For all this, Toby scouted with indignation a certain flying rumor that the chimes were haunted, as implying the possibility of their being connected with any evil thing. In short, they were very often in his ears, and very often in his thoughts, but always in his good opinion; and he very often got such a crick in his neck by staring, with his mouth wide open, at the steeple where they hung, that he was fain to take an extra trot or two afterwards to cure it.

On Christmas Eve, Toby falls asleep by the fireside, while reading a newspaper, and dreams that he is called by the chimes, and so goes up into the church-tower, which he finds peopled by dwarf phantoms, spirits, elfin creatures of the bells, of all aspects, shapes, characters, and occupations. As he gazes, the spectres disappear, and he sees in every bell a bearded figure, mysterious and awful, of the bulk and stature of the bell, — at once a figure and the bell itself. The Great Bell, or the Goblin of the Great Bell, after arraigning him for sundry instances of wrong-doing, puts him in charge of the Spirit of the Chimes, a little child, who shows him various sorrowful scenes of the future, the actors in which he knows, and some of whom are very near and dear to him. But all these scenes point the same moral, — "that we must trust and hope, and neither doubt ourselves, nor the good in one another." And when Toby breaks the spell that binds him, and wakes up suddenly with a leap that brings him upon his feet, he is beside himself with joy to find that the chimes are merrily ringing in the New Year, and that all the sin and shame and suffering and desperation which he has witnessed is but the baseless fabric of a vision. The lesson is not forgotten, however, and the New Year is made all the happier by his troubled dream.

## THE CRICKET ON THE HEARTH

### A FAIRY TALE OF HOME

**Boxer.** John Peerybingle's dog.

**Dot.** *See* Peerybingle, Mrs. Mary.

**Fielding, May.** A friend of Mrs. Peerybingle's. She is over-persuaded into consenting to bestow her hand upon Tackleton, a surly, sordid, grinding old man; but on the morning of the day appointed for the wedding, she marries Edward Plummer, a former lover, who suddenly returns after a long absence, and whom she has believed to be dead.

**Fielding, Mrs.** Her mother; a little, querulous chip of an old lady with a peevish face, and a most transcendent figure (in right of having preserved a waist like a bed-post). She is very genteel and patronizing, in consequence of having once been better off, or of laboring under an impression that she might have been, if something had happened (in the indigo-trade) which never did happen, and seemed to have never been particularly likely to happen.

**Peerybingle, John.** A large, sturdy man, much older than his wife, but "the best, the most considerate, the most affectionate, of husbands" to her.

He was often near to something or other very clever, by his own account, this lumbering, slow, honest John; this John so heavy, but so light of spirit; so rough upon the surface, but so gentle at the core; so dull without, so quick within; so stolid, but so good! O mother Nature! give thy children the true poetry of heart that hid itself in this poor carrier's breast, — he was but a carrier, by the way, — and we can bear to have them talking prose, and leading lives of prose, and bear to bless thee for their company.

**Peerybingle, Mrs. Mary,** *called* DOT from her small size. His wife, a blooming young woman, with a very doll of a baby.

**Plummer, Caleb.** A poor toymaker in the employ of Tackleton; a spare, dejected, thoughtful, gray-haired old man, wholly devoted to his blind daughter.

**Plummer, Bertha.** His daughter, a blind girl. With her father, she lives in "a little cracked nutshell of a wooden house, . . . stuck to the premises of Gruff and Tackleton like a barnacle to a ship's keel."

I have said that Caleb and his poor blind daughter lived here. I should have said that Caleb lived here, and his poor blind daughter somewhere else, — in an enchanted home of Caleb's furnishing, where scarcity and shabbiness were not, and trouble never entered. Caleb was no sorcerer, but in the only magic art that still remains to us, — the magic of devoted, deathless love. Nature had been the mistress of his study; and from her teaching all the wonder came.

The blind girl never knew that ceilings were discolored; walls blotched, and bare of plaster here and there; high crevices unstopped, and widening every day; beams mouldering, and tending downward. The blind girl never knew that iron was rusting, wood rotting, paper peeling off; the size and shape, and true proportion of the dwelling, withering away. The blind girl never knew that ugly shapes of delf and earthenware were on the board; that sorrow and faint-heartedness were in the house; that Caleb's scanty hairs were turning grayer and more gray before her sightless face. The blind girl never knew they had a master cold, exacting, and uninterested; never knew that Tackleton was Tackleton, in short, but lived in the belief of an eccentric humorist, who loved to have his jest with them, and who, while he was the guardian angel of their lives, disdained to hear one word of thankfulness.

And all was Caleb's doing; all the doing of her simple father! The consequence of this well-meant but ill-judged deception is, that Bertha comes secretly to love Tackleton with unspeakable affection and gratitude, and is nearly heart-broken on finding that he means to marry May Fielding. This compels her father to tell her the truth; to confess that he has altered objects, changed the characters of people, invented many things that never have been, to make her happier. The shock to her sensitive nature is great; but instead of losing her confidence in him, she clings to him all the more closely, and cherishes him all the more devotedly, for his innocent deceit, springing from motives so pure and unselfish.

**Plummer, Edward.** Son to Caleb, and brother to Bertha Plummer. After a long absence in the "Golden South Americas," he returns to claim the hand of May Fielding, to whom he had been engaged before leaving home. Hearing, when twenty miles away, that she has proved false to him, and is about to marry old Tackleton, he disguises himself as an old man, for the sake of observing and judging for himself, in order to get at the real and exact truth. He makes himself known to Mrs. Peerybingle ("Dot"), who advises him to keep his secret close, and not even to let Mr. Peerybingle know it, he being much too open in his nature, and too clumsy in all artifice, to keep it for him. She also offers to sound his sweetheart, and to go between them, and bring them together, which she does, and has the pleasure of seeing them married, and of expressing a hope that Tackleton may die a bachelor. Her mediation, however, becomes known, in part, to her husband, who misconstrues her actions, and suspects her of being untrue to himself. But in the end everything is satisfactorily explained, and everybody is made happy; while even the kettle hums for joy, and the cricket joins the music with its "Chirp, chirp, chirp."

**Slowboy, Tilly.** Mrs. Peerybingle's nursery-maid; a great, clumsy girl, who is very apt to hold the baby topsy-turvy, and who has a habit of mechanically reproducing, for its entertainment, scraps of current conversation, with all the sense struck out of them, and all the nouns changed into the plural number, as when she asks, "Was it Gruffs and Tackletons the toymakers, then?" and "Would it call at pastry-cooks for wedding-cakes?" and "Did its mothers know the boxes when its fathers brought them home?" and so on.

**Tackleton,** *called* GRUFF AND TACKLETON. A toy-merchant, stern, ill-natured, and sarcastic, with one eye always wide open, and one eye nearly shut.

Cramped and chafing in the peaceable pursuit of toy-making, he was a domestic ogre, who had been living on children all his life, and was their implacable enemy. He despised all toys; would n't have bought one for the world; delighted, in his malice, to insinuate grim expressions into the faces of brown paper farmers who drove pigs to market, bellmen who advertised lost lawyers' consciences, movable old ladies who darned stockings or carved pies, and other like samples of his stock in trade. In appalling masks, hideous, hairy, red-eyed Jacks in boxes, vampire kites, demoniacal tumblers who would n't lie down, and were perpetually flying forward to stare infants out of countenance, his soul perfectly revelled. They were his only relief and safety-valve.

After the marriage of his betrothed, May Fielding, to Edward Plummer (see above), he turns his disappointment to good account by resolving thenceforth to be, and by actually becoming, a pleasant, hearty, kind, and happy man.

## THE BATTLE OF LIFE

### A LOVE-STORY

**Britain, Benjamin,** *called* LITTLE BRITAIN. A small man with an uncommonly sour and discontented face; servant to Doctor Jeddler, afterwards husband of Clemency Newcome, and landlord of the Nutmeg Grater Inn. He gives this summary of his general condition: "I don't know anything; I don't care for anything; I don't make out anything; I don't believe anything; and I don't want anything."

**Craggs, Mr. Thomas.** Law-partner of Jonathan Snitchey. He seems to be represented by Snitchey, and to be conscious of little or no separate existence or personal individuality.

**Craggs, Mrs.** His wife.

**Heathfield, Alfred.** A young medical student; a ward of Doctor Jeddler's, and engaged to his younger daughter Marion. On coming of age, he starts on a three-years' tour among the foreign schools of medicine. In the very hour of his return, Marion flees from home, eloping, as it is supposed, with a young bankrupt named Michael Warden. After a time her elder sister Grace becomes Alfred's wife; and it finally transpires that Marion, though deeply loving him, discovers that Grace also loves him, and, deeming herself to be less worthy of such a husband, sacrifices her own happiness to insure her sister's. But instead of eloping with young Warden, she retires to an aunt's, who lives at a distance, where she remains secluded until after her sister's marriage has taken place.

**Jeddler, Doctor Anthony.** A great philosopher, the heart and mystery of whose philosophy is to look upon the world as a gigantic practical joke, or as something too absurd to be considered seriously by any practical man. But the loss of his favorite daughter, "the absence of one little unit in the great absurd account," strikes him to the ground, and shows him how serious the world is, "in which some love, deep-anchored, is the portion of all human creatures."

**Jeddler, Grace.** His elder daughter; married to Alfred Heathfield.

**Jeddler, Marion.** His younger daughter.

**Martha, Aunt.** Sister to Doctor Jeddler.

**Newcome, Clemency.** Servant to Doctor Jeddler; afterwards married to Benjamin Britain.

She was about thirty years old, and had a sufficiently plump and cheerful face, though it was twisted up into an odd expression of tightness that made it comical; but the extraordinary homeliness of her gait and manner would have superseded any face in the world. To say that she had two left legs, and somebody else's arms; and that all four limbs seemed to be out of joint, and to start from perfectly wrong places when they were set in motion, — is to offer the mildest outline of the reality. To say that she was perfectly content and satisfied with these arrangements, and regarded them as being no business of hers; and that she took her arms and legs as they came, and allowed them to dispose of themselves just as it happened, — is to render faint justice to their equanimity. Her dress was a prodigious pair of self-willed shoes that never wanted to go where her feet went, blue stockings, a printed gown of many colors and the most hideous pattern procurable for money, and a white apron. She always wore short sleeves, and always had, by some accident, grazed elbows, in which she took so lively an interest, that she was continually trying to turn them round and get impossible views of them. In general, a little cap perched somewhere on her head, though it was rarely to be met with in the place usually occupied in other subjects by that article of dress; but from head to foot she was scrupulously clean, and maintained a kind of dislocated tidiness. Indeed, her laudable anxiety to be tidy and compact in her own conscience, as well as in the public eye, gave rise to one of her most startling evolutions, which was to grasp herself sometimes by a sort of wooden handle (part of her clothing, and familiarly called a busk), and wrestle, as it were, with her garments, until they fell into a symmetrical arrangement.

**Snitchey, Jonathan.** Law-partner of Thomas Craggs.

**Snitchey, Mrs.** His wife.

**Warden, Michael.** A client of Messrs. Snitchey and Craggs; a man of thirty who has sown a good many wild oats, and finds his affairs to be in a bad way in consequence. He repents, however, and reforms, and finally marries Marion Jeddler, whom he has long loved.

## THE HAUNTED MAN, AND THE GHOST'S BARGAIN

### A FANCY FOR CHRISTMAS-TIME

**Denham, Edmund.** A student, whose true name is LONGFORD. He comes under the evil influence of Mr. Redlaw, and loses all sense of the kindness that has been shown him during a dangerous illness. But when a change falls upon Redlaw, his heart feels the effect also, and glows with affection and gratitude to his benefactress.

**Longford, Edmund.** *See* DENHAM, EDMUND.

**Redlaw, Mr.** A learned chemist, and a lecturer at an ancient institution in a great city. He is a melancholy but kind-hearted man, whose life has been darkened by many sorrows. As he sits brooding one night over the things that might have been, but never were, Mr. William Swidger, the keeper of the Lodge, with his wife Milly, and his father Philip, enter the room to serve his tea, and to decorate the apartment with holly in honor of Christmas.

"Another Christmas comes; another year gone!" murmured the chemist with a gloomy sigh. "More figures in the lengthening sum of recollection that we work and work at, to our torment, till Death idly jumbles all together, and rubs all out. So, Philip!" breaking off, and raising his voice as he addressed the old man standing apart, with his glistening burden in his arms, from which the quiet Mrs. William took small branches, which she noiselessly trimmed with her scissors, and decorated the room with, while her aged father-in-law looked on much interested in the ceremony.

"My duty to you, sir," returned the old man. "Should have spoken before, sir, but know your ways, Mr. Redlaw, — proud to say, — and wait till spoke to. Merry Christmas, sir! and happy

New Year! and many of 'em! Have had a pretty many of 'em myself,—ha, ha!—and may take the liberty of wishing 'em. I'm eighty-seven!"

"Have you had so many that were merry and happy?" asked the other.

"Ay, sir; ever so many," returned the old man.

"Is his memory impaired with age? It is to be expected now," said Mr. Redlaw, turning to the son, and speaking lower.

"Not a morsel of it, sir," replied Mr. William. "That's exactly what I say myself, sir. There never was such a memory as my father's. He's the most wonderful man in the world. He don't know what forgetting means. It's the very observation I'm always making to Mrs. William, sir, if you'll believe me!"

The old man reminds Mr. Redlaw of a picture of one of the founders of the institution, which hangs in what was once the great dining-hall,—a sedate gentleman, with a scroll below him, bearing this inscription, "Lord, keep my memory green!" And then the younger Mr. Swidger speaks of his wife's visits to the sick and suffering, and tells how she has just returned from nursing a student who attends Mr. Redlaw's lectures, and who has been seized with a fever.

"Not content with this, sir, Mrs. William goes and finds, this very night, when she was coming home (why it's not above a couple of hours ago), a creature more like a young wild beast than a young child, shivering upon a doorstep. What does Mrs. William do but brings it home to dry it, and feed it, and keep it till our old bounty of food and flannel is given away on Christmas morning! If it ever felt a fire before, it's as much as it ever did; for it's sitting in the old Lodge chimney, staring at ours as if its ravenous eyes would never shut again. It's sitting there, at least," said Mr. William, correcting himself on reflection, "unless it's bolted."

"Heaven keep her happy!" said the chemist aloud, "and you too, Philip! and you, William! I must consider what to do in this. I may desire to see this student: I'll not detain you longer now. Good night!"

"I thankee, sir, I thankee!" said the old man, "for Mouse, and for my son William, and for myself. Where's my son William? William, you take the lantern, and go on first through them long dark passages, as you did last year and the year afore. Ha, ha! *I* remember, though I'm eighty-seven! 'Lord, keep my memory green!' It's a very good prayer, Mr. Redlaw,—that of the learned gentleman in the peaked beard, with a ruff round his neck; hangs up, second on the right above the panelling in what used to be, afore our ten poor gentlemen commuted, our great dinner hall. 'Lord, keep my memory green!' It 's very good and pious, sir. Amen, amen!"

After the departure of these humble friends, Redlaw falls back into his train of sorrowful musings; and as he sits before the fire, an awful spectral likeness of himself appears to him. It echoes his mournful thoughts, brings each wrong and sorrow that he has suffered vividly before him, and finally offers to cancel the remembrance of them, destroying no knowledge, no result of study, nothing but the intertwisted chain of feelings and associations, each in its turn dependent on and nourished by the banished recollections.

"Decide," it said, "before the opportunity is lost!"

"A moment! I call Heaven to witness," said the agitated man, "that I have never been a hater of my kind, — never morose, indifferent, or hard to anything around me. If, living here alone, I have made too much of all that was and might have been, and too little of what is, the evil, I believe, has fallen on me, and not on others. But if there were poison in my body, should I not, possessed of antidotes, and knowledge how to use them, use them? If there be poison in my mind, and through this fearful shadow I can cast it out, shall I not cast it out?"

"Say," said the spectre, "is it done?"

"A moment longer!" he answered hurredly. "*I would forget it if I could!* Have *I* thought that alone? or has it been the thought of thousands upon thousands, generation after generation? All human memory is fraught with sorrow and trouble. My memory is as the memory of other men; but other men have not this choice. Yes: I close the bargain. Yes: I WILL forget my sorrow, wrong, and trouble!"

"Say," said the spectre, "is it done?"

"It is!"

"IT IS. And take this with you, man whom I here renounce. The gift that I have given, you shall give again, go where you will. Without recovering yourself the power that you have yielded up, you shall henceforth destroy its like in all whom you approach. Your wisdom has discovered that the memory of sorrow, wrong, and trouble is the lot of all mankind, and that mankind would be the happier in its other memories without it. Go! Be its benefactor! Freed from such remembrance from this hour, carry involuntarily the blessing of such freedom with you. Its diffusion is inseparable and inalienable from you."

The phantom leaves him bewildered, and with no memory of past wrongs or troubles. He does not know in what way he possesses the power to communicate this forgetfulness to others; but with a vague feeling of having an antidote for the worst of human ills, he goes forth to administer it. Those whom he seeks, and those whom he casually encounters, alike experience the infection of his presence. Charged with poison for his own mind, he poisons the minds of others. Where he felt interest, compassion, sympathy, his heart turns to stone. Selfishness and ingratitude everywhere spring up in his blighting footsteps. There is but one person who is proof against his baneful influence, and that is the ragged child whom Mrs. Swidger picked up in the streets. Hardship and cruelty have so blunted the senses of this wretched creature, that it grows neither worse nor better from contact with the haunted man. It is, indeed, already a counterpart of him, with no memory of the past to soften or stimulate it. Shocked by the evil he has wrought, Redlaw awakes to a consciousness of the misery of his condition. Having long taught that in the material world nothing can be spared, that no step or atom in the wondrous structure could be lost without a blank being made in the great universe, he is now brought to see that it is the same with good and evil, happiness and sorrow, in the memories of men. He invokes the spirit of his darker hours to come back and take its gift away, or, at least, to deprive him of the dreadful power of giving it to others. His prayer is heard. The phantom reappears, accompanied by the shadow of Milly, the wife of William Swidger, from whom Redlaw has resolutely kept himself aloof, fearing to influence the steady quality of goodness that he knows to be in her, fearing that he may be "the murderer of what is tenderest and best within her bosom." He learns that she, unconsciously, has the power of setting right what he has done; and he seeks her out. Wherever she goes, peace and happiness attend her. The peevish, the morose, the discontented, the ungrateful, and the selfish are suddenly changed, and become their former and better selves. Even Redlaw is restored to what he was; and a clearer light shines into his mind, when Milly tells him that, to her, it seems a good thing for us to remember wrong, *that we may forgive it.*

Some people have said since, that he only thought what has been herein set down; others, that he read it in the fire, one winter-night, about the twilight-time; others, that the ghost was but the representation of his gloomy thoughts, and Milly the embodiment of his better wisdom. *I* say nothing.

— Except this. That as they were assembled in the old hall, by no other light than that of a great fire (having dined early), the shadows once more stole out of their hiding-places, and danced about the room, showing the children marvellous shapes and faces on the walls, and gradually changing what was real and familiar there to what was wild and magical; but that there was one thing in the hall, to which the eyes of Redlaw, and of Milly and her husband, and of the old man, and of the student and his bride that was to be, were often turned; which the shadows did not obscure or change. Deepened in its gravity by the firelight, and gazing from the darkness of the panelled wall like life, the sedate face in the portrait, with the beard and ruff, looked down at them from under its verdant wreath of holly, as they looked up at it; and clear and plain below, as if a voice had uttered them, were the words,—

"Lord, keep my Memory Green."

**Swidger, George.** Eldest son of old Philip Swidger; a dying man, repentant of all the wrong he has done and the sorrow he has caused during a career of forty or fifty years, but suddenly changed by seeing Redlaw at his bedside, into a bold and callous ruffian, who dies with an oath on his lips.

**Swidger, Milly.** Wife of William Swidger; an embodiment of goodness, gentle consideration, love, and domesticity.

**Swidger, Philip.** A superannuated custodian of the institution in which Mr. Redlaw is a lecturer. He is a happy and venerable old man of eighty-seven years of age, who has a most remarkable memory. When, however, at the bedside of his dying son, he meets Redlaw (who has just closed the bargain with the ghost, in consequence of which he causes forgetfulness in others wherever he goes), he all at once grows weak-minded and petulant; but when he once more comes within the influence of his good daughter Milly, he recovers all his recollections of the past, and is quite himself again.

**Swidger, William.** His youngest son; servant to Redlaw, and husband to Milly; a fresh-colored, busy, good-hearted man, who, like his father and others, is temporarily transformed into a very different sort of person by coming in contact with his master after "the ghost's bargain" is concluded.

**Tetterby, Mr. Adolphus.** A newsman, with almost any number of small children,—usually an unselfish, good-natured, yielding little race, but changed for a time, as well as himself, into the exact opposite by Mr. Redlaw.

**Tetterby, Mrs. Sophia.** His wife, called by himself his "little woman." "Considered as an individual, she was rather remarkable for being robust and portly; but considered with reference to her husband, her dimensions became magnificent."

**Tetterby, 'Dolphus.** Their eldest son, aged ten: he is a newspaper boy at a railway station.

His juvenility might have been at some loss for a harmless outlet in this early application to traffic, but for a fortunate discovery he made of a means of entertaining himself, and of dividing the long day into stages of interest, without neglecting business. This ingenious invention, remarkable, like many great discoveries, for its simplicity, consisted in varying the first vowel in the word "paper," and substituting in its stead, at different periods of the day, all the other vowels in grammatical order. Thus, before daylight in the winter time, he went to and fro, in his little oilskin cap and cape and his big comforter, piercing the heavy air with his cry of "Morn-ing pa-per!" which, about an hour before noon, changed to "Morn-ing pep-per!" which, at about two, changed to "Morn-ing pip-per!" which, in a couple of hours, changed to "Morn-ing pop-per!" and so declined with the sun into "Eve-ning pup-per!" to the great relief and comfort of this young gentleman's spirits.

**Tetterby, Johnny.** Their second son; a patient, much-enduring child, whose special duty it is to take care of the baby.

**Tetterby, Sally.** A large, heavy infant, always cutting teeth.

It was a very Moloch of a baby, on whose insatiate altar the whole existence of this particular young brother [Johnny] was offered up a daily sacrifice. Its personality may be said to have consisted in its never being quiet in any one place for five consecutive minutes, and never going to sleep when required. . . . It roved from doorstep to doorstep in the arms of little Johnny Tetterby, and lagged heavily at the rear of troops of juveniles who followed the tumblers or the monkey, and came up, all on one side, a little too late for everything that was attractive, from Monday morning until Saturday night. Wherever childhood congregated to play, there was little Moloch making Johnny fag and toil. Wherever Johnny desired to stay, little Moloch became fractious, and would not remain. Whenever Johnny wanted to go out, Moloch was asleep, and must be watched. Whenever Johnny wanted to stay at home, Moloch was awake, and must be taken out. Yet Johnny was verily persuaded that it was a faultless baby, without its peer in the realm of England; and was quite content to catch meek glimpses of things in general from behind its skirts, or over its limp flapping bonnet, and to go staggering about with it like a very little porter with a very large parcel, which was not directed to anybody, and could never be delivered anywhere.

## THE POOR RELATION'S STORY

**Chill, Uncle.** An avaricious, crabbed old man; uncle to Michael.

**Christiana.** An old sweetheart of Michael's, to whom he imagines that he is married.

**Frank, Little.** A cousin of Michael's; a diffident boy, for whom he has a particular affection.

**Michael.** The "poor relation," and the narrator of the story, which hinges upon a fancy of *what might have been.* Premising that he is not what he is supposed to be, he proceeds, in the first place, to state what he *is* supposed to be, and then goes on to tell what his life and habits and belongings really are. He is thought to be very poor: in fact, he is rich. He is thought to be friendless; but he has the best of friends. He is thought to have been refused by a lady whom he loved: it is a mistake; he married the lady, and has a happy family around him. He is thought to live in a lodging in the Clapham Road: in reality, he lives in a castle — *in the air.*

**Snap, Betsey.** Uncle Chill's only domestic; a withered, hard-favored, yellow old woman.

**Spatter, John.** Michael's host, whom he feigns to have been first his clerk, and afterwards his partner.

## THE CHILD'S STORY

**Fanny.** One of the prettiest girls that ever was seen, in love with "Somebody."

## THE SCHOOL-BOY'S STORY

**Cheeseman, Old.** A poor boy at a boarding-school, who is a general favorite with his fellows, until he is made second Latin master; when they all agree in regarding him as a spy and a deserter, who has sold himself for gold (two pound ten a quarter, and his washing). After this, his life becomes very miserable; for the master and his wife look down upon him, and snub him; while the boys persecute him in many ways, and even form a society for the express purpose of making a set against him. One morning he is missed from his place; and it is thought at first, by the pupils, that, unable to stand it any longer, he has got up early, and drowned himself. It turns out, however, that he has come into a large fortune, — a fact which puts a very different face upon matters, making the master obsequious, and the scholars afraid for the consequences of what they have done. But "Old

Cheeseman is not in the least puffed up or changed by his sudden prosperity, addresses them as "his dear companions and old friends," and gives them a magnificent spread in the dining-room.

**Pitt, Jane.** A sort of wardrobe woman to the boys. Though a good friend to the boys, she is also a good friend to "Old Cheeseman;" and, the more they go against him, the more she stands by him. It is, therefore, only a natural thing, and one to be expected, that, when "Old Cheeseman" succeeds to his grandfather's large property, he should share it with her by making her his wife.

**Tartar, Bob.** The "first boy" in the school, and president of the "Society" formed for the purpose of annoying "Old Cheeseman."

## NOBODY'S STORY

**Bigwig Family, The.** A large household, composed of stately and noisy people, professed humanitarians, who do nothing but blow trumpets, and hold convocations, and make speeches, and write pamphlets, and quarrel among themselves.

**Nobody,** *otherwise* LEGION. The narrator of the story, which, under the guise of an allegory, contains an appeal to the governing classes in behalf of the poor, and an argument for their proper instruction and rational amusement as a means of preventing drunkenness, debauchery, and crime.

## THE SEVEN POOR TRAVELLERS

**Ben.** A waiter.

**Doubledick, Richard.** A young man who has run wild, and has been dismissed by the girl to whom he was betrothed. Made reckless by this well-deserved stroke, he enlists in a regiment of the line under an assumed name, becomes more dissipated than ever, and is constantly getting punished for some breach of discipline. Under the influence of the captain of his company, however, he becomes an altered man, rises rapidly from the ranks, and gains the reputation of being one of the boldest spirits in the whole army. At Badajos the captain falls, mortally wounded by a French officer; and from that moment Doubledick devotes himself to avenging the death of his friend, in case he should ever meet that French officer again. At Waterloo he is among the wounded, and for many long weeks his recovery is doubtful; but he is tenderly nursed by Mrs. Taunton, the mother of his lost friend, and by the young lady (Mary Marshall) to whom he had been engaged, and who now marries him. Three years afterwards he has occasion to visit the South of France, to join Mrs. Taunton (who has gone thither for her health), and escort her home. He finds her the unwitting guest of the very officer who killed her son, and whose life he has vowed to have in return. But the frank and noble demeanor of the Frenchman, the innocent happiness of his pleasant home, and the warm regard which Mrs. Taunton has come to feel for him, — all combine to suggest better thoughts and feelings; and Captain Doubledick secretly forgives him in the name of the divine Forgiver of injuries.

**Marshall, Mary.** A beautiful girl betrothed to Richard Doubledick; afterwards estranged from, but finally married to, him.

**Taunton, Captain.** The captain of the company in which Private Richard Doubledick enlists.

**Taunton, Mrs.** His mother.

## THE HOLLY-TREE

[This is the story of a gentleman, who, imagining himself to have been supplanted in the affections of a young lady, resolves to go straight to America — on his "way to the Devil." Before starting, however, he finds occasion to make a visit to a certain place on the farther borders of Yorkshire, and on the way thither he gets snowed up for a week at the Holly-Tree Inn, where he finds himself the only guest. Sitting by the fire in the principal room, he reads through all the books in the house; namely, a "Book of Roads," a little song-book terminating in a collection of toasts and sentiments, a little jest-book, an old volume of "Peregrine Pickle," and "The Sentimental Journey," to say nothing of two or three old newspapers. These being exhausted, he endeavors to while away the time by recalling his experience of inns, and his remembrances of those he has heard or read of. He further beguiles the days of his imprisonment by talking, at one time or another, with the whole establishment, not excepting the "Boots," who, lingering in the room one day, tells him a story about a young gentleman not eight years old, who runs off with a young lady of seven to Gretna Green, and puts up at the Holly-Tree. When the roads are at last broken out, and just as the disconsolate traveller is on the point of resuming his journey, a carriage drives up, and out jumps his (as he supposes) successful rival, who is running away to Gretna too. It turns out, however, that the lady he has with him is not the one with whom the traveller is in love, but her cousin. The fugitives are hastened on their way; and the traveller retraces his steps without delay, goes straight to London, and marries the girl whom he thought he had lost forever.]

**Charley.** Guest at the Holly-Tree Inn; a self-supposed rejected man; in love with Angela Leath.

**Cobbs.** The "Boots" at the Holly-Tree Inn; formerly under-gardener at Mr. Walmers's.

**Edwin.** Supposed rival of Charley, the guest at the Holly-Tree; betrothed to Emmeline.

**Emmeline.** Cousin to Angela Leath. She elopes with her lover Edwin, and is married to him at Gretna Green.

**George.** Guard of a coach.

**Leath, Angela.** The lady-love and afterwards the wife of Charley (the Holly-Tree guest), who for a time deludes himself into thinking that she prefers his friend Edwin.

**Norah.** Cousin to Master Harry Walmers, junior, with whom she runs away from home, intending to go to Gretna Green, and be married to him. She is, however, overtaken and carried home, and long afterwards becomes the wife of a captain; and finally dies in India.

**Walmers, Master Harry, junior.** A bright boy, not quite eight years old, who falls in love with his cousin, a little girl of seven, and starts with her for Gretna Green, to get married. Stopping at the Holly-Tree Inn in their journey, they are recognized by the "Boots," who had been in the service of the young gentleman's father. The landlord immediately sets off for York to inform the parents of the two little runaways of their whereabouts. They return late at night; and Mr. Walmers, —

"The door being opened, goes in, goes up to the bedside, bends gently down, and kisses the little sleeping face; then he stands looking at it for a minute, looking wonderfully like it (they do say he ran away with Mrs. Walmers); and then he gently shakes the little shoulder.

"'Harry, my dear boy! Harry!'

"Master Harry starts up and looks at his pa, — looks at me too. Such is the honor of that mite, that he looks at me, to see whether he has brought me into trouble.

"'I am not angry, my child. I only want you to dress yourself and come home.'

"'Yes, pa.'

"Master Harry dresses himself quick.

"'Please, may I' (the spirit of that little creature!), 'please, dear pa, — may I — kiss Norah before I go?'

"'You may, my child.'

"So he takes Master Harry in his hand, and I leads the way with the candle to that other bedroom, where the elderly lady is seated by the bed, and poor little Mrs. Harry Walmers, junior, is fast asleep. There the father lifts the boy up to the pillow, and he lays his little face down for an instant by the little warm face of poor little Mrs. Harry Walmers, junior, and gently draws it to him, — a sight so touching to the chambermaids, who are a peeping through the door, that one of them calls out, 'It's a shame to part 'em!'

"Finally," Boots says, "that's all about it. Mr. Walmers drove away in the chaise, having hold of Master Harry's hand. The elderly lady and Mrs. Harry Walmers, junior, that was never to be, went off next day." In conclusion, Boots puts it to me whether I hold with him in two opinions: firstly, that there are not many couples on their way to be married who are half as innocent as them two children; secondly, that it would be a jolly good thing for a great many couples on their way to be married, if they could only be stopped in time, and brought back separate.

**Walmers, Mr.** The father of Master Harry; a gentleman living at the "Elmses," near Shooter's Hill, six or seven miles from London. "Boots" thus describes him: —

He was a gentleman of spirit, and good-looking, and held his head up when he walked, and had what you may call "fire" about him. He wrote poetry, and he rode, and he ran, and he cricketed, and he danced, and he acted; and he done it all equally beautiful. He was uncommon proud of Master Harry, as was his only child; but he did n't spoil him, neither. He was a gentleman that had a will of his own, and a eye of his own, and that would be minded.

## THE WRECK OF THE GOLDEN MARY

**Atherfield, Lucy.** Child of Mrs. Atherfield, and called Golden Lucy.

**Atherfield, Mrs.** A bright-eyed, blooming young wife, going out to join her husband in California.

**Coleshaw, Miss.** A sedate young woman in black, passenger on the Golden Mary.

**Mullion, John.** A sailor who kept on burning blue lights as steadily as if they were a cheerful illumination.

**Rames, William.** Second mate of the Golden Mary.

**Rarx, Mr.** An old gentleman, a good deal like a hawk, passenger on the Golden Mary.

**Ravender, William George.** The captain of the Golden Mary, and narrator of the tale up to the point where he falls at his post.

**Smithick and Watersby.** The name of a commercial house in Liverpool, which is personated by a man; "a wiser merchant or a truer gentleman never stepped."

**Snow, Tom.** The black steward.

**Steadiman, John.** First mate of the Golden Mary, who finally, after the captain's heroic death, is in charge of the lost passengers and crew.

## THE PERILS OF CERTAIN ENGLISH PRISONERS

**Carton, Captain George.** In command. Afterward Admiral Sir George Carton, Baronet.

**Charker, Harry.** A corporal, a comrade of Gill Davis, and possessed of the one idea of Duty.

**Davis, Gilbert.** Commonly called Gill Davis, a private in the Royal Marines, and narrator of the tale.

**Drooce.** A sergeant, and the most tyrannical non-commissioned officer in his Majesty's service.

**Fisher, Mrs. Fanny.** Daughter to Mrs. Venning. A fair, slight thing.

**King, Christian George.** A Sambo fellow, fonder of "all hands" than anybody else was, who turns out to be a traitor and spy.

**Kitten, Mr.** A small, youngish, bald, botanical and mineralogical gentleman.

**Linderwood, Lieutenant.** Officer of the Christopher Columbus.

**Macey, Mr.** Brother-in-law to Miss Maryon.

**Macey, Mrs.** His wife.

**Maryon, Captain.** Captain of the sloop Christopher Columbus.

**Maryon, Marion.** His sister, afterward Lady Carton.

**Packer, Tom.** One of the rank and file.

**Pordage, Mr. Commissioner.** Sometimes styled Consul, and by himself spoken of as Government. Much attached to his diplomatic coat.

**Tott, Mrs. Isabella.** Otherwise Mrs. Belltott, widow of a non-commissioned officer.

**Venning, Mrs.** A handsome, elderly lady, with dark eyes and gray hair.

## A HOUSE TO LET

**Chops.** A dwarf whose name had been cut down to suit his stature, being originally Major Tpschoffki, of the Imperial Bulgraderean Brigade.

**Jarber.** The reader of the tale.

**Magsman, Robert.** Commonly called Toby; a Grizzled Personage in velveteen.

**Normandy.** A Bonnet at a gambling booth; but his name was n't Normandy, though he said it was.

**Peggy.** The maid.

**Trottle.** A somewhat skeptical character.

## THE HAUNTED HOUSE

**B., Master.** A former occupant of the house, who proves to have been a barber.

**Bates, Belinda.** Bosom friend of John's sister.

**Beaver, Nat.** A comrade of Jack Governor's.

**Bottles.** The deaf stable-man.

**Bule, Miss.** Of the ripe age of eight or nine.

**Governor, Jack.** Occupant of the corner room.

**Griffin, Miss.** A lady not to be intrusted with a secret.

**Herschel, John.** So called after the great astronomer.

**Herschel, Mrs.** His wife.

**Ikey.** A stable-boy; a high-shouldered young fellow, with a round red face, a short crop of sandy hair, a very broad, humorous mouth, a turned-up nose, and a great sleeved waistcoat of purple bars, with mother-of-pearl buttons, that seemed to be growing upon him, and to be in a fair way — if it were not pruned — of covering his head and overrunning his boots.

**Joby.** A sort of one-eyed tramp.

**John.** The teller of the story.

**Odd Girl.** One of St. Lawrence's Union Female orphans; a fatal mistake, and a disastrous engagement.

**Perkins.** A general dealer, not given to investigating haunted houses.

**Pipson, Miss.** Adored by Miss Bule.

**Starling, Alfred.** An uncommonly agreeable young fellow of eight and twenty.

**Streaker.** The housemaid.

**Undery, Mr.** A solicitor.

## A MESSAGE FROM THE SEA

**Clissold, Lawrence.** A debtor of Hugh Raybrock.

**Dringworth Brothers.** Bankers, America Square, London.

**Jorgan, Silas Jonas.** A New England sea-captain, but citizen of the world.

**Parvis, Arson.** A resident of Laurean.

**Penrewen.** Christian name unknown.

**Pettifer, Tom.** Who looked no more like a seaman than he looked like a sea-serpent.

**Polreath, David.** An elderly man, possibly dead.
**Raybrock, Alfred.** A young fisherman.
**Raybrock, Hugh.** Supposed lost at sea.
**Raybrock, Margaret.** His supposed widow.
**Raybrock, Mrs.** Draper and postmistress.
**Tredgear, John.** A resident of Laurean.
**Tregarthen, Kitty.** Betrothed to Alfred Raybrock.
**Tregarthen, Mr.** A Cornishman.

## TOM TIDDLER'S GROUND

**Bella.** The housemaid, Kitty's solace.
**Kimmeens, Kitty.** The pupil who stayed behind in the holidays.
**Linx, Miss.** A sharp pupil of Miss Pupford.
**Mopes, Mr.** Tom Tiddler himself.
**Pupford, Miss Euphemia.** Head of the Lilliputian college.
**Tinker, The.** Indifferent to Tom Tiddler.
**Traveller, The.** Tom Tiddler's visitor.

## SOMEBODY'S LUGGAGE

[The Christmas-tale published under this name contains an amusing description, given by a head waiter named Christopher, of the struggles, trials, and experiences of the class to which he belongs, and also an account of his purchasing a quantity of luggage left more than six years previously in Room 24 B by a strange gentleman who had suddenly departed without settling his bill, which amounted to £2 16*s.* 6*d.* Christopher pays Somebody's bill, and takes possession of Somebody's luggage, consisting of a black portmanteau, a black bag, a desk, a dressing-case, a brown-paper parcel. a hat-box, and an umbrella strapped to a walking-stick. These articles are in great part filled with manuscripts. "There was writing in his dressing-case, writing in his boots, writing among his shaving-tackle, writing in his hat-box, writing folded away down among the very whalebones of his umbrella." The writing found in the boots proves to be a very pretty story; and it is disposed of, together with the other documents, to the conductor of "All the Year Round" (Mr. Dickens), on the most satisfactory terms. The story is put in type; and a young man is sent with "THE PROOFS" to Christopher, who does not understand that they are intended to receive any corrections he may wish to make, but supposes that they are the proofs of his having illegally sold the writings. In a few days the strange gentleman suddenly reappears at the coffee-house; and Christopher, overcome with terror and remorse, makes a full confession of what he has done, lays "THE PROOFS" before him, and offers any gradual settlement that may be possible. To his amazement, the unknown grasps his hand, presses him to his breast-bone, calls him "benefactor" and "philanthropist," forces two ten-pound notes upon him, and explains, that, "from boyhood's hour," he has "unremittingly and unavailingly endeavored to get into print." Sitting down with several new pens, and all the inkstands well filled, he devotes himself, the night through, to the task of correcting the press, and is found, the next morning, to have smeared himself and the proofs to that degree, that "few could have said which was them, and which was him, and which was blots."]

**Bebelle** (a playful name for GABRIELLE). A little orphan girl, very pretty and very good; the *protégée* of Corporal Théophile and afterwards adopted by Mr. Langley.

A mere baby, one might call her, dressed in the close white linen cap which small French country-children wear (like the children in Dutch pictures), and in a frock of homespun blue, that had no shape, except where it was tied round her little fat throat; so that, being naturally short, and round all over, she looked behind as if she had been cut off at her natural waist, and had had her head neatly fitted on it.

**Bouclet, Madame.** Mr. Langley's landlady; a compact little woman of thirty-five, or so, who lets all her house overlooking the place, in furnished flats, and lives up the yard behind.

**Christopher.** Head waiter at a London coffee-house; born as well as bred to the business. He dedicates his introductory essay on "waitering" to Joseph, "much respected head waiter at the Slam-Jam Coffee-House, London, E. C., than which, a individual more eminently deserving of the name of man, or a more amenable honor to his own head and heart, whether considered in the light of a waiter, or regarded as a human being, do not exist."

**Englishman, Mr., The.** *See* LANGLEY, MR.

**Gabrielle.** *See* BEBELLE.

**Langley, Mr.,** *called* MR. THE ENGLISHMAN. A lodger at Madame Bouclet's, in the Grande Place of a dull old fortified French town.

In taking his *appartement*, — or, as one might say on our side of the Channel, his set of chambers, — [he] had given his name, correct to the letter, LANGLEY. But as he had a British way of not opening his mouth very wide on foreign soil, except at meals, the brewery [Madame Bouclet and her family] had been able to make nothing of it but L'Anglais. So Mr. the Englishman he had become, and he remained.

He is a very unreasonable man, given to grumbling, moody, and somewhat vindictive. Having had a quarrel with his erring and disobedient daughter, he has disowned her, and gone abroad to be rid of her for the rest of his life. But becoming acquainted with Corporal Théophile and his orphan charge Bebelle, and witnessing their strong affection for each other, and the deep grief of the child at the death of her friend, his heart is penetrated and softened. He adopts the forlorn little one as a trust providentially committed to him, and goes back with her to England, determined on a reconciliation with his daughter.

**Martin, Miss.** A young lady at the bar of the coffee-house where Christopher is head waiter, who makes out the bills.

**Mutuel, Monsieur.** A friend of Madame Bouclet's; a Frenchman with an amiable old walnut-shell countenance.

A spectacled, snuffy, stooping old gentleman in carpet-shoes, and a cloth-cap with a peaked shade, a loose blue frock-coat reaching to his heels, a large limp white shirt-frill, and cravat to correspond: that is to say, white was the natural color of his linen on Sundays; but it toned down with the week.

**Pratchett, Mrs.** Head chambermaid at the coffee-house where Christopher is head waiter; "a female of some pertness, though acquainted with her business." Her husband is in Australia; and his address there is "The Bush."

**Théophile, Corporal.** A brave French soldier, beloved by all his comrades; friend and protector of little Bebelle.

The corporal, a smart figure of a man of thirty, perhaps a thought under the middle size, but very neatly made, — a sunburnt corporal with a brown peaked beard. . . . Nothing was amiss or awry about the corporal. A lithe and nimble corporal, quite complete, from the sparkling dark eyes under his knowing uniform cap to his sparkling white gaiters. The very image and presentment of a corporal of his country's army, in the line of his shoulders, the line of his waist, the broadest line of his Bloomer trousers, and their narrowest line at the calf of his leg.

## MRS. LIRRIPER'S LODGINGS

[This Christmas-tale purports to be the reminiscences of a Mrs. Lirriper, a lodging-house keeper of No. 81, Norfolk Street, Strand. It sets forth the circumstances under which she went into the business, and the manner in which she has carried it on for eight and thirty years, including her trials with servant-girls, and her troubles with an opposition establishment. The chief interest of the story, however, centres around the child of Mrs. Edson, a delicate young woman, who is cruelly deserted by her husband within a few weeks after their marriage. She dies, heart-broken, in giving birth to a little boy, who is adopted by Mrs. Lirriper, and who is brought up under the joint guardianship of herself, and her friend and lodger, Major Jemmy Jackman.]

**Bobbo.** Friend and school-fellow of the hero of an extravagant story that Jemmy Lirriper tells his grandmother and godfather.

**Edson, Mr.** A gentleman from the country, who takes lodgings for himself and wife at Mrs. Lirriper's, and, after staying there for three months, cruelly deserts her under pretence of being suddenly called by business to the Isle of Man. *See further in* "Mrs. Lirriper's Legacy."

**Edson, Mrs. Peggy.** His wife; a very pretty and delicate young lady. When she discovers that her husband has abandoned her, she attempts to end her own life and that of her unborn infant by throwing herself into the Thames; but she is prevented by Mrs. Lirriper and Major Jackman, who watch and follow her, but conceal their knowledge of her intention. Desolate and heart-broken, however, she dies, not long afterwards, in giving birth to a little boy, who is adopted and brought up by Mrs. Lirriper.

**Jackman, Major Jemmy.** A gentleman who leaves Miss Wozenham's lodging-house in a rage, because "she has no appreciation of a gentleman," and takes the parlors at Mrs. Lirriper's. He becomes a warm friend of his new landlady, who reciprocates his regard. She describes him as, —

A most obliging lodger and punctual in all respects except one irregular which I need not particularly specify, but made up for by his being a protection and at all times ready to fill in the papers of the assessed taxes and juries and that, and . . . ever quite the gentleman though passionate. . . . Though he is far from tall he seems almost so when he has his shirt-frill out and his frock-coat on and his hat with the curly brims, and in what service he was I cannot truly tell you my dear whether militia or foreign, for I never heard him even name himself as major but always simple "Jemmy Jackman," and once soon after he came when I felt it my duty to let him know that Miss Wozenham had put it about that he was no major and I took the liberty of adding "which you are sir" his words were "Madam at any rate I am not a minor, and sufficient for the day is the evil thereof" which cannot be denied to be the sacred truth, nor yet his military ways of having his boots with only the dirt brushed off taken to him in the front parlor every morning on a clean plate and varnishing them himself with a little sponge and a saucer and a whistle in a whisper so sure as ever his breakfast is ended, and so neat his ways that it never soils his linen which is scrupulous though more in quality than quantity, neither that nor his mustachios which to the best of my belief are done at the same time and which are as black and shining as his boots, his head of hair being a lovely white.

The major becomes the godfather of Mrs. Edson's little boy, who is named for him; and he takes it upon himself to cultivate his mind on a system of his own, which Mrs. Lirriper thinks "ought to be known to the throne and lords and commons."

But picture my admiration when the major going on almost as quick as if he was conjuring sets out all the articles he names, and says, "Three saucepans, an Italian iron, a hand-bell, a toasting-fork, a nutmeg-grater, four pot-lids, a spice-box, two egg-cups, and a chopping-board, — how many?" and when that mite instantly cries "Tifteen, tut down tive and carry ler 'toppin-board," and then claps his hands draws up his legs and dances on his chair!

My dear with the same astonishing ease and correctness him and the major added up the tables chairs and sofy, the picters fender and fire-irons their own selves me and the cat and the eyes in Miss Wozenham's head, and whenever the sum was done Young Roses and Diamonds claps his hands and draws up his legs and dances on his chair.

The pride of the major! ("*Here*'s a mind, ma'am!" he says to me behind his hand.)

Then he says aloud, "We now come to the next elementary rule, — which is called" —

"Umtraction!" cries Jemmy.

"Right," says the major. "We have here a toasting-fork, a potato in its natural state, two pot-lids, one egg-cup, a wooden spoon, and two skewers, from which it is necessary, for commercial purposes, to subtract a sprat-gridiron, a small pickle-jar, two lemons, one pepper-castor, a blackbeetle-trap, and a knob of the dresser-drawer: what remains?"

"Toatin'-fork!" cries Jemmy.

"In numbers how many?" says the major.

"One!" cries Jemmy.

("*Here*'s a boy, ma'am!" says the major to me, behind his hand.)

Then the major goes on: —

"We now approach the next elementary rule, which is entitled"

"Tickleication," cries Jemmy.

"Correct," says the major.

But my dear to relate to you in detail the way in which they multiplied fourteen sticks of firewood by two bits of ginger and a larding-needle, or divided pretty well everything else there was on the table by the heater of the Italian iron and a chamber candlestick, and got a lemon over, would make my head spin round and round and round as it did at the time.

**Jane.** A housemaid in Miss Wozenham's service.

**Lirriper, Jemmy Jackman.** The son of Mrs. Edson, who dies in giving birth to him. He is named for Mrs. Lirriper, who adopts him, and for Major Jackman, who becomes his godfather. He grows up to be a bright, blithe, and good boy, delighting the hearts of both his guardians, who agree that he "has not his like on the face of the earth."

**Lirriper, Mrs. Emma.** The narrator of the story; a lodging-house keeper at No. 81, Norfolk Street, Strand, "situated midway between the city and St. James's, and within five minutes' walk of the principal places of public amusement."

Certainly I ought to know something of the business having been in it so long, for it was early in the second year of my married life that I lost my poor Lirriper and I set up at Islington directly afterwards and afterwards came here, being two houses and eight and thirty years and some losses and a deal of experience.

**Maxey, Caroline.** One of Mrs. Lirriper's servant-girls; a good-looking, black-eyed girl, with a high temper, but a kind and grateful heart.

**Perkinsop, Mary Anne.** A girl in Mrs. Lirriper's service, who is enticed away by an offer from Miss Wozenham of one pound per quarter more in the way of wages. Mrs. Lirriper regards her as "worth her weight in gold" for overawing lodgers, without driving them away.

**Seraphina.** The heroine of an extravagantly fanciful story related by Master Jemmy Jackman Lirriper to his "grandmother" and his godfather. She was a schoolmaster's daughter, and the most beautiful creature that ever was seen.

**Sophy,** *called* WILLING SOPHY. A poor, half-starved creature, whom Mrs. Lirriper takes into her house as a servant, and who is "down upon her knees, scrubbing, early and late, and ever cheerful, but always smiling with a black face."

I says to Sophy, "Now Sophy my good girl have a regular day for your stoves and keep the width of the airy between yourself and the blacking and do not brush your hair with the bottoms of the saucepans and do not meddle with the snuffs of the candles and it stands to reason that it can no longer be," yet there it was and always on her nose, which turning up and being broad at the end seemed to boast of it and caused warning from a steady gentleman and excellent lodger with breakfast by the week but a little irritable and use of a sitting-room when required, his words being "Mrs. Lirriper I have arrived at the point of admitting that the Black is a man and a brother, but only in a natural form and when it can't be got off."

**Wozenham, Miss.** A lodging-house keeper in Norfolk Street, not far from Mrs. Lirriper's, but on the other side of the way. There is considerable rivalry between the two establishments; and Mrs. Lirriper conceives a strong dislike to Miss Wozenham, on account of her advertising in Bradshaw's "Railway Guide," her systematic underbidding for lodgers, her enticing servant-girls away by the offer of higher wages, and her doing various other ill-natured and unfriendly acts.

## MRS. LIRRIPER'S LEGACY

[A sequel to "Mrs. Lirriper's Lodgings" (published in 1863), which met with a very warm reception from the public, and excited a general desire to know more of the old lady's experiences. The legacy is left *to* Mrs. Lirriper by the Mr. Edson who is introduced in the former part of the story as deserting his young wife shortly after marrying her, and who dies, repentant, many years after, in France, whither she goes to take care of him in his last moments, accompanied by his son Jemmy (whom he has never seen), and by her friend and adviser, Major Jackman. The benevolent conduct of this good soul to her good-for-nothing brother-in-law, Doctor Joshua Lirriper; to the obnoxious collector of assessed taxes, Mr. Buffle, on the night when his house is burnt down; and to Miss Wozenham, when that lady was in danger of having her chattels taken from her on execution,—forms the subject of the remainder of the story.]

**Buffle, Mr.** Collector of the assessed taxes. His manners when engaged in his business are not agreeable; and he has a habit of looking about, as if suspicious that goods are being removed in the dead of night by a back-door. Major Jackman knocks his hat off his head twice for keeping it on in Mrs. Lirriper's presence, when he calls at her house in the discharge of his regular duties. But when his house catches fire, and burns to the ground, he and his family are taken by the major to Mrs. Lirriper's for shelter;

and from this kindness an intimacy springs up between the two households, which is very agreeable to all parties, Mr. Buffle even going so far as to call the major his "preserver" and "best friend."

**Buffle, Mrs.** His wife; a woman who gives herself airs because her husband keeps "a one-horse pheayton."

**Buffle, Miss Robina.** Their daughter; a thin young lady with a very small appetite. She favors her father's articled young man, George, in opposition to the wishes of her parents; though they finally give their consent to the match.

**Edson, Mr.** A former lodger at Mrs. Lirriper's, and the husband of a young woman whom he cruelly deserted after living with her for a few months. Years pass by; and he is taken dangerously ill at a town in France. Finding that his recovery is impossible, he leaves all that he has to Mrs. Lirriper, who had been very kind to his poor wife, and who has brought up their child as if it were her own. On learning from the French consul in London that an unknown Englishman is lying at the point of death in Sens, and that her name is mentioned in a communication to the authorities, which is found among his papers, she sets out at once for that place with her adopted child and her friend Major Jackman. Recognizing Mr. Edson in the sick stranger, and finding him truly penitent for the grievous wrong he had done, she forgives him, and causes the boy — who does not know who the dying man is — also to say, "May God forgive you!"

**George.** A rather weak-headed young man, articled to Mr. Buffle, and enamored of his daughter.

**Gran, Mrs.** (*i. e.* MRS. LIRRIPER). A highly respected and beloved lady who resides within a hundred miles of Norfolk Street, and who figures in Jemmy Lirriper's imaginary version of the story of Mr. Edson's life.

**Jackman, Major Jemmy.** A lodger at Mrs. Lirriper's; her warm personal friend, and the godfather of her adopted child Jemmy.

**Lirriper, Doctor Joshua.** Youngest brother of Mrs. Lirriper's deceased husband. He is a dissipated scapegrace, and a systematic sponger upon his benevolent and unsuspecting sister-in-law.

Doctor of what I am sure it would be hard to say unless liquor, for neither physic nor music nor yet law does Joshua Lirriper know a morsel of except continually being summoned to the county court and having orders made upon him which he runs away from.

Joshua Lirriper has his good feelings and shows them in being always so troubled in his mind when he cannot wear mourning for his brother. Many a long year have I left off my widow's mourning not being wishful to intrude, but the tender point in Joshua that I cannot help a little yielding to is when he writes "One single sovereign would enable me to wear a decent suit of mourning for my much loved brother. I vowed at the time of his lamented death that I would ever wear sables in memory of him but alas how short-sighted is man, how keep that vow when penniless!" It says a good deal for the strength of his feelings that he could n't have been seven year old when my poor Lirriper died and to have kept to it ever since is highly creditable. But we know there 's good in all of us, — if we only knew where it was in some of us, — and though it was far from delicate in Joshua to work upon the dear child's feelings when first sent to school and write down into Lincolnshire for his pocket-money by return of post and got it, still he is my poor Lirriper's own youngest brother and might n't have meant not paying his bill at the Salisbury Arms when his affection took him down to stay a fortnight at Hatfield churchyard and might have meant to keep sober but for bad company.

**Lirriper, Jemmy Jackman.** Son of Mr. Edson, adopted by Mrs. Lirriper, and brought up under the joint guardianship of herself and Major Jackman, who is at once his godfather and his "companion, guide, philosopher, and friend." As he develops a taste for engineering, the major assists him in the construction and management of a railway, which they name "The United Grand Junction Lirriper and Jackman Great Norfolk Parlor Line," which is kept on the major's sideboard, and dusted with his own hands every morning.

"For," says my Jemmy with the sparkling eyes when it was christened, "we must have a whole mouthful of name Gran or our dear old public" and there the young rogue kissed me, "won't stump up." So the public [Mrs. Lirriper] took the shares — ten at ninepence, and immediately when that was spent twelve preference at one and sixpence — and they were all signed by Jemmy and countersigned by the major, and between ourselves much better worth the money than some shares I have paid for in my time. In the same holidays the line was made and worked and opened and ran excursions and had collisions and burst its boilers and all sorts of accidents and offences all most regular correct and pretty.

The young gentleman accompanies Mrs. Lirriper to Sens, and is present at the death of Mr. Edson; though he does not know him to be his father, and is ignorant of the facts in regard to his cruel desertion of his wife soon after marriage. Being in the habit of composing and relating stories for the amusement of his "grandmother" and godfather, and his mind dwelling on the death-bed scene he has witnessed, he frames an imaginary version of his father's history, which is wofully unlike the fact, and in which,

> In all reverses, whether for good or evil, the words of Mr. Edson to the fair young partner of his life were, "Unchanging love and truth will carry us through all."

**Madgers, Winifred.** A servant-girl at Mrs. Lirriper's; a "Plymouth sister," and a remarkably tidy young woman.

**Rairyganoo, Sally.** One of Mrs. Lirriper's domestics, suspected to be of Irish extraction, though professing to come of a Cambridge family. She absconds, however, with a bricklayer of the Limerick persuasion, and is married to him in pattens, being too impatient to wait till his black eye gets well.

**Wozenham, Miss.** A neighbor of Mrs. Lirriper's in Norfolk Street, and the keeper of a rival lodging-house. For many years, Mrs. Lirriper has been strongly prejudiced against Miss Wozenham; but on hearing that she has been "sold up," she feels so much sympathy for her, that she goes to her without delay or ceremony, expresses her regret for the unpleasantness there has been between them in the past, and cheers her up with true womanly tact and kindliness.

> I says "My dear if you could give me a cup of tea to clear my muddle of a head I should better understand your affairs." And we had the tea and the affairs too and after all it was but forty pound, and — There! she 's as industrious and straight a creeter as ever lived and has paid back half of it already, and where 's the use of saying more, particularly when it ain't the point? For the point is that when she was a kissing my hands and holding them in hers and kissing them again and blessing blessing blessing, I cheered up at last and I says "Why what a waddling old goose I have been my dear to take you for something so very different!" "Ah but I too" says she "how have *I* mistaken *you!*" "Come for goodness' sake tell me" I says "what you thought of me?" "Oh" says she "I thought you had no feeling for such a hard hand-to-mouth life as mine, and were rolling in affluence." I says shaking my sides (and very glad to do it for I had been a choking quite long enough) "Only look at my figure my dear and give me your opinion whether if I was in affluence I should be likely to roll in it!" That did it. We got as merry as grigs (whatever *they* are, if you happen to know, my dear — *I* don't) and I went home to my blessed home as happy and as thankful as could be.

## DOCTOR MARIGOLD

**Joskin.** A chuckle-headed country fellow, who volunteers a bid of twopence for Doctor Marigold's sick child, when he appears with her on the footboard of his cart.

**Marigold, Doctor.** The narrator of the story. He describes himself as "a middle-aged man, of a broadish build, in cords, leggings, and a sleeved waistcoat, the strings of which is always gone behind," with a white hat, and a shawl round his neck, worn loose and easy. He is a "Cheap Jack," or itinerant auctioneer, born on the highway, and named "Doctor" out of gratitude and compliment to his mother's accoucheur. He marries, and has one child, a little girl, but loses both daughter and wife, and continues his travels alone. Coming across a deaf-and-dumb child, however, who, he fancies, resembles his lost daughter, he adopts her, and sends her to a school for deaf-mutes, to be educated; but she falls in love with a young man who is also deaf and dumb, and he is forced to give her up. She sails for China with her husband, but returns, after an absence of a few years, bringing with her a little daughter who can both hear and talk; and the measure of the Doctor's happiness is once more full.

**Marigold, Mrs.** Wife of Doctor Marigold; a Suffolk young woman whom he courted from the footboard of his cart.

She was n't a bad wife; but she had a temper. If she could have parted with that one article at a sacrifice, I would n't have swopped her away in exchange for any other woman in England. Not that I ever did swop her away; for we lived together till she died, and that was thirteen year. Now, my lords and ladies and gentlefolks all, I'll let you into a secret; though you won't believe it. Thirteen year of temper in a palace would try the worst of you; but thirteen year of temper in a cart would try the best of you. You are kept so very close to it in a cart, you see. There 's thousands of couples amongst you getting on like sweet ile upon a whetstone in houses five and six pairs of stairs high, that would go to the Divorce Court in a cart. Whether the jolting makes it worse, I don't undertake to decide; but in a cart it does come home to you and stick to you. Wiolence in a cart is *so* wiolent, and aggrawation in a cart is *so* aggrawating.

We might have had such a pleasant life! A roomy cart, with the large goods hung outside, and the bed slung underneath it when on the road, an iron pot and a kettle, a fireplace for the cold weather, a chimney for the smoke, a hanging-shelf and a cupboard, a dog, and a horse: what more do you want? You draw off upon a bit of turf in a green lane or by the roadside;

you hobble your old horse, and turn him grazing; you light your fire upon the ashes of the last visitors; you cook your stew; and you would n't call the emperor of France your father. But have a temper in the cart flinging language and the hardest goods in stock at you; and where are you then? Put a name to your feelings.

My dog knew as well when she was on the turn as I did. Before she broke out, he would give a howl, and bolt. How he knew it was a mystery to me: but the sure and certain knowledge of it would wake him up out of his soundest sleep; and he would give a howl, and bolt. At such times I wished I was him.

At such times she does not spare her little daughter, but treats her with great cruelty. When, however, the child dies, she takes to brooding, and tries to drown remorse in liquor; but one day, seeing a woman beating a child unmercifully, she stops her ears, runs away like a wild thing, and the next day she is found in the river.

**Marigold, Little Sophy.** Their daughter; a sweet child, shamefully abused by her mother, but dearly loved by her father, to whom she is quite devoted. She takes a bad low fever, and dies in his arms, while he is convulsing a rustic audience with his jokes and witty speeches.

**Marigold, Willum.** Doctor Marigold's father; a "lovely one, in his time," at the "Cheap Jack" work.

**Mim.** A showman, who is a most ferocious swearer, and who has a very hoarse voice. He is master to Pickleson, and stepfather to Sophy, whom he disposes of to Doctor Marigold for half a dozen pairs of braces.

**Pickleson,** *called* RINALDO DI VELASCO. An amiable though timid giant, let out to Mim for exhibition by his mother, who spends the wages he receives.

He was a languid young man, which I attribute to the distance betwixt his extremities. He had a little head, and less in it; he had weak eyes and weak knees; and altogether you could n't look at him without feeling that there was greatly too much of him both for his joints and his mind.

**Sophy.** A deaf-and-dumb girl adopted by Doctor Marigold after the death of his own daughter Sophy. She becomes greatly attached to her new father, who loves her fervently in return, and is very kind and patient with her, trying at first to teach her himself to read, and then sending her to an institution for deaf mutes, to be educated. She subsequently marries a man afflicted like herself; goes abroad with him; and, after an absence of over five years, returns home with a little daughter. Doctor Marigold thus describes their meeting: —

I had started at a real sound; and the sound was on the steps of the cart. It was the light, hurried tread of a child coming clambering up. That tread of a child had once been so familiar to me, that, for half a moment, I believed I was a going to see a little ghost.

But the touch of a real child was laid upon the outer handle of the door, and the handle turned, and the door opened a little way, and a real child peeped in,—a bright little comely girl with large dark eyes.

Looking full at me, the tiny creature took off her mite of a straw hat, and a quantity of dark curls fell all about her face. Then she opened her lips, and said in a pretty voice:—

"Grandfather!"

"Ah, my God!" I cries out. "She can speak!"

"Yes, dear grandfather. And I am to ask you whether there was ever any one that I remind you of?"

In a moment, Sophy was round my neck, as well as the child; and her husband was a wringing my hand with his face hid; and we all had to shake ourselves together before we could get over it. And when we did begin to get over it, and I saw the pretty child a talking, pleased and quick, and eager and busy, to her mother, in the signs that I had first taught her mother, the happy and yet pitying tears fell rolling down my face.

## TWO GHOST STORIES

### I. THE TRIAL FOR MURDER

[Feigned to have been written by "a literary character" whom the doctor discovers in travelling about the country, and to have been intended (as well as the tales accompanying it) for the amusement of his adopted deaf-and-dumb daughter Sophy. It purports to be an account of circumstances preceding and attending a certain noted trial for murder. The narrator, who is summoned to serve on the jury, is haunted, from the time he first hears of the deed until the close of the trial, by the apparition of the murdered man. Though seen by no one else, it mingles with the jury and the officers of the court, looks at the judge's notes over his shoulder, confronts the defendant's witnesses, and stands at the elbow of the counsel, invariably causing some trepidation or disturbance on the part of each, and, as it were, dumbly and darkly overshadowing their minds.

Finally the jury returned into court at ten minutes past twelve. The murdered man at that time stood directly opposite the jury-box, on the other side of the court. As I took my place, his eyes rested on me with great attention: he seemed satisfied, and slowly shook a great gray veil, which he carried on his arm for the first time, over his head and whole form. As I gave in our verdict, "Guilty," the veil collapsed, all was gone, and his place was empty.]

**Derrick, John.** Valet to the haunted juryman.

**Harker, Mr.** An officer in charge of the jury, and sworn to hold them in safe-keeping.

Up in a corner of the Down Refreshment-Room at Mugby Junction, in the height of twenty-seven cross draughts (I 've often counted 'em while they brush the first-class hair twenty-seven ways), behind the bottles, among the glasses, bounded on the nor'west by the beer, stood pretty far to the right of a metallic object that 's at times the tea-urn, and at times the soup-tureen, according to the nature of the last twang imparted to its contents, which are the same ground-work, fended off from the traveller by a barrier of stale sponge-cakes erected atop of the counter, and lastly exposed sideways to the glare of our missis's eye,—you ask a boy so sitiwated, next time you stop in a hurry at Mugby, for anything to drink; you take particular notice that he 'll try to seem not to hear you; that he 'll appear in a absent manner to survey the line through a transparent medium composed of your head and body; and that he won't serve you as long as you can possibly bear it. That 's me.

**Piff, Miss.** One of the "young ladies" in the same Refreshment-Room.

**Sniff, Mr.** "A regular insignificant cove" employed by the mistress of the Refreshment-Room.

He looks arter the sawdust department in a back-room, and is sometimes, when we are very hard put to it, let behind the counter with a corkscrew, but never when it can be helped; his demeanor towards the public being digusting servile. How Mrs. Sniff ever come so far to lower herself as to marry him, I don't know; but I suppose *he* does; and I should think he wished he did n't, for he leads a awful life. Mrs. Sniff could n't be much harder with him if he was public.

**Sniff, Mrs.** His wife; chief assistant of the mistress of the Refreshment-Room.

She 's the one! She 's the one as you 'll notice to be always looking another way from you, when you look at her. She 's the one with the small waist buckled in tight in front, and with the lace cuffs at her wrists, which she puts on the edge of the counter before her, and stands a-smoothing while the public foams. This smoothing the cuffs, and looking another way while the public foams, is the last accomplishment taught to the young ladies as come to Mugby to be finished by our missis; and it's always taught by Mrs. Sniff.

When our missis went away upon her journey, Mrs. Sniff was left in charge. She did hold the public in check most beautiful. In all my time, I never see half so many cups of tea given without milk to people as wanted it with, nor half so many cups of tea with milk given to people as wanted it without. When foaming ensued, Mrs. Sniff would say, "Then you'd better settle it among yourselves, and change with one another." It was a most highly delicious lark.

**Whiff, Miss.** An attendant in the Refreshment-Room.

### II. THE SIGNAL-MAN

[The second Ghost Story is an account of an incident occurring on one of the branch lines leading from Mugby Junction. It is supposed to be related by "Barbox Brothers," who makes a careful study of the Junction and its vicinity, and communicates to his poor bed-ridden friend Phœbe the substance of what he sees, hears, or otherwise picks up on the main line and its five branches. Exploring Branch Line No. 1, he visits a signal-man who is stationed in a deep cutting near the entrance of a tunnel. He is a cool, vigilant, clear-headed, and educated man, who had been, when young, a student of natural history, and had attended lectures, but had run wild, misused his opportunities, gone down, and never risen again. Notwithstanding his intelligence, and his freedom from any taint of superstition, he is continually haunted by a strange apparition, which, just before any fatal accident, stands by the red light at the mouth of the tunnel, and with one hand over its eyes, as if to shut out the frightful scene about to take place, cries "Holloa! Below there! Look out! For God's sake, clear the way!" Twice has this occurred, and been followed by accident and death; and now the figure has been seen and heard again. The visitor goes away, hardly knowing how he ought to act in view of his knowledge of the man's state of mind; but he finally resolves to offer to accompany him to a wise medical practitioner, and to take his opinion.

Next evening was a lovely evening, and I walked out early to enjoy it. The sun was not yet quite down when I traversed the field-path near the top of the deep cutting. I would extend my walk for an hour, I said to myself, — half an hour on, and half an hour back, — and it would then be time to go to my signal-man's box.

Before pursuing my stroll, I stepped to the brink, and mechanically looked down from the point from which I had first seen him. I cannot describe the thrill that seized upon me, when, close at the mouth of the tunnel, I saw the appearance of a man, with his left sleeve across his eyes, passionately waving his right arm.

The nameless horror that oppressed me passed in a moment; for in a moment I saw that this appearance of a man was a man indeed, and that there was a little group of other men, standing at a short distance, to whom he seemed to be rehearsing the gesture he made. The danger-light was not yet lighted. Against its shaft, a little low hut, entirely new to me, had been made of some wooden supports and tarpaulin. It looked no bigger than a bed.

With an irresistible sense that something was wrong, — with a flashing, self-reproachful fear that fatal mischief had come of my leaving the man there and causing no one to be sent to overlook or correct what he did, — I descended the notched path with all the speed I could make.

"What is the matter?" I asked the men.

"Signal-man killed this morning, sir."

"Not the man belonging to that box?"

"Yes, sir."

"Not the man I know?"

"You will recognize him, sir, if you knew him," said the man who spoke for the others, solemnly uncovering his own head, and raising an end of the tarpaulin; "for his face is quite composed."

"Oh! how did this happen? how did this happen?" I asked, turning from one to another, as the hut closed in again.

"He was cut down by an engine, sir. No man in England knew his work better; but, somehow, he was not clear of the outer rail. It was just at broad day. He had struck the light, and had the lamp in his hand. As the engine came out of the tunnel, his back was towards her, and she cut him down. That man drove her, and was showing how it happened. Show the gentleman, Tom." . . .

"Coming round the curve in the tunnel, sir," he said, "I saw him at the end, like as if I saw him down a perspective-glass. There was no time to check speed; and I knew him to be very careful. As he did n't seem to take heed of the whistle, I shut it off when we were running down upon him, and called to him as loud as I could call."

"What did you say?"

"I said, 'Below there! Look out! Look out! For God's sake, clear the way!'"

I started.

"Ah! it was a dreadful time, sir. I never left off calling to him. I put this arm before my eyes not to see; and I waved this arm to the last; but it was no use."]

## MUGBY JUNCTION

[The hero of the story, who is also the narrator of it, is at first a clerk in the firm of Barbox Brothers, then a partner, and finally the firm itself. From being a moody, self-contained, and unhappy person, made so by the lumbering cares and the accumulated disappointments of long monotonous years, he is changed, under circumstances that awaken and develop his better nature, into a thoroughly cheerful man, with eyes and thoughts for others, and a hand ever ready to help those who need and deserve help; and thus, taking, as it were, thousands of partners into the solitary firm, be becomes "Barbox Brothers and Co."]

**Barbox Brothers.** *See* JACKSON, MR.

**Beatrice.** A careworn woman, with her hair turned gray, whom "Barbox Brothers" had once loved and lost. She is the wife of Tresham.

**Ezekiel.** "The Boy at Mugby;" an attendant in the Refreshment-Room at Mugby Junction, whose proudest boast is, that "it never yet refreshed a mortal being."

**Jackson, Mr.** A former clerk in the public notary and bill-broking firm of Barbox Brothers, who, after imperceptibly becoming the sole representative of the house, at length retires, and obliterates it from the face of the earth, leaving nothing of it but its name on two portmanteaus, which he has with him one rainy night when he leaves a train at Mugby Junction.

A man within five years of fifty, either way, who had turned gray too soon, like a neglected fire; a man of pondering habit, brooding carriage of the head, and suppressed internal voice; a man with many indications on him of having been much alone.

With a bitter recollection of his lonely childhood, of the enforced business, at once distasteful and oppressive, in which the best years of his life have been spent, of the double faithlessness of the only woman he ever loved and the only friend he ever trusted, his birthday, as it annually recurs, serves but to intensify his ever-present sense of desolation; and he resolves to abandon all thought of a fixed home, and to pass the rest of his days in travelling, hoping to find relief in a constant change of scene. It is after three o'clock of a tempestuous morning, when, acting on a sudden impulse, he leaves the train at Mugby Junction. At that black hour he cannot obtain any conveyance to the inn, and willingly accepts the invitation of "Lamps," an *employé* of the railway company, to try the warmth of his little room for a while. He afterwards makes the acquaintance of "Lamp's" daughter Phœbe, a poor bed-ridden girl; and their happy disposition, strong mutual affection, peaceful lives, modest self-respect, and unaffected interest in those around them, teach him a lesson of cheerfulness, contentment, and moral responsibility, which the experience of years had failed to impart.

On a visit, one day, to a distant town, he is suddenly accosted by a very little girl, who tells him she is lost. He takes her to his hotel, and failing to discover who she is, or where she lives, he makes arrangements for her staying over night, and amuses himself with her childish prattle, and her enjoyment of her novel situation. The little one's mother at last appears, and proves to be the woman he had loved, and who had so heartlessly eloped with his most trusted friend years before. She tells him that she has had five other children, who are all in their graves; that her husband is very ill of a lingering disorder, and that he believes the curse of his old friend rests on the whole household. Will Mr. Jackson forgive them? The injured man — now so changed from what he once was — responds by taking the child to her father, placing her in his arms, and invoking a blessing on her innocent head. "Live and thrive, my pretty baby!" he says, — "live and prosper, and become, in time, the mother of other little children, like the angels who behold the Father's face."

**"Lamps."** A railway servant employed at Mugby Junction, father of Phœbe. He is a very hard-working man, being on duty fourteen, fifteen, or eighteen hours a day, and sometimes even twenty-four hours at a time. But he is always on the bright side and the good side. He has a daughter who is bed-ridden, and to whom he is entirely devoted. Besides supplying her with books and newspapers, he takes to composing comic songs for her amusement, and — what is still harder, and at first goes much against his grain — to singing them also.

**Phœbe.** His daughter; crippled and helpless in consequence of a fall in infancy. She supports herself by making lace, and by teaching a few little children. Notwithstanding her great misfortune, she is always contented, always lively, always interested in others, of all sorts. She makes the acquaintance of Mr. Jackson ("Barbox Brothers"); and her pure and gentle life becomes the guiding star of his.

THE BOY AT MUGBY.

**Polly.** Daughter of Beatrice and Tresham; a little child found by "Barbox Brothers" in the streets of a large town.

**Tresham.** A former friend of "Barbox Brothers," who advances him in business, and takes him into his private confidence. In return, Tresham comes between him and Beatrice (whom "Barbox Brothers" loves), and takes her from him. This treachery after a time receives its fitting punishment in poverty, and loss of health and children; but "Barbox Brothers," whose awakened wrath had long seemed inappeasable, is made better at last by the discipline and experience of life, and generously forgives those who had forced him to undergo so sharp a trial.

## NO THOROUGHFARE

**Bintrey, Mr.** A lawyer, made a trustee of his business by Walter Wilding, when he surrenders his position to find the person who should have had his money.

**Defresnier & Co.** A Swiss wine-house.

**Goldstraw, Mrs.** *See* SALLY.

**Ladle, Joey.** Cellarman to Wilding & Co.

**Marguerite.** Half-niece to Obenreizer, and loved by George Vendale.

**Obenreizer.** A Swiss, agent for Defresnier & Co., wine merchants.

**Sally.** Nurse at the Hospital for Foundling Children. Afterward Mrs. Goldstraw.

**Vendale, George.** Wilding's partner, and the real Walter Wilding.

**Wilding, Walter.** A foundling, bearing the name of a real Walter Wilding, who had preceded him and been adopted. He afterward is a wine merchant, of Wilding & Co.

# HARD TIMES

## OUTLINE

### BOOK THE FIRST: SOWING

Chapter "In this life we want nothing but facts, sir; nothing but
I facts." So spoke Mr. Thomas Gradgrind to the schoolmaster, and the government inspector. Then Mr. Gradgrind proceeded
II to examine the scholars; and it appeared that Cecilia, or "Sissy" Jupe, the horse-rider's daughter, a pretty, sweet-faced girl, was unable to give the scientific definition of a horse; whereas Bitzer, a sandy-haired, freckled-faced lad, knew that this animal is graminivorous, that he has forty teeth, and numerous other facts of a like nature.

III The inspection ended, Mr. Gradgrind started homeward, thinking of his own two children, Louisa and Tom, — model children, thoroughly crammed with facts, and perfectly ignorant of fancies or fairies. But on the way he passed a circus-tent, and was horrified to find that his model children were both down on the ground trying to peer through a hole in the tent; — and Louisa was fifteen years old! Mr. Gradgrind rebuked them severely, and to Louisa he said, "What would Mr. Bounderby say? What would Mr. Bounderby say?"

IV Now Mr. Bounderby was a pompous, bustling, thriving manufacturer in Coketown, a friend of Mr. Gradgrind's. His boast was that he had come up from the gutter by his own exertions, and that he was a practical man with no nonsense or fancies about him, — a man of facts. Mr. Bounderby's advice was to
V remove Sissy Jupe from the school, as being a contaminating influence; and he, with Mr. Gradgrind, sought her father's abode. It proved to be a poor, shabby place where Jupe,
VI the clown, lived with Sissy and with Merrylegs, the performing dog. Poor Jupe had not been doing well of late; he had been hissed in the ring; and that very day he had disappeared, taking Merrylegs with him. This being the case, Mr. Gradgrind (who was really a kind-hearted man at bottom) offered to take Sissy into his family, if only, as he remarked to Bounderby, as a warning to Louisa. So Sissy said good-by to all the company,

including Sleary, the proprietor, a stout, wheezy, brandy-drinking, but kindly old soul.

VII At first she was taken to Mr. Bounderby's house, which
(Bounderby being a bachelor) was presided over by Mrs.
Sparsit, — a hook-nosed, highly connected old lady, whose mother was a Powler. Bounderby was very proud of having this aristocratic person in his train, the more so because he — so at least he said — was born in a ditch, and his mother was probably the worst woman in the world, with one exception, namely, his drunken old grandmother. Thence Sissy Jupe went to the Gradgrind mansion, partly as an attendant upon Mrs. Gradgrind, a querulous invalid.
VIII There was a kind of feeling in the family that Louisa was
destined to marry Mr. Bounderby. She disliked him; but Tom, who was now in his office, hoped that she would marry Bounderby, in order to make matters easy for him; and Tom was the only thing in the world that Louisa cared about. Sissy Jupe,
IX though of course she said nothing, thought it a horrible fate
for Louisa. Poor Sissy, by the way, was very backward in learning the facts that were taught in the Bounderby school.

X Among the workmen in Mr. Bounderby's factory was one
Stephen Blackpool, an honest, industrious man, who had been made miserable for many years by a vile, drunken wife.
XI Stephen went to his employer to inquire if he could get a
divorce; and Bounderby in his usual polite and sympathetic manner told him that he could, by special act of Parliament, and at the price of £1500, or perhaps double that amount. Stephen went off in despair, for he loved Rachael, a good, virtuous girl.

XII On his way home Stephen met a queer old lady, very
neatly dressed and respectable, who asked him many questions about Mr. Bounderby with a strange air of interest. When
XIII he arrived at his poor room, there sat Rachael, nursing his
wife, who was ill from dissipation, as tenderly as if she were
XIV the best-beloved of women. Louisa had now become a
young woman, and, at her father's suggestion, she agreed to
XV marry Bounderby. Sissy Jupe pitied her, and Louisa felt
this and tacitly resented it; and yet she was an object of pity to herself. So they were married, and Mrs. Sparsit, who per-
XVI sisted in regarding Mr. Bounderby as a victim, retired to
comfortable quarters at the bank where Tom Gradgrind and Bitzer, the light-haired, freckle-faced lad, were employed.

BOOK THE SECOND: REAPING

Chapter I One evening a handsome, languid young man of five and thirty called at the bank and asked the way to Mr. Bounderby's house. This was Mr. James Harthouse, a member of Parliament, who had come down to Coketown on political busi-
II ness. That evening he dined with the Bounderbys, and Mr. Bounderby took the occasion to dilate upon the hap'orth of stewed eels which, at eight years old, he had purchased in the streets, and upon the inferior water, specially used for laying the dust, with which he had washed them down. To Mr. Harthouse, Louisa was a puzzle. Her features were handsome, but their natural play was so locked up that it was impossible to guess at their genuine expression. She was perfectly cold and indifferent. Will nothing move her? thought Mr. Harthouse. Yes, there was something. Tom appeared. She changed as the door opened, and broke into a beaming smile. Yet he was a sullen whelp, and ungra-
III cious even to his sister. But Mr. Harthouse entertained the whelp in his room at the hotel that night, and, with the help of brandy and strong tobacco, got from him a full account of Louisa, and of her reasons for marrying Bounderby. Very soon
IV poor Stephen had another trouble on his hands: all the work-people, excepting himself, resolved to strike for higher pay; and, when he refused to join them, he became a solitary outcast, an object of hatred to his former friends and associates.
V Mr. Bounderby sent for him, and interrogated him as to the plans and designs of the striking workmen. Stephen refused to betray them; and thereupon Bounderby turned him off. Taking
VI his way sadly from the Bounderby mansion, Stephen met both Rachael and the queer little old woman already mentioned, and they both went with him to his room for a farewell cup of tea; for Stephen was obliged to seek work elsewhere. While they were there Louisa came in to express her sympathy with Stephen, and to offer him money. Tom was with her; and he took Stephen aside, and asked him to hang about the bank for an hour or two, after his work was done, on the few days that remained before his departure. Tom represented that he might want some service of Stephen; and Stephen accordingly, but with reluctance, haunted the bank after dark, but nothing came of it.
VII Mr. Bounderby had now acquired a handsome suburban residence, and Mr. James Harthouse was there a great deal, laying siege to Louisa. He managed to become a confidant of Tom (who had lost money in gambling), and of Louisa, — so far as her relations with Tom were concerned.

While affairs were in this state there came an explosion: the
VIII bank was robbed; and Stephen Blackpool, who had left town, and who had been seen lurking near the bank, was thought to be the robber.

IX After the robbery Mrs. Sparsit, whose nerves were much shaken, removed to the Bounderby mansion, where, by continual insinuations, she brought Mr. Bounderby to think that he was a much abused and neglected man. Poor Mrs. Gradgrind, who, since her marriage, had never been much alive, now faded out of existence, nursed and comforted by Sissy Jupe, on whom the whole family had come to depend, notwithstanding the lamentable deficiency in her facts.

X The robber of the bank remained undiscovered, but Tom strongly opined that it was Stephen. Mr. Harthouse agreed with him, as did most people, and the old woman who had been seen at his house was suspected of complicity. Mrs. Sparsit watched with eager eye the growing intimacy between Harthouse and Louisa; and she continued to stir up the muddy depths of Bounderby's selfish nature. "Sir," she would say, "there was wont to be an elasticity in you which I sadly miss." At last, her watching of Louisa
XI was rewarded. One evening (Bounderby being away), Harthouse came to see her, his wife. They met in the garden; and Mrs. Sparsit saw that he had his arm around Louisa's waist, and she heard him tell Louisa that he loved her. Then Louisa dismissed him, and half an hour later, although now it rained in torrents, Louisa, secretly followed by Mrs. Sparsit, left the house alone, walked to the railroad station, and took a train for Coketown,
XII where Mrs. Sparsit lost her. But Louisa went, not to her lover, but to her father's house. "Father," she cried, "your philosophy and your teaching will not save me. Save me by some other means."

BOOK THE THIRD: GARNERING

Chapter I Louisa took to her bed, and was taken care of by Sissy Jupe, who also saw Mr. Harthouse for Louisa, and, with a quiet confidence which he could not resist, asked him to leave the
II town. Mr. Gradgrind began to think that perhaps, after all, his theory of bringing up children on facts exclusively was imperfect. Mr. Bounderby, however, had no misgivings. Mrs.
III Sparsit told him that Louisa had fled with Harthouse; but when he learned the true state of affairs, he demanded that Louisa should return to his house instantly or never. She
IV remained with her father. Both Louisa and her father began to fear, though they did not say so to each other, that Tom was the thief who had robbed the bank. Rachael declared that

Stephen was innocent, that she had written to him, and that he would be back within two days to clear his name. A week passed, and still he had not come.

V And now Mrs. Sparsit distinguished herself again by capturing the mysterious old woman, and whom should she prove to be, greatly to Mr. Bounderby's shame, but his own mother, who had brought him up well and given him an education. He

VI had kept her in the background in order that he might brag about raising himself from the gutter. The next day was Sunday, and Rachel and Sissy Jupe, walking in the fields, found Stephen Blackpool lying at the bottom of a pit in which he had fallen on his way back to Coketown. He was mortally hurt, and

VII soon after he had been rescued by a gang of men, died in Rachael's arms. But first he had said to Mr. Gradgrind (he and Bounderby and many others were present): "Sir, yo' will clear me an' mak' my name good?" "How can I do so?" asked Mr. Gradgrind. "Yo'r son will tell yo' how," was the reply. Thereupon, at a hint from Sissy, Tom fled, she having given him a letter to Sleary, whose company were performing at a neighboring town. There Louisa and her father and Sissy (who had come by different routes) found him the next day, disguised as a negro groom. But while they were concocting measures Bitzer appeared, and arrested

VIII Tom. Sleary said that he could not undertake to protect Tom, but secretly he arranged with Sissy a plan for rescuing him. Sleary, with Tom and Bitzer, started to drive to the railroad, the horse being one of Mr. Sleary's best performers. They were accompanied by a learned dog, whom Mr. Sleary had instructed to keep an eye upon Bitzer. When they had gone half way, the horse (at a private signal from Sleary) stopped, and began to dance. At this moment there happened along (very strangely) Mr. Childers, one of Sleary's people, driving a very fast pony, also a professional. Tom, at a hint from Sleary, jumped down, got into the pony cart, and was driven off at the rate of fifteen miles per hour. Bitzer tried to follow, but the dog pinned him, and he was glad enough to get back in the wagon. It was a long while before the horse would stop dancing; then he went to sleep, and Sleary and Bitzer did not get back till next morning; and in the mean time Tom had escaped in a steamer from Liverpool.

IX Five years later Josiah Bounderby died in a fit. Louisa did not marry again, and Rachael never married; but Sissy Jupe's children were Louisa's pets; and Mr. Gradgrind, a white-haired, decrepit man, henceforth made his facts and figures subservient to Faith, Hope, and Charity.

# INDEX TO CHARACTERS

**Bitzer.** A light-haired and light-eyed pupil of Mr. M'Choakumchild's, in Mr. Gradgrind's model school; crammed full of hard facts, but with all fancy, sentiment, and affection taken out of him.

His cold eyes would hardly have been eyes, but for the short ends of lashes, which, by bringing them into immediate contrast with something paler than themselves, expressed their form. His short-cropped hair might have been a mere continuation of the sandy freckles on his forehead and face. His skin was so unwholesomely deficient in the natural tinge, that he looked as though, if he were cut, he would bleed white.

"Bitzer," said Thomas Gradgrind, "your definition of a horse."

"Quadruped. Graminivorous. Forty teeth; namely, twenty-four grinders, four eye-teeth, and twelve incisive. Sheds coat in the spring; in marshy countries, sheds hoofs too. Hoofs hard, but requiring to be shod with iron. Age known by marks in mouth." Thus (and much more) Bitzer.

After he leaves school, Bitzer is employed as light porter and clerk at Mr. Bounderby's bank. When Mr. Gradgrind's son, after robbing the bank, endeavors to escape, he starts in pursuit, and pounces on him just as he is about to leave his father's house for Liverpool.

"Bitzer," said Mr. Gradgrind, broken down, and miserably submissive to him, "have you a heart?"

"The circulation, sir," returned Bitzer, smiling at the oddity of the question, "could n't be carried on without one. No man, sir, acquainted with the facts established by Harvey relating to the circulation of the blood, can doubt that I have a heart."

"Is it accessible," cried Mr. Gradgrind, "to any compassionate influence?"

"It is accessible to reason, sir," returned the excellent young man; "and to nothing else." I: ii, v; II: i, iv, vi, viii, ix, xi; III: vii–ix.

**Blackpool, Mrs.** Wife of Stephen Blackpool. Soon after her marriage she takes to drinking, and goes on from bad to worse, until she becomes a curse to her husband, to herself, and to all around her. I: x–xiii; III: ix.

**Blackpool, Stephen.** A simple, honest, power-loom weaver, in Mr. Bounderby's factory. A rather stooping man, with a knitted brow, a pondering expression of face, and a hard-looking head sufficiently capacious, on which his iron-gray hair lay long and thin. His lot is a hard one. Tied to a miserable, drunken wife,

who has made his home a desolation and a mockery, and for whom he has long ceased to feel either respect or love, he finds himself unable to marry — as he would like to do, — a woman (Rachael) who has been a kind and dear friend to him for many years; and he goes to Mr. Bounderby for advice.

"I ha' coom to ask yo', sir, how I am to be ridded o' this woman." Stephen infused a yet deeper gravity into the mixed expression of his attentive face. . . .

"What do you mean?" said Bounderby, getting up to lean his back against the chimney-piece. "What are you talking about? You took her for better, for worse."

"I mun' be ridden o' her. I cannot bear 't nommore. I ha' lived under 't so long, for that I ha' had'n the pity and comforting words o' th' best lass living or dead. Haply, but for her, I should ha' gone hottering mad."

"He wishes to be free to marry the female of whom he speaks, I fear, sir," observed Mrs. Sparsit in an undertone, and much dejected by the immorality of the people.

"I do. The lady says what 's right. I do. I were a coming to 't. I ha' read i' th' papers that great fok (fair faw 'em a'! I wishes 'em no hurt!) are not bonded together for better, for worse, so fast, but that they can be set free fro' *their* misfortnet marriages, an' marry ower agen. When they dunnot agree, for that their tempers is ill-sorted, they has rooms o' one kind an' another in their houses, above a bit, and they can live asunders. We fok ha' only one room, an' we can't. When that won't do, they ha' gowd an' other cash, an' then they say, 'This for yo', an' that for me;' an' they can go their separate ways. We can't. Spite o' all that, they can be set free for smaller wrongs than mine. So I mun' be ridden o' this woman, and I wan' t' know how."

"No how," returned Mr. Bounderby.

"If I do her any hurt, sir, there 's a law to punish me?"

"Of course, there is."

"If I flee from her, there 's a law to punish me?"

"Of course, there is."

"If I marry t'oother dear lass, there 's a law to punish me?"

"Of course, there is."

"If I was to live wi' her, an' not marry her, — saying such a thing could be, which it never could or would, an' her so good, — there 's a law to punish me in every innocent child belonging to me?"

"Of course, there is."

"Now, a' God's name," said Stephen Blackpool, "show me the law to help me!"

"Hem! There's a sanctity in this relation of life," said Mr. Bounderby, "and — and — it must be kept up."

"No, no, dunnot say that, sir! 'T ain't kep' up that way, — not that way, — 't is kep' down that way. I 'm a weaver, I were in a fact'ry when a chilt; but I ha' gotten een to see wi', and eern to year wi'. I read in th' papers every 'Sizes, every Sessions — and you read too: I know it! — with dismay, how th' supposed unpossibility o' ever getting unchained from one another, at any price, on any terms, brings blood upon this land, and brings many common married fok to battle, murder, and sudden death. Let us ha' this right understood. Mine 's a grievous case, an' I want — if yo' will be so good — t' know the law that helps me."

"Now, I tell you what!" said Mr. Bounderby, putting his hands in his pockets. "There *is* such a law."

Stephen, subsiding into his quiet manner, and never wandering in his attention, gave a nod.

"But it 's not for you at all. It costs money. It costs a mint of money."

"How much might that be?" Stephen calmly asked.

"Why, you 'd have to go to Doctors' Commons with a suit, and you 'd have to go to a court of Common Law with a suit, and you 'd have to go to the House of Lords with a suit, and you 'd have to get an Act of Parliament to enable you to marry again; and it would cost you (if it was a case of very plain sailing), I suppose, from one thousand to fifteen hundred pound," said Mr. Bounderby, — "perhaps twice the money."

"There 's no other law?"

"Certainly not."

"Why, then, sir, . . . 't is a muddle," said Stephen, shaking his head as he moved to the door, — "'t is a' a muddle!"

When the Coketown operatives enter into a combination against their employers, and establish certain "regulations," Stephen refuses to join them, and they all renounce and shun him. And when Mr. Bounderby questions him about the association (styled the "United Aggregate Tribunal"), calling the members "a set of rascals and rebels," he earnestly protests that they are acting from a sense of duty, and is angrily told to finish what he 's at, and then look elsewhere for work. Leaving Coketown in search of employment, he falls into an abandoned coal-shaft ("Old Hell Shaft") hidden by thick grass, where he remains for some days, when he is accidentally discovered, and is rescued, alive, but dreadfully bruised, and so injured that he dies soon after being brought to the surface. I: x–xiii; II: iv–vi, ix; III: iv–vi.

**Bounderby, Josiah.** A wealthy Coketown manufacturer, who marries the daughter of Mr. Gradgrind.

Mr. Bounderby was as near being Mr. Gradgrind's bosom-friend as a man perfectly devoid of sentiment can approach that spiritual relationship towards another man perfectly devoid of sentiment. So near was Mr. Bounderby, — or, if the reader should prefer it, so far off.

He was a rich man, — banker, merchant, manufacturer, and what not; a big, loud man, with a stare, and a metallic laugh; a man made out of a coarse material, which seemed to have been stretched to make so much of him; a man with a great puffed head and forehead, swelled veins in his temples, and such a strained skin to his face, that it seemed to hold his eyes open, and lift his eyebrows up; a man with a pervading appearance on him of being inflated like a balloon, and ready to start; a man who could never sufficiently vaunt himself a self-made man; a man who was always proclaiming, through that brassy speaking-trumpet of a voice of his, his old ignorance and his old poverty; a man who was the Bully of humility.

A year or two younger than his eminently practical friend, Mr. Bounderby looked older; his seven or eight and forty might have had the seven or eight added to it again, without surprising anybody. He had not much hair. One might have fancied he had talked it off; and that what was left, all standing up in disorder, was in that condition from being constantly blown about by his windy boastfulness. I: iii–ix, xi, xiv–xvi; II: i–xii; III: ii–ix.

**Bounderby, Mrs. Louisa.** *See* GRADGRIND, LOUISA.

**Childers, Mr. E. W. B.** A young man, who is a member of Sleary's Circus Troupe, and is celebrated for his daring vaulting act as the Wild Huntsman of the North American Prairies.

His face, close-shaven, thin, and sallow, was shaded by a great quantity of dark hair brushed into a roll all round his head, and parted up the centre. His legs were very robust, but shorter than legs of good proportions should have been. His chest and back were as much too broad as his legs were too short. He was dressed in a Newmarket coat and tight-fitting trousers; wore a shawl round his neck; smelt of lamp-oil, straw, orange-peel, horses' provender, and sawdust; and looked a most remarkable sort of Centaur, compounded of the stable and the play-house. Where the one began, and the other ended, nobody could have told with any precision. I: vi; III: vii, viii.

**Gordon, Emma.** A member of Sleary's Circus Troupe, and a friend to Sissy Jupe. I: vi; III: vii.

MR. BOUNDERBY AND MRS. SPARSIT.

**Gradgrind, Mr. Thomas.** A retired wholesale hardware merchant.

"THOMAS GRADGRIND, sir, — a man of realities; a man of facts and calculations; a man who proceeds upon the principle that two and two are four, and nothing over, and who is not to be talked into allowing for anything over; Thomas Gradgrind, sir, — peremptorily Thomas, Thomas Gradgrind; with a rule and a pair of scales, and the multiplication-table always in his pocket, sir, ready to weigh and measure any parcel of human nature, and tell you exactly what it comes to. It is a mere question of figures, a case of simple arithmetic. You might hope to get some other nonsensical belief into the head of George Gradgrind, or Augustus Gradgrind, or John Gradgrind, or Joseph Gradgrind (all supposititious, non-existent persons), but into the head of Thomas Gradgrind — no, sir!"

In such terms Mr. Gradgrind always mentally introduced himself, whether to his private circle of acquaintance, or to the public in general.

Visiting his model school in company with a government officer of the same intensely practical, utilitarian stamp as himself, he tells the teacher, Mr. M'Choakumchild, —

"Now, what I want is facts. Teach these boys and girls nothing but facts. Facts alone are wanted in life. Plant nothing else, and root out everything else. You can only form the minds of reasoning animals upon facts: nothing else will ever be of any service to them. This is the principle on which I bring up my own children, and this is the principle on which I bring up these children. Stick to facts, sir!"

The scene was a plain, bare, monotonous vault of a schoolroom, and the speaker's square forefinger emphasized his observations by underscoring every sentence with a line on the schoolmaster's sleeve. The emphasis was helped by the speaker's square wall of a forehead, which had his eyebrows for its base; while his eyes found commodious cellarage in two dark caves, overshadowed by the wall. The emphasis was helped by the speaker's mouth, which was wide, thin, and hard set. The emphasis was helped by the speaker's voice, which was inflexible, dry, and dictatorial. The emphasis was helped by the speaker's hair, which bristled on the skirts of his bald head, a plantation of firs to keep the wind from its shining surface, all covered with knobs, like the crust of a plum-pie, as if the head had scarcely warehouse room for the hard facts stored inside. The speaker's obstinate carriage, square coat, square legs, square shoulders, nay, his very neckcloth, trained to take him by the throat with an unaccommodating grasp, like a stubborn fact, as it was — all helped the emphasis.

Mr. Gradgrind's residence is a very matter-of-fact place, called "Stone Lodge," situated on a moor within a mile or two of the great manufacturing town of Coketown.

A very regular feature on the face of the country, Stone Lodge was. Not the least disguise toned down or shaded off that uncompromising fact in the landscape. A great square house, with a heavy portico darkening the principal windows, as its master's heavy brows overshadowed his eyes, — a calculated, cast-up, balanced, and proved house. Six windows on this side of the door, six on that side; a total of twelve in this wing, a total of twelve in the other wing; four and twenty carried over to the back; a lawn and garden and an infant avenue, all ruled straight like a botanical account-book; gas and ventilation, drainage and water-service, all of the primest quality; iron clamps and girders, fire-proof, from top to bottom; mechanical lifts for the housemaids, with all their brushes and brooms: everything that heart could desire.

Mr. Gradgrind marries his eldest daughter, according to a mathematical plan which he has adopted, to Mr. Bounderby, another eminently practical man, who is not only twenty years her senior, but is in every respect unsuited to her. The result of this ill-assorted union is unhappiness not only to the wife, but to her father as well, for whom a still sharper trial is in store. His eldest son, whom he has carefully trained, becomes dissipated, robs his employer, and brings disgrace on the hitherto unblemished name of Gradgrind. In his sore trouble, Mr. Gradgrind is consoled and strengthened by two of the most unpractical people in the world, — Mr. Sleary, the manager of a circus, and Sissy Jupe, the daughter of a clown, both of whom he has repeatedly lectured on their utter want of worldly wisdom and practicality. Forced to admit that much of his misfortune is attributable to his own hard system of philosophy, he becomes a humbler and a wiser man, bending his hitherto inflexible theories to appointed circumstances; making his facts and figures subservient to Faith, Hope, and Charity, and no longer trying to grind that heavenly trio in his dusty little mills. I: i–ix, xiv–xvi; II: i–iii, vii, ix, xi, xii; III: i–ix.

**Gradgrind, Mrs.** Wife of Mr. Thomas Gradgrind.

A little thin, white, pink-eyed bundle of shawls, of surpassing feebleness mental and bodily; who was always taking physic without any effect; and who, whenever she showed a symptom of coming to life, was invariably stunned by some weighty piece of fact tumbling on her. I: iv, ix, xv; II: ix.

There was an air of jaded sullenness in . . . the girl; yet, struggling through the dissatisfaction of her face, there was a light with nothing to rest upon, a fire with nothing to burn, a starved imagination keeping life in itself somehow, which brightened its expression, — not with the brightness natural to cheerful youth, but with uncertain, eager, doubtful flashes, which had something painful in them, analogous to the changes of a blind face groping its way.

She becomes the wife of Josiah Bounderby, who says to the guests at the breakfast-table, after the marriage ceremony has been performed, —

"I have watched her bringing up, and I believe she is worthy of me. At the same time, — not to deceive you, — I believe I am worthy of her. So I thank you, on both our parts, for the goodwill you have shown towards us; and the best wish I can give the unmarried part of the present company is this: I hope every bachelor may find as good a wife as I have found; and I hope every spinster may find as good a husband as my wife has found."

The current of their wedded life does not run smooth, however. Utter incompatibility of temper, utter want of mutual love or sympathy, pave the way for a plausible acquaintance — a polished, easy man of the world — to approach her with insidious declarations of love, and to propose an elopement. Resisting the temptation, she flees to her father's house, and implores him to save her. He recommends to her husband to allow her to stay there for a while, that she may have the opportunity she so much needs for repose and reflection; but Mr. Bounderby requires that she shall return to his bed and board by the next day noon; and as she fails to do so, he refuses to have anything more to do with her, and leaves her in her father's charge. I: iii, iv, vi–ix, xiv–xvi; II: i–iii, v–xii; III: i–ix.

**Harthouse, Mr. James.** A friend of Mr. Gradgrind's; a thorough gentleman, made to the model of the time, weary of everything, and putting no more faith in anything than Lucifer. He is "five and thirty, good-looking, good figure, good teeth, good voice, dark hair, bold eyes." II: i–iii, v, vii–xii; III: ii, iii.

**Jupe, Cecilia,** *or* **Sissy.** The daughter of a clown. She has been kindly permitted to attend the school controlled by Mr. Gradgrind; but Mr. Bounderby thinks that she has a bad influence over the other children, and advises that the privilege should be withdrawn. The two gentlemen accordingly visit the "Pegasus' Arms" at Pod's End, to inform her father of their intention; but they find that Signor Jupe, — always a half-cracked man, — having got old and stiff in the joints, so that he cannot perform his parts satisfactorily, and having got his daughter into the school, and therefore, as he seems to think, got her well provided for, has run off to parts unknown. Under these circumstances Mr. Gradgrind decides to take charge of the girl, and educate and support her. She accompanies him home, and makes herself very useful and companionable in his family. When Louisa is about to fall into the meshes of Mr. Harthouse, Sissy visits that gentleman, and persuades and shames him into leaving the neighborhood; and when Mr. Gradgrind's son is about to be arrested for the robbery of Bounderby's Bank, she sends him to her father's old employer, Mr. Sleary, who conceals him, and gets him safely abroad. I: ii, iv–ix, xiv, xv; II: ix; III: i, ii, iv–ix.

**Jupe, Signor.** A clown in Sleary's circus; father of Sissy Jupe, and owner of the "highly trained performing dog Merrylegs." I: ii, iii, v, vi, ix; III: ii, viii.

**Kidderminster, Master.** A member of Sleary's Circus Troupe; a diminutive boy, with an old face, who assists Mr. Childers in his daring vaulting-act as the Wild Huntsman of the North American Prairies; taking the part of his infant son, and being carried upside down over his father's shoulder, by one foot, and held by the crown of his head, heels upwards, in the palm of his father's hand, according to the violent paternal manner in which wild huntsmen may be observed to fondle their offspring. I: vi; II: vii.

**M'Choakumchild, Mr.** Teacher in Mr. Gradgrind's model school.

He and some hundred and forty other schoolmasters had been lately turned at the same time, in the same factory, on the same principles, like so many pianoforte legs. He had been put through an immense variety of paces, and had answered volumes of head-breaking questions. Orthography, etymology, syntax, and prosody, biography, astronomy, geography, and general cosmography, the sciences of compound proportion, algebra, land surveying and levelling, vocal music, and drawing from models, were all at the ends of his ten chilled fingers. He had worked his stony way into her Majesty's most Honorable Privy Council's Schedule B, and had taken the bloom off the higher branches of mathematics and physical science, French, German, Latin, and Greek. He knew all about the water-sheds of all the world (whatever they are), and all the histories of all the peoples, and all the names of all the rivers and mountains, and all the productions, manners, and customs of all the countries, and all their boundaries and bearings on the two and thirty points of the compass. Ah! rather overdone, M'Choakumchild. If he had only learnt a little less, how infinitely better he might have taught much more! I: i–iii, ix, xiv.

**Merrylegs.** Signor Jupe's trained performing-dog. I: iii, v–viii; III: viii.

**Pegler, Mrs.** Mother of Josiah Bounderby; a mysterious old woman, tall and shapely, though withered by time. Her son, growing rich, becomes ashamed of her, and gives her thirty pounds a year to keep away from him, and not claim any relationship with him; but the secret is at last divulged, under the most ridiculous circumstances, through the agency of the inquisitive and superserviceable Mrs. Sparsit. I: xii; II: vi, viii; III: iv, v.

**Rachael.** A factory-hand; a friend of Stephen Blackpool's. I: x–xiii; II: iv, vi; III: iv–vi, ix.

**Scadgers, Lady.** Great-aunt to Mrs. Sparsit; an immensely fat old woman with an inordinate appetite for butcher's meat, and a mysterious leg, which has refused to get out of bed for fourteen years. I: vii; II: viii; III: ix.

**Slackbridge.** A trades-union agitator and orator. II: iv; III: iv.

**Sleary, Josephine.** Daughter of a circus proprietor; a pretty, fair-haired girl of eighteen, noted for her graceful Tyrolean flower-act. I: vi; II: vii.

**Sleary, Mr.** Proprietor of a "Horse-riding," or circus; a stout man, with one fixed eye and one loose eye, a voice (if it can be called so) like the efforts of a broken old pair of bellows, a flabby surface, and a muddled head, which is never sober, and never drunk. He is troubled with asthma, and his breath comes far too thick and heavy for the letter "s." I: vi, ix; III, vii, viii.

**Sparsit, Mrs.** Mr. Bounderby's housekeeper; an elderly lady highly connected, with a Coriolanian style of nose, and dense black eyebrows. Mr. Bounderby gives her a hundred a year, disguising the payment under the name of an "annual compliment." I: vii, xi, xvi; II: i, iii, vi, viii–xi; III: iii, v, ix.

# STORIES

## THE LAMPLIGHTER'S STORY

**Barker, Miss Fanny.** Niece to an old astrologer, who takes Tom Grig to be pointed out by the stars as her destined husband. He describes her as having "a graceful carriage, an exquisite shape, a sweet voice, a countenance beaming with animation and expression, and the eye of a startled fawn." She has also, he says, five thousand pounds in cash; and this attraction, added to the others, inclines Tom to marry her; but when he finds that her uncle has borrowed and spent the whole sum in an unsuccessful search for the philosopher's stone, he alters his mind, and declares that the scheme is "no go," at which the uncle is enraged, and the niece is delighted; she being in love with another young man.

**Emma.** Daughter of a crazy astrologer who has spent fifteen years in conducting fruitless experiments having for their object the discovery of the philosopher's stone. Her father designs marrying her to his partner, "the gifted Mooney;" but he utterly refuses to take her, alleging that his "contemplation of womankind" has led him to resolve that he "will not adventure on the troubled sea of matrimony."

**Galileo, Isaac Newton Flamstead.** The Christian names of the son of the crazy astrologer who takes Tom Grig to be "the favorite of the planets." He is a tall, thin, dismal-faced young gentleman, in his twenty-first year; though his father, absorbed in chimerical projects, considers him "a mere child," and has n't provided him with a new suit of clothes since he was fourteen.

**Grig, Tom.** A lamplighter, who, on going his rounds one day, is accosted by one of the strangest and most mysterious-looking old gentlemen ever seen. This person proves to be a very learned astrologer, who is on the point of discovering the philosopher's stone, which will turn everything into gold. He imagines that he has found in Tom a noble stranger, whose birth is shrouded in uncertainty, and who is destined by the stars to be the husband of his young and lovely niece. He therefore takes him into his house forthwith, and introduces him to the lady. She is greatly disturbed, and suggests that the stars must have made a mistake; but is silenced by her uncle. After this, Tom accompanies the old gentleman to the observatory, where Mr. Mooney — another scientific gentleman — casts his nativity, and horrifies him by predicting his death at exactly thirty-five minutes, twenty-seven seconds, and five-sixths of a second, past nine o'clock, A. M.,

## TO BE READ AT DUSK



## THE LAZY TOUR OF TWO IDLE APPRENTICES

**Jock.** A white-headed boy attached to an inn.

**Lorn, Mr.** Dr. Speddie's assistant.

**Speddie, Dr.** Called in to attend to Thomas Idle's sprained ankle.

## BIRTHS. MRS. MEEK, OF A SON

**Bigby, Mrs.** Mother of Mrs. Meek, and a most remarkable woman. Her son-in-law says of her, —

In my opinion, she would storm a town, single-handed, with a hearth-broom, and carry it. I have never known her to yield any point whatever to mortal man. She is calculated to terrify the stoutest heart.

**Meek, Augustus George.** Infant son of Mr. George Meek.

**Meek, Mr. George.** The narrator of the story; a quiet man, of small stature, a weak voice, and a tremulous constitution. He is made utterly miserable by the manner in which his infant child is smothered and rasped and dosed and bandaged by the nurse, aided and abetted by his wife's mother; and he is betrayed into expressing himself warmly on the subject, notwithstanding his wish to avoid giving rise to words in the family.

**Meek, Mrs.** His wife.

**Prodgit, Mrs.** Mrs. Meek's nurse; considered by Mr. Meek to be "from first to last a convention and a superstition," whom the medical faculty ought to take in hand and improve.

One afternoon . . . I came home earlier than usual from the office, and, proceeding into the dining-room, found an obstruction behind the door, which prevented it from opening freely. It was an obstruction of a soft nature. On looking in, I found it to be a female, who stood in the corner, behind the door, consuming sherry-wine. From the nutty smell of that beverage pervading the apartment, I have no doubt she was consuming a second glassful. She wore a black bonnet of large dimensions, and was copious in figure. The expression of her countenance was severe and discontented. The words to which she gave utterance on seeing me were these, "Oh! git along with you, sir, if *you* please. Me and Mrs. Bigby don't want no male parties here."

## THE GHOST OF ART

[A satire on the Art Exhibitions of the Royal Academy.]

**Parkins, Mrs.** A laundress, who invariably disregards all instructions.

## A POOR MAN'S TALE OF A PATENT

**Butcher, William.** A Chartist; friend to John.

**John.** The narrator of the story; a poor man, a smith by trade, who undertakes to obtain a patent on an invention which he has been twenty years in perfecting. He succeeds in doing so only after going through thirty-five distinct stages of obeying forms and paying fees, at a cost of ninety-six pounds, seven, and eightpence, though nobody opposes his application.

**Joy, Thomas.** A carpenter with whom John lodges in London.

## THE DETECTIVE POLICE

**Clarkson.** Counsel for Shepherdson and other thieves traced out and arrested by Sergeant Mith.

**Dornton, Sergeant.** A detective police-officer; a man about fifty years of age, with a ruddy face and a high sunburnt forehead. He is famous for steadily pursuing the inductive process, working on from clew to clew until he bags his man.

**Dundey, Doctor.** A man who robs a bank in Ireland, and escapes to America, whither he is followed and captured by Sergeant Dornton.

**Fendall, Sergeant,** A detective police-officer; a light-haired, well-spoken, polite person, and a prodigious hand at pursuing private inquiries of a delicate nature.

**Fikey.** A man accused of forgery; taken prisoner by Inspector Field.

**Mesheck, Aaron.** A Jew, who gets acceptances from young men of good connections (in the army chiefly), on pretence of discount, and decamps with the same. He is finally found by Sergeant Dornton in the Tombs prison, in New York city.

**Mith, Sergeant.** A detective police-officer; a smooth-faced man with a fresh, bright complexion, and a strange air of simplicity. He is a dab at housebreakers.

**Pigeon, Thomas.** *See* THOMPSON, TALLY-HO.

**Shepherdson, Mr.** A thief, who informs detective Mith (who, under the disguise of a young butcher from the country, has gained his confidence) that he is going "to hang out for a while" at the Setting Moon, in the Commercial Road, where he is afterwards found, and is taken into custody.

**Stalker, Mr. Inspector.** A detective police-officer; a shrewd, hard-headed Scotchman; in appearance not at all unlike a very acute, thoroughly-trained schoolmaster from the Normal Establishment at Glasgow.

**Straw, Sergeant.** A detective; a little, wiry man of meek demeanor, and strong sense, who would knock at a door, and ask a series of questions in any mild character you choose to prescribe to him, from a charity-boy upward; and seem as innocent as an infant.

**Thompson, Tally-ho,** *alias* THOMAS PIGEON. A famous horse-stealer, couper, and magsman, tracked to a lonely inn in Northamptonshire, by Sergeant Witchem, who, single-handed, arrests him, and takes him to London; though he has two big and ugly-looking companions with him at the time.

**Wield, Mr. Inspector.** A detective police-officer; a middle-aged man, of a portly presence, with a large, moist, knowing eye, a husky voice, and a habit of emphasizing his conversation by the aid of a corpulent forefinger which is constantly in juxtaposition with his eyes and nose.

**Witchem.** A detective; a short, thick-set man, marked with the small-pox, and having something of a reserved and thoughtful air, as if he were engaged in deep arithmetical calculations. He is renowned for his acquaintance with the swell mob.

## THREE "DETECTIVE" ANECDOTES

**Grimwood, Eliza,** *called* THE COUNTESS. A handsome young woman, found lying dead, with her throat cut, on the floor of her bedroom, in the Waterloo Road.

**Phibbs, Mr.** A haberdasher.

**Tatt, Mr.** A gentleman formerly in the public line; quite an amateur detective in his way. He loses a diamond pin in a scrimmage which is recovered by his friend Sergeant Witchem, who sees the man who took it, and while they are all down on the floor together knocking about, touches him on the back of his hand, as his "pal" would; and he thinks it *is* his pal, and gives it to him.

**Trinkle, Mr.** A young man suspected of the murder of Eliza Grimwood, but proved innocent.

## HUNTED DOWN

**Adams, Mr.** Clerk in the life assurance office of which Mr. Sampson is the chief manager.

**Banks, Major.** An old East India Director, who assists Mr. Sampson in rescuing Miss Niner from the toils of Mr. Julius Slinkton.

**Beckwith, Mr. Alfred.** *See* MELTHAM, MR.

**Meltham, Mr.** Actuary of the Inestimable Life Assurance Company. He falls in love with one of Mr. Julius Slinkton's nieces, a lovely girl, whose life is insured in his office. She soon dies from the effects of a slow poison secretly administered to her by her uncle; and Mr. Meltham, having become thoroughly assured of the villain's guilt, devotes himself thenceforth to the single object of hunting him down. Resigning his situation, he causes a report of his death to be put into circulation; assumes the name of Mr. Alfred Beckwith; takes rooms in the Middle Temple, opposite those of Mr. Slinkton, — to whom he is personally unknown, — and makes them a trap for him. Affecting to be a confirmed inebriate, he deludes the murderer into thinking that it would be an easy thing to obtain an insurance on his life for two thousand pounds, and then to do him to death with brandy, or, brandy not proving quick enough, with something quicker. The plotting, however, into which Slinkton is led, is well understood all along, and is counterplotted all along. The fitting time having arrived, he is confronted with the evidences of his guilt, when, finding himself brought to bay, he swallows some of the powerful poison he always carries with him, and falls down a dead man.

**Niner, Miss Margaret.** Mr. Slinkton's niece. She is saved from falling a victim to the wickedness of her uncle by the efforts of Mr. Sampson and Major Banks, who reveal to her his real character, and induce her to leave him forever.

**Sampson, Mr.** Chief manager of a life assurance company, and narrator of the story, in which he is also one of the actors.

**Slinkton, Mr. Julius.** A gentleman, educated, well-bred, and agreeable, who professes to be on the point of going into orders, but who is, in reality, a consummate hypocrite and villain. He effects an insurance for two thousand pounds on the life of Mr. Alfred Beckwith, and then attempts to poison him in order to get the money; but, being foiled in his object, he destroys himself.

In this character Dickens has drawn a portrait, only slightly idealized, of Thomas Griffiths Wainewright, well known as a coxcombical writer for "The London Magazine," under the pseudonym of Janus Weathercock. This monster actually poisoned a number of persons whose lives had been insured for large sums (among them his wife's step-sister and her mother); and in some instances he succeeded in obtaining the money. He was arrested, at last, on a charge of forgery, and sentenced to be transported to Van Diemen's Land, where he died of apoplexy, in 1852, at the age of fifty-seven. Lord Lytton has introduced him into his powerful novel of "Lucretia; or, the Children of Night."

## GEORGE SILVERMAN'S EXPLANATION

**Fareway, Adelina.** Pupil of George Silverman, who falls in love with her, and finds his love reciprocated, but resigns her to another out of pure self-depreciation and unworldliness.

**Fareway, Lady.** Her mother; widow of the late Sir Gaston Fareway, baronet; a penurious and managing woman, handsome, well-preserved, of somewhat large stature, with a steady glare in her great round eyes. She presents Mr. George Silverman to a living of two hundred a year, in North Devonshire, but imposes the condition that he shall help her with her correspondence, accounts, and various little things of that kind, and that he shall gratuitously direct her daughter's studies.

**Fareway, Mr.** Her second son; a young gentleman of abilities much above the average, but idle and luxurious, who for a time reads with Mr. Silverman.

**Gimblet, Brother.** An elderly drysalter; a man with a crabbed face, a large dog's-eared shirt-collar, and a spotted blue neckerchief, reaching up behind to the crown of his head. He is an expounder in Brother Hawkyard's congregation.

**Hawkyard, Mr. Verity,** of West Bromwich. George Silverman's guardian or patron; a yellow-faced, peak-nosed man, who is an exhorter in a congregation of an obscure denomination, among whom he is called Brother Hawkyard. He is given to boasting, and has a habit of confirming himself in a parenthesis, as if, knowing himself, he doubted his own word. Thus he tells his ward:—

"I am a servant of the Lord, George, and I have been a good servant to him (I have) these five and thirty years: the Lord has had a good servant in me, and he knows it."

From the first [says George Silverman], I could not like this familiar knowledge of the ways of the sublime, inscrutable Almighty, on Brother Hawkyard's part. As I grew a little wiser, and still a little wiser, I liked it less and less. . . . Before the knowledge became forced upon me, that, outside their place of meeting, these brothers and sisters were no better than the rest of the human family, but on the whole were, to put the case mildly, as bad as most, in respect of giving short weight in their shops, and not speaking the truth,—I say, before this knowledge became forced upon me, their prolix addresses, their inordinate conceit, their daring ignorance, their investment of the Supreme Ruler of heaven and earth with their own miserable meannesses and littlenesses, greatly shocked me.

**Silverman, George.** The narrator of the story; born in a cellar in Preston. He thus describes his parents: —

Mother had the gripe and clutch of poverty upon her face, upon her figure, and, not least of all, upon her voice. Her sharp and high-pitched words were squeezed out of her, as by the compression of bony fingers on a leathern bag; and she had a way of rolling her eyes about and about the cellar, as she scolded, that was gaunt and hungry. Father, with his shoulders rounded, would sit quiet on a three-legged stool, looking at the empty grate, until she would pluck the stool from under him, and bid him go bring some money home. Then he would dismally ascend the steps; and I, holding my ragged shirt and trousers together with a hand (my only braces), would feint and dodge from mother's pursuing grasp at my hair.

"A worldly little devil," was mother's usual name for me. Whether I cried for that I was in the dark, or for that it was cold, or for that I was hungry; or whether I squeezed myself into a warm corner when there was a fire, or ate voraciously when there was food, — she would still say, "O, you worldly little devil!" And the sting of it was, that I quite well knew myself to be a worldly little devil; worldly as to wanting to be housed and warmed; worldly as to wanting to be fed; worldly as to the greed with which I inwardly compared how much I got of those good things with how much father and mother got, when, rarely, those good things were going.

While still a small child, George loses his father and mother, who die miserably of a fever; is taken from the cellar in a half-starved state; and is handed over by the authorities to Brother Hawkyard, who, as it seems, has accepted a trust in behalf of the boy from a rich grandfather who has just died at Birmingham. After being disinfected, comfortably fed, and furnished with new clothes, he is sent to an old farm-house at Hoghton Towers, where he remains for a considerable time, and where he begins to form a shy disposition, to be of a timidly silent character under misconstruction, to have an inexpressible and even a morbid dread of becoming sordid or worldly. He is afterwards put to school, told to work his way, and, as time goes on, becomes a Foundation Boy on a good foundation, and is preached at on Sundays by Brother Hawkyard and other expounders of the same kidney. Working still harder, he at last obtains a scholarship at Cambridge, where he lives a secluded life, and studies diligently. Knowing himself to be "unfit for the noisier stir of social existence," he applies his mind to the clerical profession, and at last is presented by Lady Fareway to a living worth two hundred a year. Adelina, the only daughter of Lady Fareway, pursues her studies under his direction; and a strong but undeclared affection springs up between them. But the young clergyman, conscious that her family and fortune place him far beneath her, and feeling that her merits are far greater than his, resolves upon self-sacrifice, and quietly sets to work to turn the current of her love into another channel. For this purpose, he introduces to her Mr. Granville Wharton, another pupil of his, and contrives, in various ways, to interest them in each other. The object is accomplished, and, in little more than a year, they come before him, hand in hand, and ask to be united in marriage. As they are both of age, and as the young lady has come into possession of a fortune in her own right, he does not hesitate to do so; but the consequences to himself are disastrous. Lady Fareway has had ambitious projects for her daughter, and indignantly charges George Silverman with taking a percentage upon Adelina's fortune as a bribe for putting Mr. Wharton in possession of it. With the old cry of, "You worldly wretch!" she demands that he should resign his living, contumeliously dismisses him from her presence, and pursues him for many years with bitter animosity. But Adelina and her husband stand by him, and at length he obtains a college-living in a sequestered place, lives down the suspicions and calumnies that have dogged his steps, and pens his "Explanation."

**Sylvia.** A girl at the farm-house of Hoghton Towers, where George Silverman is placed by Mr. Hawkyard, after the death of his father and mother.

**Wharton, Mr. Granville.** Pupil of George Silverman, and married by him to Adelina Fareway.

## UNCOMMERCIAL TRAVELLER

### INDEX TO CHARACTERS

**Anderson, John.** A tramp, whose only improvidence appears to have been that he has spent the last of his little "all" upon soap. XI. *Tramps.*

**Anderson, Mrs.** His wife; a woman spotless to behold. XI. *Tramps.*

**Antonio.** A swarthy young Spanish guitar-player. V. *Poor Mercantile Jack.*

**Barlow, Mr.** An irrepressible instructive monomaniac, who knows everything, didactically improves all sorts of occasions, and presents himself in all sorts of aspects and under all kinds of disguises; so named from an all-knowing tutor in Thomas Day's juvenile story of "Sandford and Merton." XXXII. *Mr. Barlow.*

**Battens, Mr.** A virulent old pensioner at Titbull's. XXVII. *Titbull's Almshouses.*

**Bones, Mr. Banjo.** A comic Ethiopian minstrel, with a blackened face and a limp sugar-loaf hat. V. *Poor Mercantile Jack.*

**Bones, Mrs. Banjo.** His wife; a "professional" singer. V. *Poor Mercantile Jack.*

**Bullfinch.** A gentleman, who, having occasion to go to the seaside resort of Namelesston with a friend for the transaction of some business, proposes that they should dine at the Temeraire. They accordingly drive to that house, and order a little dinner, which is to be ready punctually in one hour. They return promptly, but try in vain to eat and drink what is set before them, and come to the conclusion that no such ill-served, ill-appointed, ill-cooked, nasty little dinner could be got for the money anywhere else under the sun. XXXI. *A Little Dinner in an Hour.*

**Carlavero, Giovanni.** Keeper of a small wine-shop, in a certain small Italian town on the Mediterranean. He had been a political offender, sentenced to imprisonment for life, but was afterwards released through the zealous intervention of a generous English nobleman (Lord Dudley Coutts Stuart). Desirous of testifying his gratitude to his benefactor, whom he has not seen since his liberation, he sends him by Mr. Dickens an immense demijohn of wine, the first produce of his little vineyard. With infinite difficulty this frail and enormous bottle, holding some half-dozen gallons, is safely carried to England; but the wine turns to vinegar before it reaches its destination. Yet "the Englishman," says Mr. Dickens, "told me, with much emotion in his face and voice, that he had never tasted wine that seemed to him so sweet and sound; and long afterwards the bottle graced his table." XXVIII. *The Italian Prisoner.*

**Chips.** A shipwright, who sells himself to the Devil for half a ton of copper, a bushel of tenpenny nails, an iron pot, and a rat that can speak. He gets disgusted with the rat, and tries to kill it, but does not succeed, and is punished by being subjected to a swarm and plague of rats, who finally compass his destruction by eating through the planks of a ship in which he has been "pressed" for a sailor. XV. *Nurse's Stories.*

**Cleverly, Susannah.** A Mormon emigrant; a young woman of business. XX. *Bound for the Great Salt Lake.*

**Cleverly, William.** Her brother, also a Mormon emigrant. XX. *Bound for the Great Salt Lake.*

**Cocker, Mr. Indignation.** A dissatisfied diner at the same house, who disputes the charges in his bill. XXXI. *A Little Dinner in an Hour.*

**Dibble, Mr. Sampson.** A Mormon emigrant; a very old man, who is stone-blind. XX. *Bound for the Great Salt Lake.*

**Dibble, Mrs. Dorothy.** His wife, who accompanies him. XX. *Bound for the Great Salt Lake.*

**Face-Maker, Monsieur the.** A corpulent little man with a comical face. He is heralded as "the great changer of countenances, who transforms the features that Heaven has bestowed upon him into an endless succession of surprising and extraordinary visages, comprehending all the contortions, energetic and expressive, of which the human face is capable, and all the passions of the human heart, as love, jealousy, revenge, hatred, avarice, despair." XXV. *In the French-Flemish Country.*

**Flanders, Sally.** A former nurse of the Uncommercial Traveller, and widow of Flanders, a small master-builder. XXVI. *Medicine-Men of Civilization.*

**Flipfield, Mr.** A friend of the Uncommercial Traveller's. XIX. *Birthday Celebrations.*

**Flipfield, Mrs.** His mother. XIX. *Birthday Celebrations.*

**Flipfield, Miss.** His elder sister. She is in the habit of speaking to new acquaintances, in pious and condoning tones, of all the quarrels that have taken place in the family from her infancy. XIX. *Birthday Celebrations.*

**Flipfield, Mr. Tom,** *called* THE LONG-LOST. A brother of Mr. Flipfield's. After an absence of many years in foreign parts, he returns home, and is warmly welcomed by his family and friends; but he proves to be "an antipathetical being, with a peculiar power and gift of treading on everybody's tenderest place;" and everybody wishes that he could instantly be transported back to the foreign parts which have tolerated him so long. XIX. *Birthday Celebrations.*

**Globson, Bully.** A schoolmate of the Uncommercial Traveller's; a big fat boy, with a big fat head, and a big fat fist. XIX. *Birthday Celebrations.*

**Grazinglands, Mr. Alexander.** A midland county gentleman, of a comfortable property, on a visit to London. VI. *Refreshments for Travellers.*

**Grazinglands, Mrs. Arabella.** His wife; the pride of her division of the county. VI. *Refreshments for Travellers.*

**Head, Oakum.** A refractory female pauper, who "would be very thankful to be got into a place, or got abroad." III. *Wapping Workhouse.*

**Jack, Dark.** A simple and gentle negro sailor. V. *Poor Mercantile Jack.*

**Jack, Mercantile.** A representative of the sailors employed in the merchant marine. V. *Poor Mercantile Jack.*

**Jobson, Jesse, Number Two.** A Mormon emigrant; the head of a family of eight persons. XX. *Bound for the Great Salt Lake.*

**John.** A boiler-maker, living in the neighborhood of Ratcliffe and Stepney, who obtains employment but fitfully and rarely, and is forced to live on the work of his wife. XXIX. *A Small Star in the East.*

**Kinch, Horace.** An inmate of the King's Bench Prison, where he dies.

He was a likely man to look at, in the prime of life, well to do, as clever as he needed to be, and popular among many friends. He was suitably married, and had healthy and pretty children; but, like some fair-looking houses or fair-looking ships, he took the dry rot. . . . Those who knew him had not nigh done saying, "So well off! so comfortably established! with such hope before him!"— . . . when, lo! the man was all dry rot and dust. XIII. *Night Walks.*

**Kindheart, Mr.** An Englishman of an amiable nature, great enthusiasm, and no discretion. XXVI. *Medicine-Men of Civilization.*

**Klem, Mr.** A weak old man, meagre and mouldy, who is never to be seen detached from a flat pint of beer in a pewter pot. XVI. *Arcadian London.*

**Klem, Mrs.** His wife; an elderly woman, laboring under a chronic sniff, and having a dejected consciousness that she is not justified in appearing on the surface of the earth. XVI. *Arcadian London.*

**Klem, Miss.** Their daughter, apparently ten years older than either her father or mother. XVI. *Arcadian London.*

**Mellows, Mr. J.** Landlord of the "Dolphin's Head." XXII. *An Old Stage-Coaching House.*

**Mercy.** A nurse who relates diabolical stories to the Uncommercial Traveller, when a child, with a fiendish enjoyment of his terrors. XV. *Nurse's Stories.*

**Mitts, Mrs.** A pensioner at Titbull's; a tidy, well-favored widow, with a propitiatory way of passing her hands over and under one another. XXVII. *Titbull's Almshouses.*

**Murderer, Captain.** A diabolical wretch, admitted into the best society, and possessing immense wealth. His mission is matrimony, and the gratification of a cannibal appetite with tender brides. XV. *Nurse's Stories.*

**Nan.** A sailor's mistress. V. *Poor Mercantile Jack.*

**Onowenever, Mrs.** Mother of a young lady (the Dora Spenlow of "David Copperfield," and the Flora Finching of "Little Dorrit") ardently loved by the Uncommercial Traveller in his youth.

It is unnecessary to name her more particularly. She was older than I, and had pervaded every chink and crevice of my mind for three or four years. I had held volumes of imaginary conversations with her mother on the subject of our union; and I had written letters, more in number than Horace Walpole's, to that discreet woman, soliciting her daughter's hand in marriage. I had never had the remotest intention of sending any of those letters; but to write them, and after a few days tear them up, had been a sublime occupation. XIX. *Birthday Celebrations.*

**Pangloss.** An official friend of the Uncommercial Traveller's, lineally descended from the learned doctor of the same name, who was tutor to Candide.

In his personal character he is as humane and worthy a gentleman as any I know; in his official capacity, he unfortunately preaches the doctrines of his renowned ancestor, by demonstrating, on all occasions, that we live in the best of all possible official worlds. VIII. *The Great Tasmania's Cargo.*

**Parkle, Mr.** A friend of the Uncommercial Traveller's. XIV. — *Chambers.*

**Poodles.** A comical mongrel dog, found starving at the door of the "East London Children's Hospital," and taken in and fed, since which he has made it his home. On his neck he wears a collar presented him by an admirer of his mental endowments, and bearing the legend, "Judge not Poodles by external appearances."

I find him making the round of the beds, like a house-surgeon, attended by another dog, — a friend, — who appears to trot about with him in the character of his pupil-dresser. Poodles is anxious to make me known to a pretty little girl, looking wonderfully healthy, who has had a leg taken off for cancer of the knee. "A difficult operation," Poodles intimates, wagging his tail on the counterpane, "but perfectly successful, as you see, dear sir." The patient, patting Poodles, adds, with a smile, "The leg was so much trouble to me, that I am glad it 's gone." I never saw anything in doggery finer than the deportment of Poodles when another little girl opens her mouth to show a peculiar enlargement of the tongue. Poodles (at that time on a table, to be on a level with the occasion) looks at the tongue (with his own sympathetically out) so very gravely and knowingly, that I feel inclined to put my hand on my waistcoat-pocket, and give him a guinea, wrapped in paper. XXIX. *A Small Star in the East;* XXXIII. *On an Amateur Beat.*

**Quickear.** A policeman. V. *Poor Mercantile Jack.*

**Quinch, Mrs.** The oldest pensioner at Titbull's; a woman who has "totally lost her head." XXVII. *Titbull's Almshouses.*

**Refractory, Chief.** A surly, discontented female pauper, with a voice in which the tonsils and uvula have gained a diseased ascendency. III. *Wapping Workhouse.*

**Refractory, Number Two.** Another pauper of the same character. III. *Wapping Workhouse.*

**Saggers, Mrs.** One of the oldest pensioners at Titbull's, who has split the small community in which she lives into almost as many parties as there are dwellings in the precinct, by standing her pail outside her dwelling. XXVII. *Titbull's Almshouses.*

**Salcy, P., Family.** A troupe of dramatic artists, fifteen in number, under the management of Monsieur P. Salcy. XXV. *In the French-Flemish Country.*

**Sharpeye.** A policeman. V. *Poor Mercantile Jack.*

**Specks, Joe.** An old school-fellow of the Uncommercial Traveller; afterwards a physician in Dullborough (where most of us come from who come from a country town). XII. *Dullborough Town.*

**Specks, Mrs.** His wife, formerly Lucy Green; an old friend of the Uncommercial Traveller's. XII. *Dullborough Town.*

**Squires, Olympia.** An old flame of the Uncommercial Traveller's.

Olympia was most beautiful (of course); and I loved her to

that degree that I used to be obliged to get out of my little bed in the night, expressly to exclaim to Solitude, "O Olympia Squires!" XIX. *Birthday Celebrations.*

**Straudenheim.** A shop-keeper at Strasbourg; a large-lipped, pear-nosed old man, with white hair and keen eyes, though near-sighted. VII. *Travelling Abroad.*

**Sweeney, Mrs.** A professional laundress, in figure extremely like an old family umbrella. XIV. *Chambers.*

**Testator, Mr.** An occupant of a very dreary set of chambers, in Lyon's Inn, which he furnishes with articles he finds locked up in one of the cellars, and having no owner, so far as is known to any one. He is afterwards visited, late at night, by a man considerably sodden with liquor, who examines every article, claims them all as his own, and promises to call again the next morning, punctually at ten o'clock, but who fails to do so.

Whether he was a ghost, or a spectral illusion of conscience, or a drunken man who had no business there, or the drunken, rightful owner of the furniture, with a transitory gleam of memory; whether he got safe home, or had no home to get to; whether he died of liquor on the way, or lived in liquor ever afterwards,—he never was heard of more. XIV. *Chambers.*

**Trampfoot.** A policeman. V. *Poor Mercantile Jack.*

**Ventriloquist, Monsieur the.** A performer attached to a booth at a fair. He is a thin and sallow man of a weakly aspect. XXV. *In the French-Flemish Country.*

**Victualler, Mr. Licensed.** Proprietor of a singing-house frequented by sailors; a sharp and watchful man, with tight lips, and a complete edition of Cocker's arithmetic in each eye. V. *Poor Mercantile Jack.*

**Wackley, Mr.** A coroner; a noble, patient, and humane man. XVIII. *Some Recollections of Mortality.*

**Weedle, Anastasia.** A pretty Mormon emigrant, elected by universal suffrage the beauty of the ship. XX. *Bound for the Great Salt Lake.*

**Wiltshire.** A simple, fresh-colored farm-laborer, of eight and thirty. XX. *Bound for the Great Salt Lake.*

# PLAYS, POEMS, AND MISCELLANIES

## INDEX TO CHARACTERS

### THE STRANGE GENTLEMAN

**Brown, Miss Emily.** A young lady beloved by both Mr. Trott (the Strange Gentleman) and Mr. Tinkles, but married to the latter.

**Dobbs, Miss Julia.** A wealthy woman, formerly engaged to be married to a Mr. Woolley, who died, leaving her his property, free from all incumbrances; the incumbrance of himself as a husband not being among the least. Being desperately in want of a young husband, she falls in love with a certain wild and not very strong-minded nobleman, Lord Peter, who engages to run away with her to Gretna, and be married. He fails to keep the appointment, however; and she gives her hand to Mr. Trott (the Strange Gentleman) instead.

**John.** A waiter at the St. James's Arms.

**Johnson, John.** A hare-brained mad-cap enamored of Miss Mary Wilson, with whom he starts for Gretna Green, but is temporarily detained at the St. James's Arms by his thoughtless liberality to the post-boys, which leaves him absolutely penniless. A timely loan, however, enables him to continue his journey.

**Noakes, Mrs.** Landlady of the St. James's Arms.

**Overton, Mr. Owen.** An attorney, who is mayor of the small town in which is the St. James's Arms.

**Peter, Lord.** A sprig of nobility, very wild, but not very sagacious or strong-minded, who is in love with Miss Julia Dobbs — or her handsome fortune.

**Sparks, Tom.** "Boots" at the St. James's Arms.

**Strange Gentleman, The.** *See* TROTT, MR. WALKER.

**Tomkins, Charles.** A young gentleman in love with Miss Fanny Wilson. He has arranged to run away with her to Gretna Green, and meets her for this purpose at the St. James's Arms. As he has agreed not to disclose his name, she imagines that the Strange Gentleman, staying at that house, and rumored to be insane, but whom she has not seen, is her lover. When she meets Mr. Tomkins, therefore, she acts upon the presumption that he is actually out of his head; and her conduct seems to him so strange, that he suspects her of playing him false, and works himself up into a tempest of jealousy, which only serves to confirm her belief in his lunacy. They are both, however, disabused at last, and set off, without delay, for their original destination.

**Trott, Mr. Walker,** *called* THE STRANGE GENTLEMAN. A young man desirous of marrying Miss Emily Brown, but deterred by the hostile attitude of Mr. Horatio Tinkles, who challenges him to mortal combat (on Corpse Common) for daring to think of such a thing. He accepts the challenge in a bloodthirsty note, but immediately sends another, and an anonymous one, to the mayor urging that a Strange Gentleman at the St. James's Arms be forthwith arrested, as he is bent upon committing a rash and sanguinary act. By a ludicrous blunder, he is mistaken for Lord Peter, who is expected at the same house for the purpose of meeting Miss Julia Dobbs, his intended; and who is to be seized and carried off as an insane person, in order that his relatives may not discover him. As he is being forced into the carriage, however, the lady discovers that he is unknown to her; and she refuses to accompany him. At the same moment a letter from his rival is put into his hands, saying that the challenge was a *ruse*, and that the writer is far on his way to Gretna to be married to Miss Emily Brown. Determined not to be thus balked of a wife, Mr. Trott offers himself to Miss Dobbs on the spot, is accepted, and starts *instanter* for the same place in a post-chaise and four.

**Wilson, Fanny.** A young lady affianced to Mr. Charles Tomkins.

**Wilson, Mary.** The *innamorata* of Mr. John Johnson.

## THE VILLAGE COQUETTES

**Benson, Lucy.** A beautiful village girl betrothed to George Edmunds, a humble but worthy man. Squire Norton, a man much her superior in social station, tries to lead her astray, and for a time she coquets with him; but before it is too late, she sees her error, rejects the elopement he urges, and returns to her discarded lover.

**Benson, Old.** Her father; a small farmer.

**Benson, Young.** His son; Lucy's brother.

**Edmunds, George.** A young man in love with Lucy Benson.

**Flam, The Honorable Sparkins.** Friend to Squire Norton; fascinated by Rose, a village beauty, whom he ineffectually endeavors to lead from the path of virtue, though she is at first flattered by his attentions.

**Maddox, John.** A young man attached to Rose.

**Norton, Squire.** A country gentleman, who attempts, but unsuccessfully, to seduce the fair Lucy Benson.

**Rose.** Cousin to Lucy Benson; a lovely village maiden, whom the Honorable Sparkins Flam vainly seeks to ruin.

**Stokes, Mr. Martin.** A very small farmer with a very large circle of particular friends.

## IS SHE HIS WIFE?

### OR, SOMETHING SINGULAR

**John.** Servant to Mr. Lovetown.

**Limbury, Mr. Peter.** A friend of Mr. Felix Tapkins's; made furiously jealous by the attentions his wife receives from Mr. Lovetown.

**Limbury, Mrs.** A vain, conceited woman, who carries on a flirtation with Mr. Lovetown, for the double purpose of assisting him in curing his wife of her self-tormenting suspicions, and of teaching her husband the misery of the jealous fears he has been accustomed to harbor.

**Lovetown, Mr. Alfred.** A newly-married man, perpetually yawning, and complaining of *ennui*. His wife, chagrined by his seeming indifference, determines to remove it, if she can, by wounding his vanity, and arousing his jealousy. She accordingly carries on a flirtation with a gay young bachelor (Mr. Tapkins), which perfectly effects her object. Lovetown, stung to the quick, affects a passion for Mrs. Limbury, which he does not feel, and to which she never really responds, with the double motive of obtaining opportunities of watching his wife, and of awaking any dormant feelings of affection for himself that may be slumbering in her bosom. In the carrying-on of these intrigues, many amusing misunderstandings occur; but in the end mutual explanations remove all suspicions, and re-establish the confidence and affection which have temporarily been driven away.

**Lovetown, Mrs.** His wife.

**Tapkins, Mr. Felix.** A gay, good-hearted bachelor, who has a sufficient share of vanity, and who plumes himself on his gallantry. He resides at Rustic Lodge (near Reading), a remarkable cottage, with cardboard chimneys, Grecian balconies, Gothic parapets, and a thatched roof. Such a model of compactness is this house, that even the horse can't cough without his owner's hearing him; the stable being close to the dining-room windows.

# THE MUDFOG PAPERS

## I. PUBLIC LIFE OF MR. TULRUMBLE (ONCE MAYOR OF MUDFOG)

**Jennings, Mr.** A gentleman with a pale face and light whiskers, whom Mr. Tulrumble imports from London to act as his secretary.

**Sniggs, Mr.** Predecessor of Mr. Tulrumble in the mayoralty of Mudfog.

**Tulrumble, Mrs.** Wife of Mr. Nicholas Tulrumble; a vulgar, ignorant woman.

**Tulrumble, Mr. Nicholas.** A coal-dealer, who begins life in a wooden tenement of four feet square, with a capital of two and ninepence, and a stock in trade of three bushels and a half of coals. Being industrious and saving, he gradually gets rich, marries, builds Mudfog Hall (on something which he endeavors to delude himself into thinking a hill), retires from business altogether, grows vain and haughty, sets up for a public character and a great gentleman, and finally becomes mayor of Mudfog.

Mudfog is a pleasant town . . . situated in a charming hollow by the side of a river, from which [it] derives an agreeable scent of pitch, tar, coals, and rope-yarn, a roving population in oil-skin hats, a pretty steady influx of drunken bargemen, and a great many other maritime advantages. There is a good deal of water about Mudfog; and yet it is not exactly the sort of town for a watering-place either. . . . In winter, it comes oozing down the streets, and tumbling over the fields; nay, rushes into the very cellars and kitchens of the houses with a lavish prodigality that might well be dispensed with. But in the hot summer weather it *will* dry up and turn green; and although green is a very good color in its way, especially in grass, still it certainly is not becoming to water; and it cannot be denied that the beauty of Mudfog is rather impaired even by this trifling circumstance.

Having, when in London, been present at the lord-mayor's show, Mr. Tulrumble determines to have one of his own in Mudfog, which shall equal if not surpass it. He makes arrangements, therefore, for a grand procession and dinner; but the day of his inauguration is dim and dismal, the crowd is unreasonable and derisive, the show is a failure, the dinner is flat, and Nicholas is deeply disappointed. Getting statistical and philosophical, he exerts himself to prevent the granting of a new license to an old and popular inn, called "The Jolly Boatmen," and commences a general crusade against beer-jugs and fiddles, forgetting the time when he was glad to drink out of the one, and to dance to the other. He soon finds,

II. FULL REPORT OF THE FIRST [AND SECOND] MEETING OF THE MUDFOG ASSOCIATION FOR THE ADVANCEMENT OF EVERYTHING annual, composed of copperplates, gold-leaf, and silk boards, and worked entirely by milk and water.

**Blubb, Mr.** A member who lectures learnedly upon a cranium which proves to be a carved cocoanut-shell. *See* KETCH, PROFESSOR JOHN.

**Blunderum, Mr.** Contributor of a paper, "On the Last Moments of the Learned Pig."

**Brown, Mr.** (of Edenburg). A member.

**Buffer, Doctor.** Another member.

**Carter, Mr.** President of Section D (Mechanical Science), at the first meeting of the association.

**Coppernose, Mr.** Author of a proposition of great magnitude and interest, submitted, at the first meeting of the association, to Section B (Display of Models and Mechanical Science), illustrated by a vast number of models, and explained in a treatise entitled "Practical Suggestions on the Necessity of Providing some Harmless and Wholesome Relaxation for the young Noblemen of England."

**Crinkles, Mr.** Inventor and exhibitor of a beautiful pocket-picking machine.

**Doze, Professor.** Vice-president of Section A (Zoölogy and Botany), at the first meeting of the association.

**Drawley, Mr.** Vice-president of Section A, at the second meeting.

**Dull, Mr.** Vice-president of Supplementary Section E (Umbugology and Ditchwateristics).

**Dummy, Mr.** Another vice-president of the same section.

**Fee, Doctor W. R.** A member of the association.

**Flummery, Mr.** Another member.

**Grime, Professor.** Another member.

**Grub, Mr.** President of Supplementary Section E (Umbugology and Ditchwateristics).

**Grummidge, Doctor.** A physician, who gives an account of his curing a case of monomania by the heroic method of treatment.

**Jobba, Mr.** Exhibitor of a forcing-machine on a novel plan, for bringing joint-stock railway-shares prematurely to a premium.

**Joltered, Sir William.** President of Section A (Zoölogy and Botany), at the second meeting of the association.

**Ketch, Professor John.** A member, who is called upon to exhibit the skull of the late Mr. Greenacre, which he produces with the remark, "that he'd pound it as that 'ere 'spectable section [the section of Umbugology and Ditchwateristics] had never seed a more gamerer cove nor he vos." The "professor" finds, however, that he has made a slight mistake, and has displayed a carved cocoanut instead of the skull which he intended to show.

**Kutankumagen, Doctor** (of Moscow). A physician, who succeeds in curing an alarmingly healthy man by a persevering use of powerful medicine, low diet, and bleeding, which method of treatment so far restores him as to enable him to walk about with the slight assistance of a crutch and a boy.

**Kwakley, Mr.** A member who submits the result of some ingenious statistical inquiries relative to the difference between the value of the qualification of several members of Parliament, as published to the world, and its real nature and amount.

**Leaver, Mr.** Vice-president of Section B (Display of Models and Mechanical Science), at the Oldcastle meeting.

**Ledbrain, Mr. X.** Vice-president of Section C (Statistics), at the Mudfog meeting. He reads a very ingenious paper, showing that the total number of legs belonging to one great town in Yorkshire is, in round numbers, forty thousand; while the total number of chair and stool legs is only thirty thousand. Allowing the very favorable average of three legs to a seat, he deduces the conclusion that ten thousand individuals (or one half the whole population) are either destitute of any seats at all, or pass the whole of their leisure time in sitting upon boxes.

**Long Ears, The Honorable and Reverend Mr.** A member of the association.

**Mallet, Mr.** President of Section B (Display of Models and Mechanical Science), at the second meeting.

**Misty, Mr. X.** A member.

**Misty, Mr. X. X.** Author of a communication on the disappearance of dancing bears from the streets of London, with observations on the exhibition of monkeys as connected with barrel-organs.

**Mortair, Mr.** Vice-president of Section C (Anatomy and Medicine), at the Oldcastle meeting.

**Muddlebrains, Mr.** Vice-president of Section A (Zoölogy and Botany), at the Oldcastle meeting.

**Muff, Professor.** A member of the association, remarkable for the urbanity of his manners and the ease with which he adapts himself to the forms and ceremonies of ordinary life. At the first meeting, at Mudfog, he tries some private experiments, in conjunction with Professor Nogo, with prussic acid, upon a dog. The animal proves to have been stolen from an unmarried lady in the town, who is rendered nearly distracted by the loss of her pet (named Augustus, in affectionate remembrance of a former lover), and avenges his death by a violent attack on the two scientific gentlemen, in which the expressive features of Professor Muff are much scratched and lacerated, while Professor Nogo,

besides sustaining several severe bites, loses some handfuls of hair. Professor Muff subsequently relates to the association an extraordinary and convincing proof of the wonderful efficacy of the system of infinitesimal doses. He had diffused three drops of rum through a bucketful of water, and given the whole to a patient who was a hard drinker. Before the man had drunk a quart, he was in a state of beastly intoxication; and five other men were made dead drunk with the remainder.

**Mull, Professor.** A member of the association, who criticises some of the ideas advanced by Mr. X. X. Misty in his paper on dancing bears and barrel-organ monkeys.

**Neeshawts, Doctor.** A medical member.

**Noakes, Mr.** Vice-president of Section D (Statistics), at the meeting held at Oldcastle.

**Nogo, Professor.** Exhibitor of a model of a wonderful safety fire-escape.

**Pessell, Mr.** Vice-president of Section C (Anatomy and Medicine), at the meeting at Oldcastle.

**Pipkin, Mr.** (M. R. C. S.). Author of a paper which seeks to prove the complete belief of Sir William Courtenay (otherwise Thom), recently shot at Canterbury, in homœopathy; and which argues that he might have been restored to life if an infinitesimal dose of lead and gunpowder had been administered to him immediately after he fell.

**Prosee, Mr.** A member.

**Pumpkinskull, Professor.** An influential member of the council of the association.

**Purblind, Mr.** A member of the association.

**Queerspeck, Professor.** Exhibitor of a model of a portable railway, neatly mounted in a green case, for the waistcoat pocket. By attaching this instrument to his boots, any bank or public-office clerk could transport himself from his place of residence to his place of business at the easy rate of sixty-five miles an hour. The professor explains that city gentlemen would run in trains, being handcuffed together to prevent confusion or unpleasantness.

**Rummun, Professor.** A member.

**Scroo, Mr.** Vice-president of Section B (Display of Models and Mechanical Science), at the second meeting of the association.

**Slug, Mr.** A celebrated statistician. "His complexion is a dark purple, and he has a habit of sighing constantly." He presents to Section C the result of some investigations he has made regarding the state of infant education and nursery literature among the middle classes of London. He also states some curi-

## THE PANTOMIME OF LIFE

**Do 'em.** A confederate of Captain Fitz-Whisker Fiercy, acting as his livery-servant.

**Fiercy, The Honorable Captain Fitz-Whisker.** A swindler, who struts about with that compound air of conscious superiority and general blood-thirstiness, which is characteristic of most military men, and which always excites the admiration and terror of mere plebeians. He dupes all the tradesmen in his neighborhood, by giving them orders for all sorts of articles, which he afterwards disposes of to other dealers by means of his confederate Do 'em.

## MR. ROBERT BOLTON

**Bolton, Mr. Robert.** A gentleman connected with the press. He was a young man with a somewhat sickly and very dissipated expression of countenance; but he had a knack of narration.

**Clip, Mr.** A hairdresser.

**Murgatroyd, Mr.** An undertaker.

**Sawyer, Mr.** A baker who murdered his son by boiling him in a copper.

**Thicknesse, Mr.** A large stomach surmounted by a man's head, and placed on the top of two particularly short legs.

## SKETCHES OF YOUNG GENTLEMEN

**Balim, Mr.** A young ladies' young gentleman.

**Barker, Young Mrs.** A lady who falls under the judgment of Mr. Fairfax.

**Blake, Mr. Warmint.** An out-and-out young gentleman, exceedingly aggressive in dress, speech, and manners.

**Brown, Mrs.** The hostess who permits a mistletoe in her room.

**Capper, Mr.** Mr. Mincin's host.

**Capper, Mrs.** Mr. Capper's wife, highly praised by Mr. Mincin.

**Caveton, Mr.** A "throwing-off" young gentleman.

**Dummins, Mr.** A soul congenial to Mr. Warmint Blake.

**Fairfax, Mr.** A censorious young gentleman, who always means a great deal more than he says.

**Fitz-Sordust, Colonel.** A highly charged military young gentleman.

**Greenwood, Miss.** A person who often wonders about Mr. Fairfax.

**Grey, Amelia.** A giddy girl, subject to Felix Nixon's fascinations.

## SKETCHES OF YOUNG COUPLES

### THE YOUNG COUPLE



### THE LOVING COUPLE



### THE CONTRADICTORY COUPLE

### THE COUPLE WHO DOTE UPON THEIR CHILDREN

**Saunders, Mr.** A bachelor-friend of the Whifflers.

**Whiffler, Mr. and Mrs.** A married pair, whose thoughts at all times and in all places are bound up in their children, and have no sphere beyond. They relate clever things their offspring say or do, and weary every company with their prolixity and absurdity.

### THE COOL COUPLE

**Charles.** } **Louisa.** } A husband and wife, well-bred, easy, and careless, who rarely quarrel, but are unsympathizing, and indifferent to each other's comfort and happiness.

### THE PLAUSIBLE COUPLE

**Widger, Mr. Bobtail.** } **Widger, Mrs. Lavinia.** } People of the world, who adapt themselves to all its ways, all its twistings and turnings; who know when to close their eyes, and when their ears; when to crawl upon their hands and knees; when to stoop; and when to stand upright.

### THE NICE LITTLE COUPLE

**Chirrup, Mr.** A warm-hearted little fellow, with the smartness, and something of the brisk, quick manner, of a small bird.

**Chirrup, Mrs.** His wife; a sprightly little woman, with an amazing quantity of goodness and usefulness,—a condensation, indeed, of all the domestic virtues.

### THE EGOTISTICAL COUPLE

**Sliverstone, Mr.** A clerical gentleman, who magnifies his wife on every possible occasion by launching out into glowing praises of her conduct in the production of eight young children, and the subsequent rearing and fostering of the same.

**Sliverstone, Mrs.** His wife; always engaged in praising her husband's worth and excellence.

### THE COUPLE WHO CODDLE THEMSELVES

**Merrywinkle, Mr. and Mrs.** A married pair, who have fallen into exclusive habits of self-indulgence, and forget their natural sympathy and close connection with everybody and everything in the world around them; thus depriving themselves of the best and truest enjoyment.

**Chopper, Mrs.** Mother to Mrs. Merrywinkle.

### THE OLD COUPLE

**Adams, Jane.** An aged servant, who has been nurse and story-teller to two generations.

**Crofts.** A barber.

## THE BEGGING-LETTER WRITER

**Southcote, Mr.** One of the many aliases of a professional swindler, who writes letters soliciting money for the relief of his necessities.

**Southcote, Mrs.** His wife.

## ON DUTY WITH INSPECTOR FIELD

**Bark, Bully.** A lodging-house keeper, and a receiver of stolen goods, who lives in the innermost recesses of the worst part of London.

Bark is a red villain and a wrathful, with a sanguine throat, that looks very much as if it were expressly made for hanging, as he stretches it out, in pale defiance, over the half-door of his hutch. Bark's parts of speech are of an awful sort,—principally adjectives. I won't, says Bark, have no adjective police and adjective strangers in my adjective premises. I won't, by adjective and substantive! Give me my trousers, and I 'll send the whole adjective police to adjective and substantive! Give me, says Bark, my adjective trousers! I'll put an adjective knife in the whole bileing of 'em. I 'll punch their adjective heads. I 'll rip up their adjective substantives. Give me my adjective trousers, says Bark, and I 'll spile the bileing of 'em.

**Black.** A constable, who, with his fellow-constable Green, accompanies Inspector Field to Wentworth Street to unveil its midnight mysteries.

**Blackey.** An impostor, who has stood soliciting charity near London Bridge for five and twenty years, with a painted skin, to represent disease.

**Click, Mr.** A vagabond.

**Field, Inspector.** A detective officer, who accompanies the writer, by night, to the lowest parts of London, visiting Rats' Castle (a dark, close cellar, a lodging-house for thieves, near Saint Giles's Church), the old Farm-House near the Old Mint, the sailors' dance-houses, in the region of Ratcliffe Highway, the low haunts of Wentworth Street, and revealing the worst mysteries of the great city.

**Green.** A constable, who, with another constable, named Black, acts as an escort to Inspector Field, on his visiting Wentworth Street.

**Miles, Bob.** A vagabond and jail-bird.

**Parker.** A constable who attends Inspector Field on the occasion of his visit to the "Old Mint."

**Rogers.** A constable who goes with Inspector Field to Rats' Castle.

**Warwick, The Earl of.** A thief, so called.

**White.** A constable who shows Inspector Field and his visitor the lodging-houses in Rotten Gray's Inn Lane.

**Williams.** A constable who pilots Inspector Field and his visitor to the sailors' dance-houses in the neighborhood of Ratcliffe Highway.

## OUR ENGLISH WATERING-PLACE

**Mills, Miss Julia.** A sentimental novel-reader, who figures also in "David Copperfield" as the bosom-friend of Dora Spenlow.

She has left marginal notes on the pages, as "Is not this truly touching?—J. M." "How thrilling!—J. M." "Entranced here by the magician's potent spell.—J. M." She has also Italicised her favorite traits in the description of the hero, as "His hair, which was *dark* and *wavy*, clustered in *rich profusion* around a *marble brow*, whose lofty paleness bespoke the intellect within." It reminds her of another hero. She adds, "How like B. L.! Can this be mere coincidence?—J. M."

**Peepy, The Honorable Miss.** The beauty of her day, but long deceased.

## A FLIGHT

**Compact Enchantress, The.** A French actress.

**Diego, Don.** Inventor of the last new flying-machine.

**Zamiel.** A tall, grave, melancholy Frenchman, with whom (and with other passengers) the writer takes a flying trip from London to Paris.

## OUR SCHOOL

**Blinkins, Mr.** Latin-master; a colorless, doubled-up, near-sighted man, with a crutch, who is always cold, and always putting onions into his ears for deafness, and always disclosing ends of flannel under all his garments, and almost always applying a ball of pocket-handkerchief to some part of his face with a screwing action round and round.

He was a very good scholar, and took great pains where he saw intelligence and a desire to learn; otherwise, perhaps not. Our memory presents him (unless teased into a passion) with as little energy as color; as having been worried and tormented into monotonous feebleness; as having had the best part of his life ground out of him in a mill of boys.

**Dumbledon, Master.** A parlor-boarder; an idiotic, goggled-eyed boy, with a big head, and half-crowns without end; rumored to have come by sea from some mysterious part of the earth, where his parents rolled in gold; and said to feed in the parlor on steaks and gravy, likewise to drink currant-wine.

**Frost, Miss.** A school-girl.

**Mawls, Master.** A school-boy, with manners susceptible of much improvement.

**Maxby, Master.** A day-pupil, favored by the usher, who is sweet upon one of his sisters.

**Phil.** A serving-man, with a sovereign contempt for learning.

## OUR HONORABLE FRIEND

**Tipkisson.** A sadler, a plain, hard-working man, and an opponent of "Our Honorable Friend," who is returned to Parliament (in preference to himself) as the member for Verbosity, — the best represented place in England.

## OUR VESTRY

**Chib, Mr.** (of Tucket's Terrace). A hale old gentleman of eighty-two, who is the father of the vestry.

**Banger, Captain** (of Wilderness Walk). A vestry-man, and an opponent of Mr. Tiddypot, with whom he has a Pickwickian altercation.

**Dogginson, Mr.** A vestry-man who is regarded as "a regular John Bull."

**Magg, Mr.** (of Little Winkling Street). One of the "first orators" of "Our Vestry."

**Tiddypot, Mr.** (of Gumtion House). A vestry-man. *See* BANGER, CAPTAIN.

**Wigsby, Mr.** (of Chumbledon Square). A vestry-man, who is a debater of great eminence.

## OUR BORE

**Blanquo, Pierre.** Our Bore's guide when he discovered a new valley in Switzerland.

**Callow, Mr.** An eminent physician who prescribes for our Bore.

**Clatter, Mr.** Another eminent physician who prescribes for our Bore.

**Jilkins, Mr.** The obscure practitioner who understood our Bore's case.

**Moon, Mr.** Still another eminent physician who also prescribes for our Bore.

## LYING AWAKE

**Winking Charley.** A sturdy vagrant in one of her Majesty's jails, who, like her Majesty, like the author, like everybody else, has had many astonishing experiences in his dreams.

## DOWN WITH THE TIDE

**Pea,** *or* **Peacoat.** A river policeman, with whom the writer goes down the Thames, at night, on a tour of inspection.

**Waterloo.** A toll-taker, so called, at the bridge of that name.

## THE LONG VOYAGE

**Bligh, Captain.** Master of The Bounty; turned adrift on the wide ocean in an open boat.

**Brimer, Mr.** Fifth mate of The Halsewell.

**Christian, Fletcher.** One of the officers of The Bounty; a mutineer.

**Christian, Thursday October.** A native of Pitcairn's Island; son of Fletcher Christian by a savage mother.

**Macmanus, Mr.** A midshipman on board of The Halsewell, an East-Indiaman wrecked on the island of Purbeck.

**Mansel, Miss.** A passenger on the same ship.

**Meriton, Mr. Henry.** Second mate of The Halsewell.

**Pierce, Captain.** Master of The Halsewell.

**Pierce, Miss Mary.** His daughter.

**Rogers, Mr.** Third mate of The Halsewell.

**Schutz, Mr.** A passenger in the same ship.

## OUR FRENCH WATERING-PLACE.

**Loyal Derasseur, M.** Citizen, town-councillor, and landlord. He is an old soldier, and a stanch admirer of the great Napoleon.

His respect for the memory of the illustrious general is enthusiastic. Medallions of him, portraits of him, busts of him, pictures of him, are thickly sprinkled all over the property. During the first month of our occupation, it was our affliction to be constantly knocking down Napoleon: if we touched a shelf in a dark corner, he toppled over with a crash; and every door we opened shook him to the soul. Yet M. Loyal is not a man of mere castles in the air, or, as he would say, in Spain. He has a specially practical, contriving, clever, skilful eye and hand. His houses are delightful. He unites French elegance and English comfort in a happy manner quite his own. He has an extraordinary genius for making tasteful little bedrooms in angles of his roofs, which an Englishman would as soon think of turning to any account as he would think of cultivating the desert. We have ourselves reposed deliciously in an elegant chamber of M. Loyal's construction, with our head as nearly in the kitchen chimney-pot as we can conceive it likely for the head of any gentleman, not by profession a sweep, to be. . . . M. Loyal's nature is the nature of a gentleman. He cultivates his ground with his own hands (assisted by one little laborer who falls into a fit now and then); and he digs and delves from morn to eve in prodigious perspirations — "works always," as he says, — but cover him with dust, mud, weeds, water, any stains you will, you never can cover the gentleman in M. Loyal. A portly, upright, broad-shouldered, brown-faced man, whose soldierly bearing gives him the appearance of being taller than he is. Look into the bright eye of M. Loyal, standing before you in his working blouse and cap, not particularly well shaved, and, it may be, very earthy, and you shall discern in M. Loyal a gentleman whose true politeness is ingrain, and confirmation of whose word by his bond you would blush to think of.

## OUT OF THE SEASON

**Blocker, Mr.** A grocer.

**Wedgington, Mr. B.** A singer and clog dancer, who gives an exhibition at a watering-place, after the season is over.

## THE POOR MAN AND HIS BEER.

**Bacon, Friar.** One of the most famous practical chemists of the age.

**Dreary One, The.** The writer of the sketch.

**Mangel, Ralph.** A member of the club.

**Philosewers.** The Dreary sage's companion in observation.

## HOLIDAY ROMANCE

### INDEX TO CHARACTERS

**Alicia, Princess.** The heroine of Miss Alice Rainbird's romance; eldest child of King Watkins the First, and goddaughter of the good fairy Grandmarina, who gives her a magic fish-bone, which can only be used once, but which is warranted to bring her, that once, whatever she wishes for, provided she wishes for it at the right time. The princess is a notable housewife, and is also a very motherly girl, taking sole charge of her eighteen brothers and sisters. She has great good sense, and refrains from using her magic present until some great exigency shall arise. But when, at last, her father informs her that his money is all gone, and that he has no means of getting any more, though he has tried very hard, and has tried all ways, she thinks the right time must have come for testing the virtue of her godmother's gift, and she therefore wishes it were quarter-day; and immediately it *is* quarter-day, and the king's quarter's salary comes rattling down the chimney. Moreover, her godmother appears, changes the coarse attire of the princess into the splendid raiment of a bride, and whisks her off to church, where she is married to Prince Certainpersonio, after which there is a magnificent wedding-feast.

When Grandmarina had drunk her love to the young couple, and Prince Certainpersonio had made a speech, and everybody had cried, "Hip, hip, hip, hurrah!" Grandmarina announced to the king and queen, that, in future, there would be eight quarter-days in every year, except in leap year, when there would be ten. She then turned to Certainpersonio and Alicia, and said, "My dears, you will have thirty-five children, and they will all be good and beautiful. Seventeen of your children will be boys, and eighteen will be girls. The hair of the whole of your children will curl naturally. They will never have the measles, and will have recovered from the whooping-cough before being born."

**Alicumpaine, Mrs.** One of the characters in Miss Nettie Ashford's romance; a little friend of Mr. and Mrs. Orange, whom she invites to "a small juvenile party" of grown-up people.

**Ashford, Miss Nettie.** A child of seven; pretended bride of William Tinkling, Esquire (aged eight), and author of a romance,

**Rainbird, Alice.** The "bride" of Robin Redforth, and the author of the romance of which the Princess Alicia is the heroine.

**Redforth, Lieutenant-Colonel Robin.** Cousin to William Tinkling, Esquire. He is a young gentleman aged nine, who assumes the part of a pirate, and affects to be peculiarly lawless and bloodthirsty. The romance which contains the story of Captain Boldheart is from his pen.

**Tinkling, William, Esquire.** Author of the introductory portion of the romance, and editor of the other portions. He is eight years old; and to him Miss Nettie Ashford is "married" in the right-hand closet in the corner of the dancing-school where they first met, with a ring (a green one) from Wilkingwater's toy-shop. His bride, and the bride of his friend, Lieutenant-Colonel Robin Redforth, being in captivity at the school of Drowvey and Grimmer, the two young gentlemen resolve to cut them out on a Wednesday when walking two and two. The plan fails, however; and Tinkling's bride brands him as a coward. He demands a court-martial, which is granted and assembles; the Emperor of France, the President of the United States, and a certain admiral being among the members of it. The verdict of "not guilty" is on the point of being rendered, when an unlooked-for event disturbs the general rejoicing. This is no other than the Emperor of France's aunt catching hold of his hair. The proceedings abruptly terminate, and the court tumultuously dissolves.

**Tom.** Cousin to Captain Boldheart; a boy remarkable for his cheekiness and unmannerliness.

**Watkins the First, King.** A character in Miss Alice Rainbird's romance; the manliest of his sex, and husband of a queen who is the loveliest of hers.

They had nineteen children, and were always having more. Seventeen of these children took care of the baby; and Alicia, the eldest, took care of them all. Their ages varied from seven years to seven months.

**White.** A pale bald child (a grown-up one) with red whiskers, who is a pupil in Mrs. Lemon's Preparatory School.

## PRINCE BULL: A FAIRY TALE

**Bear, Prince.** An enemy of Prince Bull; intended as a personification of Russia.

**Bull, Prince.** A powerful prince, married to a lovely princess named Fair Freedom, who brought him a large fortune, and has borne him an immense number of children.

He had gone through a great deal of fighting, in his time,

about all sorts of things, including nothing; but had gradually settled down to be a steady, peaceable good-natured, corpulent, rather sleepy prince.

Under this name the English Government is satirized, with especial reference to its bungling, inefficient prosecution of the Crimean war, and its obstinate adherence, under all circumstances, to mere official routine and formality.

**Tape.** A malicious old beldame; godmother to Prince Bull.

She was a fairy, this Tape, and was a bright red all over. She was disgustingly prim and formal, and could never bend herself a hair's breadth, this way or that way, out of her naturally crooked shape. But she was very potent in her wicked art. She could stop the fastest thing in the world, change the strongest thing into the weakest, and the most useful into the most useless. To do this she had only to put her cold hand upon it, and repeat her own name, Tape. Then it withered away.

# A DIRECTORY OF THE INHABITANTS OF DICKENS-LAND

## I

## A LIST OF PERSONS ACCORDING TO NAME AND NICKNAME

NOTE.—The numbers against the entries refer to the pages of the Dickens Dictionary, where a fuller description will be found.

# II.

## A CLASSIFIED LIST OF PERSONS ACCORDING TO OCCUPATION

NOTE. — The two following lists embrace a portion only of the names contained in Dickens's novels and shorter tales. Not a few names are omitted, as being quite unclassifiable; others, as belonging to persons, places, or things altogether insignificant; others again, because, if brought together at all, they could be so only under headings of very little interest or importance. Incomplete — designedly incomplete — as the lists are, however, it is thought that the groupings they present will be found to be both curious and useful for reference.

The tales in which the names occur may easily be ascertained by means of the List of Persons according to Name and Nickname.

**Actors.** — Master Crummles; Master Percy Crummles; Vincent Crummles; Mr. Folair; Jem Huntley; Alfred Jingle; John; Jem Larkins; Thomas Lenville; Mr. Loggins Nicholas Nickleby; Mr. Pip; P. Salcy Family; Smike; Mr. Snevellicci; Mr. Snittle Timberry; Mr. Wopsle.

**Actresses.** — Miss Belvawney; Miss Bravassa; The Compact Enchantress; Ninetta Crummles; Miss Gazingi; Mrs. Grudden; Miss Ledrook; Mrs. Lenville; Henrietta Petowker; Miss Snevellicci.

**Actuary.** — Mr. Meltham.

**Adventurers.** — Mr. Jinkins; Alfred Lammle.

**Aeronauts.** — Mr. Green; Mr. Green, junior.

**Alderman.** — Mr. Cute.

**Amanuensis.** — Caddy Jellyby.

**Americans.** — Mr. Bevan; Julius Washington Merryweather Bib; Jefferson Brick; Mrs. Jefferson Brick; Oscar Buffum; Cyrus Choke; Hannibal Chollop; Miss Codger; Colonel Diver; Doctor Ginery Dunkle; General Fladdock; Colonel Groper; Mrs. Hominy; Mr. Izzard; Mr. Jodd; Silas Jonas Jorgan; Captain Kedgick; La Fayette Kettle; Mr. Norris and family; Major Pawkins; Mrs. Pawkins; Professor Piper; Elijah Pogram; Zephaniah Scadder; Putnam Smif; Miss Toppit.

**Apprentices.** — Noah Claypole; Mark Gilbert; Hugh Graham; Sim Tappertit; Oliver Twist; Dick Wilkins.

**Architects.** — Martin Chuzzlewit; Seth Pecksniff; Tom Pinch; John Westlock.

**Articulator of bones, etc.** — Mr. Venus.

**Astrologer.** — Mr. Mooney.

**Auctioneer.** — Thomas Sapsea.

**Authors, etc.** — Theodosius Butler; Miss Codger; David Copperfield; Mr. Curdle; Mrs. Hominy; Mrs. Leo Hunter; Miss Toppit; Professor Mullit.

**Babies.** — Frederick Charles William Kitterbell; Sally Tetterby; Alexander MacStinger.

**Bachelors.** — George Chuzzlewit; Nicodemus Dumps, the Single Gentleman; John Jarndyce; Michael; Newman Noggs; Mr. Saunders; Felix Tapkins; Tackleton; Mr. Topper; Watkins Tottle.

**Bailiff.** — Solomon Jacobs.

**Ballad-seller, etc.** — Mr. Wegg.

**Bankers.** — Josiah Bounderby; Mr. Meagles; Mr. Merdle; Tellson and Co.

**Barbers.** — Crofts; Jinkinson; Mr. Slithers; Poll Sweedlepipe.

**Bar-maids.** — Becky; Miss Martin.

**Beadles.** — Mr. Bumble; Mr. Bung; Mooney; Simmons; Sownds; Sowster.
**Begging-letter writer.** — Mr. Southcote.
**Bird-fancier.** — Poll Sweedlepipe.
**Blind persons.** — Bertha Plummer; Mr. Sampson Dibble; Stagg.
**Boarding-house keepers.** — Mrs. Pawkins; Mrs. Tibbs; Mrs. Todgers.
**Boobies.** — Bentley Drummle; Edmund Sparkler.
**Boots.** — Bailey, junior; Cobbs; Tom Sparks; Sam Weller.
**Bore.** — Mr. Barlow.
**Brokers.** — Mr. Brogley; Clarriker; Fixem; Wilkins Flasher; Fascination Fledgeby; Mr. Gattleton; Frank Simmery; Grandfather Smallweed; Tom Tix.
**Burglars.** — *See* HOUSEBREAKERS.
**Butlers.** — David; Giles; Nicholas.

**Carpenters.** — Thomas Joy; Samuel Wilkins.
**Carriers.** — Mr. Barkis; John Peerybingle.
**Chambermaid.** — Mrs. Pratchett.
**Chandler.** — Tom Cobb.
**Charity-boys.** — Noah Claypole; Robin Toodle.
**Charwomen.** — Mrs. Bangham; Mrs. Blockson.
**Cheap-jacks.** — Doctor Marigold; Willum Marigold.
**Chemists.** — Thomas Groffin; Mr. Redlaw.
**Circus performers, etc.** — E. W. B. Childers; Emma Gordon; Signor Jupe; Master Kidderminster; Josephine Sleary; Mr. Sleary; Miss Woolford.
**Clergymen, etc.** — Mr. Chadband; Horace Crewler; Septimus Crisparkle; Alfred Feeder; Brother Gimblet; Verity Hawkyard; Melchisedech Howler; Mr. Long Ears; Frank Milvey; George Sliverman; Mr. Sliverstone; Mr. Stiggins; Charles Timson.
**Clerks, etc.** — Mr. Adams; Clarence Barnacle; Mr. Bazzard; Bitzer; Young Blight; Alexander Briggs; James Carker; John Carker; Frank Cheeryble; Mr. Chuckster; Chuffey; Mr. Clark; Bob Cratchit; Mr. Dobble; Walter Gay; Tom Gradgrind; William Guppy; Uriah Heep; Mr. Jones; Mr. Jackson; Mr. Jinks; Tim Linkinwater; Jarvis Lorry; Mr. Lowten; Mr. Mallard; Wilkins Micawber; Augustus Minns; Mr. Morfin; Nicholas Nickleby; Newman Noggs; Nathaniel Pipkin; Thomas Potter; Bartholomew Smallweed; Putnam Smif; Mr. Smith; Robert Smithers; Horatio Sparkins; John Spatter; Dick Swiveller; Mr. Tiffey; Tom; Alfred Tomkins; Mr. Tupple; John Wemmick; Mr. Wicks; Reginald Wilfer; Mr. Wisbottle. *See also* PARISH CLERKS.
**Clients.** — Mr. Watty; Michael Warden; Amelia; Mike.
**Coachmen, etc.** — William Barker; George; Joe; Martin; Sam; William Simmons; Tipp; Tom; Tony Weller; William.
**Coal-dealer.** — Nicholas Tulrumble.
**Collectors.** — Mr. Buffle; Mr. Lillyvick; Mr. Pancks; Mr. Rugg.
**Companions.** — Mrs. General; Mary Graham; Kate Nickleby.
**Constables.** — Black; Darby; Green; Daniel Grummer; Rogers; White; Williams.
**Convicts.** — Alice Brown; Compeyson; John Edmunds; Kags; Abel Magwitch.
**Corn-chandlers.** — Octavius Budden; Wilkins Micawber; Uncle Pumblechook.
**Coroner.** — Mr. Wackley.
**Costumer.** — Solomon Lucas.
**Cricketers.** — Mr Dumkins; Luffey; Peter Magnus; Mr. Podder; Mr. Staple; Mr. Struggles.
**Cripples.** — Phœbe; Tiny Tim; Fanny Cleaver; Gruff and Glum; Mr. Wegg.

**Dancing-masters.** — Mr. Baps; Signor Billsmethi; Prince Turveydrop.
**Deaf-mute.** — Sophy Marigold.
**Detectives.** — Mr. Inspector Bucket; Sergeant Dornton; Sergeant Fendall; Inspector Field; Sergeant Mith; Mr. Nadgett; Rogers; Inspector Stalker; Sergeant Straw; Mr. Tatt; Inspector Wield; Witchem.
**Distiller.** — Mr. Langdale.
**Dogs.** — Boxer; Bull's-eye; Diogenes; Jip; Merrylegs; Poodles.

**Dressmakers.** — Fanny Cleaver (dolls' dressmaker); Miss Knag; Madame Mantalini; Amelia Martin; Kate Nickleby; Miss Simmond.

**Drivers.** — *See* COACHMEN, etc.

**Drunkards.** — Mrs. Blackpool; Mr. Dolls; John; Krook; Warden.

**Drysalters.** — Brother Gimblet; Verity Hawkyard.

**Dustman.** — Nicodemus Boffin.

**Dwarfs.** — Chops; Quilp; Miss Mowcher.

**Editors, etc.** — Jefferson Brick; Colonel Diver; Mr. Pott; Mr. Slurk.

**Emigrants.** — Susannah Cleverly; William Cleverly; Dorothy Dibble; Sampson Dibble, Jessie Jobson; Wiltshire; Anastasia Weedle.

**Engine-driver.** — Mr. Toodle.

**Engineers.** — Daniel Doyce; Edwin Drood.

**Fairies.** — Grandmarina; Tape.

**Farmers.** — Old Benson; John Browdie; Godfrey Nickleby; Martin Stokes.

**Fishermen.** — Ham Peggotty; Daniel Peggotty.

**Footmen.** — Mercury; Muzzle; John Smauker; Thomas Towlinson; Tuckle Whiffers.

**Fops.** — Fascination Fledgeby; Mr. Mantalini; Mr. Toots.

**Forgers.** — Mr. Fikey; Mr. Merdle.

**Frenchmen.** — Bebelle; Blandois (*or* Rigaud); Madame Bouclet; the Compact Enchantress; Charles Darnay (*or* Evrémonde); Lucie Darnay; Ernest Defarge; Thérèse Defarge; Monsieur the Face-maker; Théophile Gabelle; Gaspard; Mademoiselle Hortense; Jaques (One, Two, Three, Four, Five); Lagnier (*or* Rigaud); M. Loyal Derasseur; Alexander Manette; Lucie Manette; Monsieur Mutuel; St. Evrémonde; P. Salcy Family; Corporal Théophile; the Vengeance; Monsieur the Ventriloquist.

**Gamblers.** — Joe Jowl; Isaac List; Miss Betsey Trotwood's Husband; Little Nell's Grandfather.

**Gamekeeper.** — Martin.

**Gardeners.** — Mr. Cheggs; Hunt; Wilkins.

**Gentlemen.** — Mr. Tite Barnacle; Sir Joseph Bowley; Mr. Brownlow; Sir John Chester; Sir Thomas Clubber; Hon. Mr. Crushton; Sir Leicester Dedlock; The Hon. Sparkins Flam; Mr. Alexander Grazinglands; Mr. Grimwig; Geoffrey Haredale; Sir Mulberry Hawk; Master Humphrey; Sir William Joltered; Hon. Mr. Long Ears; Nicholas Nickleby; Squire Norton; Samuel Pickwick; Mr. John Podsnap; Sir Matthew Pupker; Jack Redburn; Sir Barnet Skettles; the Hon. Wilmot Snipe; Sir Hookham Snivey; the Hon. Mr. Snob; the Hon. Bob Stables; Mr. Melvin Twemlow; Mr. Wardle.

**Germans.** — Baron and Baroness von Koëldwethout; Straudenheim; Baron and Baroness von Swillenhausen.

**Giants.** — Gog; Magog; Pickleson.

**Governesses.** — Mrs. General; Miss Lane; Ruth Pinch.

**Green-grocers.** — Harris; Tommy; Richard Upwitch.

**Grocers.** — Jacob Barton; Mr. Blocker; Joseph Tuggs.

**Groom.** — Thomas.

**Guards.** — George; Joe.

**Haberdashers.** — Mr. Omer; Mr. Phibbs.

**Hangman.** — Ned Dennis.

**Hop-grower.** — Mr. Chestle.

**Horse-jockey.** — Captain Maroon.

**Hostlers.** — Bottles; Hugh; Ikey; Mark Tapley.

**Housebreakers.** — Toby Crackit; Bill Sikes.

**Housekeepers.** — Mrs. Bedwin; Miss Benton; Molly; Mrs. Pipchin; Miss Pross; Mrs. Rouncewell; Peg Sliderskew; Mrs. Sparsit; Esther Summerson; Mrs. Tickit; Agnes Wickfield.

**Hypocrites.** — Mrs. Heep; Uriah Heep; Charity Pecksniff; Mercy Pecksniff; Seth Pecksniff; Julius Slinkton.

**Impostor.** — Blackey.
**Invalids.** — Bill Barley; Mrs. Clennam; Mrs. Crewler; Mr. Gobler; Mrs. Gradgrind; Mrs. Skimpole; Mr. Tresham.
**Inventors.** — Mr. Crinkles; Don Diego; Daniel Doyce; John; Professor Queerspeck; Mr. Tickle.
**Irishman.** — Frederick O'Bleary.
**Ironmaster.** — Mr. Rouncewell.
**Italians.** — Giovanni Carlavero; John Baptist Cavalletto.

**Jailer.** — Mr. Akerman.
**Jews.** — Barney; Fagin; Aaron Mesheck; Mr. Riah.
**Judge.** — Mr. Justice Stareleigh.
**Juggler.** — African Knife-swallower; Sweet William.
**Jurymen.** — Thomas Groffin; Richard Upwitch.

**Laborers.** — Bayton; Will Fern; Joe; Wiltshire.
**Ladies.** — Princess Alicia; Lady Bowley; Lady Clubber; Lady Dedlock; Mrs. Gowan; Baroness von Koëldwethout; Mrs. Merdle; Lady Fareway; Lady Scadgers; Lady Skettles; the Hon. Mrs. Skewton; Lady Snuphanuph; Lady Tippins; Baroness von Swillenhausen.
**Lamplighter.** — Tom Grig.
**Landladies.** — Mrs. Bardell; Mrs. Billickin; Madame Bouclet; Mrs. Craddock; Mrs. Crupp; Mrs. Lirriper; Mrs. Lupin; Mrs. MacStinger; Mrs. Noakes; Miss Abbey Potterson; Mary Ann Raddle; Mrs. Tibbs; Mrs. Todgers; Mrs. Whimple; Mrs. Williamson; Miss Wozenham.
**Landlords.** — Bark; The Black Lion; James George Bogsby; Christopher Casby; M. Loyal Derasseur; James Groves; W. Grubble; Captain Kedgick; Mr. J. Mellows; Mr. Licensed Victualler; John Willet.
**Laundresses.** — Mrs. Dilber; Mrs. Parkins; Mrs. Stubbs; Mrs. Sweeney.
**Law-stationers.** — Mrs. Harris; Mr. Snagsby.
**Law-student.** — Percy Noakes.
**Law-writers.** — Captain Hawdon; Tony Jobling.
**Lawyers.** — Mr. Bintrey; Sally Brass; Sampson Brass; Samuel Briggs; Serjeant Buzfuz; Sydney Carton; Clarkson; Thomas Craggs; Mr. Dodson; Mr. Fips; Mr. Fogg; Hiram Grewgious; Uriah Heep; Mr. Jaggers; Mr. Jorkins; Conversation Kenge; Mortimer Lightwood; Percy Noakes; Joseph Overton; Owen Overton; Solomon Pell; Mr. Perker; Mr. Phunkey; Mr. Rugg; Mr. Skimpin; Jonathan Snitchey; Serjeant Snubbin; Francis Spenlow; Henry Spiker; Mr. Stryver; Mr. Tangle; Thomas Traddles; Mr. Tulkinghorn; Mr. Vholes; Mr. Wickfield; Eugene Wrayburn.
**Locksmith.** — Gabriel Varden.
**Lodging-house Keepers.** — Bully Bark; Mrs. Billickin; Mr. Bulph; Mrs. Lirriper; Miss Wozenham.
**Lords.** — *See* NOBLEMEN.
**Lunatics.** — Mr. Dick (Richard Babley); The Gentleman in Small-clothes; Miss Flite.

**Magistrates.** — Alderman Cute; Mr. Fang; Mr. Nupkins; Mr. Commissioner Pordage.
**Manufacturer.** — Josiah Bounderby.
**Matrons of Workhouses.** — Mrs. Corney; Mrs. Mann.
**Mayors.** — George Nupkins; Joseph (*or* Owen) Overton; Mr. Sniggs; Mr. Tulrumble.
**Medical Students.** — Ben Allen; Alfred Heathfield; Jack Hopkins; Bob Sawyer.
**Member of Congress.** — Elijah Pogram.
**Members of Parliament.** — William Buffey; Cornelius Brook Dingwall; Mr. Gregsbury; Sir Matthew Pupker; Sir Barnet Skettles; Honest Tom; Hamilton Veneering. *See also* NOBLEMEN.
**Merchants.** — Barbox Brothers (Mr. Jackson); Cheeryble Brothers; Clarriker; Arthur Clennam; Mr. Dombey; Mr. Fezziwig; Mr. Thomas Gradgrind; Mr. Murdstone; Mr. Miles Owen; Herbert Pocket; Mr. Quinion; Scrooge; Walter Wilding.
**Messengers.** — Jerry Cruncher; Jenkinson; Mr. Perch.
**Military Men.** — Captain Adams; Matthew Bagnet; Major Bagstock; Captain Bailey;

Major Banks; Captain Boldwig; Colonel Bulder; General Cyrus Choke; Major Hannibal Chollop; Colonel Chowser; Captain Doubledick; Captain Dowler; General Fladdock; Tom Green; Colonel Groper; Gruff and Glum; Captain Hawdon; Captain Helves; Captain Hopkins; Major Jemmy Jackman; Captain Kedgick; the Recruiting Sergeant; George Rouncewell; Lieutenant Slaughter; Wilmot Snipe; Lieutenant Tappleton; Captain Taunton; Corporal Théophile; Joe Willet.

**Milliners.** — Miss Knag; Madame Mantalini; Amelia Martin.

**Misers, etc.** — Uncle Chill; Christopher Casby; Anthony Chuzzlewit; Jonas Chuzzlewit; Arthur Gride; Ralph Nickleby; Scrooge; Bartholomew Smallweed; Grandfather Smallweed.

**Mistresses.** — Alice Brown; Little Em'ly; Mistress Alice; Nan; Nancy.

**Murderers.** — Jonas Chuzzlewit; Gaspard; Bradley Headstone; Mademoiselle Hortense; Captain Murderer; Rigaud; Mr. Rudge; Bill Sikes; Julius Slinkton; William Warden.

**Musical Performers.** — Antonio; Matthew Bagnet; Banjo Bones; Mrs. Banjo Bones; Mr. Brown; Mr. Cape; Frederick Dorrit; Mr. Evans; Mr. Harleigh; John Jasper; Miss Jenkins; Signor Lobskini; Miss A. Melvilleson; Master Wilkins Micawber; Lætitia Parsons; Little Swills; Mr. Tippin; Mrs. Tippin; Miss Tippin; Mr. and Mrs. B. Wedgington.

**Nautical-instrument maker.** — Solomon Gills.

**Newsmen, etc.** — Adolphus Tetterby; 'Dolphus Tetterby.

**Noblemen, etc.** — Lord Decimus Tite Barnacle; Prince Bear; Lord Boodle; Prince Bull; Prince Certain Personio; Cousin Feenix; Baron von Koëldwethout; Monseigneur; Lord Mutanhed; Lord Peter; Marquis St. Evrémonde; Count Smorltork; Lord Snigsworth; Lord Lancaster Stiltstalking; Baron von Swillenhausen; Lord Frederick Verisopht; King Watkins the First.

**Notaries.** — Abel Garland; Mr. Witherden.

**Nurses.** — Mrs. Bangham; Mrs. Blockitt; Dawes; Sally Flanders; Flopson; Sairey Gamp; Mercy; Millers; Betsey Prig; Mrs. Prodgit; Mrs. Thingummy; Mrs. Polly Toodle; Mrs. Wickham.

**Old Maids.** — Miss Barbary; Berinthia (*or* Berry); Rosa Dartle; Volumnia Dedlock; Miss Havisham; Miss Lillerton; Miss Jane Murdstone; Miss Anastasia Rugg; Miss Skiffins; Judy Smallweed; Miss Clarissa Spenlow; Miss Lavinia Spenlow; Miss Lucretia Tox; Miss Wade; Rachael Wardle; Miss Witherfield.

**Orators.** — Mr. Edkins; Mr. Magg; Mr. Slackbridge.

**Orphans.** — Johnny; Lilian.

**Pages.** — Alphonse; Withers.

**Painters.** — Henry Gowan; Miss La Creevy.

**Parish-clerks.** — Solomon Daisy; Nathaniel Pipkin; Mr. Wopsle.

**Paupers.** — Anny; Little Dick; Mrs. Fibbetson; Martha; John Edward Nandy; Oakum Head; Chief Refractory; Refractory Number Two; Old Sally; Mrs. Thingummy; Oliver Twist.

**Pawnbrokers.** — David Crimple; Mr. Henry; Pleasant Riderhood.

**Pensioners.** — Mr. Battens; Mrs. Quinch; Mrs. Saggers.

**Pew-opener.** — Mrs. Miff.

**Philanthropists.** — Bigwig Family; Luke Honeythunder; Mrs. Jellyby; Mr. and Mrs. Pardiggle; Mr. Quale; Miss Wisk.

**Philosophers.** — Doctor Jeddler; Mr. Mooney.

**Physicians.** — Bayham Badger; Mr. Chillip; Ginery Dunkle; Doctor Grummidge; Doctor Haggage; John Jobling; Doctor Kutankumagen; Doctor Lumbey; Alexander Manette; Mr. Pilkins; Parker Peps; Doctor Soemup; Joe Specks; Doctor Toorell; Doctor Wosky. *See also* SURGEONS.

**Pirate.** — Lieutenant-Colonel Robin Redforth.

**Pickpockets.** — *See* THIEVES.

**Pilot.** — Mr. Bulph.

**Plasterer.** — Thomas Plornish.

**Poets.** — Mr. Slum; Augustus Snodgrass; Mrs. Leo Hunter.

**Policemen.** — Sergeant Dornton; Inspector Field; Mr. Inspector; Sergeant Mith; Parker; Peacoat; Quickear; Sharpeye; Inspector Stalker; Trampfoot; Williams; Sergeant Witchem.

**Politicians.** — Lord Boodle; Horatio Fizkin; Major Pawkins; Mr. Rogers; Samuel Slumkey.

**Pony.** — Whisker.

**Porters, etc.** — Bullamy; "Lamps;" Tugby; Toby Veck.

**Postmasters.** — Tom Cobb; Monsieur Gabelle.

**Postmistress.** — Mrs. Tomlinson.

**Pot-boy.** — Bob Gliddery.

**Prisoners.** — Mr. Ayresleigh; John Baptist Cavaletto; the Chancery Prisoner; William Dorrit; Charles Evrémonde; Doctor Haggage; George Heyling; Captain Hopkins; Horace Kinch; Mr. Martin; Wilkins Micawber; Mr. Mivins; Neddy; Mr. Price; Rigaud; Mr. Simpson; Smangle; Mr. Walker; Mr. Willis.

**Prostitutes.** — Bella; Bet; Emily; Martha Endell; Eliza Grimwood; Nan.

**Pugilist.** — The Game Chicken.

**Pupils.** — Adams; Belling; Bitherstone; Bitzer; Mrs. Black; Bobbo; Bolder; Briggs; Rosa Bud; Cobbey; David Copperfield; Cripples; George Demple; Dumbledon; Miss Edwards; Richard Evans; Adelina Fareway; Miss Ferdinand; Miss Frost; Miss Giggles; Bully Globson; Graymarsh; Harry; Charley Hexam; Miss Jennings; Johnson; Helena Landless; Jemmy Jackman Lirriper; Mary Anne; Mawls; Maxby; Mobbs; John Owen; Miss Pankey; Miss Reynolds; Miss Rickitts; Miss Shepard; Barnet Skettles, junior; Smike; Miss Smithers; Sophia; Joe Specks; Steerforth; Bob Tartar; Tomkins; Toots; Tozer; Traddles; Granville Wharton; White.

**Ranger.** — Phil Parkes.

**Raven.** — Grip.

**Receivers of Stolen Goods.** — Bully Bark; Fagin; Joe; Mr. Lively.

**Reporter.** — David Copperfield.

**Resurrectionist.** — Jerry Cruncher.

**Rioters.** — Ned Dennis; Hugh; Barnaby Rudge; Sim Tappertit.

**Robe-maker.** — Mr. Jennings.

**Saddlers.** — Old Lobbs; Tipkisson.

**Seamen, etc.** — Old Bill Barley; Captain Boldheart; William Boozey; Mr. Bulph; Captain Bunsby; Captain George Carton; Captain Cuttle; Dando; Gilbert Davis; Dark Jack; Mercantile Jack; Captain Silas Jonas Jorgan; John Mullion; Job Potterson; Captain Purday; Captain William George Ravender; John Steadiman; Lieutenant Tartar.

**Secretaries.** — Ferdinand Barnacle; Mr. Fish; Mr. Gashford; John Harmon; Mr. Jennings; Lafayette Kettle; Jonas Mudge; Mr. Wobbler.

**Servants.** — I. *Male.* Benjamin Britain; Brittles; Deputy; John Derrick; Do'em; Jeremiah Flintwinch; Old Glubb; John Grueby; James; Joe (the Fat Boy); John; Littimer; the Native; Kit Nubbles; Peak; Pepper; Phil; Pruffle; Tom Scott; Sloppy; Smike; Phil Squod; William Swidger; Mark Tapley; Tinkler; Robin Toodle; Job Trotter; Tungay; Samuel Weller. — II. *Female.* Jane Adams; Agnes; Anne; Barbara; Becky; Berinthia; Betsey; Biddy; Charlotte; Clickitt; Mary Daws; Emma; Affery Flintwinch; Flowers; Goodwin; Guster; Hannah; Mademoiselle Hortense; Jane; Janet; Winifred Madgers; the Marchioness; Martha; Mary; Mary Anne; Caroline Maxey; 'Melia; Miss Miggs; Clemency Newcome; Susan Nipper; Mary Anne Paragon; Clara Peggotty; Mary Anne Perkinsop; Phœbe; Priscilla; Mrs. Rachael; Sally Rairyganoo; Robinson; Rosa; Tilly Slowboy; Betsey Snap; Sophia; Willing Sophy; Tamaroo; Tattycoram.

**Sextons, etc.** — Bill; Old David; Gabriel Grub.

**Sharpers.** — *See* SWINDLERS.

**Sheriff's Officers.** — Blathers; Dubbley; Duff; Mr. Namby; Mr. Neckett; Mr. Scaley; Mr. Smouch; Tom.

**Shipwright.** — Chips.

**Shoe-binder.** — Jemima Evans.

**Shopkeepers.** — Giovanni Carlavero; Mrs. Chickenstalker; Mrs. Chivery; Augustus Cooper; Ernest Defarge; Little Nell's Grandfather; Mrs. Plornish; Pleasant Riderhood; Straudenheim; Mrs. Tugby.

**Showmen, etc.** — Tom Codlin; Mr. Grinder; Mr. Harris; Mrs. Jarley; Jerry; Mim; Vuffin.

**Shrews.** — Mrs. Bumble; Mrs. Joe Gargery; Mrs. MacStinger; Mrs. Marigold; Miss Miggs; Mrs. Raddle; Sarah; Mrs. Snagsby; Mrs. Sowerberry; Fanny Squeers; Mrs. Squeers; Mrs. Varden.

**Smiths.** — Richard; Joe Gargery; Dolge Orlick; John.

**Spaniard.** — Antonio.

**Spendthrift.** — Edward Dorrit.

**Spies.** — Roger Cly; Solomon Pross.

**Sportsman.** — Nathaniel Winkle.

**Statisticians.** — Mr. Filer; Mr. Kwakley; Mr. X. Ledbrain; Mr. Slug.

**Stenographer.** — David Copperfield.

**Steward.** — Mr. Rudge; Job Potterson.

**Stoker.** — Mr. Toodle.

**Stone-mason.** — Durdles.

**Straw-bonnet maker.** — Jemima Evans.

**Street-sweeper.** — Jo.

**Student.** — Edmund Denham.

**Sugar-baker.** — Gabriel Parsons.

**Suitors in Chancery.** — Richard Carstone; Ada Clare; Miss Flite; Mr. Gridley; John Jarndyce.

**Surgeons.** — Mr. Knight Bell; Mr. Dawson; Mr. Lewsome; Mr. Losberne; Doctor Payne; Doctor Slammer; Allan Woodcourt. *See also* PHYSICIANS.

**Swindlers, etc.** — Blackey; Mr. Bonney; Do 'em; Fitz-Whisker Fiercy; Alfred Jingle; Mr. Jinkins; Alfred Lammle; Mr. Merdle; Rigaud; Zephaniah Scadder; Montague Tigg; Job Trotter; Captain Walter Waters; Mr. Wolf.

**Tailors.** — Mr. Omer; Mr. Trabb; Alexander Trott.

**Tapster.** — David Crimple.

**Taxidermist.** — Mr. Venus.

**Teachers, etc.** — Cornelia Blimber; Doctor Blimber; Mr. Blinkins; Old Cheeseman; Mr. Creakle; Mr. Cripples; Amelia and Maria Crumpton; Mr. Dadson; Miss Donny; Miss Drowvey; Mr. Feeder; Miss Grimmer; Miss Gwynn; Bradley Headstone; Betty Higden; Latin-Grammar Master; Mrs. Lemon; Mr. M'Choakumchild; Mr. Marton; Charles Mell; Miss Monflathers; the Misses Nettingall; Nicholas Nickleby; Emma Peecher; Professor Piper; Mr. Sharp; Wackford Squeers; Doctor Strong; Miss Tomkins; Miss Twinkleton; the Misses Wackles. *See also* GOVERNESSES.

**Temperance Reformers.** — Anthony Humm; Jonas Mudge; Brother Tadger.

**Thieves.** — Charley Bates; Bet; Tom Chitling; Noah Claypole; John Dawkins (the Artful Dodger); Doctor Dundey; Aaron Mesheck; Nancy; Mr. Shepherdson; Bill Sikes; Tally-ho Thompson; Earl of Warwick.

**Toadies.** — Mr. Boots; Mr. Brewer; Mr. and Mrs. Camilla Mrs. Coiler; Mr. Flamwell; Georgiana; Mr. Pluck; Sarah Pocket; Mr. Pyke.

**Tobacconist.** — Miss Chivery.

**Toy-maker.** — Caleb Plummer.

**Toy-merchant.** — Tackleton.

**Tramps.** — John Anderson; Mrs. Anderson.

**Turner.** — Mr. Kenwigs.

**Turnkeys, etc.** — Mr. Akerman; Bob; John Chivery; Young John Chivery; Solomon Pross; Tom Roker.

**Umbrella-maker.** — Alexander Trott.

**Undertakers.** — Mr. Joram; Mr. Mould; Mr. Omer; Mr. Sowerberry; Tacker; Mr. Trabb.

**Usurers.** — Anthony Chuzzlewit; Arthur Gride; Ralph Nickleby; Grandfather Smallweed.

**Vagabonds, etc.**—John Anderson; Mr. Chick; Bob Miles; Edward Twigger; Winking Charley.

**Valets.**—*See* SERVANTS.

**Verger.**—Mr. Tope.

**Vestrymen.**—Mr. Chib; Captain Banger; Mr. Dogginson; Mr. Magg; Mr. Tiddypot; Mr. Wigsby.

**Waiters.**—Archbishop of Greenwich; Ben; Christopher; Ezekiel; Jack; John; Miss Piff; William Potkins; Mrs. Sniff; Thomas; Miss Whiff; William.

**Watermen.**—Dandy; Jesse Hexam; Mr. Lobley; Roger Riderhood; Tommy.

**Weaver.**—Stephen Blackpool.

**Wharfinger.**—Mr. Winkle, senior.

**Wheelwright.**—Mr. Hubble.

**Widowers.**—Mr. John Dounce; John Podgers; Tony Weller.

**Widows.**—Barbara's Mother; Mrs. Bardell; Mrs. Bedwin; Mrs. Billickin; Mrs. Bloss; Mrs. Brandley; Mrs. Briggs; Mrs. Budger; Mrs. Clennam; Mrs. Coiler; Mrs. Copperfield; Mrs. Corney; Mrs. Crisparkle; Lady Fareway; Mrs. Fielding; Flora Finching; Sally Flanders; Mrs. General; Mrs. Gowan; Edith Granger; Mrs. Gummidge; Mrs. Guppy; Mrs. Heep; Mrs. Jiniwin; Mrs. Markleham; Mrs. Maplesone; Mrs. Mitts; Mrs. Nickleby; Mrs. Nubbles; Mrs. Pegler; Mrs. Skewton; Mrs. Sparsit; Mrs. Starling; Mrs. Steerforth; Mrs. Taunton; Lady Tippins; Mrs. Tisher; Mrs. Wardle; Mrs. Woodcourt.

# III.

## NAMES OF PLACES, CORPORATIONS, SOCIETIES, AND LITERARY PRODUCTIONS

**Church.**— Little Bethel.

**Corporations, etc.** — Anglo-Bengalee Disinterested Loan and Life Insurance Company; Circumlocution Office; Eden Land Corporation; Human Interest Brothers; Inestimable Life Assurance Company; United Grand Junction Lirriper and Jackman Great Norfolk Parlor Line; United Metropolitan Improved Hot Muffin and Crumpet Baking and Punctual Delivery Company. *See* Societies.

**Literary Productions.** — Considerations on the Policy of removing the Duty on Beeswax; Last Moments of the Learned Pig; Ode to an Expiring Frog; Speculations on the Sources of the Hampstead Ponds, with some Observations on the Theory of Tittlebats; the Thorn of Anxiety.

**Newspapers.** — Eatanswill Gazette; Eatanswill Independent; New York Rowdy Journal.

**Places** (*various*). — Ball's Pond; Borrioboola Gha; Chinks's Basin; Chumbledon Square; Cloisterdam; Dingley Dell; Dullborough; Eatanswill; Eden; Great Winglebury; Grogzwig; Haven of Philanthropy; Mill Pond Bank, Chinks's Basin; Mugby Junction; Muggleton; Namelesston; New Thermopylæ; Oldcastle; Old Hell Shaft; Old Mint; Pavilionstone; Plashwater Weir Mill; Pocket-Breaches; Pod's End; Poplar Walk; Port Middlebay; Princess's Place; Rats' Castle; Stagg's Garden; Stiffun's Acre; Tom-all-alone's; Tucket's Terrace; Verbosity; Wilderness Walk.

**Political Parties.** — Eatanswill Buffs; Eatanswill Blues.

**Public Houses.** — Black Boy and Stomach-ache; Black Lion; Blue Boar; Blue Dragon; Boot-jack and Countenance; the Bush; the Crozier; Dolphin's Head; Golden Cross; Good Republican Brutus of Antiquity; Great White Horse; Holly-Tree; Jolly Bargemen; Jolly Boatmen; Jolly Sandboys; Jolly Tapley; Lighterman's Arms; Marquis of Granby; Maypole; National Hotel; Nutmeg-grater; Original Pig; the Peacock; Pegasus' Arms; Pig and Tinderbox; St. James's Arms; Saracen's Head; Setting Moon; Six Jolly Fellowship Porters; Slamjam Coffee-House; Sol's Arms; the Temeraire; Three Cripples; Three Jolly Bargemen; Traveller's Twopenny; Valiant Soldier; White Hart; White Conduit House; White Horse Cellar; Winglebury Arms.

**Residences, etc.** — Abel Cottage; Amelia Cottage; Blunderstone Rookery; Boffin's Bower; Chesney Wold; the Den; the Elmses; Fizkin Lodge; the Growlery; Gumtion House; Harmony Jail; Hoghton Towers; Manor Farm; Mudfog Hall; Norwood; Oak Lodge; Rose Villa; Rustic Lodge; Satis House; Stone Lodge; the Warren; Wooden Midshipman.

**Schools.** — Dotheboys Hall; Minerva House; Nuns' Houe; Salem House; Westgate House.

**Sciences.** — Ditchwateristics; Umbugology.

**Shop.** — Wooden Midshipman.

**Societies.** — All-Muggleton Cricket Club; Finches of the Grove; Convened Chief Composite Committee of Central and District Philanthropists; Glorious Apollos, Infant Bonds of Joy; Ladies' Bible and Prayer-book Distribution Society; Master Humphrey's Clock; Mr. Weller's Watch; Pickwick Club; 'Prentice Knights; Social Linen Box Committee; Superannuated Widows; United Aggregate Tribunal; United Bull-Dogs; United Grand Junction Ebenezer Temperance Association; Watertoast Association of United Sympathizers.

**Vessels.** — The Beauty; the Cautious Clara; the Family; the Royal Skewer; the Scorpion; the Screw; the Son and Heir.

# A CONDENSED BIBLIOGRAPHY OF THE WRITINGS OF CHARLES DICKENS

BASED UPON THE FULL BIBLIOGRAPHY PREPARED BY RICHARD HERNE SHEPHERD

1833–1835

Stories and Sketches contributed to *The Monthly Magazine, or British Register of Politics, Literature, Art, Science, and the Belles Lettres.* New Series. London: published by A. Robertson; afterwards by Cochrane and Macrone, and by James Cochrane and Co. Vols. xvi. to xix.

A Dinner at Poplar Walk. — December, 1833.
  Republished under the title of "Mr. Minns and his Cousin."
Mrs. Joseph Porter, "over the way." — January, 1834.
Horatio Sparkins. — February, 1834.
The Bloomsbury Christening. — April, 1834.
The Boarding House. — May, 1834.
The Boarding House, No. II. — August, 1834.
The Steam Excursion. — October, 1834.
Passages in the Life of Mr. Watkins Tottle. Chapter First. — January, 1835.
*Ib.* Chapter Second. — February, 1835.

Sketches of London (signed "Boz"), in the *Evening Chronicle.* 1835.

Hackney-Coach Stands. — Saturday, January 31.
Gin Shops. — Saturday, February 7.
Early Coaches. — Thursday, February 19.
The Parish. — Saturday, February 28.
"The House." — Saturday, March 7.
London Recreations. — Tuesday, March 17.
Public Dinners. — Tuesday, April 7.
Bellamy's. — Saturday, April 11.
Greenwich Fair. — Thursday, April 16.
Thoughts about People. — Thursday, April 23.
Astley's. — Saturday, May 9.
Our Parish. — Tuesday, May 19.
The River. — Saturday, June 6.
Our Parish. — Thursday, June 18.
The Pawnbroker's Shop. — Tuesday, June 30.
Our Parish. — Tuesday, July 14.
The Streets — Morning. — Tuesday, July 21.
Our Parish — Mr. Bung's Narrative. — Tuesday, July 28.
Private Theatres. — Tuesday, August 11.
Our Parish. — Thursday, August 20.

Scenes and Characters (signed "Tibbs"), printed in *Bell's Life in London*, 1835.

Seven Dials. — September 27.
Miss Evans and "the Eagle." — October 4.
The Dancing Academy. — October 11.
Making a Night of it. — October 18.
Love and Oysters. — October 25.
  Entitled in the collected "Sketches," "Misplaced Attachment of Mr. John Dounce."
Some Account of an Omnibus Cad. — November 1.
The Vocal Dress-Maker. — November 22.
  Entitled in the collected "Sketches," "The Mistaken Milliner."
The Prisoners' Van. — November 29.
The Parlour. — December 13.
  Entitled "The Parlour Orator" in the collected "Sketches."
Christmas Festivities. — December 27.
  Entitled in the collected "Sketches," "A Christmas Dinner."

1836

THE SAME.

The New Year. — January 3.
The Streets at Night. — January 17.

The Tuggs's at Ramsgate (with two illustrations by Seymour). — A Little Talk about Spring, and the Sweeps (with an illustration by R. W. Buss). — *The Library of Fiction, or Family Story-Teller; consisting of original Tales, Essays, and Sketches of Character.* London: Chapman and Hall.

SKETCHES BY "Boz." New Series. (*Morning and Evening Chronicle.*)

Meditations in Monmouth Street. — *M. C.* Saturday, September 24.
Scotland Yard. — *M. C.* Tuesday, October 4; *E. C.* Wednesday, October 5.
Doctors' Commons. — *E. C.* Wednesday, October 12.
Vauxhall Gardens by Day. — *M. C.* and *E. C.* Wednesday, October 26.

SKETCHES BY "Boz;" ILLUSTRATIVE OF EVERY-DAY LIFE AND EVERY-DAY PEOPLE. In Two Volumes. Illustrations by George Cruikshank. London: John Macrone.

SUNDAY UNDER THREE HEADS. As it is; As Sabbath Bills would make it; As it might be made. By Timothy Sparks. London: Chapman and Hall.

THE STRANGE GENTLEMAN. A Comic Burletta. In Two Acts. By "Boz." First performed at the St. James's Theatre, on Thursday, September 29, 1836. London: Chapman and Hall.

THE VILLAGE COQUETTES. A Comic Opera. In Two Acts. By Charles Dickens. The Music by John Hullah. London: Richard Bentley. 1836.

1837

SKETCHES BY "Boz;" ILLUSTRATIVE OF EVERY-DAY LIFE AND EVERY-DAY PEOPLE. The Second Series. London: John Macrone.

IS SHE HIS WIFE? OR, SOMETHING SINGULAR! A Comic Burletta. In One Act. By "Boz."

THE POSTHUMOUS PAPERS OF THE PICKWICK CLUB. Being a faithful Record of the Perambulations, Perils, Travels, Adventures, and Sporting Transactions of the Corresponding Members. Edited by "Boz." With forty-three illustrations by R. Seymour, R. W. Buss, and Hablot K. Browne ("Phiz"). In twenty monthly parts, commencing April, 1836, and ending November, 1837 (Parts 19 and 20 forming a double number). London: Chapman and Hall.

1837-1839

CONTRIBUTIONS TO "BENTLEY'S MISCELLANY," 1837-1839. London: Richard Bentley.

Public Life of Mr. Tulrumble, once Mayor of Mudfog. January, 1837.
Stray Chapters by "Boz." Chapter 1. The Pantomime of Life. March, 1837.
Stray Chapters by "Boz." Chapter 2. Some particulars concerning a Lion. May, 1837.
Editor's Address on the Completion of the First Volume, signed "Boz," and dated "London, June, 1837."
pp. 397-413. Full Report of the First Meeting of the Mudfog Association for the Advancement of Everything. October, 1837.
Address, dated "30th November, 1837."
Mr. Robert Bolton, the "Gentleman connected with the Press." August.
Full Report of the Second Meeting of the Mudfog Association for the Advancement of Everything. September.
Familiar Epistle from a Parent to a Child aged two years and two months, signed "Boz." February, 1839.

1838

THE LAMPLIGHTER. A Farce.

Only 250 copies privately printed (1879) from the manuscript copy in the Forster Collection at South Kensington; each copy numbered.

OLIVER TWIST; OR, THE PARISH BOY'S PROGRESS. Commenced in the second number of *Bentley's Miscellany*, in February, 1837, and concluded in March, 1839. Published in three volumes, post 8vo, in October, 1838, six months in advance of its completion in the *Miscellany*, with twenty-four illustrations by George Cruikshank. London: Richard Bentley.

SKETCHES OF YOUNG GENTLEMEN. Dedicated to the Young Ladies. With six illustrations by "Phiz" (H. K. Browne), small 8vo. London: Chapman and Hall.

MEMOIRS OF JOSEPH GRIMALDI. Edited by "Boz." With twelve illustrations by George Cruikshank. In two volumes, post 8vo. London: Richard Bentley.

1839

THE LIFE AND ADVENTURES OF NICHOLAS NICKLEBY. With 39 illustrations by "Phiz;" and portrait of the author after Maclise, engraved by Finden. In twenty monthly parts, demy 8vo, commencing April, 1838, and ending October, 1839, — parts 19 and 20 forming a double number. London: Chapman and Hall.

Notice of Mr. John Gibson Lockhart's pamphlet, "The Ballantyne Humbug handled." — *Examiner*, March 31.

1840

SKETCHES OF YOUNG COUPLES. With an urgent Remonstrance to the Gentlemen of England (being Bachelors or Widowers) on the present alarming crisis. By the Author of "Sketches of Young Gentlemen." With six illustrations by "Phiz" (H. K. Browne). London: Chapman and Hall.

Notice of Hood's "Up the Rhine." Printed in *The Examiner.*

1840–1841

MASTER HUMPHREY'S CLOCK. With illustrations on wood by George Cattermole, H. K. Browne, George Cruikshank, and Daniel Maclise. In eighty-eight weekly numbers, imperial 8vo, commencing April 4, 1840, and ending November 27, 1841, and in twenty monthly parts, — forming three volumes. London: Chapman and Hall.
BARNABY RUDGE began at p. 229 of Vol. II and ended at p. 420 of Vol. III.

1841

The Fine Old English Gentleman. New Version (to be said or sung at all Conservative dinners). — *Examiner*, Saturday, August 7.

The Quack Doctor's Proclamation. — *Examiner*, Saturday, August 14.

Subjects for Painters. After Peter Pindar. — *Examiner*, Saturday, August 21.

The Lamplighter's Story. — Printed in *The Pic-Nic Papers by various hands, edited by Charles Dickens.* With illustrations by George Cruikshank. London: Henry Colburn.

1842

Circular Letter on International Copyright with America, dated "Devonshire Terrace, July 7, 1842," and signed "Charles Dickens."

Prologue to Mr. Westland Marston's Play, "The Patrician's Daughter." Written by Mr. Charles Dickens, and spoken by Mr. Macready. — *Sunday Times*, December 11.

AMERICAN NOTES FOR GENERAL CIRCULATION. By Charles Dickens. In two volumes. London: Chapman and Hall.

1843

To the Editor of *The Times*. — Letter dated "Devonshire Terrace, Sunday, Jan. 15," *The Times*, Monday, January 16, 1843.
In contradiction of a misstatement made in a criticism of "American Notes" (by the late James Spedding), published in the *Edinburgh Review* of January, 1843.

A CHRISTMAS CAROL IN PROSE. Being a Ghost Story of Christmas. With illustrations by John Leech. London: Chapman and Hall.

1844

THE LIFE AND ADVENTURES OF MARTIN CHUZZLEWIT — HIS RELATIONS, FRIENDS, AND ENEMIES. Comprising all his wills and his ways: with an Historical Record of what he did and what he did n't; showing, moreover, who inherited the family plate, who came in for the silver spoons, and who for the wooden ladles: the whole forming a complete Key to the House of Chuzzlewit. Edited by Boz. With 40 illustrations by H. K. Browne. In twenty monthly parts, demy 8vo, commencing January, 1843, and ending July, 1844, — parts 19 and 20 forming a double number. London: Chapman and Hall.

A Word in Season. Printed in *The Keepsake* for 1844, edited by the Countess of Blessington. London: Longmans.

Letter to the Committee of the Metropolitan Drapers' Association, dated "Devonshire Terrace, March 28, 1844." Printed in *The Student and Young Men's Advocate, a Magazine of Literature, Science, and Art.* London: Aylott and Jones.

Threatening Letter to Thomas Hood, from an Ancient Gentleman. By favour of Charles Dickens. Printed in *Hood's Magazine and Comic Miscellany*. May.

Evenings of a Working Man, being the occupation of his scanty leisure. By John Overs. With a Preface relative to the Author, by Charles Dickens. London: T. C. Newby.

1845

THE CHIMES: a Goblin Story of some Bells that rang an Old Year out and a New Year in. By Charles Dickens. Illustrated by Maclise, Doyle, Leech, and Clarkson Stanfield. London: Chapman and Hall.

1846

THE CRICKET ON THE HEARTH. A Fairy Tale of Home. By Charles Dickens. Illustrated by Maclise, Doyle, Clarkson Stanfield, Leech, and Landseer. London: Bradbury and Evans.

CONTRIBUTIONS TO THE "DAILY NEWS:"—

The British Lion. A New Song, but an Old Story. Signed "Catnach."—Saturday, January 24.

Crime and Education. Letter, dated "Wednesday morning, Feb. 4, 1846."—Wednesday, February 4.

The Hymn of the Wiltshire Labourers.—Saturday, February 14.

Letters on Social Questions—Capital Punishment. Three letters.—Monday, March 9, Friday, March 13, and Monday, March 16.

PICTURES FROM ITALY. The Vignette Illustrations on wood, by Samuel Palmer, pp. 270. London: Bradbury and Evans.

The substance of this volume appeared originally in the *Daily News*, from January to March, 1846, under the title of "Travelling Letters. Written on the Road. By Charles Dickens."

THE BATTLE OF LIFE. A Love Story. Illustrated by Maclise, Doyle, Leech, and Clarkson Stanfield. London: Bradbury and Evans.

1848

DEALINGS WITH THE FIRM OF DOMBEY AND SON, WHOLESALE, RETAIL, AND FOR EXPORTATION. With forty illustrations by H. K. Browne. In twenty monthly parts, commencing October, 1846, and ending April, 1848,—parts 19 and 20 forming a double number. London: Bradbury and Evans.

Notice of "The Drunkard's Children," a Sequel to "The Bottle," in eight plates, by George Cruikshank.—*Examiner*, July 8.

Notice of "The Rising Generation," a series of twelve drawings on stone, by John Leech.—*Examiner*, December 30.

THE HAUNTED MAN AND THE GHOST'S BARGAIN. A Fancy for Christmas Time. With frontispiece and title engraved on wood after John Tenniel, and fourteen other woodcut illustrations by Stanfield, Leech, Frank Stone, and John Tenniel. London: Bradbury and Evans.

1849

To the Editor of *The Times*.—Two Letters on Public Executions, Wednesday, November 14, and Monday, November 19.

1850

THE PERSONAL HISTORY, ADVENTURES, EXPERIENCE, AND OBSERVATION OF DAVID COPPERFIELD, THE YOUNGER, OF BLUNDERSTONE ROOKERY. Which he never meant to be published on any account. With forty illustrations by H. K. Browne. In twenty monthly parts, commencing May, 1849, and ending November, 1850,—parts 19 and 20 forming a double number. London: Bradbury and Evans.

CONTRIBUTIONS TO "HOUSEHOLD WORDS:"—

A Preliminary Word.—March 30.
A Child's Dream of a Star.—April 6.
The Begging-Letter Writer.—May 18.
A Walk in a Workhouse.—May 25.
The Ghost of Art.—July 20.
The Detective Police.—July 27. August 10.
Three Detective Anecdotes.—September 14.
A Poor Man's Tale of a Patent.—October 19.
A Christmas Tree.—December 21.
What Christmas is, as we grow older.—Printed in the extra number for Christmas, 1851.

1851

MR. NIGHTINGALE'S DIARY. A Farce, in One Act. London, 1851. Bradbury and Evans, Printers, Whitefriars. (Privately printed.)

CONTRIBUTIONS TO "HOUSEHOLD WORDS:"—
Births. "Mrs. Meeks of a Son."—February 22.
A Monument of French Folly.—March 8.
Bill Sticking.—March 22.
The Guild of Literature and Art.—May 10.
On Duty with Inspector Field.—June 14.
Our English Watering-Place.—August 2.
Whole Hogs.—August 23.
A Flight.—August 30.
One Man in a Dockyard.—September 6. Written jointly by Charles Dickens and R. H. Horne.
Our School.—October 11.

1852

CONTRIBUTIONS TO "HOUSEHOLD WORDS:"—
A Plated Article.—April 24.
Our Honourable Friend.—July 31.
Our Vestry.—August 28.
Our Bore.—October 9.
Lying Awake.—October 30.
Trading in Death.—November 27.
The Poor Relation's Story } Christmas number.
The Child's Story }

To be Read at Dusk. Printed in *The Keepsake*, edited by Miss Power. London: David Bogue.

1852–1854

A CHILD'S HISTORY OF ENGLAND.
Vol. I. England from the ancient times to the death of King John. 1852.
Vol. II. England from the reign of Henry III. to the reign of Richard III. 1853.
Vol. III. England from the reign of Henry VII. to the Revolution of 1688. 1854.
London: Bradbury and Evans.

Divided here into thirty-seven chapters, but originally into forty-five, which appeared at irregular intervals in *Household Words;* the first chapter in the number for January 25, 1851, and the last in the number for December 10, 1853.

1853

BLEAK HOUSE. With forty illustrations by H. K. Browne. In twenty monthly parts, commencing March, 1852, and ending September, 1853. London: Bradbury and Evans. 1853.

CONTRIBUTIONS TO "HOUSEHOLD WORDS:"—
Down with the Tide.—February 5.
The Noble Savage.—June 11.
Frauds on the Fairies.—October 1.
The Schoolboy's Story } Christmas number.
Nobody's Story }
The Long Voyage.—December 31.

1854

HARD TIMES. For these Times. By Charles Dickens. London: Bradbury and Evans.

Originally published in weekly instalments in *Household Words*, commencing April 1, and concluding August 12, 1854.

CONTRIBUTIONS TO "HOUSEHOLD WORDS:"—
The late Mr. Justice Talfourd.—March 25.
Our French Watering-Place.—November 4.
The Seven Poor Travellers.—Christmas Number.

1855

CONTRIBUTIONS TO "HOUSEHOLD WORDS:"—
Prince Bull: a Fairy Tale.—February 17.
By Rail to Parnassus.—June 16.
Out of Town.—September 29.
The Holly-Tree.—Christmas Number.

1856

CONTRIBUTIONS TO "HOUSEHOLD WORDS:"—
A Nightly Scene in London. — January 26.
Proposals for a National Jest-Book. — May 3.
Out of the Season. — June 28.
The Wreck. — Christmas Number.
Child's Hymn, printed in "The Wreck of the Golden Mary." — Christmas Number.

1857

LITTLE DORRIT. With forty illustrations by H. K. Browne. In twenty monthly parts, commencing December, 1855, and ending June, 1857, — parts 19 and 20 forming a double number. London: Bradbury and Evans.

CONTRIBUTIONS TO "HOUSEHOLD WORDS:"—
Curious Misprint in the Edinburgh Review. — August 1.
The Lazy Tour of Two Idle Apprentices. — October. [With Wilkie Collins.]
The Perils of Certain English Prisoners. — Christmas Number.

1858

CONTRIBUTIONS TO "HOUSEHOLD WORDS:"—
Personal. — June 12.

This is the statement which Dickens thought it necessary to publish respecting his separation from his wife, and the groundless rumors that were abroad in connection with it.

A House to Let. — Christmas Number.

1859

A TALE OF TWO CITIES. In Three Books. By Charles Dickens. London: Chapman and Hall.

Published in weekly instalments in *All the Year Round*, commencing in the first number, April 30, 1859, and ending in the thirty-first, November 26, 1859.

The Poor Man and his Beer. — *All the Year Round*, April 30.
The Blacksmith. A Trade Song. — *All the Year Round*, April 30.
A Last Household Word. — *Household Words*, May 28.

HUNTED DOWN. A Story in Two Portions. — Printed in *The New York Ledger* of August 20 and 27 and September 3, 1859.

Leigh Hunt. A Remonstrance. — *All the Year Round*, December 24.
In reference to the current and not altogether unfounded idea that Leigh Hunt was the original of Harold Skimpole in "Bleak House."

The Haunted House. — *All the Year Round*. Christmas number.

1860

A Message from the Sea. — *All the Year Round*. Christmas number.

1861

THE UNCOMMERCIAL TRAVELLER. London: Chapman and Hall.

GREAT EXPECTATIONS. In Three Volumes. London: Chapman and Hall.
Originally published in weekly instalments in *All the Year Round*, from December 1, 1860, to August 3, 1861.

To the Editor of *The Times*. — *The Times*, London, Saturday, January 12.
Refers to a dramatized version of his Christmas story, "A Message from the Sea," announced for performance without his sanction at the Britannia Theatre.

The Election for Finsbury. To the Editor of the *Daily News*. — *Daily News*, London, Saturday, November 23.

Tom Tiddler's Ground. — *All the Year Round*. Christmas number.

1862

Somebody's Luggage. — *All the Year Round*. Christmas number.

1863

The Earthquake. — To the Editor of *The Times*. — *The Times*, Thursday, October 8.
Mrs. Lirriper's Lodgings. — *All the Year Round*. Christmas number.

1864

In Memoriam: W. M. Thackeray. — *Cornhill Magazine*, February.
Mrs. Lirriper's Legacy. — *All the Year Round*. Christmas number.

1865

OUR MUTUAL FRIEND. With 40 illustrations by Marcus Stone. In 20 monthly parts, commencing May, 1864, and ending November, 1865, —parts 19 and 20 forming a double number. In two volumes. London: Chapman and Hall.

Dr. Marigold's Prescriptions. —*All the Year Round.* Christmas number.

1866

LEGENDS AND LYRICS. By Adelaide Anne Procter. With an Introduction by Charles Dickens. London: Bell and Daldy.

History of "Pickwick." —*Athenæum*, March 31, April 7.

Respecting Seymour and his illustrations of the first two numbers of *The Pickwick Papers.*

Mugby Junction. —*All the Year Round.* Christmas number.

1867

The late Mr. Stanfield. —*All the Year Round*, June 1.

To the Editor of *The Times.* — *The Times*, London, Wednesday, September 4.

Referring to the erroneous reports current about his health.

No Thoroughfare. —*All the Year Round.* Christmas number. Written conjointly with Mr. Wilkie Collins, in nearly equal portions. The only portions furnished exclusively by Dickens were the "Overture" and the "Third Act;" Mr. Collins contributing to Acts First and Fourth, and writing the whole of the Second.

NO THOROUGHFARE. A Drama, in Five Acts and a Prologue. By Charles Dickens and Wilkie Collins. As first performed at the New Adelphi Theatre, London, December 26, 1867. New York: Robert M. de Witt.

1868

THE UNCOMMERCIAL TRAVELLER. By Charles Dickens. With illustrations. London: Chapman and Hall, 1868. pp. 172.

Contains eleven new papers from *All the Year Round*, besides those published in former edition.

George Silverman's Explanation. In nine chapters. — *The Atlantic Monthly*, Boston, January, February, and March, 1868.

Holiday Romance. In Four Parts. Printed in *Our Young Folks, an Illustrated Magazine for Boys and Girls*, Boston, January, March, April, and May, 1868. With four full-page illustrations drawn by Sir John Gilbert, and initial-letter illustrations to each part by G. G. White and S. Eytinge, junior.

1868, 1869

NEW UNCOMMERCIAL SAMPLES. Printed in *All the Year Round*, New Series.

- Aboard Ship. — December 5, 1868.
- A Small Star in the East. — December 19, 1868.
- A Little Dinner in an Hour. — January 2, 1869.
- Mr. Barlow. — January 16, 1869.
- On an Amateur Beat. — February 27, 1869.
- A Fly-Leaf in a Life. — May 22, 1869.
- A Plea for Total Abstinence. — June 5, 1869.

1869

Landor's Life. A notice of Mr. John Forster's Life of Walter Savage Landor. —*All the Year Round*, July 24.

On Mr. Fechter's Acting. — *The Atlantic Monthly*, Boston, August.

1870

THE MYSTERY OF EDWIN DROOD. — With twelve illustrations by S. L. Fildes, and a portrait engraved on steel from a photograph taken in 1868. In six monthly parts, commencing April, 1870, and ending September, 1870, pp. viii. 190. London: Chapman and Hall.

1882

THE PLAYS AND POEMS OF CHARLES DICKENS. With a few Miscellanies in Prose. Now first collected. Edited, prefaced, and annotated by Richard Herne Shepherd. In Two Volumes. London: W. H. Allen and Co.